Nonhuman Photography

Nonhuman Photography

Joanna Zylinska

The MIT Press
Cambridge, Massachusetts
London, England

This book was set in Stone Sans and Stone Serif by Toppan Best-set Premedia Limited.

Library of Congress Cataloging-in-Publication Data

Names: Zylinska, Joanna, 1971- author.
Title: Nonhuman photography / Joanna Zylinska.
Description: Cambridge, MA : The MIT Press, [2017] | Includes bibliographical references and index.
Identifiers: LCCN 2017010149 | ISBN 9780262037020 (hardcover : alk. paper)
ISBN 9780262552622 (paperback)
Subjects: LCSH: Photography--Philosophy. | Hidden camera photography. | Electronic surveillance. | Automatic machinery. | Extinction (Biology)
Classification: LCC TR183 .Z95 2017 | DDC 770--dc23 LC record available at https://lccn.loc.gov/2017010149

Contents

Acknowledgments

The seeds for this book were planted with the inaugural professorial lecture on nonhuman photography that I gave at Goldsmiths, University of London, in March 2014. I am grateful to my Goldsmiths colleagues and students for ongoing support and inspiration, in particular Lisa Blackman, Sean Cubitt, Natalie Fenton, Julian Henriques, and Sarah Kember. Many other institutions and organizations have generously invited me to present material from this project as it unfolded: Aalto University, Centre Culturel International de Cerisy, Coventry University, the Center for 21st Century Studies at the University of Wisconsin–Milwaukee, Courtauld Institute of Art, European Communication Research and Education Association (ECREA), Institut National d'Histoire de l'Art (INHA), the International Media Art Biennale WRO 2015, Katholieke Universiteit Leuven (KU Leuven), King's College London, Lincoln University, Lund University, New York University Abu Dhabi, Onassis Cultural Centre, Polish Academy of Sciences, Princeton University, Universidad de las Américas Puebla, the Universities of Bergen, Copenhagen, Greenwich, Kent, Minnesota, Oregon, Westminster, and the West of England, and the Winchester School of Art. I received invaluable feedback at all of those places, which helped me improve the manuscript immensely.

I am truly grateful to many individuals who have inspired me and helped me develop the ideas contained in this book. I would especially like to thank Clare Birchall, Dave Boothroyd, Ting Ting Cheng, Theodoros Chiotos, Gabriela Méndez Cota, Alberto López Cuenca, David Cunningham, Ewa Domańska, Mika Elo, Richard Grusin, Kamila Kuc, Max Liljefors, Nina Sellars, Doug Sery, Jonathan Shaw, Stelarc, Frederik Truyen,

Ross Varney, Michael Wamposzyc, Bernadette Wegenstein, and Paul Wombell. I am also very grateful for the generosity of many artists whose work has long served as inspiration for me, and who have kindly allowed me to reproduce their images in this book: Bonamy Devas, Véronique Ducharme, Juliet Ferguson, Alexa Horochowski, Pieter Hugo, Tong Lam, Lindsay Seers, and Richard Whitlock. As always, a special thank-you goes to Gary Hall.

Introduction: Capturing the End of the World

At the very beginning of the twenty-first century, a professional photographer with an interest in environmental issues named James Balog decided to record glacier retreat, a phenomenon that is considered the most visible indicator of climate change in the world today (figure 0.1). To realize his project, Balog invested in a number of Nikon DSLR cameras, which he subsequently customized with microcomputers to enable them to capture images over a period of several years, in different weather conditions. The cameras were then installed in high-resistance cases and soldered onto rocks. Exposed to extremely harsh weather in Iceland, Alaska, and the Arctic, these cameras recorded, for years on end, the transformations of the geo- and hydrosphere. Upon retrieving them, Balog uploaded the data from the cameras' memory cards onto his computer, and then edited the still images into time-lapse videos that illustrated the progressive ice loss from glaciers. Subsequently developed into the Emmy-winning and Oscar-nominated documentary *Chasing Ice* (2012), the project has been promoted worldwide via a series of events under the umbrella of "the Anthropocene"—i.e., the present time interval, going back to at least the Industrial Revolution, in which the human has been recognized as a geological agent that has had irreversible impact upon the Earth.[1] The project has also served as a driver for the activities of the Earth Vision Institute, a donor-funded organization headed by Balog whose goal is to help global citizens see the impact of environmental change and envisage a better tomorrow.

The above anecdote encapsulates all of the key concerns of *Nonhuman Photography*. On the one hand, the production process involved in shooting the multiyear collection of images of glaciers from high vantage points in extreme weather conditions signals that today, in the age of CCTV, drone media, medical body scans, and satellite imaging, photography is

Figure 0.1
Four screengrabs by Joanna Zylinska from the Earth Vision Institute's time-lapse video of the receding Columbia Glacier in Alaska, 2007–2014, http://earthvision institute.org/share-this/columbia-glacier-alaska/.

increasingly decoupled from human agency and human vision. Yet I will also argue throughout the book that *even those images that are produced by the human*, whether artist or amateur, *entail a nonhuman, mechanical element*. By this I mean that these images involve the execution of technical and cultural algorithms that shape our image-making devices as well as our viewing practices. On the other hand, the glacier project demonstrates how photography is increasingly mobilized to document and illustrate the precariousness of the human habitat, and also how—through advertising, campaign posters, and Instagram—it is tasked with helping us imagine a better tomorrow and a better life for ourselves. *In its conjoined human-nonhuman agency and vision, photography thus functions as both a form of control and a life-shaping force.*

All-encompassing in the workings of traffic control cameras, smart phones, and Google Earth, photography can therefore be described as a technology of life: it not only represents life but also shapes and regulates it—while also documenting or even envisioning its demise. Thanks to the proliferation of digital and portable media as well as broadband connectivity, photography has become pervasive and ubiquitous: we could go so far as to say that our very sense of existence is now shaped by it. In the words of Susan Sontag, "To live is to be photographed, to have a record of one's life, and therefore to go on with one's life oblivious, or claiming to be oblivious, to the camera's nonstop attentions."[2] This altered role and agency of the photographic medium calls for a new understanding of photography, I suggest, beyond its traditional humanist frameworks and perceptions. *Nonhuman Photography* analyzes this new ontological—and political—conjuncture, as well as possible ways of negotiating it, while also refusing to submit to the conventional "human versus machine" narrative. Through this, *it outlines a posthumanist philosophy of photography, anchored in the sensibility of what has become known as "the nonhuman turn."*

There are good reasons why a new conceptual framework for understanding photography as part of a wider media context may be needed. Even though photography has become embedded in our everyday lives on so many different levels, the traditional scholarly and curatorial way of discussing this medium still maintains a relatively narrow set of humanist and human-centric frameworks and discourses on the topic: photography as art or photography as social practice. The first framework is rooted in the methodology of art history, and is encapsulated by numerous histories of photography, typically narrated as stories of the evolution of the medium featuring those rare singular actors identified as "artists."[3] In the art historical view, photographs are positioned as discrete objects that yield themselves to being framed and displayed, individually or in series, on flat surfaces in galleries and other cultural institutions. They are then analyzed in aesthetic, semiotic, and economic terms, for example, in terms of how they affect us, what they mean, and what their value is. The second framework through which photography tends to be interpreted is sociological. It offers a contextual perspective that studies not only how people take and make photographs, but also what they do with photographs: how they store images in family albums, how they join camera clubs, how "professionals" differ from "amateurs," how they all contribute to the emergence of "popular taste" about photography.[4] New ethnographies of the digital which are cognizant of the multiplicity of photographic practices that transcend their visual aspect to embrace phatic communication, narrative orality, and sensory-tactile experience very much inscribe themselves in this trend.[5] The area of photography as professional practice—mainly in the documentary and photojournalistic tradition, but also in fashion and advertising—falls in between these two traditional frameworks, with the market once again acting as an adjudicator of appropriate categorization.[6]

Nonhuman Photography adopts a different, and arguably more complex and more multifaceted, perspective in its treatment of photography: that of posthumanist media theory. By this I mean a media-theoretical framework that combines insights from media, communications, and cultural studies with those of continental philosophy and cultural theory, while also raising questions about the human subject as the anchor and main reference point of analysis. In other words, my book positions photography first and foremost *as a medium*, one that is subject to dynamic and ongoing processes of mediation—only some of which involve humans. Treating photography as a set of processes rather than just objects, it draws on theories of mediation, media ecology, and posthumanism with a view to overcoming the entrenched humanism of the traditional debates on the medium so far. Written by a theorist-practitioner, *Nonhuman Photography* incorporates my various photographic projects as accompaniments to (rather than just illustrations of) the argument, in order to stage a different mode of thinking *about* and *with* media, one that involves the simultaneous production *of* media. Writers, students, media practitioners, and artists attempting to both theorize things and make things will hopefully find in it a number of pointers and openings toward a wider debate on how to do and make media (studies) today. The book also has a companion website (www.nonhuman.photography) that allows readers to see, in color, movement, and high resolution, many of the image-based projects discussed here.

Exploring the nonhuman aspects of photography while also building on the work of media theory, including theories of media ecology (Vilém Flusser, John Durham Peters, Siegfried Zielinski), posthumanist philosophy (Karen Barad, Henri Bergson, Claire Colebrook, Gilles Deleuze and Félix Guattari, Donna Haraway, Tim Ingold), and traditional photography theory (Roland Barthes, Geoffrey Batchen, André Bazin, Joan Fontcuberta, Michael Fried, John Tagg), *Nonhuman Photography* ultimately aims to sketch out a conceptual framework for understanding image-based media, visuality, and perception. Through this framework, it challenges the typical orientation of photography theory toward indexicality, representation, and the preservation of memory traces. It also shifts attention to the nonrepresentational acts of photographic creation. Moving away from typical associations between photography, mourning, and death (as found in Roland Barthes's *Camera Lucida*, for example), the book positions *photography as a formative practice of life*. Although its method is not faithfully or perhaps even recognizably "Deleuzian," *Nonhuman Photography* aims to do for photography what Deleuze and Guattari did for cinema, in terms of acknowledging photography's ontological force and its significance as a life-shaping medium. Its argument is therefore intended to be both affirmative and critical: in analyzing "nonhuman photography" as a cultural condition in which visual enhancement, algorithmic logic, and mediated perception enable different modes of visuality and self-identification, it also raises ethico-political questions about the camera eye's inhumane or even antihuman interventions. To sum up, the goal of this book is thus to expand the human-centric concept of photography by embracing imaging practices from which the human is absent—as its subject, agent, or addressee. The notion of "nonhuman photography" proposed here encapsulates three different yet interconnected conceptual planes:

(1) the rather frequently encountered yet often uncanny-looking photographs that are not *of* the human (depopulated expansive landscapes, say);
(2) photographs that are not *by* the human (contemporary high-tech images produced by traffic control cameras, microphotography, and Google Street View, but also outcomes of deep-time "impressioning" processes, such as fossils);
(3) photographs that are not *for* the human (from QR codes and other algorithmic modes of machine communication that rely on photographic technology through to perhaps still rather cryptic-sounding photography "after the human").

The link that I posit between photography and the Anthropocene—and, more broadly, between photography, biology, and geology—highlights the interweaving of the matter (and materiality) of chemistry, minerals, fossil fuels, and the sun, but also of us humans, with this particular medium. In his introduction to *The Nonhuman Turn*, Richard Grusin identifies this eponymous "turn" with a decentering of the human as the datum point of the humanities, and with a shift of attention toward questions concerning our human engagement—as well as material entanglement—with nonhuman entities and issues "from climate change, drought, and famine; to biology, intellectual property, and privacy; to genocide, terrorism, and war."[7] In a similar vein, Elizabeth Ellsworth and Jamie Kruse have recently postulated something called "the geological turn."[8] By this they mean an increasingly widespread turn toward the geologic as a source that explains and inspires cultural responses to conditions of the present moment. All these authors intimate that the recognition of the vital role played by nonhuman agents in the life of our planetary system needs to shape our understanding of the radical changes brought on by the modern way of life.

What are these changes? As Elizabeth Kolbert has explained in her well-known article in *National Geographic* titled "Enter the Anthropocene—Age of Man," "Probably the most significant change, from a geological perspective, is one that's invisible to us—the change in the composition of the atmosphere. Carbon dioxide emissions are colorless, odorless, and in an immediate sense harmless. But their warming effects could easily push global temperatures to levels that have not been seen for millions of years."[9] We could thus say that there is something in the air at the moment—and this something is a mixture of cosmic dust and human-induced pollution. In other words, *the Anthropocene describes the changing condition of photography and photomedia because it becomes visible to us through altered light—and through the particulate matter that is reflected in it.* But the Anthropocene also serves as an articulator of a new crisis: a crisis of life itself, both as a biological and social phenomenon. Yet, while scientists are still debating whether the designation of a new epoch is justified, the Anthropocene has already been renamed by cultural and political theorists as the Anthrobscene, Capitalocene, Chthulucene, Eurocene, Plantationocene, and Technocene, with questions being raised about the viability of its underpinning structure that "does not exist outside structures of mourning."[10] So even though we are not anywhere near solving the climate issues, in humanities debates we already find ourselves post-Anthropocene.[11] Yet, problematic as the term now is, it may be worth staying in its shadow a little longer, for political and ethical reasons. Mindful of these problems, we should therefore perhaps figure the Anthropocene first and foremost "as a critical zone rather than one grand evil mess that includes all of humanity."[12]

One of the main reasons I propose to link the light of photography and the shadow of the Anthropocene is that, as demonstrated by the opening anecdote of the photographing of a receding glacier, many responses to the planetary crisis signaled by the term "Anthropocene" have been visual. In addition to science-led projects such as Balog's, we can also mention here large-scale art photographs of the damaged environment by Andreas Gursky or Edward Burtynsky, the critical photographic project *The Last Pictures* by Trevor Paglen, or the many visual works included in *Grain Vapor Ray: Textures of the Anthropocene* published by the MIT Press in 2015. I will indeed discuss many of these representations and visualizations of climate change and ecological disasters via the trope of "posthuman landscapes." But I also aim to expand this "representationalist" approach[13] to suggest that the concept of "nonhuman photography" can help us see and understand, in a new way, both the photographic medium and ourselves as partly constituted by this medium.

My claim about photography's vital importance in the age of a global crisis of life at various levels thus constitutes the book's philosophical axis. As I stated earlier, photography is a formative practice of life not only because it represents our lives in various ways but also because it actually shapes life. It does so through images but also through various kinds of material impressions it activates—and also through the forms of perception it generates. In a philosophical gesture akin to the one made by Siegfried Zielinski in *Deep Time of the Media*, my argument here *expands the notion of photography beyond "things that humans do with cameras" to embrace imaging processes from which the human is absent*—microphotography, space photography, drone-mounted cameras. Yet, by way of a conceptual experiment, I also want to take a step further to read human cultural practices as only one section of longer-term processes occurring across "naturecultures." This will allow us to *see photography as occurring precisely across what Zielinski calls "deep time," as forms of stabilized perception and impression that occur across various media, such as stone, clay, wax, or even skin in tanning—and to consider photographs in terms of fossils*. The recognition of the formative role of light across different time periods (in fossils, imprints, photograms, analog film frames, digital snapshots) will also help us shift the debate on photography beyond the analog-digital binary. For me, it is this moment of *temporary stabilization which signals a cut in time* that differentiates photography from moving media, such as film or video—and that, notwithstanding its kinship with other photomedia, points to photography's ontological singularity.

There are some interesting predecessors to this nonhuman mode of thinking in media, communications, and cultural studies: for example, in the work of Canadian scholar Harold Innis, which reads railroads and trade routes as part of the wider communications system.[14] We could also look to Welshman Raymond Williams's linking of culture to the transformation of substance at the biological level, beyond the control or even influence of the human.[15] Last but not least, communications scholar John Durham Peters's 2015 book, *The Marvelous Clouds: Toward a Philosophy of Elemental Media*, argues that "media theory is about environments and infrastructures as much as about messages and content" and that we need "to think of the media as environmental, as part of the habitat."[16] But the interdisciplinary conjuncture of media, communications, and cultural studies can also remind us why it *makes sense* for embodied humans of the early twenty-first century to zoom in on this sliver of geological unfolding we call "history" to try to make sense of it, using the conceptual and material tools at our disposal. It can therefore help us recalibrate the human in relation to geological scales, without losing sight of the significance of that narrow stretch of temporality we call "culture"—and of how we have arrived at it. Indeed, it is the question of seeing—and unseeing—things we take for granted that the interdisciplinary conjuncture of media, communications, and cultural studies has the correct apparatus to address, which is why it provides a useful rejoinder to philosophical, art historical, and sociological frameworks that deal with images and viewpoints. This attempt to "unsee" the seemingly obvious is precisely what I aim to achieve in *Nonhuman Photography*, by offering the notion of "nonhuman vision" as an alternative vantage point from which to understand ourselves and what we humans have called "the world," in all its nonhuman entanglements. With this, the book responds to Nicholas Mirzoeff's injunction to "recognize how deeply embedded in our very sensorium and modern ways of seeing the Anthropocene-aesthetic-capitalist complex of modern visuality has become."[17]

And thus chapter 1, "Nonhuman Vision," poses a challenge to the traditional tenets of the self-focused, capital- and fossil-fueled, masculinist I, who is supposedly in control of his own vision and (world)view. It also explores the possibility of developing some better modes of seeing and imagining both the present and the future. Drawing on the work of Donna Haraway, Vilém Flusser, and James Gibson, it outlines an ecological model of perception as a more embodied, immersive, and entangled form of image and world formation. This model opens up a passageway to being-with, and thus offers a promise of a better ethics and a more responsible politics. It does this by exploring the revolutionary potential of the photographic medium at a time when, for many, photography has become synonymous with image deluge, banality, and narcissism. The chapter is followed by images from my project *Active Perceptual Systems*.

Chapter 2, "The Creative Power of Nonhuman Photography," continues with the argument that nonhuman photography does not just mean photos taken by agents that are not human, such as CCTV cameras, body scanners, or space satellites, and posits that all photography is to some extent nonhuman. While this nonhuman aspect of photography can no doubt produce inhumane practices, I also suggest that it is precisely in its nonhuman aspect that photography's creative, or world-making, side can be identified. Rather than therefore contribute to recent jeremiads about photography—in which it is seen as supposedly dying in the digital era because it is no longer authentic or material enough, or imploding due to its excessiveness and banality, as evidenced on Instagram and in the much-maligned selfie phenomenon—I argue that it is precisely through focusing on its nonhuman aspect that we can find life in photography.

It is the existence of images, and, in particular, light-induced mechanical images known as photographs, *after the human* that is the main focus of chapter 3. The "after the human" designation references the present imagining of this disappearance of the human world as a prominent visual trope in art and other cultural practices. Such "ruin porn" has some historical antecedents: from the sublime romantic landscapes of ruined abbeys, all the way through to paintings such as *Rotunda* by Joseph Gandy, commissioned by John Soane, the architect of the Bank of England, and depicting the aforesaid bank as a ruin even before it was built. Yet the visualization of ruins has gained a new inflection in the Anthropocene, a period that is said to be suffering from a dual "eco-eco" crisis: the current global economic crisis and the impending—and irreversible—ecological crisis. We can think here of the haunting images of Detroit but also of TV series imagining our demise as a species, such as History channel's *Life after People*. Extending the temporal scale beyond that of human history by introducing the horizon of extinction will allow me to denaturalize our political and aesthetic frameworks through which we humans understand ourselves. It will also help me take some steps toward visualizing a post-neoliberal world *here and now*.

In chapter 4, "Photography and Extinction," the horizon of extinction serves as a reference point against which I aim to think the ontology of photography and its agency: what photography can do with and to the world, what it can cast light on, and what the role of this light (or, more broadly, light as such seen through the photographic lens) is in approaching questions of life and death on a planetary scale. Considering the history of photography as part of the broader nature-cultural history of our planet, I trace parallels between photographs and fossils, and propose to understand photography as a light-induced process of fossilization occurring across different media. Photography thus can be said to bear a material record of life rather than just its memory trace. But I also turn to photography's original reliance on the natural light emanating from the sun to explore what photographic practice can tell us about energy sources, and about our relation to the star that nourishes our planet. I do this via an engagement with photographers who have consciously adopted the horizon of extinction as their workspace—from the nineteenth-century geologist-photographer William Jerome Harrison through to contemporary artists such as Hiroshi Sugimoto. I also look at practices in which the work of the sun has been taken on as both a topic and a medium, including the postdigital work of Penelope Umbrico.

Chapter 5, "Ecomedia between Extinction and Obsolescence," builds a link between geological and technical perspectives on media by developing parallels between biological extinction and technical obsolescence. It addresses the current transformations in our media landscape, whereby many objects traditionally considered stable or fixed—photographs, imaging systems, technological networks—are radically changing both their identity and their visibility. In this context, the photographic image is seen as existing in a dynamic set of entangled media relations, and hence as a process rather than as a discrete object. This rethinking of photography in more dynamic and processual terms leads to a broader discussion of producing, curating, studying, and looking at images in the currently transforming media landscape—but also of the constantly updated apparatuses that are producing these images. Picking up the Anthropocene thread, I suggest that we should not worry so much about the (frequently pronounced) death of photography but rather about the multiple deaths of cameras and other equipment—and about the piles of e-waste resulting from those "deaths." The chapter includes a series of images from my artwork *The Vanishing Object of Technology*.

In suggesting that perhaps "we have always been digital," chapter 6 attempts to move the debate on photography beyond the analog-digital binary—and beyond the instrumental, industry-imposed focus on the technical future of the medium. Exploring anxieties over the challenge digitization poses to our established notions of art, culture, and the media, it also questions some of the ways of defending these established notions and values via multiple strategies of remembrance, archiving, and data storage. Although photographic arts—in particular, Tacita Dean's found-image project *Floh*—provide a focal point for the discussion, the argument focuses on sociocultural and political, as much as aesthetic, issues. The "amateur" becomes for me a pivotal concept in trying to rethink the relationship between media production, media consumption, and art, and in considering what it means to both photograph and archive photographs "seriously" in the age of digital cameras, Flickr, Pinterest, and the ubiquitous Delete button. The chapter incorporates images from my artwork *We Have Always Been Digital 2.0*.

Looking at laser-enabled photographic modeling of worlds past and future, the conclusion to the book aims to reclaim "life" in photography, beyond and outside the human control of the photographic apparatus and the photomedia it produces. But it is also a historically located, human-anchored tribute to photography as a mode of *thinking, sensing, and seeing across time*.

For cost reasons, the color photographs featured in this book have been converted to black-and-white. However, a free-access companion website features the key images and projects discussed in the book, including those from my own practice. There readers will be able to see works analyzed in *Nonhuman Photography* in color, access film and animation clips, and follow additional leads. They will also be able to find links to some of the images that I was unable to reproduce in the book, either due to the difficulty of obtaining permissions or because several artists' representatives wanted control over what I wrote about the works. (Chapter 6 discusses in more detail issues of accessing, curating, reproducing, and licensing images in the digital age.) Please visit the online gallery for an augmented experience of "nonhuman photography": www.nonhuman.photography

1 Nonhuman Vision

The view from where, exactly?

The term "nonhuman vision" perhaps most readily furnishes readers' imagination with images of CCTV cameras, Google Earth, satellites, and drones. And, indeed, this chapter does take as its starting point processes of perception in which the very act of seeing something, and its subsequent temporary fixing into an image, are performed by a nonhuman agent, even if their addressee is determinedly human. The term may also bring up visual acts where the human is more explicitly positioned as part of the sighting process in real time: endoscopy, microphotography, or night photography. In those latter cases, detailed images obtained via technical apparatuses such as electronic microscopes or cameras equipped with a CCD sensor featuring very high ISO sensitivity enable access to realms that normally remain hidden from human sight. The role of such apparatuses is thus to enhance limited and partial human vision. Yet it is not my aim in this chapter to celebrate uncritically any such technological enhancements to, or even replacements for, human vision, because, as Donna Haraway bluntly states with reference to examples such as magnetic resonance imaging, home and office video display terminals, and satellite surveillance systems, "Vision in this technological feast becomes unregulated gluttony: [the] eye fucks the world to make techno-monsters."[1] Technologically enhanced vision is therefore still human, and most definitely humanist, in that it reinforces the visual mastery and material dominance of the observer: it is like the eye of a slave owner glancing over his plantation or a general scanning the battlefield,[2] only better. However, just as it is not my intention to gush over technological enhancements to human vision, neither is it to promote any kind of visual Luddism as yet another installment in man's (or woman's) struggle against technology. So, even though this chapter does start by looking at the machinic aspects of vision that challenge the limitations of the human senses and that produce images which defy human perception, it proposes the concept of "nonhuman vision" as an ethico-political response to what Haraway calls the "god trick" of infinite vision, a masculinist gaze of domination and occupation "seeing everything from nowhere."[3] Importantly, as the examples just cited demonstrate, nonhuman vision is not directly opposed to its human counterpart. As pointed out by John Johnston, "Among the inherited oppositions that continue to impose limits on reflection about vision and visual culture today, that which opposes the human to the technical is perhaps the most visibly widespread and invisibly pernicious."[4] Therefore, rather than counterpoise human vision with a machinic one,[5] the chapter will *position the human as part of a complex assemblage of perception in which various organic and machinic agents come together—and apart—for functional, political, or aesthetic reasons.*

In addition to being about perception and vision, this chapter is also about viewpoints—that is, about actual points and positions from which what we humans refer to as "the world," or "the environment," is apprehended and from which knowledge is constructed. It is thus also about scale, proclaiming as it does the need to reintroduce structure and framing to seemingly vast posthumanist vistas, if we early twenty-first-century human thinkers and observers are to make any meaningful argument about them. Writers such as Martin Jay and Jonathan Crary, as well as Haraway herself, have variously argued that vision is historically constructed. Yet the construction of vision *as vision* does not occur separately from other developments: it is part and parcel of the all-encompassing and indivisible process of mediation "that is simultaneously economic, social, cultural, psychological, and technical."[6] From this perspective, the chapter recognizes that something unique *has* occurred to human perception and the associated ways of grasping the world in the last couple of decades, with the unprecedented extrapolation of vision to apparatuses big and small—to an extent that, as Crary puts it in *Techniques of the Observer*,

> Most of the historically important functions of the human eye are being supplanted by practices in which visual images no longer have any reference to the position of an observer in a "real," optically perceived world. If these images can be said to refer to anything, it is to millions of bits of electronic mathematical data.

> Increasingly, visuality will be situated on a cybernetic and electromagnetic terrain where abstract visual and linguistic elements coincide and are consumed, circulated, and exchanged globally.[7]

Yet the historical specificity of data-driven images and nonhuman scales in perception aside, my position in this chapter stops short of embracing the radical discontinuity and disruption of perception as a result of the extension of visuality across various scales. Instead, I aim to develop an argument about *the inherent nonhumanity of all vision*, while also zooming in on some recent technological and sociopolitical developments around vision and perception to illustrate this point and consider its consequences.

Nonhuman vision as an ethico-political pointer

There are good reasons why we may want to adopt nonhuman vision as an ethico-political pointer. We can reference here the recent explicit recognition that the human vision and human viewpoint are too narrow and too parochial, a realization that has occurred across different disciplines, countries, social groups, and media in light of the debates on climate change, extinction, and the Anthropocene. The exploration of nonhuman vision as outlined in this chapter therefore needs to be seen as not just a description of events but also as a normative proposition. *Embracing nonhuman vision as both a concept and a mode of being in the world will allow humans to see beyond the humanist limitations of their current philosophies and worldviews, to unsee themselves in their godlike positioning of both everywhere and nowhere, and to become reanchored and reattached again*. Nonhuman vision is therefore not just about reflexivity; it is rather about introducing concern about our point of view, and an account of it, into our conceptual and visual framework, while removing from it the privileging and stability of the humanist standpoint. It is about inviting the view of another to one's spectrum of visuality, to the point of radically disrupting this spectrum. This approach borrows from what Haraway has called a "partial standpoint," one that allows for the production of situated knowledge—and for giving an account of this knowledge. Lessons about such partial standpoints can be learned from other beings and entities—dogs, pigeons, insects, satellites, and space probes—as demonstrated, for example, in Jana Sterbak's video *Waiting for High Water*, screened as part of her 2005 Venice show, "Through the Eyes of the Other." The poetic yet somewhat menacing images, shaky in their

Figure 1.1
Bird's-eye view from Dr. Julius Neubronner's miniature pigeon camera, with the pigeon's wing tips visible on the edges of the top image, ca. 1908. Public domain.

execution and sporting slanted horizons as well as unusual camera angles, were captured by three video cameras placed on the head of Sterbak's Jack Russell terrier, Stanley. The footage presents a unique view of the city of Venice on the brink of flooding. The low-rise embodied canine perspective deprives the human observer of the solid grounding offered by binocular human vision; it also imposes "an awareness of the physical basis of sight, which is now recognized as something deeply subjective that cannot possibly be separated from the body."[8]

Sterbak's project echoes early experiments with attempting—and inevitably failing—to see "through the eyes of the other" by Dr. Julius Neubronner, who in 1908 patented a miniature pigeon camera activated by a timing mechanism (figure 1.1). "Spectators in Dresden could watch the arrival of the camera-equipped carrier pigeons, and the photos were immediately developed and turned into postcards which could be purchased."[9] Haraway herself has learned about partial standpoints, as she admits,

> in part [by] walking with my dogs and wondering how the world looks without a fovea and very few retinal cells for color vision but with a huge neural processing and

> sensory area for smells. It is a lesson available from photographs of how the world looks to the compound eyes of an insect or even from the camera eye of a spy satellite or the digitally transmitted signals of space probe-perceived differences "near" Jupiter that have been transformed into coffee table color photographs. The "eyes" made available in modern technological sciences shatter any idea of passive vision; these prosthetic devices show us that all eyes, including our own organic ones, are active perceptual systems, building on translations and specific ways of seeing, that is, ways of life. There is no unmediated photograph or passive camera obscura in scientific accounts of bodies and machines; there are only highly specific visual possibilities, each with a wonderfully detailed, active, partial way of organizing worlds.[10]

Borrowing from the intimations of posthumanist theory, my earlier statement that *all vision is to some extent nonhuman* should be understood as meaning that even we humans see in ways that are more than just *uniquely* human. Devices such as satellites or drones only foreground this inherent nonhumanity of all vision. Drawing on feminist intimations of Haraway and others, I thus want to position "nonhuman vision" as a *better* way of looking, not just in an optical but also in an ethico-political sense.

The liberation of the I/eye

The aim of this chapter is therefore to challenge the traditional tenets of the liberal, self-focused, masculinist "I," who is supposedly in control of his own vision and (world)view. Importantly, the postulation of the nonhumanism of all vision needs to be differentiated from statements about vision's potential inhumanism. The aim of the former is to explore the possibility of developing some better modes of seeing and (re)imagining both the present and the future. This vision of nonhuman vision will therefore be of use to us in posing important political questions: If a liberation of the I/eye is to occur, what forms of subjectivity and perception does it require? And to what extent can the posthumanist framework help us develop a better vision for the human, if this human is to unsee himself in his own narcissistic parochialism and develop what we could call a truly ecological vision of selfhood? Drawing on the work of Vilém Flusser and James Gibson, I will move to outline an ecological model of perception as a more embodied, immersive, and entangled form of image and world formation. This model will open up a passageway to being-with, and thus will offer a promise, even if not a guarantee, of a better ethics and a more responsible politics. It will do this by exploring the revolutionary potential of the photographic medium, at a time when photography seems to have become democratized beyond the point of banality, by looking at various *image envisioners*, artists as well as amateurs.

Perception and vision are vast topics, which have been addressed from various angles by both the humanities and the sciences over the course of centuries. The discussion offered here will therefore not aim to be exhaustive; instead, it will borrow insights from the interdisciplinary heritage of visual studies and media studies to say something specific about the medium that arguably organizes that which is both extremely familiar to us and uniquely abstract: photography. Given that photography converts the dynamism of vision into two-dimensional flat impressions of the flow of time, its mode of working has often been treated as secondary or even lifeless by those in visual and media studies. It is cinema that has been positioned instead as allowing special access to, or even modeling, the experience of life.[11] Yet it is precisely in this moment of carving and hence abstracting time that the potential of photography will be identified as *a medium that slows down time and can teach us humans to look at ourselves and our environment differently*. As Rebekah Modrak puts it in *Reframing Photography*, photography is "about actions involving looking. It's the act of reproducing an image an endless number of times. ... It's about pausing something that has life and movement so that we can watch it when it's still. It's about creating movement through fixed images."[12] This chapter will therefore sketch out a critical vitalist framework for understanding photography as a quintessential practice of life, one that exceeds its human articulations and (re)presentations. Retracing the experiments with photography that go back nearly two centuries, I also want to take some steps toward narrating what could be described as a nonrepresentational and nonhuman history of the medium (to be developed further in chapter 3), as a challenge to its more familiar, and more dominant, humanist counterpart. Photography will thus function here as an expanded case study through which I will try to envisage some more ethical and more politically enabling ways of seeing the world, and thus also of living with/in it.

Photography beyond humanism

The humanist argument about photography and image making is reflected in the widely disseminated stories about the image deluge we are said to be producing today, as a result of which there is supposedly nothing left for us to see or know. We can hear echoes of these stories in such headline-grabbing statements as: Every two minutes, we take more pictures than did the whole of humanity in the 1800s! Every day, 350 million photos are uploaded to Facebook! There are over twenty billion photos on Instagram! And it's estimated that humankind has taken 3.8 trillion pictures so far![13] The accuracy of such statements should be taken with a grain of salt, not least because of the rapid changes these platforms and the practices associated with them are undergoing, as well as the relative impossibility of measuring accurately the activities they are referencing. However, numerical accuracy is not the primary concern of those who make such proclamations. By drawing on the rhetorical strategies of the mathematical sublime, they are first of all interested in creating a shock effect among their audiences, dazzling us with numbers that are difficult to grasp—whose role is to act as "clickbait," to instigate the purchase of an app or a device, or perhaps even to cause a moral panic.

It is not only generators of media hype, salespeople, and "life as it used to be" morality peddlers who treat us to narratives about visual excess. In a similar vein, media and visual studies scholars have interpreted the production and consumption of images in the digital age in terms of affective labor: a form of work that is seemingly limitless, yet that remains unaccounted for and hence ultimately unrewarded, even if it is temporarily satisfying on a personal level. Indeed, clicking and sharing are never-ending tasks we are all mobilized to perform if we are to keep up with the times, or at least with the timelines of our friends' and families' lives. Marxist critic Jonathan Beller, writing primarily about cinema but also extending his argument to social media, argues that, in the current culture of visual excess, "in accord with the principles of late capitalism, to look is to labor."[14] He goes on to suggest, "With the rise of [the] internet grows the recognition of the value-productive dimensions of sensual labor in the visual register. Perception is increasingly bound to production."[15] Beller is rather pessimistic about the possibility of escaping from this factory of late modern visuality, set up as a narcissistic hall of mirrors. The fact that, at the time of writing, the most popular tags on Instagram include #love, #me, #cute, #follow, and #selfie seems to corroborate his thesis.[16]

Yet it may be worth turning at this point to photography critic Lyle Rexer, who refuses to be swayed either by excessively optimistic or excessively pessimistic stories about the supposed image deluge—or, more importantly, by their humanist underpinnings. Instead, in his book *The Edge of Vision: The Rise of Abstraction in Photography,* Rexer attempts to reconfigure photography as a medium of nonhuman vision. He encourages us to engage, slowly and meticulously, with various kinds of abstract images instead, i.e., with "photographs without pictures," also called "photographs that withhold,"[17] because they invite us to practice a "way of looking that doesn't privilege the subject of the photograph."[18] The reasons for this visual exercise are not just academic: Rexer aims to promote what he terms "novel seeing," in which photography "is not a looking at or a looking through but a *looking with.*"[19] For Rexer, "The photograph itself is a piece of performance art, and the performer is light—its passing through and encountering things in the world."[20] His revisionist rereading of the traditional narrative that photography is about looking at traces of light, and hence originally about the sun, rather than about decoding human-made signs and symbols, reveals his deeper ontological and ethical ambitions for the medium. He writes, "We feel throughout the history of photography a chafing at its limits, an impatience with mere visuality, and a wish for some more intimate expression of the world's relation—but one somehow made available through the eyes."[21] Rexer's sentiment about the photographic medium is akin to my own desire that shapes this book. It is a desire to position photography as a zoetic, life-giving, and world-making force, albeit one that entails the enactment of (at times violent) actions of the cut that need to be performed in order to still time. The ethical dimension of photography can be confronted and engaged by its human subjects when they respond to those cuts by means of *looking-with* (or even *becoming-with*) an image. If it seems to some readers like too large a philosophical claim, the proposition of photography's zoetic ontology and relational ethics could perhaps be seen instead in terms of an artistic performance: as an articulation of a possibility, or an attempt to engender a different language about, and a new perception of, the familiar technology and practice.

As mentioned before, nonhuman vision in photography is therefore not opposed to the human mode of seeing but rather forms its constitutive aspect, even if at times this is unseen or repressed. But this aspect is also one that has been present in the history of photography from its beginning. Joseph Nicéphore Niépce's *View from the Window at Le Gras* (1826 or 1827) (figure 1.2), which is considered to be the first photographic image ever

Figure 1.2
Enhanced version of Joseph Nicéphore Niépce's *View from the Window at Le Gras,* 1826 or 1827. Public domain.

made, took eight hours to expose. Niépce had positioned a camera obscura on the upper floor of his country home. Within the camera he placed a polished pewter plate coated with a type of asphalt called bitumen of Judea—a light-sensitive material that hardened on being exposed to daylight. The plate was then washed in a mixture of lavender oil and petroleum, revealing a faint yet clearly traceable image of the buildings and landscape surrounding Niépce's estate, Le Gras.

As Bill Anthes explains,

> The required eight-hour exposure produced a visual paradox: sunlight and shadow can be seen on two sides of structures at left and right—the "pigeon house" or upper loft of Niépce's home, and the sloped roof of a barn with a bakehouse in the rear. As such, Niépce's landmark image presages something that will be true of all the photographs produced in the centuries following his invention: the camera has recorded a view that, for all its apparent veracity, is a scene which the human eye could never see.[22]

The first image in the history of photography therefore presents a distinctly nonhuman vision, while also enacting a nonhuman agency at the heart of its production.

Such a nonhuman mode of seeing *and* doing will arguably shape the whole of subsequent photographic practice, as well as the early discourse about this practice—even though, with the increasing focus on human subjects and on the representational aspects of the image in the second half of the twentieth century, this mode will recede into the background of the narrative about the photographic medium. This is why it is important to highlight that, working within a similar time frame as Niépce, English scientist Henry William Fox Talbot—who, alongside his French contemporary, also laid claim to the coveted title of "the inventor of photography"[23]—described the photographs gathered in his book *The Pencil of Nature* (1844–1846) as having been "impressed by Nature's hand."[24] Talbot foregrounded not only the nonhuman impressioning of paper by light as the fundamental aspect of every photographic act but also the nonhuman vision of the camera obscura's eye. He associated the camera obscura with detachment and the lack of passion, and thus of moral vision, as manifest in its inability to tell the difference between human and nonhuman entities: "the instrument chronicles whatever it sees, and certainly would delineate a chimney-pot or a chimney-sweeper with the same impartiality as it would the Apollo of Belvedere."[25]

Even war photography, later subsumed by the humanist aspirations of the documentary practice—which is somewhat erroneously premised on the causal link between perception, empathy, and moral action—has nonhuman antecedents. English photographer Roger Fenton traveled to the Crimea in 1854 to record the events of the ongoing military conflict. However, due to the weight and size of his equipment, as well as the limitations of the photographic technology at the time, he was constrained in the kinds of images he was able to capture. The need for long exposure times may explain why some of the most memorable photos of the conflict—such as his vast and melancholy *Valley of the Shadow of Death*—have a distinctly nonhuman feel. Interestingly, it is now widely suspected that Fenton had altered the vistas captured in that photograph by adding the cannonballs to the desolate landscape for effect. This constructionist approach, coupled with the vision dislodged from a singular human observer, was carried on to Fenton's postwar photography, as Rexer comments:

> Take for example his work *The Long Walk, Windsor* (1860), whose path splits the image in two and disappears into the empty, overexposed sky. The photograph organizes a perspective that is, strictly speaking, not human, an extreme version of the

vanishing point that actual experience would have contradicted. Fenton reveals to us now what the connoisseurs of his century did not understand: that photography was quintessentially a conceptual art, not a quotation at all but a visual reconstruction of reality, a simulacrum with a difference. Insofar as they reconstruct reality, photographs withhold a measure of it.[26]

Visual experimentation of this kind increased with the development of camera technology at the end of the nineteenth century. Attempts to slow down time and break it into singular instances, normally invisible to the human eye, drove the work of motion photographers such as Étienne-Jules Marey and Eadweard Muybridge, whose images of movement led to the overall sense that the universe itself was "expanding with machine-aided human vision" and that "there were orders of reality yet to be disclosed."[27]

The attempt to find new perspectives that would further challenge established ways of seeing, literally and figuratively, was taken up by many European artists in the early twentieth century. In the images of Russian photographer Alexander Rodchenko, Modrak writes, "transmission towers soar into the sky from a worm's-eye point of view, horns trumpet directly overhead, and we float over crowds and stairways as though seeing with a bird's eye."[28] The insect and bird perspective was meant to allow for a displacement of fixed relations and arrangements, whether on the material or sociopolitical level. Bauhaus professor László Moholy-Nagy went so far as to label "photography's ability to exceed human vision with radical points of view achieved by cameras, and with experimental processes using light and photographic chemistry,"[29] a "New Vision." The embracing of nonhuman perspectives in photography by central and eastern European avant-gardes was more than just an aesthetic experiment: the gesture carried an explicit revolutionary agenda. By breaking with representationalism and aiming to shock viewers with radical new angles and vistas, photographers such as Rodchenko and El Lissitzky endowed the photographic medium with the power to transform reality—or at least with their belief in that power. This belief then resurfaced in the work of media theorist Vilém Flusser, to whom I will turn later in my attempt to rethink and reimagine photography and its discourses today. It is also worth pointing out that the avant-garde experiments with photography most likely received conceptual and technical impetus from the early scientific photography of the day. In the introduction to *Revelations: Experiments in Photography*, a catalog accompanying the exhibition on the influence of science photography on modern and contemporary photographic art, which was a collaboration between the National Media Museum in Bradford and the Science Museum in London, Ben Burbridge goes so far as to suggest that the nascent scientific imagining in areas such as microphotography or radiography in the early twentieth century "helped to introduce a radically abstract vocabulary into the field of fine-art photographic practice."[30] The exhibition's co-curator Greg Hobson in turn states that, since its early days, photography has been able to "lend form to things that were not normally visible to the human eye—providing them with the appearance of something permanent and solid, or at least bound by shape and structure."[31] Hobson's definition captures both the inherent world-making function of photography as a medium that gives form, or stabilizes, the world in motion, and the medium's inherent nonhuman aspect.[32]

My brief sketch of the nonhuman side of the history of photography hopefully demonstrates that there is something rather conservative about the discourse of the photographic medium that has dominated the field of both professional practice (in its artistic and journalistic guises) and amateur pastime in the twentieth century, when photography's transformative ambitions were overshadowed by the conviction that the medium was close to "truth." Rexer traces back the emergence of this conviction and approach—which he terms "a broadly documentary catechism for photography"[33]—to the curatorial vision of North American institutions such as MoMA and the Metropolitan Museum of Art in New York City in the 1960s, when work of artists such as Diane Arbus and Robert Frank helped establish the photographic medium as art, while also curbing its experimental tendencies. The nonhuman, mechanical, and transformative vision as practiced by the followers of the avant-garde tradition never entirely disappeared from the picture, but it did recede into the background in the mid-twentieth century, with the representational approaches coming to stand in for the medium itself.

Improvements in camera technology and color printing no doubt contributed to the strengthening of this link between photography and verisimilitude—and thus to the forgetting of the fact that early photographs were "translations, not transcriptions."[34] If not strictly black and white, the first photographic images were monochrome, with the image established through the play of shadows and lights on a photosensitive surface. Subsequent developments such as the popularization of color photography as well as the increased affordability of the medium and its portability have obfuscated this moment of visual translation by positing an equivalence between an image and its representation. And thus, "As Alan Sekula ... has pointed out, it is the most natural thing in the world for someone to open their wallet and produce a photograph saying 'this is my dog.'"[35] This broadly documentary approach to photography finds a continuation in the amateur use of images on social media. Formal experimentation with filters on Instagram and other sharing platforms only serves to highlight the relatively narrow scope of available subjects and viewpoints, which have all been preprogrammed and preseen by the camera's and editing software's algorithms. The images on Flickr, a platform with arguably more creative ambitions for the medium and its audience, as demonstrated by a quick look at the "recent photos" on any given day, also tend to fall into one of several preestablished and hence visually legitimated representational categories, such as portraiture, landscape, or still life.

Nonhuman versus inhumane photography

It can perhaps be argued that the domination of the humanist tradition in the discourses about photography as well as in its practices in recent decades springs from an attempt to offset the anxiety some feel about photography's mobilization for all kinds of inhumane practices. Although I am using this latter term cautiously—as any theorist of posthumanism worth his or her salt would—I am seeing its value as an indicator of wider social concerns about photography's role and function today. Inhumane practices are practices which are shaped by the cybernetic logic of performance and functionality, but from which responsibility to and for the human as a living, breathing assemblage of culturally specific values, desires, and passions remains distinctly absent. The decision not to publish images of victims in the aftermath of the Hiroshima and Nagasaki bombings out of the unwillingness to disturb the American public illustrates how inhumane values can be perpetuated in and on behalf of photography, even if on the surface such decisions are presented as signs of "humanism" and "care." As Modrak writes: "[I]n the weeks after the bombings, U.S. newspapers and magazines reproduced aerial views of the demolished cities and photographs of the mushroom cloud, images that effectively distanced Americans from the specifics of human suffering and focused on the scientific and military victories of the bomb itself."[36] Yet photography's possible complicity with inhumane practices does not apply only to wartime events. As demonstrated by the contributors to the collection *Seeing from Above: The Aerial View in Visual Culture* edited by Mark Dorrian and Frederic Pousin, the aerial view has become a "symbol of modernity" per se,[37] with the aerial image, as encapsulated by Google Earth, being "the most prominent manifestation and stimulant of this voracious contemporary appetite for views from above."[38] In a separate publication—a 2008 article titled "Mindless Photography"—photography theorist John Tagg also extends this problematic of aerial perception to the highly technologized and seemingly prosperous Western world of the early twenty-first century—a world which knows no warfare within its own territories. I will discuss Tagg's argument in more detail in the following chapter, but, for now, I would like to highlight briefly two developments involving the expansion of photography and photo imaging beyond the human visual capacity that have caused particular distress to Tagg: the regulation of urban traffic by CCTV-controlled systems and the surveillance of space by satellites equipped with cameras. Tagg claims that such practices instantiate an "inorganic machine regime,"[39] as a result of which "photography loses its function as a representation of the ego and the eye."[40] It also establishes a "circuit of mindless assemblage," whose primary role is to "capture the viewer as a function of the State."[41] Nearly a decade later, this instrumental function of image capture is not only executed by the state (although, as we now know thanks to Edward Snowden's revelations, various modern states have become extremely efficient in executing it), but it has also been taken up by Silicon Valley–based technological corporations such as Google, Facebook, and Twitter. In this global networked setup, images arrive to us as data which is then assigned visual characteristics and converted, or rather translated, into what we humans recognize as photographs. It is in this sense that "the activities of visuality are enacted prior to, or beyond, representation."[42]

Tagg laments the fact that the photograph no longer touches the body the way it did in the old *punctum* model, when an individual image affected the viewer beyond the semiotic meaning it conveyed. Today, even if it does travel through the body, as electricity and data, the image is "emptied of any content of palpable sensation."[43] Rob Coley adopts a similar tone in his essay "The Horror of Visuality" when he argues that "a monstrous control operates in the form of computational stimuli, functioning socially and biologically, infiltrating bodily relations so as to cultivate an addiction to its influence."[44] It would perhaps be easy to dismiss Tagg's concern as just a manifestation of his unreformed humanism (and, indeed, I will put this challenge to him later in the book). Yet Tagg's turn to the age-old anxiety about technology seems to have found an unwitting resonance with many contemporary theorists of new media, including Coley, who, after Julian Assange and Snowden, have realized that the promises of a horizontal, collaborative, and truly sharing society made in the early days of the Internet have now been overshadowed by a much darker ensemble of hierarchy and enclosure, and by the monetization of subjectivity on both affective and cellular levels. Indeed, we know now, Coley writes, "that the vast majority of data intercepted from fiber-optic cables is unexamined by humans. It is software that sieves metadata, that conducts complex pattern analysis, that searches for 'triggers.' ... Here, as Deleuze warned us ... , the individual becomes the 'dividual,' the network subject, depersonalized as packets of potential."[45]

This sentiment has been reflected in the emergence of what could be called "noir theory": writing in the shadow of the double eco-eco crisis,[46] when the precariousness of the human has been exposed not just economically but also existentially, as a species. What Tagg identified in 2008 was, therefore, a premonition of a new nonhuman visuality which has a definitive inhumane touch: one that reduces the human to a source of digital capital in social media or treats the human as a visual disturbance in Google Street View (GSV) imagery (see figure 1.3)—or as an accident in drone warfare. As Jon Rafman, a photographer who first came to fame after turning surreal scenes he had found in Google Street View captures into photographic objects, has commented: "I saw GSV ... in some way as the ultimate conclusion of the medium of photography: the world being constantly photographed from every perspective all the time."[47]

Beyond paranoid scholarship

The changed setup of visuality notwithstanding, there is arguably something rather disabling about this form of "paranoid scholarship" as espoused by the likes of Beller and Tagg. This mode of writing, drawing on familiar modernist tropes of decay and demise—be it of the human's connection to his authentic self and his true desire, or of the human species' connection

Figure 1.3

Joanna Zylinska, *Park Road*, London, 2011 (developed as part of the "Excavating Utopia" exhibition for the Look2011 Liverpool International Photography Festival). Park Road is the most common street name in the United Kingdom. There are over a dozen Park Roads in London alone: from the leafy and wealthy thoroughfare bordering Regent's Park in NW1 through to the urban and suburban byways of E10 and SE25. Using Google Street View, I have "visited" these different Park Road locations in order to create a multilayered portrait of the mediated city, always under surveillance. The close-up photographs zoom in on the intimate moments of life as it unfolds on "Park Road, London."

to the natural environment—glosses over the theorist's own pleasure at wallowing in the crisis, and at drawing vital energy for his (and it is, indeed, usually *his*) critical activity. Similar arguments about the alienation of the human I/eye by the media have been put forward before, with connections being made between television watching and laziness, or computer games and violence. Can posthumanist theory offer us tools to develop a more prudent response to this anxiety about the disembodied yet all-embracing condition of the networked media, one that does not involve reinvesting value in the ever so fragile yet also singular and hence individualistic modern subject—a subject who is said to *have the right* to freedom, happiness, and "the look"? Could we think of a standpoint that does not see the critic's mind as a disembodied entity, capable of rising above the networks of data and images while assessing everyone else's entrapment in them? After all, this "god trick" of adopting a view from the top only ends up reconfirming the humanism of its subject, a *primus inter pares* who can elevate himself above the general malaise by the bootstraps of his critical faculties.

As an alternative, I want to propose a different modality of seeing the world around us, one that does not give up on criticality but that operates in a less detached, more immersive way. Sarah Kember and I have previously termed this modality "critical attention." It is a disposition that entails an ethical openness to the world, but also a mindful and corporeal embeddedness in it. In this mode, the view of the situation always comes from within the enfolding of matter (at hand). Critical attention "transcends human-centered intentionality by foregrounding the 'entangled state of agencies' at work in any event" and acknowledges that "what we are referring to as 'human' is only a distinct entity 'in a relational, not an absolute, sense' because, as Barad explains, 'agencies are only distinct in relation to their mutual entanglements; they don't exist as individual elements.'"[48] By itself, critical attention is not a guarantee of any transformation occurring within an established material and sociopolitical setup, but it is a necessary first step in unseeing and hence unknowing those arrangements. Naturally, there are limitations to what such an unseeing and unknowing of the human standpoint can achieve, given that it is being performed by this very human, even if in the spirit of challenging the humanist legacy.

Inspired by the work of Deleuze and Guattari, media theorists have offered various responses to the encroaching visual and nonvisual control by global communication networks. Those responses do not usually posit a disembodied critical eye/I which can rise above its material arrangements to make pronouncements about it. Instead, they put forward a tactic of "circuit-breaking," which is to arise from within the system itself, and which involves creating noise or a glitch within that system. For example, Rob Coley argues that "Vigilant, surreptitious, or false behaviours, which impair algorithmic control, might allow some room to manoeuvre. ... Any countervisuality must be immanent to the weird and noisy middle of mediation."[49] *The question therefore is not whether to be inside or outside the network—whether to tweet or not to tweet, to post on Instagram or not—because such spatial differentiations do not apply in the interlinked era in which we are all becoming (social) media.*[50] *The question, rather, is how to envision a new mode of thinking and acting in the world in which we humans are increasingly positioned as a function of images and media—as their producers, consumers, distributors, clients, corporeal apparatuses, kinesthetic machines, and reflexive surfaces.*

Circuit-breaking envisioners as new revolutionaries

This is precisely the problem posed by Vilém Flusser in his book *Into the Universe of Technical Images*, a poignant analysis of how photographs, television broadcasting, and other mechanically produced images are contributing to "a mutation of our being-in-the-world."[51] The basis of Flusser's argument is the opposition he proposes between traditional images (which are made up of "surfaces") and technical images (which are mosaics assembled from particles). Produced by an apparatus and driven by computational logic, a technical image is a "blindly realized possibility."[52] Flusser harbors no illusions about the human ability to manage the process of producing or even perceiving such images long-term, even if the apparatus—*unlike* the universe, as Flusser is keen to point out—"is subject to human control."[53] But "in the longer term, the autonomy of the apparatus must be liberated from human beings" and behave the way all systems do—i.e., aim toward entropy, or heat death.[54] Yet Flusser's philosophy is not deterministic, even if he rejects any straightforward notion of "free will" and other similar humanist niceties. Acknowledging that information logic shapes the universe and its constituent parts and particles, he identifies the uniqueness of the human in the human's ability and willingness to actively oppose "the implacable tendency of the universe toward disinformation."[55] He also outlines a role (albeit temporary) for envisioners, i.e., "people who try to turn an automatic apparatus against its own condition of being automatic."[56]

The automaticity of photography is executed not only on the level of algorithm—with the majority of cameras manufactured today being able to choose the "correct" exposure, light temperature (aka white balance), and focus—but also on the level of framing. Indeed, on picking up a camera and looking through a viewfinder or at an LCD screen, we are entering the flat perspectival vision that only began to be passed off as natural in Renaissance painting. This point of view is determined by the lens, which is positioned as an extension of the human eye—although it could more accurately be described as the eye's constriction, or "tunneling." As Richard Whitlock, a contemporary photographic artist who has attempted to challenge the visual domination of perspectival vision in his practice, argues:

> Under perspective, the dominant visual mode today, we find ourselves distanced from the things around us and from each other. We become onlookers, outsiders to a world in which objects become things to be to be looked at and studied. We look at them and examine them with impunity, since they belong in a different world. Under perspective nothing returns our gaze, nothing looks us squarely in the face, unless it be positioned at the vanishing-point, in which case it will have vanished.[57]

Experimentation with perspective becomes for Whitlock more than an aesthetic endeavor. Just as it was for Russian constructivists such as Rodchenko, for Whitlock it is an epistemological and ethico-political task, one that challenges the mastery of the vanishing-point vision and reminds us that there are other ways of constructing the world. Whitlock's eight-minute looped moving image *The Street*, composed of many photographs and videos, depicts a nondescript yet visually pleasant street in Thessaloniki, Greece (figure 1.4). Initially we think we are just looking at a photo of an urban corner surrounded by relatively low-rise city mansions, on a sunny day. But then our brain quickly registers visual incongruity: the whole cityscape seems located on one plane, as if it had been folded to eliminate any sense of distance or depth. We also start noticing movement occurring in selected sections of the frame: people bustling about on balconies, laundry fluttering in the wind, cars and bicycles passing in front of our eyes and receding into the background ... except there is no background and the objects that move away retain their size. While the scene looks realistic at first glance, on being seen properly, it starts to resemble a medieval painting, in which

Figure 1.4
Still from Richard Whitlock, *The Street*, HD video, 2012. Courtesy of the artist.

several temporalities are unfolding at the same time, inviting the viewer to travel with her eyes from one scene to another, without offering a linear trajectory between them. The flattened perspective ends up disappointing the (modern) eye that seems to know how to look at the world, and at photographic images of this world, but it also offers the viewer something else in return: an excitation resulting from the brain being pushed to unthink that it knows what it is seeing. *The Street* ends up generating what the artist himself has called "an extraordinary vitality," or an enhanced sensation of life itself—rather than just a mimetic representation of life. While Whitlock is adamant that the project is *not* a direct commentary on the Greek financial crisis unfolding at the time of its production—which is why the collapsed perspective should not be seen as a metonymy for the foreshortening of Greece's political and economic future by the European Union, with its rigid decisions about the management of the Greek debt—he does agree that art should challenge established viewpoints, whether they are about traditional cinematographic vision or "Greek profligacy."[58]

Whitlock thus seems to have become a Flusserian envisioner: someone who has been freed by the apparatus he uses "from the pressure for depth" and who is therefore capable of devoting his "full attention to constructing images."[59] Working with the algorithm, while also being worked by it, envisioners do not step outside the world that they describe: their creations are always born *in medias res*, i.e., in the midst of the technical setup. The liberatory role of the artist as creator is clearly acknowledged by Flusser, but its performance does not involve rage against the machine. Only by becoming nonhuman, by letting him- or herself be ruled by the system, can the envisioner unleash "a wholly unanticipated power of invention."[60] Flusser explains: "For envisioners, those who produce technical images, stand against the world, pointing toward it to make sense of it."[61] They inform the world, or give it form. This conscious in-forming activity is opposed by Flusser to the sheer act of taking images: not every image maker is an in-former; not every photographer is an envisioner. Google's "search by image" feature, introduced in 2011, which, thanks to its pattern recognition algorithm, allows users to find images across the web that bear visual similarities to the one they input into the search box, brings this fact home rather poignantly. As curator and writer Katrina Sluis provocatively teases:

> Think your #srsly #cute #scottishfold #cat is unique? Think your enhanced high-dynamic-range photo of the Franz Josef glacier viewed from the altar window of

Waiho church in the South Island of New Zealand is unique? Think again. The grouping, aggregating and tracking online of images "visually" made it possible to discover images that were *just like yours*, and escape the image-language problem of previous archival taxonomies.[62]

It is not that the photo of the envisioner's cat will necessarily stand out from the Google image grid, or that his or her Instagram feed will be better curated. Rather, a true envisioner, as envisioned by Flusser, should be able to break the feedback loop between the image and the receiver that generates ever new versions of the system's predictable outputs, while also making images themselves "fatter and fatter."[63] This act will need to involve interrupting the ceaseless flow of likes and retweets, of tags and mirror images—in other words, of all those acts of digital creation which forfeit more insubordinate forms of creativity and which thus end up colonizing their users' attention, turning it into affective capital for the still insatiable Giant Tech Monster. Actively promoting dialogical, rewired images, envisioners have the potential to become new revolutionaries, capable of producing "new information, improbable situations."[64] Flusser is not being naïve in imagining what may sound like "a revolution by a camera phone," albeit one used by a circuit-bending artist. Writing in 1985, he is already acutely aware that "it is possible to miss the deadline"[65]—hence the urgency of his vision to reenvision image making as a nonhuman practice of creation, before it becomes truly inhumane: "For the way telematics gadgets are used now, to produce empty chatter and twaddle on a global scale, a flood of banal technical images, definitively cements in place all the gaps between isolated, distracted, key-pressing human beings. Soon there will be nothing more we can say to one another, so now is the moment to talk it over."[66] Have we not left it too late?

British artist Erica Scourti seems to be starting from a similar standpoint, even if the tenor of her work is less dramatic and more playful. Her project *So Like You* developed for Brighton Photo Biennial 2014 responds precisely to this obesity of images today, with everyone's photos from birthday parties, beach holidays, or London looking more or less the same. Rather than take on the role of a digital demiurge who would in-form us *ex nihilo*, Scourti works not only with the apparatus and its code but also with its clients, products, and outcomes. Taking as its starting point selected snapshots from her own family album—the kinds of images most of us have stowed away in the attic, drawer, or, especially the younger among us, on our computer hard drives and Facebook—as well as letters and other personal memorabilia, she runs them through the aforementioned "search by image" function provided by Google to recognize patterns and discover similarities within the web's visual trove. In the process, she collects strangers' images to create multiple mirror versions of her own life—which loses its singularity and becomes a replication of cultural (as well as genetic) code. Yet Scourti's project does not entail a complete abdication of authority and decision making to the machine. The creative gesture is still very much at work here, but it lies in re-forming the perception of what counts as human uniqueness, and of the forms of freedom afforded to us by the apparatuses—cameras, servers, Google, but also the historically and biologically constructed visual apparatus, the environment in which we see and image things, and even the biological makeup of that "we." *So Like You* therefore fits into a certain legacy of the modernist, and humanist, gesture of pointing to an object (a urinal, say) or a visual array and turning it into something else. The artist's gesture is both informative and performative in this case, i.e., it rearranges the seen object's established role, setup, and legacy with a view to making it look different and say something different to us. But it also serves as a premonition of a new era for images, when, as Sluis writes, "a photograph's value might not lie in the specificity of its content but rather in its legibility to machines and the data generated around it. This reflects a paradigm shift in which there is less value to be extracted from individual images than from the relations between them. These relations tell us much about audience sentiment, patterns of consumption and potential future demand for images."[67] So much, then, for the "free" image storage offered by many online platforms today! In the era of images getting fatter and fatter, the free lunch is not being had by their makers, nor, contrary to the rhetoric of the day, is it even being *shared*: it is, rather, being enjoyed, in private, by the few Big Data companies who are getting more and more gluttonous.

Could an envisioner make the Giant Tech Monster choke? Bonamy Devas may be just the man for the job. Working in the tradition of glitch artists who break the established circuits of communication by introducing a malfunction into the system, he has developed *Photographic Tai Chi*, a project whose aim is to fool the cell phone camera's algorithm (figure 1.5). Devas invites audiences to join him in his exercise in circuit bending. The process involves some actual exercise: participants are asked to move their

Figure 1.5
Bonamy Devas, from *Photographic Tai Chi*, 2015. Courtesy of the artist.

bodies in a tai chi–like manner and then photograph each other with the panorama function of their camera switched on, while also trying to do everything one is not supposed to do when shooting panoramas: shake the camera vigorously, move it up and down as well as back and forth, wiggle. The images produced take on all sorts of shapes and sizes, depending on the individual phone's algorithm. They are visually reminiscent of cubist experiments, with their broken lines of vision, multiple viewpoints, and surreal connections between elements. Yet they also differ from modernist masterpieces precisely because of their networked character. The artist encourages the participants to enter what Flusser imagines as a "dialogue" and share the results of their experiments, offline and online. He also participates in the game himself. "By tagging the images #phototaichi and sharing via Instagram, a dispersed, crowd-sourced, evolving, post-human digital entity emerges from the feed,"[68] says Devas. Through this, he can perhaps be said to be taking a step toward what Flusser called "a society of artists"—players who engage in moves and countermoves in order to reprogram the apparatus. Revolutionary engagement today, according to this cybernetics-inspired critic of technology, has to begin "with the silly telematic gadgets. It is these that must be changed and changed in ways that suit their technology. Should this be successful, the centers will collapse of their own accord."[69] Just as China seems scared of Falun Gong, should Silicon Valley, "our new default provider of infrastructure for all basic services,"[70] not be scared of Photographic Tai Chi?

The haptic eye

The projects discussed above seem to open up possibilities not only for telling a different story of photography, one that goes beyond its most conservative, representational, and naturalistic goals, but also for *rethinking perception as unfixed, nonlinear, embodied, and mobile.* Drawing on insights from current theories of, and narratives about, perception, I aim to take some further steps in my effort to shift the understanding of photography and vision beyond their humanist associations and affinities. Interestingly, art history, philosophy, and other humanities fields which have been concerned with vision may prove to be at least as useful in this interrogation as science-based disciplines. This is because scientists working on perception seem to be rather wary of dealing with the conceptual and the conjectural, thus typically limiting their analyses to the mechanics of vision and its psychophysical and physiological aspects. For example, the key textbook of psychology, *Sensation and Perception* by E. Bruce Goldstein, while providing an accessible account of perception as "conscious sensory experience" which "occurs when the electrical signals"[71] representing the object we see are transformed by our brains into our experience of seeing that object, nonetheless pronounces in its opening pages that "we still don't understand perception."[72] Goldstein offers a detailed account of the *mechanics* of perception by explaining: "Perception is determined by an interaction between bottom-up processing, which starts with the image on the receptors, and top-down processing, which brings the observer's knowledge into play."[73] He also claims that recognition and action form its inherent components. Yet, when it comes to making a leap from explaining the mechanics of perception to explaining how nerve impulses, or sodium and potassium molecules flying across a membrane, become transformed into actual perceptual experience—i.e., the perception of a person's face or the experience of the color red—Goldstein admits defeat, not just by himself but by his fellow scientists. He states, "Although researchers have been working to determine the physiological basis of perception for more than a century, the hard version of the mind-body problem is still unsolved. The first difficulty lies in figuring out how to go about studying the problem."[74] For this reason, many researchers focus instead on the physiological problem of the *neural correlate* of consciousness (where consciousness can be roughly seen to stand in for our experiences).

It is therefore to philosophers and visual theorists that we should turn in an attempt to rethink perception, not only because such scholars are more willing to take on open-ended questions but, most importantly, because they approach perception as a cultural problem and not just a physiological one. As Crary has poignantly argued, perception and vision "have no autonomous history. ... [W]hat determines vision at any given historical moment is not some deep structure, economic base, or world view, but rather the functioning of a collective assemblage of disparate parts on a single social surface. It may even be necessary to consider the observer as a distribution of events located in many different places."[75] An art historian by training, Crary does an excellent job in tracing back the changing ideas of perception and vision across Western history to demonstrate how the dominant model of vision as linear, based on a straight ray of light emanating from God—even if it is not scientifically accurate[76]—has shaped our modern understanding of perception. He cites the camera obscura, "with its monocular aperture," as becoming "a more perfect terminus for a cone of vision, a more perfect incarnation of a single point than the awkward binocular body of the human subject."[77] The camera obscura thus ended up stabilizing perception for centuries to come. It was only in the early to mid nineteenth century that the increased physical and conceptual mobility of the human subject in the world encouraged some new articulations of the human's relationship to, and cognizance of, his or her environment. Yet Crary also manages to trace an alternative, even if suppressed, history of perception, which he terms the "anti-optical notion of sight,"[78] with thinkers as diverse as Berkeley, Goethe, and Schopenhauer pointing to more subjective and more sensuous aspects of vision, and hence to its inherent tactility. While the stereoscope opened up the possibility of embracing the physical side of the act of perception, this possibility was overcome by that of the photographic camera, which managed to remap and subsume the phenomenological and the tactile within the optical.

Yet it is important to emphasize here that it is not photography as such that led to this withdrawal and reductionism, but rather its unbroken association with the linearity and fixity of vision. Crary explains that photography "recreated and perpetuated the fiction that the 'free' subject of the camera obscura was still viable. Photographs seemed to be a continuation of older 'naturalistic' pictorial codes, *but only because* their dominant conventions were restricted to a narrow range of technical possibilities (that is, shutter speeds and lens openings that rendered elapsed time invisible and recorded objects in focus)."[79] However, as I have tried to show throughout this chapter, photography from its beginning has developed a parallel trajectory of nonnaturalistic experiments, working against the equipment's technical limitations or even embracing them as modes of artistic expression. When representationalism is not the main goal of image making, the camera's technology does not have to be seen as "restricted" and "narrow" but can rather be embraced as facilitating a different way of imaging. But, with the technological developments in optics and electronics, the naturalistic set of visualizing conventions became the norm, thus firming up the dominant understanding of photography as a practice of representation.

My effort to remap vision as nonhuman, decentered, and distributed has by no means been driven by a desire to elide the human form from the history of photography. Even though the "pure perception of modernism," as Crary puts it, was premised on "the denial of the body, its pulsings and phantasms, as the ground of vision,"[80] the story of nonhuman vision I have been telling here by casting light on nonhuman and nonrepresentational photography has in fact been *an attempt to reclaim vision's embeddedness and embodiment*—and thus to reinsert the human back into the picture beyond the strict subject-object dichotomy. Yet grasping vision as distributed allows us to sever the "ray of light" believed to connect the human observer in a straight line with the divine on the one hand and with the perceived object on the other. This gesture has been in step with Haraway's intimation that "Vision can be good for avoiding binary oppositions."[81] I would thus like to insist, together with Haraway, "on the embodied nature of all vision and so reclaim the sensory system that has been used to signify a leap out of the marked body and into a conquering gaze from nowhere."[82] We could perhaps go so far as to embrace what Haraway calls, after coral and ethnography researcher Eva Hayward,[83] "the haptic visual," whereby vision is figured "as touch, not distance, as entwined with, or negatively curving in loops and frills, not surveying from above."[84] There is a clear ethical imperative in this kind of material-conceptual refiguration of visuality "as a becoming-with or being-with, as opposed to surveying-from."[85]

Interestingly, architecture has been at the forefront of developing alternative theories of perception that go beyond the linear visual model, as it is an explicitly visual and sensual practice, focused on the relationship between bodies, buildings, and environments. In his tellingly titled book *The Eyes of the Skin: Architecture and the Senses*, Finnish architect, educator, and writer Juhani Pallasmaa argues against the denigration of the body in perception. Resisting the traditional positioning of the eye outside time and history by many philosophers, and the subsequent adoption of this model by artists and architects—a culmination of which can be found in the visual distancing of certain forms of modernism, with buildings designed to be looked at rather than dwelled in—Pallasmaa develops his theory of the eye as skin instead. His theory of vision as haptic rather than just ocular revisits the suppressed sensuous dimension of architectural history, going back all the way to ancient Greek architecture, with its "haptic sensibility." He argues that "The sense of sight may incorporate, and even reinforce, other sense modalities."[86] In this framework, the eye is dethroned from its function as the ultimate source of knowledge and arbiter of meaning in the world. It is rather redefined as just one of the senses, with all of them seen as "extensions of the sense of touch—as specializations of the skin."[87] Interestingly, one of the architectural designs by Pallasmaa himself that returns most often in his book (and in its afterword by Peter MacKeith) as both a concept and an image is that of a door handle: a seemingly innocuous architectural detail that is also a literal invitation to touch the building. We could therefore conclude that Pallasmaa's theory of the haptic eye is close to my concept of nonhuman vision because it repositions seeing as an active and dynamic process of sensuous interaction between surfaces. While stripping linear, ocular perception of its dominant role in cognition and world making, it also enriches our understanding of how perception works by pointing to the fact that we are already *of the world*—and that we emerge *with it.*[88]

Pallasmaa's ideas develop from the ecological theory of perception outlined by psychologist James Gibson in the mid-1950s. Premised on the assumption that the point of observation is mobile rather than fixed, Gibson's theory moves away from the model of perception as the transmission of an image from an object to the eye (or the brain). Instead, he understands vision as a panoramic perceptual system, with both the eye and the brain being parts of that system. This model is a direct opposite of what Haraway described as a "god trick" of infinite vision "from nowhere": in Gibson's ecological model of perception, "to perceive the world is to coperceive oneself."[89] According to Gibson, vision is kinesthetic, requiring a movement of the perceiving agent's body and delivering simultaneous information about, and awareness of, "the world" and "the self in the world."[90] There is an ethical dimension to Gibson's proposition: concerned that we modern humans "live boxed-up lives,"[91] he is intent on returning us to ways of seeing that are, if not entirely nonhuman, then at least premodern-adult-human: those of our ancestors, children, and animals. Importantly, Gibson is keen to liberate us from the fixities of not just our viewpoints but also our standpoints, and to get us to look around, literally. This involves challenging the camera/shutter model of perception because, in his understanding (supported by scientific research), our eyes are never fixed: "The eyes normally search, explore, or scan, and there are seldom fewer than several saccadic jumps per second. They look at but do not fixate."[92] Being in constant movement—following in a smooth way, searching

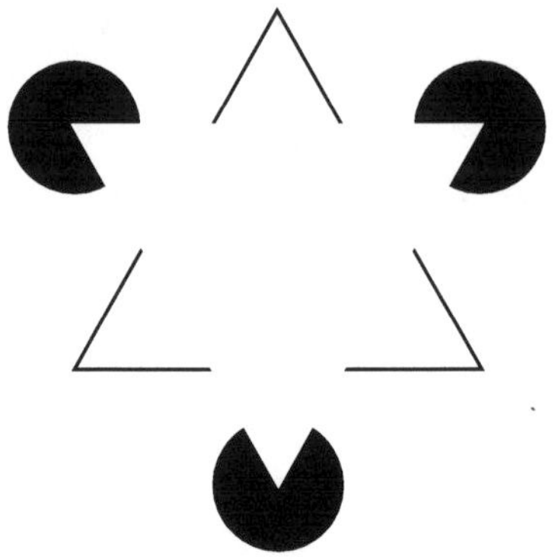

Figure 1.6

Fibonacci, *Kanizsa Triangle*. Such "kanizsa figures," named after researcher Gaetano Kanizsa, trigger "the percept of an illusory contour by aligning Pac-Man-shaped inducers in the visual field, such that the edges form a shape" ("Illusory Contours," https://en.wikipedia.org/wiki/Illusory_contours), 2007, license: CC BY-SA 3.0.

in a jerky manner, and experiencing a small low-frequency tremor—our eyes are "drawn to hard edges"[93] as points of stoppage on this inevitably blurry journey of perceptive movement. Rebekah Modrak explains: "The eye and brain are accustomed to using contours as a way to understand the environment." Even though nothing in the world is actually made up of lines and edges, "the eye and brain have evolved systems that encode these differentiating signals and process the information in such a deceptively casual manner that we start to believe that edges and lines are visible components of the 'real world.'"[94] We could therefore go so far as to suggest that *our visual apparatus introduces edges and cuts into the imagistic flow: it cuts up the environment so that we can see it, and then helps us stitch it back together again* (figure 1.6). With this idea, we arrive at the concept of perception as active, or even world-making, rather than just secondary and responsive.

The ethical force of the cut

In light of the analysis above, I would like to suggest that vision itself can be understood as photographic. Similar propositions have been made before, but they were premised on a very different model of both vision and photography, with the act of seeing considered as purely mechanical, the eye as a passive vehicle of image production, and photography, to cite Susan Sontag, as "an act of non-intervention."[95] The aim of this chapter has been to challenge such passive models and to position photography as a zoetic, life-giving force. It has also been to return life and movement to the very process of human perception—a process which needs to become (again) other-than-human if it is to be truly liberated from its physical and conceptual constraints. We are entering here the realm of photography understood not as a passive recording of the world but as an active process of shaping it through making cuts in the imagistic flow. Photography can play a key role in the liberation of vision from its conceptual and physical rigidity by allowing us to take stock of the imagistic flow—and of the insertions made in it by our visual and cognitive apparatus. So, rather than follow the "flow of images equals the flow of life" line of thinking, which has led some theorists—from Bergson and Deleuze through to Gibson—to proclaim that "Moviemakers are closer to life than picture makers,"[96] I want to return to photography here as a quintessential practice of both life and the cut. The cover of Henri Cartier-Bresson's photobook *The Decisive Moment*, featuring a paper gouache cutout by Henri Matisse, serves as a telling illustration of this point. Even though the humanist narrative of Cartier-Bresson's eponymous idea, as encapsulated in his rather conventional photographs of "the Occident" and "the Orient,"[97] promotes the idea of the photographer as a self-contained focused eye that can isolate chance events and grab them, Matisse's cover returns us to the mechanical aspect of photography as the practice of cutting undertaken in alliance with various apparatuses: the eye, the brain, the camera. This is to say, cutting is not a purely human-centric process because its driving mechanism exceeds human control, but there do, of course, exist instances of cutting which the human subject can make her own, and of which she can give an account. Drawing attention to the cut is therefore also a way of reintroducing the moment of ethico-political decision into the perceptive flow. As Kember and I have argued in *Life after New Media*, "The process of cutting is one of the most fundamental and originary processes through which we emerge as 'selves' as we engage with matter and attempt to give it (and ourselves) form. Cutting reality into small pieces—with our eyes, our bodily and cognitive apparatus, our language, our memory, and our technologies—we enact separation and relationality as the two dominant aspects of material locatedness in time."[98] If vision is indeed nonhuman and if its liberation can be achieved only through displacing it from its humanist anchorings and models, we need a cut to be more than just a technique—one that we encounter not only in photography but also in film making, sculpture, writing, or, indeed, any other technical practice that involves transforming matter: it must also be seen as an ethical imperative ("Cut!").[99] Given that perception involves the insertion of edges and lines into the flow of vision, a process that is to a large extent nonconscious and not just human, we may need to introduce reflection to this process and pose the question of whether it is possible to recut the world anew, to a different size and measure, beyond the "god trick" of the straight line and the visual gluttony of the insatiable eye fuck.

Nonhuman photography: A postscript

The images that make up the *Active Perceptual Systems* project (figure 1.7) were taken over a period of two years with an automated "intelligent" wearable camera called the Autographer. Originally designed as a mnemonic device for people with Alzheimer's, the Autographer was subsequently remarketed by the OMG Life company as a media gadget tool for the "always-on" generation. On selected days between 2014 and 2016, I wore the camera in various everyday situations: on a city walk, in a holiday resort, in an art gallery, in a lecture theater (when talking about nonhuman photography), at home. Inconspicuous due to its resemblance to a small necklace yet clearly visible, the camera randomly took photographs at frequent intervals. I then uploaded the photos to my computer. My decision to wear the camera on a given day, switch it on, and then select and process the images (originally taken in color) was coupled with the decision of the camera algorithm regarding *what* to photograph and *when*. The machinic behavior was nevertheless influenced by the way I moved my body, enacting a form of immersive, corporeal perception that broke with the representationalist linearity of perspectival vision while also retaining human involvement in the multiple acts of image capture. The human element was also foregrounded in the subsequent editing activities: I was faced with over 18,000 images from which I chose several dozen. The selection process was akin to making careful incisions in the image flow, with a view to setting up narrative connections—some of which were not necessarily present in the original sequence. In an age of constant surveillance—from CCTV cameras installed in city centers, on public transport, and in shopping malls, through to self-monitoring via the constant recording of our lives with cell phones—*Active Perceptual Systems* is designed as a commentary on this incessant fabrication of images: *of us*, but also *by us*. It also raises the question of whether, in the age of "image obesity," the creative photographer can be seen as first and foremost an editor: a Flusserian in-former who provides structure to the imagistic flow *after* the images have been taken.

Figure 1.7
Joanna Zylinska, from *Active Perceptual Systems*, 2014–2016.

Figure 1.7 (continued)

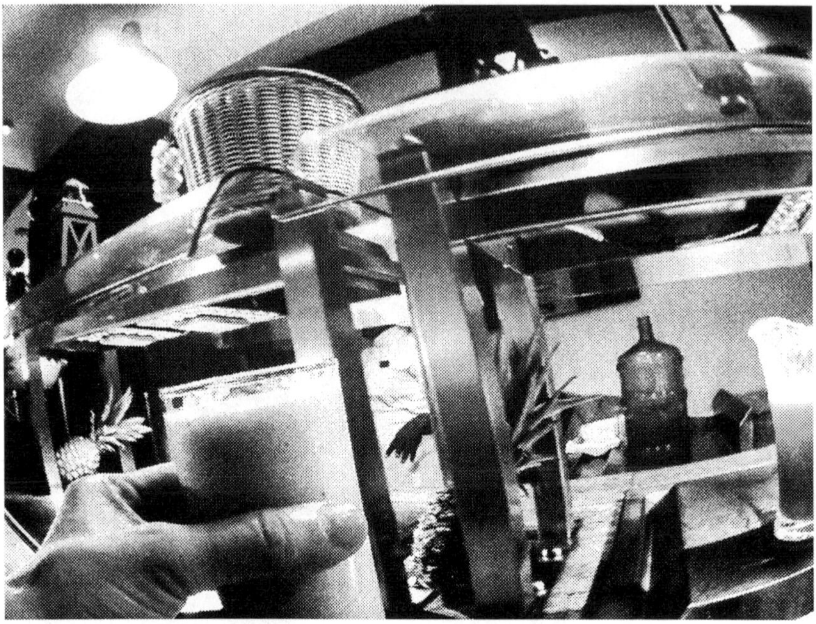

Figure 1.7 (continued)

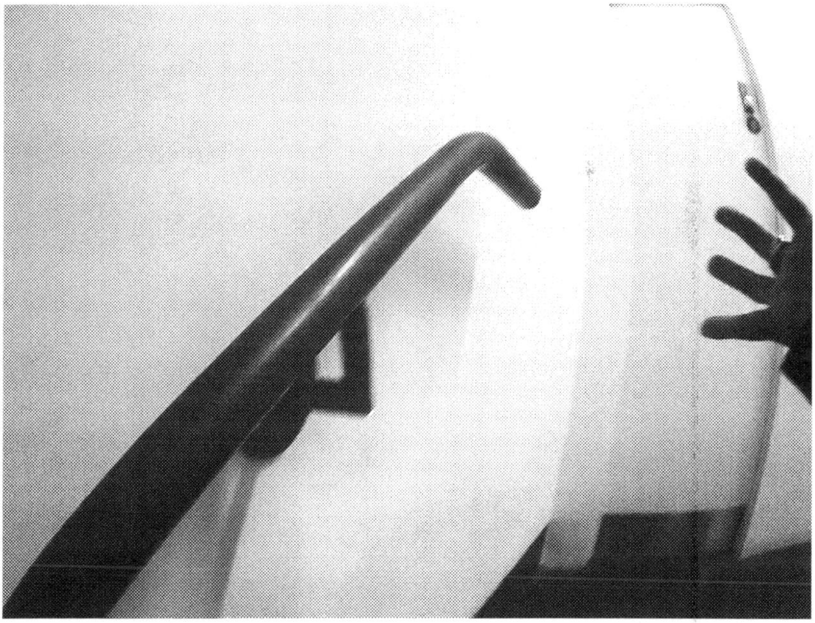

Figure 1.7 (continued)

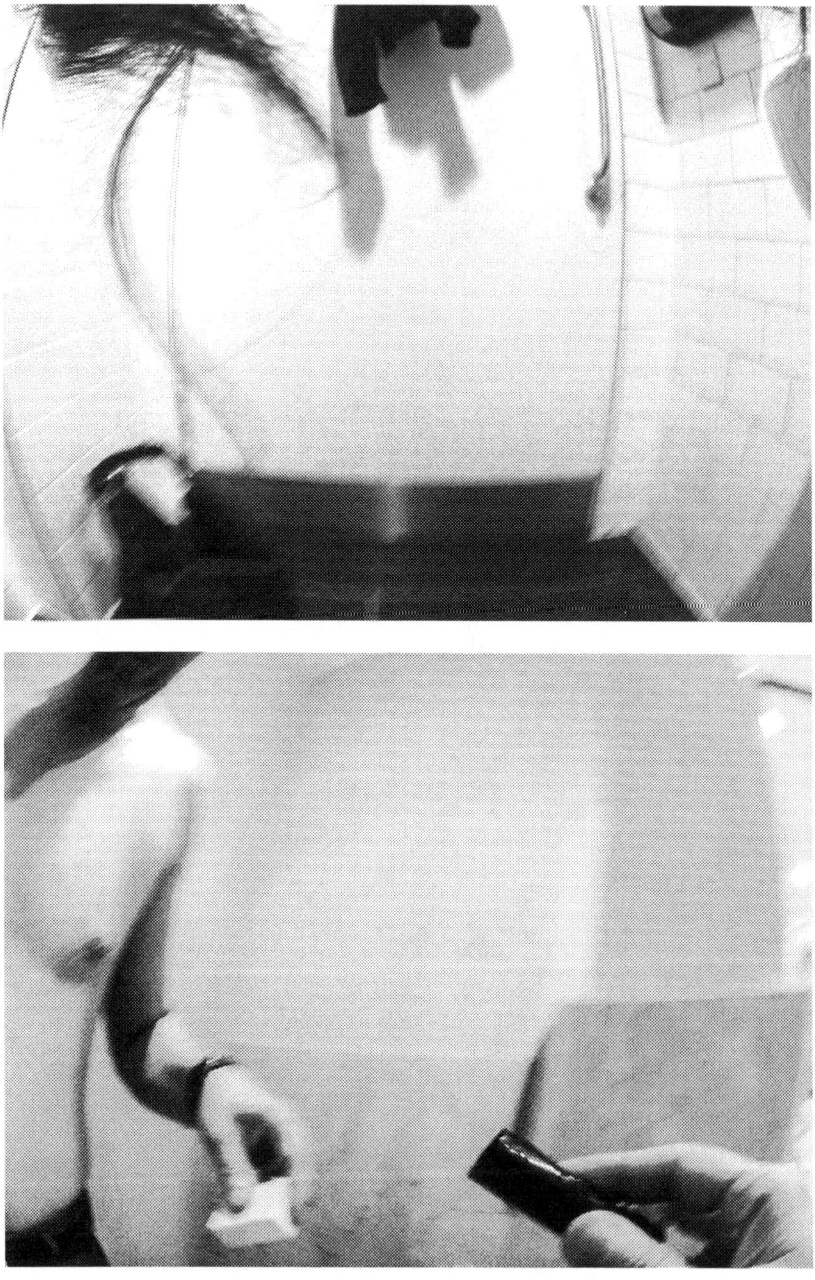

Figure 1.7 (continued)

2 The Creative Power of Nonhuman Photography

iEarth

This chapter offers a philosophical exposition of the concept of "nonhuman photography" that forms the axis of the book. It also explores the photographic medium's creative, or life-making, power. As I explained in the preface, "nonhuman photography" embraces three different but often entwined ontological categories: photographs that are not *of*, *by*, or *for* the human. Yet the ultimate aim of this chapter, and the book as a whole, is not just to enumerate examples; rather, it is to suggest that there is more to photography than meets the (human) eye and that *all photography bears a nonhuman trace*. With this perhaps still somewhat cryptic proposition in mind, let us take a short detour from philosophizing to look at a photographic project of mine as a way to provide a bridge from the previous chapter on nonhuman vision—as well as to introduce the key ideas behind the argument that follows.

Titled *iEarth* (figure 2.1), the project offers a vision of natural spaces that are actually (wo)man-made while also bearing an imprint of a technological tool. Manufactured from a children's diorama kit, these "unnatural landscapes" (in their original online gif version) dazzle with color and lushness, displaying the kind of greenery that is more associated with media representations of nature than with "nature itself." The bird's-eye view of the landscapes evokes the perspective of satellite images of different locations, both remote and familiar, which we associate with Google Earth or Microsoft's Virtual Earth—a viewing position I discussed in the previous chapter under the rubric of "nonhuman vision." This particular perspective has a double function: it denaturalizes the familiar while also creating an illusion of immediacy, proximity, and visual mastery. Technology is mobilized on a

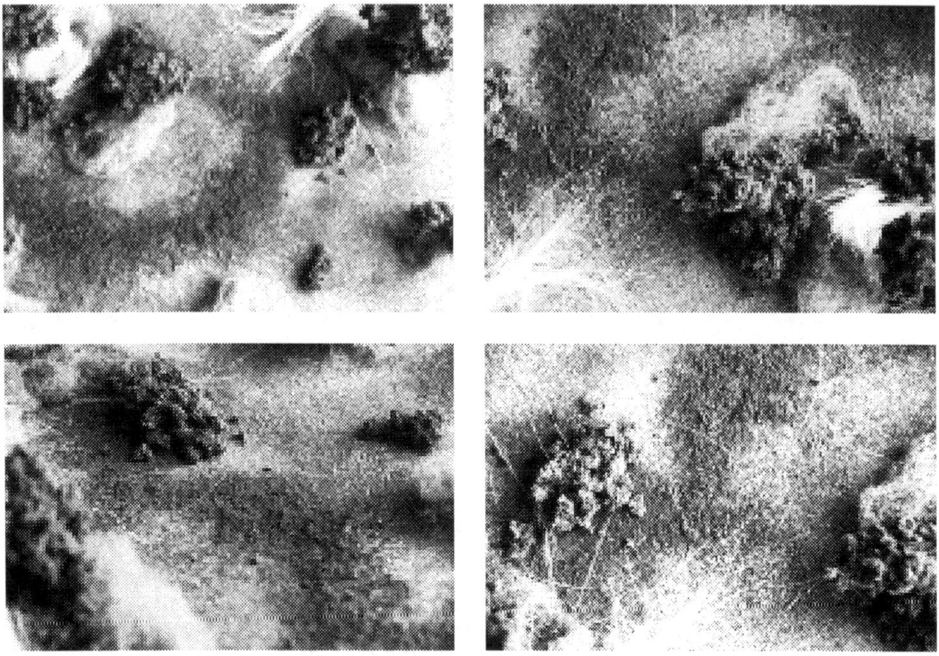

Figure 2.1
Joanna Zylinska, stills from *iEarth*, 2014. For the gif version, see Joanna Zylinska, "iEarth," *ADA: A Journal of Gender, New Media, and Technology* 5 (May 2014), http://adanewmedia.org/2014/07/issue5-zylinska/.

number of levels in this project: in the crafting of the diorama, the taking of the image, the pixelation of the photographs, and then, in the last instance, the gif animation. Pixelation and animation are more than just a visual or conceptual gimmick here: their implementation was intended to destabilize the relationship between "nature" and "artifact," between "the real" and "the virtual," in the constitution of the diorama landscapes. Yet instability is, of course, already inherent in the very concept of "landscape"—a concept which is one of the cornerstones of traditional photography. Besides, *iEarth* is not actually a landscape but rather *a photograph* (or rather a series of photographs) *of an approximation of a landscape*, and hence a copy of a copy—without an original. The work suggests that *photographic re/presentation, be it analog or digital, is always already technological*, and also that what we think of as "landscape" or "nature" comes to us via the physical and technological effort of capturing, carving, molding, and freezing, by means of a whole sequence of technological tools such as ploughs, tractors, excavators, secateurs, easels, paintbrushes, and cameras. "The cut," as previously argued, is therefore essential both to temporarily stabilize the world into entities and to make temporarily stable, light-induced images (aka photographs) out of the flow of duration.

This somewhat serious-sounding philosophical agenda is underpinned by a more playful desire on my part to poke fun with this work at the monumentalization of nature in the work of meditative "large-format" landscape photographers, such as Andreas Gursky and Edward Burtynsky—and at the "view from nowhere" perspective they often adopt. The "now you see it, now you don't" aspect introduced by the pixelation and gif animation, coupled with what may look like excessive acceleration or even computer error, is aimed to push the viewer to engage with these images physically, through squinted eyes. The aesthetics of *iEarth* thus issues an injunction: the viewer has to become actively involved in the process of seeing by moving her head, blinking, or even looking away from the dizziness caused by this pseudo-sublime, one we can associate with the oft-frustrating and jaggy visuality of the early Internet. The homonymy between the "I" and the "eye" in *iEarth* is a commentary on our practices of looking at the world but also on our narcissism when engaging with it. The brandlike title was chosen to remind us that "nature" has become a commodity, a product we fetishize and yearn for. With this, *iEarth* perhaps inscribes itself ironically in what Sarah Kember has termed "iMedia," with the posited presence of the polyvalent "I" appended to a brand being "an illusion that refuses to be revealed."[1] The subject of iMedia is thus "isolated in the production and consumption of their own media":[2] an illusion that extends to the narcissistically endowed humanist vision of the Earth that is often seen as existing for "our" dominion, benefit, and pleasure. Just like Dziga Vertov's kino-eye, *iEarth* also foregrounds the technical process of the production of the world through biological and photographic vision. Through this process, it can perhaps help us look at the Earth—which for us humans tends to stand for "the world"—and at ourselves on this Earth, with a different eye.

Seeing our planet from afar has by now become a familiar device for creating an illusion of telluric unity (aka "globalization"). We can think here of two iconic images: the 1968 *Earthrise* and the 1972 *Blue Marble* (figures 2.2 and 2.3). In his illuminating article "Earth Imaging: Photograph, Pixel, Program," Chris Russill explains how these two photographs were implemented

Figure 2.2
Earthrise (rotated), taken during the Apollo 8 mission, 1968, courtesy of NASA. Public domain.

by Stewart Brand, publisher of the *Whole Earth Catalog*—a countercultural magazine-cum-product review manifesting a unique mix of West Coast environmentalism and entrepreneurship—to conjure up a particular image of both present and future. Brand's incorporation of the two images into his publication was aimed at creating a collective vision of humanity while also allowing this humanity to see "itself from outside": a vision intended to evoke a sense of responsibility for this "delicate jewel in vast immensities of hard-vacuum space." "Suddenly humans had a planet to tend to," declared Brand.[3] Russill is particularly intrigued by the visual mechanisms involved in conveying this message, arguing that Brand "rooted earth imaging in a

Figure 2.3
The Blue Marble, taken during the Apollo 17 mission, 1972, courtesy of NASA. Public domain.

narrow history dominated by the episodic adventures of the space exploration paradigm."[4] He goes on to show that this view from above that is supposed to establish a commonality actually ends up being what I termed in the previous chapter, with Haraway's help, a "view from nowhere." Indeed, not a single astronaut on Apollo 17, from whom the image originated, actually did *see* the Earth as depicted in the *Blue Marble* image, as they were unable to position their bodies close enough to the window to look out: instead, the images captured had been shot "from the hip."[5] More interestingly, they all subsequently claimed individual authorship of that image. There was also, perhaps unsurprisingly, a lot of technical manipulation involved in the production of the two photographs. On receiving the raw data from the space cameras, the image processors at NASA labs adjusted and "reoriented" the copies obtained; they also chose the color scheme "to align with cultural expectations for popular consumption."[6] While the evenly lit Earth in the *Blue Marble* is the result of the adjustment of lights and shadows as well as tight cropping,[7] the image of *Earthrise* as we know it has been shifted from a portrait to a landscape orientation in order to create an illusion of the Earth "rising" over the moon, with a view to subjugating the nonhuman eye of the space camera to the visual mastery of the human.

The rationale behind these manipulations, Russill argues, was to repress "the strangeness and difficulty in seeing the earth,"[8] a perceptual shift that was supposed to help promote the environmental agenda. We cannot actually *see* environmental damage or climate change—to really "see" them, we would need to capture electromagnetic radiation that is illegible to the human, or map the rise in ocean temperatures over a prolonged period of time and then translate the data streams obtained into diagrams, graphs, and other kinds of visualizations[9]—and yet images like *Earthrise* and the *Blue Marble* constitute the Earth as a graspable object while issuing a veiled threat of "it" being taken away from "us."[10]

The "pixel image" of the Earth included in Al Gore's consciousness-raising environmental documentary *An Inconvenient Truth* (2006) and adopted from astronomer Carl Sagan's "Pale Blue Dot" visualization of our planet as an insignificant blurry square captured by Voyager 1 from the distance of around 6 billion kilometers is a case in point (figure 2.4), even though, through its nonrepresentational aspect, it seemingly stands in contrast to the two photographs discussed above. As Russill highlights, "The 'whole earth' fills most of the frame and suggests the priority of the global in understanding our earthly condition. Sagan's dot, on the other hand, hints at a cosmic zoom by adopting a perspective of an interstellar machine probe."[11] Yet the fantasy of the human grasp of "the object" (be it the Earth or climate change) is manifested by both the photos and the pixel, reduced in scale to allow us to see this "it," and take control. All three images are therefore very much part of the logic of Kember's iMedia. They adopt nonhuman vision as attempts at visual mastery, thus repressing the strangeness of what is being perceived, while reducing *what is being perceived* to *an object of perception*—and hence also possession, (technical and biological) manipulation, and, ultimately, human-charged salvation. What the actual

Figure 2.4
The Pale Blue Dot, taken by the Voyager 1 space probe at the request of astronomer Carl Sagan, 1990, courtesy of NASA, annotated by Joanna Zylinska. Public domain.

standpoint for this salvation is and how we should go about embarking upon it remain unknown: in images like this, reduced to our human scale and viewpoint, the human ends up enlarging *him*self as an occupier and owner of the actual, nonironic "iEarth."[12] The proto-Anthropocene sensibility is thus already reduced to a belief that, as Nicholas Mirzoeff suggests, "somehow the war against nature that Western society has been waging for centuries is not only right; it is beautiful and it can be won"[13]—because, at the end of the day, we can hold the Earth in our hand, or shrink it to a pale blue dot. The somewhat excessive pixelation of my (definitely ironic) *iEarth* can therefore perhaps be read as an invitation to look otherwise: not from close up or far away but rather (from) askew, and also through, with, and as part of. It can also signal an attempt to recut and reframe Al Gore's "pixel as family portrait," to use Russill's apt term, in nonhumanist terms in order to open up a less masterful and less self-aggrandizing visuality of the Anthropocene, with its unequal distribution of shadows and lights.

Photography as philosophy

iEarth and its more serious visual predecessors are not meant to serve as direct illustrations of the concept of nonhuman photography this chapter outlines. However, they do lead us to a wider problematic of human-nonhuman relations, and raise the politico-ethical question of human responsibility in a world in which the agency of the majority of actants—such as wind, meteorites, rain, or earthquakes—goes beyond that of human decision or will, even if it may be influenced by human action. The question of human responsibility in the universe, in which we are quintessentially entangled on both a cellular and a cosmic level (with all of us being "made of starstuff," as Carl Sagan remarked in his documentary TV series *Cosmos*), is an important one. *Even if*, unlike Stewart Brand, *we cannot be entirely sure what this fragile human "we" actually stands for, the responsibility to face, and give an account of, the unfoldings of this world—which is made up of human and nonhuman entities and relations—belongs to us humans in a singular way*. Philosophy, in particular ethics, has typically been a way of addressing the problem of responsibility.[14] But written linear argument is only one mode of enquiry through which this problem can be approached. Alongside philosophical writing, in recent years I have been attempting to experiment with other, less verbal modes of addressing ethical and political issues: those enabled by art, and more specifically photography—of which the *iEarth* project is an example. These experiments have been driven by one overarching question: Is it possible to *practice philosophy as a form of art*, while also *engaging in photography and image making as ways of philosophizing*? The reason photography may lend itself to this kind of cross-modal experimentation is because of its ontological, or world-making (rather than *just* representational), capabilities. We can turn here for support to literary critic Walter Benn Michaels, who, while upholding "the impossibility (and the undesirability) of simply denying the indexicality of the photograph,"[15] also argues, "It is precisely because there are ways in which photographs *are not* just representations that photography and the theory of photography have been so important."[16] My proposition about photography's ontological capabilities entails a stronger claim than the one made by Michael Fried in the conclusion to his book, *Why Photography Matters as Art as Never Before*. There, photography as practiced by representatives of what Fried calls "the anti-theatrical tradition," such as Jeff Wall, Thomas Struth, or Berndt and Hilda Becher, is positioned as "an ontological medium" because it "makes a positive contribution" to ontological thought via its engagement with issues such as absorption and worldhood.[17] While for Fried photography just *makes philosophy better*, my claim in this book is that *photography makes philosophy*, full stop—and also, more importantly, that *photography makes worldhood*, rather than just commenting on it.

It may seem at this point that what was meant to be an account of nonhuman photography is revealing itself to be quite strongly attached to the concept of the human—as philosopher, photographer, or art critic. This is true, because there is nothing more humanist than any unexamined singular gesture of trying to "move beyond the human." My ambition here, as in my other work,[18] is therefore to explore the possibility of continuing to work with the concept of the human *in light of the posthumanist critique*,[19] taking the latter seriously as both an injunction and a set of possibilities. The reasons for this proposed retention of the human have nothing to do with any kind of residual humanism or species nostalgia. Instead, they spring from the recognition of *the strategic role of the concept of the human as a temporary stabilization in any kind of artistic, creative, political, or ethical project*, while also remembering that in many works of critical theory the human has been revealed to be nothing more than a fantasy of unity. This fantasy has involved the occlusion of the human's dependency, both material and conceptual, on other living and nonliving entities and processes. Seen as too Eurocentric and masculinist by postcolonial and feminist theory, the human has also been revealed by various science disciplines to be just an arbitrary cutoff point in the line of species continuity on the basis of characteristics shared across the species barrier: communication, emotions, or tool use. This (non- or posthumanist) human which my book retains as the anchor point of its inquiry is thus premised on the realization that we are in (philosophical) trouble as soon as we start speaking about the human, but it also recognizes the historical entanglement of this concept and the way it has structured our thinking, philosophy, and art for many centuries.[20] So, onto a posthumanist theory of nonhuman photography, as articulated by a human, all too human, philosopher-photographer ...

Toward nonhuman photography (and all the way back)

To anchor our discussion of nonhuman photography in scholarly debates, I want to look at two important texts in photography theory in which the relationship between human and nonhuman agents, technologies, and imaging practices has been addressed explicitly: the 2008 essay by John Tagg titled "Mindless Photography" briefly mentioned in the previous chapter, and a 2009 book by Fred Ritchin, *After Photography*. Tagg's essay is a commentary on the supposed withering of the critical paradigm in photographic practice and its interpretation, a paradigm articulated by Victor Burgin in his 1984 seminal text *Thinking Photography* and subsequently adopted by many scholars and students of photography. In his article Tagg references two then-recent phenomena which, in his view, had radically altered the relationship between photography and the human: (1) the CCTV system introduced in 2003 to monitor the implementation of a traffic congestion charge in central London, and (2) the visual rendering of data captured by a radio telescope, in June 2005, of solar dust cloud radiation in the Taurus Molecular Cloud, where the data represented an event that "took place in 1585, or thereabouts."[21] While in the 1970s and early 1980s "photography was framed as a site of human meanings that called the human into place," the more recent developments cited by Tagg are said to have undermined "this confident assumption."[22] Tagg seems disturbed by the fact that, in the London traffic surveillance system, the relationship between the embodied human subject and the technical apparatus has been irrevocably broken, with the technological circuit which consists of "cameras, records, files and computers"[23] doing away with visual presentation, "communication, psychic investment, a subject, or even a bodily organ"[24]—until the visual data concerning the car with a given number plate that has missed the congestion charge payment reaches the court. Tagg is similarly troubled by the severance of the relationship between photography and human sensation, between stimulus and response, in space photography. (Unlike Stewart Brand, he does not find it reassuring to be able to hold whole planets, including our own "Blue Marble," in our gaze.) Instead, Tagg goes so far as to suggest that in those new technological developments,

> photography loses its function as a representation of the ego and the eye and even as a pleasure machine built to excite the body. In place of those figures, photography is encountered as an utterly dead thing; mindless in a much blunter sense than imagined [by Burgin]. ... [It is] driving towards a systemic disembodiment that, accelerating in the technologies of cybernetics and informatics, has sought to prepare what has been hailed as the "postbiological" or "posthuman" body for its insertions into a new machinic enslavement.[25]

Photography that is unable to provide stimulation and pleasure for the human is then immediately linked by Tagg with mindlessness, emptiness, and ultimately death. With this articulation, Tagg may seem to be engaging in a belated attempt to rescue photography from its long-standing association with mortality, and to retrospectively postulate *the possibility that photography can act as a life-giving force*. However, this no doubt radical possibility, briefly hinted at in the passage cited above, is immediately withdrawn. Photography does not deliver life to the human anymore and, for Tagg, it is only the human that can be both life's subject and its arbiter. This is, of course, a familiar philosophical gesture, first enacted by Aristotle, whereby technology is reduced to a mere tool for human existence, survival, or improvement and is then assessed on the basis of how well it performs this function (rather than being understood as a dynamic network of forces, as Michel Foucault and Bernard Stiegler respectively suggest, or as an "intrinsic correlation of functions"[26] between the human and the apparatus, as Vilém Flusser apprehends it). Conceived in these instrumental terms, as the human's opponent and enemy—and not part of the originary techno-logic that brings forth the human in the world, and the world itself as a space occupied by human and nonhuman entities—photography must inevitably fail.

It would be unfair not to mention the political motivation that underpins Tagg's argument. His concern with "machinic enslavement" is driven by what he sees as the deprivation of the human subject of both corporeal integrity and political subjectivity as a result of the encroachment on our lives of those new photo-imaging technologies, in which "there is nothing to be seen."[27] This concern no doubt has become even more pressing in the era of global networked surveillance enacted by the likes of the NSA, GCHQ, Facebook, and Google. Yet to blame photography for the immoral and inhumane actions of its developers or users is to misidentify the enemy, while also weakening the power of a political critique developed in its ambit. In his essay Tagg takes some significant steps toward analyzing the changes occurring in photographic practice at the beginning of the twenty-first century but then recoils in horror from the brink of his own analysis. What could have served as a stepping stone toward developing both a radical posthumanist photography theory *and* a radical posthumanist political analysis ends up retreating into a place of nostalgia for the human of yesteryear, one who was supposedly in control of both his personal body and the body politic but who can now only tilt at windmills—which are turning into drones in front of his very eyes.

If only Tagg had allowed himself to hear the exhortation from another photography theory radical, Fred Ritchin! Admittedly, Ritchin's work is not free from the sense of nostalgia espoused by Tagg: in *After Photography* Ritchin reveals that he misses the time when people believed in images and when images could be used to solve conflicts and serve justice. Yet, even though his book opens with a rather dispiriting account of the changes occurring to the photographic medium and its representationalist ambitions, it ends with an affirmation of *life in photography*. Dazzled by the horizon of scale revealed by telescopy and physics, much as Tagg was, Ritchin nevertheless admits that "in the digital-quantum world, it might be just possible ... to use an emerging post-photography to delineate, document, and explore the posthuman. To dance with ambiguity. To introduce humility to the observer, as well as a sense of belonging. To say yes, and simultaneously, no."[28]

(Always) nonhuman photography

It is precisely in this critical-philosophical spirit, of saying yes, and simultaneously, no, that my opening proposition that *all photography is to some extent nonhuman* should be read. While I am concerned about ways in which the nonhuman aspect of photography can produce inhumane practices, I also want to suggest that *it is precisely in its nonhuman aspect that photography's creative, or world-making, side can be recognized*. Therefore, rather than contribute to recent jeremiads about photography and its supposed loss of authenticity and materiality, or its visual excess and self-involved banality, I argue that it is precisely through focusing on its nonhuman aspect that we can find life in photography. This line of argument is partly indebted to the work of Flusser, who, in *Towards a Philosophy of Photography*, writes: "The photographic apparatus lies in wait for photography; it sharpens its teeth in readiness. This readiness to spring into action on the part of apparatuses, their similarity to wild animals, is something to grasp hold of in the attempt to define the term etymologically."[29] Flusser builds here on the Latin origins of the term "apparatus," which derives from *apparare*, "make ready for" (as a combination of the prefix *ad-*, "toward," and *parare*, "make ready"). This leads him to read photography as facilitated by, or even proto-inscribed in, the nexus of image capture devices, various chemical and electronic components and processes, as well as sight- and technology-equipped humans. Blaise Aguera y Arcas finds it remarkable that Flusser should describe the camera as having a "program" and "software" when he was writing his philosophy of photography in 1983, given that the first digital camera was not available until 1988. "Maybe it took a philosopher's squint to notice the programming inherent in the grinding and configuration of lenses, the creation of a frame and field of view, the timing of the shutter, the details of chemical emulsions and film processing. Maybe, also, Flusser was writing about programming in a wider, more sociological sense," offers Aguera y Arcas.[30]

Flusser's conceptualization of photography challenges the humanist narrative of invention as an outcome of singular human genius by recognizing the significance of the technological setup in the emergence of various sociocultural practices. This is not to say that these practices function *outside* the human but rather that the concepts of self-contained human intentionality and sovereign human agency may be too limited to describe the emergence of specific technological processes at a particular moment in time. Flusser's idea seems to be (unwittingly) reflected in Geoffrey Batchen's proposition outlined in *Burning with Desire* that photography was invented—seemingly repeatedly, by Nicéphore Niépce, Louis Daguerre, Hippolyte Bayard, and William Henry Fox Talbot, among others—due to the fact that in the early nineteenth century there already existed a desire for it. This desire manifested itself in the proliferation of discourses and ideas about the possibility of capturing images and fixing them, and of the technologies—"the camera obscura and the chemistry necessary to reproduce"[31] the images taken with it—that would facilitate such a development. We could therefore perhaps go so far as to say that the photographic apparatus, which for Batchen contains but also exceeds a discrete human component, was awaiting the very invention of photography.

The ideas about the photographic apparatus discussed above will eventually point me not just toward rethinking the photographic medium but also toward a possibility (one that has been withheld by Tagg) of a posthumanist political analysis. For now, taking inspiration from Flusser, and building on the point made by Aguera y Arcas, I want to suggest that human-driven photography—where an act of conscious looking through a viewfinder or, more frequently nowadays, at an LCD screen held at arm's length—is only one small part of what goes on in the field of photography, even though it is often made to stand in for photography as such. The execution of human agency in photographic practice, be it professional or amateur, ostensibly manifests itself in decisions about the subject matter (the "what") and about ways of capturing this subject matter with a digital or analog apparatus (the "how"). Yet in amateur, snapshot-type photography, these supposed human-centric decisions are often affective reactions to events quickly unfolding in front of the photographer's eyes. Such reactions happen too quickly, or we could even say *automatically*, for any conscious processes of decision making to be involved—apart from the original decision to actually have, bring, and use a camera (or a camera phone), rather than not. This automatism in photography also manifests itself in the fact that these kinds of "snap" reactions are usually rechanneled through a whole database of standardized, preprogrammed, preexisting image frames, whose significance we are already familiar with and which we are trying to recreate in a unique way, under the umbrella of so-called individual experience: "toddler running toward mother," "girl blowing out a candle on a birthday cake," "couple posing in front of the Taj Mahal." It is in this sense that, as Flusser has it, "weddings conform to a photographic program."[32]

Similar representationalist ambitions accompany many professional photographic activities, including those performed by photographic artists or those undertaken by photojournalists who aim to show us, objectively and without judging, what war, poverty, and "the pain of others," to borrow Susan Sontag's phrase,[33] are "really" like. Even before any moment of making a picture actually occurs, fine art photographers tend to remain invested in the modernist idea of an artist as a human agent with a particular vocation, one whose aesthetic and conceptual gestures are aimed at capturing something unique, or at least capturing it uniquely, with an image-making device. And thus we get works of formal portraiture; images of different types of vegetation or geological formations that are made to constitute "landscapes"; still-life projects of aestheticized domesticity, including close-ups of kitchen utensils, fraying carpets, or light traces on a wall; and, last but not least, all those works that can be gathered into that ragbag called "conceptual photography."[34] In this way, images inscribe themselves in a cybernetic loop of familiarity, with minor variations to style, color, and the (re)presented object made to stand for creativity, originality, or even "genius."

The automated image

Through the decisions of artists and amateurs about their practice, photography becomes an act of *making something significant*, even if not necessarily *making it signify something* in any straightforward way. Photography is thus a practice of focusing on what is in its very nature multifocal, of literally casting light on what would have otherwise remained obscure, of carving a fragment from the flow of life and turning it into a splinter of what, post-factum, becomes known as "reality." Traditionally, this moment of selection—referred to as "decisive" by followers of the documentary tradition in photography, such as Henri Cartier-Bresson—was associated with the pressing of the button to open the camera's shutter. However, with the introduction of the Lytro camera into the market in 2012, the temporality of this seemingly unique and transient photographic moment has been stretched into both the past and the future. The original Lytro camera captured the entire light field rather than a single plane of light, thus allowing the photographer to change and readjust the focus on a computer in postproduction. Interestingly, Lytro was advertised as "The only camera that captures life in living pictures"—a poetic formulation which was underpinned by the constant industry claim to "absolute novelty," but which merely exacerbated and visualized the inherent instability of *all* photographic practice and *all* photographic objects. Lytro was thus just one more element in the long-term humanist narrative about "man's dominion over the earth," a narrative that drives the progressive automatization of many of our everyday devices, including cameras, cars, and refrigerators. In 2015, the company itself shifted focus—from attempting to alter the focus of singular images to the development of Lytro Immerge: an end-to-end system for capturing light fields for use in creating virtual reality (VR) content, "providing lifelike presence for live action VR through six degrees of freedom."[35] And thus, giving us an illusion of control over technology by making cameras smaller and more intimate, and domestic equipment more user-friendly, the technoscientific industry actually exacerbates the gap between technology and the human by relieving us from the responsibility of getting to know and engage with the increasingly software-driven "black boxes." The renewed interest in VR—a multisensory experience which is supposed to envelop us and feel "real" by being played out in front of our eyes on a screen built into a personal headset—shown not only by Lytro, Inc., but also by many other technology companies, such as Facebook (via its Oculus Rift), Google, Samsung, and Sony, provides an apt illustration of this desire to "keep the box black."

In light of the dominance of the humanist paradigm in photography, a paradigm that is premised on the supposed human control of both the practice of image making and its equipment, it is important to ask what gets elided in such conceptualizations. Of course, I am not the only one who is asking this question: the problem of nonhuman agency in photography has been explored by other theorists, artists, and curators. One photography event that brought many of these ideas to the fore was *Drone: The Automated Image*, a series of shows taking place under the umbrella of the photography biennale Le Mois de la Photo in Montreal, curated by Paul Wombell, in 2013.[36] The uniqueness of this thirteenth edition of the Montreal biennale lay not so much in highlighting the machinic aspect of photographic and video practice, as this aspect had already been mobilized in the early days of photography—for example, in the works of Alexander

Figure 2.5
Véronique Ducharme, *Encounters*, 2012–2013. Courtesy of the artist.

Rodchenko or László Moholy-Nagy. *Drone: The Automated Image* (which was concerned with much more than just drones) took one step further on this road toward not just nonhuman but also posthumanist photography by actually departing from the human-centric visualization process. In many of the works shown, the very act and process of capture were relegated to a computer, a camera mounted atop a moving vehicle, a robot, or a dog. To mention just one example, Canadian artist Véronique Ducharme presented a photography-based installation called *Encounters*, consisting of images taken by automatic hunting cameras (figure 2.5). As the artist explained:

Over the course of one year, automatic cameras, installed in various parts of the Quebec landscape, recorded images from the forest. The images included animals, sunrise, wind and other actants susceptible of triggering the shutter of the cameras. These digital images, including the "mistakes" of the cameras (i.e., blacked-out or overexposed images) were then transferred onto slide film in order to be projected in the gallery space using slide projectors. Accompanied by its rhythmic mechanical click, each machine has been programmed to sporadically and unpredictably project the images around the space, leaving the viewer entangled within the dialogue created by the machines and the images.[37]

Figure 2.6
Juliet Ferguson, *Stolen Images*, 2011. Courtesy of the artist.

Ducharme's project offers a thought-provoking intervention into the debate about (human) intentionality in photography theory, whereby intentionality is seen as both a condition and a guarantee of the medium being considered a form of art.[38] Photographic agency is distributed here among a network of participants, which includes not just nonhuman but also inanimate actors—even if "the beholder" of the installation is still envisaged to be a human gallery-goer.

Ducharme's work has similarities with another project which foregrounds and remediates nonhuman photographic agency without reneging on its human dimension: *Stolen Images* by British photographer Juliet Ferguson (figure 2.6), published in the London independent photography magazine *Flip* in 2012 and online in *Photomediations Machine* in 2013. Accessing CCTV cameras using appropriate search terms via Google as part of her journalism job, Ferguson was able "to see through the all-seeing eyes of the CCTV camera places" what she would not have had access to in the real world—without leaving her sofa.[39] The process led her to reflect "on what it means to take a photograph" and to pose the following questions: "The majority of the cameras I used I could pan, zoom and focus. Is this any less photography than someone using a fully automatic camera and taking a picture from a designated panorama point at a beauty spot? Does photography demand a presence or are photographs taken using appropriated cameras controlled from another country in another time zone just as valid as 'created' images?"[40] Ferguson reveals that, in the process, she began "to see a certain beauty in the images as they became removed from their original intention of surveillance. Instead, they offered a unique perspective on the ebb and flow of a day, from a vantage point and rigidity that ordinary photography doesn't offer."[41]

The photographic condition

Ducharme's *Encounters* and Ferguson's *Stolen Images* demonstrate that art practice is merely part of a wider *photographic condition*, with things photographing themselves, without always being brought back to the human spectrum of vision as the ultimate channel of perception and of things perceived. Naturally, humans form part of this photographic continuum—as artists, photojournalists, festival organizers, computer programmers, engineers, printers, Instagram users, and, last but not least, spectators. However, what these two projects make explicit is that *we are all part of that photographic flow of things being incessantly photographed*, and of trying to make interventions from within the midst of it. In this way, Ducharme's and Ferguson's projects fall into a category that we might term *insignificant photography*—not in the sense that they are mindless (as Tagg would perhaps have it), irrelevant, and of no consequence, but rather *in the sense of allowing us to see things that have been captured almost incidentally and in passing, with the thematic "what" not being the key impulse behind the execution of the images*. It is worth emphasizing that this idea of insignificant photography has not just come to the fore with the development of networked digital technologies but was actually present in the early discourse of photography, even if that early discourse tended to confine photography's nonhuman aspect to the fairly conservative idea of "objective observation." Steve Edwards explains:

> Throughout its history, the camera has repeatedly been seen as an objective machine that captures information without any interference from the artist. ... In the early years of photography this was an often repeated theme: it was assumed that the sun made the picture, or the camera did, or even that the object in question depicted itself (Talbot spoke of his country pile, Lacock Abbey, as the first building "that was ever yet known to have drawn its own picture").[42]

The separation between the mechanism of photography as "objective observation" and the human-centric notion of the "intentionality" of the photographer has been used as a disciplinary device in art history: as signaled before, the elevation of photography to the status of art has been premised upon it.[43] It is this separation that the work of many contemporary photographers such as Ducharme and Ferguson troubles to a significant extent.

So what is meant by this notion of the photographic condition, and does the postulation of its existence stand up to philosophical and experiential scrutiny? To explore these questions, let us start from a very simple proposition: *there is life in photography*. If living in the so-called media age has become tantamount to being photographed on a permanent basis, with our identity constituted and verified by the ongoing development of our photo galleries and photo streams on mobile phones, tablets, and social media platforms such as Facebook, Instagram, Tumblr, and Pinterest, not to mention the thousands of security cameras quietly and often invisibly registering our image when we pass through city centers, shopping malls, and airports, then, contrary to its more typical Barthesian association with the passage of time and death, photography can be understood more productively as a life-making process. Photography lends itself to being understood in a critical vitalist framework due to its positioning in a network of dynamic relations between present and past, movement and stasis, flow and cut. In making cuts into duration, in stabilizing the temporal flow into entities, photography is inherently involved with time. Significantly, for vitalist philosophers such as Henri Bergson and Gilles Deleuze, time, duration, and movement stand precisely for life itself. As Bergson provocatively asks, "But is it not obvious that the photograph, if photograph there be, is already taken, already developed in the very heart of things and at all the points of space?"[44] Photography's proximity to life is therefore revealed in its temporal aspect, which is enacted in photography's dual ontology, whereby it can be seen as both object and practice, as both snapshot and all the other virtual snapshots that could potentially have been there, and, last but not least, as both being something here and now, and being something always unfolding into something else. It is also in this dual ontology that the nonhuman side of photography comes to the fore, performed as it is through agents as diverse as CCTV, drone cameras, satellites, endoscopy equipment, and webcams, as well as camera- and mobile-phone-sporting humans.

My notion of the photographic condition has affinities with the Deleuze-inspired concept of "camera consciousness" developed by Anthony McCosker with regard to drones. McCosker proposes we move beyond seeing drones primarily as "unruly aerial objects with the capacity for privacy-invasive imaging" and approach them instead "as experience and as provocation to reconsider wireless networks, visuality and camera-conscious sociality."[45] This more relational mode of approaching human-machinic entanglements, beyond the moral panic about technology's threat to "us"—even if not beyond the *political* concern about drones' role in redefining relations of sociality, intimacy, and control—paves the way for a new understanding of visuality prompted by the machinic vision of the disembodied eye. In this reconceptualization, "camera consciousness" begins to stand for "a broader cultural condition and logic bound up in the dual sense of visual augmentation and anxiety over altered modes of visibility and mediated perception."[46] Yet anxiety does not mean a priori repudiation: indeed, McCosker is clear that a new consciousness to emerge from a different—intensified, distributed, and networked—relation with technical objects is needed if we are to truly grasp the singularity of the visual experience today, in both its constraining and enabling guises: "Hence with drones we can also ask: what are the new kinds of perception and action or control made possible by our human-technical assemblages?"[47] Summing up, we should reiterate that to acknowledge the life-making aspect of photography is not necessarily to condone the politically suspicious yet increasingly widespread technologies of ubiquitous surveillance, control, and loss of privacy enabled by various kinds of cameras. Much has already been written about the latter, with little acknowledgment so far of the *vital* potentiality of photography—which, in an ontological sense, *does not have to* be an agent of control, even if it at times plays this role. There is, therefore, a danger of moralizing photography in academic and public discourses *before its potential has been truly explored.* The foregrounding of the inherently creative power of photography as a practice, and of the camera consciousness as a distributed and networked experience facilitated by the new visual setup, is therefore part of the philosophical argument of this chapter, although issues of politics never disappear from its agenda.

Photography and life

The on-off activity of the photographic process, which carves life into fragments while simultaneously reconnecting them to the imagistic flow, may allow us to conclude not only that *there is life in photography*, but also that *life itself is photographic*. Interestingly, Claire Colebrook explains this process of creative becoming in and of life by drawing on the very concept of image production, or "imaging." She writes: "All life, according to Bergson and to Deleuze after him, can be considered as a form of perception or 'imaging' where there is not one being that apprehends or represents another being, but two vectors of creativity where one potential for differentiation encounters another and from that potential forms a relatively stable tendency or manner."[48] This idea has its root in Bergson's *Matter and Memory*, where our experience of the world, which is always a way of sensing the world, comes in the form of images. We should mention here that, on the whole, Bergson is somewhat hesitant about the role played by images in cognition: in *Creative Evolution*, he dismisses them as mere "snapshots" of perception, post-factum reductions of duration and time to a sequence of the latter's frozen slices.[49] It may therefore seem strange that my attempt to say something new about photography revisits the work of a philosopher who only used the concept of photography negatively, to outline a "better"—i.e., more intuitive and more fluid—mode of perception and cognition. However, my argument here, as in my previous work,[50] is that Bergson's error is first and foremost media-specific and not philosophical per se: namely, he misunderstands photography's inherently creative and dynamic power by reducing it to a sequence of already fossilized artifacts, with the mind fragmenting the world into a sequence of "snapshots." For this reason, I want to suggest that, putting their mystical underpinnings aside, we can mobilize Bergson's *philosophical* writings on duration understood as a manifestation of *élan vital* to rethink photography as a quintessential practice of life. Indeed, photography is one possible (and historically specific) enactment of the creative practice of imaging, with the cuts into duration it makes always remaining connected to the flow of time. If we accept the fact that cutting—whether with our visual or conceptual apparatus—is inevitable to the processes of making sense of the world, then we can see any outcomes of the photographic cut, i.e., photographs and other products of the image-making process, as temporary stabilizations of the flow of duration that still bear a trace of life—rather than as frozen and ultimately deadly mementoes of the past. It is important to point out that, in order to recognize any kind of process *as a process*, we need to see it against the concept of a temporary stabilization, interruption, or cut into this process. A photograph is one possible form such stabilizations take, and a rather ubiquitous one at that. It is precisely because of its ubiquity and its increasingly intuitive technological apparatus that it serves as a perfect illustration of Bergson's ideas—or rather, of my own "differentiated reading" of Bergson. Bergson himself foregrounds this mutually constitutive relationship between process and stoppage when he says, "Things are constituted by the instantaneous cut which the understanding practices, at a given moment, on a flux of this kind, and what is mysterious when we compare the cuts together becomes clear when we relate them to the flux."[51] This supposition allows us to see photography as an ultimately salutary and creative force in managing the duration of the world by the human as a species with limited cognitive and sensory capacity.

Bergson aside, there are also more "vernacular" reasons for describing photography as a quintessential practice of life. Over the last few decades, the photographic medium has become so ubiquitous that our very sense of existence is shaped by it. We regularly see ourselves and others represented by the photographic medium, in both its formal and informal guises—from the documentation of our life in its fetal stage via medical imaging, through to the regular recording of our growth and maturation in family, school, and passport photographs; the incessant capture of the fleeting moments of our life with phone cameras; and the subsequent construction of our life's "timeline" on social media. We also make sense of the world around us through seeing it imaged. While photography used to be something that others did—professionals equipped with large machines that allowed them to capture a better image of the world out there, advertisers trying to sell us chunks of that world, photojournalists dispatched to the world's remote corners that few of us could regularly access—we can safely say that, in the age of the camera phone and wireless communication, we are all photographers now, with our consciousness becoming that of the camera in a more literal sense as well.

Yet we are all not just photographers today: *we have also become distributors, archivists, and curators of the light traces immobilized on photosensitive surfaces*. As Victor Burgin aptly points out, "the most revolutionary event in the recent history of photography is not the arrival of digital cameras as such, but rather the broadband connection of these cameras to the Internet—in effect turning every photograph on the Web into a potential frame in a boundless film."[52] One could perhaps go so far as to say that the availability of relatively low-cost storage and networked distribution of digital data has changed the very ontology of the photographic medium. *Photographs function less as individual objects or as media content to be looked at and more as data flows to be dipped or cut into occasionally.* The intensity and volume of photographic activity today, and the very fact that it is difficult to do anything—order food, go on holiday, learn about the Moon, have sex—without having it visualized in one way or another, before, during, or as part of the experience, gives credence to Sontag's formulation that "the photographs are us."

Even though this photographic condition does have a very particular, culturally specific enactment in the age of the digital camera and "the networked image," could we return to our original point to suggest that there is a deeper logic, or tendency, in photography that takes the medium beyond its specific cultural incarnations, be it digital or analog? Chapter 4 will trace this relationship back to deep time, through a parallel reading of photographs and fossils. For now, I would like to highlight that the notion of the creative role of the imaging process in life has also been manifested in the work of radical biologists, such as Lynn Margulis. As she put it in a book coauthored with her son Dorian Sagan, "All living beings, not just animals, but plants and microorganisms, perceive. To survive, an organic being must perceive—it must seek, or at least recognize, food and avoid environmental danger."[53] This act of perception, which involves the seeking out and recognition of something else, involves the making of an image of that something else (food, predator, sexual partner), one that needs to be at least temporarily fixed in order for the required proximity—for consumption or sex—to be accomplished. We could perhaps therefore suggest that imaging is a form of proto-photography, planting the seed of the combined human-machinic "desire" explored by Batchen that came into its own in the early nineteenth century. It is precisely through images that novelty comes into the world, which is why images should not be reduced to mere representations, Colebrook argues, but should rather be understood as creations, "some of which are philosophical, some artistic, some scientific."[54] To put this another way, the creative impulse of life takes it beyond representation as a form of picturing what already exists: instead, *life is a creation of images in the most radical sense, a way of temporarily stabilizing matter into forms*. Photographic practice as we conventionally know it, with all the automatism it entails, is just one instantiation of this creative process of life.

If all life is indeed photographic, the notion of the photographic apparatus that embraces, yet also goes beyond, the human becomes fundamental to our understanding of what we have called the "photographic condition." To speak of the photographic apparatus is, of course, not just to argue for a straightforward replacement of the human vision with a machinic one, but rather to recognize the mutual intertwining and co-constitution of the organic and the machinic, the technical and the discursive, in the production of vision, and hence of the world. In her work on the use of apparatuses in physics experiments, philosopher and quantum physicist Karen Barad argues that such devices are not just "passive observing instruments; on the contrary, they are productive of (and part of) phenomena."[55] We could easily apply this argument to photography, where the camera as a viewing device, the photographic frame both in the viewfinder and as the circumference of a photographic print, the enlarger, the computer, the printer, the photographer (who, in many instances, such as surveillance or speed cameras, is replaced by the camera-eye), and, last but not least, the discourses about photography and vision *that produce them as objects for us humans* are all active agents in the constitution of a photograph. In other words, they are all part of what we understand by photography.

Becoming a camera

As signaled earlier, it is not just philosophy that help us envisage this nonhuman, machinic dimension of photography: photographic, and, more broadly, artistic practice is even better predisposed to enact it (rather than just provide an argument *about* it). A series of works by British artist Lindsay Seers is a case in point. Exhibited, among other places, at Matt's Gallery in London as *It Has to Be This Way* in 2009, and accompanied by an aptly titled book, *Human Camera*, Seers's ongoing project consists of a number of seemingly autobiographic films. These are full of bizarre yet just-about-believable adventures occurring to their heroine, all verified by a body of "experts"—from doctors and critics through to family members—that

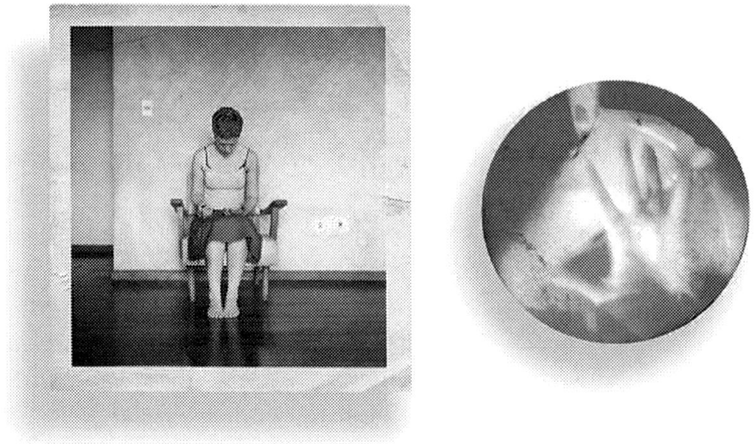

Figure 2.7
Lindsay Seers, *Optogram (mouth camera)*, 2010. Courtesy of the artist.

appear in the films but also leave behind "evidence" in the form of numerous written accounts, photographs, and documentary records. In one of the films, a young girl, positioned as "Lindsay Seers," is living her life unable to make a distinction between herself and the world, or between the world and its representations. The girl is gifted with exceptional memory so, like a camera that is permanently switched on, she records and remembers practically everything. "It is as if I was in a kaleidoscope, a bead in the mesmerising and constantly shifting pattern. Everything was in flux, every single moment and every single object rewritten at every turn," as "Lindsay Seers" recalls in a short piece called "Becoming Something" included in *Human Camera*.[56] This terrifyingly magnificent gift is lost once the girl sees a photograph of herself. She then spends her adult life clothed in a black sack, photographing things obsessively. In this way, she is literally trying to "become a camera" by making photographs on light-sensitive paper inserted into her mouth, with the images produced "bathed in the red light" of her body (figure 2.7). This ambition is later replaced by an attempt to "become a projector" by creating things ex nihilo through the emanation of light. Some of Seers's films presented in the show are screened in a black hut modeled on Thomas Edison's *Black Maria*, his New Jersey film studio that was used for projection as well as photography. With this, Seers invites us not just to witness her process of becoming a camera but also to enter a giant camera ourselves, to literally step into the world of imaging, to reconnect us to the technicity of our own being.

Although Bergson's argument about life as a form of imaging is posited as transhistorical, we can add a specific inflection to it by returning to Flusser, and, in particular, his study of the relation between the human and the technical apparatus. For Flusser, that relation changed significantly in the years after the Industrial Revolution, when "photographers [were] inside their apparatus and bound up with it. ... It is a new kind of function in which human beings and apparatus merge into a unity."[57] Consequently, human beings now "function as a function of apparatuses,"[58] limited as they are to the execution of the camera's program from the range of seemingly infinite possibilities which are nevertheless determined by the machine's algorithm. Arguably, humans themselves are enactors of such a program, a sequence of possibilities enabled by various couplings of adenine, cytosine, guanine, and thymine, arranged into a double helix of life. To state this is not to postulate some kind of uncritical technological or biological determinism that would remove from "us" any possibility of action—as artists, photographers, critics, or spectators—and any responsibility for the actions we take. It is merely to acknowledge our kinship with other living beings across the evolutionary spectrum, with our lives remaining subject to biochemical reactions that we cannot always understand, control, or overcome (from blushing through to aging and dying). Just as "the imagination of the camera is greater than that of every single photographer and that of all photographers put together,"[59] the imagination of "the program called life" in which we all participate (and which is an outcome of multiple processes running across various scales of our planet) far exceeds our human imagination. Such a recognition of our entanglement as sentient and discursive beings in complex biological and technical networks is necessary if we are to become involved, seriously and responsibly, in any kind of photography, philosophy, or other critical or everyday activity in which we aim to exercise "free will."

Re-forming the world

By reconnecting us to the technical apparatus, by letting us explore our machinic kinship, artists such as the appropriately named Seers and the other image makers discussed in this chapter are all engaged (even if they are not always up-front about it or perhaps even entirely aware of it) in exploring the fundamental problem that many philosophers of technology who take science seriously have been grappling with: Given that "there is no place for human freedom within the area of automated, programmed and programming apparatuses," how can we "show a way in which it is nevertheless possible to open up a space for freedom"?[60] Such an undertaking is very much needed, according to Flusser, "because it is the only form of revolution open to us."[61] As discussed in the previous chapter, Flusser points to "envisioners"—that is, "people who try to turn an automatic apparatus against its own condition of being automatic"[62]—as those who will be able to undertake the task of standing "against the world," by pointing "at it with their fingertips to inform it."[63] In this perspective, codification and visualization are seen as radical interventions into the world, and ways of re-*forming* it, rather than as ways of dehumanizing it, as Tagg seemed to suggest.

Any prudent and effective way of envisaging and picturing a transformation of our relation to the universe must thus be conducted not in terms of a human struggle against the machine but rather in terms of our mutual co-constitution, as a recognition of our shared kinship. This recognition of the photographic condition that encompasses yet goes beyond the human, and of the photographic apparatus that extends well beyond our eyes and beyond the devices supposedly under our control, should prompt us human philosophers, photographers, and spectators to mobilize the ongoing creative impulse of life, in which the whole world is a camera, and put it to creative rather than conservative uses. The conceptual expansion of processes of image making beyond the human can also allow us to work toward escaping what Colebrook calls the "privatization of the eye in late capitalism,"[64] where what starts out as a defense of our right to look often ends up as a defense of our right to look at the small screen. In challenging the self-possessive individualism of the human eye, photography that seriously and consciously engages with its own expansive ontological condition and its nonhuman genealogy may therefore be seen as a truly revolutionary practice. Indeed, the concept and practice of nonhuman photography reconnects us to other beings and processes across the universe, including those of the Taurus Molecular Cloud. Photography in its nonhuman guise serves as a reminder that the short moment in natural history when the human species has folded "the world around its own, increasingly myopic, point of view,"[65] and that has allowed it to become "seduced, spellbound, distracted and captivated by inanity,"[66] should not obscure the wider horizon of our openness to the world, our relationality with it through originary perception. The concept of nonhuman photography can therefore serve as both *a response to "man's tendency to reify himself"*[67] and *an opening toward a radical posthumanist political analysis*. It can serve in both ways by highlighting that there is more than just one point of view and that, by tearing the myopic eye from the perspective-driven bipedal body and embracing the distributed machinic-corporeal vision, it may be possible to see the drone as more than just a killing machine—although, of course, there are no guarantees.[68]

3 Photography after the Human

After what?

The title of this chapter may at first glance seem absurd or even pointless. My ongoing proposition to consider photography as always bearing a nonhuman trace notwithstanding, readers may still wonder about the legitimacy of situating what common sense dictates to be a distinctly human cultural practice in a nonhuman future, and may also question the very need for such an exercise. To explain this conceptual entry point, I would like to inscribe the argument to be outlined here within a wider framework of current posthumanist perspectives, where what is being reimagined is both the notion of the human and the notion of the world that supposedly exists for and in agreement with this human. In this framework, imagination and visualization become tools in decentering the human as the rationale for, and pivot point of, the universe: the human is viewed instead as one of many transitory species, existing in a series of dynamic relations with other nonhuman entities and processes in the geo- and biosphere. Yet this human is also recognized as being endowed with a set of traits such as reflexivity, purposefulness, and language; traits that—even if not *uniquely* human—do translate into a set of historically specific practices such as storytelling, philosophizing, and image making. As already stated, the main concern of this chapter is the existence of images, and, in particular, light-induced mechanical images known as photographs, *after the human. The "after the human" designation does not refer only to the straightforward material disappearance or conceptual overcoming of the human at some point in the future, then, but also to the present imagining of that disappearance as a prominent visual trope in art photography and other cultural practices.* The concept of human extinction, of there being a geological time in which the human is no more, expands the temporal scale of the problematic under discussion. It also opens up the question of the survival of photographic and other imagistic artifacts, as well as the viability of the continuation of image-making processes, in a world from which humans (or at least *most* humans) are gone.

Photography as a practice of life

But let us start with some futurology. William Bornefeld's 1996 science fiction novel *Time and Light* offers an interesting conceptual gateway for our discussion because it considers photography in a postapocalyptic context while also interrogating photography's powers beyond its supposed ability to represent. The novel is set in an unspecified time, inside a five-mile-long domed city called Fullerton, in which the last survivors of an undetermined nuclear disaster have reconstructed a miniature semblance of the bourgeois society of yesteryear, with all its hierarchies and exclusions. Deemed "The Family of Man," Fullerton's residents resemble a bad copy of the people depicted in Edward Steichen's celebrated 1955 photographic exhibition at MoMA of that same title. The aim of Steichen's exhibition was to showcase the commonalities among cross-cultural human experience while also promoting the values of *pax Americana*. In the essay titled "The Great Family of Man" included in *Mythologies*, Roland Barthes described the exhibition, which subsequently toured to Paris, as presenting a "moralized and sentimentalized" idea of a community and thus perpetuating a myth of a "human essence," while also obscuring the historical, geospecific, and ethnic fault lines that divided humanity.[1] Designating such attempts at what we might term "cultural geology" as politically disabling in their misguided search for eternal truths about humankind, Barthes rallied against "the solid rock of a universal human nature."[2] He ended the essay with a warning: "I rather fear that the final justification of all this Adamism is to give to the immobility of the world the alibi of a 'wisdom' and a 'lyricism' which only makes the gestures of man look eternal the better to defuse them."[3]

The illuminated domed city of Fullerton in Bornefeld's novel seems to have been processed through a Barthesian critical filter. Its "Great Family of Man" is revealed as being powered by its invisible underbelly: an underground world full of depraved and dirty workers—very unlike those noble working men and women from Steichen's images—whose sole purpose in life is to provide fuel and energy for the smooth running of the city above. The postindustrialism of Fullerton is therefore being fed by the steam-and-manpower industrialism of this hidden underground world, which serves as its bloodline. Fullerton's geospatial arrangements reveal a nexus of socio-political issues that structure it. Jussi Parikka points out that the underground lies "at the crux of technical imaginary of modernity" as both "the place of hell"—through the hard labor of mining, excavation, and deadly vapors—and "a place of technological futures."[4]

Fullerton's society operates according to a number of prohibitions, the most prominent of which is an absolute ban on photography and other forms of imaging. The justification for this rule is as follows:

> It was told that at one time in its early history the dome society had been excessively visual with a great emphasis on looking at things including pictures in printed books; but it was decided a long time ago that a visual society was in a constant state of imbalance and agitation due to stress on the optic nerve, and produced discord, especially harmful in the small controlled dome atmosphere; therefore, visual paraphernalia was phased out and then totally eliminated.[5]

The novel itself is constructed around twelve photographs which we never see, but which hint at famous images from the history of photography in the Western world. Those photographs serve as prompts for various developments in the narrative. Bundled into a package, they arrive one day in the hands of its main protagonist, Doctor Noreen, who violates societal expectations by not reporting his discovery. After having literally seen traces of light, Noreen is pushed to commit further acts of insubordination, which include his descent to Fullerton's underbelly to shake the dome from the bottom up. At times bizarre in its imagery and less than convincing in its plot, Bornefeld's book succeeds on a different level: it articulates a defense of the ontology of photography as a zoetic, life-transforming medium, one that can agitate and animate a different life—rather than just critique the present one, the way documentary photography does.

It is perhaps not too much of an overstatement to suggest that, to understand a given society, we should look not just at the images it produces of itself but also at its very relationship to photography and image making. As Joan Fontcuberta illuminates in his aptly titled *Pandora's Camera: Photogr@phy after Photography*, "the products of the camera are materials that transcend the merely documentary as a discourse of verification, and take on instead a symbolic value that we do well to analyse in attempting to judge the regimens of truth that every society assigns itself."[6] Bornefeld seems to suggest that the survival of photography is vital to the survival of a human society, because images are what can give life back to an enclosed and paralyzed community—although, in themselves, they do not carry any guarantee of a better world. Importantly, this is a very different story of photography from the more common narrative we have inherited from Barthes's *Camera Lucida* (more about that in chapter 4), in which photography is inherently marked with death. Bornefeld's consideration of this survival-extinction dyad with regard to both humans and photographs draws attention to the fact that photography's powers are never just representational, regardless of whether we are talking about purposeful and staged photographic practice, amateur snapshots, or even automatic recordings by unmanned cameras placed in car parks, on drones, or in the Hubble Space Telescope. In every one of these cases, photography's power is first and foremost creative: it produces what we humans refer to as "life" by carving out an image from the flow of duration and stabilizing it in a certain medium.

We could perhaps therefore reiterate, building on the argument outlined in this chapter so far as well as in the previous one, that *photography is a quintessential practice of life*. Photography records life, remembers life, or even creates it, bringing forth images, traces, and memories of the past while also transforming the latter into a different—clearer, more stable, less perishable—version of itself. Attending to this life-forming power of photography, however, involves needing to go beyond the established tradition of understanding perception and cognition in Western culture as agential processes controlled by the human, even if at times delegated to nonhuman automata. It also requires giving up on the molecular notion of the human—and, indeed, of photographs as outcomes of human production—for the sake of outlining instead what we might term a relational ontology of mediation, from which (human and nonhuman) photographers, photographs, and photography itself emerge only through temporary resolutions and cuts. Mediation is to be understood here as a dynamic and hybrid process in which economic, social, cultural, psychological, and technical forces converge and intra-act, producing a variety of temporary stabilizations. Some of those stabilizations will take the form we conventionally understand as "media": scanners, cameras, photographs. As Sarah Kember and I have argued in *Life after New Media: Mediation as a Vital Process*, which postulates the primacy of the notion of mediation for understanding our human becoming with media and technology, it is "precisely in its efforts to arrest duration, to capture or still the flow of life—beyond singular photographs' success or failure at representing this or that referent—that photography's vital forces are activated."[7] This inherent "lifeness" of photography has the potential to *animate* the human. A similar vision is outlined by Bornefeld, both in the novel's plot and in the author's note at the end—which describes photographs as having "a life of their own."[8]

Ruin lust

The sci-fi imaginings notwithstanding, there is yet another meaning of this "after the human" designation encompassed by our discussion, one that paves the way for a more radical imagining of the abstraction of life and death in a temporal sense, while also holding the horror of extinction at bay. I am referring here to the recent proliferation, in art and especially in photography, of the practice of *imagining and imaging a certain future "after the human" from the viewpoint of the here and now* (figure 3.1). Variously

Figure 3.1
Shane Gorski, *Wasteland*, from the Detroit Public Schools Book Depository set, 2008, Flickr, License: CC BY-ND 2.0.

referenced as "ruin lust" or "ruin porn," such (re)presentations of the vanishing of the world as we know it by artists, and the pleasurable and painful wallowing by viewers in the images of decay that show the world as it soon will be, have some clear historical antecedents. These stretch from the sublime romantic landscapes of ruined abbeys by the likes of Giovanni Battista Piranesi and Hubert Robert, all the way through to paintings such as Joseph Gandy's *Rotunda*, commissioned by John Soane, the architect of the Bank of England, and depicting that bank as a ruin even before it was built.[9] At the same time, this visual practice has gained a new inflection in a period in which the global economic crisis of the last decade and the impending climate catastrophe have come to be experienced and articulated with an ever increasing intensity: we can think here of the seductive and haunting images of Detroit, a financially bankrupt North American city with a glorious industrial and architectural past, which widely proliferate on the Internet. Incidentally, it is not just the fossil fuels that are said to have become depleted in the current era: according to writer and activist Arundhati Roy, democracy, too, has been "used up, together with the other resources of our planet."[10] For Roy, the global crisis also entails a crisis of political imagination, signaling as it does the inability to reimagine our current geopolitical formation beyond the tired clichés of our elected governments.

Many accounts and images of the current global crisis—a crisis that extends beyond, even if never exceeds, the domain of finance to embrace areas such as healthcare, air quality, the climate, and politics itself—use the trope described by Ursula Heise as "the rhetoric of decline," interweaving elegy and tragedy not only to point to the decline of nature but also to signal anxiety about our present culture's narrative of modernization.[11] Brian Dillon even goes so far as to suggest that "Ruins seem ... intrinsic to the projects of modernity and, later, Modernism."[12] Tate Britain's 2014 exhibition "Ruin Lust" (figure 3.2) inscribes itself in this rhetoric. As explained on the show's website, the term refers to a long-term fascination with representations of ruination "through both the slow picturesque decay and abrupt apocalypse." The exhibition was partly inspired by a 1953 book by Rose Macaulay titled *Pleasure of Ruins*, in which the author contrasted the horrifying ruins that were widely encountered in the aftermath of World War II with the much more pleasant, historical, and historicized ruins upon which nature has exerted its softening touch, such as Pompeii and the Parthenon. The good ruin of the past, "a fantasy, veiled by the mind's dark

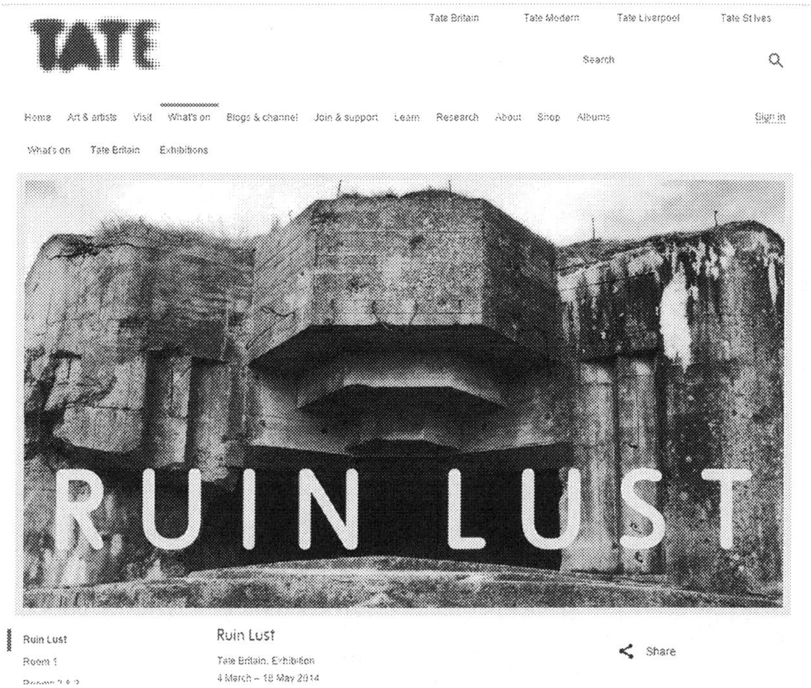

Figure 3.2
"Ruin Lust," Tate Britain, March 4 to May 18, 2014, screengrab of Tate website by Joanna Zylinska, 2014.

imaginings,"[13] had offered Macaulay a contrast to, and a relief from, the unbearable ruins that spoke of the more recent atrocities. Relics depicted in "Ruin Lust," from Turner's *Tintern Abbey* (1794) through to John Savage's photographic series *Uninhabited London* (1977–2008), function as a mournful reminder of the passage of time—individual, historical, and cosmic. The exhibition was framed, both in its publicity and in the actual entrance space of the gallery, by a magisterial image by Jane and Louise Wilson, *Azeville* (2006), showing one of the many abandoned World War II coastal bunkers along the Atlantic Wall defense fortification in Normandy. A black-and-white photograph covering the whole of the wall facing the entrance to the exhibition space, it depicts a huge building in a state of decay which looks like a squatting giant, the black hole of its entryway resembling a gaping mouth. Shot with a large-format camera to capture as much detail as possible, the image gains a certain visual tenderness due to the layer of vegetation covering the building's top, like some sort of incongruous thinning hair, or perhaps a hat on top of a giant head. Dismaying as this idea may seem, are we allowed to read this image as a depiction of a moment in time when the wartime ruin has moved beyond its sheer horror, to enter Macaulay's space of the picturesque and the pleasant? To suggest this may be the case is not to diminish the trauma and destruction generated by World War II, but is only to point out that all sorts of catastrophic events eventually lend themselves to both monumentalization and aestheticization, as a way of containing the shared trauma and moving on. And, to follow this line of thought, if even the images of Nazi ruination or 9/11 destruction (as evidenced, for example, in Joel Meyerowitz's evocative book of photographs, *Aftermath: World Trade Center Archive*)[14] are now becoming "good ruins" and entering the space of the picturesque (or at least the pictorial), what kinds of horror do they stand *in place of*? What kind of apocalyptic event would then constitute their "bad ruin" counterpart? Are the good ruins of exhibitions and events such as Tate Britain's "Ruin Lust" or the British Council's *A Clockwork Jerusalem* at the 2014 Venice Architecture Biennale actually attempts to confront *and* ward off the total ruination and annihilation of the earth, the human, and life as we know it, in both economic and biological senses?

Visualizing the eco-eco disaster

We can indeed argue that the urgency of the recent set of calamitous events in our global economic and ecological systems, dubbed an "eco-eco disaster" by Tom Cohen and a "great acceleration" by J. R. McNeill and Peter Engelke,[15] is precisely what has ushered in this new set of visualization codes and practices—perhaps in an attempt to hold off the political and ecological apocalypse by enclosing and enframing it in a series of horrifying yet ultimately digestible images. Popular culture, especially mainstream film and TV, have long been at the forefront of turning catastrophe into visual entertainment as a form of relief: we can mention classic movies such as *The Day the World Ended* (1955), *Armageddon* (1998), and *Children of Men* (2006), as well as TV series such as ABC's *Invasion* (2005–2006). Yet, arguably, something has changed of late: a new sense of *total* disaster and *total* obliteration, without any notion of heroism or hope, is being ushered in by more recent productions such as the History Channel's *Life after*

People and HBO's *The Leftovers*. Ecological cataclysms and the irreversible human-induced changes to the structure and dynamics of our planet have also become a frequent aesthetic trope in art, and fine art photography in particular. We can think here of projects such as Andreas Gursky's monumental studies of commerce, global tourism, and the environment (*Dubai World*, *Bangkok*, or *Ocean*, to name but a few), or the equally large-scale photographs arranged into series titled *Oil*, *Australian Mines*, and *Water* by Edward Burtynsky. These mainly desolate landscapes by Gursky and Burtynsky imagine a world in which the human is no more, although a human artist is still, of course, performing both the imagining and the accompanying imaging. The "after the human" designation, which is one of the main concerns of this chapter, functions in their images predominantly as a certain aesthetic and visual trope. It thus references ruination and extinction as a particular art historical mode of re/presentation and aestheticization. And, like all art historical tropes and trends, despite the irreversibility of the change it depicts, it is likely to pass long before the human has either solved the global economic or environmental crisis—or, indeed, has become extinct. Yet since this visual trope is very much with us at the moment, it may be worth dwelling in and on the ruins for a while, with a view to imagining what could perhaps be described as "better ruination": not in the sense of Macaulay's picturesque but rather in an attempt to reimagine our relation to the world just before the ruin, in the little time we have left.

This is precisely how Jason McGrath proposes to read the work of Canadian-based photographer Tong Lam.[16] Lam's 2013 book *Abandoned Futures: A Journey to the Posthuman World* and his exhibition "Unreal Estate" from the same year depict derelict spaces in China: unfinished and abandoned theme parks, shopping malls, and housing projects now overgrown by vegetation. McGrath locates Lam's deanthropomorphized gaze in the political context of China's march toward postindustrialization: "A rusted old locomotive, an abandoned factory: some of the modern ruins of Lam's photos are reminders of a now mostly suppressed alternative modernity, an abandoned future of liberation from capitalism itself."[17] McGrath reads Lam's images as an exposition of the failure of the mentality of limitless growth. The coupling of the crisis of the American-Chinese dream of unrestrained consumerism with the human abode's inability to sustain that dream in all its actualizations also serves as a reminder—one that is issued to us historically located humans—of the deep time that encapsulates and

Figure 3.3
Tong Lam, *An outdated and abandoned theme park in Chengdu, Sichuan Province*, 2013. Reproduced with permission.

exceeds the temporality of our existence as both individuals and a species. According to McGrath, "The posthuman gaze at modernist ruins reminds us that, no matter how many new objects we produce, consume, and discard, those objects will in many cases far outlive us and the purposes to which we put them. The fake sphinx may go unappreciated by any human observer, but its head will continue to make a fine perch for a bird" (figure 3.3).[18] This look at human history from the perspective of cosmic time need not be seen as a sign of political quietism or planetary-scale existentialist paralysis of the "why do anything if we are all going to become extinct?" kind. Rather, it can introduce a certain humility into our political frameworks, from which a new image of the world, and of ourselves in this world, can then emerge.

This mode of (re)imagining the known is not restricted to popular culture or to fine art. The subcultural practice of urban exploration, as investigated in Bradley Garrett's 2013 heavily illustrated book *Explore Everything: Place-hacking the City*, relies on photography not just to document the visited ruins but also to depict the "after the human" landscape that for now

Figure 3.4
Dennis Skley, *Time isn`t passing ... [Urban Explorer]*, 2012. Flickr, License: CC BY-ND 2.0.

remains obscured from public view, but which offers a chilling premonition of things to come, for all of us (figure 3.4). Garrett—who is both an urban explorer and an academic—rebuts accusations that urban exploration is just a rite-of-passage pastime for affluent youths, for whom ruins are slightly edgier and more exciting versions of theme parks, places they can always leave in order to return to their cozy upper middle-class abodes. Instead, Garrett foregrounds a darker and more philosophical dimension of this practice. "Residing in the ruin, or even the construction site," he writes, "triggers affective associations, leading to a crisis of memory as one realises that everything is always already being lost. The reliance on photography, then, is an effort to capture not that transition, but the experience of being present in the flow of time."[19]

Imag(in)ing a postcapitalist world

Garrett's statement can help us comprehend a unique role that photography—as a device capable of stopping time and conjuring things out if it—plays in the human engagement with ruination. The philosopher of duration Henri Bergson claims, "We do not think real time. But we live it, because life transcends intellect."[20] Time cannot be grasped, then, either with a camera or the intellect, because to capture time truly would mean to stop it. Instead, time can only be experienced and enacted, repeatedly. The imaging process presents itself as primary and ontological here. We could perhaps go so far as to say that *through photography the world becomes something for us,* and then does it over and over again. We could then ask, together with the anthropologist Tim Ingold, "Could it be that images do not stand for things but rather help you find them?"[21] This idea can be traced back to Bergson's *Matter and Memory,* in which he argues that our experience of the world, which is made up of sensations, takes place through images. "And by 'image' we mean," explains Bergson, "a certain existence which is more than that which the idealist calls a representation, but less than that which the realist calls a thing—an existence placed half-way between the 'thing' and the 'representation.'"[22] To put this another way, the creative impulse of life takes life beyond representation as a form of picturing what already exists: instead, life is a creation of images in the most radical sense, a way of temporarily stabilizing matter into forms. Photographic practice as we conventionally know it is just one instantiation of this creative process of life. If, after Bergson, time, aka "duration," equals creative evolution and hence life itself,[23] we are once again presented with the vision of photography as effectively enacting and allowing one to sense, rather than just represent, what I earlier called "lifeness."[24] It may seem paradoxical that it is by capturing something as potentially lifeless as ruination and decay that the practice of photography is able to create this life-enhancing sensation. Yet it is not only by sensing life but also by being able to envisage its alternative arrangements and articulations (the way Bornefeld's novel and Lam's photographs also attempt to do) that the photographic trope of ruination can lend itself to a *planned world-making purpose*—which is another name for politics. As Garrett suggests, drawing on Susan Buck-Morss's account of Walter Benjamin's *Arcades Project,* "the image of the 'ruin' is emblematic not only of the fragility of capitalism but also of its inevitable destruction. ... As people become more curious about what a post-capitalist world would look like, urban explorers can supply imaginative depictions."[25]

These combined spatiotemporal senses of the "after the human" designation addressed here arrange themselves into an articulation not only of a particular visual sensibility but also, therefore, of a certain ethico-political responsibility. Visualization becomes a way of engaging with a political and existential problem of great magnitude—even if it does not yet offer any specific and definitive solutions. It is precisely here that art and photography have the potential to become truly ethical (rather than just moral or, worse, moralizing and moralistic), as they can depict and outline this human-nonhuman relationality *qua* responsibility. This line of thought develops from my book *Minimal Ethics for the Anthropocene*,[26] the aim of which was to think seriously about human (and nonhuman) extinction, and about the kinds of ethics and politics that are ushered in by the horizon of extinction. It is thus linked to an attempt to imagine what is still principally an abstract concept for us: not just the death of ourselves as individuals but also the death of all of us *as a species*. The Anthropocene can serve as a thought device to help us visualize the multiple event of extinction—but also to intervene in the timeline of the extinction of various species. The term itself names a new geological period in which the human's impact upon the geomorphological and biological setup of planet Earth has become both momentous and irreversible, via processes such as excavation, deforestation, urbanization, and globalization. It is also a period that is experiencing a mass extinction of various species as a result of anthropogenic factors. Even though scientists are still debating the accuracy of this term, many philosophers, cultural theorists, and artists have adopted the Anthropocene as a driving concept in recent initiatives: Berlin's Haus der Kulturen der Welt ran a two-year Anthropocene Project in 2013–2014 which culminated in the publication by the MIT Press of a three-volume set, *Grain Vapor Ray: Textures of the Anthropocene*,[27] while the Serpentine Gallery in London put on an event in 2014 called "Extinction Marathon: Visions of the Future." Both of these attempted to investigate, by means of critical discourse as well as artistic practice, how the understanding of planetary processes can offer inspiration to reimagine the ways in which humans are living on earth.

I should mention that some have questioned whether the concept of the Anthropocene is politically conservative, as it seemingly apportions blame to this nebulous entity called "the human" without providing a more detailed account of the inequalities of power and capital involved in our having an impact upon the planet. Yet obviously not all humans, or even all groups of humans, have exerted the same amount of agency in enacting these changes: just as global derivatives traders have contributed more to the economic crisis than, say, subprime mortgage buyers, international oil petroleum companies have contributed more to the eco-pollution of the Niger Delta than have local farmers. As Etienne Turpin indicates in the introduction to his edited collection *Architecture in the Anthropocene*, the Anthropocene is a kind of grand leveler, because it "implicates all humanity equally in the production of a geophysical stratigraphy that is, and has been—since the 'beginning' of the era, which is also a matter of debate—asymmetrically produced according to divisions of class, race, gender and ability."[28] Rather than read this statement as depoliticizing, we could see it as pointing to an inherent element of justice that such a deep-time perspective entails: in the Anthropocene framework, even the very rich cannot escape extinction. At the risk of sounding flippant, I want to suggest that bringing this framework to bear on global capitalism is the only way to show definitively that this particular systemic arrangement will inevitably die out! I realize this statement may fill some readers with glee and others with horror, and that not everyone's horizon of conceptual or spiritual fulfilment involves the death of capitalism. Yet wherever one stands politically, the concept of the Anthropocene can become a powerful tool in shaking up politics-as-we-know-it, across the whole political spectrum. This is because—as many scientists have pointed out by highlighting the increase in the earth's temperatures, the rise of ocean levels, and the depletion of fossil fuels—carrying on as before is no longer an option.[29] Again, no matter what one's political stance, it would be hard to deny that the Anthropocene thesis is almost a perfect antidote to the politics of the status quo: it is also the first science-backed account of the death of the postindustrial capitalism of the globalized world—as well as the death *of* that world.[30] This is not to suggest that we should all therefore just sit back and wait for extinction to happen, or extinguish all hope for material and political change in the near term, contemplating the ruin porn while wallowing in our own transience. Still, extending the temporal scale beyond that of human history by introducing the horizon of extinction can be an important first step in visualizing a post-neoliberal world *here and now*, even if further steps will require us to shorten this scale again. In a 2003 essay for the *New Left Review*, Fredric Jameson recalled a saying that "it is easier to imagine the end of the world than to imagine the end of capitalism," yet he suggested: "We can now revise that and witness the attempt to imagine capitalism by way of imagining the end of the world."[31] The neo-cyberpunk landscapes of China's Pearl River Delta and London's South Bank, with their empty money boxes in the sky for some future investors, are a premonition of the world after the human, in which a row of decaying high rises will be overgrown by posturban vegetation. Yet to say this is not to indulge in some more ruin porn. The framework of the Anthropocene can instead be mobilized to help us take some steps toward imagining what Rory Rowan has termed "a *better* geo-social future," beyond both the "secularized eschatology of catastrophism" and the "sunny machismo" of much of current Left politics.[32]

The temporal scaling of photography

As already mentioned, numerous attempts have, of course, been made to domesticate the abstraction of extinction (including, or rather especially, human extinction) via all sorts of science fiction and artistic visualizations. And photography has been particularly prolific in engaging with the Anthropocene. Indeed, I want to suggest that photography is uniquely placed when it comes to exercising what might be termed the geological sensibility and reimagining the eco-eco disaster. There are two reasons for this. First, *the activity and presence of light as an enabler and enforcer of temporary stabilization and as a marker of the passage of time offers a different perspective on the problems of extinction, climate change, and the depletion of natural resources*. As discussed above, photography allows us to apprehend time as duration precisely by making incisions in its flow: it gives us a concept of the flow, while also enacting incisions in it. We could suggest that photography becomes a supplement to process philosophy in that it foregrounds moments when things stabilize, when they *become things*. Even though these moments of stabilization and isolation are temporary and impermanent—no matter whether they are enacted on a mirror-like surface of metallic silver, paper covered with silver halide, or a CCD sensor—they scale down the "deep time" of nonhuman history to the human measure of duration and perception, while also reconnecting us to a temporal flow of matter and energy. Photography thus becomes a device for us to look at the world, a world we are constantly making (and unmaking). Significantly, light not only represents change in the world but also becomes a carrier of that change: we can think here, for example, of Nadav Kander's photographic series *Dust* (2014), which captures the radioactive ruins of secret cities on the border between Kazakhstan and Russia. These "empty landscapes of invisible dangers," to use the artist's own phrase,[33] feature dilapidated or collapsing buildings, with overgrown shards of concrete arranging themselves into absurd apocalyptic sculptures. Enveloped in gentle pinkish-bluish haze and glow, the cities of Priozersk and Kurchatov are an inversion of William Bornefeld's Fullerton. Strangely encysted in domes made from beautiful dispersed light, they contain radiation, contamination, and ruination. Because light is always coupled with dust, clouds, rain, and other elements, it becomes visible to us humans in this very coupling.[34] As James Gibson puts it in *The Ecological Approach to Visual Perception*, "We never see light, only illuminations."[35] In Kander's series, photographs become not just carriers of traces of light but also reminders of our deadly solar economy, with its inextricable link to fossil fuels. (The next chapter will develop this point by tracing the parallels between photographs and fossils, in an attempt to rethink our relationship to light, the sun, and the energy sources at our disposal.)

There is also another sense in which photography yields itself particularly well to zooming in on the "after the human" perspective. This has to do with its inherently nonhuman ontology and status, whereby, as already intimated in chapter 2, the human-driven practice conventionally known as photography is part of a wider "photographic condition." Photography has always been nonhuman because it has been shaped by what Vilém Flusser has identified as "the photographic apparatus" that supposedly "lies in wait for photography"[36] and that leaves an algorithmic mark on it—one executed by the machine, the cultural conventions of photographic representation, or human photographers' DNA. This nonhuman trace is not decisive—that is to say, it does not *determine* which images will or will not be taken, or whether they will be taken at all, but it does affect the so-called nature of both photographic technique and photographic practice. *The photographic condition whose existence I postulate refers to various living and nonliving things—such as, say, satellites in the sky or cells in our body—participating in the process of imaging across many levels and scales.* As mentioned in the previous chapter, biologist Lynn Margulis claims that the principal characteristic of all living organisms is their ability to perceive, i.e., to recognize and make an image of something. Imaging is therefore positioned—not just by Margulis but also by many philosophers (and proto-philosophers) of posthumanist thought, such as Henri Bergson, Gilles Deleuze and Félix Guattari, as well as Claire Colebrook—as a fundamentally creative process of life. Seen in this light, photography can be said to be ontological, or world-making, establishing as it does what I have earlier termed the "photographic condition," which exceeds human photographic practices. *It is this dual proposition—that, since its very inception, photography has always been nonhuman, and that the human-driven practice conventionally known as photography is part of a wider photographic condition—that underpins my effort to think photography "after the human" (i.e., beyond its traditional humanism and human-centrism).* Therefore, rather than understand the photographic projects under discussion in this piece (or, indeed, any other photographic works) as complete(d) photographs to be inspected and interpreted, we should think of them as nodes "in a matrix of trails to be followed by observant eyes."[37] Through this idea, we are introduced to a different mode of understanding artistic practice, beyond a split between viewer and image, mind and world, and into a dynamic and ongoing movement of intra-actions. That movement, according to Ingold, "is nothing less than life itself, and it is the impulse of life that gives rise to the forms we see."[38] If all life is imagistic or photographic, we do not actually *need* photography to enact it for us. Yet photography in its various guises, both amateur and artistic, is particularly well placed to bring this image-making condition of life to light. Looking at the photographs that imagine the world "after the human" as discussed in this chapter, but also arguably looking *at any other* less apocalyptic photographs, "[w]e cannot help but imagine these scenes as eventually having no human observer at all; rather than a modern subject apprehending such objects, there will be only the objects themselves 'prehending' one another," as McGrath writes.[39] In spite of my earlier reservation, I seem to have returned here to Barthes's argument outlined in *Camera Lucida*, in which photographs of other humans serve as reminders of their inevitable death. Seen in the Anthropocene framework, photography does indeed remind us of the passage of time across larger scales: it brings home the fact that there will be a time not just after the life of our mother, say, but also after the life of any other human on earth. Yet, in a twist to Barthes's argument, photography also incises time to bring forth things, here and now: it therefore both *makes life*, and can *make life better.*

But how can photography perform this role with regard to the "eco-eco" crisis discussed in this chapter? Arguably, this kind of total yet distributed event can never be looked at just from outside: it can only be sensed and apprehended. Even though the "after the human" imagery analyzed so far can potentially act as a trigger for various humans to intervene in the precarious conditions of planetary life, as already said, it also poses the danger of impeding the understanding of the crisis by abstracting it into a series of limited photographic tropes: "emptiness," "abandonment," "eerie landscape," "ruin." With this in mind, let us take a look at some more interventionist attempts to deal with the issue of climate change, where photography is being mobilized not just to imagine the Anthropocene but also to halt it.

How would you photograph a mammoth?

The first category of images I want to focus on relates to what could be described as representationalist "rescuism": an attempt to prevent extinction with a techno-fix. The resurrection biology project is a case in point. This movement, proudly embracing a conservationist agenda, has featured prominently in the media due to its plans to revive the passenger pigeon (*Ectopistes migratorius*), which became extinct in the early twentieth century. The possibility of bringing back mammoths has also been raised. Perhaps unsurprisingly, photography has been instrumental in selling the idea of de-extinction to the public. In March 2014, the *New York Times Magazine* published a series of de-extinction images by Stephen Wilkes, headed by the ominous announcement, "The Mammoth Cometh."[40] Wilkes is an American photographer who, interestingly enough, is principally known for his photographs of ruined landscapes and abandoned structures. His foray into species rescuism resulted in a series of stunning photos of several now-gone animals, all looking uncannily alive. No doubt keen for the public to know that the production process did not rely on any computer-generated imagery but only used traditional photographic techniques, plus a mastery of light, Wilkes was happy to discuss his method openly. And thus we learn that the image of the passenger pigeon (extinct in 1914) was taken in the Museum of Comparative Zoology at Harvard University, while the Tasmanian tiger (last spotted in Tasmania in 1930) came from the Mammalogy Department at the American Museum of Natural History, with the stuffed animal pictured against the background of a printed transparency from the photographer's prior visit to Australia. The eponymous woolly mammoth, extinct about 4,000 years ago, was captured at the Royal BC Museum in Victoria, British Columbia. "The fun part of the project," confessed Wilkes, "was pushing the boundaries of what is real and what is fake, creating an illusion. As well as understanding the tricks that make the mind think something is alive."[41]

In producing the images, Wilkes resorted to old-school lighting and background simulation tricks to achieve the effect of *liveness*. Yet in the digital era, photography increasingly merges with visualization and data rendering, using algorithms and earlier representational frameworks to envisage new ones. This is why the seemingly absurd question of how you would photograph a mammoth is offered a nonabstract answer in the form of de-extinction images. Photography is tasked in de-extinction efforts with providing us with images of the life forms we have lost but seemingly want back. The problem with the de-extinctionist mode of thinking is that it sees organisms as individual entities that can simply be reinserted into various environments, rather than as mutually constituted with them. It thus slides over the issue of our human responsibility toward the biosphere by focusing on singular successes of the survival and revival of "charismatic megafauna": the useful and the cute.[42] Ignoring the complex relations and processes that organize cross-species populations, the de-extinction project reduces any efforts to supposedly "conserve" and bring back certain species to a human exercise in species vanity, a capital-fueled effort to beget life in a godlike manner. Matter is reduced here to a mere substrate for human creation, albeit one that requires a good dose of venture capital for this process of creation to be carried through.[43] Photography, in turn, becomes a mere visualization tool in this game of techno-fixes, losing its lifeness in an attempt to beget life.

The very last pictures in the universe

So how can we reimagine and reinvent life (and death) otherwise, beyond the instrumental, the narcissistic, and the pointless? How can we move beyond representationalism in photography to imagine the Anthropocene better? I would like to see these as more than just technical questions that call for an engineering solution. Instead, in what follows I want to explore the practical possibility of ushering in different kinds of images that exceed the rather conservative efforts of bio-resurrectionists. American artist Trevor Paglen poses similar questions by way of framing his 2012 project *The Last Pictures*. Citing biologist Susan Oyama, Paglen wonders how we can envisage and capture the abstraction that is the ecological collapse given that "the things that most threaten us are those for which there are no images." He asks:

> What does a picture of global warming look like? (A terrified polar bear on a piece of melting ice?) What does rampant resource depletion look like? (A clear-cut

rainforest?) What sort of picture signifies ecological destruction? (An aerial image of an oil spill?) What is a photograph of economic inequality? (Portraits juxtaposing the lives of rich and poor?) What does a picture of capitalism look like? (A factory spewing filth into the sky? A day trader in front of computer terminal?)[44]

The Last Pictures, developed in collaboration with the Creative Time agency and a number of engineers and scientists, involved sending into space a golden disk etched with one hundred images that are indicative, even if not representative, of what we understand as humanity. Attached to the EchoStar XVI communications satellite, the disk thus became "a future alien artifact."[45] For Paglen, the project is not "a grand representation of humanity" or "a portrait of life on earth," but rather a "collection designed to transcend the Anthropocene and to transcend deep time itself. A collection of pictures designed for the time of the cosmos."[46] Paglen knows the chances that some future civilization will find this artifact are almost nil. However, the point of *The Last Pictures* is not to convey something as complex and simultaneously abstract as humanity—even though the history of photography and the history of space travel are full of examples of similar misguided ambitions, from Edward Steichen's exhibition "The Family of Man" to Carl Sagan's collection of images sent with the *Voyager* mission and dubbed a "Rosetta Stone for aliens" by author Mike Davis.[47] For Paglen, the gesture is more meaningful than any future act of interstellar deciphering, because the very idea of meaning "itself breaks down in the vastness of time."[48] Nothing manifests the abstract scales of time as poignantly as a plastic coffee cup which, Paglen comments, "is meant to be sipped for a few minutes but its Styrofoam takes more than a million years to biodegrade."[49] The plastic cup then becomes another "hyperobject," to use Timothy Morton's term (i.e., an object that is "massively distributed in time and space relative to humans").[50] Alongside the photograph of the fake sphinx from Tong Lam's photographs, "unappreciated by any human observer" even though "its head will continue to make a fine perch for a bird,"[51] the image of the Styrofoam cup serves as a time machine for us humans, one that helps us not only to imagine ourselves gone but also to see the limitations of our own "this-worldly" horizon and perspective.

"Photography after the human," understood in the multiple senses engaged in this chapter, must not be seen as a pointless intellectual or artistic exercise. Rather, it is an important ontological and ethical challenge, as it can help us create, here and now, a vision of a world which is not human (i.e., which is not *of* or *for* the human). Built upon the abstraction of our human death and eventual extinction, a world picture of this kind shatters the traditional images of this world, along with those representational practices that have driven the humanist and human-centric tradition of photography and image making. Claire Colebrook, one of the most interesting thinkers of extinction—and of the human restrictions on being able to think oneself out of and beyond extinction—outlines a posthumanist theory of imaging that goes beyond any kind of melancholia or mourning. She writes:

> A certain thought of delimited extinction, the extinction of humans, opens up a variability or intrusion of a different side of the image. This is a geological, post-anthropocene or disembodied image, where there is some experimental grasping at a world that would not be the world for *a* body, nor the world *as* body. ... In the era of extinction we can go beyond a self-willing self-annihilation in which consciousness destroys itself to leave nothing but its own pure non-being; we can begin to imagine imaging for other inhuman worlds. That is to say: rather than thinking of the post-human, where we destroy all our own self-fixities and become pure process, we can look positively to the inhuman and other imaging or reading processes.[52]

The introduction of that inhuman perspective will allow us to reorient our embodied human eye that is stuck in its own present spectacle by cutting into the flow of time and speculating about this flow's future direction.[53] In liberating vision from the constraints of the embodied human eye, with its established set of visual relations and the limited directionality of its outlook, a possibility arises of glimpsing another setup, or rather, of glimpsing it differently. This seemingly minimal intervention (when compared, say, with direct action or political engagement) can actually have earth-shattering consequences, because it plants in our human minds a radically different set of images and imaging practices, one that transcends the subjectivism of the human eye. Unseeing ourselves and what we are calling "the world" in this way must be a first step in any kind of concrete and responsible reconfiguration of our here and now.

4 Photography and Extinction

Extinction as an affective fact

Building on the argument of the previous chapter on photography after the human, I now propose to focus on the concept of extinction as a reference point against which we can think the ontology of photography and its agency. In what follows, I will consider what photography can do with and to the world, what it can cast light on, and what the role of this light (or, more broadly, of light *as such*, seen through the photographic lens) is in approaching questions of life and death on a planetary scale. Under the umbrella of "the Anthropocene," the previous chapter dealt with imagining the irreversible changes to the bio- and geosphere brought forth by the human, changes that are expected to precipitate the disappearance of the human as a species. It also discussed some of the ways of imaging ecological disasters in visual arts and, specifically, in photography—as both a warning against environmental excesses by humans and a call for us humans to consider our political responsibility for our future. I suggested there that envisaging and portraying the world *after the human* is a conceptual device that could help us come to terms with our transience as individuals and as a species, while also placing before us the urgent task of having to slow down the speed of human (and nonhuman) extinction, and the processes that lead to it, while there is still time. The aim of this chapter is to slow down this imaginary passage toward the vanishing of the human and of life as we know it in order to consider what it would mean to *dwell under the horizon of extinction,* and to envisage what we are calling the world "after extinction," in a different sense: not at a time when various species, including the one we are narcissistically most invested in—ourselves—have disappeared, but rather at a time when extinction has entered the conceptual and visual

Figure 4.1
Joanna Zylinska, still from *Exit Man*, 2017.

horizon of the majority of global citizens in one way or another (figure 4.1). Extinction will thus be positioned as a looming affective fact: something to be sensed and imagined *here and now*.[1]

Thinking photography under the horizon of extinction will allow me to draw two temporal lines in the history of this particular medium: one extended toward the past, the other—toward the future. *If we consider the history of photography as part of the broader natural-cultural history of our planet, as I propose to do here, we will be able to trace parallels between photographs and fossils, and read photography as a light-induced process of fossilization occurring across different media.* Seen from this perspective, photography will be presented as containing an actual material record of life rather than just its memory trace. But I will also go back to photography's original embracing of the natural light emanating from the sun to contemplate to what extent photographic practice can tell us something about energy sources, and about our relation to the star that nourishes our planet, and thus, about life as solar survival. I aim to do this via an engagement with photographers who have consciously adopted the horizon of extinction as their workspace—from the nineteenth-century geologist-photographer William Jerome Harrison through to contemporary artists such as Hiroshi Sugimoto and Alexa Horochowski. I will also look at the postdigital practice of Penelope Umbrico, in which the work of the sun has been taken up as both a topic and a medium.

How to grasp geological change

In a certain sense, we have *always* lived in a time "after extinction" and hence under its horizon. In a paper published in 2008, US scientists David Wake and Vance Vredenburg reminded the scholarly community that five mass extinctions had taken place during the history of our planet, each time wiping out significant populations of living beings. The first one supposedly occurred "during the late Ordovician period, some 450 million years ago, when living things were still mainly confined to water."[2] The most devastating mass extinction took place in the Permian period around 250 million years ago, while the most recent and familiar one—which wiped out the dinosaurs and the ammonites, among other species—arrived "at the close of the Cretaceous period."[3] Having analyzed extinction rates among amphibians across geological epochs, Wake and Vredenburg concluded that "an event of a similarly catastrophic nature was currently under way."[4] This event-to-be, brought to the awareness of a wider public by science journalist Elizabeth Kolbert in her eponymous book, has gained the moniker "the Sixth Extinction."

All these scientific attempts to identify and count extinctions notwithstanding, it is worth emphasizing that extinction is primarily a process rather than an event: it is an inextricable part of the natural selection that drives evolution. Indeed, on studying the marine fossil record, David Raup and Jack Sepkoski, paleontologists from the University of Chicago, argued as early as 1984 that, "in addition to the five major mass extinctions, there had been many lesser extinction events."[5] This is why geologists also talk about "background extinction"—a relatively prolonged course of action unfolding across scales of cosmic time, with the average "background extinction rate" of mammals roughly calculated as 0.25 per million species-years.[6] Mass extinctions are instances during which the rate of this process is considerably disturbed, i.e., when a "significant proportion of the world's biota" is eliminated "in a geologically insignificant amount of time."[7] Mass extinctions can therefore be described as moments of intensification on the timeline of continuous expiratory duration. They are significant not only because they represent a curious scientific anomaly but also because of their consequences for the biological makeup of our planet. In what seems to be a reconciliation between the earlier position on extinction as a gradual process called uniformitarianism and catastrophism, present-day geology "holds that conditions on earth change only very slowly, except when they don't."[8]

Even though we have always lived "after extinction," extinction did not enter our human conceptual spectrum until the eighteenth century. As Kolbert points out, "Aristotle wrote a ten-book *History of Animals* without ever considering the possibility that animals actually had a history."[9] Brought in to provide an explanation for the existence of fossils for which no living correlates could be found, the concept of extinction "challenged predominant Christian notions of the Great Chain of Being in which Nature was understood as a complete whole, created by God without gap or imperfection."[10] Curiously, the theory of extinction, or of the existence "of the world previous to ours"—as outlined by the French naturalist Georges Cuvier at the turn of the eighteenth century—was established as a fact several decades before the acceptance of evolution. Even more curiously, Cuvier actually opposed the theory of evolution. It was only with Darwin that extinction started to be seen as part of the evolutionary process, although, unlike his rivals at the time, Darwin himself foregrounded the "smoothness" of this process rather than the geologically significant disruptions to it. This checkered history of the acceptance of the concept of extinction explains why the horizon of extinction under which we currently find ourselves is epistemologically precarious. Indeed, awareness of extinction as a biogeological fact does not seem to have become fully embraced by the human population—or it has perhaps just receded to our collective unconscious. Biologist Ilkka Hanski claims that our present grasp of significant geological and environmental transformations is limited due to our "cognitive incapacity to perceive large-scale and long-term changes."[11] And, as "the apparent stability of the current state of the world is deceiving our senses,"[12] we have not only failed to develop a responsible long-term response to climate change but have also so far foreclosed on the possibility of ushering in any kind of cosmic geopolitics. "Most of the time," writes Hanski, "we only perceive and worry about what is going on around us, although we occasionally spare a thought for the relatively near future."[13]

This is why the looming prospect of the human-influenced Sixth Extinction is something we can so easily remove from our consciousness, even if we have heard the facts, seen the diagrams and simulations, and studied the data. In this context, *dwelling under the horizon of extinction without turning our gaze away from it presents itself as an ethical task, I suggest, as well as a condition of any meaningful long-term politics that exceeds the parochialism of the current parliamentary and nation-state political models.* But if we are to devise a truly cosmic political project—for the humans of here and now, but also for their human and nonhuman descendants—we need to force ourselves to combat our cognitive and sensory limitations in order to grasp extinction not just as a concept but also as a set of material conditions. The exercise in imagining extinction, including the extinction of our own species, undertaken as part of this chapter, could perhaps be a first step in this process. Naturally, there is something self-defeating about this exercise in philosophizing across cosmic scales: it forces us to acknowledge that, after the extinction of the human, once the rats or the microbes have inherited the Earth, there will be no one to do philosophy or art—at least in the way we humans have shaped these practices. I do not mean to suggest that the event of human extinction will be more dramatic for the ecosphere as a whole than the previous extinctions (dinosaurs will, of course, have "cared" much more than we do about the Cretaceous-Tertiary mass extinction, which *we* have branded the "first"); rather, I wish to reintroduce the human standpoint into the theorization of extinction as a concept and a problem. I am proposing to do this not in order to inject a dose of humanism into our debate but precisely in order to avoid what Donna Haraway has criticized as a "view from nowhere"—a view which ends up smuggling back the (usually white, straight, male) human into the debate under the umbrella of its supposed nonhuman perspective.[14] With this reservation in mind, I would like to pick up the exhortation issued by the Center for 21st Century Studies at the University of Wisconsin–Milwaukee to "think of the event of extinction not as destructive or final, but as generative,"[15] and to consider what happens to writing, theory, and philosophy—but also to art and photography—as vehicles for enabling a radically different set of arrangements for the world (i.e., a radically different politics) *after thinking the event of extinction*. Jan Zalasiewicz, a convener of the Anthropocene Working Group at the International Commission on Stratigraphy, claims that the extraordinary geological significance of our current period in which the human has become an agent of geological change will be reflected in the fossils left to future generations.[16] Kolbert aptly highlights this idea with this rather humbling image: "a hundred million years from now, all that we consider to be the great works of man—the sculptures and the libraries, the monuments and the museums, the cities and the factories—will be compressed into a layer of sediment not much thicker than a cigarette paper."[17] Geological significance always implies the insignificance of *any* event when it is seen on a cosmic scale.

Geomedia

The material manifestation of this geological significance is of particular interest to me here precisely because it allows us to confront the transience of our human needs, attachments, desires, and memories with the more permanent record of human and nonhuman life that endures in time. If we think in terms of deep history, we can say that the past leaves an imprint of itself in the rocks, or even—although this may perhaps still seem to be an association too far—that the past photographs itself. In what follows, I will argue that the link between fossilization and photography is more than just a metaphor and that this conceptualization can tell us something new both about the photographic medium and about its conditions, *which are also the conditions of our existence*: *light, energy, the sun*. This proposition brings us back to one of the key lines of argument of the present chapter, and of the book as a whole: namely, that photography as a conventionally recognized human practice is just part of what we earlier termed the *photographic condition* of the universe.

Thinking about media in geological terms inscribes itself in what Jussi Parikka identifies as the wider "drive toward geological and geophysical metaphors in media arts and technological discussions."[18] This drive can be explained by the fact that science itself "implicitly perceived the earth as media," analyzing fossils as it did, and still does, in terms of "records," "indices," and "biofilms."[19] Writing, reading, and interpretation therefore seem to reside at the very heart of what have become known as the earth sciences.[20] Indeed, John Durham Peters explains that for both Darwin and his close friend Charles Lyell—known as the founder of geology—"the earth is a recording medium," even if a "profoundly fallible one. At best it inscribes ruins, enigmas, and hieroglyphics; at worst, blank stretches of oblivion. In their conviction that history can be memorialized only in fragments, Lyell and Darwin form one strand in a modern conversation about the nature of media inscription."[21] For Peters, such historico-geological interpretations inevitably involve distortions that result from temporal transmissions across deep time. He reminds us: "Knowledge is necessarily historical, even in sciences where history might seem irrelevant. The universe is a text, a distorted text, that comes from afar—a classic hermeneutical situation."[22] This conclusion should not be misread as an attempt to "reduce" everything to textuality, the way proponents of materialist thinking sometimes tend to dismiss references to language, but should rather be seen as an intimation that the universe presents itself to us through the tropes, tools, and media we ourselves have forged as part of our becoming-human. (It *may* indeed present and reveal itself entirely differently to different species or classes of beings, but our knowledge of that presentation will be limited to the material and conceptual tools at our disposal, including our very concept of "knowledge.") For this reason, drawing on Jacques Derrida's philosophy, Gary Hall explains that the currently championed opposition between textuality and materiality is actually something of a red herring, because "a written mark, for it to be capable of being understood, must have a sense of permanence. This means it must be possible for it to be materially or empirically inscribed. In short, the condition of writing's very possibility is the material."[23] It is thus impossible to separate the materiality of photography from what our human history has designated as "photographic practice," with all of the values, ideas, and narratives about it—to which I am also contributing with this text, of course, even if my book is also an attempt to expand the concept of photography beyond its association with that historically specific human activity.

Photography as "drawing with light" has been intrinsically connected with inscription from its early days, yet the actual process of making a mark on the surface was originally seen as a function of a nonhuman agent. In the aptly titled *The Pencil of Nature,* one of the first commercially available books of photography, initially published in installments between 1844 and 1846, William Henry Fox Talbot writes that "the plates of this work have been obtained by the mere action of Light upon sensitive paper. They have been formed or depicted by optical and chemical means alone, and without the aid of any one acquainted with the art of drawing. They are impressed by Nature's hand."[24] Significantly, it is the human-specific "art" aspect of the practice, one associated with a unique, historically acquired skill, and not its "drawing" part, that Talbot highlights as remaining in opposition to human activity. The leaving of marks can be cultivated, but, as Talbot himself discovered in the context of his self-avowed inability to draw well, nature beats the human in precision. As illustrated by the examples of images of landscapes, people, architecture, and still lifes included in *The Pencil of Nature*, the eye of the camera is both more accurate and more powerful than the human eye.[25] Talbot was very much aware of the fragility of the resultant photographic recording; indeed, he put much effort precisely into trying to reduce this fragility and to fix an image on paper. But the very idea of light acting as "the pencil of Nature," making semipermanent inscriptions to be detected and interpreted by others, positions photography in its nascent state alongside the then newly emergent discipline of geology (as Lyell's *Principles of Geology* was published between 1830 and 1833), resulting in photographs being seen as thin fossils.

Let us dwell for a moment on this link between photography and geology as different forms of temporal impression by turning to the work of William Jerome Harrison, a nineteenth-century English scientist, teacher, and writer. Harrison authored two seemingly unrelated volumes that reflected his personal and professional interests: *A Sketch of the Geology of Leicestershire and Rutland* (1877) and *History of Photography* (1887).[26] In his intricate reading of Harrison's work, Adam Bobbette shows how, for Harrison, "photography and geology are constituted by similar processes."[27] Full of painstaking detail but perhaps rather tame conceptually, Harrison's prose in *History of Photography* occasionally raises from the everyday to quasi-sublime heights in an attempt to say something bigger about the material at hand. And thus, among the thorough accounts of the different methodologies of the dry and wet photographic processes, Harrison boldly pronounces that "There is nothing new under the sun—especially in photography."[28] This link is not just metaphorical: "Harrison characterizes the protagonists of the art form as apprentices of impressions. According to his assessment, 'impressioning' is a process as ancient as the tanning of human skin under the sun, or the bleaching of wax by the sun. In each case, the sun has created an impression on a body. For Harrison, this was the earliest and most basic form of photography."[29]

Specifically, Harrison looks at the working processes of one of the many simultaneous inventors of photography, Nicéphore Niépce. We can see a clear link between photography and fossilization in Niépce's account of photography (called heliography, or "sun-writing," by him), in which light "acts chemically upon bodies" and "augments the natural consistency of some of these bodies," "solidifies them even; and renders them more or less insoluble."[30] This link becomes even more evident in Harrison's noting that "Niépce studied lithographic forms of image reproduction, the geological implications of which are evident: *litho* [*sic*][31] is Greek for stone, and *lithography* is the process of imprinting an image onto a stone. ... Niépce considered, radically, that light could be substituted for human labour as the agent for copying images into stone."[32] We could conclude that Harrison saw the history of photography as literally a geological history. Peters makes this point even more explicitly, arguing: "Harrison's discovery is this: light's transmission is also a recording. The endless record is found in the motion of light through outer space. The transmissions of light across the cosmos constitute a mobile archive. Recording (saving time) and transmission (bridging space) are indistinguishable in his picture."[33] Harrison therefore can be described as the first narrator of the nonhuman history of photography. Indeed, in the closing words of *History of Photography,* he considers the photographic process to be part of the geological history of the Earth, pointing out "how beautifully it exemplifies the theory of evolution, process rising out of process."[34] Photography is thus revealed to be also coupled with extinction. And fossils lie at the very origin of the history of photography in yet another and more literal sense: one of the first photographs presented by Niépce's competitor Louis-Jacques-Mandé Daguerre as evidence of his newly discovered photographic process featured rows of fossils (figure 4.2). Daguerre's 1839 *Shells and Fossils,* showing deep-time artifacts carefully arranged into a sculptural grid reflecting light at various angles, placed photography in its very nascence between science and art, while also hinting at its geological entanglement.

In making the connection between photography and fossilization, and thus extinction, Harrison not only pinpoints the nonhuman element of the photographic inscription, but also seems to intimate that photography *has always been there,* in cosmic deep time. It "just" needed to be discovered and then fixed for a little longer—rather than invented. If photography and fossilization are both practices of "the impression of softer organisms onto harder geological forms," then *photography is not a new process but, instead, a "modern, mediated extension"*[35] *of the ancient-long "impressioning" activity enabled by light, soil, and various minerals*. The human element comes into the picture, literally, as the "apprentice to impressions enabled by the technical-material apparatus of the camera, plate, chemicals and light."[36] As Bill Anthes points out, this process of nonhuman impressioning by light was also "demonstrated, with gruesome effect, by the shadows of passersby

Figure 4.2
Louis-Jacques-Mandé Daguerre, *Shells and Fossils*, 1839. Public domain.

etched permanently into the granite buildings near the hypocenter of the blast when the United States detonated an atomic bomb over the Japanese city of Hiroshima during World War Two; the blast of light imprinted permanent photograms of passersby onto buildings and pavements."[37]

Photography beyond the tomb

This step into deep time—on Harrison's part, but also my own—can be seen as an *attempt to go beyond the history of photography as part of human history, a history that is driven primarily by human motivations and needs*. The key representative of that humanist approach to the history of photography would be André Bazin's argument in "The Ontology of the Photographic Image," in which he links photography, along with other plastic arts, with the "practice of embalming the dead,"[38] as a way of achieving victory over time by stowing the body away "in the hold of life."[39] Even though something approaching a geological vocabulary of "impressions" enters Bazin's discourse, with photography being described as "a kind of decal or transfer," resembling "a fingerprint" and contributing "something to the order of natural creation,"[40] he ultimately connects the process to the human's "deep need" to have the last word in the argument with death. It is precisely this understanding of photography as both an attempt to overcome death and a constant reminder of it that set the tone for the discourse on this medium in the twentieth century. No text made this link more explicit and conserved it for future scholars of photography more strongly than the celebrated *Camera Lucida* by Roland Barthes.[41] Barthes's slim volume is a protracted meditation on the death of his mother, prompted by seeing a photograph of her, and, more broadly, on images as affective devices that become placeholders for melancholia and mourning. Yet this narrative, as well as the very choice of images in *Camera Lucida*, arguably end up confining photography to a permanent struggle against death. The photographic medium ultimately becomes here a memory aid and a mausoleum, with life preserved as a death mask. An attempt to tell a "deep history" of photography as part of the history of the Earth—a history that transcends human desires and needs—the way I have endeavored to do here, through Harrison's work, can allow us to outline a different approach to the photographic medium and process. If we recognize that the Earth is "a source of invention through the entanglements of form and matter,"[42] while the sun is a source of energy and ultimately life on this Earth, we can read photography as partaking of their vibrant and life-giving (rather than just life-conserving) properties.

Fossilization of time

From the perspective of cosmic time, fossilization can be seen not just as the preservation of life but also as the transmission of its evolutionary principle, with all the nonlinear unpredictability and diversity it entails. It is therefore perhaps apposite to try, together with Claire Colebrook, to "Imagine a species, after humans, 'reading' our planet and its archive: if they encounter human texts (ranging from books, to machines to fossil records) how might new views or theories open up?"[43] For Colebrook, such a text would operate as "a force or disturbance not felt by the organism but witnessed after the event in its having always already occurred."[44] One attempt to envisage such an archive was undertaken by Japanese photographer Hiroshi Sugimoto in the exhibition "Aujourd'hui, le monde est mort [Lost Human Genetic Archive]" held at the Palais de Tokyo in 2014.

The concept of fossilization underpins the whole of Sugimoto's oeuvre. As the artist has explained in a TV interview with PBS:

Fossils work almost the same way as photography: as a record of history. The accumulation of time and history becomes a negative of the image. And this negative comes off, and the fossil is the positive side. This is the same as the action of photography. So, that's why I am very curious about the artistic stage of imprinting the memories of the time record. A fossil is made over 450 million years; it takes that much time. But photography, it's instant. So, to me, photography functions as a fossilization of time.[45]

An attempt to preserve time as a record of the past that nevertheless carries a trace of life is arguably part of *all* photographic practice. Yet in Sugimoto's work, fossilization as a way of recording time gains a unique visual and conceptual inflection, becoming more than just a figure of speech. As explained in a leaflet accompanying his show "Still Life" (London, 2014), the fossil is both a historical fact and a photographic conceit for the artist, serving as "a living record and point of departure into history, crystalizing a moment in time into a singular object." Sugimoto is principally known for his restrained, minimalist images that record the passage of time: for example, his series called *Theaters* (1978–present), shot in old-style cinemas, captures a whole movie in a single frame by leaving the shutter open over its duration and thus rendering it as a glaring white rectangle; while *Seascapes* (1980–present) features the lines of the horizon as places where water meets air. Then there are his *Dioramas* (1976–2012), which engage the topic of fossilization even more explicitly. The series consists of elegant black-and-white images of the natural world, taken with a large-format camera inside natural history museums. What on the surface looks like classical images of open vista landscapes and wild animals is actually a very subtle rendering of the artifice that goes by the name of "nature." The painted backgrounds, 3D foregrounds, and stuffed fauna create a slightly uncanny vision of wildlife, from which "the only thing absent is life itself"—not because photography mummifies and entombs life per se, but because the object photographed had been dead for a long time. Appropriately, thirteen large-format photos from the *Diorama* series were exhibited at London Pace Gallery (November 21, 2014–January 24, 2015) in the aforementioned show called "Still Life," with its title a playful riff on the art historical desiccation of life *from life*.

"Lost Human Genetic Archive" dispels with the minimalism and visual elegance of Sugimoto's earlier work by presenting the visitor with an

Figure 4.3
Website of Palais de Tokyo promoting Sugimoto's exhibition, screengrab by Joanna Zylinska, 2015.

extremely rich and diverse collection of objects amassed by the artist over time and arranged into a series of tableaux.[46] The exhibition addresses the topic of the Anthropocene, so readily taken up by various artists today. Yet Sugimoto's project seems to have sprung from more than just a recent fad: after all, he has been interested in ways of constructing, and responding to, "the natural world" since the early days of his practice. The recent Anthropocene sensibility seems to have just intensified this interest, or cast different light on it. "Intensity" is indeed the sensation that most adequately sums up the experience of visiting the show. Placed somewhere between Dante's Inferno and an enormous toy store (with both Barbie dolls and sex dolls on display!) (figure 4.3), the cavernous basement of Palais de Tokyo was a delightful space to explore, presenting a *Wunderkammer* for the age of extinction in which new things popped up from every crevice and around every corner, on their way to going out with a bang. Each little room in the show staged an alternative "just after the extinction" scenario, throwing light on different aspects of the process. "Yes, we are going to die," Sugimoto-the-roguish-curator-of-doom seemed to want to remind us, "but what a blast we've had—and yet," he frowned, "look what a mess we've made." (Just think of the plastic needed to make all these different dolls!) This dual emotion of playfulness and melancholia was conveyed by the conflicting visuality of the setup: the visitors wandered around in a corrugated metal mazelike structure, constantly presented with amazing objects: the Shinto god of thunder Kaminari-sama, astronauts' poo, fossils from the Cambrian to the Eocene, one of Sugimoto's own *Seascapes*. In a statement that was perhaps a variation on the established trope of the sublime in art, whereby the work evokes pleasure and pain for aesthetic as well as moral effect, Sugimoto mischievously declared: "Imagining the worst conceivable tomorrows gives me tremendous pleasure."[47]

There is more to this phrase than just a manic hysteria in the face of an event about which we cannot do much, a kind of Anthropocene-era laughter at a time when tears seem like a belated response to the done deal. Many times in the show, in the context of various end-of-life scenarios, Sugimoto reiterated the statement, "The world died today. Or maybe yesterday, I don't know ... " As the *Guardian* critic Adrian Searle has explained: "Echoing the beginning of Albert Camus's 1942 novel *The Stranger*, which begins with almost the same words ('Mother died today. Or maybe yesterday ... '), the phrase keeps recurring, leitmotif and chorus. Swapping 'mother' with 'world' implies a final, universal end of fertility and the breaking of the primal bond. It's also fun."[48] The exploratory fun offered by the artist to the visitors to this Lunapark of the Anthropocene, full of excess and toys and stuff everywhere, carried with it a serious message: "Where is this human race heading, incapable of preventing itself from being destroyed in the name of unchecked growth?"[49] With this opulent exhibition, the artist still managed to put his trademark minimalism at the center of the work—but this was minimalism conceived as an ethico-political decision, not an aesthetic affectation, one that was aimed to challenge our (including the artist's own) desire to consume, conserve, and collect.

The contestation of both modernism and the accompanying minimalism as merely aesthetic choices has become a powerful trope for many other artists who are consciously working under the horizon of the eco-eco disaster. US-based artist Alexa Horochowski's visually restrained if conceptually rich project *Club Disminución* (Club of Diminishing Returns), instigated during her residency at Casa Poli in Chile in 2012–2013, offers an interesting counterpart to Sugimoto's opulent archive. *Club Disminución* takes to task the modernist dream of an ideal society which was to be arrived at through developments in technology and engineering in addition to the progress of the human mind. Casa Poli, a minimalist, cement cube, stands on a jagged cliff overlooking the Pacific, over a narrow cave, thus both foregrounding and suspending the differentiation between the (hu)man-made and what this human calls "nature," between architecture and land. In an essay on Horochowski's project, Christina Schmid suggests that "Casa Poli reads both as a tribute to Le Corbusier's stark architecture and to the site itself, strangely in keeping with a place swept clean of all but the most resilient vegetation."[50] By blurring the boundaries between development and evolution, Horochowski has opened a rift in the modernist narrative of the seamless unification between citizens and their environment, with the promised Corbusian order resulting in a haunted space, exposed to the elements. Staying in this modernist masterpiece, literally perched at the edge of the world, the artist polluted its visual and conceptual purity with the objects and materials found outdoors: rubbish, fossils, kelp. This last material provides a conceptual thread for the *Club Disminución* show, first staged in 2014 at The Soap Factory in Minneapolis—one of the many places of traditional industrial production now regenerated into "cultural industries" zones. Kelp (*Durvillaea antarctica*) or *cochayuyo*, as it is called in Chile, is a shore seaweed that resembles a thick cable and that arranges itself into unusual quasi-sculptural tangles. Attracted to its rubbery texture and its strange beauty, Horochowski started collecting the plant in large amounts during the early stages of the project, and then hung it in various places in the white modernist cube of Casa Poli. As a plant that could easily pass for a technological object, cochayuyo thus became an inspiration for her to interrogate the intertwining of nature and culture, extinction and obsolescence. The "diminishing returns" refers in part to Horochowski's seemingly pointless activities such as straightening the kelp, drying it, and fitting it into cuboid shapes.

The visitors to Horochowski's exhibition at The Soap Gallery were greeted by large-screen videos showing this cable-like product, with images cut and

Figure 4.4
Alexa Horochowski, from *Club Disminución*, 2014. Image courtesy of the artist.

mirrored on screen to form a kaleidoscope of poetic movement. Rippling and revolving before our eyes, the videos offered a poignant reflection on the regurgitation of naturecultures, always with diminishing returns. In the show, the products of nature and culture were rendered indistinguishable in what became a meditation on human pursuits in a world that escapes human control the more we try to order and own it. These were accompanied by another playful take on modernist visual art: cubelike structures which may have been made of kelp, cable, or metal wire. Even if we touched them, we were not entirely sure of their material. "Natural objects, flotsam, and 'naturalized' garbage, combined with studio-generated objects" arranged themselves into what the artist has described as "a posthuman natural history of the future," whereby "a fossil of a credit card [one of the most intriguing objects in the show (figure 4.4)] heralds a postconsumer future, beyond the era of the Anthropocene."[51] This particular artifact raises an intriguing question: what will future generations make of the fossils of those small embellished plastic rectangles that the humans of the late capitalist era have endowed with so much value? Yet Horochowski offers us more than the familiar lamentation over the passing of man and his worldly wealth. Schmid writes that the artist's "more-than-vaguely vaginal imagery suggests a gendering of the dialogue: macho modernism's tragic-heroic quest for mastery"[52]—so evident in the jeremiads by the various Anthropocene-era male prophets of doom and gloom, who seem to take delight in pronouncing our imminent death[53]—"quavers, about to be engulfed and swallowed up by an entirely different sensibility."[54]

Club Disminución envisages a future beyond the human. Just as in Tong Lam's photographs (discussed in chapter 3) of the fake sphinx's head, unappreciated by the human, that makes "a fine perch for a bird,"[55] this is a future when piled-up kelp hints at "a life beyond human purpose."[56] The project thus becomes a quintessential example of "art after the human," still appreciated "as art" from our human position of here and now, yet appreciated precisely for its placement against the horizon of extinction. In its playful reflection on the passage of time, *Club Disminución* seems to be "encouraging the United States to join the club of formerly great nations and have-beens who lament the waning of past glories. Celebrating diminishing economic opportunity anticipates the twilight on the horizon: come, have a seat amid the lengthening shadows."[57] Yet Schmid insists—and I would agree with her—that "*Club Disminución* is not a depressing show," although it may be a melancholic one, disturbing and disorienting as it does our typologies and classificatory systems. "Calmly and not without humor … , Horochowski proposes that we dare look into the dark," Schmid concludes. "We can face the sunset, her work argues. *Club Disminución* gathers in the fading light and dwells, affectionately, in the lengthening shadows of the human age."[58]

On how to face the sunset

So, if we humans can never face the sun, what does it mean for us to be able to face the sunset? This question has been addressed, although from a slightly different vantage point, by photo artist Penelope Umbrico, perhaps best known for her large-scale project *Suns (From Sunsets) from Flickr* (figure 4.5). Begun in 2006 (when "sunset" was the most tagged word on the image-hosting website Flickr), the project explores ideas of originality and replication in the culture of online sharing. The artist zooms in on a snapshot she finds that features a sunset, cuts out the sun from it, resizes it, and adds it to the ever growing grid of burnt-out white globes (a testament to the majority of users' relying on their cameras' automatic exposure, without compensating for the contrast of this particular scene) placed against

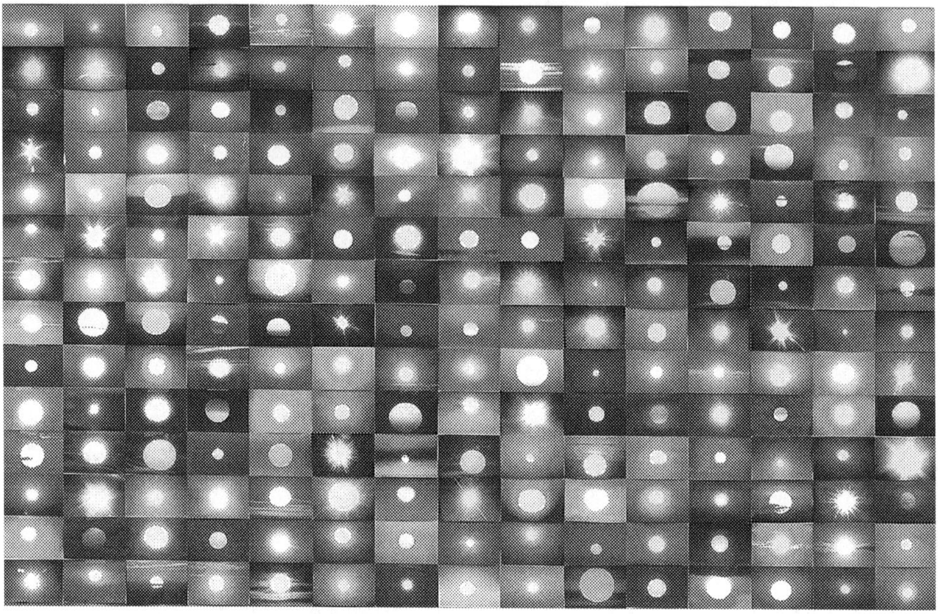

Figure 4.5
Penelope Umbrico, *Suns (From Sunsets) from Flickr*, 2006–ongoing. Screengrab by Joanna Zylinska, 2015.

an orange-red background. These sun tapestries are then displayed as large printouts on gallery walls, but they also return to the Internet in different guises—as small grids, a screensaver, a set of virtual postcards available in the virtual environment Second Life.

Umbrico's principal interest is not the banal visuality of the sunset but rather participation in the collective practice of sharing something you cannot claim authorship over. She also admits to being interested in the sun as our light source, and in the transformations this light source is undergoing, as both image and matter:

I thought it peculiar that the sun, the quintessential giver of life and warmth, constant in our lives, symbol of enlightenment, spirituality, eternity, all things unreachable and ephemeral, omnipotent provider of optimism and vitamin D ... and so ubiquitously photographed, is now subsumed to the internet—this warm singular object made multiple in the electronic space of the web, and viewed within the cool light of the screen.[59]

Alongside her exploration of digital environments, Umbrico's concerns are aligned with the traditional perception of photography as a practice of drawing with light, and with the energetic transformations its geological actions undergo on the Internet. In what sounds like a playful rebuttal of the more solemn tenor of certain philosophical propositions about the death of the sun, Umbrico pronounces that "the sun is dead but we make our own light"[60]—and then goes off to rephotograph the suns from Flickr as displayed on the screen with her iPhone, and to explore the new light effects produced in the process. The result is a follow-up project, *Sun/Screen* (2014), in which sunset-like hues merge with a moiré pattern caused by the superimposition of the pixel grids, meshes, or dot patterns upon an image. The image then emits an uncannily beautiful light, which does not belong to the sun any more, but which is not entirely *ours* either. Yet our human perception, with its specific visual apparatus and its color recognition capabilities, is required to acknowledge this very denaturalization of the sun into a moiré pattern. In other words, the denaturalized sun needs the human body to experience this denaturalization: otherwise, the process and the concept, and even the artwork, do not make sense—even if they can still take place beyond or outside the human.

Umbrico's seriously playful projects can be seen as an unwitting response to the philosophical problem posed by French philosopher Jean-François Lyotard in his essay "Can Thought Go On without a Body?," first published in 1987 and included in *The Inhuman*. Lyotard declares that the "sole serious question facing humanity today"[61] is the solar explosion that awaits us in 4.5 billion years, as a result of which "everything," including thought which can think this "everythingness," will come to an end. The sun's death presents itself to us as the ultimate event of extinction and thus as the ultimate sublime. It stands for the most dramatic and final *horror vacui*, the horror of there being nothing at all, but also for the end of the sublime as the end of "the human," and of the human's philosophical horizon, with its acquired terms of reference. As Lyotard points out, "after the sun's death there won't be a thought to know that its death took place."[62] Yet the universe of course *will* "know" about this death; it will "see," "record," and no doubt "respond" to it, but in a language that far exceeds human communication models and structures. Having outlined this somewhat bleak yet still rather remote prospect of the total annihilation of life, Lyotard then proceeds to mock the efforts undertaken by the cyberneticists of technocapitalism to "make thinking materially possible after the change in the condition of matter" by shifting life to other galaxies in order to liberate it from the throes of the dying sun. This process seems desperately grotesque as, for Lyotard, embodiment constitutes the very condition of thought: our "software"—mind, philosophy, language—is codependent on, i.e., constituted by and constitutive of, our hardware (the body). However, imagining the solar demise—that is, conducting philosophy under the shadow of not just individual human death but also the extinction of humankind—reminds us that the Earth is a "transitory ... arrangement of matter/energy."[63] It also casts different light on our "local" human wars and conflicts—not to mention "philosophical debates" and "passions."[64]

The serious tenor of the essay changes when Lyotard adopts a persona he calls "SHE" in the second part of the piece. As Jerry Aline Flieger puts it, "'She' insists that a certain human capacity is associated with a field of vision that is not the sweep of satellite surveillance but which is limited to a human sphere."[65] Even if we see embodiment as epiphenomenal rather than fundamental in the development of the human, SHE allows us to recognize that, rather than entertain fantasies of extricating human intellect from its material shell, we would be better off getting to the bottom of the desexualized yet so-very-gendered dream of disembodied posthuman thought. From this point of view, the actual disaster that should concern us would involve the disappearance not of the solar system as our matrix of reference but rather of the body, i.e., the extinction of the human as we know it—*while we are still around.* Accusing philosophers of extricating matter from their writings, Lyotard reminds us at the same time that the materiality of the human and of the universe as we know it needs to be read alongside its technicity, with matter being taken "as an arrangement of energy created, destroyed and recreated over and over again, endlessly."[66] He pinpoints:

As anthropologists and biologists admit, even the simplest life forms, infusoria (tiny algae synthesized by light at the edges of tidepools a few million years ago [now termed Protista]) are already technical devices. Any material system is technological if it filters information useful to its survival, if it memorizes and processes that information and makes inferences based on the regulatory effect of behavior—that is, if it intervenes on and impacts its environment, so as to assure its perpetuation at least. A human being is not different in nature from an object of this type.[67]

Lyotard thus reads the emergence of life in early microorganisms as a technical process. With this, he goes beyond the humanist logic of originary technicity that has shaped the work of many other French philosophers, such as Bernard Stiegler, whereby it is the human that is seen as constituted by, and emerging with, technicity (fire, tools, language). For Lyotard, technicity is already the condition and driving force of primordial life, long before the emergence of the human. Picking up on this idea, I want to suggest that *the process of the emergence of life also reveals itself to be inherently photographic, because light is needed to initiate photosynthesis, i.e., to make a lasting change on an organism, and then to trigger further changes*. Yet, even if we continue pursuing this expanded understanding of photography as a nonhuman process that exceeds human acts involving cameras and photosensitive material (as we have been in this book so far), we are nevertheless returned here, with Lyotard, to the phenomenological experience of light cast upon a human body, located on the Earth which is still being lit by its middle-aged sun. Indeed, for Lyotard, corporeality is the condition of knowledge but also of the phenomenological experience that enables and conditions openness, generativity, and generosity—and that allows for the transmutation of the technical action of transmitting and receiving information into an ethical act. This returns us to the issue of the human's inability to face the sun, yet still having to take on the task of facing the sunset. The death of the sun, the universe, and the extinction of everything we know and do not know is thus repositioned here from an ontological to an ethico-political problem. Being able to face the sunset also means coming to terms with the problem of energy—and of the depletion of resources not only in the solar domain but also in the more parochial, terrestrial (or, more specifically, subterranean) realm. Being able to *share* the sunset, as Umbrico does, hints at the possibility of thinking, even if not yet actually implementing, a more generous, less exploitative, mode of engaging with those resources.

Fossil *non*sense

It is precisely humans' *(mis)management of energy sources as fossil fuels* that is referenced as one of the symptoms of the Anthropocene, a state of events that has resulted in the change of the composition of the atmosphere—and thus in the alteration of the nature of the light that reaches us through it.

Figure 4.6
Joanna Zylinska, still from *Exit Man*, 2017.

As Kolbert writes, citing the chemist Paul Crutzen (the original author of the term "Anthropocene"), "Owing to a combination of fossil fuel combustion and deforestation, the concentration of carbon dioxide in the air has risen by forty percent over the last two centuries, while the concentration of methane, an even more potent greenhouse gas, has more than doubled."[68] Facing the sunset is therefore a way of suspending what Finnish philosopher Tere Vadén has called "fossil sense":[69] an assumption that, because things have been a certain way for the last 150 years—with the intertwined logic of economic growth and fossil fuel exploitation shaping our modern way of life—they will always be this way. Fossil sense is therefore actually *non*sense: it is an example of thinking that encapsulates the "derangements of scale"[70] and that involves a forgetting of the deep time of history, fueled by myopic self-interest and species narcissism (figure 4.6). Vadén claims that our lives are so intertwined with fossil fuels that "[o]ur desires are the desires of oil, our dreams the dreams of coal."[71] The modern human is himself fossil-fueled, with the very core of not just his physical but also his economic and sociopolitical identity being shaped by hydrocarbons. To extend the concept and metaphor we have been working with, we can go so far as to suggest that, while our own bodies are made of the (same) starstuff, they now also carry a record of industrially processed hydrocarbons: shards of coal, remnants of oil. Or, indeed, that we ourselves have become a photograph—and a fossil—of our way of life. As Antti Salminen puts it in his poignantly titled essay, "Photography in the Age of Fossil Nihilism," "When a life form lives off fossil fuel, it will gradually become fossilized itself."[72] Salminen continues:

> There is something distinctly un-dead about this image [of modern man being "made of oil from top to toe"]: if it is the case that the modern humane and self-conscious identity was based on an enormous volume of ancient metabolic waste from (marine) organisms, the Western man modernized the world using energy generated from the countless deaths of non-human beings. Ultimately, behind this image too lies the sun's gaping madness, the source of all the earth's energy, excluding tide, geothermal energy, and fission. A culture based on subjective individuality is structurally dependent on the vast amounts of energy, which it consumes entirely subconsciously, in volumes that a human being, left to his own devices, could never hope to match.
>
> In other words: the subject cannot be sustained through manual labor alone. The subject's very existence and ongoing survival is contingent upon energy borrowed from oil, a light distilled from death. In order to have the energy to be a subject, to be modern, we humans must sift through layers of ancient, non-human death. The modern man, in his current individualized incarnation, is, quite literally, a fossil brought to life by the death of the sun.[73]

Living under the cloud of oil fumes and global pollution, like characters from William Bornefeld's novel *Time and Light* inhabiting a domed city of Fullerton discussed in chapter 3, we seem to have forgotten about the sun. Grand as this proposition may sound, I want to suggest that photography can be mobilized to address the present fossil crisis in two ways: by expanding the temporal perspective from which this issue is normally seen (or *not seen*, as the case may be), and by helping us outline a different, less deadly solar economy. Some claim that photography can most easily undertake this task by serving as a record of the terrible damage done to the environment. We can reference here, for example, the series called *Oil* by Edward Burtynsky, which features large-scale images of oil fields in Azerbaijan, the United States, and Canada; discarded or burning tire piles in California; and oil refineries. These predominantly bird's-eye view images of what, from above and afar, look like digitally enhanced landscape paintings for the HDR age,[74] with their rich colors, billowing clouds, and a remarkable amount of detail, are intermingled with equally large images of ruined car factories, shot face-on. Burtynsky admits that what began "out of a sense of awe at what we as a species were up to" has ended up as a meditation on our conflicting relationship to oil "as both the source of energy that makes everything possible, and as a source of dread, for its ongoing endangerment of our habitat."[75] This kind of representational art is no doubt important in being able to visualize environmental destruction and our damaging relationship to various sources of energy, including the sun. Yet there is also a danger that these conventionally beautiful images, even if shot "under the light of the black sun,"[76] will actually cause what Nicholas Mirzoeff has called "a loss of perception," and thus perpetuate our *forgetting about the sun*—with beauty acting as an anesthetic against the urgency of the environmental situation.[77] As the increasing proliferation of images of disaster and suffering in various media testifies, there is no evidence that perception is a trigger for (moral) action. Indeed, sentimentalism or moral outrage aside, visual oversaturation may actually lead to nonaction. Scientist Ilkka Hanski argues that, due to the way our sensual and cognitive apparatus has evolved, we humans "are only able to perceive a small region of space and a short length of time."[78] We could therefore conclude, perhaps a little crudely, that evolution has made it impossible for us to *truly* see evolution—and hence also extinction: or rather, that once we have seen it, it is very easy for these kinds of long-term events to disappear from our visual and conceptual horizon.

Thus, we should not overestimate the role of documentary and representational photography that takes environmental issues as its topic. To state this is not to argue for photography's inherent weakness, however. Indeed, the argument of this chapter—and of the book as a whole—is that photography is a quintessential practice of life, not just in the sense that it records our lives nonstop, on both a micro and a macro level, but also in the deeper philosophical sense of encompassing life as duration through making incisions in it. In other words, *all* photography, with its capacity to capture light and make it act upon surfaces, acts as a cue for the goings-on of deep time, well beyond human control and human existence. Salminen goes so far as to suggest: "In the fossil nihilist age, photography acts as a reminder of the sun, to which the fossil man can turn for little else than leave to simply expire."[79]

It is here, in this image of photography as a reminder of the sun, and thus of life itself, that the two temporal lines of this chapter—one orientated toward the past, the other toward the future—come together. *Photography as an embalmer and carrier of imprints testifies to the continued existence of solar energy and to its photosynthesis-enabling capabilities.* To say this is not to rewrite the traditional narrative about photography as being about life *rather than* death in any straightforward and naïve way. Yet rhetorically placing photography under the horizon of extinction—a horizon under which it has arguably unfolded on a material level since time immemorial—has allowed us to come out on the side of life, and to think fossils beyond the currently dominant fossil nihilism. In the closing pages of his book *Flight Ways: Life and Loss at the Edge of Extinction* Thom van Dooren develops an idea that could be described as "ethical mourning": a way of responding responsibly to the horizon of extinction by telling stories about ongoing extinctions. Of course, we need more than just stories of extinctions past, even if telling such stories can play an important and salutary role for our current biosphere. Fossils and/as photographs can therefore be seen as more than just forms of *memento mori*: they are also ethical injunctions, pointing and reaching out to life, in both its actual and virtual forms. Citing grief counsellor and philosopher Thomas Attig, van Dooren writes that "In choosing to grieve actively, we choose life."[80] This is precisely where photography as a process of fossilization that keeps a record of time becomes an ethical task, a form of countermourning the passage of time by casting light on solar light. By turning and returning to the sun, we can take first steps toward envisaging a new energetics, one that develops a more ethical relationship to fossils as "layers of ancient, non-human death." Photography as an original practice of light, now undertaken under the glow of electricity as often as under the glow of the sun, can get us to engage with light anew—even though, in its present digital setup, it is also, in Salminen's words, "contingent upon energy borrowed from oil, a light distilled from death."

5 Ecomedia between Extinction and Obsolescence

Death in media-ecological niches

This chapter adopts a media-ecological perspective to explore parallels between biological extinction and technical obsolescence. It is set against the background of the current transformations in our media landscape, whereby many objects traditionally considered stable or fixed—photographs, imaging systems, technological networks—are radically changing both their identity and their visibility. In this context, the photographic image can be said to exist in a dynamic set of entangled media relations, and hence be seen as a process taking place in a network of material-cultural infrastructures rather than regarded as a discrete object.[1] This rethinking of photography in more dynamic and media-ecological terms encourages a broader discussion of producing, curating, studying, and looking at images today—but also of the constantly updated apparatuses that are helping produce these images. Picking up the Anthropocene thread, I want to suggest that, *instead of becoming too preoccupied with the frequently pronounced "death of photography," we should turn our attention to the multiple deaths of cameras and other equipment—and to the piles of e-waste resultant from those "deaths."* The argument of this chapter is anchored in the notion of "photographic fossils"[2]—remnants of our human history of making images that will continue long into a posthuman future as discarded techno-trash, materials decomposing in the air, soil, and oceans, as well as cosmic debris. Through this media-geological exploration of various sites of our fossilized media past, I offer a meditation, across different temporal scales, on our human relation to devices and materials that we create and discard, on the desire for new products that fuels so-called innovation, and on the politics, ethics, and aesthetics of waste. The argument outlined here, speculating as it does on photography's nonhuman *future*, provides a follow-up to the nonhuman *history* of photography outlined in the previous chapter.

Returning to the concept of extinction discussed earlier in the book, the chapter zooms in on a set of processes associated with the becoming-extinct of media technology, i.e., with technological obsolescence, decay, and death. However, if the relationship between *physis* and *tekhne*, or nature and artifice, is itself a product of the human mind and thus a cultural imprint upon temporal unfoldings that are just different in scale and duration rather than in kind,[3] then extinction and obsolescence can perhaps be treated as two facets of the same phenomenon. This argument draws inspiration from Stanisław Lem's 1964 philosophical treatise *Summa Technologiae*, in which this Polish writer, best known for his science fiction novels, postulates two types of evolution: biological and technical. Identifying a technical tendency in the bio-logic of life, he argues: "Every technology is actually an artificial extension of the innate tendency possessed by all living beings to gain mastery over their environment, or at least not to surrender to it in their struggle for survival."[4] Lem goes on to identify a number of parallels between biological and technical evolution:

> It is not only that the first amphibians were similar to fish, while the mammals resembled small lizards. The first airplane, the first automobile, or the first radio owed its appearance to the replication of the forms that preceded it. The first birds were feathered flying lizards; the first automobile was a spitting image of the coach with a guillotined shaft; the airplane had been "copied" from the kite (or even the bird), the radio from the already existing telephone.[5]

In tracing conceptual and material parallelism between extinction and obsolescence, I would nevertheless like to signal that the proposition to interpret what may more obviously present itself as an insatiable capitalist desire for innovation in evolutionary terms is not aimed at naturalizing, and hence depoliticizing, the production process. On the contrary, my goal here is to highlight precisely the mobilization of what we could call a "banalized Darwinism" which reduces the undetermined zigzags of evolution to a linear progression in order to justify the constant need for technological upgrade. Adopting the ecological—and geological—perspective in my study of media technologies, including photography, will also allow me to draw attention to the hubris behind the innovation agenda that fuels the global economy, and that produces seemingly infinite amounts of technological fossils in the process. The intensified outpouring of variations of the same merchandise at a particular moment in the production cycle is a case in point.

To illustrate this process, let us look at the camera stock available at the time of writing (April 2016) from the Japanese optical equipment manufacturer Canon. Its list of interchangeable lens digital cameras includes EOS-1D X Mark II, EOS-1D X, EOS-1D C, EOS M10, EOS M3, EOS 7D Mark II, EOS 6D, EOS 80D, EOS Rebel T6s (called 760D outside the US); EOS Rebel T6i (750D outside the US), EOS Rebel T6 (1300D outside the US), EOS Rebel T5 (1200D outside the US), EOS Rebel T5i (700D outside the US), EOS Rebel SL1 (100D outside the US), EOS 60D, EOS 60Da, EOS 5D Mark III, EOS 5DS, and EOS 5DS R. This list is accompanied by eighteen variations of Canon's advanced compact PowerShot models and three entry-level IXUS models. Even though results for the financial quarter for Canon Inc. show that its overall operating profit is up 7.6% year over year, in 2015 the company recorded its net income at 49.2 billion yen, 15.6% lower than the previous year, year over year. The Imaging Resource website explains that these figures "tell a story we've been hearing for a number of years now—sales are down and not necessarily looking any brighter. ... Canon's camera sales are a continually sinking ship, but what stands out and confirms what we've all but known is that the sales of lower-end compact cameras are not just falling, but taking a nosedive. Year-over-year, compact camera sales are down a whopping 29% [while] interchangeable lens cameras are ... down 17%."[6] The current Canon provision, with its seemingly endless issuing of variations of the same product (and similar analyses could be conducted for Canon's competitors, such as Nikon or Sony), seems to reflect what Lem has described as "elephantiasis, so typical of the predecline blossom of dying evolutionary branches."[7] Lem goes on to compare the last zeppelins of the 1930s, or the last exemplars of the steam-driven freight train before it was made obsolete by diesel and electric locomotives, with the atlantosauruses and brontosauruses of the Cretaceous period, where the size of provision—be it in terms of the actual dimensions, market share, or "evolutionary radiation"—is the last breath of life before the line's extinction or obsolescence (in our case, before the ultimate victory of the camera phone in the majority of media-ecological niches).

To accompany this industry-based perspective, in his cultural history of photography, Jakub Dziewit analyzes the behavior of members of Internet forums dedicated to photography by drawing on naturalistic rhetoric.

He describes these amateur photographers as "breeders" of personalized and rarefied collections, which consist of carefully chosen camera and lens specimens. Many photographers posting on such forums display an almost organic commitment to growing their collections, coupled with a conviction about the superiority of their specimens over those of the other posters—as manifested in the overzealous defense of their brand/genus, with all its characteristics. This desire is rarely driven by the ambition to take better pictures—indeed, relatively few photographs get posted on equipment forums, such as dpreview—rather, it is focused on achieving the perfection of the breed. It is precisely the aspiration to develop the ideal breed of photographic equipment, which Dziewit compares with a desire to breed the perfect Arabian horse, that he believes underpins the efforts of many users.[8] The affective attachment to the process of cultivating one's collection tends to overshadow any economic, political, or ethical issues: indeed, any discussion of those, limited to frequent threads about whether it is moral to use Amazon's generous return policy to test equipment and return it if it is simply not to one's liking, usually gets foreclosed rather quickly, or leads to flame wars. The majority of discussants on camera forums, posting predominantly from the relatively affluent regions of the world, seem unwilling to acknowledge the fact that, as Gay Hawkins puts it, "The capacity to overconsume is a minority privilege that masks not only the conditions of production—but also the ecological consequences of an economy driven by the logic of growth at all costs."[9] Yet what I offer here is not just a study of exuberant media consumers in the world "out there." This minority privilege is also something that I, as a passionate photographer, frequent buyer of photographic equipment, reader of industry magazines on the topic, and user of its Internet forums, find myself very much enveloped in. Its interrogation here is therefore designed as a way of turning the critical mirror back on myself as both media scholar and equipment geek to raise the ethico-political problem of photographic obsolescence in the wider context of our changing media ecologies.

Shallow media geology

There already exists much scholarship in media studies on the ecological aspects of media obsolescence. One can mention here Sean Cubitt's *Eco-Media*, Richard Maxwell and Toby Miller's (rather human-centric) *Greening the Media*, Jennifer Gabrys's *Digital Rubbish*, and Jussi Parikka's *A Geology of Media* as well as his edited "living book" *Medianatures*.[10] Drawing on aspects of this research, with its extensive tracing of specific material deposits such as "plastics, wood, plywood, copper, aluminum, silver, gold, palladium, lead, mercury, arsenic, cadmium, selenium, hexavalent chromium and flame retardants" that make up media components,[11] I will *retell the story of the photographic ecomedia as an embodied story of human perception and human responsibility for the universe whose tiny corner we presently occupy*. The term "ecomedia" builds on work by Cubitt, who, in an attempt to make "a contribution to ecological politics,"[12] introduced the concept in his eponymous book to examine how popular culture deals with environmental themes, but my use of this term extends its scope to more nonhuman and post-natural contexts.[13] For me, "ecomedia" stands for media that is concerned with ecological themes while also revealing its own entanglement with bio-technical ecologies of our planet that transcend what we conventionally understand as media networks. In this view, we humans are an inherent part of those media ecologies—rather than merely media producers or users who represent ecological themes in a certain way, and who affect "nature" positively or negatively. Ecomedia, the way I see it, pursues what I would call, after Timothy Morton, an "ecology without nature"[14]—an ecological predisposition that does not evoke a discrete prelinguistic realm of natural resources separate from the human, and requiring protection against human activities. To say this is *not* to proclaim that there is nothing outside human cognition or perception, but rather that the human notion of nature is already a truncated set of concepts and material entities, carved out along human cognitive and sensory lines. (To try to "unthink" this notion, consider the following: What would "nature" would look like for a dolphin, a mycelium network, or a stone?)

With this approach, I aim to update my earlier work in *Minimal Ethics for the Anthropocene* (2014) by focusing on several specific geophysical locations. Whereas in that book I considered a more general position on ethics as a way of living a good life when life itself was declared to be under a unique threat, while also reflecting on what counted as goodness in those circumstances,[15] my method here is that of an amateur geologist-philosopher-artist, one whose dirty process involves an affective-material excavation of the past mixed with a textual and visual speculation about the future. My way of working differs from the more brazen, albeit more ambitious, exploratory pursuits in which (predominantly male) media archaeologists and media geologists thrust their probes into deep time across cosmic scales, offering a God's-eye view of the universe's geological, biological, and art historical strata. What I aim to do here is much more modest in scope in that it offers a "view from somewhere" of a universe that "exceeds and incorporates" me—and within which I am only temporally at home.[16] Tentatively described as "shallow media geology," my excavatory pursuits will lead me to look around, probe the folds of matter at hand, play with the dust, check out the dirt under my fingernails. Specifically, the chapter will dig into three localized material and conceptual "fossil sites": (1) the global: photographic images of e-waste by Pieter Hugo, in which photography is mobilized to tell a wider story of ecomedia; (2) the national: displays of old photographic equipment at the National Media Museum in the north of England which serve as a memento to both the medium and the geographical region that hosts them; (3) the domestic: everyday media infrastructures that preserve and enable photomedia setups and their networks.

The untimely death of photography

Before we embark on our dig, we should tackle one of the biggest myths about photography itself: its regularly pronounced obsolescence and death. The foundations of this myth need to be looked at not just because they tell us something about our investments in, and disavowals of, different media and art forms (which the next chapter will address in more detail), but also because they provide some actual building material for our media pasts and futures—and for our stories about them. Those suffering from medium nostalgia misrecognized as fondness for medium specificity—represented in this chapter by theorist Nick Mirzoeff, artist Tacita Dean, and journalist Antonio Olmos—initially greeted the arrival of digitization as the premonition of the analog medium's death. And thus in the 1999 edition of *An Introduction to Visual Culture*, Mirzoeff concluded, "After a century and a half of recording and memorializing death, photography met its own death some time in the 1980s at the hands of computer imaging."[17] (A foremost theorist of the complexities of visual culture and an advocate for its vibrancy, Mirzoeff has significantly revised this position in his subsequent works—as evident in his idea of "Photography 2.0.")[18]

Tacita Dean, commenting on the waning of the traditional 35mm film (which was both subject and matter of her 2011 Tate Modern installation "Film") rather than on photography as such, issued the following lament: "This beautiful medium, which we invented 125 years ago, is about to go. ... How long have we got? I hope we've got a year left. It's that critical."[19] London-based Mexican photojournalist Antonio Olmos, in turn, commented as late as 2013 that "Photography has never been so popular, but it's getting destroyed. There have never been so many photographs taken, but photography is dying."[20] Chapter 6, which zooms in on Dean's artistic practice and the critical discourses surrounding it, probes what is behind such pronouncements and what it is that their authors are actually afraid of losing (evidence? truth? depth? authenticity?). It also outlines a different trajectory of the photographic medium, and a less hysterical story about it, in light of digitization. For now, I want to pick up on the 2013 post in the *New York Times*'s blog *Bits*, which rebuked claims of the last rites supposedly being read for photography—this time because it was being replaced by online video technology—with a statement that "the reports of the death of photography have been greatly exaggerated."[21] The *Times*'s skepticism relates to the way in which the human mind is said to construct memories around single images, rather than moving sequences. Photographs stay with us, literally: they are mnemonic devices that mark the passage of time and help us build narratives around them.

Also, if we track the ongoing changes to the photographic market and what is often seen as the progressing decline of the traditional photographic apparatus, we can raise further questions about this story of photography's premature demise. Drawing on its analysis of the data from Japan-based CIPA (Camera & Imaging Products Association), the online photography platform PetaPixel has concluded that, even though "the sales of dedicated cameras have been shrinking by double digit figures each of the following years," with traditional camera companies such as Canon recording diminishing profits, as discussed earlier, if you "[m]ix in data for smartphone sales," the growth of camera sales has been phenomenal.[22] The shrinking of the media-ecological niche of amateur cameras—both advanced amateur DSLRs and low-end point-and-shoots, not to mention film cameras—has occurred at the expense of the growth of functionality and, more important, instant accessibility of camera phones. Camera phones are therefore an example of what Robert Capps of *Wired* magazine has called "good enough tech." According to Capps, the overall acceleration and increasing connectivity of our everyday lives has altered what we expect of our portable devices: "We now favor flexibility over high fidelity, convenience over features, quick and dirty over slow and polished." As a result, "companies that focus on traditional measures of quality—fidelity, resolution, features—can become myopic and fail to address other, now essential attributes like convenience and shareability. And that means someone else can come along and drink their milk shake."[23] This perhaps explains why well-established names in camera manufacturing such as Olympus, Pentax, Minolta, or Kodak have either entirely disappeared or considerably reduced their market share. We have also witnessed firmer embedding into the camera market of electronics manufacturers such as Sony, Panasonic, and Samsung, companies whose successes in the photographic domain can be explained by their involvement in the production of affordable mirrorless cameras that are smaller than their DSLR counterparts and are also "good enough"—or, in many cases, better—to replace them. Then there are newcomers such as GoPro, whose unique product, a head- or bike-mountable rugged camera, allows adventure buffs to take pictures and videos of themselves in action. The combined geology and futurology of photography has to take into account Internet-enabled and thus networked smartphones and other "good enough" hybrid devices as well as the whole media ecologies in which they participate: "the camera" as a 35mm analog film-fed, standalone object is no longer indicative of the supposed health or decline of the medium.

Yet something obviously *is* disappearing—and then reappearing again, transformed into a different shape, form, and medium. The changing media landscape is being driven by the ethos of planned obsolescence that has been with us since the 1930s but that has intensified in the era of plastic, networked culture, and "the digital." But, rather than pursue the narrative of "never-ending technological evolution and progress," I want to follow Jennifer Gabrys in adopting a "perspective of transience" in order to trace "continual cycles of novelty and obsolescence" and the impact of those cycles upon our "material cultures, economies, and imaginaries."[24] Transient photomedia ecologies, I suggest, open up a different viewpoint through which we can see ourselves inhabiting what we call the world—and to grasp its "naturecultural" transformations. As John Durham Peters points out, "Media are not only about the world; ... they *are* the world."[25]

Those media ecologies also issue a call to us humans to give an account of the thickenings of matter around us—of what we see, make, and make obsolete. Together with Peters, I am working here with an expanded understanding of the concept of media borrowed from early Canadian media theory, which understood media in terms of infrastructures, not just communication devices. Peters argues that it was only in the twentieth century that "media" "came to mean the mass media of radio and television, cinema, newspapers, magazines, and sometimes books, but the term never completely lost its environmental meaning; indeed, mass media were so pervasive and elemental that they could fit nicely into the long lineage of medium as ambiance, and some, such as McLuhan and his followers, sought a more expansive (and ancient) notion of media ecology."[26] From that earlier, "infrastructural" understanding of media, he deduces, with McLuhan's help, an ethical call. Unlike the moralism of much of contemporary environmental theory,[27] this is first and foremost *a call for "media awareness,"*[28] *born out of a desire to awaken the somnambulists who ignore their technological habitats from their "media narcosis."*[29] The ethical call of photomedia, however, even if originally issued by the media themselves, needs to be picked up and augmented by a media theorist. Or, to put it another way, a media theorist, in this view, is someone who is already attentive, open to the demand of media, to its rustling ontology and changing temporality. It is therefore also someone who hears—and smells—media rot.

Site I: Pieter Hugo's *Permanent Error*

This media-theoretical role does not have to be played *only* by those who deal in the medium of linear language: philosophers, writers, storytellers. Visual artists and in particular photographers have made a significant contribution to the general understanding of the Anthropocene and related media-ecological problems by bringing to the fore issues of media decay. South African photographer Pieter Hugo's project *Permanent Error*,[30] consisting of a series of large-format photographs taken at the electronic waste dump called Agbogbloshie on the outskirts of the Ghanaian capital Accra, is a case in point (figures 5.1 and 5.2). The images are portraits of predominantly male young workers, shot against the background of burning e-junk being transformed into sublimely menacing tongues of black smoke. The muted color palette of beiges, browns, and rusty reds, coupled with the

Figure 5.1
Pieter Hugo, *Yakubu Al Hasan, Agbogbloshie Market, Accra, Ghana 2009*, C-print. © Pieter Hugo. Courtesy of Stevenson, Cape Town/Johannesburg, and Yossi Milo, New York.

stillness of the sitters (or, more appropriately, standers), gives Hugo's photos a sense of preindustrial timelessness, making them look like retrofitted stills from a bizarre square-format video game in which all action has somehow expired. The viewer's eye lingers over some intriguing detail: a bird's-nest wire bundle on a man's head, a white apron, the pointy ribs of a beautifully formed white cow. We may be tempted to interpret these images as examples of the aestheticization of poverty for the visual pleasure of first-world spectators—or perhaps as representations of the inhumane labor conditions in Africa, aimed at evoking moral outrage in (and delivering

Figure 5.2
Pieter Hugo, *Al Hasan Abukari, Agbogbloshie Market, Accra,* Ghana 2009, C-print. © Pieter Hugo. Courtesy of Stevenson, Cape Town/Johannesburg, and Yossi Milo, New York.

moral redemption for) those who look at them in Western art galleries. However, as photography writer Sean O'Toole points out, "*Permanent Error* is not singularly a record of privation and toil. Hugo is a fabulist, a wonderfully accomplished one at that. He is also, more prosaically, someone who notices things."[31]

The images do indeed reveal the gloomy story of wealthy economies' media rot that has been deposited out of our sight and mind, in poorer regions of the world. The billowing smoke does point to the carcinogenic activity of burning electronic debris in order to extract copper and precious metals out of its plastic carcasses, even if the moodily beautiful two-dimensional flattening of the scene excises the stench of animal and mineral putrefaction. The youth of the workers and the thinness of the animals does signal the precarity of life and labor in soil that is contaminated with "lead, mercury, thallium, hydrogen cyanide and PVC."[32] Yet, commenting on Hugo's practice of using actors in his previous works and thus foregrounding the eerily performative aspect of these documentary but also "stagey" images, O'Toole encourages us to read them beyond "poverty porn":

> Irrespective of the opinion his photos prompt—because looking without some form of thought or consciousness is just dumb gawping—it bears stating, without any desk thumping theatrics, that Hugo's magnetic portraits demand attention. They are, quite simply, hard to ignore. The compulsion to look, to not turn away, is, I think, an outcome of his work's pin-sharp formalism, craftsman-like finesse, acute silence and exaggerated pageantry, the latter often an outcome of simply placing a human subject within a square frame.[33]

Permanent Error makes a demand on us, unwittingly perhaps mobilizing the Levinasian framework of ethics as a demand to respond to the alterity of the other. For Emmanuel Levinas, we, i.e., human witnesses faced with events unfolding before our eyes, are being called to respond. We are being called to acknowledge that something is occurring outside our conceptual and material horizon; that an "otherwise than being"—a place of absolute alterity that cannot be subsumed by the conceptual categories at our disposal—accuses and makes a demand on us.[34] It is not too much of a leap to suggest that photography stages an ethical situation per se because, as Victor Burgin explains, its signifying system already occupies a particular point of view—that of "the technical apparatus itself."[35] Even the most human-centric and humanist photography therefore bears a nonhuman trace. And it is precisely this nonhuman position that is "bestowed upon the spectator."[36] *With any kind of photograph, we are looking at a scene that has been carved out for us; we arrive at the scene which has already been seen.* This moment of finding ourselves at the scene, at the always already seen, is precisely the context from which Levinas develops his philosophy of alterity and his ethics of dealing with what exceeds our visual or conceptual grasp. Ethics as responsibility for the infinite alterity of the other is not a result of some transcendental imperative for him, but rather emerges from what may be described as a pragmatic condition of finding oneself seen by the other, i.e., arriving into the world which the other already inhabits.

Working with the Levinasian framework, I also want to suggest that Hugo's project opens up Levinas's theory to the nonhuman agency of an ethical demand.[37] Unlike in Levinas, it is not just the *human face* that reaches to us from the pictures—although in many of the portraits the gaze of the featured worker reaches and pierces that of the viewer on the other side of the photo panel. I would argue that it is the image itself—the material artifact of the photograph—that touches us and calls us to responsibility. To say this is to highlight something different than just a moral response to the representation of human suffering, as a result of which we are supposedly elevated and driven to perform a good deed. Indeed, I am rather skeptical about these kinds of moralistic responses, given how fleeting they tend to be. We can think, for instance, of the highly emotional reactions to the photograph of a drowned three-year-old Syrian boy named Aylan Kurdi, whose body washed up on a Turkish beach as his family tried to reach Europe in September 2015. Published by worldwide media, the image "spread to 20 million screens around the world in just 12 hours."[38] Researchers at the University of Sheffield's Visual Social Media Lab conducted a study of this photograph's travels in order to demonstrate how "a single image transformed the debate on immigration."[39] Yet merely a few months later, any emotional stirrings evoked by the photograph gave way to much more hostile sentiments toward refugees, with the initial hospitable response withdrawn and any sense of responsibility withheld.

The argument I am beginning to sketch out here about the ethical demand of the image differs from the humanist and human-centric ethics of images outlined by Lillie Chouliaraki and Bolette B. Blaagaard, for whom "The ethics of images is ... a crucial aspect of the public cultures of the West as the primary mechanism of moral education through which the West becomes the witness of other people's suffering. This is because the realities that images represent work not only to depict the world as it is but also to evoke emotions and visions about how the world might or should be."[40] Chouliaraki and Blaagaard's argument is premised on the assumption that commonality exists among all humans and that humanitarianism is a naturally ensuing response to representations of suffering. It is very much the *content* of those images, i.e., what they represent or even perform, that is crucial, according to these authors, in teaching the public a lesson in moral response and moral behavior. However, I would argue that the potential collapse of the distinction between morality and its ugly twin, moralism,[41] poses a danger of making this kind of Western "ethics of images" anti-ethical in the last instance, with moral sentiment easily giving way to boredom, disillusionment, or even rage. (Again, responses to images and stories about refugees and immigrants provide a good illustration of this affective cycle.)

Going back to Hugo's images, I would therefore venture that something else is making a demand in them, apart from their content. The visual pleasure of the compositionally elegant photographs is broken by a cut of the horizon that slices the image into seemingly incompatible sections. We could describe it as a ninety-degree flip of a line that cuts across Baruch Barnett Newman's paintings whereby, in spite of the impending chaos, Lyotard writes, "the flash of the *Tzim-tzum*, the zip, takes place, divides the shadows, breaks down the light into colours like a prism, and arranges them across the surface like a universe."[42] I would thus like to make a more minimal suggestion about the ethical claim of images than the one issued by Chouliaraki and Blaagaard. Hugo's photographs do indeed call upon us and call us to responsibility, but not by asking us to devise a whole new environmental ethics of human and nonhuman relations; instead, they challenge our—or, indeed, my—*ethos*, or what Levinas calls "my place under the sun."[43] Ethos here, after Gay Hawkins and Rosalyn Diprose (whom Hawkins quotes extensively), stands for both "habitat" and "habitual way of life," "dwelling" and "character." Ethics as ethos is therefore first and foremost concerned with "modes of being in the world," with being embodied *in* the world.[44] In *Ethics of Waste*, Hawkins poses the following question: "Could our most visceral responses to waste be a source of new ethical practices?"[45] In light of the etymological discussion above, it is important to note that she is not looking for new morals but rather for new habits—that is, new ways of inhabiting spaces of media—and of us living *with* and *as* media. Seen in this light, ecomedia images of this kind become a fossil site for a media geologist who wants to do something other than either take delight in the aesthetic or moralize. The images *impress* themselves upon her, push to be read *in context*; they also open up to other territories, conversations, and sites. *Permanent Error* thus emerges as a site of fossilization, but not only in the sense of recording and preserving "media fossils" in the form of discarded electronics: it also enacts the process of "impressioning" upon our media archaeologist, whereby impressioning (also called fossilization), as we learned from the previous chapter via photographer and geologist Jerome Harrison, is in itself a photographic process. The images thus show us that *there is photography in photography*—just as, in Serbian artist Bojan Šarčević's video, there is water in the water.[46] The active act of looking becomes a way of carving a space between the viewer and the image surface—but it also carries a risk of drowning.

Kaja Silverman suggests that the human look is always fueled by a fantasy of omnipotence, where powers residing elsewhere in the field of vision are overlooked at the expense of the masterly capture of a scene. We can see this mastery posited by Silverman in iterations of the train of thought that is no doubt traversing many a viewer's mind: "This is such a moving scene ... The man's face has so much dignity ... Thank God I'm not an Agbogbloshie worker ... My laptop is so slow and will probably need changing soon ... Isn't it terrible, having to inhale deadly media vapors!" Silverman acknowledges that "there is nothing we can consciously do to prevent certain projections from occurring over and over again, in an almost mechanical manner."[47] Yet she also calls on viewers to work though the originary impulses, desires, and fantasies involved in "just looking,"[48] and try to look again, "productively." This countervisual strategy of what we might term "affect override" constitutes for her an important ethical task. Silverman writes: "The ethical becomes operative not at the moment when unconscious desires and phobias assume possession of our look, but in a subsequent moment, when we take stock of what we have just 'seen,' and attempt—with an inevitably limited self-knowledge—to look again, differently."[49] I therefore want to reiterate my earlier claim that photography itself—as a medium, genre, and material object—resists and undoes this tendency toward scoptophilic possession, and that it lays an ethical horizon before us. There is no such thing as just looking at photographs[50] because, before we can look, we are always already looked at: the photograph has looked at us. In the glossiness of its paper, the tonality of its surface, and the materiality of its frame or screen, the photograph possesses a nonhuman agency of its own, which it unwittingly mobilizes to take away what Burgin calls "our command of the scene." Burgin writes: "To remain long with a single image is to risk the loss of our imaginary command of the look, to relinquish it to that absent other to whom it belongs by right—the camera. The image then no longer receives our look, reassuring us of our founding centrality, it rather, as it were, avoids our gaze, confirming its allegiance to the other."[51] Letting oneself be unsettled by an image, being temporarily thrown out of our habitus, signals the possibility of an ethical opening—although of course there can be no assurances of the subsequent occurrence of an ethical act.

Site II: National Media Museum

Let us now step away from the precipice of a singular image to take in a larger vista: that of the photographic medium itself, together with its histories, practices, apparatuses, and institutions. My geological pursuits take me to a zone where photography as both a medium and a monument to this medium can be encountered and experienced: the National Media Museum (NMM) in Bradford in the north of England. NMM holds the largest collection of photographic artifacts—both photo-imaging equipment and the outcomes of various historical photographic processes—in the United Kingdom. I visited the museum in March 2016 for a "shallow dig" for photographic fossils, hoping to have an experiential-affective encounter with cameras old and new (figure 5.3). Rather than plan in advance what I was going to investigate, I decided to wait and see what was to be seen, to let the material impress itself upon me, to speak to me, and maybe even tell me a story.

In approaching NMM as a site of both historical memory and material e-waste, I was following Gabrys's suggestion that

> Some of the best places to witness the unwitting decay of electronics are in the very spaces where they would be preserved. Many electronics relegated to museums undergo such a rapid scale and rate of demattering that preservation is rendered problematic. Preservation becomes another word for managed decay, for a delay within the extended process of disposal. The museum may also be construed as a space of disposal.[52]

I therefore wanted to discover not only what NMM displays but also what it does *not* show, and was also curious to see how the lines between showing and not showing were drawn on a curatorial and practical level. With this, I was interested in learning how the museum tells the story of photography through its apparatuses old and new.

The photography exhibition at NMM is staged in a basement space called Kodak Gallery, which was launched in 1989 to celebrate the 150th

Figure 5.3
Self-portrait in the Small Object Store of the National Media Museum in Bradford, 2016. Photo by Joanna Zylinska.

anniversary of the photographic medium. Yet, due to its cryptlike positioning and shadowy interior, it is tinged with a certain nostalgia about the analog medium's—and Kodak's own—heyday. The very first exhibit the visitor sees upon entering the space is an ochre wall called "Capturing Light," with the title inscribed, in gold, on what looks like a classical frieze (figure 5.4). Underneath are panels featuring information about the nature of light, about the camera obscura as an aid to draftsmen across centuries, and about the discovery of the light-responsive aspect of chemicals such as silver salts that eventually allowed an image obtained with a camera obscura to be fixed on a photosensitive surface. I cannot help but see the similarity between the black-and-white information panels, with their neoclassical patterned ornamental framing, and Central European–style obituaries that are usually posted around the building and living area of a deceased person. Indeed, the whole wall, surrounded by a burgundy carpet featuring a white Persian geometric frieze, has something of a funeral parlor about it. This association is further exacerbated by the placing of a small physical exhibit

Figure 5.4
The "Capturing Light" wall in the National Media Museum, Bradford. Photo by Joanna Zylinska.

behind a dark glass pane in the center of the wall. A wooden box resembling an urn or a tiny coffin on closer inspection turns out to be a "portable reflex camera obscura c 1800" (figure 5.5).

The overall narrative about photography outlined through the Kodak Gallery is straightforwardly linear, as is often the case in traditional institutions of knowledge. After the brief introduction to the early days of photography via the sepulchral wall described above, visitors are presented with early box cameras, including the world's first commercially produced camera, the Giroux "Daguerreotype," as well as Fox Talbot's small camera obscuras affectionately called "mousetraps" by his wife Constance. At the risk of pushing this sequence of funereal associations too far, the small cameras are neatly arranged in long brown wooden cabinets which very much look like open caskets we have seen in both fairy tales and real life, with

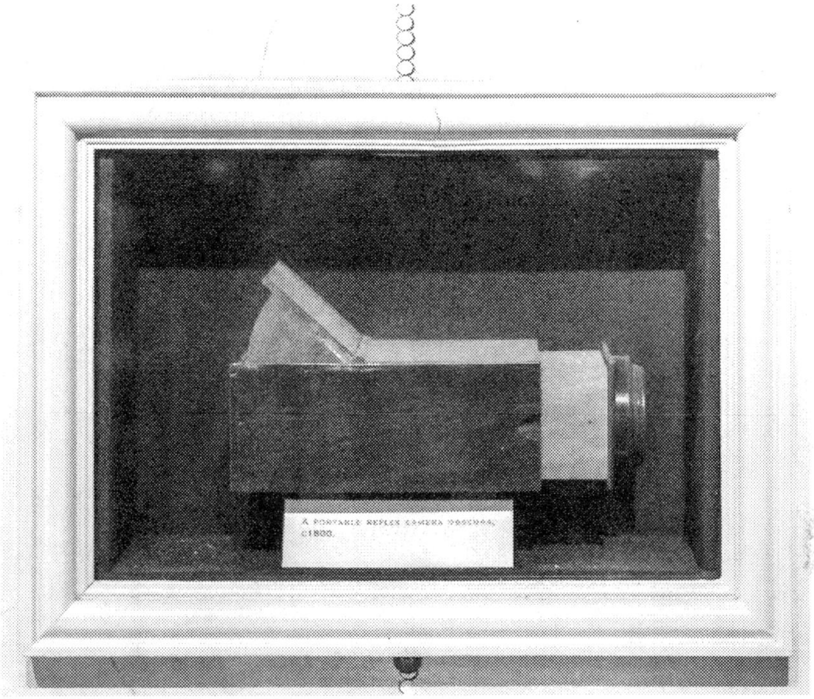

Figure 5.5
Close-up of the "Capturing Light" wall: a portable reflex camera obscura c. 1800. Photo by Joanna Zylinska.

the photographic equipment on show suspended between the anticipation of Sleeping Beauty and the dashed hopes of Lenin (figure 5.6). Theodor Adorno was indeed correct in pointing out that "Museum and mausoleum are connected by more than phonetic association." For Adorno, "The German word '*museal*' [museumlike], has unpleasant overtones. It describes objects to which the observer no longer has a vital relationship and which are in the process of dying. They owe their preservation more to historical respect than to the needs of the present. ... Museums are like the family sepulchers of the works of art."[53]

The strangely devivified story of photography at NMM is not told solely through its equipment: the cameras on display are accompanied by various other artifacts, such as a reproduction of Fox Talbot's first negative (because "[t]he original is too fragile to be displayed and is kept safe and secure in our archives"), showing a latticed window in Lacock Abbey, and a "modern

Figure 5.6
Early cameras on display in the National Media Museum. Photo by Joanna Zylinska.

replica of the first heliograph made by Niépce" around 1926, which I discussed in chapter 2. The exhibition also encompasses that quintessential genre of monumental reenactment—a diorama—which mummifies the past as permanent present. In the words of photographer Hiroshi Sugimoto, who has developed an extensive series of diorama images shot in the American Museum of National History (discussed in chapter 4), "However fake the subject, once photographed, it's as good as real."[54] In NMM the past is mummified as present twice over, as the diorama in question is a reenactment of a daguerreotype, also on display, featuring "Jabez Hogg photographing Mr Johnson in Richard Beard's Studio, ca 1843" (figure 5.7). The display also features a model of a photographic daylight studio that made photography desirable among upper and middle classes,[55] before moving on to show the popularization of the medium with the Kodak Brownie. There is a premonition of things to come, with multiple iterations of the Brownie

Figure 5.7
Close-up of a diorama at the National Media Museum, incorporating glass reflections. Photo by Joanna Zylinska.

being accompanied by displays of dusty rows of faded equipment, of closed camera stores, and of the ironically self-reflexive exhortation "Adapt or die" featured in one of the glass cases (figures 5.8 and 5.9). The Brownie display is somewhat excessive, resembling what we may call an exuberant evolutionary radiation that signals the last gasp on the medium's evolutionary trajectory before its extinction—that is, its move to the "digital."

During my visit I was fortunate to be offered a tour of the museum's storage rooms. I was particularly keen to look at the spaces where "photographic fossils" are stowed away, but I also appreciated being able to see them as part of the wider media infrastructures in various states of preservation and decay. The storage rooms at NMM serve as a perfect illustration of Gabrys's insight into the politics of archiving:

> Often, the museum and archive collect and stow away objects that have for most purposes been disposed of and removed from the spaces of everyday circulation. The museum collects objects in storage, much the same as the electronics lingering in closets, attics, and warehouses; but the objects in the museum must be

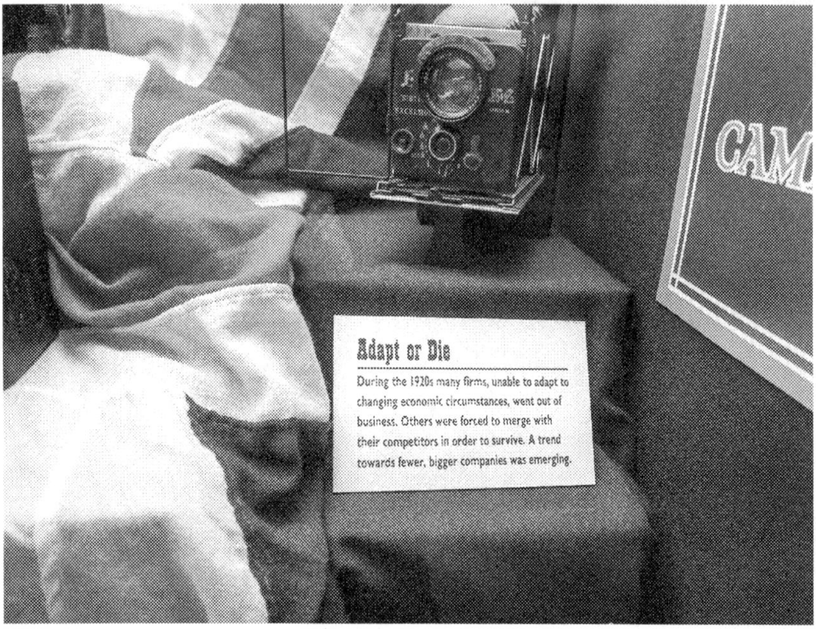

Figures 5.8 and 5.9
Ominous-looking signs ("Adapt or Die" and "Closed") in the Kodak Gallery at the National Media Museum, featuring various iterations of the Kodak Brownie. Photos by Joanna Zylinska.

continually sorted and deaccessioned in order to make way for new objects. Moreover, the migration of archived materials to digital formats has shortened the life of most museum objects, tied as they are to the life of electronic data.[56]

This negotiation between preservation and decommissioning, between use value and obsolescence, is clearly visible in NMM's attempts to establish some kind of relationship between chaos and order, with the Large Object Store and Small Object Store vying for the rare visitor's attention with two different types of aesthetics. The first room is reminiscent of a jumble sale, with intriguing pieces of equipment large and small, such as box cameras, tripods, reflectors, and projectors gathered under the vintage "Kodak supplies" sign (figure 5.10). I was mesmerized by the space, basking in its warm light and dusty atmosphere. It felt as if I'd found myself on a decommissioned film set, with action having moved on elsewhere, while there was still so much fun to be had in this place! I was keen to wander around the tangled semisculptural arrangements of machines and cables, to run my

Figures 5.8 and 5.9 (continued)

Figure 5.10
Large Object Store, National Media Museum. Photo by Joanna Zylinska.

fingers along the assembled objects, to play with a domestic table lamp with a fringed yellow shade. But then it was time to move on to the Small Object Store, which turned out to be the exact opposite of the first storage room (figure 5.11). Clinically tidy and linearly structured, it hosted long rows of refrigerator-like metal cabinets containing now obsolete cameras and other image-making equipment. The majority of apparatuses in the cabinets were multiple iterations of film cameras, from large-format machines to portable 35mm devices.

Perhaps surprisingly, the digital is very much an afterthought in the photographic exhibition at NMM. (The museum does feature a new permanent gallery called "Life Online" which offers a more contemporary—even if not necessarily more informative—take on digital cultures. Its aim is to "showcase the evolution of internet and computing technology" via a "range of inspiring interactives and fun games.") Yet "the digital" is also where things get really interesting in the underground Kodak Gallery because digitality is already staged here as obsolescence. Unwittingly echoing the

Figure 5.11
Small Object Store, National Media Museum. Photo by Joanna Zylinska.

ironic statement by Lem that "[n]othing ages as fast as the future,"[57] visitors' encounter with the digital—a technology that, as we know (but are not explicitly told in the Kodak gallery), precipitated Kodak's self-inflicted downfall—involves a relatively small mauve glass case headed by the slogan "The Digital Revolution" in a blocky old-fashioned typeface. Several early-model Kodak cameras are displayed, including Kodak DC20, DC40, and DC2010 Digital Zoom Camera, shown alongside Sony's Mavica, featuring a floppy disk for its camera memory, as well as Apple's first foray into digital imaging, the binoculars-resembling QuickTake 150. Yet the information that it was a Kodak engineer, Steve Sasson, who first "proposed the idea of a 'filmless camera'"[58] in 1975 is nowhere to be found. This omission is perhaps explained by the now rather embarrassing fact that, on being presented with Sasson's demonstration, Kodak executives were unable to comprehend "why anyone would ever want to look at images on a TV screen."[59] They were also unwilling to invest in what looked like a threat to their main source of revenue at the time: print film. Kodak Gallery at NMM sidesteps this unfortunate yet also decisive chapter in Kodak's history, as it does the company's 2012 filing for bankruptcy and its subsequent shedding of its core film and digital business to focus on commercial imaging. Kodak's unfinished story of its own obsolescence is rather telling. The company's demise was partly inaugurated by the very gesture to construct a Kodak Gallery nearly three decades ago, long before the financial troubles of the company made themselves known. The decision to install such a gallery thus started the process of monumentalization, with historically arranged displays of past artifacts always, inevitably, being a testament to failure.[60] Gabrys contends that "Any museum or archive in which electronics are held is a collection of repeated obsolescence and breakdown," yet she also goes on to argue that "failure is only one part of this story. Whether in a state of decay or preservation, obsolete devices begin to express tales that are about something other than technical evolution cases full of cameras old and new."[61]

It is therefore perhaps possible to retrace the exhibition path at NMM in search of an alternative story of photography, one that would be not so much about the explicit obsolescence of the analog medium and the implicit extinction of the company that thrived on it but rather about our wider cultural desires, economic investments, social frustrations, and political disappointments. "Failure presents the fossils of forgotten dreams, the residue of collapsed utopias," writes Gabrys. "Through the outmoded, it is possible to move beyond those more 'totalizing' aspects of technology, such as progress, teleological reasoning, or the heroism of invention."[62] Interestingly, the photographic fossils on display, both in the storage rooms and in the main part of the museum, present a very Western, even US-centric, story of photography. But at the same time, they also foreground a failure of the American Dream, with its belief in technological progress and infinite consumer spending, and its promise of growing affluence for all, translated into a version of universal happiness. For me, as someone who grew up on the other side of the Iron Curtain, the photographic display at NMM offers an interesting trip down somebody else's memory lane. I am rather surprised that, apart from a few scattered Eastern European devices, there is almost no recognition in the exhibition of the parallel technological developments, and of the sociocultural narratives that accompanied them, in other parts of the world. Looking at glass cases full of German Rolleiflexes, Kodak Brownies, and Japanese Nikons, I remembered my first-ever camera: a Soviet 35mm manually operated Smena 8M, produced by LOMO. This was followed in 1989 by a more advanced Zenith TTL model, which automatically measured light reflected from an object through its lens, and then, two years later, an East German Praktika. All these Eastern bloc devices were eventually superseded by a Canon purchased with scholarship money when I was an exchange student at the University of Groningen in the Netherlands in 1993. The painfully expensive Canon broke after just six months when its electronic module failed irreparably, planting in me the first seeds of doubt about the combined narrative of technological progress and Western technological supremacy.

These reflections about technological progressivism evoked by my visit to NMM are unfolding against a unique temporal horizon: a period when the museum itself is undergoing a significant repositioning in its core mission (figure 5.12). In February 2016 it announced that around 400,000 objects from its three-million-strong photography collection would be transferred to the Victoria and Albert Museum in London, while NMM

Figure 5.12
The exterior of the National Media Museum. Photo by Joanna Zylinska.

changes its focus and agenda. "The move reinforces Director Jo Quinton-Tulloch's new focus on STEM (science, technology, engineering, and maths) at the National Media Museum, heralded by a new £1.5 million interactive light and sound gallery due to open in March 2017," proclaims the museum's website.[63] From this vantage point, NMM reveals itself to be a "fossil of forgotten dreams," with photography, especially in its artistic guides, being slowly elided from the cultural spectrum. The first steps in that direction had already been taken in 2006, when the institution formerly known as the National Museum of Photography, Film and Television changed its name to the National Media Museum. Yet this more recent shift in the museum's planned operations is particularly significant as it has occurred against the wider background of cuts to the funding of public cultural institutions—universities, libraries, research councils, parks, festivals—in the United Kingdom and elsewhere. The museum directorate's turn to STEM, so familiar to the academic community, is therefore perhaps understandable in the current climate of the economic depletion of public coffers, a situation which is reflected in the undermining of arts and humanities as both academic disciplines and repositories of cultural practices, at the expense of the supposedly more useful—and potentially more profitable, or at least "fundable"—science subjects.

Of course, contrary to the story of photography's obsolescence narrated by NMM, with its limp last chapter called "The Digital Revolution," the photographic medium has never been as exuberant as it has become in this era of the networked camera in which we have all become photographers. Nevertheless, the museum's Kodak Gallery (which will no doubt undergo a reconfiguration sometime soon) presents photography as an industrial cultural practice belonging to a bygone era of mechanical reproduction. Photography as art is not entirely disappearing from the United Kingdom's cultural landscape, though—it is "just" relocating to London, the capital city that has a monopoly on British culture in all its different guises, and that is still seen as worth investing in. The fact that London's biggest industry is the finance sector, and that the majority of newly built high-rise properties serve as moneyboxes in the sky for an international elite who often never even visit their investments, testifies to the wider cultural politics of the United Kingdom. London is seen as exciting to international buyers not only thanks to the country's relative economic and political stability and its propitious corporate tax regime, but also because it has a nebulous aura of "culture." It therefore pays to invest in London, to furnish it with cultural products that are seen as fossils elsewhere, because London is still capable of turning those fossils into economic fuel. With this, London offers a contrast to the location of NMM, Bradford—a city with a glorious industrial past in textiles, in particular wool. Like many other places in the north of England, Bradford has suffered years of unemployment and underinvestment as a result of the collapse of heavy industry. Its spectacular Victorian architecture, like its museum, is also a fossil of a manufacturing-era utopia when regional networks of wool, coal, and iron ore ensured a balanced development and growth across the British Isles. Bradford is now positively multicultural, except that what conventionally counts as "culture" is being siphoned off to London, with the region's multiculturalism reduced to an "immigration problem." It is therefore understandable why Simon Cooke, Conservative leader of the opposition at Bradford Council, has described the decision to transfer art photography to V&A "an appalling act of cultural vandalism."[64] *This is perhaps what the ruination of the eco-eco crisis of the Anthropocene looks like on a regional scale, with whole tranches of culture, understood as Raymond Williams's "ways of life,"*[65] *becoming extinct.* It is perhaps also strangely apposite that my guided tour around the museum's storage rooms should have been conducted by a curator who has just been laid off as part of NMM's repositioning of its core mission.[66]

Site III: The vanishing object of technology

The site of my third "shallow dig" in this chapter shifts from the international and national contexts of media e-waste and media fossils to focus on the changing ecology of our domestic technical setups. By this I mean something quite specific: the gradual disappearance of cables, leads, and wires from behind our computers, music systems, TV sets, kitchen equipment, and other domestic devices that rely on the continuous supply of electricity for their functioning. In line with my geological approach, I am not going to offer a materialist analysis of the economics behind the altered nature of global design, production, and distribution of technical equipment; or a culturalist reading of what such altered technological setups mean for us (even though both types of analysis could no doubt tell us something interesting about what we designate as "the world" as well as about the way in which we perceive "it" in its multiple unfoldings). Instead, by way of some very shallow digging, I want to propose a poetic meditation on, and mediation of, the aesthetic of such workaday entanglements. As I suggested along with Sarah Kember in *Life after New Media*, "mediation" can become an alternative framework for "understanding and articulating our being in, and becoming with, the technological world, our emergence and ways of intra-acting with it, as well as the acts and processes of temporarily stabilizing the world into media, agents, relations, and networks."[67]

The etymological similarity between "meditation" and "mediation" is not accidental. Both terms contain the prefix "med-," which means "to measure, limit, consider," and both refer to the practice of limitation and suspension—of analysis and critique as distanced modes of engagement with the world. Mediation entails recognizing one's locatedness *within* the media, being always already mediated—a state of events that pertains to us humans as much as it does to other entities from which we attempt to differentiate ourselves. However, by engaging in any philosophical or creative activity, by trying to think, write about, or otherwise capture the material entanglements around us (of which we are part), it is necessary to perform an act of *découpage*, to make a cut through the flow of particles, things, and images, to "measure, limit and consider" what perhaps in its very nature escapes measurement. It is precisely from such dual spatial positioning—of being in the middle of "this aggregate of images" that Bergson calls "the universe,"[68] and of trying to carve some specific images out of it that capture a unique technical sensibility—that my poetic mediation arises.

In offering an intertwined textual and visual engagement with a unique moment in the history of technology, I aim to enact a way of philosophizing with a camera as much as with a pen or keyboard. While the photographs included in the Site II section of this chapter serve as *illustrations of* my visit to NMM and my subsequent argument, the relationship between text and image changes in Site III. The images presented here constitute an inherent part of the argument itself, with the textual part serving as their supplement (figure 5.13). The project started in early 2011, when I began photographing tangles of cables and wires in domestic and office settings as well as taking notes about the setups captured. The drive for this work came from the increasing inconvenience I was experiencing when having to carry my laptop, iPad, cell phone, and camera charger, all spouting long leads—an inconvenience made even more pronounced through frequent travel and through having half of my luggage space taken up by a bunch of wires. But I also became ever more fascinated by the tangled dusty arrangements behind both my own and other people's desks and media consoles, with numerous devices such as monitors, speakers, external hard drives, printers, scanners, DVD or Blu-ray players, satellite or cable TV boxes, additional USB ports, extensions, and other pieces of equipment (some of which may have become obsolete but which cannot really be removed for fear of disrupting the setup) all connected to form a wiry sculptural mess.

The project is meant to offer more than just a nostalgia trip inspired by the supposedly vanishing technology; a retro-fashion tribute aimed at reminiscing about "old media" just for the sake of it. Nor do I want it to be a celebration of the brave new world of improved technological design, or even a prediction of wirelessness as a new technological condition, as interrogated by Adrian Mackenzie in the book of the same title.[69] My ambitions are much more minimal: I just want to stabilize that moment of the gradual *disappearance of wires from our human view*, to make it a moment worth contemplating, to see what happens before it happens.

The curators of the (now defunct) 20minutesintothefuture website have no doubt that this is indeed what is happening right now. They boldly pronounce:

> Wired connections will exist for only the largest of machines, the common man will never need to use a wire for connectivity or indeed for power. The cable tie will [be] found only in museums. The disappearance of cables from our lives is inevitable. We already have working prototypes of devices using wireless electricity and wireless charging. We've been using Wi-fi for many years now and the approaching introduction of 4G/LTE networks means that entire cities can have wireless access to fast broadband. We are already decreasing the number of cables we need by designing devices according to standards, thus e.g. most modern phones and portable devices can be charged using a USB cable—no need to have a separate cable/adapter for each one.[70]

This kind of futuristic rhetoric is fueled by the desire of the technoscientific industry to make technology friendlier and supposedly "more intelligent"—which often amounts to attempts to disguise any visible technological aspects of machines in an effort to make them look and behave more "like us." Thus, the Swedish furniture manufacturer IKEA has collaborated with the Chinese electronics company TCL to offer a furniture-TV called UPPLEVA. "One of the central value proposition[s is] the disappearance of cables (or at least hiding them better) and a better integration of the TV in the furniture,"[71] explains Mark Laperrouza. Such undertakings

Figure 5.13

Joanna Zylinska, *The Vanishing Object of Technology II*, 2012.

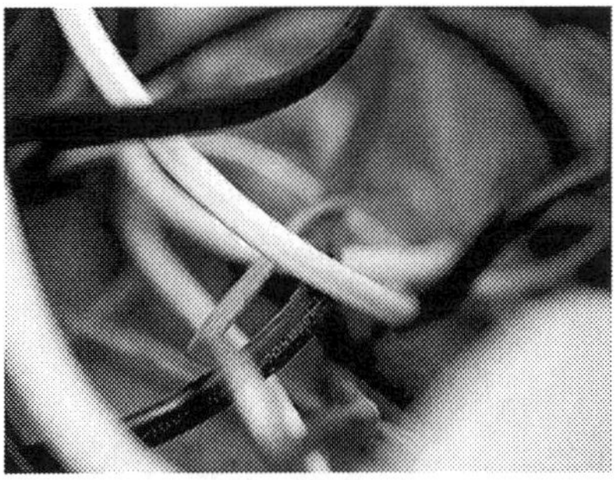

Panasonic Quintrix SR TV
Philips Cinema Center Speaker CS710
Philips Super Audio CD and Digital A/V Surround Receiver
Technics AV Control Stereo Receiver SA-EX100
Technics Stereo Cassette Deck RS-TR474
Technics Compact Disc Player SL-PG480A
Philips CD Sound Machine AZ1832B
Micromod UHF Audio/Video Modulator
Samsung Digital TV Tuner DSB-S305G

Dell Optiplex 745 Computer with Ethernet Connection
Dell 1708FP1 Monitor
HP LaserJet 1012 Printer
Alcatel-Lucent IP Touch PhonePhase Lighting Cables for Studio Lighting

Panasonic Quintrix SR TV
Philips Cinema Center Speaker CS710
Philips Super Audio CD and Digital A/V Surround Receiver
Technics AV Control Stereo Receiver SA-EX100
Technics Stereo Cassette Deck RS-TR474
Technics Compact Disc Player SL-PG480A
Philips CD Sound Machine AZ1832B
Micromod UHF Audio/Video Modulator
Samsung Digital TV Tuner DSB-S305G

Toshiba 32WLT58 LCD Colour TV
Aiwa FX2800 Video Cassette Recorder
Philips DVP5960 DVD Player
Virgin Media Cisco Systems 1TB TiVo box
Virgin Media Super Hub VMDG480
Sennheiser HDR120 Wireless Headphones with Battery Charging Stand

Figure 5.13 (continued)

Toshiba 32WLT58 LCD Colour TV
Aiwa FX2800 Video Cassette Recorder
Philips DVP5960 DVD Player
Virgin Media Cisco Systems 1TB TiVo box
Virgin Media Super Hub VMDG480
Sennheiser HDR120 Wireless Headphones with Battery Charging Stand

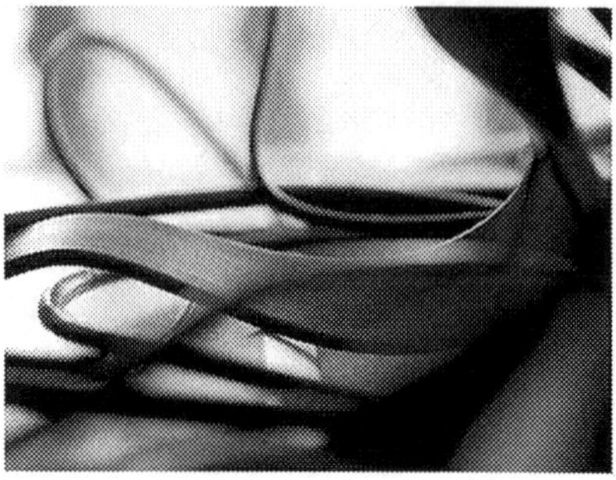

Toshiba 32WLT58 LCD Colour TV
Aiwa FX2800 Video Cassette Recorder
Philips DVP5960 DVD Player
Virgin Media Cisco Systems 1TB TiVo box
Virgin Media Super Hub VMDG480
Sennheiser HDR120 Wireless Headphones with Battery Charging Stand

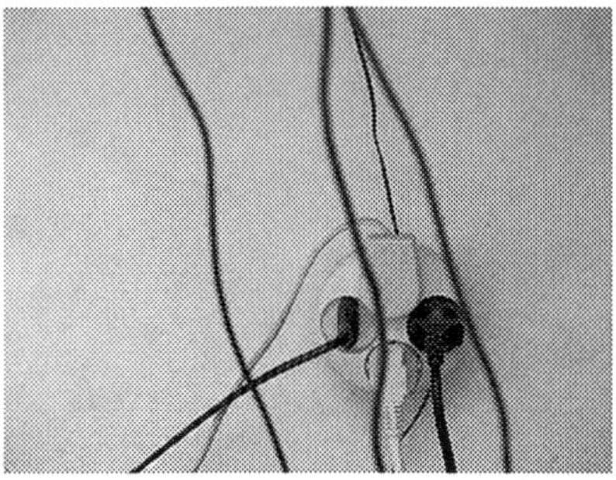

Toshiba Portege R500 Laptop and Adapter PA-1750-09
Dell MOC5U0 Mouse
Hewlett Packard LaserJet 1018 Printer
Multiplug Extension DPM PP30
Transonic Intermarket NHS40 Speakers
Magnum HI-GI Audio center NHS-75MK2
Wall Lamp made by Antoni Przeworski Co.

Netgear 54 Mbps Wireless ADSL 2 Modem Router DG834G v.4
Western Digital External Hard Drive
Hewlett Packard HP PSC 1410 Printer-Copier-Scanner
Computer Amplified Speaker System No Name

Figure 5.13 (continued)

usually end up mystifying the technological process even further as a result of the delegation of our everyday existence to "the experts," i.e., designers and technocrats, as already predicted by Jean-François Lyotard in his report on the state of knowledge for the government of Quebec, subsequently published in 1979 as *The Postmodern Condition*.[72]

Significantly, the "vanishing cable" ambition only applies to smaller domestic and small office settings. As the BBC reported in 2012, "For the first time since 2001, client PC shipments have declined sequentially for three consecutive quarters and have been below historical averages for the last seven quarters,"[73] while more and more people now rely on portable electronic devices to perform the few functions they do every day—social networking, text messaging, online shopping, email. Even so, Google was involved in financing an undersea cabling system called Unity between Japan and the United States, which was completed in 2010. Together with Facebook, it is now developing the Pacific Light Cable Network which will directly connect Los Angeles to Hong Kong by 2018. As Mackenzie poignantly indicates, "Wirelessness struggles against wires, and the extensive tying and knotting of wires called 'networks.'"[74]

It is precisely this extensive tying and knotting of wires as stabilized into unwitting sculptural objects that is of interest to me. We could perhaps say that such wire tangles are part of an "accidental aesthetics," understood as something that emerges over time, as a result of the historical accumulation of various technical objects to which those wires are attached, of those wires being kicked around or rearranged with someone's foot while she is sitting at a desk or vacuuming, coupled with the accumulation of layers of dust and grime on their surfaces. If conscious aesthetic decisions are ever made about wire arrangements, such decisions are usually focused on minimizing the visibility and presence of the wires: on gathering them into a wire holder, pushing or pinning them behind furniture or along skirting boards. Wire tangles and knots thus serve as a testament to the everyday struggle between order and chaos in everyday media ecologies. They are intrusions into the oft minimalist or functionalist arrangements of living or work spaces, a material reminder of the excess of the everyday that cannot be swept away. They reveal a unique slippery-obstinate tactility, one we encounter when trying to tidy them up or tidy up around them—that is, when trying to bring order into what is inherently a disorderly arrangement. But cables and wires are also a way of domesticating entanglement, stilling it, making it present. We could therefore perhaps go so far as to say that this aesthetic presencing of the wired tangle has an ethical dimension, too: it is a demand placed on the human inhabitant of domestic or office spaces by second-rate objects connected to other objects. And even though aesthetic arrangements are something that has caught my attention, literally and photographically, it is the ethical call of these arrangements that is really of primary concern to me.

This idea of the ethical call of objects expands on my argument from *Bioethics in the Age of New Media,* in which I positioned bioethics as an originary philosophy, situated even before ontology. That idea was inspired by the work of Levinas, although, as already mentioned in this chapter, I parted ways with him over the humanist limitations of his ethics, whereby a primordial responsibility exerted upon me always came from human others. In my bioethics, understood as an "ethics of life," the human is called upon to respond to an expanded set of obligations that affect her, make an impression on her, allow for her differentiation from the world around her, and demand more than just a reaction. This is to say that while I do recognize, together with other theorists of posthumanist thought, that "it is not all about us," I also acknowledge the singular human responsibility *to make a decision to respond*—or to withhold such a response. The bioethics of expanded obligations thus becomes a way of taking responsibility for the world around us and of addressing the tangled ecology of everyday connections and relations.[75]

This is where imagistic practice such as, for example, photographic work performed with a camera stops being just an aesthetic endeavor, and where it opens a passageway to ethics. To say this is not to suggest that image-based practice such as mine is ethical per se or that it entails a moral lesson for us all. My claim, to return to my earlier formulation, is much more minimal than that: it is a way of signaling that turning images of wired tangles into photographs is a way of visualizing these acts of the presencing of the world, this demand that objects in the world place upon us, and also of carving and slicing the world in a particular way as an inevitably violent yet also pragmatic gesture of arranging it into particular objects and setups. Photography can be a way of reminding ourselves that *there are setups* in the first place by stabilizing and hence creating them *as setups*—such as the particular ones seen here, which we have coordinated at a certain scale by connecting equipment in this and that way—and yet the photographic process is open to so many different influences and activities: production; transfer of particles of electricity; linkage to objects, systems, and bodies we are not familiar with or cannot even envisage. With this, photography takes over from our human perception the task of "cut[ting] inert matter into distinct bodies."[76] It is precisely the relationship between flux and setup, between duration and cut, that, according to Bergson, organizes or even makes the world for us. He posits that "things are constituted by the instantaneous cut which the understanding practices, at a given moment, on a flux of this kind, and what is mysterious when we compare the cuts together becomes clear when we relate them to the flux."[77] The wired tangles are then more than just symbols: they are actual bundles of duration and stoppage, foregrounding some processes and connections while also hinting at other invisible ones across different scales. They are a reminder to us that there is life behind a machine; that, as Jane Bennett puts it, "deep within is an inexplicable vitality or energy, a moment of independence from and resistance to us and other bodies: a kind of thing-power."[78] If, as announced in a think piece in *New Statesman*, "Today if you are not often wired, you do not exist,"[79] the knots and entanglements of cables may prompt us to enquire what such different forms of being wired entail, and may tell us that it *does* matter who and what we are connected to, when, and why. They may also ask us to account for the kinds of ecologies we exist in and help shape.

As helpless as during the last ice age

So-called technological progress carries with it various kinds of debris: broken promises, discarded ideas, obsolete machines, decomposing infrastructures. "Using technologies as its organs," writes Lem, "man's homeostatic activity has turned him into the master of the Earth; yet he is only powerful in the eyes of an apologist such as himself. Faced with climactic disturbances, earthquakes, and the rare but real danger of the fall of meteorites, man is in fact as helpless as he was during the last ice age."[80] Of course we now know that some of the climactic disturbances we face are actually the consequence of our attempt to exert mastery over the Earth, yet this knowledge, as Lem correctly observes, still leaves us helpless. We simply do not know what to do with the mess we have made. Is seeing media fossils as a cosmic remorse the best we can hope for? Or can ecomedia become part of a solution that involves revisualizing the world as a more ethical space, making it more habitable and more resilient not just for us but also for future humans—and future nonhumans? Renouncing any fantasy of returning to the purity of nature, we should perhaps rather conclude, after Hawkins, that [w]aste is *inevitable*." If this is indeed the case, then "how we deal with this, what sort of calculations and values we create to make this incontrovertible fact meaningful,"[81] becomes a most pressing ethico-political task.

6 We Have Always Been Digital

Digital futures

It is commonplace to state that digital technology has played a significant role in the transformation of the photographic landscape, from the practices and modes of production of commercial and art photography through to amateur practice as well as photojournalism. As a result of the proliferation of photo-sharing platforms such as Flickr, Instagram, and Tumblr, amateur photographers can post their work next to that of seasoned professionals, while the very legitimacy of those traditional skills- and income-based divisions is being put into question. The convergence of different media has resulted in cell phones doubling as both still and video cameras.[1] Photo imaging is now also arguably faster, more immediate, and more accessible than ever, both financially and geographically, with photographs becoming modes of communication, or forms of "digital touch," rather than continuing to serve primarily as objects of visual appreciation.[2] This transformation in media use and distribution has been fueled by the vacuously optimistic slogan "Everyone is creative!"[3] Promoted by advocates of the neoliberal paradigm of cultural industries, in which creativity is positioned as a tradeable commodity, this slogan seems to have been embraced wholeheartedly by the YouTube and Instagram generation[4]—to some extent naïvely perhaps, yet partly also in defiance of the media giants that promote a top-down model of cultural production. Contributing free labor to those platforms while also getting various forms of connectivity and sociality in return, "everyday creatives" have become key agents in altering the increasingly interconnected processes of media production, distribution, and consumption today, and thus in shaping a new future for media institutions and media networks.

As part of this transformation, the very ontology of the photographic object has become much more multiple, fluid, distributed, networked, and, with the proliferation of practices such as interface photography and QR codes, often not even aimed at the human viewer. As Asko Lehmuskallio and Edgar Gómez Cruz point out, "Automation processes, algorithmic photography, metadata and big data are only some of the keywords recently used for describing changes in photography."[5] The context for this final chapter of the book is provided by this very transformation of the media environment in the digital age. However, my aim here is to explore deeper issues and anxieties that digitization has raised over not just *photography's future* but also *the human future* by looking at how stories about various media often serve as an articulator of wider anxieties and crises. I also intend to query some of the ways of envisaging and enacting this future via multiple strategies of representation, archiving, and data storage. Although I will be looking at the problem of digitization through the lens of photographic arts, my concerns in this chapter are sociocultural, political, and economic as much as they are aesthetic. The chapter thus takes a step back from my considerations of the future "after the human" in the earlier parts of this book to look at what we might term "the near future." Yet deeper concerns about the material and economic precariousness of our planet and its human and nonhuman inhabitants, and about ways of envisaging it in and with the photographic medium, are still very much at the heart of this chapter.

But this will not be yet another discussion of the advantages and disadvantages of digitality. Even though digital technology as applied to the photographic medium functions as an entry point for the argument presented here, and even though this chapter carries with it a subtle warning against any kind of antidigital hysteria, I am not proposing to see the conversion (photographic or other) of information into binary code as a good or value in itself, or suggesting that we must all be fascinated—or, equally, horrified—by it as a technical process or cultural phenomenon. But what we *do* need to do is reflect on others' as well as our own desires and affective investments that have shaped not only the discourse around digitality but also the material processes of image capture, encoding, archiving, reproduction, and distribution in the digital age. "In any case," as Geoffrey Batchen observes in *Each Wild Idea*, "even if we continue to identify photography with certain archaic technologies, such as camera and film, those technologies are themselves the embodiment of the idea of photography or, more accurately, of a *persistent economy of photographic desires and concepts*."[6] So this chapter is first of all about affect rather than technology—where "affect" means more than *just* emotion located in a singular skin-bound subject, and stands instead for "something that perhaps escapes or remains in excess of the practices of the 'speaking subject.'"[7] The term is largely inherited from the Deleuzian project of trying to grasp and articulate "all of the incredible, wondrous, tragic, painful and destructive configurations of things and bodies as temporarily mediated, continuous events."[8] It names passions and actions enveloping a variety of human-nonhuman configurations and intra-actions taking place, in our case, in the photographic milieu. Affect and technology are therefore never entirely separate, as Batchen's earlier book, *Burning with Desire: The Conception of Photography*, poignantly illustrates.

This "persistent economy of photographic desires and concepts" clearly comes into play in the assessment of the photographic industry by Steve Macleod, creative director at one of London's leading art printers, Metro. In an interview with Simon Denison, Macleod complains: "For too many years we have seen digital as the great white hope for photography but there was actually nothing wrong with what we had. It wasn't broke so why try fixing it?"[9] To defend photography in its earlier, or what Batchen calls "archaic," forms, Macleod resorts to the rather ambiguous term "fixing." He expresses his desire *not to fix*—that is, not to repair—things, because there was nothing "wrong" with the photographic state of events in the first place. But he also reveals his contradictory ambition *to fix* images precisely the way they used to be developed (i.e., by dissolving the remaining silver halide grains that were not turned into black metallic silver in the developing process), at the time that it was still possible to stop the incessant flow of data. This (impossible) fixation of photography, both analog and digital, opens it onto another metaphor that is associated with cultural production in late postindustrial capitalism: that of "liquidity."

Liquid culture

The term "liquidity" carries a certain sense of melancholia—to be heard, for example, in Marshall Berman's famous phrase "all that is solid melts into air," which he borrows from Marx. In a similar vein, sociologist Zygmunt

Bauman wrote for many years about "liquid modernity," "liquid life," "liquid love," and "liquid fear."[10] For Bauman, all these liquid states seemed to be opposed to some fantasy period in the past, when social relations, individual emotions, and worldly affects were supposedly much more solid and stable. Images of liquidity—in the form of sea waves, ocean depths, floods, and drowning—are also frequently mobilized to convey a general sense of planetary catastrophe, especially that related to climate change.[11] However, rather than join this mournful chorus, I want to argue here for an *inherent liquidity of culture* and its objects—including photographs. Liquidity provides us with a model for understanding cultural objects as permanently *unfixed* and *unfixable*. It also helps us move beyond the ontological concerns that have occupied photography scholars from the medium's inception (that is, the perennial "What is photography?" question) toward photography's acts, affects, and temporal effects. Such an attempt to redefine photography in terms of its inherent liquidity does not situate us outside the ontological framework, because any such redefinition inevitably entails saying something about photography's being, but it opens up a rather different set of questions through which photography can be approached and understood. The notion of liquidity also allows us to address the problem of memory and archiving in relation to photography without the anxiety, technophobia, or hysteria that have often accompanied discussions about the future of this medium.[12] What changes in this particular articulation is not a cultural object as such—a photograph, or even the discipline or practice of photography—because these are understood here to have *always* been unstable, liquid, and only ever stabilized temporarily. What changes instead is our way of understanding this object, and of speaking about it.

One recent development drawing on this idea of the inherent liquidity of culture is the Liquid Books project initiated by Gary Hall and Clare Birchall in collaboration with the Open Humanities Press, an international open-access publishing collective whose mission is to make leading works of contemporary critical thought freely available worldwide.[13] Liquid Books is a series of experimental digital "books" which are published under the conditions of open editing and free content. As such, readers are free to annotate, tag, edit, add to, remix, reformat, reversion, reinvent, and reuse any of the books in the series—and, indeed, they are encouraged to do so. This project, Hall and Birchall explain, "is decentering the author and editor functions by making everyone potential authors/editors."[14] It also raises broader questions about the extent to which "the ability of users to remix, reversion and reinvent such liquid 'books' actually renders untenable any attempt to impose a limit and a unity on them as 'works.'"[15] Moreover, the Liquid Books project makes us query what the potential consequences of such "liquidity" are "for those of our ideas that depend on the concept of the 'work' for their effectivity": those concerning attribution, citation, copyright, intellectual property, and so on.[16] The reader cannot "finish" and hence claim to "know" such a liquid book in quite the same way as she perhaps can with a conventional print-on-paper text.

Could we think along similar lines to embrace the idea of liquid photographs, liquid exhibitions, and liquid galleries?[17] To some extent, Flickr and other online photo-sharing sites[18] encourage such a process of liquidization, with their multiple tagging systems, comment boxes, and even open competitions, in which participants are encouraged to reprocess a raw file in many different ways. But what kind of future for photography is this conceptual transformation offering? Will such a process of liquidization not lead in the end to photography's liquidation, its disappearance in the flickers of the constant data flow? Shouldn't we, then, try to "fix" it somehow? The final part of this chapter will discuss a publishing-archiving project I have been involved in called *Photomediations: An Open Book*, which builds on the Liquid Books series discussed above and which explores the questions posed here in the context of photographic and archival practice. But, for now, I would like to probe deeper some of the conceptual assumptions behind photographic liquidity in its past, present, and future forms.

Photographic flow

Most narratives oriented toward the future cannot avoid an emotional, if not literal, excursion into the past. Or, to put it differently, any plan or project to build an archive—which is by itself future-driven, as it is a way of conserving the past, or at least a version of it, for the upcoming generations—requires a trip down memory lane. In my own exploration of photography's future, I now want to turn to complex passions, or affective investments, of both artists and art critics, as manifested in the recent interest in found images in their "material" guises, i.e., old and often anonymous photos salvaged from flea markets, car trunk sales, and family attics, and then repurposed for art projects. I am putting "material" in quotation marks to query the oft uncritical use of the term "materiality" with regard to analog photography, which is then set against the supposed immateriality of the digital. This (mis)perception is only possible if one ignores the materiality of the screen on which one views digital images, the materials that make up the camera or cell phone which are part of its system of production, the network cables that participate in its transfer, etc. However, my interest in this section of the chapter is precisely in the materiality of the analog photographic object, and in the immaterial affects invested in this object by many photographers and viewers of images. Taking as my framing device Tacita Dean's 2001 art book *Floh*—whose title means "flea" in German, but which also resonates with the words "flow" and "flaw" in English—and Mark Godfrey's 2005 article, "Photography Found and Lost: On Tacita Dean's *Floh*," I will explore the extent to which Dean's art project, based on images she came across at German flea markets, displays a certain nostalgia toward the world of yesteryear, an imagined place that tells us as much about the artist's idea of the past (and the present) as it does about the past itself. Even though Godfrey positions Dean's work as emerging precisely "at a moment when the flood or blizzard or jumble is being tamed, cleaned up, and organized—at the moment of digitalization,"[19] Dean's project, together with Geoffrey's comments on it, are not actually about digit(al)ization as such.[20] I would go so far as to suggest that Dean's *Floh* and Godfrey's interpretation of it are not even so much *about photography*. Instead, they can be read as symptomatic of broader anxieties concerning modernity, anxieties that find their way into the celebration of the analog, the dusty, and the dead. Perhaps unsurprisingly, Godfrey's and Dean's political and aesthetic preference is actually much more for the modernity of Siegfried Kracauer and Walter Benjamin—with what I would call its historicized and hence "ordered mess"—rather than for the more unordered and messy postindustrial modernity of today.[21] Digitization, as we shall see later on, functions as a screen for the projection of these fantasies and anxieties about a particular idea of modernity—and, more importantly from a political viewpoint, about its social and economic consequences. *The analog image* and *the found object*—both as concepts and as material entities—serve as anchors for the increasingly precarious self that is trying to locate itself in a world where the roles of the producer and consumer of media images (but also, more broadly, the role of the self as a cultural and economic agent) are becoming increasingly ambiguous and uncertain.

However, the aim of this analysis is not to *correct* Dean's and Godfrey's reading of "the found image." Indeed, my engagement with Dean's *Floh* springs first of all from a certain work of seduction that her project has inflicted on me. I find myself mesmerized by the ascetic beauty of her found photographs, the pastel, painterly colors of the reproduced images, the amazing quality of Steidl's printing, the elegance of the book's pale-green linen cover. I am also enticed by the clearly not accidental and hence rather uncanny choice and arrangement of the untitled snapshots: two photographs on facing pages of two white Audis parked alongside each other, one with (presumably) the drivers standing next to their vehicles, the other showing just the cars; two shots of a woman in an oversized hat with a wide brim and a coat with rather large lapels; a single photo of a group of young men and women in what appear to be military uniforms, with the faces of two women in the last row mysteriously gouged away with a blue pen.[22] It is out of this affective seduction that my intellectual interrogation of *Floh* arises. I desperately want Dean's project to be more than a beautiful object of nostalgia, a mere presentation of "aspects of photography that will soon be gone," or only "an example of a mode of photographic *finding* that is nearing extinction."[23] Neither is the aim of my argument to claim that various art projects that engage with found images can all simply be reduced to their authors' anxiety, or that every desire to find traces of the past, and to collect and archive them, is merely a cover for a longing for order, meaning, and locatedness in a universe which is ultimately "indifferent" (although some archiving projects may indeed be motivated by such longing). Also, we must recognize that the use of "the found image" in art has not been uniform: we can think here of projects as diverse as Gerhard Richter's *Atlas*, Walid Ra'ad's work with The Atlas Group, or Thomas Ruff's *Jpegs*. There is something specific, however, about Dean's engagement with found images that reveals the artist's nostalgic attachment to the past, coupled with her sense of discomfort about what is to come. An affective frame for this reading is provided by the artist's confession in her profile featured in *The Guardian* in 2009: "Pet hate: Digital photography."[24]

Archive fever

The recent theoretical turn to the idea of the archive in art criticism, as evidenced by publications such as *The Archive* edited by Charles Merewether and Okwui Enwezor's *Archive Fever: Uses of the Document in Contemporary Art,* has demonstrated a number of complex ideas and concerns over the relationship between the past, the present, and the future, and, in particular, over memory and its preservation. As Merewether puts it in the introduction to his volume, the archive functions "as the means by which historical knowledge and forms of remembrance are accumulated, stored and recovered."[25] We can see from this description that archiving is an effort undertaken by an individual or institution—an artist, an amateur historian, a museum—not only to preserve the past but also to construct a certain version of this past and a memory of it, by including certain objects and traces while excluding others. It is also an effort to shape a future by preparing a cultural repository from which historians and artists will be able to draw. Of course, the process of constructing an archive, as we can see in Dean's flea market project, is never fully conscious: it is underpinned by the collector's own unacknowledged passions, desires, preferences, and omissions. As Freud explains in his essay "A Note upon the Mystic Writing-Pad," "an unlimited receptive capacity and a retention of permanent traces seem to be mutually exclusive properties in the apparatus which we use as substitutes for our memory."[26] An archive is as much a form of institutionalized forgetting and of the erasure of traces as it is a practice of their preservation, and thus of remembrance. Therefore, *Floh* is not providing a random collection of images which leapt at Dean like fleas while she was browsing through bins full of discarded photos at German markets and which she later placed in her book. Instead, we are presented with an archive of conscious and unconscious choices, decisions, and affective reactions that are gathered under the heading of "randomness" (itself perhaps a synonym for the flea market?).

The word "archive" (from the Greek, *arkhē*), as we learn from Jacques Derrida's opening words to his *Archive Fever,* signals both a commencement and a commandment, and thus a requirement for authority, order, and the law.[27] But at the same time, it points to the fundamental absence of any such transcendental law and order. Otherwise, why would philosophers have been so preoccupied with tracing and identifying *arkhē* as the organizing principle of the world (water for Thales, air for Anaximenes) if it had already been there, waiting for them to get hold of it? What is more, if order was already there, if it was to be found easily, why institute the commandment to archive, store, and hence remember and re-remember things? An archive, *any* archive, is born out of a fundamental recognition of transience, of the passage of time, and thus also of what I am calling, for the purposes of this chapter, liquidity. This awareness of transience perhaps explains the anxiety or even panic behind many archiving projects. My argument may look Heraclitean or, to give it a more contemporary inflection, Deleuzian, but even if everything is indeed in flux or flow, I want to emphasize that temporary material stabilizations do matter to singular, culturally framed embodied subjects, who will use various strategies to apply cuts to this flow in an effort to make (sense of) the world, and of themselves in this world. Archives are examples of such stabilizations, which is why their cultural signification—including the signification of the desire to archive this and not that at a particular moment in time—must be subject to careful analysis.

Significantly, Benjamin Buchloh argues that a "mnemonic desire" to remember, preserve, and archive traces of the past is "activated especially in those moments of extreme duress in which the traditional material bonds between subjects, between subjects and objects, and between objects and their representation appear to be on the verge of displacement, if not outright disappearance."[28] He is writing here about two periods that instigated what Hal Foster calls "an archival impulse":[29] the time of Aby Warburg's 1925–1929 *Mnemosyne Atlas* (i.e., the era of the withering of the "European humanist") and that of Richter's *Atlas* (i.e., postwar German culture, unable to come to terms with Nazism and throwing itself insanely into consumerism). Just as those two atlases were not, in the first place, *about* photography or imaging in the broader sense, neither is Dean's. The upheaval she is trying to capture with *Floh* seems to have to do with a broader reworking of the relations of production and consumption in the digital age, but also with the radically changing position of the artist in the age of user-generated media, collaborative and net art, and the elevation of the amateur: the blogger, the hacker, the YouTube and Vimeo "movie director." At a deeper level, the present time is also a period in which the human's relationship to his or her environment as both home and protective envelope has changed. In the Anthropocene, a sensibility which is very much part of Dean's work (as evident in her films, such as *Disappearance at Sea*, about an ill-fated sea voyage, and *JG*, exploring connections between J. G. Ballard's short story "The Voices of Time" and Robert Smithson's earthwork and film *Spiral Jetty*), "the home" has first and foremost become a site of loss and longing.

Always already digital

If Dean's *Floh* project, but also perhaps her practice at large, is indeed situated "at the moment of digitalization," as Godfrey suggests, it is worth asking to what extent the *Floh* archive she has constructed is an attempt to erase digital traces that are imprinting themselves on our visual imaginary with ever greater intensity from "art history proper," and an effort to keep art history a certain way: intact, orderly (even if apparently random), dead. There is something both heroic and tragic in this undertaking. It is heroic because Dean takes up the baton from many earlier artists as preservers of value and the past, as keepers, against all odds, of a certain world that (allegedly) once was. However, this effort is also tragic—but not because digital imagery has really flooded the public imagination to such an extent that to fight its proliferation with a few faded analog snapshots seems amusingly futile. It is tragic because it is based on the fundamental misrecognition of digitality as being somehow different from photography per se, as something that has arrived only after analog photography was already fully formed.

Batchen provides us with a very different framework for understanding not only the history but also the ontology of photography. Revisiting the early photographic processes and looking at the narratives and artifacts that accompany them, he argues that W. H. Fox Talbot's lace photographs—or, more specifically, photogenic drawing contact print negatives—conjure the "electronic flow of data that the photographic image has become today."[30] Consequently, Batchen positions them as a "fledgling form of informational culture."[31] *If we thus read digitality as the interlacing of an ON/OFF pattern that is translated, or rather transcoded, into different material media—light-sensitive papers, silicon chips, and so forth—we can see that photography, even at its very inception, reveals itself to be always already digital.* Indeed, photography always consists of a recording of a binary pattern: the presence and absence of light—even though, in its analog "encoding," this presence-absence dualism reveals itself to a human viewer as visual contiguity. The frequent use of lace in Talbot's photographic experiments was also a harbinger of another feature of the digital era: lossless reproducibility. As Batchen explains, "Talbot's photographs of lace were often produced using the same specimen, as if to show that his medium was capable of a repeatable, even mechanical reproduction of a given set of visual data."[32]

Yet this repeatability can also pose a threat. In a rather symptomatic passage, a tone of anxiety or even hysteria creeps into Godfrey's otherwise reasoned scholarly argument, as evidenced in the following account he provides of the condition of the photographic medium in the digital era:

> [W]hat is crucial here is the impact of digitalization on the amateur treatment of photography both at the moment of exposure and at the moment of storage. Digitalization discourages people from saving or printing out "mistaken" photographs—they can be erased from a camera's memory before they have physical presence, erased without any superstitious misgivings. All this might be heralded in the name of cleanliness, affordability, and efficiency, but the implications of digital handling are potentially troublesome: "To be actually able to delete an image in the moment of its inception is quite an enormous thing," Dean comments. "It pushes beyond democracy and becomes almost totalitarian. It [parallels the way] society is trying to organize itself to get rid of anything that is dysfunctional or not up to the standard. It's a horrifying concept to me if I think about it."[33]

The whole complex network of processes connected to the representation and transmission of data through binary code, when applied to the context of digital photography, seems to be reduced here by Godfrey—and Dean (whose words Godfrey draws on to support his lament)—to a fascist attempt to cleanse and order the world. It also implies, rather naively, a bizarre kind of technological determinism, i.e., a belief that if a technology itself allows a user to delete data almost instantly, then every user will automatically do so. This belief, which ascribes the overriding power to change users' behavior to technology itself, is also coupled with a conviction that all users have developed a sense of the photographic standard, and that they are willing and able to evaluate what counts as dysfunctionality. But what presents itself to Godfrey and Dean as a terrifying result of "digital eugenics," I see merely as a different set of possibilities in photographic practice—possibilities as yet undetermined. This is not to say that some users will not be employing the Delete button on their digital cameras or phones frequently or even obsessively; but only to contend that the results of this deletion of data will be as accidental, unforeseen, subject to the "random floe,"[34] and hence as far from totalitarian, as those of analog photographic practice. A quick browse through any amateur photo-hosting website or social media platform, from Flickr through to Instagram and Facebook—sites which are full of such "mistakes" and "dysfunctionalities" resulting from poor framing, blown highlights, camera shake, excessive Photoshop manipulation, or over-the-top Instagram filter use—provides experiential, if not scientific, support to my argument.

Also, the same processes connected with the selection of data were already in operation with analog photography on a number of levels: many photographers used to decide (and still do) which frame to print by evaluating the negative on a light box. Many waded through their test strips or the "print-and-develop" packages they received from a one-hour lab around the corner in order to choose "the keepers" and discard those that did not match "the standard." Of course there were always those photographers for whom an accidental multiple exposure or an unexpected camera shake conjured much more interesting results than those resulting from the application of the dominant norms of "the photographic standard," a standard that advised correct exposure, the rule-of-thirds framing, and impeccable sharpness. However, this preference for a different aesthetic among the photographic avant-garde—both institutionalized and amateur—has been the case with digital, as much as analog, photography.

Does this mean that nothing has changed in the digital era? Not at all. The material process of selecting data takes place differently with analog and digital photography; different things get discarded and lost (film strips and print snaps versus memory cards and USB sticks). The possibility of digging out old faded analog prints from bins at flea markets will undoubtedly become less ubiquitous in the age of digital photography. But it is not only *finding images* in this way that will become less likely. Rather, the space of the flea market itself is under threat in a culture where goods are becoming obsolescent faster and faster, and where global production and trading practices alter the nature of their flow. We should not be too hasty in announcing the demise of the flea market, though: after all, commercial initiatives such as eBay or noncommercial ones such as Freecycle can be seen as its new incarnations in the Internet age.[35]

Beyond digital hysteria

What perhaps predominantly concern Godfrey and Dean are thus the conditions of global capitalism, with its striving toward uniformity, efficiency, and totalization, more than the end of analog photography or the disappearance of the flea market for images. Yet, even though a similar political concern is close to my own heart, I am still puzzled by the inward-looking, even narcissistic, drive of their "high art" project, one which seems to be driven by a desire to preserve a particular role and position for both the artist and the art critic. As Godfrey puts it toward the end of his article, "At the moment of its obsolescence, analog photography ... is [to Dean] like a structure that initially held utopian promise, but despite nineteenth-century hopes for the medium, it became—in the hands of its amateur users—a chaotic floe, as often treated rationally as it was superstitiously, as often prone to mistakes as it was able to capture an intended image for posterity."[36] Here perhaps lies the clue to understanding what Dean's project is actually all about. Motivated by fear of the amateur photographer with her hobbyist excesses, Dean takes on the heroic role of attempting to stop this madness of imag(in)ing-without-end, by introducing some kind of ban, barrier, or dam, in the shape of her art book, to tame this incessant proliferation. This proliferation was already initiated in the early twentieth century, when, thanks to Kodak, photography became a pastime available to most people in industrialized countries. Digital photography is thus a continuation of users' practices enacted with the analog medium; only it is faster, even less permanent, and even more excessive. Commenting on the final image in Dean's book, in which a man stands alone on a sand dune against a church, with the landscape elements turning out to belong to a painted backdrop of a stage set, Godfrey (reluctantly?) admits that "analog images were every bit as tricky as digital manipulations."[37]

At the same time, analog photography is perhaps the last moment when this tide of crazy amateur imaging can be halted; when the artist can still attempt to intervene without herself being drowned by the "floe" of images found and lost. This may explain why Dean prefers her photographs and her sources frozen, immobilized in the bins at flea markets, neatly stowed away in a place that shouts "debris," waiting for the artist to lend them a revitalizing touch and gaze, to choose them from among others, to restore life to them. It is the repetition of the Duchampesque gesture of pointing at things on Dean's part that designates these few select everyday snapshots as "art," even before they find their way to her beautifully printed volume. In this way, even if photography has become deskilled, the position of the artist as designator and legislator of what counts as art is confirmed. In the process of working with found images in this particular fashion, Dean takes on the role of the artist as a guarantor of the authority of "good choices" in culture, a gatekeeper of quality, but also a magician who—through careful selection, through the application of the "less is more" principle—transforms trash into gold. Yet, ironically, Dean's own art project is part of the very same mechanical cycle of media production and exchange that she and Godfrey criticize in so-called mass culture. As Martha Langford has observed, not without irony, "Today, 4,000 people can refer to their signed copy of *Floh* as 'my Tacita Dean.'"[38]

Even though I am aware it may read like a denouncement of Dean and Godfrey, this chapter is actually an attempt on my part—as a philosopher and media theorist who is also a photographer—to come to terms with anxieties similar to those troubling Godfrey and Dean. These can be formulated as a set of questions: How do we continue photographing "seriously" in the digital era? How do we deal with the amateur photographer who "masquerades" as an artist? Can we see photo-sharing websites such as Flickr and Instagram as twenty-first-century versions of the flea market? How do we cope with digital excess, the über-democratic proliferation of equipment as well as interesting (and not-so-interesting) imagery? How do we decide what to delete and what to keep? Hal Foster offers a defense of this "archival impulse"[39]—which he identifies in the work of Dean but also in that of Thomas Hirschhorn and Sam Durant—in the following terms: "Perhaps the paranoid dimension of archival art is the other side of its utopian ambition—its desire to turn belatedness into becomingness, to recoup failed visions in art, literature, philosophy and everyday life into possible scenarios of alternative kinds of social relations, to transform the no-place of the archive into the no-place of a utopia."[40] The archival impulse behind Dean's *Floh* can thus perhaps be read as a paranoid but ultimately salutary effort to do (a minimal) something rather than nothing, to keep going rather than freeze, and to try to turn the data and image flow into a more manageable data stream.

From lace to code

So, indeed, *how can we continue engaging "seriously" with photographs today, as image makers, curators, and archivists, without becoming too paralyzed by the anxieties brought on by the digital age?* I would like to showcase two different interventions into the nexus of photographic affects, ideas, and fixations developed from my own scholarly and artistic practice, as an attempt to think and work through this supposed liquidity of culture. *Even if, as I*

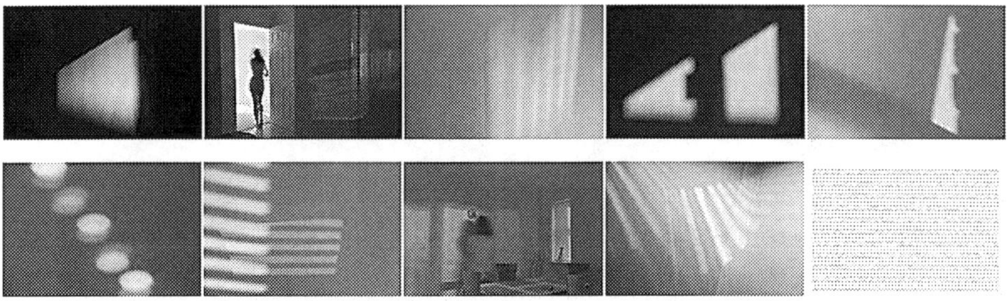

Figure 6.1
Joanna Zylinska, *We Have Always Been Digital*, 2009.

suggested at the opening of this chapter, all photographs are inherently liquid, I wish to interrogate whether we can shoot and curate in a way that visualizes this liquidity and makes it explicit. Wouldn't such an attempt inevitably involve working *against the archive*, as it were? This is another way of saying: can we create images and collections that challenge the concept of a fixed repository while also inevitably hinting at the need (and desire) for some kind of closure, or cut, to the liquid flow of data? Could being trapped in and by the archive be seen as a state of possibility, not an impasse, one that inevitably requires some physical and conceptual readjustment, a movement-with and within?

The first project, a diptych titled *We Have Always Been Digital II*, revisits, for the purposes of this book, a series of images I originally made in 2009 (figure 6.1).[41] The purpose of that original series was to explore digitality as the intrinsic condition of photography, both in its past and present forms. The images highlight the formal role of light in the constitution of a pattern, suggesting that the seemingly contiguous analog aesthetics of light, as captured on various surfaces, is underpinned by what Batchen has identified as the ON/OFF logic of information culture—which, as discussed earlier, he traced back to the work of one of photography's inventors, Fox Talbot. This ON/OFF logic is visualized as a pattern, enacted as a play of shadows and lights—or, in other words, as lights' presence and absence. The nine images of light patterns displayed on the wall, furniture, and human body were taken with a DSLR camera. They are accompanied by a tenth panel featuring a sequence of 0s and 1s which I randomly typed. That last image hints at the computational logic of both photography and the world at large,[42] while also withholding any possibility of their meaningful decoding.

Figure 6.2
William Henry Fox Talbot, *Lace*, from *The Pencil of Nature*, 1845. Public domain.

In making that original project, I was inspired not only by Talbot's photogenic drawings of lace (figure 6.2) but also by his photograph of light falling through the window panels in Lacock Abbey (figure 6.3), a set of images Talbot allegedly sent to his friend Charles Babbage, the inventor of the differential engine (i.e., the first computer). Yet, as Batchen has aptly observed, Talbot's pictures are not so much images of lace or a window, but rather photographs of the object's "patterning, of its regular repetitions of smaller units in order to make up a whole."[43] With this reading, Batchen seems to have proposed an analogy between the invention of photography and the invention of computing as two ways of capturing a pattern in different media. Interestingly, when introducing the lace picture in *The Pencil of Nature* as "the first example of a negative image," Talbot outlined a number of oppositions through which the early history of photography became subsequently framed: negative versus positive; black versus white; absent versus present—even if the image itself broke the rigidity of these

Figure 6.3
William Henry Fox Talbot, *Window in the South Gallery of Lacock Abbey*, made from the oldest photographic negative in existence, 1835. Public domain.

oppositions precisely through the fuzziness of its boundary lines and light traces. He wrote:

The ordinary effect of light upon white sensitive paper is to *blacken* it. If therefore any object, as a leaf for instance, be laid upon the paper, this, by intercepting the action of the light, preserves the whiteness of the paper beneath it, and accordingly when it is removed there appears the form or shadow of the leaf marked out in white upon the blackened paper; and since shadows are usually dark, and this is the reverse, it is called in the language of photography a *negative* image.

> This is exemplified by the lace depicted in this plate; each copy of it being an original or negative image: that is to say, directly taken from the lace itself. Now, if instead of copying the lace we were to copy one of these negative images of it, the result would be a *positive* image of the lace: that is to say, the lace would be represented *black* upon a *white* ground. But in this secondary or positive image the representation of the small delicate threads which compose the lace would not be quite so sharp and distinct, owing to its not being taken directly from the original. In taking views of buildings, statues, portraits, &c. it is necessary to obtain a *positive* image, because the negative images of such objects are hardly intelligible, substituting light for shade, and vice versa.[44]

We could suggest that Talbot moved beyond analog human perception to highlight a deeper algorithmic logic at work in image making, a logic that would later be embraced by code writers and digital camera manufacturers to replicate the look of "traditional" photographs. Interestingly, in the 2000s, digital camera manufacturers went to great trouble to ensure that photos produced with their equipment looked "less digital." Yet this desire to reproduce the original analog look as closely as possible, to the point of deceiving the (expert) viewer, relied on the precise execution of computation so that, through its binary logic, the analog visuality of early photographs could be mimicked perfectly. This is why it is not so much of a leap to suggest not only that *we have always been digital*, but also, conversely, that *we have never stopped being analog*. The fascination with "Fuji colors" in the latest iteration of Fuji digital cameras, whose jpegs are said to perfectly replicate the look of popular Fuji films such as Astia and Provia without the need to postprocess the raw files, provides another illustration of this historical zigzagging between analog and digital. (Incidentally, Fuji cameras—to which I myself have a somewhat irrational affective attachment—first gained popularity among "serious hobbyists" due to their adoption of the traditional rangefinder look, if not functionality, thus signaling to both the outside world and the inner amateur circle that their users were *serious* about their pastime, that they were not *just* amateurs.)

In an attempt to probe this idea of perennial digitality further, I recently revisited my earlier photographic series *We Have Always Been Digital* to look at both the light patterns and the algorithmic patterns underpinning the images. Rather than attempting to discover any kind of ontological truth or technological essence behind them, I was interested in highlighting processes of translation and abstraction that were involved in *all* forms of

Figure 6.4
Joanna Zylinska, *We Have Always Been Digital II*, 2016.

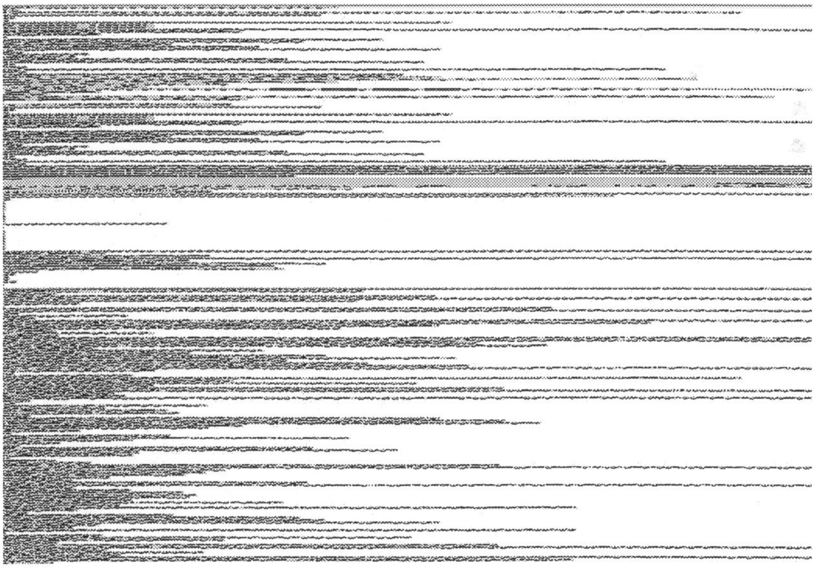

Figure 6.5
Joanna Zylinska, *We Have Always Been Digital II*, 2016.

photographic practice. I also aimed to bring focus to the black-boxing of technology that we tend to associate with digital devices but that was already at work—perhaps inevitably, given the nature of light-sensitive materials—with early large-format cameras, which were literally black boxes. In the second iteration of *We Have Always Been Digital*, I thus overlaid the nine original photographs from the first series in Photoshop to create an abstract composite image showing a textured palimpsest of light traces appearing on different surfaces (figure 6.4). The visual latticework obtained, corresponding perhaps to Talbot's *Lace*, engages the analog and continuous nature of light while also becoming more abstract than the individual images from the first series. I then opened the composite jpeg file in a PC program called Notepad to reveal its code, which I then pasted (almost in its entirety) into a separate panel. The image obtained became the second part of a diptych to accompany the composite photograph (figure 6.5). This code-displaying image offered a different kind of abstraction, outlining a pattern which, at the scale and in the format in which it was presented, gained an alternative legibility for the human spectator: the image had been transformed from a command aimed at a machine with the goal of executing a visualization, to a visual abstraction presented in barely legible black marks on a white surface and arranged into another kind of latticework. The black-and-white conversion of the image added another layer of translatability to the process, while also foregrounding the fact that, as discussed in chapter 1, photographs have *always* been translations—and not transcriptions—of reality.

An *an*archive of photomediations

The second intervention I want to discuss revisits the idea of the photographic archive in the digital age, in an attempt to think about the liquidity of culture beyond fear-inducing concepts such as image deluge and data flood. Titled *Photomediations: An Open Book* (figure 6.6),[45] the 2014–2017 project—which I led in collaboration with Kamila Kuc, Jonathan Shaw, Ross Varney, Michael Wamposzyc, and Gary Hall—has involved redesigning a coffee-table book as an online experience with a view to producing a creative multiplatform resource for various audiences. *Photomediations: An Open Book* uses open (libre) content, drawn from various online repositories

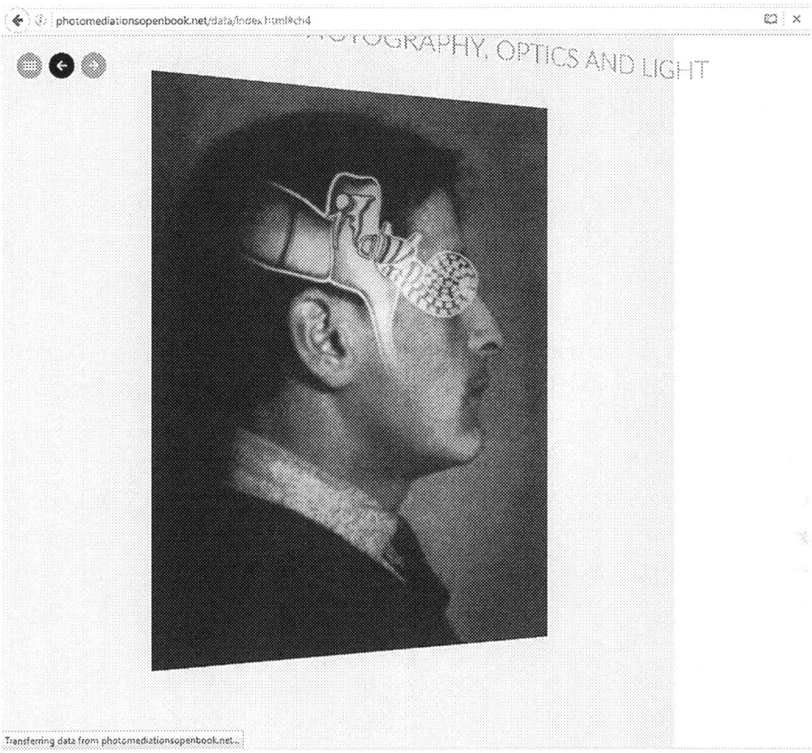

Figure 6.6
Turning a page online in *Photomediations: An Open Book*: www.photomediationsopenbook.net. Image featured on the page: Bill Domonkos, *George*, 2014. (Domonkos combined footage from the Prelinger Archive with a photograph from The Library of Congress.) Source: Public Domain Review / The Library of Congress. License: CC BY-SA.

(Europeana, Wikipedia Commons, Flickr Commons), and tagged with open licenses. Through a comprehensive introduction[46] and four curated chapters on light, movement, hybridity, and networks that include over two hundred images, *Photomediations: An Open Book* tells the story of the dynamic relationship between photography and other media. In the spirit of the Liquid Books project discussed earlier, the book's four main chapters are then followed by three "open" chapters to which readers can contribute content: a social space, an online exhibition, and a reader. With an invitation issued to all readers to enrich and remix its various sections as well as individual images, the book challenges, as Kamila Kuc has put it in her article "A Curated Object and a Disruptive e-Anarchive," "the hegemonic structures of a traditional repository, where ... the haunting spectrum of history is too often shaped into a politically comfortable fiction."[47] Through this open approach on the level of both form and content, the book aims to enact a different history of photography in and for the digital age. A version of the reader, featuring academic and curatorial texts on photomediations, has also been published in a standalone book format by Open Humanities Press (figure 6.7).

Kuc explains, "Through its unique hybrid format, *Photomediations* enacts a shift from the idea of the book, and hence the archive, as a repository of documents and thus of knowledge, to the idea of the archive as a dynamic tool of knowledge production."[48] Similar to Dean's construction of the *Floh* archive, our curatorial work on the book embraced serendipity, playfulness, and visual correspondences in bringing together a vast array of divergent images from various open repositories (figures 6.8 and 6.9). In this way, *Photomediations: An Open Book* moves toward becoming "a living archive of innovative knowledge production rather than ... a repository of old material"[49]—even though old images from known and unknown histories of photography were still very much of interest to us when putting together the collection.

With this anarchival impulse, to use Foster's term,[50] which manifests itself in a search for obscure traces and a lack of desire for completion, our *Photomediations* book offers a response to the inadequacy of the rigid formulations and categories through which photography has traditionally been perceived and approached, proposing instead that it may be time to radically transform, rather than just expand, its very notion. The concept of photomediations that underpins our open book is therefore offered as a richer and more potent conceptual alternative. To think in terms of photomediations is to try to outline a different narrative about the medium, one that remains more attuned to its radically changing ontology. The notion of photomediations aims to cut across the traditional classification of photography as suspended between art and social practice in order to capture the dynamism of the photographic medium today, as well as its kinship with other media—and also with *us as media*. The framework of photomediations adopts a process- and time-based approach to images by tracing the technological, biological, cultural, social, and political flows of data that

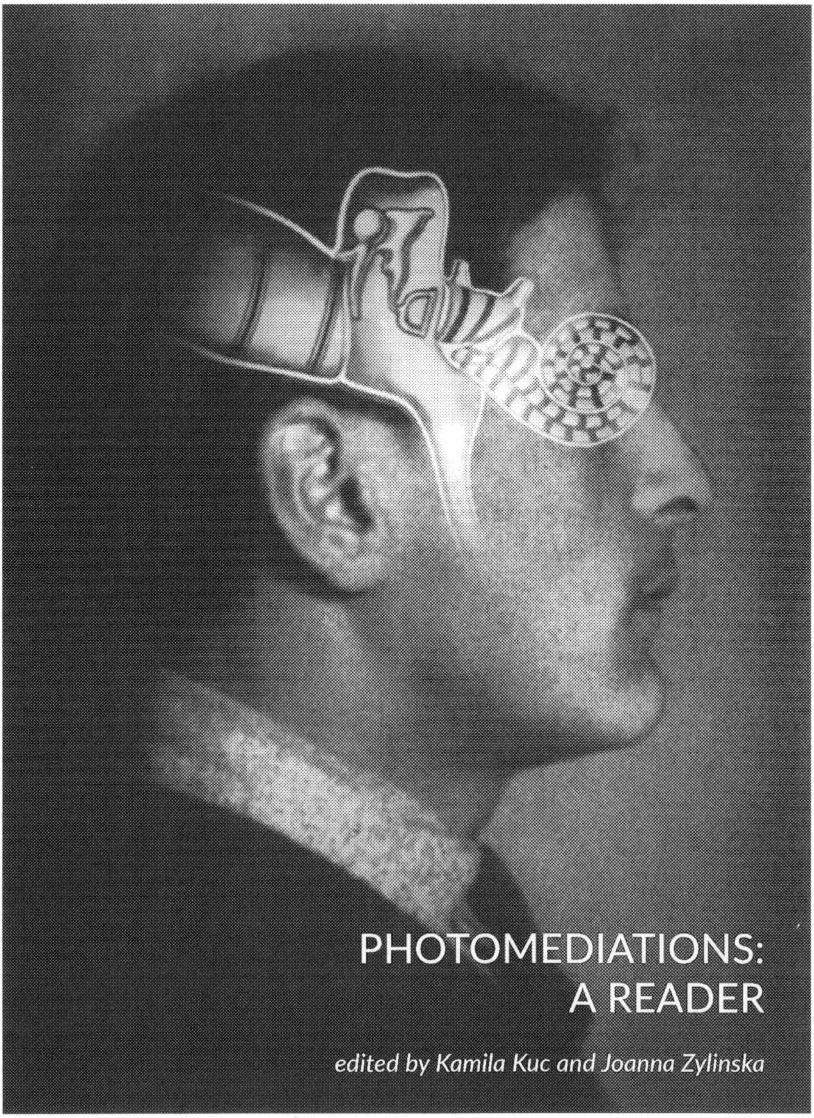

Figure 6.7
Cover of *Photomediations: A Reader*, available as an open access pdf and a printed book, http://www.openhumanitiespress.org/books/titles/photomediations/.

Figure 6.8
The Ostrich, *Fractal Landscape*, 2002. A fractal landscape randomly generated with a custom-programmed algorithm and rendered using Terragen, Wikimedia Commons. License: CC BY 3.0.

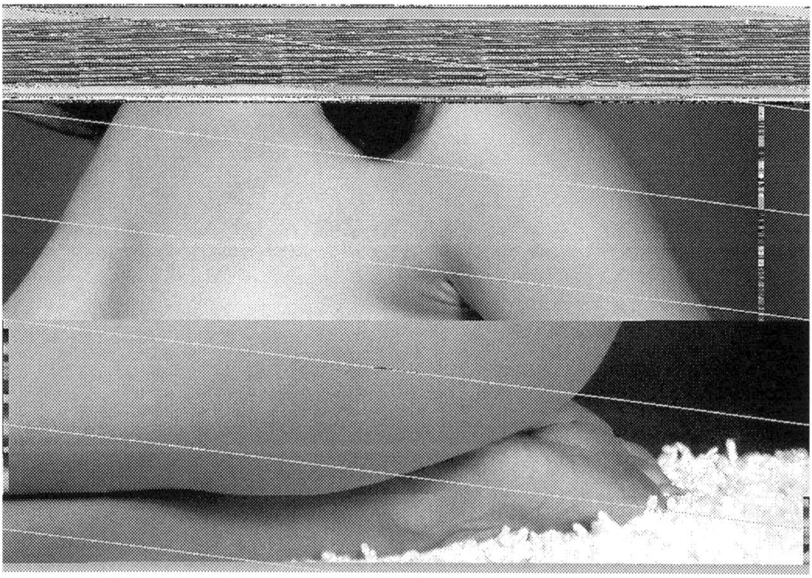

Figure 6.9
mikrosopht [deleted], *Glitch 127*, 2007. Glitch image of the body, created by utilizing a temporary browser image caching error, Flickr. License: CC BY 2.0.

produce photographic objects.[51] Etymologically, the notion of photomediations brings together the hybrid ontology of "photomedia" and the fluid dynamism of "mediation." Allowing us to sidestep the technicist distinction between analog and digital photography, as well as—more radically perhaps—that between still and moving images, the concept of photomedia foregrounds instead what is common to various kinds of light-based practices under discussion. As Jai McKenzie argues, "regardless of technological change, light is a constant defining characteristic of photomedia intrinsically coupled with space and time to form explicit light-based structures and experiences."[52] For McKenzie, photomedia encapsulate not just photographic cameras but also cinema, video, television, mobile phones, computers, and photocopiers. This definition takes cognizance of the fact that, to cite Jonathan Shaw, over the last decade the photographic apparatus has been "reunited with its long lost child, the moving image, ... (arguably) ... having given birth to it many years ago."[53] The concept of mediation, in turn, highlights precisely this intertwined spatial and temporal nature of photography, pointing as it does to a more processual understanding of media that has recently been taken up by scholars and artists alike. We could perhaps go so far as to conclude that *the photograph as such never just exists on its own*. Instead, what emerges are *multiple and ongoing processes of photomediation*. Photography can therefore be seen as an active practice of cutting through the flow of mediation, where "the cut" operates on a number of levels: perceptive, material, technical, and conceptual. In other words, photography can be described as a practice of making cuts in the flow of imagistic data, of stabilizing data as images and objects. Performed by human and nonhuman agents alike, with the latter including the almost incessantly working CCTV cameras, Google Street View equipment, and satellite telescopes, those cuts participate in the wider process of imaging the world.

Although *Photomediations: An Open Book* is an open platform, it certainly does not associate openness with an "anything goes" approach (or, worse, "everything is up for grabs"). Part of the academic movement of "radical open access" that promotes open access to knowledge and culture,[54] the platform advocates informed and responsible curatorial activity. It also recognizes the need, in the current media landscape, for singular ethical and political decisions to be made, over and over again, with regard to both the medium and its institutions, such as publishers, galleries, online spaces, and intellectual property and copyright. Media historian Siegfried Zielinski identifies "[p]ermutation, combinatorics, poetry from a machine; cutting up, taking apart, and putting together again" as gestures that the literary avant-garde in the 1960s used "to creatively attack the bourgeois tradition of the post-war manufacturing of culture."[55] In the early twenty-first-century culture of a supposed deluge of images and texts, predefined camera programs, and Instagram, an avant-garde gesture can perhaps lie first and foremost in efforts to remap the visual landscape—and to rewrite its discourses. Rather than pursue the possibility of taking an original photo of a wedding or a unique selfie, we would be better off engaging in the creative activity of photography by trying to arrange different routes through the multilayered landscape of photomediations. The editorial and curatorial paths proposed in our project are only one possible way of tracing such a new story of photography. They are also an invitation extended to others to engage with *Photomediations: An Open Book* and to mark their own photomediations routes in an anarchival spirit like the one that drove our original efforts.

What's to be done?

Where will this anarchival spirit lead us? Is the recognition of the inherent liquidity of photography, of the perennial photographic flow that the digital age makes even more visible and perhaps overwhelming, therefore also an injunction against the archive and against archiving; an acknowledgment of the futility and ultimate stupidity of the archival impulse which is only going to make us crazy? Not necessarily. In exploring the philosophical limitations of photographic containment throughout this chapter, I have been in agreement with Derrida when he says in the closing pages of *Archive Fever* that we are "in need of archives." To recognize this need means for Derrida "never to rest, interminably, from searching for the archive right where it slips away. It is to run after the archive, even if there's too much of it, right where something in it anarchives itself."[56] Recognizing this need also means, I want to suggest, responding to this injunction to archive, to store things, to repeat, to remember—which is always at the same time an injunction to bury things, to forget about them.

Photography is just one of many cultural practices where such a dual injunction to remember and forget, to store things and throw them away, is enacted. But in its physical two-dimensionality, its anchoring in the index (no matter how much of a fantasy that anchoring is), and its existence in the mappable parallel trajectories of art, commerce, and amateurism, photography becomes a comfortable space in which one can suffer from archive fever. To borrow a phrase from a letter written by Louis Daguerre to Nicéphore Niépce in 1828, it allows us to "burn ... with desire"[57]—a desire for order, for representation, for archivization, for memory, for the graspable other who can at least temporarily be mine, for the world I can hold in my hand or on my cell phone screen—without incinerating ourselves to death. To shift metaphors, whether archived in family albums, on social networking platforms such as Instagram or Snapchat, or in projects based on "found images" such as Dean's *Floh* or our *Photomediations: An Open Book*, photography provides a safe space for exploring the liquidity of culture without drowning in its fast-moving waters. It is in this sense that we can talk about photography's "lifelike"[58] status: not because its digitized objects yield themselves to processes of self-organization, self-replication, and autonomy in the same way that other forms of so-called "artificial life" do, but because both in its amateur and art forms, it is capable of carving out new passageways in life, and of life, by moving us, and making us move, in a myriad ways.[59] Interestingly, a recent survey of occupations that are likely to become obsolete as a result of computerization places "Photographic Process Workers and Process Machine Operators" at 99% probability of disappearance, and "Camera and Photographic Equipment Repairers" at 97%—while the likelihood of the job of "Photographers" disappearing is only 0.02%.[60] It thus appears that photography's future will remain entangled with the human future for a little while longer yet.

Conclusion: Postphotography?

As I was putting finishing touches to this book in the summer of 2016, a news item caught my eye reporting the discovery of an extensive preindustrial urban settlement in Cambodia that far exceeded the familiar boundaries of the Angkor Wat temple complex. By "firing lasers to the ground from a helicopter," archaeologists were able to produce "extremely detailed imagery of the Earth's surface,"[1] while revealing in the process a highly sophisticated water management system created during the Angkorian Empire (figure 7.1). The report was of interest to me not only because the discovery of the latent imagistic and material layer underneath the Cambodian jungle was accomplished by mobilizing the techniques and methods of "nonhuman photography," but also because it offered an actual dispatch from the end of the world—a trace of a civilization long gone, whose presence nevertheless revealed itself to the nonhuman vision of an airborne laser scanner. Where the human eye, both in its flat and elevated positions, could see only thick vegetation, the so-called lidar[2] survey's eye was able to penetrate through the surface to identify the geometric patterns of earth mounds that archaeologists could subsequently read as the early Khmer society's urban infrastructure. The patterns most likely represented a complex water management system, as well as giant quarries, from the early to mid-Angkor period (ninth to thirteenth centuries CE).

The ability of laser imaging technology to penetrate through thick jungle and uncover traces of past societies allowed archaeologists to revisit their prior theories about the rise and decline of civilizations, while also revealing "long term patterns of human-environment interactions at the regional scale."[3] We could conclude that nonhuman photography lets us humans see the nonhuman shaping of civilizations: the role of water and other resources, the impact of surrounding ecologies on the development

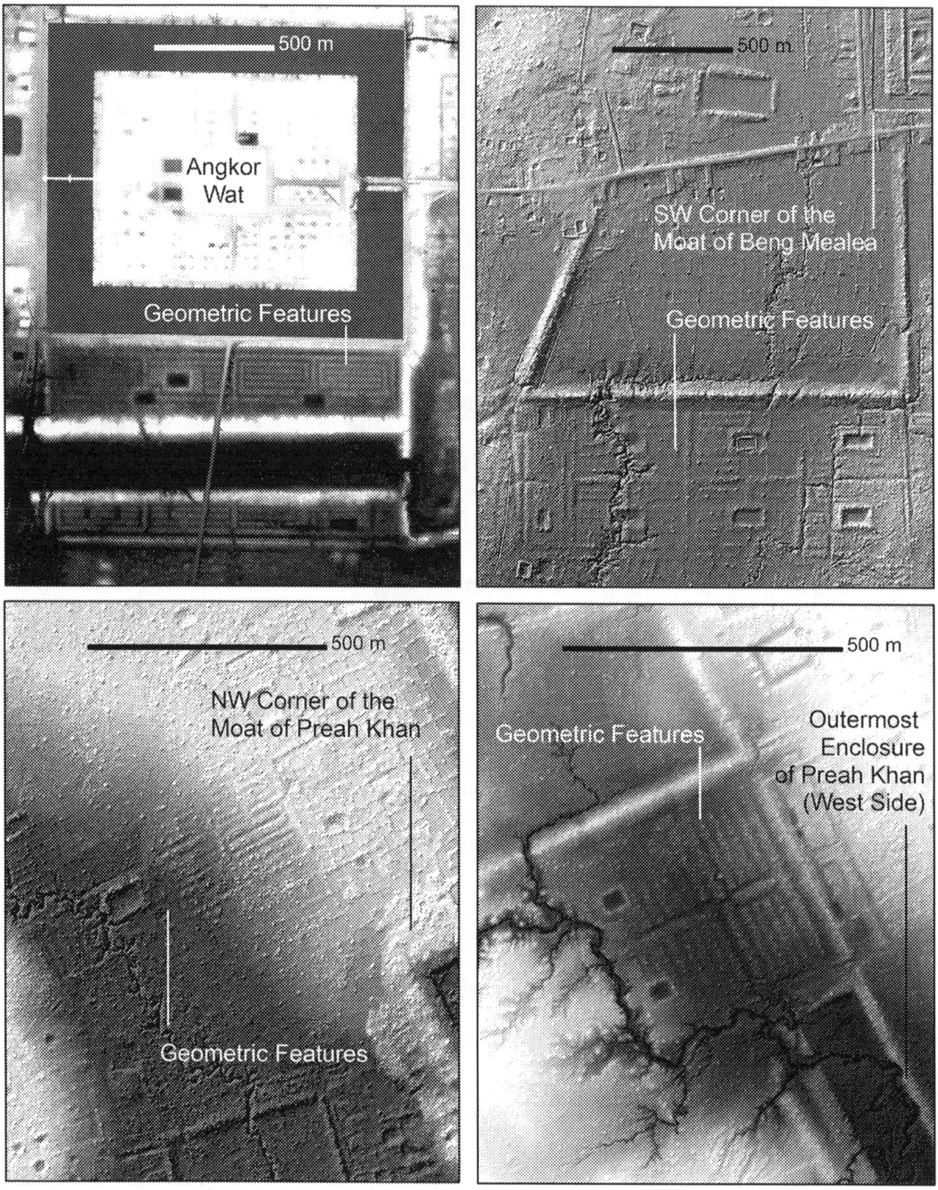

Figure 7.1

Unexplained, geometric linear patterns associated with major temples across northwest Cambodia. Imagery consists of airborne laser scanning-derived bare-earth models, overlain by a semitransparent hillshade model, CC BY 4.0. (Evans, "Airborne Laser Scanning.")

of those civilizations. It also, in this particular case, challenges the image of medieval Southeast Asian urban architecture as primarily consisting of civic-ceremonial centers made up of temples and other ritualistic spaces. "The engineered landscape of Sambor Prei Kuk is … clearly more extensive, densely-inhabited and more complex than previously believed,"[4] writes the author of the project's report, Damian Evans. The identification of what looks like a "loop" in the highway system in the laser scanner–derived photos calls for a radical reassessment of our understanding of the overland transportation and communication between major centers of the era—as well as of the role of Angkor itself. (Just because *we* modern humans have discovered the Angkor Wat temple complex first does not mean that it *was* the center of the Khmer civilization, and the more extensive image sets now available raise doubts about its exclusive role.) More interestingly, the images also seem to offer an imagistic record of premodern traces of the Anthropocene. Evans points out that the photographs "speak directly to evolving debates about the decline of the classical Angkorian Empire, in which it has been argued that increasing complexity and urbanisation in the 11th to 13th centuries generated large populations of non-rice-producing inhabitants who would have been heavily reliant on elaborate state-sponsored water management systems for the production [of] consistent yields of rice."[5] Early Khmer societies seem to have been actively involved in the profound and repeated transformation of "the landscapes in which they lived and inherited from their predecessors," a process that "took place over millennia at a regional scale."[6]

The laser images can thus be said to allow us to *re*imagine the end of the world—not just in the future but also in the past—by prompting us to reassess the theory of the collapse of the Angkorian Empire as a result of invasion by neighbors, and to see it instead as "a more gradual demographic decline due to the breakdown of the water management system and the absence of the food security it provided."[7] These kinds of ultramodern photographs of the past provide us with "a more complex understanding of how large-scale socio-ecological processes may create systemic vulnerability" to environmental events.[8] Nonhuman photography can thus be deployed to denaturalize nature while also offering a better, more accurate, and more entangled account of human-nonhuman relations. Indeed, high-resolution airborne laser scanning is capable of "showing that the extent of anthropogenic changes to 'natural' landscapes during the past few thousand years has so far been substantially underestimated."[9]

The actual technology involved in the lidar survey is also worth looking at: it is a combination of various photomedia devices, including the aforementioned airborne laser scanner (Leica ALS70 HP) and a digital camera (60 megapixel Leica), as well as sophisticated modeling software used in postproduction to interpret the data obtained. The scanner, mounted to a helicopter skid pad, pulses the terrain at regular intervals during flight. As explained by a feature in *The Guardian*,

> The time the laser pulse takes to return to the sensor determines the elevation of each individual data point. The data downloaded from the ALS is calibrated and creates a 3D model of the information captured during the flights. In order to negate tree foliage and manmade obstacles from the data, any sudden and radical changes in ground height are mapped out, with technicians who have models of the terrain fine-tuning the thresholds in processing these data points. Once completed, the final 3D model is handed over to the archaeologists for analysis, which can take months to process into maps.[10]

Nonhuman photography here is therefore very much dependent on the human element: engineers, photographers, pilots, coders, archaeologists, data scientists. This human-nonhuman assemblage has, of course, permeated and shaped photography since its very beginning, as I have attempted to demonstrate throughout this book, but the coupling is foregrounded much more explicitly in these kinds of high-resolution, software-driven photomediations. In the lidar process, laser scanning technology that emits light comes together with photography that captures that light to create a new field called *photogrammetry*: the science of making measurements from photographs. In addition to involving the capture of light reflected from various surfaces, this technology entails 3D modeling on the basis of the data acquired from the laser and the camera. Transcending the analog-digital binary in its mode of operation, the lidar survey at the same time raises an important question: Are we still dealing with photography here, or have we perhaps arrived at something that could be termed postphotography?

The concept of postphotography has appeared in recent years in an attempt to capture the transformations of the medium "in the age of the Internet and mobile phone."[11] We can mention here the catalog-book published on the occasion of the "postphotography" exhibition, "From Here On," held at Rencontres d'Arles in 2013,[12] or the 2014 photo book *Post-Photography: The Artist with a Camera* by journalist Robert Shore, which has gathered the work of fifty artists working with photography in ways other than *just* taking pictures. Shore's artists are instead "metaphotographers who can make sense of the billions of images being made."[13] Yet rather than follow any such linear shift toward a supposed post-medium condition, I am more inclined to side with Edgar Gómez Cruz, who, while remaining aware of the radical changes the photographic medium and its context are undergoing, nevertheless favors an expansion of the definition of photography and not its overcoming. For Gómez Cruz, it makes sense to retain an ontological continuity with the photographic medium's earlier incarnations, provided we are prepared to challenge the rather limiting representationalist understanding of photography and focus instead on its creative, interfacial role in both making marks and establishing connections. "By understanding photography as an assemblage of 'surface-marking technologies' we move away from a semiotic/indexical understanding of images and could increasingly relate everyday photography with other kinds of image-processes, for example scientific imagery," he suggests.[14] *The reconceptualization of photography in algorithmic and computational terms*[15] *in the early twenty-first century invites us to see the photographic image as first of all a node in the networked sequence of human-nonhuman processes of connection, identification, translation, and, last but not least, invention.* However, if we are prepared to accept that photography since its early days has been both inventive (as evidenced, for instance, in its monochromatic legacy that entailed a process of creative translation) and nonhuman (with Talbot's Lacock Abbey as the first building that took its own picture),[16] then the current developments merely foreground its *original* nonhuman entanglement and kinship—to be seen in fossils, analog snapshots, and lidar-produced photomaps. Photography based on algorithms, computers, and networks merely intensifies this condition, while also opening up some new questions and new possibilities.

The possibility of seeing both into the past and into the future—of seeing life before and after the human (including before and after particular groups of humans), but also before and after our nonhuman counterparts (glaciers, forests, empires)—is also an instance when nonhuman visuality turns into a human-centric responsibility. As a practice of incision, photography can help us redistribute and re-cize the human sensible[17] to see other traces, connections, and affordances—to let us humans perceive and experience the world otherwise. Nonhuman photography can allow us to unsee ourselves from our parochial human-centered anchoring, and encourage a different vision of both ourselves and what we call the world. Adam Brenthel poignantly emphasizes that "We do not really need to artificially produce realistic images of storm surges and the drowning of a world because we already saw first hand the effects that Hurricane Katrina had on … the streets of Louisiana."[18] Rather than in representing, the transformative role of nonhuman photography may thus perhaps lie in foregrounding the flow of duration (which for Bergson, and Deleuze after him, stands for life itself), while also showing us the cuts and incisions through which things stabilize in the world. *Photography is therefore never just about cuts: it is also about reconnecting us to the current of life—and about making us feel alive, over and over again.*

Roberto Huarcaya's project *Amazograms—90 meters of Bahuaja Sonene* (figures 7.2 and 7.3) channels this very sentiment. Originally made in 2014, it was displayed in the Peruvian pavilion during the 15th Venice Architecture Biennale two years later. The display consisted of long sequences of photosensitive paper onto which, in a manner evocative of Talbot's early photograms, the Amazonian forest had been contact-printed directly, with

Figure 7.2
Joanna Zylinska, close-up of the installation of Roberto Huarcaya's *Amazograms—90 meters of Bahuaja Sonene* in the Peruvian pavilion during the 15th Venice Architecture Biennale in 2016.

Figure 7.3
Joanna Zylinska, close-up of the installation of Roberto Huarcaya's *Amazograms—90 meters of Bahuaja Sonene* in the Peruvian pavilion during the 15th Venice Architecture Biennale in 2016.

the help of a small flashlight and the full moon. The long paper strips had subsequently been developed in the water of the nearby river, with the contaminated liquid taken back to Lima in order to dispose of it safely. Huarcaya's *Amazograms,* images of the forest that has taken its own picture, carry a trace of life in that fundamental biological sense: as vegetation, oxygen, light, and water. They are a form of impermanent fossil which offers a deep-time link between the ancient world of the Amazon with its indigenous knowledges, and its modern function as a frontier, a resource—and a task. This ninety-meter-long "undulating ribbon in fragile equilibrium"[19] can serve as a lifeline, as well as a marker of the time lost. In *Amazograms* photography reveals itself as a nonhuman mode of geological tracing with light, across different time scales. But it also comes to the fore as a human-centric practice that has the potential to reenergize us by encouraging us to look at the sun and the moon—and to sense, embrace, *and rethink* our sources of energy and light.

Notes

Introduction

1. For example, on December 2, 2015, Balog presented a talk-cum-screening titled "Human Tectonics: Ice, Fire, and Life in the Anthropocene" at an event hosted by The Royal Photographic Society at the Regent Street Cinema in London.

2. Susan Sontag, "Regarding the Torture of Others," *New York Times*, May 23, 2004, http://www.nytimes.com/2004/05/23/magazine/regarding-the-torture-of-others.html.

3. Art historical narratives of this kind span from Beaumont Newhall's modernist classic *The History of Photography from 1839 to the Present*, first published in 1939 (New York: Museum of Modern Art, 1982, 5th ed.), through to Michael Fried, *Why Photography Matters as Art as Never Before* (New Haven: Yale University Press, 2008).

4. Pierre Bourdieu's book *Photography: A Middle-Brow Art* (Stanford: Stanford University Press, 1990) has served as initial inspiration for the development of this sociological framework.

5. Elizabeth Edwards's review article "Objects of Affect: Photography Beyond the Image," *Annual Review of Anthropology* 41 (2012): 221–234, is in a way exemplary of this approach. On the one hand, it seems to embrace the Latourian model that has made its way into anthropology, whereby "the social saliency of objects and their efficacy is activated by networks of humans and nonhumans, people and things" (223), and Edwards also makes quite a radical proposition that "photographs cannot be understood through visual content alone but through an embodied engagement with an affective object world, which is both constitutive of and constituted through social relations" (221). On the other hand, the article ends up reaffirming the discreteness of the ontological categories it seemingly hybridizes by returning to the human as both the arbiter of sense and the ultimate addressee and reference point of photographs—as evident in the following question that summarizes Edwards's review: "Underlying all these positions ... is the central ethnographic question, why do photographs as 'things' matter to people?" (224). It is worth mentioning in this

context the collection *Digital Photography and Everyday Life: Empirical Studies on Material Visual Practices*, edited by Edgar Gómez Cruz and Asko Lehmuskallio (London: Routledge, 2016). While many of the articles in the book, guided by the opening question, "*What do ordinary people do with their cameras and personal pictures, as part of everyday life?*" (Richard Chalfen, foreword, xv), inscribe themselves in the human-centric and humanist narrative about the photographic medium, the two editors—both in the joint introduction and in their respective contributions—have also taken some bold steps toward shifting photography into different terrains and modes of thought. Thus, Gómez Cruz outlines a theory of nonrepresentational photography, demonstrating how "photographic technologies are increasingly being used not (only) as a representation or performance but as a techno-visual interface between objects, information, networks, environments, databases and people" ("Photo-genic Assemblages," 230)—as evident, for example, in QR codes that function as translators between material objects, databases, and occasionally also humans. Lehmuskallio picks up this line of argument, in turn, to discuss the functioning of cameras as sensors in wearable or remotely controlled camera technology. Here, "a database of thousands of recorded images might be used for modelling social networks or geolocation information" (Lehmuskallio, "The Camera as a Sensor among Many," 245–246), providing an example of what I am referencing in this introduction as photography that is not "*for* the human."

6. The material outlined in this paragraph has been reworked from Joanna Zylinska, "Photomediations: An Introduction," in Kamila Kuc and Joanna Zylinska, eds., *Photomediations: A Reader* (London: Open Humanities Press, 2016), 7–17.

7. Richard Grusin, introduction to Grusin, ed., *The Nonhuman Turn* (Minneapolis: University of Minnesota Press, 2015), vii.

8. Elizabeth Ellsworth and Jamie Kruse, eds., *Making the Geologic Now: Responses to Material Conditions of Contemporary Life* (Brooklyn, NY: Punctum Books, 2012).

9. Elizabeth Kolbert, "Enter the Anthropocene—Age of Man," in Ellsworth and Kruse, *Making the Geologic Now*, 31; originally published in *National Geographic Magazine*, March 2011.

10. Tom Cohen and Claire Colebrook, preface to Tom Cohen, Claire Colebrook, and J. Hillis Miller, *Twilight of the Anthropocene Idols* (London: Open Humanities Press, 2016), 11.

11. Claire Colebrook has gone so far as to argue that "we have *always* been post-Anthropocene" ("We Have Always Been Post-Anthropocene: The Anthropocene Counter-Factual," https://www.academia.edu/12757260/We_Have_Always_Been_Post-Anthropocene, author's manuscript, undated, emphasis mine).

12. Cohen and Colebrook, preface, 11.

13. For Karen Barad, representationalism is characterized by "the belief in the ontological distinction between representations and that which they purport to represent [whereby] ... that which is represented is held to be independent of all practices of representation." See Barad, *Meeting the Universe Halfway: Quantum Physics and the Entanglement of Matter and Meaning* (Durham: Duke University Press, 2007), 46. This belief ignores the role of the technical apparatus in the shaping of images, and hence also of our knowledge of the world—and our picture of it.

14. See, for example, Harold A. Innis, *The Fur Trade in Canada: An Introduction to Canadian Economic History* (Toronto: University of Toronto Press, 1930) and *The Bias of Communication* (Toronto: University of Toronto Press, 1951).

15. See Raymond Williams, "Culture Is Ordinary," in Anne Gray and Jim McGuigan, eds., *Studying Culture* (London: Arnold, 1997), 5–15.

16. John Durham Peters, *The Marvelous Clouds: Toward a Philosophy of Elemental Media* (Chicago: University of Chicago Press, 2015), 4.

17. Nicholas Mirzoeff, "Visualizing the Anthropocene," *Public Culture* 26, no. 2 (2014): 213.

Chapter 1

1. Donna Haraway, "Situated Knowledges: The Science Question in Feminism and the Privilege of Partial Perspective," *Feminist Studies* 14, no. 3 (Autumn 1988): 581.

2. In *The Right to Look*, Nicholas Mirzoeff associates these two examples with the emergence of modern visuality. He argues that "what is being visualized is too substantial for any one person to see and is created from information, images, and ideas. This ability to assemble a visualization manifests the authority of the visualizer. In turn, the authorizing of authority requires permanent renewal in order to win consent as the 'normal,' or everyday, because it is always already contested." Nicholas Mirzoeff, *The Right to Look: A Counterhistory of Visuality* (Durham: Duke University Press, 2011), 2. See also Haraway, "Situated Knowledges," 582.

3. Haraway, "Situated Knowledges," 581.

4. John Johnston, "Machinic Vision," *Critical Inquiry* 26 (Autumn 1999): 27–48, 27.

5. Instead, the chapter adopts an expanded and hybrid concept of machinic vision outlined by John Johnston (ibid.). For Johnston, machinic vision "presupposes not only an environment of interacting machines and human-machine systems but a field of decoded perceptions that, whether or not produced by or issuing from these machines, assume their full intelligibility only in relation to them" (27). The concept of "the machinic," derived from Deleuze, signifies "the type of working relationship among the heterogeneous elements and relations defined by an assemblage" (28). It is opposed to the concept of machine-like vision espoused, for example, by

Paul Virilio, which inscribes itself in a "catastrophic narrative tracing a Fall" from natural perception into technology (30).

6. Sarah Kember and Joanna Zylinska, *Life after New Media: Mediation as a Vital Process* (Cambridge, MA: MIT Press, 2012), xv.

7. Jonathan Crary, *Techniques of the Observer: On Vision and Modernity in the Nineteenth Century* (Cambridge, MA: MIT Press, 1990), 2.

8. Kassandra Nakas, "Jana Sterbak," website documenting the exhibition project "Becoming Animal, Becoming Human / Animal Perspectives," 2009, http://becoming-animal-becoming-human.animal-studies.org/html/sterbak.html.

9. "Dr Julius Neubronner's Miniature Pigeon Camera," *The Public Domain Review*, not dated, http://publicdomainreview.org/collections/dr-julius-neubronners-miniature-pigeon-camera/. I am grateful to Kamila Kuc for pointing me to this work via *Photomediations: An Open Book*.

10. Haraway, "Situated Knowledges," 583.

11. Chapter 3 in my book co-written with Sarah Kember, *Life after New Media*, discusses in detail the relationship between photography, cinema, and life in the work of Henri Bergson and Gilles Deleuze, in an attempt to "salvage" photographic ontology and photographic thinking from being dismissed too easily by vitalist philosophy.

12. Rebekah Modrak with Bill Anthes, *Reframing Photography: Theory and Practice* (London: Routledge, 2011), xliii.

13. These statements have been taken from various tech blogs and news feeds from between 2012 and 2015 (buzzfeed, popphoto.com, mybilliondollarapp.com). Their accuracy should not be taken literally, not least because of the rapid changes the platforms discussed are undergoing and the relative impossibility of measuring accurately what they are pronouncing. However, numerical accuracy is not their authors' primary concern: they are more interested in creating a shock effect among their readers, dazzling them with difficult to grasp numbers and acting as "clickbait."

14. Jonathan Beller, *The Cinematic Mode of Production: Attention Economy and the Society of the Spectacle* (Hanover, NH: University Press of New England, 2006), 2.

15. Ibid.

16. As listed on the website http://top-hashtags.com/instagram/ on April 21, 2015.

17. Lyle Rexer, *The Edge of Vision: The Rise of Abstraction in Photography* (New York: Aperture, 2013), 9.

18. Ibid., 11.

19. Ibid.

20. Ibid., 12.

21. Ibid.

22. Anthes, in Modrak with Anthes, *Reframing Photography*, 112.

23. This is a rather crowded field. Alongside Niépce and Talbot, Frenchmen Hippolyte Bayard and Louis Daguerre, as well as several other scientists, were clamoring for the title. In *Burning with Desire: The Conception of Photography* (Cambridge, MA: MIT Press, 1997), Geoffrey Batchen explains this outbreak of multiple and parallel photographic inventions at the end of the nineteenth century as due to the existence of a "desire" for photography, which manifested itself in a widespread interest in fixing images as well as the adequate maturation of the technological assemblage that enabled this process. Chapter 2 develops this point further.

24. H. Fox Talbot, *The Pencil of Nature* (London: Longman, Brown, Green and Longmans, 1844), Project Gutenberg online edition, n.p.

25. Ibid.

26. Rexer, *The Edge of Vision*, 32.

27. Ibid., 52.

28. Modrak with Anthes, *Reframing Photography*, 42.

29. Ibid., 45.

30. Ben Burbridge, introduction to Burbridge, ed., *Revelations: Experiments in Photography* (London: Mack in association with Media Space, 2015), 23.

31. George Hobson, foreword to Burbridge, *Revelations*, 7.

32. In the essay "All That Is Solid Melts into Air: Early Scientific Photography and Modern Art" (in Burbridge, *Revelations*, 119), Burbridge cites Moholy-Nagy's declaration made in *Painting, Photography, Film* that "photography should not emulate human vision in a reproductive fashion." Instead, Moholy-Nagy claimed it needed to "'make visible existences which cannot be perceived or taken in by our optical instrument, the eye.'"

33. Rexer, *The Edge of Vision*, 133–134.

34. Ibid., 29.

35. Cited in Terence Wright, *The Photography Handbook*, 2nd ed. (London: Routledge, 2004), 2.

36. Modrak, in Modrak with Anthes, *Reframing Photography*, 200. Also, Joan Fontcuberta argues: "The mainstream media and institutions purvey a paternalistic discourse designed to cocoon us from the harshness of the world, imposing the distance that will prevent the catastrophe and suffering from offending our immature

sensibility. All that is left are scraps of formalism or hypocritical humanitarianism, the spectacle of the pain that we do nothing to lessen." Fontcuberta, *Pandora's Camera: Photogr@phy after Photography* (London: Mack, 2014), 157.

37. Gilles Tiberghien, "Robert Smithson and Aerial Art," in Mark Dorrian and Frederic Pousin, eds., *Seeing from Above: The Aerial View in Visual Culture* (London: IB Tauris, 2013), 277.

38. Mark Dorrian, "On Google Earth," in Dorrian and Pousin, *Seeing from Above*, 295.

39. John Tagg, "Mindless Photography," in J. J. Long, Andrea Noble, and Edward Welch, eds., *Photography: Theoretical Snapshots* (London: Routledge, 2009), 29.

40. Ibid., 25.

41. Ibid., 29.

42. Rob Coley, "The Horrors of Visuality," in Kamila Kuc and Joanna Zylinska, eds., *Photomediations: A Reader* (London: Open Humanities Press, 2016), 291.

43. Tagg, "Mindless Photography," 21.

44. Coley, "The Horrors of Visuality," 290.

45. Ibid., 301.

46. This concept has been proposed by Tom Cohen in "Introduction: Murmurations—'Climate Change' and the Defacement of Theory," in Cohen, ed., *Telemorphosis: Theory in the Era of Climate Change*, vol. 1 (Ann Arbor: Open Humanities Press, 2012), 13–42.

47. Cited in Carol Squiers, *What Is a Photograph?* (New York: International Center of Photography and DelMonico Books, 2014), 41. In a similar vein, Mark Dorrian claims that "Google knows more about the United Kingdom's citizens than does MI5, the state security agency," thus aiming to fulfill the "dream of total knowledge, which is also a kind of total seeing" ("On Google Earth," 294).

48. Kember and Zylinska, *Life after New Media*, 186.

49. Coley, "The Horrors of Visuality," 304. Coley turns here to McKenzie Wark's *Telesthesia*, a book which for Coley "gives shape to such a tactic by calling for the identification of weird moments, anomalous irruptive events, when the paradoxes of control reveal an 'after image,' a peripheral glimpse of the monster" (292).

50. See Trebor Scholz, "Becoming Facebook," in D. E. Wittkower, ed., *Facebook and Philosophy* (Chicago: Open Court, 2010), and chapter 6, "Face-to-Facebook, or the Ethics of Mediation" in Kember and Zylinska, *Life after New Media*.

51. Vilém Flusser, *Into the Universe of Technical Images*, trans. Nancy Ann Roth (Minneapolis: University of Minnesota Press, 2011), 5.

52. Ibid., 16.

53. Ibid., 19.

54. Ibid.

55. Ibid., 18.

56. Ibid., 19.

57. Richard Whitlock, "Non-perspectival Photography: Towards a Post-digital Visuality," *Photomediations Machine*, May 18, 2014, http://photomediationsmachine.net/2014/05/18/non-perspectival-photography-towards-a-post-digital-visuality/.

58. See Gregory Sholette, "Richard Whitlock's 'The Street': An Interview," *Afterimage Online: The Journal of Media Arts and Cultural Criticism*, November 7, 2013, n.p., http://vsw.org/afterimage/2013/11/07/video-and-interview-i-richard-whitlocks-the-street/.

59. Flusser, *Into the Universe of Technical Images*, 36.

60. Ibid., 37.

61. Ibid., 45.

62. Katrina Sluis, "Authorship, Collaboration, Computation? Into the Realm of Similar Images," in Kuc and Zylinska, *Photomediations*, 285.

63. Flusser, *Into the Universe of Technical Images*, 53.

64. Ibid., 67.

65. Ibid., 86.

66. Ibid.

67. Sluis, "Authorship, Collaboration, Computation?," 289.

68. Bonamy Devas, "Photographic Tai Chi," *Photomediations Machine*, May 22, 2015, n.p., http://photomediationsmachine.net/2015/05/22/photographic-tai-chi/.

69. Flusser, *Into the Universe of Technical Images*, 86.

70. Evgeny Morozov, "Facebook Isn't a Charity: The Poor Will Pay by Surrendering Their Data," *Observer*, April 26, 2015, 28.

71. E. Bruce Goldstein, *Sensation and Perception*, 8th ed. (Belmont, CA: Wadsworth Cengage Learning, 2010), 8.

72. Ibid., 4.

73. Ibid., 10.

74. Ibid., 39.

75. Crary, *Techniques of the Observer*, 6.

76. See chapters 1–3 in Goldstein, *Sensation and Perception*.

77. Crary, *Techniques of the Observer*, 53.

78. Ibid., 60–62.

79. Ibid., 133–136, emphasis added.

80. Ibid., 136.

81. Haraway, "Situated Knowledges," 581.

82. Ibid.

83. Eva Hayward, "Fingeryeyes: Impressions of Cup Corals," *Cultural Anthropology* 25, no. 4 (2010): 577–599. In her study of cup corals, Hayward attends to the interplay of vision and touch, invoking as she does "fingeryeyes to articulate the in-between of encounter, a space of movement, of potential: this haptic-optic defines the overlay of sensoriums and the inter- and intrachange of sensations. Fingeryeyes, in this instance, is the transfer of intensity, of expressivity in the simultaneity of touching and feeling" (581).

84. Haraway in "Anthropocene, Capitalocene, Chthulucene: Donna Haraway in Conversation with Martha Kenney," in Heather Davis and Etienne Turpin, eds., *Art in the Anthropocene: Encounters among Aesthetics, Politics, Environments and Epistemologies* (London: Open Humanities Press, 2015), 258.

85. Ibid.

86. Juhani Pallasmaa, *The Eyes of the Skin: Architecture and the Senses*, 3rd ed. (London: John Wiley & Sons, 2012), 29.

87. Ibid., 45.

88. In a similar vein, Hayward argues that "our eyes are contiguous with—not divisible from—the body's sensorium. Embodied vision is necessarily accreted by the other senses and their amplification. In this way, sight is of the body, not just in the body, and this effects a distributed sensuousness" ("Fingeryeyes," 582).

89. James Gibson, *The Ecological Approach to Visual Perception* (Boston: Houghton Mifflin, 1979), 141.

90. Ibid., 187.

91. Ibid., 203.

92. Ibid., 212. Argentinian artist Mariano Sardon's *Morphologies of the Gaze* (2012) offers a poetic illustration of this phenomenon. The project consists of a series of video portraits, constructed by the superimposition of lines over images of faces which represent the eye movements of various people looking at those faces. The

"200 Gazes Looking around Them" (200 miradas recorriendo sus rostros) series, which is part of this project, "connects information, technology and neuroscience with regard to how we perceive and construct the world. When looking at someone's face, each person performs a unique sequence of eye movements. In the work, the eye movements of a person looking at a face were drawn over an image of the observed person. The eye movements of each person looking were recorded for a period of time by a special eye-tracking device used in a neuroscience lab. This test was undertaken by 200 people. The image of each face was subsequently reconstructed, mapping all the eye movements of each person looking. The videos produced show how the image of a face is constructed over time by the gaze of 200 people. The image of a face that emerges is therefore a collective construction, made up from gazes of different people." Web text for the biennale of new media art, Transitio_MX05 Biomediaciones, held in Mexico City, September 20–29, 2013.

93. Modrak, in Modrak with Anthes, *Reframing Photography*, 10.

94. Ibid., 11.

95. Susan Sontag, quoted in ibid., 3.

96. Gibson, *The Ecological Approach to Visual Perception*, 293.

97. Jai McKenzie takes issue with Cartier-Bresson's conviction that a photographer supposedly "hunts down, recognises and captures with their camera these 'chance' moments; that the photograph somehow stands for a larger sequence of events. According to Flusser this is not the case; the image only demonstrates the program of the apparatus and not a decisive moment." McKenzie, *Light and Photomedia: A New History and Future of the Photographic Image* (London: IB Tauris, 2014), 58.

98. Kember and Zylinska, *Life after New Media*, 75. See also my *Bioethics in the Age of New Media* (Cambridge, MA: MIT Press, 2009), 30, in which I first proposed the concept of "the cut" as a structuring device in ethical thinking.

99. See Kember and Zylinska, *Life after New Media*, 71.

Chapter 2

An earlier and shorter version of this chapter came out in Mika Elo, Marc Goodwin, Marko Karo, and Merja Salo, eds., *Photographic Powers* (Helsinki: Aalto ARTS, 2015). License: CC BY 4.0.

1. Sarah Kember, *iMedia: The Gendering of Objects, Environments and Smart Materials* (Basingstoke: Palgrave Macmillan, 2016), 8.

2. Ibid., 10.

3. Stewart Brand, cited in Chris Russill, "Earth Imaging: Photograph, Pixel, Program," in Stephen Rust, Salma Monani, and Sean Cubitt, eds., *Ecomedia: Key Issues* (London: Routledge, 2016), 233.

4. Russill, "Earth Imaging," 236.

5. See ibid., 237.

6. Ibid., 239. Elizabeth A. Kessler's *Picturing the Cosmos: Hubble Space Telescope Images and the Astronomical Sublime* (Minneapolis: University of Minnesota Press, 2012) offers an intriguing account of the processes of data translation and interpretation in space photography. She describes their alignment with various familiar visual tropes, so that, in space photos made available to us by NASA and other agencies, galaxies end up looking like nineteenth-century landscape photography.

7. Russill writes: "When the light of the Blue Marble is digitized, made calculable, and rendered visually as a sequence of images, it suggests that endless images are 'latent' in the imaging process, and that our perception is dependent on how light is abstracted by a computer program. The representation of the earth is a function of the desired technical resolution, and not at all what our eyes would see from space" ("Earth Imaging," 244–245).

8. Ibid., 240.

9. For a critical interrogation of the scientific visualizations of the geomorphological changes our world is undergoing—changes to its temperature, ice caps, water levels, and composition of air that, taken together, stand for what science describes as "climate change"—see Adam Brenthel, *The Drowning World: The Visual Culture of Climate Change* (Lund: Lund University, 2016). Brenthel examines scientific reports and other texts and artifacts that deal with climate change to highlight the multiple messages that come through attempts at scientific communication. The two main chapters of the book are structured around two key images that are frequently mobilized to communicate climate change: the image of Planet Earth floating in dark space known as the *Blue Marble* (discussed in this chapter), and an image of the sea or ocean that segues into images of waves, floods, and total immersion or even submersion. Such images usually appear on the covers of science reports, to shock and awe us, while a more scientific message about climate change is conveyed through the use of maps, diagrams, and graphs in the main body of such reports. Brenthel claims, "When graphs and diagrams are used in out-reach material, they most often refer to things that can be measured such as weight, concentration, length, and so on. There is a[n] inclination toward the tangible when the changing world is explained to the lay viewer." However, he also states that "the really essential 'things' that need to be communicated to promote public awareness and understanding of climate change are the opposite: interconnections, time, risk, uncertainty, potentiality, unknown states of the world, i.e., non-things. All these 'non-things' are challenging to depict in a way that [would] make them recognizable to the lay viewer and there are few symbols that can be used to signify them" (22).

10. Russill, "Earth Imaging," 229.

11. Ibid.

12. Tom Cohen and Claire Colebrook argue: "Not only has the narrative of humans as a destructive species generated the imperative to survive—if 'we' discover ourselves to be an agent of destruction, then 'we' must re-form, re-group and live on; the very critical motifs or idols that offered another way of thinking about the future became the means for a hyper-humanism." Cohen and Colebrook, preface to Tom Cohen, Claire Colebrook, and J. Hillis Miller, eds., *Twilight of the Anthropocene Idols* (London: Open Humanities Press, 2016), 9. For a critique of the masculinist assumptions behind Anthropocene solutionism, see Joanna Zylinska, *Minimal Ethics for the Anthropocene* (Ann Arbor: Open Humanities Press, 2014).

13. Nicholas Mirzoeff, "Visualizing the Anthropocene," *Public Culture* 26, no. 2 (2014): 217.

14. In my books *Bioethics in the Age of New Media* (Cambridge, MA: MIT Press, 2009), *The Ethics of Cultural Studies* (London: Continuum, 2005), and *Minimal Ethics for the Anthropocene*, I explored this question of responsibility by taking some steps toward outlining a nonprescriptive, nonmoralistic, content-free ethics which nevertheless entails a deep sense of ethical obligation.

15. Walter Benn Michaels, "Photographs and Fossils," in James Elkins, ed., *Photography Theory* (London: Routledge, 2007), 447.

16. Ibid., 445.

17. Michael Fried, *Why Photography Matters as Art as Never Before* (New Haven: Yale University Press, 2008), 347.

18. See chapter 5 in Zylinska, *Minimal Ethics for the Anthropocene.*

19. Although the tradition of posthumanist critique in the humanities extends as far back as the work of Charles Darwin and Sigmund Freud, and includes writings by authors such as Michel Foucault, Jacques Derrida, and Donna Haraway, some of the recent key texts that critically expound the concept of posthumanism include N. Katherine Hayles, *How We Became Posthuman: Virtual Bodies in Cybernetics, Literature, and Informatics* (Chicago: University of Chicago Press, 1999); Cary Wolfe, *What Is Posthumanism?* (Minneapolis: University of Minnesota Press, 2009); Rosi Braidotti, *The Posthuman* (Cambridge: Polity, 2013); and Stefan Herbrechter, *Posthumanism: A Critical Analysis* (London: Bloomsbury, 2013).

20. For a discussion of the humanist blind spot in much of so-called posthumanist theory, see Gary Hall, *Pirate Philosophy: For a Digital Posthumanities* (Cambridge, MA: MIT Press, 2016)—especially chapter 4.

21. John Tagg, "Mindless Photography," in J. J. Long, Andrea Noble, and Edward Welch, eds., *Photography: Theoretical Snapshots* (London: Routledge, 2008), 21.

22. Ibid., 24.

23. Ibid., 19.

24. Ibid., 21.

25. Ibid., 25.

26. Cited from a letter written by Flusser in Siegfried Zielinski, *[... After the Media]: News from the Slow-Fading Twentieth Century*, trans. Gloria Custance (Minneapolis: Univocal, 2013), 114. Zielinski explains that, for Flusser, "the apparatus does what the human wants it to do, and the human can only want what the apparatus is able to do" (114).

27. Tagg, "Mindless Photography," 24.

28. Fred Ritchin, *After Photography* (New York: W. W. Norton, 2009), 183.

29. Vilém Flusser, *Towards a Philosophy of Photography*, trans. Anthony Mathews (London: Reaktion Books, 2000), 21–22.

30. Blaise Aguera y Arcas, "Art in the Age of Machine Intelligence," *Medium*, February 23, 2016, https://medium.com/artists-and-machine-intelligence. Aguera y Arcas continues: "Be this as it may, for today's cameras, this is no longer a metaphor. The camera in your phone is indeed powered by software, amounting at a minimum to millions of lines of code. Much of this code performs support functions peripheral to the actual imaging, but some of it makes explicit the nonlinear summing-up of photons into color components that used to be physically computed by the film emulsion. Other code does things like removing noise in near-constant areas, sharpening edges, and filling in defective pixels with plausible surrounding color, not unlike the way our retinas hallucinate away the blood vessels at the back of the eye that would otherwise mar our visual field. The images we see can only be 'beautiful' or 'real-looking' because they have been heavily processed, either by neural machinery or by code (in which case, both), operating below our threshold of consciousness. In the case of the software, this processing relies on norms and aesthetic judgments on the part of software engineers, so they are also unacknowledged collaborators in the image-making. There's no such thing as a natural image; perhaps, too, there's nothing especially artificial about the camera."

31. Geoffrey Batchen, *Burning with Desire: The Conception of Photography* (Cambridge, MA: MIT Press, 1997), 25.

32. Vilém Flusser, *Into the Universe of Technical Images*, trans. Nancy Ann Roth (Minneapolis: University of Minnesota Press, 2011), 56.

33. See Susan Sontag, *Regarding the Pain of Others* (New York: Picador, 2003).

34. There are, of course, many ways of systematizing art photography, with additional categories and subcategories—such as "abstraction," "architecture," or "nude"—being listed frequently. The quick typology proposed here does not aim to be comprehensive or scholarly: rather, my aim is to highlight the traditional categories used by professional fine art photography exhibitions and competitions, as well

as amateur artist photo-hosting sites. The last category, "conceptual photography," is perhaps the most open and the most contentious. I am using the term here in the expanded sense it has gained on many art photography websites. To cite from one of them, Fotoblur (http://www.fotoblur.com, accessed February 24, 2017), conceptual photography is a "genre of photography in which the artist makes a photograph of a concept or idea."

35. Lytro, https://www.lytro.com.

36. The present chapter arose out of a catalog essay I wrote for this exhibition: Joanna Zylinska, "All the World's a Camera: Notes on Nonhuman Photography," in Paul Wombell, ed., *Drone: The Automated Image* (Bielefeld: Kerber, 2013).

37. Véronique Ducharme, "Encounters," February 15, 2014, *Photomediations Machine*, http://photomediationsmachine.net/2014/02/15/encounters/.

38. For the exposition of this argument, developed in response to the writings of Michael Fried on the work of Thomas Demand, see Michaels, "Photographs and Fossils," 443–444.

39. Juliet Ferguson, "Stolen Images," April 29, 2013, *Photomediations Machine*, http://photomediationsmachine.net/2013/04/29/stolen-images.

40. Ibid.

41. Ibid.

42. Steve Edwards, *Photography: A Very Short Introduction* (Oxford: Oxford University Press, 2006), 19.

43. Fried's *Why Photography Matters as Art as Never Before* espouses this point of view.

44. Henri Bergson, *Matter and Memory*, trans. Nancy Margaret Paul and W. Scott Palmer (London: George Allen & Unwin, 1911), 31.

45. Anthony McCosker, "Drone Media: Unruly Systems, Radical Empiricism and Camera Consciousness," *Culture Machine* 16 (2015), online.

46. Ibid.

47. Ibid.

48. Claire Colebrook, *Deleuze and the Meaning of Life* (London: Continuum, 2010), 11.

49. Bemoaning our suppression of intuition—which can offer us a more accurate and less fragmented picture of the world—Bergson highlights in *Creative Evolution* (New York: Random House, 1944) our overreliance on the intellect in the cognitive process: "Instead of attaching ourselves to the inner becoming of things, we place ourselves outside them in order to recompose their becoming artificially. We take snapshots, as it were, of the passing reality, and, as these are characteristic of the

reality, we have only to string them on a becoming, abstract, uniform and invisible, situated at the back of the apparatus of knowledge, in order to imitate what there is that is characteristic in this becoming itself. Perception, intellection, language so proceed in general. Whether we would think becoming, or express it, or even perceive it, we hardly do anything else than set going a kind of cinematograph inside us" (362).

50. This section develops some of the ideas discussed in chapter 3 of Sarah Kember and Joanna Zylinska, *Life after New Media: Mediation as a Vital Process* (Cambridge, MA: MIT Press, 2012).

51. Bergson, *Creative Evolution*, 172.

52. Victor Burgin, "Mutating Photography," in Chantal Pontbriand, ed., *Mutations: Perspectives on Photography* (Göttingen: Steidl, 2011), 144.

53. Lynn Margulis and Dorian Sagan, *What Is Life?* (Berkeley: University of California Press, 2000), 27.

54. Colebrook, *Deleuze and the Meaning of Life*, 23.

55. Karen Barad, *Meeting the Universe Halfway: Quantum Physics and the Entanglement of Matter and Meaning* (Durham: Duke University Press, 2007), 142.

56. Lindsay Seers, *Human Camera* (Birmingham, UK: Article Press, 2007), 36.

57. Flusser, *Towards a Philosophy of Photography*, 27.

58. Ibid., 26.

59. Ibid., 30.

60. Ibid., 91–92.

61. Ibid., 82.

62. Flusser, *Into the Universe of Technical Images*, 19.

63. Ibid., 45.

64. Colebrook, *Deleuze and the Meaning of Life*, 17.

65. Claire Colebrook, *Death of the PostHuman: Essays on Extinction*, vol. 1. (Ann Arbor: Open Humanities Press, 2014), 22.

66. Ibid., 15.

67. Ibid.

68. For a playful, tactical media-style exploration of what a drone would do in times of peace, see IOCOSE's project, *Drone Selfies*, 2014, http://photomediationsmachine.net/2014/08/06/drone-selfies/.

Chapter 3

An earlier version of this chapter was originally published in the journal *Photographies*, 9, no. 2 (2016), 167–186, DOI: 10.1080/17540763.2016.1182062.

1. Roland Barthes, *Mythologies*, trans. Annette Lavers (London: Paladin Books, 1973), 100.

2. Ibid., 101.

3. Ibid., 102.

4. Jussi Parikka, *Geology of Media* (Minneapolis: University of Minnesota Press, 2015), 14.

5. William Bornefeld, *Time and Light* (Clarkston, GA: Borealis, 1996), 43.

6. Joan Fontcuberta, *Pandora's Camera: Photogr@phy after Photography* (London: Mack, 2014), 7.

7. Sarah Kember and Joanna Zylinska, *Life after New Media: Mediation as a Vital Process* (Cambridge, MA: MIT Press, 2012), 72.

8. Bornefeld, "Author's Note," *Time and Light*, 418.

9. See Bradley L. Garrett, *Explore Everything: Place-hacking the City* (London: Verso, 2013), 54.

10. Arundhati Roy, "Is There Life after Democracy?," *Dawn.com*, May 7, 2009. http://www.dawn.com/news/475778/is-there-life-after-democracy.

11. Ursula K. Heise, "Lost Dogs, Last Birds, and Listed Species: Cultures of Extinction," *Configurations* 18, no. 1–2 (Winter 2010): 52.

12. Brian Dillon, "Decline and Fall," *Frieze*, no. 130 (April 2010), http://www.frieze.com/article/decline-and-fall. See also Brian Dillon, *Ruin Lust* (London: Tate Publishing, 2014).

13. Rose Macaulay, *Pleasure of Ruins* (London: Thames and Hudson, 1984), 454–455.

14. Joel Meyerowitz, *Aftermath: World Trade Center Archive* (London: Phaidon Press, 2006).

15. Tom Cohen, "Introduction: Murmurations—'Climate Change' and the Defacement of Theory," in Cohen, ed., *Telemorphosis: Theory in the Era of Climate Change*, vol. 1. (Ann Arbor: Open Humanities Press, 2012), 14; J. R. McNeill and Peter Engelke, *The Great Acceleration: An Environmental History of the Anthropocene since 1945* (Cambridge, MA: Harvard University Press, 2016).

16. See the artist's website for more images from the exhibition and the book: Tong Lam, http://visual.tonglam.com/.

17. Jason McGrath, "Apocalypse, or, the Logic of Late Anthropocene Ruins," *Cross-Currents: East Asian History and Culture Review*, E-Journal no. 10 (March 2014): 115, http://cross-currents.berkeley.edu/e-journal/issue-10.

18. Ibid., 117.

19. Garrett, *Explore Everything*, 54.

20. Henri Bergson, *Creative Evolution*, trans. Arthur Mitchell (1911; repr., New York: Random House, 1944), 53.

21. Tim Ingold, *Being Alive: Essays on Movement, Knowledge and Description* (London: Routledge, 2011), 197.

22. Henri Bergson, *Matter and Memory*, trans. Nancy Margaret Paul and W. Scott Palmer (London: George Allen & Unwin, 1911), vii.

23. See Bergson, *Creative Evolution*.

24. See Kember and Zylinska, *Life after New Media*, 83.

25. Garrett, *Explore Everything*, 64–65.

26. Joanna Zylinska, *Minimal Ethics for the Anthropocene* (Ann Arbor: Open Humanities Press, 2014).

27. Katrin Klingan et al., eds., *Grain Vapor Ray: Textures of the Anthropocene* (Cambridge, MA: MIT Press, 2015).

28. Etienne Turpin, "Who Does the Earth Think It Is, Now?," in Turpin, ed., *Architecture in the Anthropocene* (Ann Arbor: Open Humanities Press, 2013), 3.

29. As Naomi Klein highlights in *This Changes Everything*, many climate change deniers do not actually deny climate change as such, but rather adopt denialism as a stand because it supports their economic interests. See Naomi Klein, *This Changes Everything: Capitalism vs. the Climate* (New York: Simon and Schuster, 2014).

30. The potential nuclear annihilation of our planet, itself enabled by science, was arguably a predecessor of the science-backed theory of the death of capitalism, and everything else, in the Anthropocene. However, there was a certain reversibility to the arrival of nuclear war—which today looks more remote than it did in the 1950s and 1960s. The narrative about the Anthropocene, in turn, is premised on the epoch's irreversibility, and on the "deep time" inevitability of the extinction of the human (and of other species), even if efforts are being solicited—and made—to lessen the impact of climate change across the current human time scale. I am grateful to Gary Hall for raising this point with me.

31. Fredric Jameson, "Future City," *New Left Review* 21 (May–June 2003), http://newleftreview.org/II/21/fredric-jameson-future-city.

32. Rory Rowan, "Extinction as Usual? Geo-Social Futures and Left Optimism," in "Supercommunity," special issue, *e-flux journal* 65 (May–August 2015): 7.

33. Flowers Gallery, press release for the exhibition "Dust" by Nadav Kander, Flowers Gallery London, September 10–October 11, 2014.

34. Gibson writes: "It should be remembered that light comes from the whole sky as well as from the sun, and from other reflecting surfaces as well. Light reverberates between the sky and the earth and between surfaces." James J. Gibson, *The Ecological Approach to Visual Perception* (Boston: Houghton Mifflin, 1979), 29.

35. Ibid., 54.

36. Vilém Flusser, *Towards a Philosophy of Photography*, trans. Anthony Mathews (London: Reaktion Books, 2000), 21–22.

37. Ingold, *Being Alive*, 197.

38. Ibid., 178–179.

39. McGrath, "Apocalypse, or, the Logic of Late Anthropocene Ruins," 116.

40. Nathaniel Rich, "The Mammoth Cometh," *New York Times Magazine*, February 27, 2014, http://www.nytimes.com/2014/03/02/magazine/the-mammoth-cometh.html.

41. Quoted in "How Do You Light a Woolly Mammoth?," *The 6th Floor*, November 1, 2014, http://6thfloor.blogs.nytimes.com/2014/02/28/under-cover-how-do-you-light-a-woolly-mammoth/.

42. Heise, "Lost Dogs, Last Birds, and Listed Species," 60.

43. See Zylinska, *Minimal Ethics for the Anthropocene*, 110.

44. Trevor Paglen, *The Last Pictures* (Berkeley: University of California Press, 2012), 13.

45. Ibid., 7.

46. Ibid., xiii.

47. Ibid., 12.

48. Ibid., 11–12.

49. Ibid., xii.

50. Timothy Morton, *Hyperobjects: Philosophy and Ecology after the End of the World* (Minneapolis: University of Minnesota Press, 2013), 1.

51. McGrath, "Apocalypse, or, the Logic of Late Anthropocene Ruins," 117.

52. Claire Colebrook, *Death of the PostHuman: Essays on Extinction*, vol. 1. (Ann Arbor: Open Humanities Press, 2014), 27–28.

53. Ibid., 14.

Chapter 4

A shorter version of this chapter was originally presented at the "After Extinction" conference at the Center for 21st Century Studies (C21), University of Wisconsin–Milwaukee, April 30–May 2, 2015. The shorter essay is forthcoming in a conference-based volume edited by Richard Grusin and published by the University of Minnesota Press.

1. I am borrowing the concept of "affective fact" from Brian Massumi. Extinction yields itself to being interpreted through this concept *not* because it stands in opposition to some *actual* facts (such as climate change, deforestation, or depletion of energy sources), but because it affects us mainly as a threat of things to come. Threat, for Massumi, is "affectively self-causing." Brian Massumi, "The Future Birth of the Affective Fact: The Political Ontology of Threat," in Melissa Gregg and Gregory J. Seigworth, eds., *The Affect Theory Reader* (Durham: Duke University Press, 2010), 52–54.

2. Quoted in Elizabeth Kolbert, *The Sixth Extinction: An Unnatural History* (London: Bloomsbury, 2014), Kindle edition, n.p.

3. Ibid.

4. Ibid. The exact temporality of this "currently" may need to be interrogated further. As Yuval Noah Harari points out, "*Homo sapiens* drove to extinction about half of the planet's big beasts long before humans invented the wheel, writing, or iron tools." Harari, *Sapiens: A Brief History of Humankind* (London: Harvill Secker, 2014), 72.

5. Kolbert, *The Sixth Extinction.*

6. Ibid.

7. Ibid.

8. Ibid.

9. Ibid.

10. Cited from the call for papers for the C21 Annual Conference: After Extinction, University of Wisconsin Milwaukee, April 30–May 2, 2015.

11. Ilkka Hanski, "The World That Became Ruined," in "Science and Society," special issue, *EMBO Reports* 9 (2008): S34.

12. Ibid.

13. Ibid.

14. See Donna Haraway, "Situated Knowledges: The Science Question in Feminism and the Privilege of Partial Perspective," *Feminist Studies* 14, no. 3 (Autumn 1988): 575–599.

15. Call for papers for "After Extinction," the C21 Annual Conference, University of Wisconsin–Milwaukee, April 30–May 2, 2015.

16. Referenced in Kolbert, *The Sixth Extinction.*

17. Kolbert, *The Sixth Extinction.*

18. Jussi Parikka, *The Anthrobscene* (Minneapolis: University of Minnesota Press, 2014), Kindle edition. See also Jussi Parikka, *A Geology of Media* (Minneapolis: University of Minnesota Press, 2015).

19. Parikka, *The Anthrobscene.*

20. As Claire Colebrook argues, "The fossil record opens a world *for us*, insofar as it allows us to read back from the brain's present to a time before reading." Colebrook, *Death of the PostHuman: Essays on Extinction*, vol. 1 (Ann Arbor: Open Humanities Press, 2014), 23.

21. John Durham Peters, "Space, Time, and Communication Theory," *Canadian Journal of Communication* (online), 28, no. 4 (2003): n.p.

22. Ibid.

23. Gary Hall, *Pirate Philosophy: For a Digital Posthumanities* (Cambridge, MA: MIT Press, 2016), 106.

24. H. Fox Talbot, *The Pencil of Nature* (London: Longman, Brown, Green and Longmans, 1844), Project Gutenberg online edition.

25. "[T]he operator himself discovers on examination, perhaps long afterwards, that he has depicted many things he had no notion of at the time." "[T]he eye of the camera would see plainly where the human eye would find nothing but darkness." Ibid., n.p.

26. W. Jerome Harrison, *A Sketch of the Geology of Leicestershire and Rutland* (Sheffield: William White, 1877); W. Jerome Harrison, *History of Photography* (New York: Scovill Manufacturing Company, 1887).

27. Adam Bobbette, "Episodes from a History of Scalelessness: William Jerome Harrison and Geological Photography," in Etienne Turpin, ed., *Architecture and the Anthropocene* (Ann Arbor: Open Humanities Press, 2013), 51.

28. Harrison, *History of Photography*, 107.

29. Bobbette, "Episodes from a History of Scalelessness," 52.

30. Harrison, *History of Photography*, 19.

31. The correct word is *lithos* (*λίθος*).

32. Harrison, *History of Photography*, 52.

33. Peters, "Space, Time, and Communication Theory."

34. Harrison, *History of Photography*, 129. The linearity of Harrison's evolutionary narrative reflects the understanding of evolution as logical progression and betterment across time, rather than, as Stanisław Lem put it nearly eighty years later, "a chaotic and illogical designer [that] does not accumulate its own experiences." Stanisław Lem, *Summa Technologiae*, trans. Joanna Zylinska (Minneapolis: University of Minnesota Press, 2014), 339–340.

35. Bobbette, "Episodes from a History of Scalelessness," 53.

36. Ibid.

37. In Rebekah Modrak with Bill Anthes, *Reframing Photography: Theory and Practice* (London: Routledge, 2011), 115. The website of the International Shadows Project, an anonymous global art project which commemorates the Hiroshima atrocities in various parts of the globe, explains: "When the atomic bombs detonated over Hiroshima and Nagasaki, people within 300 meters of the hypocenters were instantly vaporized by the intense heat, leaving nothing behind but faint 'shadows' on nearby walls, pavement, and other stone and concrete surfaces that weren't vaporized with them. Survivors traced these shadows with chalk, and the tracings have become a symbol for state terrorism and nuclear annihilation." International Shadows Project, "Hiroshima, August, 1988," http://www.thing.net/~grist/l&d/shadows/sh88int.htm.

38. André Bazin, "The Ontology of the Photographic Image," *Film Quarterly* 13, no. 4 (Summer 1960): 4.

39. Ibid., 5.

40. Ibid., 8.

41. See Roland Barthes, *Camera Lucida* (New York: Hill and Wang, 1981).

42. Bobbette, "Episodes from a History of Scalelessness," 53.

43. Colebrook, *Death of the PostHuman*, 39.

44. Ibid.

45. Interview with PBS, *Memory*, channel Art21, release date: July 14, 2011, transcript published on Archinect Blogs, http://archinect.com/windscreens/to-me-photography-functions-as-a-fossilization-of-time.

46. "Lost Human Genetic Archive" was not the first show in which Sugimoto explored the history of the human against the horizon of deep time. In 2005–2006, he staged an exhibition called "History of History" at the Japan Society in New York, in which his own photographs were displayed alongside other artifacts: scrolls, wood sculptures, and, most interestingly for us here, fossils. The appearance of fossilized ammonites, trilobites, and sea lilies in the exhibition was most apposite, according to the artist, given that fossils are "the oldest form of art" and a kind of "pre-photography," providing a genealogy for his art. From the vantage point of deep time, photography can therefore be seen as "the first art, prehistoric, prehuman." See Walter Benn Michaels, "Photographs and Fossils," in *Photography Theory*, ed. James Elkins (London: Routledge, 2007), 431, 432.

47. Cited in Adrian Searle, "Hiroshi Sugimoto: Art for the End of the World," *Guardian*, May 16, 2014, http://www.theguardian.com/artanddesign/2014/may/16/hiroshi-sugimoto-aujordhui-palais-de-tokyo-paris-exhibition.

48. Ibid.

49. Exhibition description on the Palais de Tokyo website, "Aujourd'hui, le monde est mort [Lost Human Genetic Archive]: Hiroshi Sugimoto," http://www.palaisdetokyo.com/en/event/aujourdhui-le-monde-est-mort-lost-human-genetic-archive.

50. Christina Schmid, "A Club at the End of the World," October 16, 2014, MN Artists website, http://www.mnartists.org/article/club-end-world.

51. Ibid.

52. Ibid.

53. For a critique of the masculinism of the dominant discourses of and debates on the Anthropocene, see Joanna Zylinska, *Minimal Ethics for the Anthropocene* (Ann Arbor: Open Humanities Press, 2014).

54. Schmid, "A Club at the End of the World."

55. Jason McGrath, "Apocalypse, or, the Logic of Late Anthropocene Ruins," *Cross-Currents: East Asian History and Culture Review*, e-journal no. 10 (March 2014), 117, http://cross-currents.berkeley.edu/e-journal/issue-10.

56. Schmid, "A Club at the End of the World."

57. Ibid.

58. Ibid.

59. http://www.penelopeumbrico.net/index.php/project/suns/.

60. Penelope Umbrico, talk at The Photographers' Gallery, London, January 16, 2015.

61. Jean-François Lyotard, *The Inhuman*, trans. Geoffrey Bennington and Rachel Bowlby (Cambridge: Polity Press, 1991), 9.

62. Ibid.

63. Ibid., 10.

64. Ibid.

65. Jerry Aline Flieger, "The Listening Eye: Postmodernism, Paranoia, and the Hypervisible," *Diacritics* 26, no. 1 (1996), 97.

66. Lyotard, *The Inhuman*, 9.

67. Ibid., 12. In a line of argument that parallels that developed by Lyotard, historian Yuval Noah Harari provides the following account of the energy conversion process that has entangled various classes of beings through history, including plants, animals, humans, and stars: "Humans had only one machine capable of performing … energy conversion tricks: the body. In the natural process of metabolism, the bodies of humans and other animals burn organic fuels known as food and convert the released energy into the movement of muscles. Men, women and beasts could consume grain and meat, burn up their carbohydrates and fats, and use the energy to haul a rickshaw or pull a plough. Since human and animal bodies were the only energy conversion device available, muscle power was the key to almost all human activities. Human muscles built carts and houses, ox muscles ploughed fields, and horse muscles transported goods. The energy that fuelled these organic muscle-machines came ultimately from a single source—plants. Plants in their turn obtained their energy from the sun. By the process of photosynthesis, they captured solar energy and packed it into organic compounds. Almost everything people did throughout history was fuelled by solar energy that was captured by plants and converted into muscle power" (Harari, *Sapiens*, 335).

68. Kolbert, *The Sixth Extinction*.

69. Tere Vadén, "Fossil Sense," *Mustarinda*, Helsinki Photography Biennial Edition HBP14 (2014): 99.

70. Timothy Clark, "Derangements of Scale," in Tom Cohen, ed., *Telemorphosis: Theory in the Era of Climate Change*, vol. 1 (Ann Arbor: Open Humanities Press, 2012).

71. Vadén, "Fossil Sense," 101.

72. Antti Salminen, "Photography in the Age of Fossil Nihilism," *Mustarinda*, Helsinki Photography Biennial Edition HBP14 (2014): 66.

73. Ibid., 69.

74. HDR stands for "high-dynamic-range" imaging. It is a technique of multiply exposing one scene, focusing alternately on shadows and highlights, to reproduce a

greater dynamic range of luminosity than in traditional photography. It results in intensely colorful images which sometimes border on the psychedelic and kitsch.

75. Edward Burtynsky, http://www.edwardburtynsky.com/site_contents/Photographs/Oil.html.

76. Salminen, "Photography in the Age of Fossil Nihilism," 66.

77. Nicholas Mirzoeff argues, "As we learn how to look at the (Western, imperial) artwork via aesthetics a paradox results: the conquest of nature, having been aestheticized, leads to a loss of perception (aesthesis), which is to say, it becomes an anaesthetics. ... The aesthetics of the Anthropocene emerged as an unintended supplement to imperial aesthetics—it comes to seem natural, right, then beautiful—and thereby anaesthetized the perception of modern industrial pollution." Mirzoeff, "Visualizing the Anthropocene," *Public Culture* 26, no. 2 (2014): 220.

78. Hanski, "The World That Became Ruined," S34.

79. Salminen, "Photography in the Age of Fossil Nihilism," 70.

80. Thom van Dooren, *Flight Ways: Life and Loss at the Edge of Extinction* (New York: Columbia University Press, 2014), 144.

Chapter 5

1. For an exposition of this idea, see Daniel Rubinstein and Katrina Sluis, "A Life More Photographic: Mapping the Networked Image," *Photographies* 1, no. 1 (March 2008), 9–28.

2. This idea has affinities with Jussi Parikka's concept of "media fossils": "bodies of dying media technology [that] are not disappearing as part of the soil but constitute a defining mix in terms of their chemicals, hardware elements, metals, and more." In Parikka, *A Geology of Media* (Minneapolis: University of Minnesota Press, 2015), 114–115.

3. See Tim Ingold, "Beyond Biology and Culture: The Meaning of Evolution in a Relational World," *Social Anthropology* 12, no. 2 (2004), 209–221, and Joanna Zylinska, *Minimal Ethics for the Anthropocene* (Ann Arbor: Open Humanities Press, 2014), 50–57.

4. Stanisław Lem, *Summa Technologiae*, trans. Joanna Zylinska (Minneapolis: University of Minnesota Press, 2013), 4.

5. Ibid., 15–16.

6. "And Now, Canon's Real Q3 2015 Financial Results," Imaging Resource, October 30, 2015, http://www.imaging-resource.com/news/2015/10/30/and-now-canons-real-q3-2015-financial-results.

7. Lem, *Summa Technologiae*, 16.

8. See Jakub Dziewit, *Aparaty i obrazy: w stronę kulturowej historii fotografii* (Katowice: Grupa Kulturalna, 2014), 176–177.

9. Gay Hawkins, *The Ethics of Waste: How We Relate to Rubbish* (Lanham, MD: Rowman and Littlefield, 2005), 113.

10. See Sean Cubitt, *EcoMedia* (Amsterdam: Rodopi, 2005); Richard Maxwell and Toby Miller, *Greening the Media* (Oxford: Oxford University Press, 2012); Jennifer Gabrys, *Digital Rubbish: A Natural History of Electronics* (Ann Arbor: University of Michigan Press, 2011); Jussi Parikka, *A Geology of Media* and his *Medianatures* (London: Open Humanities Press, 2013).

11. These components are to be found in "metal, motor/compressor, cooling, plastic, insulation, glass, LCD, rubber, wiring/electrical, concrete, transformer, magnetron, textile, circuit board, fluorescent lamp, incandescent lamp, heating element, thermostat, brominated flame retardant (BFR)–containing plastic, batteries, CFC/HCFC/HFC/HC, external electric cables, refractory ceramic fibers, radioactive substances and electrolyte capacitors (over L/D 25 mm)." V. N. Pinto, cited in Jussi Parikka, "Introduction: The Materiality of Media and Waste," in *Medianatures*, n.p.

12. Cubitt, *EcoMedia*, 1.

13. Cubitt's *EcoMedia* is premised on a concept of "the green world" (also called the "natural world," 4), which is seen as separate from the human—with *techne*, in the form of apparatuses and language, mediating between the two realms. For me, those relations are more entangled and interwoven, because I see technology as originary rather than mediatory. Yet there seems to be more of a recognition of this human-nonhuman entanglement in the 2016 essay collection *Ecomedia: Key Issues* edited by Cubitt with Stephen Rust and Salma Monani. The editors acknowledge not only that we "[h]umans are animals," but also that "we share the world in common with one another and with other nonhuman organisms and processes." This leads them to conclude that "media, society, and the environment are materially embedded in natural resource use and abuse" (2)—an approach that also informs my position in this book. I am therefore very much on board with their proposition to "understand media as particular concentrations of flows of minerals and energy" (5). Stephen Rust, Salma Monani, and Sean Cubitt, "Introduction: Ecologies of Media," in Rust, Monani, and Cubitt, eds., *Ecomedia: Key Issues* (London: Routledge, 2016).

14. See Timothy Morton, *Ecology without Nature: Rethinking Environmental Aesthetics* (Cambridge, MA: Harvard University Press, 2007).

15. See Zylinska, *Minimal Ethics*, 11.

16. For a more thorough critique of this "Big History" approach which "claims to cover all disciplines and offers what is, in fact, a whistle-stop tour of physics, astronomy, geology, and biology" (229), see Sarah Kember and Joanna Zylinska, "Media

Always and Everywhere: A Cosmic Approach," in Ulrik Ekman et al., eds., *Ubiquitous Computing, Complexity, and Culture* (New York: Routledge, 2015), 224–234. In response, Kember and I propose a "just right" Goldilocks approach, in which "What matters is her [Goldilocks'] (sense of) perspective, her view from somewhere of a universe of cosmic media that exceeds and incorporates her—and within which she is only temporally at home" (234).

17. Nicholas Mirzoeff, *An Introduction to Visual Culture* (London: Routledge, 1999), 86.

18. Nicholas Mirzoeff, "Photography 2.0," *Occupy 2012* blog, http://www.nicholasmirzoeff.com/O2012/2012/01/22/photography-2-0/.

19. Cited in Charlotte Higgins, "Tacita Dean's Turbine Hall Film Pays Homage to a Dying Medium," *Guardian*, October 10, 2011, http://www.theguardian.com/artanddesign/2011/oct/10/tacita-dean-film-turbine-hall.

20. Cited in Stuart Jeffries, "The Death of Photography: Are Camera Phones Destroying an Artform?," *Guardian*, December 13, 2013, http://www.theguardian.com/artanddesign/2013/dec/13/death-of-photography-camera-phones.

21. Nick Bilton, "The Death of Photography Has Been Greatly Exaggerated," *Bits*: The New York Times's blog, July 5, 2013, http://bits.blogs.nytimes.com/2013/07/05/the-death-of-photography-has-been-greatly-exaggerated/.

22. Michael Zhang, "This Is What the History of Camera Sales Looks Like with Smartphones Included," PetaPixel, April 9, 2015, http://petapixel.com/2015/04/09/this-is-what-the-history-of-camera-sales-looks-like-with-smartphones-included/.

23. Robert Capps, "The Good Enough Revolution: When Cheap and Simple Is Just Fine," *Wired*, August 24, 2009, http://www.wired.com/2009/08/ff-goodenough.

24. Gabrys, *Digital Rubbish*, vii.

25. John Durham Peters, *The Marvelous Clouds: Toward a Philosophy of Elemental Media* (Chicago: University of Chicago Press, 2015), 21.

26. Ibid., 48.

27. For a critical discussion of this point, see Hawkins, *The Ethics of Waste*, 1–13, 38.

28. Peters, *The Marvelous Clouds*, 38.

29. Ibid.

30. Pieter Hugo, *Permanent Error* (Munich: Prestel Art, 2011).

31. Sean O'Toole, "Permanent Error," *Mahala*, May 5, 2011, http://www.mahala.co.za/art/permanent-error/.

32. Michael Stevenson, "Permanent Error," project description on the Stevenson gallery website, 2010, http://archive.stevenson.info/exhibitions/hugo/index2010.htm.

33. O'Toole, "Permanent Error."

34. See Emmanuel Levinas, *Otherwise than Being: Or Beyond Essence*, trans. Alphonso Lingis (Pittsburgh: Duquesne University Press, 1998). For an introduction to his philosophy of alterity, see Emmanuel Levinas, "Ethics as First Philosophy," in *The Levinas Reader*, ed. Sean Hand (Oxford: Blackwell, 1989).

35. Victor Burgin, "Looking at Photographs," in Burgin, ed., *Thinking Photography* (London: Macmillan, 1982), 146.

36. Ibid.

37. As I argued in *Bioethics in the Age of New Media* (Cambridge, MA: MIT Press, 2009), Levinas's ethical theory undoubtedly suffers from an anthropocentric bias, which is evident in the excessive weighting he gives to the logos, or rather perhaps in the too narrow conception of the logos as human word, as discourse between equals. I want to suggest, however, that Levinas's "error" is first of all scientific and historical rather than philosophical per se, in that he does not consider seriously the limitations of his own concept of the human as a speaking being with a face, rather than a sentient being reaching to—and touched by—the other in a myriad different ways. His commitment to the difference and singularity of the human seems to blind him to the discursive limitations of his own language through which ethical responsibility toward the other is justified. Because do we really know with whom we can enter into a discourse (a refugee? a cat? a computer bot?) and what this "entering into a discourse" (58) actually means?

38. "Aylan Kurdi: How a Single Image Transformed the Debate on Immigration," University of Sheffield website, December 14, 2015, https://www.sheffield.ac.uk/news/nr/aylan-kurdi-social-media-report-1.533951.

39. Ibid.

40. Lillie Chouliaraki and Bolette B. Blaagaard, guest editorial in "The Ethics of Images," special issue, *Visual Communication* 12, no. 3 (2013): 254.

41. On the differences and similarities between morality and moralism, see Wendy Brown, *Politics out of History* (Princeton: Princeton University Press, 2001), 30–31.

42. Jean-François Lyotard, *The Inhuman*, trans. Geoffrey Bennington and Rachel Bowlby (Cambridge: Polity Press, 1991), 86.

43. My "place in the sun"—a Blaise Pascal–inflected concept Levinas proposes in "Ethics as First Philosophy" (82–85)—is always a usurpation. For Levinas, this place is never originally "mine": it already belongs to the other who precedes me, and whom I may have oppressed, starved, or driven away. Therefore, no matter how

invested we are in the illusion of our own self-sufficiency and power, we always find ourselves standing before the face of the other, which is both our accusation and a source of our ethical responsibility. See also Zylinska, *Bioethics in the Age of New Media*, 55.

44. Hawkins, *The Ethics of Waste*, 25.

45. Ibid., 24.

46. Bojan Šarčević, *It Seems That an Animal Is in the World as Water in the Water*, 1999. These projects offer a way of looking at our media environment from amid those environments, while also challenging Marshall McLuhan's conviction that such a viewpoint offers limited knowledge. McLuhan argued: "One thing about which fish know exactly nothing is water, since they have no anti-environment which would enable them to perceive the element they live in." Marshall McLuhan and Quentin Fiore, *War and Peace in the Global Village* (New York: McGraw-Hill, 1968), 175. Yet, as John Durham Peters argues, "fish probably know a lot about water's temperature, clarity, currents, weather, prey, and so on," although he goes on to explain that McLuhan's point was that "they did not recognize it as water. It was just background, the stuff that slides into infrastructural obliviousness" (*The Marvelous Clouds*, 55). Yet, contra McLuhan, we could perhaps suggest that photography does indeed allow, even if it does not guarantee, a discernment of temporary boundaries and cuts between image and viewer, content and form, time stoppage and temporal flow. And it is precisely in the event of such a cut and such a realization—which is corporeal and haptic and not just cognitive—that an ethical attitude toward media is activated.

47. Kaja Silverman, *The Threshold of the Visible World* (London: Routledge, 1996), 173.

48. I am referencing here James Elkins's argument that "Looking immediately activates desire, possession, violence, displeasure, pain, force, ambition, power, obligation, gratitude, longing. ... [T]here seems to be no end to what seeing is, to how it is tangled with living and acting. But there is no such thing as just looking." Elkins, *The Object Stares Back: On the Nature of Seeing* (San Diego: Harcourt, 1996), 45.

49. Silverman, *The Threshold of the Visible World*, 173.

50. See Elkins, *The Object Stares Back*, 45.

51. Burgin, "Looking at Photographs," 152.

52. Gabrys, *Digital Rubbish*, 107.

53. Theodor W. Adorno, *Prisms*, trans. Samuel and Shierry Weber (Cambridge, MA: MIT Press, 1981), 175.

54. Hiroshi Sugimoto, http://www.sugimotohiroshi.com/diorama.html.

55. As Naomi Rosenblum explains in *A World History of Photography*, "By the time it was announced in 1839, Western industrialized society was ready for photography. The camera's images appeared and remained viable because they filled cultural and sociological needs that were not being met by pictures created by hand. The photograph was the ultimate response to a social and cultural appetite for a more accurate and real-looking representation of reality, a need that had its origins in the Renaissance." Rosenblum, *A World History of Photography*, 3rd ed. (New York: Abbeville Press, 1997), 15.

56. Gabrys, *Digital Rubbish*, 107.

57. Stanisław Lem, "Dwadzieścia lat później" [Twenty Years Later], in Lem, *Summa Technologiae*, 4th exp. ed. (Lublin, Poland: Wydawnictwo Lubelskie, 1997), 327; translation mine.

58. Audley Jarvis, "How Kodak Invented the Digital Camera in 1975," Techradar, May 9, 2008, http://www.techradar.com/news/cameras/photography-video-capture/how-kodak-invented-the-digital-camera-in-1975-364822, accessed May 18, 2016.

59. Ibid.

60. Cultural theorist Will Straw suggests that "the sites in which unwanted cultural commodities (old records, books, etc.) accumulate are, at one level, museums of failure." Cited in Gabrys, *Digital Rubbish*, 104.

61. Gabrys, *Digital Rubbish*, 104.

62. Ibid., 106.

63. "National Media Museum Invests in Science and Technology—Transferring Art of Photography Collections to the V&A," NMM website, February 2, 2016, http://www.nationalmediamuseum.org.uk/aboutus/pressoffice/2016/february/national-media-museum-transfers-photography-collections-to-v-and-a.

64. Hannah Furness, "V&A Accused of 'Cultural Rape' after Bradford Museum Loses Photo Collection," *Telegraph*, February 2, 2016, http://www.telegraph.co.uk/news/uknews/12136008/VandA-accused-of-cultural-rape-after-Bradford-museum-loses-photo-collection.html.

65. See Raymond Williams, "Culture Is Ordinary," in Anne Gray and Jim McGuigan, eds., *Studying Culture* (London: Arnold, 1997), 5–15.

66. I want to express my thanks to Iain Logie Baird, associate curator (television and radio) at the National Media Museum, for giving me a guided tour of NMM's storage rooms during my visit in March 2016 as well as offering a peek into the museum's politics and economics.

67. Sarah Kember and Joanna Zylinska, *Life after New Media: Mediation as a Vital Process* (Cambridge, MA: MIT Press, 2012), xv.

68. Henri Bergson, *Matter and Memory*, trans. Nancy Margaret Paul and W. Scott Palmer (London: George Allen & Unwin, 1911), 3.

69. See Adrian Mackenzie, *Wirelessness: Radical Empiricism in Network Cultures* (Cambridge, MA: MIT Press, 2010).

70. "20 Minutes into the Future," curated by Maciej Baron and David de la Peña, Creative Technologists at Saatchi & Saatchi London, http://20minutesintothefuture.co.uk/?cat=1, accessed August 5, 2012.

71. Mark Laperrouza, "TCL+IKEA=UPPLEVA," *Lift Lab* blog, posted April 20, 2012, http://liftlab.com/think/marc/2012/04/, accessed April 21, 2012.

72. See Jean-François Lyotard, *The Postmodern Condition*, trans. Geoff Bennington and Brian Massumi (1979; Minneapolis: University of Minnesota Press, 1984).

73. "PC Sales Weaken on Economic Woes and Mobile Devices," *BBC News Technology*, July 20, 2012, http://www.bbc.co.uk/news/technology-18921585.

74. Mackenzie, *Wirelessness*, 8.

75. This paragraph has been reworked from Zylinska, *Minimal Ethics*.

76. Henri Bergson, *Creative Evolution*, trans. Arthur Mitchell (1911; New York: Random House, 1944), 248–249.

77. Ibid., 272.

78. Jane Bennett, *Vibrant Matter: A Political Ecology of Things* (Durham: Duke University Press, 2010), 12.

79. Santiago Zabala, "I'm Wired, Therefore I Exist," *New Statesman*, July 29, 2012, http://www.newstatesman.com/sci-tech/sci-tech/2012/07/im-wired-therefore-i-exist.

80. Lem, *Summa Technologiae*, 5.

81. Hawkins, *The Ethics of Waste*, 122.

Chapter 6

Parts of this chapter were published as: Joanna Zylinska, "On Bad Archives, Unruly Snappers and Liquid Photographs," *Photographies* 3, no. 2 (August 2010): 139–153.

1. Edgar Gómez Cruz argues: "It would probably be safe to affirm that, for many people, photography is a more commonly used function of the mobile phone than making a call, and it is equally safe to say that people are taking more photos with mobile phones than with other kinds of camera. The audio capabilities of mobile phones seem to be less important that the visual ones. Photography has gone from being a medium for the collection of important memories to an interface for visual

communication. ... [V]ernacular uses of photo-technologies are incorporating practices that move away, not only from traditional uses of photography, but even from representational realms. Photography is increasingly being used as an interface, without even involving an image." Gómez Cruz, "Photo-genic Assemblages: Photography as a Connective Interface," in Edgar Gómez Cruz and Asko Lehmuskallio, eds., *Digital Photography and Everyday Life: Empirical Studies on Material Visual Practices* (London: Routledge, 2016), 229.

2. For a reading of photography as "a socio-technical practice" rather than only an "aesthetic object," see Paul Frosh, "The Gestural Image: The Selfie, Photography Theory and Kinaesthetic Sociability," in Kamila Kuc and Joanna Zylinska, eds., *Photomediations: A Reader* (London: Open Humanities Press, 2016), 251–267.

3. "Everyone is creative" was used as an opening line in the UK government's Green Paper (i.e., a tentative proposal document) titled "Culture and Creativity: The Next Ten Years," issued by the Department for Culture, Media and Sport in 2001.

4. A 2012 film, *PressPausePlay*, produced by House of Radon, a creative agency based in Stockholm, and made freely available on Vimeo, encapsulates this message about the increase in creative opportunities for everyone thanks to cheaper and more accessible technology. It features interviews with many artists, actors, musicians, and other "creatives"—including Moby, Lena Dunham, Seth Godin, and Sean Parker. The film can be found at http://vimeo.com/34608191.

5. Asko Lehmuskallio and Edgar Gómez Cruz, "Why Material Visual Practices?," in Gómez Cruz and Lehmuskallio, *Digital Photography and Everyday Life*, 7.

6. Geoffrey Batchen, *Each Wild Idea: Writing Photography History* (Cambridge, MA: MIT Press, 2001), 140, emphasis added.

7. Lisa Blackman and Couze Venn, "Affect," *Body and Society* 16, no. 1 (2010): 9.

8. Felicity J. Colman, "Affect," in Adrian Parr, ed., *The Deleuze Dictionary* (Edinburgh: Edinburgh University Press, 2005), 11.

9. Quoted in Simon Denison, "Printing Revolution," *Source*, no. 60 (Autumn 2009): 41–42.

10. See Zygmunt Bauman, *Liquid Modernity* (Cambridge: Polity, 2000); Zygmunt Bauman, *Liquid Love* (Cambridge: Polity, 2003); Zygmunt Bauman, *Liquid Life* (Cambridge: Polity, 2005); Zygmunt Bauman, *Liquid Fear* (Cambridge: Polity, 2006); Zygmunt Bauman, *Liquid Times* (Cambridge: Polity, 2006).

11. For an exposition of this idea, see Adam Brenthel, *The Drowning World: The Visual Culture of Climate Change* (Lund: Lund University, 2016).

12. The chapter aptly titled "Epitaph" in Geoffrey Batchen's *Burning with Desire: The Conception of Photography* (Cambridge, MA: MIT Press, 1997), 206–216, provides a

useful summary of such hysterical reactions to digitization and of moribund predictions about photography's future.

13. See Open Humanities Press, http://www.openhumanitiespress.org, Liquid Books series, http://liquidbooks.pbworks.com.

14. Gary Hall and Clare Birchall, "Introduction to Version One Point Zero," in Hall and Birchall, eds., *New Cultural Studies: The Liquid Theory Reader* (Ann Arbor: Open Humanities Press, 2009), http://liquidbooks.pbworks.com/New+Cultural+Studies:+The+Liquid+Theory+Reader.

15. Ibid.

16. Ibid.

17. The Liquid Reader project, which I have been running with my students on the MA Digital Media at Goldsmiths since early 2010 under the Liquid Books aegis, consists of an attempt to actively involve students in producing an innovative, student-centered, customizable learning tool which allows them to participate in curriculum design. The Reader includes links, texts, annotations, and blog snippets. As part of the Reader, we have also developed a "gallery-in-a-book." At the beginning of the course, students were asked to work on a series of photographs. We agreed that the photographs could be taken with a cell phone camera, a DSLR, a film camera, or any other image-capturing device. The only rule was that they had to be somehow related to one another, via content, form, or method. This online "gallery-in-a-book" has become part of the Liquid Reader. The project has raised some interesting questions for our classroom discussion: Can a book "contain" an art gallery? Is everyone an artist and a media producer today? What would Barthes and Foucault say? The project was originally undertaken with grant support from the ADM-HEA (Art, Design and Media Subject Centre at the Higher Education Academy) and Goldsmiths's GLEU (Goldsmiths' Learning Enhancement Unit).

18. The Liquid Book project as described above and the mainstream photo-sharing websites such as Flickr, SmugMug, or Instagram are based on rather different cultural assumptions about the nature of media production, ownership, and labor. The former is first and foremost driven by socially and politically significant "open access" and "open scholarship" agendas; the latter commercial (even if not yet always profitable) platforms do not make any such claims.

19. Mark Godfrey, "Photography Found and Lost: On Tacita Dean's *Floh*," *October* 114 (Fall 2005): 113.

20. The process of turning information into code seems so unstable that scholars and artists themselves are at a loss regarding what to call it: for some it is "digitization" (the term I prefer), for others—"digitalisation" (in the United Kingdom) or "digitalization" (the latter term being used by Godfrey). Google seems to favor "digitization" (with US spelling), but it also allows "digitizing."

21. I am more comfortable with the understanding of modernity along the lines developed by Jean-François Lyotard in *The Postmodern Condition*: "[m]odernity, *in whatever age it appears*, cannot exist without a shattering of belief and without discovery of the 'lack of reality' of reality, together with the invention of other realities" (Minneapolis: University of Minnesota Press, 1984), 77, emphasis added. Modernity stands here for a modality rather than for a particular artistic period or style. In this sense it cannot be overcome by postmodernity because the latter is always already implied by it.

22. See Tacita Dean, *Floh* (Göttingen: Steidl, 2001).

23. Godfrey, "Photography Found and Lost," 114.

24. Andrew Pulver, "Artist and Photographer Tacita Dean's Best Shoot," *Guardian*, September 16, 2009, https://www.theguardian.com/artanddesign/2009/sep/16/photography-tacita-dean-best-shoot.

25. Charles Merewether, introduction to Merewether, ed., *The Archive* (London: Whitechapel; Cambridge, MA: MIT Press, 2006), 10.

26. Sigmund Freud, "A Note upon the 'Mystic Writing-Pad,'" in *The Standard Edition of the Complete Psychological Works of Sigmund Freud*, vol. 19, ed. James Strachey (London: Hogarth Press, 1961), 227–228.

27. See Jacques Derrida, *Archive Fever*, trans. Eric Prenowitz (Chicago: University of Chicago Press, 1996), 1.

28. Benjamin H. D. Buchloh, "Gerhard Richter's *Atlas*: The Anomic Archive," in Merewether, *The Archive*, 95.

29. Hal Foster, "An Archival Impulse," in Merewether, *The Archive*, 143.

30. Geoffrey Batchen, "Electricity Made Visible," in Wendy Hui Kyong Chun and Thomas Keenan, eds., *New Media, Old Media* (London: Routledge, 2006), 33.

31. Ibid., 30.

32. Batchen, *Each Wild Idea*, 169.

33. Godfrey, "Photography Found and Lost," 113–114.

34. Ibid., 114.

35. Freecycle is "a grassroots and entirely nonprofit movement of people who are giving (& getting) stuff for free in their own towns. It's all about reuse and keeping good stuff out of landfills." See Freecycle, http://www.freecycle.org.

36. Godfrey, "Photography Found and Lost," 117.

37. Ibid.

38. Martha Langford, "Strange Bedfellows: Appropriations of the Vernacular by Photographic Artists," *Photography and Culture* 1, no. 1 (July 2008): 80.

39. Foster, "An Archival Impulse," 143.

40. Ibid., 156.

41. This project was exhibited as part of the "Solid States/Liquid Objects" show, held together with Nina Sellars in the Shifted Gallery, Melbourne, in August 2009, and was also included in the "Media and the Senses" exhibition at Goldsmiths, University of London, in May 2011. Selected images from it were published in an earlier version of this chapter, in Zylinska, "On Bad Archives, Unruly Snappers and Liquid Photographs"; and then in Sarah Kember and Joanna Zylinska, *Life after New Media: Mediation as a Vital Process* (Cambridge, MA: MIT Press, 2012).

42. This is a reference to the theory of the computational universe as discussed by N. Katherine Hayles in *How We Became Posthuman: Virtual Bodies in Cybernetics, Literature, and Informatics* (Chicago: University of Chicago Press, 1999): "Some theorists, notably Edward Fredkin and Stephen Wolfram, claim that reality is a program run on a cosmic computer. In this view, a universal informational code underlies the structure of matter, energy, spacetime—indeed, of everything that exists. The code is instantiated in cellular automata, elementary units that can occupy two states: on or off. Although the jury is still out on the cellular automata model, it may indeed prove to be a robust way to understand reality. Even now, a research team headed by Fredkin is working on showing how quantum mechanics can be derived from an underlying cellular automata model" (11). The theory assumes that all matter is computational, i.e., that it entails differentiation between present and absent bits of information.

43. Batchen, *Each Wild Idea*, 169.

44. H. Fox Talbot, *The Pencil of Nature* (London: Longman, Brown, Green and Longmans, 1844), Project Gutenberg online edition, n.p.; italics his.

45. *Photomediations: An Open Book* was a collaboration between scholars from Goldsmiths, University of London, and Coventry University. It was part of Europeana Space, a grant project funded by the European Union's ICT Policy Support Programme under GA no. 621037.

46. Some of the ideas discussed in this section have been borrowed from that introduction. For the full text, see Joanna Zylinska, "Photomediations: An Introduction," in Kuc and Zylinska, *Photomediations: A Reader*, 7–17.

47. Kamila Kuc, "A Curated Object and a Disruptive e-Anarchive," *Photomediations Machine*, October 20, 2015, http://photomediationsmachine.net/2015/10/20/a-curated-object-and-a-disruptive-e-anarchive/.

48. Ibid.

49. Ibid.

50. Foster argues that "archival art is as much preproduction as it is postproduction: concerned less with absolute origins than with obscure traces (perhaps 'anarchival impulse' is the more appropriate phrase), these artists [i.e., artists working with Internet archives and databases] are often drawn to unfulfilled beginnings or incomplete projects—in art and in history alike—that might offer points of departure again" (Foster, "An Archival Impulse," 144).

51. This idea has been based on Kember and Zylinska, *Life after New Media*.

52. Jai McKenzie, *Light and Photomedia: A New History and Future of the Photographic Image* (London: IB Tauris, 2014), 1.

53. Jonathan Shaw, "Hybridity and Digital Transformations," in Shaw, ed., *NewFotoScapes* (Birmingham: Library of Birmingham, 2014), 4.

54. See Gary Hall, *Digitize This Book! The Politics of New Media, or Why We Need Open Access Now* (Minneapolis: University of Minnesota Press, 2008), and Janneke Adema and Gary Hall, "The Political Nature of the Book: On Artists' Books and Radical Open Access," *New Formations*, no. 78 (Summer 2013): 138–156.

55. Siegfried Zielinski, *[... After the Media]: News from the Slow-Fading Twentieth Century*, trans. Gloria Custance (Minneapolis: Univocal, 2013), 58.

56. Derrida, *Archive Fever*, 91.

57. Cited in Batchen, *Burning with Desire*, viii.

58. Sarah Kember, "The Virtual Life of Photography," *Photographies* 1, no. 2 (September 2008): 180.

59. In his *Creative Evolution* (New York: Random House, 1944), a book which became foundational for many later philosophical works on affect and vitality, including those of Deleuze and Massumi, Henri Bergson defines life as a nonpredetermined movement and a "tendency to act on inert matter" (79). However, even if life is movement, a way of working upon what he terms "solids," Bergson also emphasizes our tendency to "cut up" matter and "carve out" objects from this flow of life (124–125)—a tendency that, I argue, is also a survival strategy against the excessive vitality that can become too overbearing.

60. This study, conducted by Carl Benedikt Frey and Michael Osborne and published by Oxford University Press in 2013, has been cited by Maxfield Weir in "Our Photographic Future: Vision and Action in a Dematerialised World," in the catalog for the exhibition "Photography: [De]Materialised," Oxford House Gallery, London, April 2015.

Conclusion

1. Lara Dunston, "Revealed: Cambodia's Vast Medieval Cities Hidden beneath the Jungle," *Guardian*, June 11, 2016, https://www.theguardian.com/world/2016/jun/11/lost-city-medieval-discovered-hidden-beneath-cambodian-jungle.

2. "Lidar" stands for *li*ght *d*etection *a*nd *r*anging.

3. Damian Evans, "Airborne Laser Scanning as a Method for Exploring Long-Term Socio-ecological Dynamics in Cambodia," *Journal of Archaeological Science* 74 (October 2016): 164–175, doi:10.1016/j.jas.2016.05.009, available online.

4. Ibid.

5. Ibid.

6. Ibid.

7. Ibid.

8. In gathering this understanding, writes Evans in "Airborne Laser Scanning," "archaeologists will be much better prepared to address one of the core issues facing studies of societal resilience in the face of hydroclimatic instability. ... By considering humans and their environment as dynamic coupled systems, future programs based on regional-scale ALS acquisitions might analyse the precise articulation between those two systems, moving away from mono-causal explanations and environmental determinism towards more sophisticated models of socio-ecological systems that acknowledge their full complexity."

9. Ibid.

10. Dunston, "Revealed."

11. I am referencing here the book-catalog titled *From Here On: PostPhotography in the Age of Internet and the Mobile Phone* by Joan Fontcuberta et al. (Barcelona: RM Verlag, 2013). It was originally published for the exhibition "From Here On" presented at Arts Santa Monica in Barcelona, Spain, and then at Rencontres d'Arles in 2013—where it gained much more publicity. The exhibition and book were curated by five renowned international photography curators: Joan Fontcuberta, Martin Parr, Erik Kessels, Clément Chéroux, Joachim Schmid. It was an interesting undertaking that addressed precisely the developments that have taken place in photography around the use of new technologies—while also being an excellent candidate for the *Congrats, you have an all male panel!* Tumblr, http://allmalepanels.tumblr.com/.

12. See above.

13. Robert Shore, "Introduction: Post-Photography Is ...," in *Post-Photography: The Artist with a Camera* (London: Laurence King, 2014), 11.

14. Edgar Gómez Cruz, "Photo-genic Assemblages: Photography as a Connective Interface," in Edgar Gómez Cruz and Asko Lehmuskallio, eds., *Digital Photography and Everyday Life: Empirical Studies on Material Visual Practices* (London: Routledge, 2016), 238.

15. See Daniel Rubinstein and Katrina Sluis, "A Life More Photographic: Mapping the Networked Image," *Photographies* 1, no. 1 (March 2008), 9–28; and Asko Lehmuskallio, "The Camera as a Sensor among Many: The Visualization of Everyday Digital Photography as Simulative, Heuristic and Layered Pictures," in Gómez Cruz and Lehmuskallio, *Digital Photography and Everyday Life*.

16. See Steve Edwards, *Photography: A Very Short Introduction* (Oxford: Oxford University Press, 2006), 19.

17. This idea builds on Jacques Rancière's concept of "the distribution of the sensible" as the organization of the experiential field that delimits its members' positions within it, and their responses to it. It is a way of making certain things visible and others invisible, which prompts Rancière to argue that "Politics revolves around who has the ability to see and the talent to speak, around the properties of spaces and the possibilities of time." Rancière, *The Politics of Aesthetics: The Distribution of the Sensible*, trans. Gabriel Rockhill (London: Continuum, 2014), 13. On the idea of recutting the field of the sensible as a political gesture, see also Clare Birchall, "Shareveillance: Subjectivity between Open and Closed Data," *Big Data and Society* 3, no. 2 (July–December 2016): 1–12.

18. Adam Brenthel, *The Drowning World: The Visual Culture of Climate Change* (Lund: Lund University, 2016), 173.

19. Cited from the leaflet "Our Amazon Frontline" distributed in the Peruvian pavilion at the 15th Venice Architecture Biennale.

Bibliography

"20 Minutes into the Future." Curated by Maciej Baron and David de la Peña, Creative Technologists at Saatchi & Saatchi London, n.d. http://20minutesintothefuture.co.uk/?cat=1 (accessed on April 21, 2012; no longer available).

Adema, Janneke, and Gary Hall. "The Political Nature of the Book: On Artists' Books and Radical Open Access." *New Formations* 78 (2013): 138–156.

Adorno, Theodor W. *Prisms*. Trans. Samuel and Shierry Weber. Cambridge, MA: MIT Press, 1981.

Aguera y Arcas, Blaise. "Art in the Age of Machine Intelligence." *Medium*, February 23, 2016. https://medium.com/artists-and-machine-intelligence.

Barad, Karen. *Meeting the Universe Halfway: Quantum Physics and the Entanglement of Matter and Meaning*. Durham: Duke University Press, 2007.

Barthes, Roland. *Camera Lucida*. New York: Hill and Wang, 1981.

Barthes, Roland. *Mythologies*. Trans. Annette Lavers. London: Paladin Books, 1973.

Batchen, Geoffrey. *Burning with Desire: The Conception of Photography*. Cambridge, MA: MIT Press, 1997.

Batchen, Geoffrey. *Each Wild Idea: Writing Photography History*. Cambridge, MA: MIT Press, 2001.

Batchen, Geoffrey. "Electricity Made Visible." In *New Media, Old Media*, ed. Wendy Hui Kyong Chun and Thomas Keenan. London: Routledge, 2006.

Bazin, André. "The Ontology of the Photographic Image." *Film Quarterly* 13 (4) (Summer 1960): 4–9.

Beller, Jonathan. *The Cinematic Mode of Production: Attention Economy and the Society of the Spectacle*. Hanover: University Press of New England, 2006.

Bennett, Jane. *Vibrant Matter: A Political Ecology of Things*. Durham: Duke University Press, 2010.

Bergson, Henri. *Creative Evolution*. Trans. Arthur Mitchell. 1911; New York: Random House, 1944.

Bergson, Henri. *Matter and Memory*. Trans. Nancy Margaret Paul and W. Scott Palmer. London: George Allen & Unwin, 1911.

Berman, Marshall. *All That Is Solid Melts into Air*. Harmondsworth, UK: Penguin, 1982.

Bilton, Nick. "The Death of Photography Has Been Greatly Exaggerated." *Bits*, the New York Times's blog, July 5, 2013. http://bits.blogs.nytimes.com/2013/07/05/the-death-of-photography-has-been-greatly-exaggerated/.

Birchall, Clare. "Shareveillance: Subjectivity between Open and Closed Data." *Big Data and Society* 3 (2) (2016): 1–12.

Blackman, Lisa, and Couze Venn. "Affect." *Body and Society* 16 (1) (2010): 7–28.

Bobbette, Adam. "Episodes from a History of Scalelessness: William Jerome Harrison and Geological Photography." In *Architecture and the Anthropocene*, ed. Etienne Turpin, 45–58. Ann Arbor: Open Humanities Press, 2013.

Bornefeld, William. *Time and Light*. Clarkston, GA: Borealis, 1996.

Bourdieu, Pierre. *Photography: A Middle-Brow Art*. Trans. Shaun Whiteside. Stanford: Stanford University Press, 1990.

Braidotti, Rosi. *The Posthuman*. Cambridge: Polity Press, 2013.

Brenthel, Adam. *The Drowning World: The Visual Culture of Climate Change*. Lund: Lund University Press, 2016.

Brown, Wendy. *Politics out of History*. Princeton: Princeton University Press, 2001.

Buchloh, Benjamin H. D. "Gerhard Richter's *Atlas*: The Anomic Archive." In *The Archive*, ed. Charles Merewether. London: Whitechapel; Cambridge, MA: MIT Press, 2006.

Burbridge, Ben, ed. *Revelations: Experiments in Photography*. London: Mack in Association with Media Space, 2015.

Burgin, Victor. "Looking at Photographs." In *Thinking Photography*, ed. Victor Burgin. London: Macmillan, 1982.

Burgin, Victor. "Mutating Photography." In *Mutations: Perspectives on Photography*, ed. Chantal Pontbriand. Göttingen: Steidl, 2011.

Chalfen, Richard. Foreword. In *Digital Photography and Everyday Life: Empirical Studies on Material Visual Practices*, ed. Edgar Gómez Cruz and Asko Lehmuskallio. London: Routledge, 2016.

Capps, Robert. "The Good Enough Revolution: When Cheap and Simple Is Just Fine." *Wired*, August 24, 2009. http://www.wired.com/2009/08/ff-goodenough.

Chouliaraki, Lillie, and Bolette B. Blaagaard. Guest editorial. In "The Ethics of Images," special issue, *Visual Communication* 12 (3) (2013): 253–259.

Clark, Timothy. "Derangements of Scale." In *Telemorphosis: Theory in the Era of Climate Change*, vol. 1, ed. Tom Cohen, 148–166. Ann Arbor: Open Humanities Press, 2012.

Cohen, Tom. "Introduction: Murmurations—'Climate Change' and the Defacement of Theory." In *Telemorphosis: Theory in the Era of Climate Change*, vol. 1, ed. Tom Cohen, 13–42. Ann Arbor: Open Humanities Press, 2012.

Cohen, Tom, and Claire Colebrook. Preface. In *Twilight of the Anthropocene Idols*, ed. Tom Cohen, Clare Colebrook, and J. Hillis Miller. London: Open Humanities Press, 2016.

Colebrook, Claire. *Death of the PostHuman: Essays on Extinction*. Vol. 1. Ann Arbor: Open Humanities Press, 2014.

Colebrook, Claire. *Deleuze and the Meaning of Life*. London: Continuum, 2010.

Colebrook, Claire. "We Have Always Been Post-Anthropocene: The Anthropocene Counter-Factual," n.d. https://www.academia.edu/12757260/We_Have_Always_Been_Post-Anthropocene.

Coley, Rob. "The Horrors of Visuality." In *Photomediations: A Reader*, ed. Kamila Kuc and Joanna Zylinska, 290–310. London: Open Humanities Press, 2016.

Colman, Felicity J. "Affect." In *The Deleuze Dictionary*, ed. Adrian Parr. Edinburgh: Edinburgh University Press, 2005.

Crary, Jonathan. *Techniques of the Observer: On Vision and Modernity in the Nineteenth Century*. Cambridge, MA: MIT Press, 1990.

Cubitt, Sean. *EcoMedia*. Amsterdam: Rodopi, 2005.

Dean, Tacita. *Floh*. Göttingen: Steidl, 2001.

Denison, Simon. "Printing Revolution." *Source*, no. 60 (Autumn 2009): 40–43.

Derrida, Jacques. *Archive Fever*. Trans. Eric Prenowitz. Chicago: University of Chicago Press, 1996.

Devas, Bonamy. "Photographic Tai Chi." *Photomediations Machine*, May 22, 2015. http://photomediationsmachine.net/2015/05/22/photographic-tai-chi/.

Dillon, Brian. "Decline and Fall." *Frieze*, no. 130 (April 2010). http://www.frieze.com/article/decline-and-fall.

Dillon, Brian. *Ruin Lust*. London: Tate Publishing, 2014.

Dorrian, Mark. "On Google Earth." In *Seeing from Above: The Aerial View in Visual Culture*, ed. Mark Dorrian and Frederic Pousin, 290–308. London: IB Tauris, 2013.

"Dr Julius Neubronner's Miniature Pigeon Camera." *The Public Domain Review*, n.d. http://publicdomainreview.org/collections/dr-julius-neubronners-miniature-pigeon-camera/.

Ducharme, Véronique. "Encounters." *Photomediations Machine*, February 15, 2014. http://photomediationsmachine.net/2014/02/15/encounters/.

Dunston, Lara. "Revealed: Cambodia's Vast Medieval Cities Hidden beneath the Jungle." *Guardian*, June 11, 2016. https://www.theguardian.com/world/2016/jun/11/lost-city-medieval-discovered-hidden-beneath-cambodian-jungle.

Dziewit, Jakub. *Aparaty i obrazy: W stronę kulturowej historii fotografii*. Katowice: Grupa Kulturalna, 2014.

Edwards, Elizabeth. "Objects of Affect: Photography Beyond the Image." *Annual Review of Anthropology* 41 (2012): 221–234.

Edwards, Steve. *Photography: A Very Short Introduction*. Oxford: Oxford University Press, 2006.

Elkins, James. *The Object Stares Back: On the Nature of Seeing*. San Diego: Harcourt, 1996.

Ellsworth, Elizabeth, and Jamie Kruse. *Making the Geologic Now: Responses to Material Conditions of Contemporary Life*. Brooklyn, NY: Punctum Books, 2013.

Enwezor, Okwui. *Archive Fever: Uses of the Document in Contemporary Art*. New York: International Center of Photography; Göttingen: Steidl, 2008.

Evans, Damian. "Airborne Laser Scanning as a Method for Exploring Long-term Socio-ecological Dynamics in Cambodia." *Journal of Archaeological Science* 74 (October 2016): 164–175, doi:10.1016/j.jas.2016.05.009, available online.

Ferguson, Juliet. "Stolen Images." *Photomediations Machine*, April 29, 2013. http://photomediationsmachine.net/2013/04/29/stolen-images.

Flieger, Jerry Aline. "The Listening Eye: Postmodernism, Paranoia, and the Hypervisible." *Diacritics* 26 (1) (1996): 90–107.

Flowers Gallery. Press release for the exhibition *Dust* by Nadav Kader, Flowers Gallery London, September 10–October 11, 2014.

Flusser, Vilém. *Into the Universe of Technical Images*. Trans. Nancy Ann Roth. Minneapolis: University of Minnesota Press, 2011.

Flusser, Vilém. *Towards a Philosophy of Photography*. Trans. Anthony Mathews. London: Reaktion Books, 2000.

Fontcuberta, Joan. *Pandora's Camera: Photogr@phy after Photography*. London: Mack, 2014.

Fontcuberta, Joan, et al. *From Here On: PostPhotography in the Age of Internet and the Mobile Phone*. Barcelona: RM Verlag, 2013.

Foster, Hal. "An Archival Impulse." In *The Archive*, ed. Charles Merewether. London: Whitechapel; Cambridge, MA: MIT Press, 2006.

Furness, Hannah. "V&A Accused of 'Cultural Rape' after Bradford Museum Loses Photo Collection." *Telegraph*, February 2, 2016. http://www.telegraph.co.uk/news/uknews/12136008/VandA-accused-of-cultural-rape-after-Bradford-museum-loses-photo-collection.html.

Freud, Sigmund. "A Note upon the "Mystic Writing-Pad." In *The Standard Edition of the Complete Psychological Works of Sigmund Freud*, ed. James Strachey, vol. 19. London: Hogarth Press, 1961.

Fried, Michael. *Why Photography Matters as Art as Never Before*. New Haven: Yale University Press, 2008.

Frosh, Paul. "The Gestural Image: The Selfie, Photography Theory and Kinaesthetic Sociability." In *Photomediations: A Reader*, ed. Kamila Kuc and Joanna Zylinska, 251–267. London: Open Humanities Press, 2016.

Gabrys, Jennifer. *Digital Rubbish: A Natural History of Electronics*. Ann Arbor: University of Michigan Press, 2011.

Garrett, Bradley L. *Explore Everything: Place-hacking the City*. London: Verso, 2013.

Gibson, James. *The Ecological Approach to Visual Perception*. Boston: Houghton Mifflin, 1979.

Godfrey, Mark. "Photography Found and Lost: On Tacita Dean's *Floh*." *October* 114 (Fall 2005): 90–119.

Goldstein, E. Bruce. *Sensation and Perception*. 8th ed. Belmont, CA: Wadsworth Cengage Learning, 2010.

Gómez Cruz, Edgar. "Photo-genic Assemblages: Photography as a Connective Interface." In *Digital Photography and Everyday Life: Empirical Studies on Material Visual Practices*, ed. Edgar Gómez Cruz and Asko Lehmuskallio, 228–242. London: Routledge, 2016.

Gómez Cruz, Edgar, and Asko Lehmuskallio, eds. *Digital Photography and Everyday Life: Empirical Studies on Material Visual Practices*. London: Routledge, 2016.

Grusin, Richard. Introduction. In *The Nonhuman Turn*, ed. Richard Grusin. Minneapolis: University of Minnesota Press, 2015.

Hall, Gary. *Digitize This Book! The Politics of New Media, or Why We Need Open Access Now*. Minneapolis: University of Minnesota Press, 2008.

Hall, Gary. *Pirate Philosophy: For a Digital Posthumanities*. Cambridge, MA: MIT Press, 2016.

Hall, Gary, and Clare Birchall. "Introduction to Version One Point Zero." In *New Cultural Studies: The Liquid Theory Reader*, ed. Gary Hall and Clare Birchall. London: Open Humanities Press, 2009. http://liquidbooks.pbworks.com/New+Cultural+Studies:+The+Liquid+Theory+Reader.

Hanski, Ilkka. "The World That Became Ruined." In "Science and Society," special issue, *EMBO Reports* 9 (2008): S34.

Harari, Yuval Noah. *Sapiens: A Brief History of Humankind*. London: Harvill Secker, 2014.

Haraway, Donna. "Situated Knowledges: The Science Question in Feminism and the Privilege of Partial Perspective." *Feminist Studies* 14 (3) (Autumn 1988): 575–599.

Haraway, Donna, and Martha Kenney. "Anthropocene, Capitalocene, Chthulucene: Donna Haraway in Conversation with Martha Kenney." In *Art in the Anthropocene: Encounters among Aesthetics, Politics, Environments and Epistemologies*, ed. Heather Davis and Etienne Turpin. London: Open Humanities Press, 2015.

Harrison, W. Jerome. *History of Photography*. New York: Scovill Manufacturing Company, 1887.

Harrison, W. Jerome. *A Sketch of the Geology of Leicestershire and Rutland*. Sheffield: William White, 1877.

Hawkins, Gay. *The Ethics of Waste: How We Relate to Rubbish*. Lanham, MD: Rowman and Littlefield, 2005.

Hayles, N. Katherine. *How We Became Posthuman: Virtual Bodies in Cybernetics, Literature, and Informatics*. Chicago: University of Chicago Press, 1999.

Hayles, N. Katherine. *My Mother Was a Computer: Digital Subjects and Literary Texts*. Chicago: University of Chicago Press, 2005.

Hayward, Eva. "Fingeryeyes: Impressions of Cup Corals." *Cultural Anthropology* 25 (4) (2010): 577–599.

Heise, Ursula K. "Lost Dogs, Last Birds, and Listed Species: Cultures of Extinction." *Configurations* 18 (1–2) (Winter 2010): 49–72.

Herbrechter, Stefan. *Posthumanism: A Critical Analysis*. London: Bloomsbury, 2013.

Higgins, Charlotte. "Tacita Dean's Turbine Hall Film Pays Homage to a Dying Medium." *Guardian*, October 10, 2011. http://www.theguardian.com/artanddesign/2011/oct/10/tacita-dean-film-turbine-hall.

Hobson, Greg. Foreword. In *Revelations: Experiments in Photography*, ed. Ben Burbridge. London: Mack in Association with Media Space, 2015.

Horochowski, Alexa. "Club Disminución." *Photomediations Machine*, January 13, 2015. http://photomediationsmachine.net/2015/01/13/club-disminucion/.

"How Do You Light a Woolly Mammoth?" *The 6th Floor*, November 1, 2014. http://6thfloor.blogs.nytimes.com/2014/02/28/under-cover-how-do-you-light-a-woolly-mammoth/.

Hugo, Pieter. *Permanent Error*. Munich: Prestel Art, 2011.

Ingold, Tim. *Being Alive: Essays on Movement, Knowledge and Description*. London: Routledge, 2011.

Ingold, Tim. "Beyond Biology and Culture: The Meaning of Evolution in a Relational World." *Social Anthropology* 12 (2) (2004): 209–221.

Innis, Harold A. *The Bias of Communication*. Toronto: University of Toronto Press, 1951.

Innis, Harold A. *The Fur Trade in Canada: An Introduction to Canadian Economic History*. Toronto: University of Toronto Press, 1930.

Jameson, Fredric. "Future City." *New Left Review* 21 (May–June 2003). http://newleftreview.org/II/21/fredric-jameson-future-city/.

Jarvis, Audley. "How Kodak Invented the Digital Camera in 1975." Techradar, May 9, 2008. http://www.techradar.com/news/cameras/photography-video-capture/how-kodak-invented-the-digital-camera-in-1975-364822.

Jeffries, Stuart. "The Death of Photography: Are Camera Phones Destroying an Artform?" *Guardian*, December 13, 2013. http://www.theguardian.com/artanddesign/2013/dec/13/death-of-photography-camera-phones.

Johnston, John. "Machinic Vision." *Critical Inquiry* 26 (Autumn 1999): 27–48.

Kember, Sarah. *iMedia: The Gendering of Objects, Environments and Smart Materials*. Basingstoke, UK: Palgrave Macmillan, 2016.

Kember, Sarah. "The Virtual Life of Photography." *Photographies* 1 (2) (September 2008): 175–203.

Kember, Sarah, and Joanna Zylinska. *Life after New Media: Mediation as a Vital Process*. Cambridge, MA: MIT Press, 2012.

Kember, Sarah, and Joanna Zylinska. "Media Always and Everywhere: A Cosmic Approach." In *Ubiquitous Computing, Complexity, and Culture*, ed. Ulrik Ekman et al., 224–234. New York: Routledge, 2015.

Kessler, Elizabeth A. *Picturing the Cosmos: Hubble Space Telescope Images and the Astronomical Sublime*. Minneapolis: University of Minnesota Press, 2012.

Klein, Naomi. *This Changes Everything: Capitalism vs. the Climate*. New York: Simon and Schuster, 2014.

Klingan, Katrin, et al., eds. *Grain Vapor Ray: Textures of the Anthropocene*. Cambridge, MA: MIT Press, 2015.

Kolbert, Elizabeth. "Enter the Anthropocene—Age of Man." In *Making the Geologic Now: Responses to Material Conditions of Contemporary Life*, ed. Elizabeth Ellsworth and Jamie Kruse, 28–32. Brooklyn, NY: Punctum Books, 2012. [Originally published in *National Geographic*, March 2011.]

Kolbert, Elizabeth. *The Sixth Extinction: An Unnatural History*. London: Bloomsbury, 2014. Kindle edition.

Kuc, Kamila. "A Curated Object and a Disruptive e-Anarchive." *Photomediations Machine*, October 20, 2015. http://photomediationsmachine.net/2015/10/20/a-curated-object-and-a-disruptive-e-anarchive/.

Kuc, Kamila, and Joanna Zylinska, eds. *Photomediations: A Reader*. London: Open Humanities Press, 2016.

Lam, Tong. *Abandoned Futures: A Journey to the Posthuman World*. Carpet Bombing Culture, 2013.

Langford, Martha. "Strange Bedfellows: Appropriations of the Vernacular by Photographic Artists." *Photography and Culture*. 1 (1) (July 2008): 73–94.

Laperrouza, Mark. "TCL+IKEA=UPPLEVA." *Lift Lab* blog, posted April 20, 2012. http://liftlab.com/think/marc/2012/04/ (no longer available).

Lehmuskallio, Asko. "The Camera as a Sensor among Many: The Visualization of Everyday Digital Photography as Simulative, Heuristic and Layered Pictures." In *Digital Photography and Everyday Life: Empirical Studies on Material Visual Practices*, ed. Edgar Gómez Cruz and Asko Lehmuskallio, 243–266. London: Routledge, 2016.

Lehmuskallio, Asko, and Edgar Gómez Cruz. "Why Material Visual Practices?" In *Digital Photography and Everyday Life: Empirical Studies on Material Visual Practices*, ed. Edgar Gómez Cruz and Asko Lehmuskallio, 1–16. London: Routledge, 2016.

Lem, Stanisław. "Dwadzieścia lat później" [Twenty Years Later]. In S. Lem, *Summa Technologiae*, 4th exp. ed. Lublin, Poland: Wydawnictwo Lubelskie, 1997.

Lem, Stanisław. *Summa Technologiae*. Trans. Joanna Zylinska. Minneapolis: University of Minnesota Press, 2013.

Levinas, Emmanuel. "Ethics as First Philosophy." In *The Levinas Reader*, ed. Sean Hand. Oxford: Blackwell, 1989.

Levinas, Emmanuel. *Otherwise than Being: Or Beyond Essence*. Trans. Alphonso Lingis. Pittsburgh: Duquesne University Press, 1998.

Lyotard, Jean-François. *The Inhuman*. Trans. Geoffrey Bennington and Rachel Bowlby. Cambridge: Polity Press, 1991.

Lyotard, Jean-François. *The Postmodern Condition*. Trans. Geoff Bennington and Brian Massumi. Minneapolis: University of Minnesota Press, 1984.

Macaulay, Rose. *Pleasure of Ruins*. London: Thames and Hudson, 1984.

Mackenzie, Adrian. *Wirelessness: Radical Empiricism in Network Cultures*. Cambridge, MA: MIT Press, 2010.

Margulis, Lynn, and Dorian Sagan. *What Is Life?* Berkeley: University of California Press, 2000.

Massumi, Brian. "The Future Birth of the Affective Fact: The Political Ontology of Threat." In *The Affect Theory Reader*, ed. Melissa Gregg and Gregory J. Seigworth, 52–54. Durham: Duke University Press, 2010.

Maxwell, Richard, and Toby Miller. *Greening the Media*. Oxford: Oxford University Press, 2012.

McCosker, Anthony. "Drone Media: Unruly Systems, Radical Empiricism and Camera Consciousness." *Culture Machine* 16 (2015) (online).

McGrath, Jason. "Apocalypse, or, the Logic of Late Anthropocene Ruins." *Cross-Currents: East Asian History and Culture Review*, e-journal no. 10 (March 2014): 113–119. http://cross-currents.berkeley.edu/e-journal/issue-10.

McKenzie, Jai. *Light and Photomedia: A New History and Future of the Photographic Image*. London: IB Tauris, 2014.

McLuhan, Marshall, and Quentin Fiore. *War and Peace in the Global Village*. New York: McGraw-Hill, 1968.

McNeill, J. R., and Peter Engelke. *The Great Acceleration: An Environmental History of the Anthropocene since 1945*. Cambridge, MA: Harvard University Press, 2016.

Merewether, Charles, ed. *The Archive*. London: Whitechapel; Cambridge, MA: MIT Press, 2006.

Merewether, Charles. Introduction to *The Archive*, ed. Charles Merewether. London: Whitechapel; Cambridge, MA: MIT Press, 2006.

Meyerowitz, Joel. *Aftermath: World Trade Center Archive*. London: Phaidon Press, 2006.

Michaels, Walter Benn. "Photographs and Fossils." In *Photography Theory*, ed. James Elkins, 431–450. London: Routledge, 2007.

Mirzoeff, Nicholas. *An Introduction to Visual Culture*. London: Routledge, 1999.

Mirzoeff, Nicholas. *The Right to Look: A Counterhistory of Visuality*. Durham: Duke University Press, 2011.

Mirzoeff, Nicholas. "Visualizing the Anthropocene." *Public Culture* 26 (2) (2014): 213–232.

Modrak, Rebekah, with Bill Anthes. *Reframing Photography: Theory and Practice*. London: Routledge, 2011.

Morozov, Evgeny. "Facebook Isn't a Charity: The Poor Will Pay by Surrendering Their Data." *Observer*, April 26, 2015, 8.

Morton, Timothy. *Ecology without Nature: Rethinking Environmental Aesthetics*. Cambridge, MA: Harvard University Press, 2007.

Morton, Timothy. *Hyperobjects: Philosophy and Ecology after the End of the World*. Minneapolis: University of Minnesota Press, 2013.

Nakas, Kassandra. "Jana Sterbak." Website documenting the exhibition project "Becoming Animal, Becoming Human / Animal Perspectives," 2009. http://becoming-animal-becoming-human.animal-studies.org/html/sterbak.html.

"National Media Museum Invests in Science and Technology—Transferring Art of Photography Collections to the V&A." NMM website, February 2, 2016. http://www.nationalmediamuseum.org.uk/aboutus/pressoffice/2016/february/national-media-museum-transfers-photography-collections-to-v-and-a.

Newhall, Beaumont. *The History of Photography from 1839 to the Present Day*. 5th ed. New York: Museum of Modern Art, 1982.

O'Toole, Sean. "Permanent Error." *Mahala*, May 5, 2011. http://www.mahala.co.za/art/permanent-error/.

Paglen, Trevor. *The Last Pictures*. Berkeley: University of California Press, 2012.

Pallasmaa, Juhani. *The Eyes of the Skin: Architecture and the Senses*. 3rd ed. London: John Wiley and Sons, 2012.

Parikka, Jussi. *The Anthrobscene*. Minneapolis: University of Minnesota Press, 2014. Kindle edition.

Parikka, Jussi. *A Geology of Media*. Minneapolis: University of Minnesota Press, 2015.

Parikka, Jussi. "Introduction: The Materiality of Media and Waste." In *Medianatures*, ed. Jussi Parikka. London: Open Humanities Press, 2013.

Peters, John Durham. *The Marvelous Clouds: Toward a Philosophy of Elemental Media*. Chicago: University of Chicago Press, 2015.

Peters, John Durham. "Space, Time, and Communication Theory." *Canadian Journal of Communication* [online] 28 (4) (2003).

Pulver, Andrew. "Artist and Photographer Tacita Dean's Best Shoot." *Guardian*, September 16, 2009. https://www.theguardian.com/artanddesign/2009/sep/16/photography-tacita-dean-best-shoot.

Rancière, Jacques. *The Politics of Aesthetics: The Distribution of the Sensible*. Trans. Gabriel Rockhill. London: Continuum, 2014.

Rexer, Lyle. *The Edge of Vision: The Rise of Abstraction in Photography*. New York: Aperture, 2013.

Rich, Nathaniel. "The Mammoth Cometh." *New York Times Magazine*, February 27, 2014. http://www.nytimes.com/2014/03/02/magazine/the-mammoth-cometh.html.

Ritchin, Fred. *After Photography*. New York: W. W. Norton, 2009.

Rosenblum, Naomi. *A World History of Photography*. 3rd ed. New York: Abbeville Press, 1997.

Ross, Andrew. *Nice Work If You Can Get It: Life and Labor in Precarious Times*. New York: New York University Press, 2009.

Rowan, Rory. "Extinction as Usual? Geo-Social Futures and Left Optimism." In "Supercommunity," special issue, *e-flux journal* 65 (May–August 2015): 1–11.

Roy, Arundhati. "Is There Life after Democracy?" *Dawn.com*, May 7, 2009. http://www.dawn.com/news/475778/is-there-life-after-democracy.

Rubinstein, Daniel, and Katrina Sluis. "A Life More Photographic: Mapping the Networked Image." *Photographies* 1 (1) (March 2008): 9–28.

Russill, Chris. "Earth Imaging: Photograph, Pixel, Program." In *Ecomedia: Key Issues*, ed. Stephen Rust, Salma Monani, and Sean Cubitt, 228–250. London: Routledge, 2016.

Rust, Stephen, Salma Monani, and Sean Cubitt. "Introduction: Ecologies of Media." In *Ecomedia: Key Issues*, ed. Stephen Rust, Salma Monani, and Sean Cubitt. London: Routledge, 2016.

Salminen, Antti. "Photography in the Age of Fossil Nihilism." *Mustarinda*, Helsinki Photography Biennial Edition HBP14 (2014): 65–70.

Schmid, Christina. "A Club at the End of the World." October 16, 2014. MN artists website, http://www.mnartists.org/article/club-end-world.

Scholz, Trebor. "Becoming Facebook." In *Facebook and Philosophy*, ed. D. E. Wittkower. Chicago: Open Court, 2010.

Searle, Adrian. "Hiroshi Sugimoto: Art for the End of the World." *Guardian*, May 16, 2014. http://www.theguardian.com/artanddesign/2014/may/16/hiroshi-sugimoto-aujordhui-palais-de-tokyo-paris-exhibition.

Seers, Lindsay. *Human Camera*. Birmingham, UK: Article Press, 2007.

Shaw, Jonathan. "Hybridity and Digital Transformations." In *NewFotoScapes*, ed. Jonathan Shaw. Birmingham, UK: Library of Birmingham, 2014.

Sholette, Gregory. "Richard Whitlock's *The Street*: An Interview." *Afterimage Online: The Journal of Media Arts and Cultural Criticism* November 7, 2013. http://vsw.org/afterimage/2013/11/07/video-and-interview-i-richard-whitlocks-the-street/.

Shore, Robert. *Post-Photography: The Artist with a Camera*. London: Laurence King, 2014.

Silverman, Kaja. *The Threshold of the Visible World*. London: Routledge, 1996.

Sluis, Katrina. "Authorship, Collaboration, Computation? Into the Realm of Similar Images." In *Photomediations: A Reader*, ed. Kamila Kuc and Joanna Zylinska, 283–289. London: Open Humanities Press, 2016.

Sontag, Susan. *Regarding the Pain of Others*. New York: Picador, 2003.

Sontag, Susan. "Regarding the Torture of Others." *New York Times*, May 23, 2004. http://www.nytimes.com/2004/05/23/magazine/regarding-the-torture-of-others.html.

Squiers, Carol. *What Is a Photograph?* New York: International Center of Photography and DelMonico Books, 2014.

Stevenson, Michael. "Permanent Error." 2010. Project description on the Stevenson gallery website, http://archive.stevenson.info/exhibitions/hugo/index2010.htm.

Sugimoto, Hiroshi. Interview with PBS, Art21, 2011. Transcript published on *Archinect* blog, http://archinect.com/windscreens/to-me-photography-functions-as-a-fossilization-of-time.

Tagg, John. "Mindless Photography." In *Photography: Theoretical Snapshots*, ed. J. J. Long, Andrea Noble, and Edward Welch, 16–30. London: Routledge, 2008.

Talbot, H. Fox. *The Pencil of Nature*. London: Longman, Brown, Green and Longmans, 1844. Project Gutenberg online edition.

Tiberghien, Gilles. "Robert Smithson and Aerial Art." In *Seeing from Above: The Aerial View in Visual Culture*, ed. Mark Dorrian and Frederic Pousin, 277–289. London: IB Tauris, 2013.

Turpin, Etienne. "Who Does the Earth Think It Is, Now?" In *Architecture in the Anthropocene*, ed. Etienne Turpin, 3–10. Ann Arbor: Open Humanities Press, 2013.

University of Sheffield. "Aylan Kurdi: How a Single Image Transformed the Debate on Immigration." December 14, 2015. https://www.sheffield.ac.uk/news/nr/aylan-kurdi-social-media-report-1.533951/.

Vadén, Tere. "Fossil Sense." *Mustarinda,* Helsinki Photography Biennial Edition HBP14 (2014): 99–101.

van Dooren, Thom. *Flight Ways: Life and Loss at the Edge of Extinction.* New York: Columbia University Press, 2014.

Weir, Maxfield. "Our Photographic Future: Vision and Action in a Dematerialised World." In catalog for the exhibition "Photography: [De]Materialised," Oxford House Gallery, London, April 2015.

Whitlock, Richard. "Non-perspectival Photography: Towards a Post-digital Visuality." *Photomediations Machine,* May 18, 2014. http://photomediationsmachine.net/2014/05/18/non-perspectival-photography-towards-a-post-digital-visuality/.

Williams, Raymond. "Culture Is Ordinary." In *Studying Culture,* ed. Anne Gray and Jim McGuigan, 5–15. London: Arnold, 1997.

Wolfe, Cary. *What Is Posthumanism?* Minneapolis: University of Minnesota Press, 2009.

Wright, Terence. *The Photography Handbook.* 2nd ed. London: Routledge, 2004.

Zabala, Santiago. "I'm Wired, Therefore I Exist." *New Statesman,* July 29, 2012. http://www.newstatesman.com/sci-tech/sci-tech/2012/07/im-wired-therefore-i-exist.

Zhang, Michael. "This Is What the History of Camera Sales Looks Like with Smartphones Included." PetaPixel, April 9, 2015. http://petapixel.com/2015/04/09/this-is-what-the-history-of-camera-sales-looks-like-with-smartphones-included/.

Zielinski, Siegfried. *[... After the Media]: News from the Slow-Fading Twentieth Century.* Trans. Gloria Custance. Minneapolis: Univocal, 2013.

Zielinski, Siegfried. *Deep Time of the Media: Toward an Archaeology of Hearing and Seeing by Technical Means.* Trans. Gloria Custance. Cambridge, MA: MIT Press, 2006.

Zylinska, Joanna. "All the World's a Camera: Notes on Nonhuman Photography." In *Drone: The Automated Image,* ed. Paul Wombell. Bielefeld: Kerber, 2013.

Zylinska, Joanna. *Bioethics in the Age of New Media.* Cambridge, MA: MIT Press, 2009.

Zylinska, Joanna. "The Creative Power of Nonhuman Photography." In *Photographic Powers,* ed. Mika Elo and Marko Karo, with Marc Goodwin. Helsinki: Aalto ARTS, 2015.

Zylinska, Joanna. *The Ethics of Cultural Studies*. London: Continuum, 2005.

Zylinska, Joanna. *Minimal Ethics for the Anthropocene*. Ann Arbor: Open Humanities Press, 2014.

Zylinska, Joanna. "On Bad Archives, Unruly Snappers and Liquid Photographs." *Photographies* 3 (2) (August 2010): 139–153.

Zylinska, Joanna. "Photomediations: An Introduction." In *Photomediations: A Reader*, ed. Kamila Kuc and Joanna Zylinska, 7–17. London: Open Humanities Press, 2016.

Index

Sadie Brower Neakok, An Iñupiaq Woman

Sadie Brower Neakok

An Iñupiaq Woman

❖ ❖ ❖

MARGARET B. BLACKMAN

UNIVERSITY OF WASHINGTON PRESS

Seattle and London

First paperback edition, 1992
Printed in the United States of America

Library of Congress Cataloging-in-Publication Data
Blackman, Margaret B.
Sadie Brower Neakok, an Iñupiaq woman.
Bibliography: p.
Includes index.
1. Neakok, Sadie Brower, 1916– 2. Eskimos—Alaska—Biography. 3. Judges—Alaska—Biography. 4. Eskimos—Government relations. 5. Indians of North America—Government relations. I. Title
E99.E7N363 1989 979.8'7[B] 88-33959
ISBN 0-295-97180-0

The paper used in this publication meets the minimum requirements of American National Standard for Information Sciences—Permanence of Paper for Printed Library Materials, ANSI Z39.48-1984.

For Sadie's family

and the people of the North Slope Borough

Contents

Preface

Clad in a blue velveteen fancy parka she had made herself, hands clasped behind her back after the fashion of Iñupiat[1] women who have carried a lifetime of small children on their backs, Sadie Brower Neakok walked through the doors of Barrow High School on August 14, 1984. She had come at the urging of my husband Ed Hall, who had, with the help of Craig Gerlach and myself, organized a two-week archæology and oral history field school for Barrow High School students. The North Slope Borough Field School was modeled loosely on the *Foxfire* projects, and we hoped in the course of two weeks to introduce students to the rich resources of local history and prehistory, and to provide them with a basic framework for investigating the North Slope heritage. Accordingly, we selected two elders—a man[2] and a woman—who would be willing to work with me and to be interviewed about their lives by the twelve students. We needed elders who were at ease speaking English because the students were ethnically mixed (Iñupiat, white, Hawaiian, Filipino), and because I speak no Iñupiaq.

Sadie was a perfect choice for the task. Fluent in English and a former teacher in the Barrow schools, she was quite comfortable in the role of life history subject. More important, because of her various public service roles in the community over a forty-year period, Sadie had much to offer on Barrow history. She described the first airplane landing in Barrow in 1926, the tragic crash of Will Rogers and Wiley Post in 1935, the construction of the U.S. Navy base and DEW-line station (Defense Early Warning) outside of town, the protest over subsistence hunting regulations in the 1960s, the problems Barrow natives faced with the introduction of the white man's legal system, and more. She was equally descriptive about her own life. During the

two-week field school the students came to imagine this diminutive, wispy-haired woman in the many different garments reflecting the rich and varied roles she has assumed during her life: the homemade skin clothing of her early childhood; the alien hat and fashionable dresses of her San Francisco high school years; the roomy work parkas under which she carried each of her thirteen babies; the special clothing she had to wear as a volunteer nurse attending TB patients; and the judicial robes of Barrow's magistrate. We listened to Sadie as an advocate for better education, improved health and sanitation in Barrow, and native rights, but we came to see her equally as the wife of an Iñupiaq hunter and the mother to a large family.

Sadie was born in Barrow in 1916, the sixth child of Asianggataq, an Iñupiaq woman, and her white husband Charles Brower. Brower, a whaler and fur trader who managed the first land-based whaling station in the Arctic and operated a trading store in Barrow for almost sixty years, is well known to students of the Alaskan Arctic through his memoirs, *Fifty Years Below Zero*. Sadie and her nine brothers and sisters were raised with a mixture of Iñupiat and white traditions. They ate white man's meals as well as native food, spoke English and Iñupiaq, and learned respect for Iñupiat ways; but they hewed to the white man's clock and to their father's evening curfews, and they were sent Outside[3] for a white man's education. Despite the schooling that prepared them for life Outside, all but one came back to Barrow to live.[4]

Sadie continued on to college, completed two years, and returned to Barrow to put her education to use—first as a Bureau of Indian Affairs (BIA) schoolteacher, then as a volunteer health aide, a welfare worker, and finally as Barrow's magistrate, a position she held for twenty years. In private life she became the wife of Nate Neakok, an Iñupiaq hunter who, she states emphatically, never went to school, "but knew more than I did, a college student, a teacher." Over the next twenty-three years, Sadie gave birth to thirteen children, and she and Nate took in numerous others temporarily as foster children.

Sadie's accomplishments as a public servant have not gone unheralded, as is evident in the several honors that adorn her kitchen walls: Alaska Native Woman of the Year (twice), Soroptimist Woman of the Year in 1974 ("I didn't know what 'Soroptimist' meant," exclaimed Sadie, "but I knew it couldn't be bad with 'optimist' behind it."),[5] and awards for outstanding community service. In 1969 she was one of two

Alaskan natives called to Washington, D.C., to serve on a special White House conference on nutrition and the high cost of living, and in May of 1987 Sadie was recognized by the University of Alaska with an honorary doctorate of laws. In addition to her community work, Sadie's domestic achievements were acknowledged when she was voted Alaska's Mother of the Year in 1968. Retired officially since 1977, and in actuality since 1980, Sadie is only now recovering from long-term health problems. Even so, her expertise is still called upon in various projects like the field school or, more recently, the 1986 North Slope Borough Elders' Conference on native law ways. "It's time, though," she says, "for younger people to start taking over for me."

A small group of field school students met each afternoon and interviewed Sadie for about two and a half hours at the high school library.[6] Mornings were devoted to discussing oral history interviewing and to composing interview questions. The students were divided, alphabetically, into four groups. So that a succession of student groups, each with limited time, could collect the outlines of a life history, each group focused on a segment of Sadie's life—childhood, teen-age years, early adulthood, and later years. As each new group met, I apprised them of what the preceding day's group had learned. At the conclusion of the field school, the students and I had collected approximately seventeen hours of life history tapes from Sadie. Unfortunately, the field school was too brief to enable students to transcribe and edit the tapes and see them to a final product. The duration of the project was sufficient, however, to indicate that after seventeen hours much of Sadie Neakok's life story was still untold.

Life histories, as the oral narratives of individual lives, are collected for various reasons. We take for granted that the lives of important individuals are worth recording for posterity: vicariously we enjoy their successes and suffer through or revel in their scandals—their fame or infamy. As a counterpoint to ethnography, the life history gives an insider's personal view of another culture. More recently, life history (and oral history generally) has given voice to those who might otherwise not be heard—the ordinary, the disadvantaged, women, minorities.

The initial reasons for collecting Sadie's life history were linked to the North Slope Borough Field School. As a respected and knowledge-

able elder in the community who related well to students, Sadie could provide student interviewers not only with experience in interviewing but also with a story—her own and the community's—that would hold their interest. As her life history unfolded, other reasons for pursuing it presented themselves. Trader baron Charles Brower had dominated the North Slope political-economic landscape for some fifty years, and his descendants continue to do so today. Sadie's life story could open a window onto this important family and provide a logical sequel to her father's life story. Sadie viewed the project accordingly. Years ago she had been approached about writing her own sequel to *Fifty Years Below Zero*. At one time she had even been sent a tape recorder and tapes by the University of Alaska to record her life story, but motherhood and career had left no time for such reminiscences. "My time was just absorbed in family and community life. I never could complete it; so I sent all the equipment back."

A community activist for more than half her three score and eleven years, Sadie has played a critical role in the shaping of modern Barrow. She sees herself in the role of helper/teacher, and so do the Iñupiat of Barrow, who dubbed her *Ikayuqti Iñugmiñun*—"a helper to her people." "Sometimes," exclaims Sadie, reflecting on her long career of public service, "I think I'm the mother to this whole town." Regarding motherhood, Sadie's is a portrait of one woman who appears to have had it all—a life of community service, the opportunity and responsibility to put one's education to use in a challenging career, marriage, and a family several times larger than any imagined by modern women struggling to balance the demands of motherhood and a career. Of equal interest is Sadie's bicultural upbringing and the advantages and disadvantages it has conferred upon her throughout life.

Not least important, especially to a younger generation increasingly cut adrift from the old, oral histories and life histories are powerful reminders that not all history and not all lives worth reading about are to be found in mainstream textbooks used in high school classrooms. Fifty-seven years ago, Sadie experienced the dissonance between life and classroom more jarringly than do today's native students in Barrow, but it is still there. "When I went Outside," she says, "I didn't know what a president was, or his cabinet, Congress, all those things. . . . 'Important' dates . . . had no significance to me; why should I remember all these? They were people and events that had no bearing on my

life." As one who brought her Outside education back home and applied it, Sadie Neakok is a role model for today's North Slope young people, many of whom will find jobs as North Slope Borough government employees. With this in mind, Sadie's story in book form continues her tradition of public service to the northern community. Furthermore, Sadie's life story addresses the relative dearth of life history literature on Eskimo women, particularly contemporary women.[7]

At the field school's conclusion in late August of 1984, Sadie and I discussed continuing the project the following summer with the idea of eventual publication. She was amenable and interested, so I returned to Barrow for two weeks in late July and early August of 1985. This time our interviews were conducted at Sadie's large kitchen table, in the relatively quiet afternoon hours between the conclusion of lunch and the preparation of dinner, a time selected by Sadie. Nonetheless, there was still considerable activity about the house. Sadie's sons or her husband would occasionally come in to rattle through the drawers of the tall tool chest, looking for a wrench, exciting the "record level" needle on my tape recorder. "The Price is Right" usually played from the living room TV at the beginning of our interviews; grandchildren and children came and went; the honeybucket man arrived one day to collect the household's waste. Visitors dropped in, particularly at first as Sadie had just returned from a lengthy hospital stay. The citizens' band radio (CB) was usually on, so the Neakoks could keep in touch with family members inland at their fish camp, and we were occasionally interrupted by one of their voices crackling over the air waves. All this activity enhanced rather than disrupted the interviews, providing me with a glimpse of Sadie's household and the rhythm of its afternoons.

Our interviewing again proceeded in chronological order, and we completed twenty-one hours of interviews. In addition, we studied Sadie's scrapbooks, photo albums, college yearbook, and drawerful of awards. In Barrow, Fairbanks, and Anchorage I interviewed five other individuals—two judges, an attorney, Sadie's former law clerk, and the field auditor for the Alaska Court System—each of whom had worked with Sadie in her capacity as magistrate.

Sadie's narrative in chapters 2 through 9 represents a blend of the two summers' interviews, plus incidental material from brief interviews in 1986 and 1987. Past experience in life history research had proven to

me that a life history cannot be written without follow-up interviews *after* the basic structure of the book has been laid out. Accordingly, I returned to Barrow in July of 1986 to spend a few days with Sadie reviewing the questions I had accumulated as the manuscript had progressed. Sadie and Nate were preparing to fly inland to retrieve a boat their son had cached, and they had to be ready whenever the search-and-rescue helicopter was available. "I'll give you as much time as I have," Sadie promised, and we completed seven hours of interviews in the two days before she left.

Although the chapters had been sent to Sadie for comment as they were completed, this was her first opportunity to see the entire manuscript. Before my arrival Sadie had returned to me one chapter with answers to my questions, but unfortunately the medication she was taking for her blood-clotting problems had hampered her vision. Reading gave her excruciating headaches. Needless to say, she had made little headway on the stack of chapters that lay on her kitchen table. Sadie was hopeful that she would be able to read again by the end of the summer, but we also tentatively arranged to have the final draft of the manuscript read to her by Dave Libbey, anthropologist and oral history archivist for the North Slope Borough in Barrow. Fortunately, Sadie was able to review the manuscript herself in December of 1986, and her comments and additions were incorporated into the final version. In the summer of 1987, when I returned to Barrow to participate in a second field school for Barrow High School students, I discussed with Sadie points that reviewers of the manuscript had raised. Much of this material is treated in the Epilogue. Life history research and the methodology behind Sadie's life history are discussed in the Appendix.

⁂

Lighting a cigarette, Sadie sat in her kitchen chair, her back against the wall. I pulled up a chair beside her, placing the tape recorder and microphone between us on the table that had recently been cleared of the lunch dishes. I began with one of the questions on my list for the day, settling in for another engrossing interview session that would bring me back the following afternoon with a new list of questions.

Sadie's speech is animated. She is a storyteller who often reenacts conversations and the feelings that accompanied them. She punctuates

her speech with exclamatory remarks and laughter, emphatically jabbing her cigarette in the ashtray. Her large expressive hands are frequently in motion when she talks, and now and then, as she recalls a particularly troubling incident, she pauses to rest her head on her hands. The people and events she describes take form as Sadie relives the past in the telling. Sadie is remarkably comfortable when being interviewed, and her answers to questions are invariably both thoughtful and direct. As her story takes shape, her clear sense of her place in Barrow's history becomes evident, a factor having great impact on the final configuration of her life story. Fittingly, Sadie's story begins with a historical consideration of her place, although those who are already familiar with Barrow and the North Slope may wish to skip directly to her narrative.

There is no singular precedent for the presentation of life history material, save that as much of it as possible should be in the subject's own words. Sadie's life history is told in two voices, hers (predominantly) and mine. Our respective words are distinguished by different type styles. As author/editor I have elected to preface Sadie's story by placing it in its cultural and historical context, and occasionally to interrupt her narrative with my own remarks or those of others who know the North Slope Iñupiat, with the intent of providing a broader context for her story.

Margaret B. Blackman

Acknowledgments

A life history such as this one depends on the time and assistance of many people in different places and positions, and I extend my thanks to all who have helped me bring the manuscript to fruition.

For archival assistance, I am indebted to Renee Blahuda, Verda Carey, Philip Cronenwett, Phyllis DeMuth, Kristine Haglund, Joyce Justice, Jann Laiti, and Margaret Rich.

To Jim Dusen, photographer at SUNY Brockport, goes the credit for preparing the photographic prints; Norm Frisch, also of SUNY Brockport, prepared the map of Alaska. Bill Hess, who has done considerable photography on the North Slope, supplied prints of Barrow, Sadie, and Iñupiat whalers.

In Barrow, the North Slope Borough provided funding for the field school project in 1984. The North Slope Borough also assisted with my expenses in the summer of 1985 and with publication costs. Sherie Steele of the borough's TV studio showed me video materials relevant to the project, and Dixie Figgins shared historical materials relating to the Presbyterian church. Roger Harms, principal of Barrow's high school, gave us use of the school for interviewing and loaned us equipment for duplicating tapes. Special thanks are owed the field school students—pictured and identified in the insert following page 174—with whom I began this project. In Juneau, friends Lynn and Skip Wallen kindly housed me while I did research in the Alaska State Library.

Sue Sullivan and Lynne Fullerton transcribed the many hours of interviews. Lynne's thoughtful editing and expert instruction on the intricacies of formatting the manuscript on my computer are also much appreciated. Student help was proffered by Dominick D'Aunno,

who proofread and photocopied the manuscript, and by Jenny Marchant, who spent hours in the library answering last minute research questions.

I would have had great difficulty rendering Sadie's life history materials on her years as magistrate without the help of Alaska Court System personnel. I am especially appreciative of the time and information given by the five court-system people I interviewed: Charlotte Brower, Stephen Cline, Robert Coats, Michael Jeffery, and Marjorie Lori. In addition, Carol Baekey of Magistrate Services provided me with copies of the magistrate training materials, Teresa Carns of the Judicial Council searched the council's minutes for information pertaining to Sadie and provided information on the functions of the council.

Several people have read the manuscript, or parts of it, and I have benefited from their expertise: Stephen Cline, Stephen Conn, Craig Gerlach, Edwin S. Hall, Jr., Michael Jeffery, Dave Libbey, Edna MacLean (who also provided assistance with the orthography), Leona Okakok, William Schneider, Charles Smythe, and Rosita Worl. Margaret Lantis and Catharine McClellan offered helpful commentary for preparing the final draft of the manuscript. I have especially benefited from William Schneider's thoughts on the life history process, and I thank him also for loan of the Neville Jacobs interviews with Sadie and other oral history materials in the University of Alaska's Oral History Archives.

Dave Libbey, as resident anthropologist in Barrow and the North Slope Borough's archivist, was of immeasurable help in this project. He photographed the dedication of the new Alaska Court System building, photocopied and documented Sadie's family photos, and sought answers to several last minute questions about modern Barrow.

My original debt for this project is to my spouse and colleague, Ed Hall, who created the field school project and "found" Sadie for us. I have relied not only on his support and interest throughout the project but also on his extensive library of Arctic materials, much of which ended up on my side of the office we share.

Then there is my daughter, Meryn Hall, who became a seasoned traveler at age two and a half, worked puzzles and colored while I interviewed, endured the uncertainties of strange day-care centers in faraway places, played by my desk or sat on my lap as I wrote, and

collected pretend "life histories" on a plastic ruler covered with a scrap of fabric. In her own way she has taught me much about the life history enterprise.

Although oral historians increasingly produce life histories of individuals who are ordinary citizens, it takes an unusual person to submit to the rigors of life history interviewing, particularly when there are multiple interviewers. Sadie is that sort of special person. She participated in the field school out of civic pride and duty, at a time when her health was failing, and she submitted to interviews the following summer as she recuperated from surgery. Not only was her life story inherently interesting, but her affability and caring made each interview session an event to look forward to. My thanks, too, to her family for their patience and understanding.

All royalties accruing from sale of this publication will go to Sadie Neakok.

Sadie Brower Neakok, an Iñupiaq Woman

I

Home: The Northernmost Outpost

Barrow is a town that leaves a strong impression on the Outsider. As the northernmost city in the western hemisphere, the largest Eskimo community in North America, oil boomtown, and seat of the largest "county" government in the United States, Barrow is the sort of place that attracts modern-day curiosity seekers. Writers who journey to the "top of the world" commonly dwell on its remoteness (five hundred air miles north of Fairbanks), the three months of winter darkness and the week-long summers, the high cost of living, the alcohol problems, and the clash of Eskimo and white cultures. Some apply catchy epithets, summing up Barrow as "a ghetto on ice," "the caboose of the world," and "an Alaskan tragedy." Those who spend more time see Barrow through somewhat different eyes. Writes David Boeri (1983:193) in *People of the Ice Whale*, Barrow has become "the focal point of Eskimo adjustment to the modern world, the crossroads of contact with big money, western culture, and industrialization." Whatever its problems and the unappealing features it presents to the unprepared Outsider, Barrow is "home" to 1,800 Iñupiat.

Much of what is Barrow today is new. Barely one hundred years ago at this writing, the first white settler—Sadie Neakok's father—arrived to take up permanent residency in this Eskimo community; in 1986 nearly 40 percent of Barrow's residents were non-native.[1] The sudden wealth from the Prudhoe Bay oil strike, which has, among other things, brought improved housing, subsidized utilities, and ultramodern schools, began to affect Barrow Iñupiat only after 1972. Forty years before that, as Sadie herself so amply demonstrates, the people of Barrow had a very limited understanding of money, and all they knew of the vast oil resources were the asphalt chunks they dug out of oil seeps

to heat their drafty frame homes. Today, the pickup trucks, three-wheelers, modern buses, front-loaders, dump trucks, and the water and sewage trucks that service the community's homes rumble over gravel roads that were surveyed only twenty-five to thirty years ago. Just twenty years ago transportation in Barrow was primarily by dog team (in 1986 the only native-owned dog team in town belonged to a dog musher). Twenty-five years ago the one telephone in town was operated by Wien Airlines, whose small planes landed on the sand spit in front of Sadie's house. Today one can long-distance direct-dial Sadie Neakok or almost any other resident of Barrow, and jet planes from Anchorage/Fairbanks service Barrow twice daily. The rapidity of change in Barrow seems staggering, but it is not unique; this pattern is repeated throughout the Arctic.

Other features of Barrow bespeak its still strong Iñupiat heritage. Most noticeable, perhaps, is the native language. Announcements and news are broadcast over radio and TV in Iñupiaq as well as in English; information pamphlets on jury duty and other mysteries of the Alaska Court System are rendered in Iñupiaq; and conferences held in Iñupiaq are sponsored by the borough, bringing modern technology to the service of preserving the wisdom of the elders for younger generations. Barrow's three well-stocked grocery stores notwithstanding, fish and *ugruk* (bearded seal) meat hang to dry in the summer sun from the ubiquitous racks beside the houses. A native student participating in a summer archæological dig misses a day of work to go walrus hunting with his father; an *umiaq*[2] rests upside down next to a plexiglass-covered bus stop. The sleek city buses themselves take shotgun-toting Iñupiat six miles north of town to "Shooting Station," where enormous flocks of eider ducks fly to and from their summer feeding grounds.

The focal point of Iñupiat subsistence, the bowhead whale, consumes the interest of townspeople from late April into May, when whaling crews of village men are camped out on the ice by the open leads. If they are successful in their quest, the town gathers on a sunny day in late June for the annual *Nalukataq* or whale feast. The current mayor of the borough as well as his predecessors have been whaling captains; as magistrate, Sadie Neakok managed to find time to sew the requisite new clothing for members of her husband's whaling crew and to mend their tent. David Boeri (1983) noticed that even the cabs in town may not run in the spring because their drivers are out on the ice,

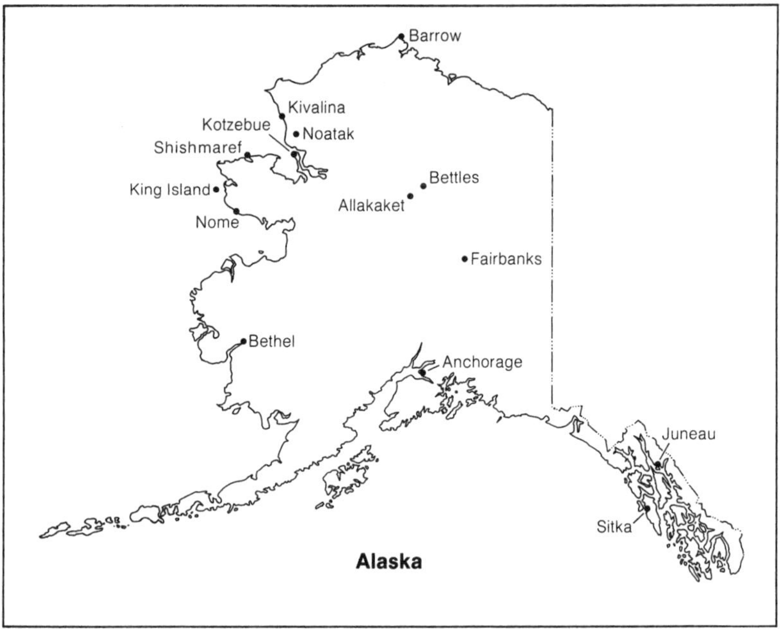

hunting whales. Perhaps most important in regard to Iñupiat culture and its future, the modern borough government has, during its fifteen years of existence, consistently acted as an advocate for Iñupiat interests, balancing income-producing development with native concern for the land and its natural resources.

The Outside visitor to this northernmost American city arrives by jet from Anchorage or Fairbanks. Upon disembarking, tourists on a package tour immediately board the white "Tundra Tours" buses owned by the native regional corporation; they don pile-lined nylon parkas to protect themselves from the cold, windy Arctic summers. The community has become accustomed to tourists since the first plane load arrived in Barrow in 1954, and the Iñupiat have benefited financially from the sale of arts and crafts and the performances of their dancers.

Tour groups are housed at the Top of the World Hotel, owned and operated by a native regional corporation, and they take their meals at the adjoining Mexican restaurant (authentic, with south-of-the-border cooks and waiters), whose owner is also the proprietor of a fleet of

water and sewage trucks. Three other hotels in town compete with Top of the World for the steady influx of temporary workers, government representatives, researchers, tourists, and others; and a Chinese-style restaurant (owned by Koreans), a fast food "barn," two cafés, and two pizza parlors offer a change of pace from Pepé's North of the Border cuisine.

Other signs of the times are evident in this Arctic outpost: at the "Arcticade" local teen-agers gather to try their skill at the familiar arcade games; at the Top of the World Hotel a photo concession offers the one-hour developing service that has become standard in tourist meccas, and the Arctic Hair and Tanning Salon guarantees California suntans even during the dark Arctic winter.[3] Presumably this last business caters mainly to the white population of town; Sadie may not have been alone in her initial but misguided delight that Barrow finally had a local hide tannery!

During Sadie's childhood, every out-of-town visitor was known to all the locals soon after arrival, and most ended up staying at her father's trading station. In smaller villages, even today, an Outsider is taken note of the moment he or she steps off the plane, but one can stroll Barrow's downtown streets "without arousing more than a glance" (Boeri 1983:197). That Barrow is more city than village is evident in the four large buildings that dominate the town's center: the three story Alaska Court System building, completed in the summer of 1985; the Arctic Slope Regional Corporation building, built in the mid-1970s in the wake of native land claims; *Stuaqpak* ("Big Store"), a supermarket/department store; and the North Slope Borough office building. Other than these and a few other buildings throughout town, the highest structures rising from the flat tundra are the T-shaped electrical poles that traverse the city's gravel streets.

Seen from the air, facing the Chukchi Sea with the expanse of tundra behind it, Barrow appears to cling to the land's very edge. The paved runway to its modern airport marks the southern edge of town. The city's multiple streets give way to a narrow tongue of gravel road trending northeast towards Point Barrow twelve miles in the distance. A mile beyond Barrow towards the point is the satellite community of Browerville, named for the town's first white resident, trader/whaler Charles Brower. Mattie's Cafe in Browerville operates out of one of the buildings that comprised Brower's trading station.[4] Four miles

farther out the gravel road, an enclave of military Quonset huts squats in neat rows surrounding the labyrinthine administrative building that until 1980 served as the Naval Arctic Research Laboratory. This naval installation, together with its gravel landing strip, was constructed towards the end of World War II as a base operations camp for oil exploration in National Petroleum Reserve No. 4, which surrounds Barrow on three sides.[5] The military presence is reiterated in the complex of buildings beyond the landing strip that mark the DEW-line station. A mile or so beyond the DEW-line site the gravel road peters out, giving way to the jumble of plywood shacks and canvas tent frames of "Shooting Station" or "Duck Camp," a favorite spot for hunting in summer when eider ducks fly close over the land. This is the last stop on the city bus line. One can, with a four-wheel-drive vehicle, motor beyond Duck Camp to the northernmost edge of land in the United States. The remains of a large Eskimo village that existed here until the 1930s have now all but washed into the sea.

Barrow, Browerville, and Shooting Station lie amidst the rich remains of the Iñupiat past. Birnirk, the best-known site of a culture that flourished around A.D. 600, occupies a now-grassy expanse at Duck Camp. For seventy years Iñupiat have dug in the eroding bluffs of Barrow and Browerville for the remains of the old cultures, encouraged in the early years by trader Charles Brower and by explorer Vilhjalmur Stefansson, who paid for artifacts with chewing gum in 1912. Archæological remains have also been turned up incidentally by Iñupiat while quarrying oil-soaked sod (from ancient kitchen areas) for fuel and while mining archæological areas for scrap metal—exchanged for staples—during World War I (Hall 1981). A latter-day Iñupiat pothunter discovered in 1982 the human remains of what has come to be known as Barrow's "frozen family"—two mummified humans, three partial skeletons, and the well-preserved contents of their sod house—apparently crushed by a surge of sea ice in a fall storm some three hundred years before contact with Euro-Americans.[6] That house and its contents were situated near what is today designated the "Utqiagvik Preserve," the grassy acreage of tumbled-in house mounds near the southwestern edge of the town ancestral to modern Barrow.

According to Charles Brower, Utqiagvik was in 1884 "the largest Eskimo settlement on the Alaska coast." Located "on a bluff fifty feet above the sea," Utqiagvik numbered "dozens of igloos" and "three

dance houses where every night [during the dark months] the Eskimos would congregate and have their native dances" (n.d.:143–45). Though the first to settle there permanently, Brower was by no means the first white man to see Utqiagvik. A British expedition, under the direction of F. W. Beechey in the *Blossom*, explored the northern coast of Alaska in 1826 as far as Icy Cape, and a small barge from the *Blossom*, commanded by Officer Thomas Elson, met Iñupiat off Point Barrow, but decided not to land due to the apparent hostility of the natives. In 1852 the men of the British ship *Plover* were the first white people to overwinter with the Barrow Eskimos. John Simpson, the ship's surgeon, gave the earliest population figures for the area, counting forty sod houses at Utqiagvik[7] and fifty-four at Nuvuk, the village at the tip of Point Barrow (Simpson 1875).

John Murdoch (1892:79), at Barrow from 1881–83 as naturalist on the International Polar Expedition, elaborated on the settlement pattern of Utqiagvik: "The village . . . occupies a narrow strip of ground along the edge of the cliffs of Cape Smyth, about 1,000 yards long, and extending some 150 yards inland. The houses are scattered among the hillocks without any attempt at regularity and at different distances from each other, sometimes alone, and sometimes in groups of two contiguous houses, which often have a common cache frame. . . . All the houses agree in facing south. Besides the dwellings there are in Utkiavwin [Utqiagvik] three and in Nuwuk two of the larger buildings used for dancing, and as workrooms for the men." The photographer on the International Polar Expedition took what must be the earliest photograph of Utqiagvik.

Though the large number of houses at these settlements testified to the bounty of the coastal zone, the Iñupiat were anything but sedentary. The subsistence activities of a family throughout the year might take it over hundreds of square miles, along the coast, inland, and back to the coast again.[8] If hunting had been good at other seasons, only minimal subsistence hunting might be undertaken during the darkest months of winter, but when the sun reappeared above the horizon in February, some villagers would travel inland to base camps along the Chipp/Ikpikpuk, Meade, and other rivers, where they fished through the river ice and hunted caribou. Others would remain along the coast to hunt seals through the sea ice. By April the people would congregate at the coastal villages to prepare for spring whaling.

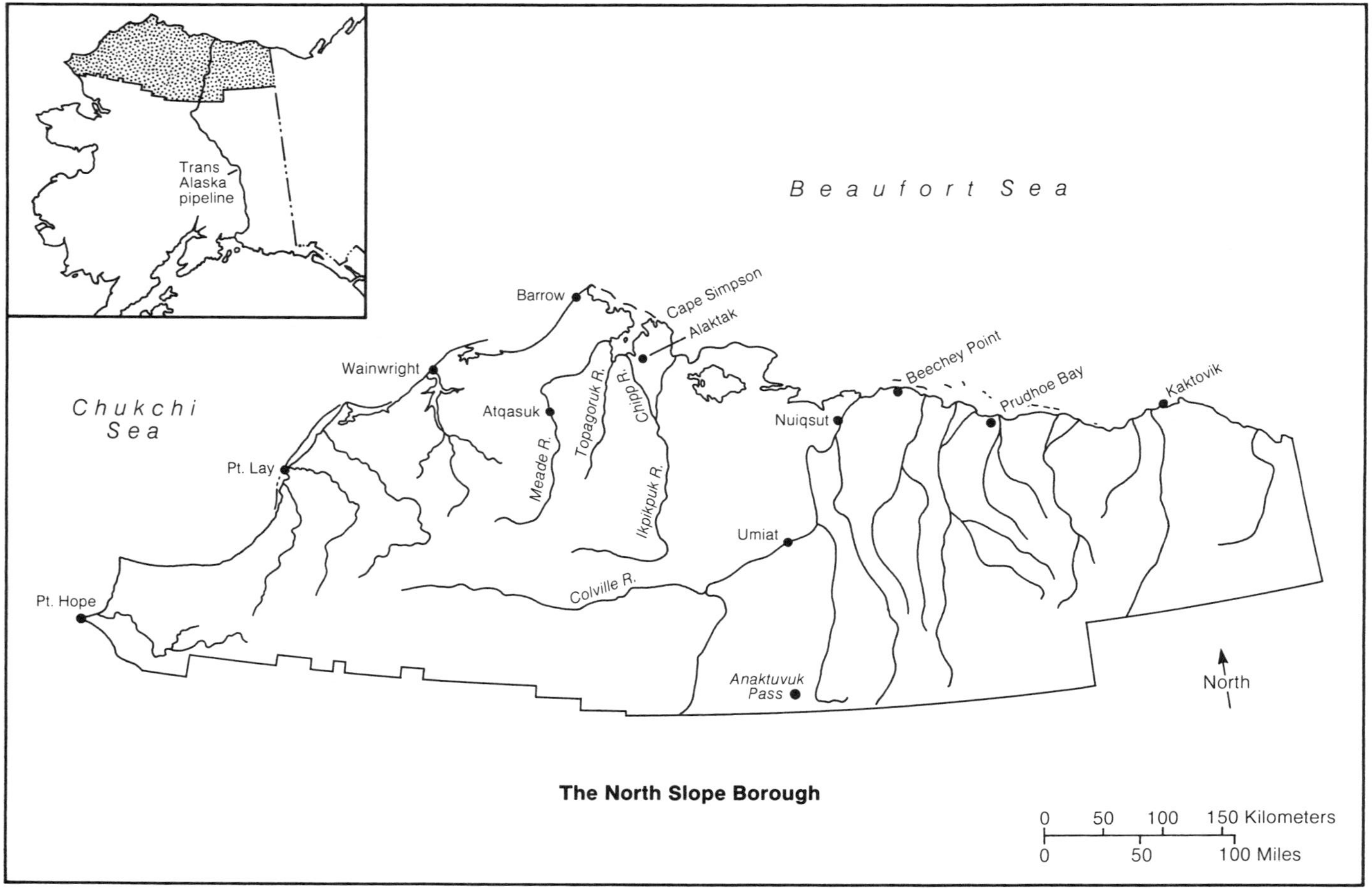

The North Slope Borough

Whaling took place towards the end of April and throughout May as migrating bowhead appeared in the open leads of the Chukchi Sea. Whale hunters stationed on the ice by the leads would also hunt *ugruk* (bearded seal), seals, and walrus as the opportunity arose. A successful whaling season was celebrated in late June with a whale feast or *Nalukataq*, during which the successful whaling captains shared the bounty of their catch, dances were performed, and the daring were tossed high in the air from stretched walrus skins. Charles Brower, who witnessed and participated in many such celebrations during his long association with Iñupiat whaling, reports that the *Nalukataq* of 1900 at Barrow was "the best I ever saw," lasting a record ten days.[9]

Following *Nalukataq*, the people again dispersed, and from June to September there was great diversity in subsistence activities. Some families camped along the shore to hunt seal; others went to inland camps where they fished and hunted caribou; still others set up permanent summer camps at Shooting Station. In late June and early July many Barrow Iñupiat traveled eastward to the Colville River Delta and beyond to trade with Eskimos of other groups. In late July walrus were hunted offshore in the open water, but by early August attention turned landward as young caribou were sought for winter clothing. By late September most families had returned to the village. The women sewed skin clothing for the coming winter and the men fixed and stored any hunting gear that might not be used during the cold months. In the fall, short forays might be made inland to fish or hunt caribou. With the coming of the ice in late fall, sealing became the main activity.

Oddly enough, the ill-fated exploring expedition of Sir John Franklin in 1845 set the stage for changes in Iñupiat life that transpired in the following half-century. Three of the ships detailed by the British to search for Franklin and his men had contact with the Barrow people, and one of them—the *Plover*—overwintered at Barrow from 1852 to 1854. The policy of the search ships was to establish friendly relations between Eskimos and whites, in the event that the lost explorers would be found by natives and become dependent upon them. Even more important than their protracted contact with the Iñupiat at Barrow were the commercial ramifications of the search for Franklin. Although the first commercial whaling vessel had passed into Arctic waters in 1848, it was the returning search vessels that informed whalers of the rich whaling grounds in the Arctic and proved the

ice-laden waters penetrable. "From that time, and for more than a half a century, Barrow served as a major port of call for the commercial whalers of the Arctic fishery" (Sonnenfeld 1956:210).[10]

Whale blubber was sought commercially as both illuminant and lubricant before development of the Pennsylvania oil fields in the 1860s, but the subsequent market for "whalebone" or baleen kept as many as seventy-five ships a season in the waters off Barrow. This plasticlike material that grows in long plates from the upper jaw of the bowhead found multiple uses in the western world as corset stays, foundations for hoop skirts, buggy whips, umbrella ribs, fishing rods, components in the construction of chair seats and backs, billiard cushion springs, and mattress stuffing. By 1870 the Arctic fishery accounted for about 67 percent of the ships, 75 percent of the oil, and 83 percent of the baleen obtained in the North Pacific whale fishery. The season was very short—from mid-August to the beginning of October—and, until the 1890s, ships generally did not winter over in the Arctic but followed the bowhead west and south on its return migration in the fall. The application of steam power to whaling vessels in the 1880s[11] lengthened the time they could spend whaling in Arctic waters and increased their eastward range during the short whaling season.

A decline in the number of whales and a subsequent rise in the price of baleen led to a search for ways to conserve cost and maximize profit. One solution was the establishment of shore-based whaling stations from which crews could take whales during the spring migration in a fashion similar to the Iñupiat; a second strategy was for ships to overwinter in the Arctic in a protected harbor. The latter was adopted after discovery of the feeding grounds of the bowhead in 1889 near the MacKenzie Delta. In 1890 the first ships wintered over at Herschel Island in the Canadian Arctic, and by the mid-1890s there were as many as fifteen ships and five hundred men stationed there. Shore-based whaling proved even more successful. Two major whaling stations were established along the northern Alaskan coast: the first at Barrow in 1884, followed by one at Point Hope in 1887.[12] The shore stations employed Eskimos as whaling crew in addition to the few whites hired by the whaling companies, and they adopted the Eskimo method of hunting from small craft off the shore-fast ice in the spring.

By 1894 there were two shore-based whaling companies in Barrow[13]

controlling a total of twenty-eight whaling crews. Competition for native crew members was intense, particularly for harpooners and steersmen, and by 1908 some of the more affluent natives themselves were maintaining five or six crews. Barrow natives prospered during the boom years of commercial whaling, receiving annually from their employers approximately $200 worth of supplies in payment. Wrote Stefansson, who observed the scene just before the baleen market crashed:

> The whaling season in the spring is six weeks, and is six weeks of fairly easy work at that. For all the rest of the year the men have nothing to do,—are their own masters, and can go wherever they like, while their employers must not only pay them a year's wages for six weeks' work, but also furnish them houses to live in, usually, and rations for the entire year. Of course the men are expected to get their own fresh meat, which they do by seal and walrus hunting, and by cutting in the whales,—only the bone [baleen] of which goes to their employers. The employer supplies them with cloth for garments, and such suitable provisions as flour, tea, beans, rice, and even condensed milk, canned meats and fruits. Each man each year gets, among other things, a new rifle with loading tools and ammunition. . . . The pay-day of the Point Barrow Eskimo comes in the spring, and . . . the people scarcely know what to do [with their bounty of goods]. So they load them into their skin boats and take them east along the coast, to [trade] them at any point in the Colville or at Flaxman Island. [1912:60–61]

Both overwintering and shore-based whaling took their toll on the bowhead population. As the numbers of whales declined, the price of baleen increased, reaching a high of $6.50 per pound.[14] And as the price of baleen rose, so did the impetus to find a cheaper substitute. Charles Brower reported from Barrow in 1910 that "the Herman was the only ship to come in this summer. To my surprise they brought me word that bone was unsaleable [*sic*]" (n.d.:638). When Brower went Outside that fall he talked with a New Jersey manufacturer in an attempt to find out what had happened to the whalebone market. "[H]e kindly showed me how they made bone for corsets using a small thin piece of steel covering it with rubber and vulcanizing it" (n.d.:645). "I was sure," Brower adds, "that bone was gone for good." He was right. Brower (n.d.:658) wrote sadly of the end of commercial whaling at Barrow. In the spring of 1913, he notes in his autobiography, "Jack [Hadley] and I went out because we did not know what to do other-

wise. It had been our habit so long we did not seem right not to go on the flaw [floe]."

For the Iñupiat, the commercial whaling vessels and crew offered their first real glimpse of western culture and technology. At times that contact seemed transitory, while at other times the Barrow people found the crews of several stranded whaling ships living in their very backyards.[15] The whalers introduced western goods to the Iñupiat, the most important of which were the cheap guns they brought with them to trade for baleen, ivory, and fresh meat. By the time Brower reached Barrow in 1886, the rifle had replaced the bow and arrow for land hunting and was being used in sealing as well. Twenty years later, guns were cheap and plentiful in Barrow, being part of the annual provisions supplied whaling crews by their employers. Stefansson (1912:61) remarked after his 1908 trip to Barrow, "There are few Eskimo who will use a rifle more than one year . . . and you see rifles and shotguns, which our most fastidious sportsmen would consider good as new, lying around on the beach, thrown away by Eskimo who have no realization of their value because of the ease with which they have always obtained them in the past." The numerous ships that were wrecked in the Arctic ice provided another source of goods and, according to eyewitnesses, the Iñupiat became skilled at expropriating wrecks. The razing of the *Daniel Webster* in 1880 by the villagers of Nuvuk was probably characteristic of many.[16] Commented John Muir:

> The Point Barrow Eskimos, keenly familiar with the actions of the winds and currents on the movements of the ice, watched the struggling ship, and came aboard before the ice had yet closed upon her, like wolves scenting their prey from afar. Many a wreck had they enjoyed here, and now, sure of yet another, they ran about the ship examining every moveable article, and narrowly scanning the rigging and sails with reference to carrying away as much as possible of the best of everything, such as the sails, lead pipe for bullets, hard bread, sugar, tobacco, etc., in case they should have but a short time to work. . . . As soon as she was given up, the Eskimos climbed into the rigging, and dexterously cut away and secured all the sails, which they value highly for making sails for their large traveling canoes [*umiat*] and for covers their summer huts. Then they secured as much lead as possible. . . .
>
> The ship was then about five miles from the Eskimo village, and the natives were allowed to assist in carrying everything that had been saved.

> Under the circumstances, in getting over the five miles of ice with such riches, they, like white men, reasoned themselves into the belief that everything belonged to them, even the chronometers and sextants. Accordingly, at the village a general division was made in so masterly a manner that by the time the officers and crew reached the place their goods had vanished into a hundred-odd dens and holes; and when hungry, they asked for some of their own biscuits, the natives complacently offered to sell them at the rate of so much tobacco apiece. Even the chronometers had been divided, it is said, after being taken apart, the wheels and bits of shining metal being regarded as fine jewelry for the young women and children to wear. [1917:188–89]

Among the goods liberated from the *Daniel Webster* by the Iñupiat was a keg of rum. Before 1880 the Iñupiat had become accustomed to trading for alcohol, and in their scavenging more than thirty wrecked ships from 1871 "[they] came across the medicine chest and as they had been used to buying alcohol from [the whalers], they imagined that anything in a bottle was whiskey. They drank everything that was liquid" (Brower n.d.:142). "In trying all that the medicine chests contained many were poisoned, so many dying in one village that it was abandoned, and never used again. This was the village of Nu-na-reah, south of Point Belcher two miles" (n.d.:230). By 1888 Point Hope natives had learned to distill "hootch," and a group of them who came to Utqiagvik seeking employment as whaling crew members with Brower's station taught the Utqiagvik people how to distill alcohol.

Brower himself contributed to the enterprise, trading flour and molasses—the primary ingredients in hootch—to natives during the lean winter of 1889–90 for caribou meat, and although he does not say so in his writings, according to some Barrow elders, Brower got his start with the whaling station by trading whiskey to Utqiagvik natives in the years before 1890.[17] Later, however, Brower crusaded against alcohol consumption and smashed stills in an attempt to eradicate the village of the deadly brew. In 1897 he cut off the sugar and molasses rations of more than a hundred commercial whalers who were stranded in Barrow for the winter when some of them set up several Eskimos with stills. The guilty sailors confessed, sugar rations were resumed, and "the Eskimo quit from that time, never since has a bit been made in this village" (Brower n.d.:530).

The whalers were presumably the major vectors of influenza and

other diseases that killed off large numbers of natives between 1851 and 1902. Simpson (1875:237–38) notes that forty people died of the flu at Nuvuk during the winter of 1851–52. Murdoch (1892:54), who followed Simpson by thirty years, also remarked on the population decline and, commenting on the prostitution of native women to whalers, suggests that venereal disease was introduced through these contacts. In 1900, a few days after *Nalukataq*, the natives contracted from whalers who had stopped at Barrow en route to Herschel Island "some kind of sickness like the flue we had a few years ago" (Brower n.d.:565). The inland people who had come to the coast to trade were hardest hit. On the advice of their shamans, they started inland, dying en route "all along the coast and up the rivers" (Brower n.d.:565). "That was," wrote Brower, "the end of the eskimo living inland." In 1902 another disaster hit as a measles epidemic wiped out 126 of the Barrow population. Despite the toll disease took among the Barrow people, Stefansson (1912:66) suggests the population remained more or less constant from 1880 to the second decade of the twentieth century due to the immigration of Eskimos, attracted by the prosperity of the whaling industry from areas as far flung as St. Lawrence Island, the MacKenzie Delta, and the headwaters of the Colville, Noatak, and Kobuk Rivers.[18]

The commercial whalers of the nineteenth century brought changes to Iñupiat whaling practices which are still in evidence today. Charles Brower may have been the only white man who went whaling with Iñupiat[19] using exclusively aboriginal whaling gear. In the 1870s Eskimos began using modern whaling gear (darting guns, shoulder guns)[20] obtained from whalers and from wrecked whaling ships. Though Iñupiat whalers at Barrow blamed use of the white man's gear for a bad year in 1882 (and thus they reverted to use of the stone-bladed harpoon in 1883), the new equipment soon replaced everything but the traditional *ugruk* bladder floats and the skin boats. At first, though, the Iñupiat were highly suspicious of white whaling methods. Brower recalled their mistrust in 1886 when shore-based commercial whaling began at Barrow:

> Every day . . . we talked of what we expected to do in the spring, mostly catching whales, it got so at last that we had them dead along the ice letting the Eskimo cut them for us, all we wanted was bone. The Eskimo could have the blubber for working for us. I think at times we had as many

> as 10 or 12 tied up at one time in our minds. In everything we did the Eskimo found fault with, saying if we did thus and so the whales would never come along the ice. First they objected to our hammering after the sun came, the whales would hear us, whales could hear a long distance. Our gear was wrong; they had never used that kind, it was pe-li-lak, forbidden by the old time doctors. Tents were out of the question, as for cooking on the ice, that was not to be thought of. We, of course, could not do as they wanted us to. Our boats were wooden whale boats, we planned to stay with them all the season, maybe not coming in at all until whaling was over. When they found out we were getting extra footgear to take with us, that was the limit, then they knew we would never get a whale. [n.d.:267]

Yet, two seasons later (1888) Brower reports that that year's whaling had been the last when many Iñupiat had kept to the old customs. The changes were not all one-sided, however, for shore-based Yankee whalers quickly abandoned the heavy wooden New England whaling boats during spring whaling in favor of the lighter Eskimo *umiaq*.

The commercial whalers were the most important agents of change in northern coastal Alaska. They provided an introduction to western technology and goods and brought permanent changes to native whaling and hunting practices. On the negative side, the industry was responsible for the depletion of the bowhead, the introduction of alcohol, and the diseases that so reduced the native population. Whaling left its mark in yet another significant way as whalers like Jim Allen, Charles Brower, George Leavitt, Fred Hopson, and Tom Gordon took Iñupiat wives and fathered large families. Their mixed-blood children, in many instances, were destined for a life different from that of other Iñupiat. Sadie Brower Neakok is one of perhaps fifty such first-generation native Alaskan children of New England whalers.

In 1890 the Presbyterian church sent its first missionary, L. M. Stevenson, to begin a mission and school at Utqiagvik. Stevenson's initial concern was the traffic in liquor. Liquor, he noted, was the primary item for which natives traded whalebone[21] and it also fueled the prostitution of native women and girls. Believing he would get little assistance from the government in halting the liquor traffic, Stevenson (1892) lamented, "The only remaining course is to educate the people so that they will stop of themselves." Education remained his top priority, and he began school in a small room of the U.S. Government

Refuge Station constructed the year before at Barrow for stranded whalers. Although the pupils were reportedly eager to learn, especially English (which had made virtually no inroads during the commercial whaling presence), the subsistence activities of the Iñupiat and their consequent mobility made for a very short school year. Stevenson noted that on April 14, 1891, "the report of 'whales seen in the lead' set everyone wild with excitement, nearly breaking up the school. All the pupils large enough left immediately to hunt whales, and a few weeks after the remaining boys and girls left to drive the dog teams that were transporting the whalebone and meat to the village from the edge of the ice, from 12 to 20 miles out to sea" (U.S. Bureau of Education 1893:964).

A school and mission house were erected in 1894,[22] and in 1896 H. R. Marsh, a medical student, arrived in Barrow to replace Stevenson and to take on the additional task of ministering to the medical needs of the Barrow people. Marsh learned the Iñupiaq language well enough to preach in it, introduced hymns translated into the native language by Canadian missionaries, formally organized the church in 1899, and performed the first baptisms (Spencer 1959:380). Marsh also became responsible for supervision of the reindeer herd, which was introduced to Barrow in 1898 as relief food for the stranded commercial whalers.[23] In that capacity he also supervised the training of native apprentice herders.[24]

The impact of the missionaries was manifold. They introduced the English language through formal instruction of children; their medical efforts saved lives through the treatment of disease and assistance in difficult childbirth cases; and, as missionaries elsewhere have succeeded in doing, they eventually undercut the authority of the shamans, who, though powerful, were a constant source of fear and anxiety among their own people (Spencer 1959:381).[25] Brower (n.d.:568) remarked that in the winter of 1900–01 the shamans "made their last endeavor to keep some control over the Eskimo. [When their attempts failed] they tried another tack saying they had received messages from above, telling them of a wonderful new religion better for the Eskimos than the white man's. For awhile each had a small following, eventually they lost all their prestige." Later he adds, "This year [1900–01] we lost the last of the devil doctors" [one converted to Christianity, the other hung himself] (n.d.:572).

Much of the Christian doctrine and teachings assimilated by the Barrow people derived not from the missionaries in their presence, but from other sects with which they had indirect contact. Stefansson (1912:38–39) likened the adoption of Christianity among the Eskimos to the spread of "a habit or a fashion," which reached the Barrow people from both Point Hope to the west and the Colville River to the east. Not surprisingly, the form Christianity took represented a synthesis of old and new beliefs and rituals. Despite the eventual demise of the shamans, for example, the new Christianity was interpreted within a context of shamanism. Missionaries were believed, like shamans, to acquire their power directly from a spirit source—God, in this case—and, like shamans, some missionaries were deemed effective and others, feckless. Unfortunately for the Reverend Marsh, he was compared to an ineffectual shaman because "his prayers could not be relied upon to control wind and weather, but that was no reason for supposing that other missionaries were equally powerless" (Stefansson 1912:432–33). On this and other counts, the people of Barrow requested that the Board of Home Missions replace Marsh.[26] Following a similar course of logic, the prohibitions espoused by the church became taboos in the traditional sense, the most rigorously adopted of which was the Sabbath. A cook in the employ of one of the two whaling stations at Barrow attributed the origin of the Sabbath taboo in 1893 to "a couple of Christian Natives from far inland in a southeast direction. They made several speeches about God and Christ to the people. From that time on all the people have begun to notice our Sabbath day. They call it 'Sawakutl Pehchok,' that is, 'a day of no work'" (Abe 1893).[27] Stefansson reports how this taboo affected whaling:

> they would commence on Saturday afternoon to pull back their boats from the edge of the ice and get everything ready for the Sabbath observance. Saturday evening the men themselves would abandon temporarily their boats and gear, on the outer edge of the shore ice, to go ashore and remain there all day Sunday. It usually took them half of Monday to get everything ready for work again. In this manner they lost two days out of every seven from a harvest season of only six weeks in the year.[1912:91]

Brower blamed this practice on the missionaries, complaining, "It may be the only day during the season they have a chance to get their meat and blubber to last them for a year, still they haul their boats back and

all come in to church." Because of the critical importance of whaling to Iñupiat subsistence, however, even the Reverend Marsh exhorted them not to abandon whaling on Sundays, which only increased his disfavor among the people. As Sadie notes in her narrative, the Sunday taboos still held sway when she was growing up. In fact, they remained in effect until the late 1940s, when the Navy oil exploration program hired native workers on a seven-day work week.

The missionaries endeavored to eradicate old customs as well as institute new ones. In the winter of 1900–01 the winter dances in the *qargi* or dance house were halted at missionary behest. Wrote Brower (n.d.:573), "the missionaries did not think [the *qargi*] a good place for the young people to congregate nights, there being no restrictions on any of them, and no doubt they often did what they had been told not to do. So the old dance houses were all demolished and used for fuel. It did not stop the younger people from doing as they had always done. They simply went somewhere else." Eventually the church became the center for socializing, and a bored Charles Brower (n.d.:670) noted in 1913: "Outside of our business there was not anything of interest going on these days, the Eskimo were so religious, that the only thing that interested them were their meetings, at the church, nearly every night there was one of some kind. Never was there any more dancing or story telling as there had been in the first years. Even their games did not seem to be played with the zest that they had been used to showing."

The demolishing of the dance houses for fuel is related to another missionary-induced change—the adoption of frame houses. Both Brower and Stefansson believed the change a great mistake, and Brower tried to persuade natives not to buy lumber. "I knew," he said, "they would not be as comfortable in a small frame house as they were in their own style igloos that had taken them centuries to develop" (n.d.:573). The frame houses were poorly insulated and ventilated and required heating by a stove. As a result, Barrow and environs were soon scoured clean of driftwood; the people looked to coal, the nearest source of which was some fifty miles away, to blubber, to asphalt-soaked sod from natural oil seeps, to blubber-impregnated soil from the kitchen areas of house ruins, and to anything else—like the remains of old dance houses—that would keep the stove going. Houses were cold when fuel supplies were low or were overheated when fuel was

available; they were airless from attempts to chink them from drafts. Due to new-found Christian modesty, Eskimos no longer stripped to the waist indoors (in the sod houses, outer clothing was left in the entryway), but remained overdressed in overheated and poorly ventilated houses. These conditions, along with overcrowding (which the missionaries had hoped to avoid with the new-style housing), set the stage for the rapid transmission of respiratory illnesses.[28]

As elsewhere that missions were established, the church set standards of morality, focusing on the sexual habits of the Iñupiat, discouraging the marriage of pubescent girls and the offering of women to visitors, performing marriages in the church, and so forth. By the time that Sadie Neakok was married in 1940, the standards seem to have been quite stern, and the church membership—the Presbyterian elders in particular—had become arbiters of right and wrong.

In 1921, Mollie Greist, a nurse and the wife of the Presbyterian missionary doctor, formed the "Mothers Club." Through its auspices she gave instruction on hygiene, baby care, and the use of sewing machines. The Mothers Club still exists in Barrow today as a service organization.[29] Church and school personnel worked in concert to effect changes in hygiene, introducing the concepts of regular bathing and laundering. Weekly inspections of village homes were conducted; the neatest proudly displayed a "Cleanest Home of the Week" banner. As a teacher and later as a welfare worker in Barrow, Sadie Neakok was much involved in these activities in the 1930s and 1940s.

Molly and Henry Greist had arrived in 1921 to staff the new Barrow hospital, erected by the Board of Home Missions of the Presbyterian church. Taken over in the 1950s by the U.S. Public Health Service, it eventually encompassed surgical and childbirth facilities, an X-ray department, a laboratory, and a pharmacy. Today its staff includes a dentist and social worker in addition to the resident doctors and nurses.

The educational horizons for Alaskan natives were limited in the early years. A policy statement made in 1911 sums up the position taken by the federal government, which, in 1894, took over from the churches the education of native Alaskans:

> The work of the Bureau of Education in Alaska, which is conducted for the benefit of adults as well as children, is practical in character, emphasis being placed on the development of domestic industries, household arts,

personal hygiene, village sanitation, morality, and the elementary English subjects. [U.S. Bureau of Education, cited in Sonnenfeld 1956:366]

Practical instruction began with mathematics and English. Charles Hawkesworth, a teacher at Barrow from 1908 to 1911, was the first to apply classroom lessons directly to life at Barrow. Concerned with Charles Brower's monopoly on goods and supplies and with the lack of a standard of value for those goods, Hawkesworth (1908) tried to break Brower's hold on the village economy through educating the children: "I wanted to get the children as soon as possible acquainted with values . . . in whalebone, lumber, furs, provisions, and in all articles of trade. . . . The need, pressing need of this school is to give education in comparative values." In their drawing classes, Hawkesworth's pupils planned houses for their own families. "First they would draw the plan on a certain scale and have the paper show each joist and timber required and then figure out in detail the cost of the lumber and sundries needed and also the cost of the freight for landing the materials at Barrow" (Hawkesworth 1910). Although he gave primary emphasis to arithmetic, and the children came to prefer that subject, he also had the children keep simple diaries and write stories in English.

English usage was reinforced by a Tuesday social evening at the schoolteacher's residence. Mrs. Hawkesworth "formed a gathering into a club and had the various officers elected and the usual ballot formed for three months at a time. In this club all the members had practice in talking English, and in speaking pieces, singing songs, playing games and in the way we had of carrying on our municipal and national governments" (Hawkesworth 1910). He adds that this was the most enjoyable event of the school week. By Hawkesworth's time, industrial and domestic arts had become part of the school curriculum. Accordingly, he put the boys to work making and engraving names on wooden grave markers, while his assistant teacher Annie Coodalook instructed the girls in sewing.

When Sadie Neakok became a teacher at Barrow in 1939, she followed a tradition established by Annie Coodalook, the first native teacher hired at Barrow. Native teachers were particularly important in dealing with the youngest students, most of whom spoke no English when they began school. Hawkesworth asserted: "An assistant Native teacher is as necessary as a white man, yes more so for the younger

ones and the Primer classes. Ten new inland children, who have never before seen white people, were registered. They quickly learned the names of English objects through association with their own Eskimo names which Annie could give them" (1910).

By all accounts, church and school could claim success in their endeavors by 1910, as the children were eager learners and the Barrow population were devoted churchgoers. The Iñupiat life style, however, particularly in the years following the end of commercial whaling, was not compatible with either regular school or church attendance. By 1914, commercial interests in the North Slope area had turned from whaling to furs, particularly Arctic and red fox furs, which were in demand for coats Outside. The fur trade proved lucrative for the next fifteen or so years, and H. Liebes and Company, which was in partnership with Charles Brower at Barrow, opened fur trading stations at Wainwright, Beechey Point, Barter Island, and Demarcation Point. Though whaling continued to be important to Iñupiat subsistence, furs provided the wherewithal to obtain much-needed goods and supplies, and winter traplines took Barrow trappers far afield of the village for extended periods of time.[30]

Nonetheless, the church had a strong hold on its membership, and Brower, whose livelihood now depended on the sale of furs, complained in 1920: "I had to almost force many to even leave the village during the trapping season. The missionaries wanted them to stay around so they could attend church three times every week. I thought that they could be religious out in the country as well as here and still make a living. We finally got them to trap as they found there was no credit [at the store] for those that did not try and do something for themselves" (n.d.:694). Parents wishing their children to attend school left them in the village with grandparents while they tended their traplines. Sadie remarked, "The grandparents were very valuable to the children. They were the ones that raised the kids, not the real parents. I've seen that many times; it was like that when I was growing up."

Trappers from Barrow were not totally dependent on Brower's trading station, for fur prices were high in the 1920s and there were other posts to the east of Barrow where they could be traded. The fur shipments and prices peaked in 1925 and again in 1929, but after a particularly bad winter in 1927–28, Liebes decided to close the Alaskan branch of its fur trading business. The various stations were sold one by

one, though Brower remained in partnership with Liebes until 1938, when he assumed full ownership of the Cape Smythe Whaling and Trading Company.

The Depression visited hard times upon Barrow. Fuel was in short supply and fur prices were at an all time low, resulting in a subsequent loss of store credit. Many Barrow people are reported to have migrated inland in 1936 to take advantage of resources there. Though the caribou herd was slowly beginning to rebound from a population low, relatively few were available close to the coast.[31] Were it not for the reindeer herds many people might have starved to death.

Reindeer herding had been introduced to the Alaskan Arctic in 1892 as a replenishable replacement for the declining caribou herds and as a home industry that would, through the sale of meat and other products, provide a source of income for the native people. Additionally, it was hoped that sled-trained deer might replace carnivorous dogs, which compete with humans for food resources. The first reindeer arrived in Barrow in 1898, sent as part of a relief mission to aid the crews of seven wrecked whaling ships who were stranded there for the winter. Only part of the herd was slaughtered to help feed the crews; the remainder (125) formed the nucleus of the Barrow reindeer herd, which, as it increased, was apportioned among native herders. Although ultimately the reindeer herding program failed at Barrow due to a variety of causes,[32] reindeer were particularly important to subsistence during the Depression years when other resources failed.

In February of 1940 Charles Brower wrote to his friend A. M. Bailey at the Denver Museum of Natural History: "This has been the worst year I have ever put in at Barrow. No furs and what few we have there is no sale for at prices that does not pay to collect them. Then all the village has been sick with the measles and are just beginning to get around again. Everyone has been hungry and I am broke trying to keep things going" (Brower 1940*a*). By August the situation was no better, and regulations on subsistence hunting presaged the Outside controls that Barrow people would face a generation later. Brower again unloaded to Bailey:

> There has been no ice here or down the coast for over a month and a half so there is no hunting—no seals and of course no walrus. All the natives are getting hungry. There is plenty of caribou just a little way from here to the east but the restrictions are so that no one is allowed to kill them.[33]

> Now the Department of the Interior through the Biological Survey has issued hunting licenses to the eskimo and every duck, ptarmigan, deer, moose or sheep that they kill has to be reported. They are of course allowed to kill a few only in case of starvation but they have no clothing and meat now. The reindeer has been so desimated [*sic*] by over killing and the wolves during the past few years that now the reindeer service is trying to increase the herds. No deer are to be killed except a few for sale. No owner in the herd can have deer killed for himself but if he wants any skins that are killed has to buy them back from the reindeer company. They have nothing to buy with so all are hard up for meat and clothing. It is pitiful to see the kids around with nothing on but rags that a ragpicker would pass by. . . .
>
> A few of the Eskimo will leave here to hunt deer [caribou] saying they will take a chance with the game commission. I can't stop them for they will not listen. I was appointed wildlife agent but can do nothing as they will not listen and say the deer are theirs for food and clothing and always have been. I certainly wish that I had quit here about ten years ago for there is no pleasure here anymore.
>
> There has been a taboo on grizzlies. The last year or so unlawful to kill them and if one is killed by the natives for food he can't sell the skin and I have to get a special permit for sending one out to some museum or university. I suppose seals will next be protected. Excuse the kick but I can't help it. Things are rotten.[1940*b*]

In a letter written the next year to Stefansson, Brower (1941) concluded, "I don't think that religion and education accomplished much for them. All most [all] of them are poverty stricken." Brower lived just long enough to see the beginning of the emergence of the Barrow people from poverty during the last years of the war.

In 1940 there were only a handful of wage-paying jobs in Barrow for Iñupiat. Wage-earners included a few janitorial workers at the hospital and school, nurse's aides, weather observers for the U.S. Meteorological Station, airplane mechanic's assistants, storekeepers, and two schoolteachers, one of whom was Sadie Neakok. A coal mine, opened at Meade River in 1942–43 to supply fuel for Barrow homes, employed natives to run the mine. There was seasonal work as longshoremen when the annual supply ships unloaded, and as guides for hunting and exploring parties. Oil exploration at the end of the war, however, really opened up wage labor to local native people.

Charles Brower in 1886 had been the first white man to see the oil seeps near Cape Simpson; he had had a sample assayed in San Francisco but had remarked, "[It was] so far away that it was of no use to anyone." In 1923 an executive order set apart 37,000 square miles of territory, including the oil seep lakes, as National Petroleum Reserve No. 4. Interest in NPR, or "Pet-4," developed during World War II as the country looked for a supplementary source of fuel for naval operations in the Pacific Theater. Some Iñupiat helped in the construction of a military airfield just north of Barrow in 1944, and many more turned to the production of native arts and crafts, which they sold to the some two hundred Navy Seabees brought in to construct "Camp Barrow" in 1944.[34] Brower (1944) said of the Navy presence, "I have lived here a long time but at last civilization has caught up with me. Since the navy took over here everything is on the move. What they are doing I can't write about for at the present time everything is censored but plenty is going on." In 1946 a civilian contractor (ARCON) took over from the Seabees; in addition to the three hundred or so men at its camp, ARCON employed Iñupiat labor from the summer of 1946 until the end of operations in the fall of 1953.

The main barrier to native employment was the high incidence of TB in the Barrow population, and native applicants were required to submit to a complete physical examination. Because of the potential for long-term employment of natives in the area, a study of TB in the Barrow-Wainwright area was undertaken in 1948. Children were vaccinated, and active cases were isolated. Sonnenfeld (1956:530–31) comments, "the needs of the defense program precipitated long needed public health activity which might otherwise have continued at the snail's pace which the lack of personnel and appropriations had previously imposed."[35] Much work at the base was seasonal—during the summer—and the work week was typically seven days with time-and-a-half paid for overtime. With employment at the Navy base, the old taboo against work on the Sabbath formally came to an end after nearly a half-century.

According to Sadie, almost all the able-bodied men in the village from age sixteen on up were employed at the base in on-the-job training. Nate Neakok, Sadie's husband, worked there as a mechanic for several years; his initiation into wage labor was not uncommon:

> They [Barrow people] didn't know anything about machinery and carpentry. I remember Nate telling me when he came from his first job, "That boss of mine wanted me to go and start that cherry picker and drive it, and I didn't know which end to start with, let alone how to start it." And he said he fiddled around with that cherry picker until the thing started, and he didn't know how to stop it, and he ran right through one of the buildings—the old shops. And when he finally got it stopped, he thought sure that's the end of his job. But when he turned around, his boss was laughing at him.

Over two hundred Barrow natives were employed during the seven years of oil exploration. In general the turnover was quite high, as the average length of employment was only two to five-and-a-half months. A few, however, including Nate Neakok, were employed on a long-term basis.

Wage labor brought unprecedented money into Barrow. It was an asset to whaling because of the need to purchase whaling gear and the practice of native whaling captains supporting their crews during whaling season. Sonnenfeld (1956) reports an increase in the number of crews which took part in whaling during the years of ARCON employment, and a record number of whales (seventeen) taken in 1953, the last year of operations. At the same time the new money brought its problems. "Kids didn't know where to spend the money," Sadie commented. "We didn't have a bank. . . . They were spending the money as fast as it was coming in, buying out the stores." Wage labor also attracted Iñupiat from other communities, particularly Wainwright, seventy-five miles southwest of Barrow: "There were people from all over starting to come into Barrow," Sadie remembered. "And there was no housing. It was terrible. And some of them became welfare recipients, looking for jobs, and that's how Barrow grew so fast."

Grow, it did. Between 1939 and 1950 the population had increased by 300 percent. In response to the population growth, the Alaska Native Service launched a housing program, assisted by the Navy's free shipment of lumber. Approximately one hundred frame homes were built between 1947 and 1953. During the same period, streets were surveyed in Barrow, and, with the assistance of ARCON, a village generator was installed and a sanitary waste disposal program was initiated (which consisted of hauling 55-gallon drums filled with waste out on the ice to be taken away by ocean currents).

The period of employment at the Navy base was an especially important one for Barrow natives. Sonnenfeld (1956:560), who conducted his research on Barrow subsistence during the last year of ARCON operations, concluded, "If nothing else, ARCON employment gave the Eskimo a taste of modern living and, in this sense, allowed him a choice. He could either remain primarily a hunter and trapper, or else, through employment, associate himself with a more 'western' type of living, which implied as well an association of dependence." Contemporary observers of Barrow life style might disagree that the choice was either/or; indeed, by the late 1970s it appeared that one could do both.

Oil exploration was brought to a temporary close in 1953, though the defense presence and some employment for local natives remained. The Air Force took over the old Navy base when construction of the DEW-line station began in 1954. The Arctic Research Laboratory (ARL), operated by the Navy and the University of Alaska to conduct biological and geological Arctic research, was the other occupant of the camp four miles north of Barrow. ARL (later, NARL; see note 4, this chapter) moved onto the base with eight full-time employees in 1947 and grew to more than sixty before the end of its thirty-three years of operation. The laboratory was a minor source of employment for Barrow natives; usually seven to eight Iñupiat worked there as assistants. The base was decommissioned in 1981 and the facility was turned over to the village corporation that was formed after land claims. Today only about thirty people are employed at NARL, to maintain the base and operate the gas fields that supply natural gas to the town (Alaska Consultants 1983:12).

Construction of the DEW-line system began the year following the closing of oil exploration operations. In all, seventeen Distant Early Warning stations were built across the Alaskan Arctic, and Barrow was a center for construction activities. For the next several years, employment was available for Barrow natives at higher wages than those offered by ARCON in the preceding years.

Following the war and the creation of the airstrip, regular air service to Barrow was mostly military, but the base strip also served as a landing field for the first mail- and passenger-service planes operated by Wien Airlines. Early air service on DC-3s to Fairbanks was once a week. Sadie, who traveled perhaps more than other villagers, recalled, "When

the plane would land up there [at the base] we would have to take whatever vehicle—dog team, weasel,[36] or whatever we could find—and go up there and fly out. We didn't have cars then. If you were late for your flight, you had to wait another week to go out." She remembered in particular trying to catch the plane for a trip to Washington, D.C.; the four-and-a-half mile ride to the airport took two hours on Nate's weasel. "Our weasel broke down, and my poor white dress, it had blotches of oil from trying to help Nate put that darn machine back together."

Wien Airlines in 1954 began what has become an important industry for the local community. That summer a hotel was completed, and Wien Airlines arranged scheduled tours of Barrow, bringing in some two to three hundred tourists that first season. In thirty-plus years the tourist business has increased twenty-fold. Occasionally some tourists sneak away from the scheduled activities, like the group who, on the hotel clerk's recommendation, showed up in the summer of 1984 at Sadie's for a taste of *maktak*.[37] "I get quite involved in tourism," Sadie commented. "It's just that people that have worked up here feel at ease telling the tourists, 'Well, maybe Sadie can help you.' So they end up at my house."

At the time of statehood in 1959, Barrow had the appearance of a small town. Though there were no phones in the village yet, generators owned by the Bureau of Indian Affairs (BIA) provided electricity to the hospital and school, and the native cooperative store distributed power to homes from its generator. Black-and-white TV—consisting of month-old tapes from Seattle and Anchorage broadcast over a single local channel—was still several years in the future. The town boasted two movie theaters, a café, a beauty shop, a couple of stores, and three churches.[38] The mail came in twice a week by plane; news of the world was received on the ubiquitous radio; direct communication with Outside was via short-wave radio at the "wireless station," and transportation about town or out into the tundra was by dog team. Village children attended the BIA school through the eighth grade, but only a small percentage went on to high school, which required leaving the village for one of the BIA boarding schools—Chemawa in Oregon or, more likely, Mt. Edgecombe in Sitka. Statehood brought with it the incorporation of Barrow as a city, and a plethora of rules and regulations new to the Barrow people. In 1960 the newly appointed

state judicial officer, Magistrate Sadie Neakok, opened court at her kitchen table.

The 1960s ushered in an era of growing ethnic consciousness. In 1961 Barrow people collectively and successfully protested enforcement of the Migratory Bird Act of 1916, which prohibited the hunting of waterfowl during the only season these birds were present in the Arctic (see pp. 180–84). The fall following the "duck-in," northern and northwestern Iñupiat village leaders met in Barrow at a conference, "Iñupiat Paitot" (People's Heritage), to discuss their common problems. Aboriginal subsistence and land rights emerged as top concerns. In 1966 the Arctic Slope Native Association, a regional grouping of North Slope villages, was organized in Barrow for the purpose of resolving native land claims (see Gallagher 1974). Native land claims on the North Slope had become a pressing issue in the wake of the state of Alaska's lease sales in the Prudhoe Bay area between 1964 and 1967, and the Arctic Slope Native Association emerged as one of the most powerful regional organizations comprising the statewide Alaska Federation of Natives, also founded in 1966. The discovery of oil on the North Slope in 1968 heightened the land-claims issue and eventually led to enactment of the Alaska Native Claims Settlement Act (ANCSA) in 1971.[39]

Alaskan natives eligible under the provisions of ANCSA were organized into one of twelve (later thirteen) regional corporations, and those not claiming urban areas as their place of residence were additionally enrolled in a village corporation. Land and money of the settlement (44 million acres and $962 million) were disbursed through the corporations, the idea being that corporations—especially the regional ones, which were required to be profit-making—would wisely invest their assets for the benefit of their shareholders and would be self-sustaining. The Iñupiat of the North Slope were enrolled in the Arctic Slope Regional Corporation (ASRC), whose membership included that of the parent organization, Arctic Slope Native Association.[40]

Under ASRC's wing are the village corporations of the eight villages located on the North Slope. ASRC has invested most of its settlement monies in subsidiaries doing business on the North Slope (which has meant jobs locally for Iñupiat). As the regional corporations (but not village ones) own subsurface rights to land, ASRC's 5.6 million acres have been viewed in terms of their potential development and some

have been leased to oil companies for exploration. The village corporation of Barrow, Ukpeagvik Iñupiat Corporation (UIC), controls about 200,000 acres. Both corporations have been moderately successful and, while the individual shareholder may not have benefited in any noticeable way financially, the corporations have given the Iñupiat a measure of control over the land, providing as well local jobs and experience in business management.[41] Nonetheless, throughout Alaska, native people have perceived serious problems with ANCSA. Their discontent has grown as the December 1991 date that marks the expiration of certain provisions of the act draws nearer.

A review of ANCSA, which heard evidence from native peoples throughout the state, was commissioned in 1983 by the Inuit Circumpolar Conference, an international organization of Eskimo peoples, and was largely funded by the North Slope Borough (see below). The report, authored by Canadian law professor Thomas Berger, was instrumental in the passage of legislation in December 1987 to amend certain features of the act; on February 3, 1988, "ANCSA Amendments of 1987" became Public Law 100–241.[42]

Despite the importance of the regional and village corporations, the Iñupiat have gained more control over their destiny through their regional government, the North Slope Borough. Through the formation of a borough encompassing all of the North Slope and recognized by the state in 1972, the Iñupiat acquired jurisdiction over 51 million additional acres of land. The impetus for formation of the borough came from recognition that such a government had taxation powers within its boundaries; the North Slope oil industry comprises today the tax base for the borough. In 1974 the borough received a home-rule charter from the state which allows it to assume all powers not expressly forbidden by state law. These include tax collection, education, planning, and zoning (Peat, Marwick, Mitchell & Co. 1978:284). Through general elections the borough has acquired such additional special powers as sewage, light, power, heat, water, transportation, housing, police, historic site preservation, and others.

The borough encompasses some 88,000 square miles of territory, includes eight villages, and serves a population of approximately 8,300, about 65 percent of whom are Iñupiat.[43] The borough government is headed by an elected mayor (who has always been Iñupiaq) serving a three-year term, and an elected assembly of seven members. The

borough has a massive capital improvements program, initiated in 1974 and fueled by its millions in tax dollars and the sale of municipal bonds. To date the program has assisted all North Slope Borough villages, providing new housing and public buildings, road construction, improved sewage and sanitation, and updated fuel delivery systems. When the Bureau of Indian Affairs turned responsibility for education over to the borough in 1975, new schools were constructed in every village. Barrow High School, with its swimming pool, indoor track, television studio, machine shops, and computer laboratory is the showpiece of them all. Home rule for the borough has also brought local/regional control over schools; the seven-member North Slope Borough School Board (presently, all Iñupiat), makes decisions on programmatic as well as budgetary issues.

The North Slope Borough is the major employer in Barrow (and the other villages); in 1982, 44 percent of the jobs in Barrow were with the North Slope Borough.[44] In addition to its role as employer, the borough is the guardian of the Iñupiat lifeway. The borough's Commission on Iñupiat History, Language and Culture has undertaken as its mission the inventory of all traditional land-use areas within the borough and the recording and preservation of Iñupiat language and culture. The commission has periodically brought together North Slope elders for conferences on topics ranging from oil spills to traditional law, and, in accordance with its mission, has sponsored oral history and archæological research. The North Slope Borough's comprehensive plan for land use and its coastal-zone management program give top priority to preserving and enhancing Iñupiat culture and the natural resources that sustain that lifeway.

Over its short life the borough has had its troubles. Its per capita indebtedness is higher than that of any other city in Alaska, higher in fact than that of the entire state. Many wonder what will be the borough's future when the last petroleum resources have been extracted from North Slope oil and gas fields. The borough has had leadership problems as well. Although a number of non-natives serve in high administrative advisory capacities, the borough leadership is drawn from a small pool of capable and educated natives, most of whom also hold executive positions in other North Slope institutions—the regional or village corporations, the Whaling Captains Association, various firms that contract with the borough for construction, and so forth.

The wearing of such multiple hats creates conflicts of interest. More seriously, in the spring of 1984 the North Slope Borough was rocked by scandal; the then mayor was accused of awarding payoffs and illegal contracts to Outside firms who curried his favor. Picked up by the national press, the scandal was called by the *Wall Street Journal* "a painful lesson for a culture caught between ancient tribal ways and the ways of the 20th century America" (Wells 1985). A new administration, which has tightened its own financial belt and has supported the ongoing investigation of the old, has helped to restore faith in the government both to borough residents and financial investors. Faith in the North Slope Borough is important, for more than anything else, the borough has given the Iñupiat of the North Slope a sense of self-determination and confidence in their future.

In the wake of the momentous changes in Barrow, an Iñupiat way of life still survives. It is manifest in the summertime hunters offshore in their *umiat*, the babies piggybacked inside their mothers' colorful handmade parkas, and the Iñupiaq names of buildings and streets. Its least visible manifestations are its most important: the sharing of resources, the networks of kin ties, the native ceremonies, and, perhaps most of all, the value of the land and sea and all the associations "place" has in the Iñupiat collective and individual history. Whatever the outcome, it is clear that Barrow and the North Slope have become a testing ground where the success of the wedding of modern government, western technology, and big money with the values Iñupiat place on their heritage and traditional lands will be decided. In the recent history of Barrow a few determined individuals, like Sadie Neakok, have been dedicated to making that marriage work. As Sadie has often remarked, "Sometimes I feel like the mother to this whole town." Indeed, she has nurtured Barrow and its people—provisioning, teaching, guiding, disciplining—for forty years.

2

The Northernmost American and His Family

To the outside world Charles Brower was known as America's most northerly pioneer and the Alaskan Arctic's longest non-native resident. To the Iñupiat of Barrow and environs he was a white umialik, *a rich man and a whaling captain, who helped revolutionize whaling and introduced a steady supply of the white man's goods into the community. He was fifty-three when Sadie, his sixth child, was born.*

Brower grew up in New York City and neighboring New Jersey. He was groomed for education at Annapolis but ran off to sea at age thirteen instead. By the time he was seventeen he had been to Australia, South America, and India. In 1884 Brower signed on with the San Francisco–based Pacific Steam Whaling Company to sail to Corwin Bluff, east of Cape Lisburne, Alaska, to open up coal fields there to fuel the company's steam-driven whaling vessels in the Arctic. "We were to stake all we could of it," he notes, "and if we could get enough each year, to supply the steamers. We were also to trade with the Eskimos for furs, whalebone,[1] and ivory" (Brower n.d.:115).

Brower helped construct a small building at the Corwin Coal Mine to house the stakers, and, eager to see more of the country, he set out in December of 1884 with an Eskimo guide for Cape Smythe (Barrow) where the company had taken over a station built three years before by the U.S. Arctic Exploring Expedition.[2] Brower's contract gave him the freedom to explore the country, as long as he relinquished everything he acquired in trade to the company; so, that first year he saw not only the area between Lisburne and Barrow but also traveled west and south along the coast to Point Hope, Cape Krusenstern, to what is now Kotzebue, and inland to Noatak.

After a year in the Arctic, Brower "left the ice for home," explaining, "I wanted to quit and start somewhere else, Africa by preference" (n.d.:200–1), but the Pacific Steam Whaling Company persuaded him to stay with the company and put him to work in their San Francisco shipyard for the winter.

In 1886 Brower was asked to go to Barrow to take charge of the whaling station there. "I did not care to go back to Alaska, and refused; they, however, would not take no for an answer, so that I finally told them that if my chum George Leavitt would go, and would take charge of their station I would go along as assistant. Never thinking he would accept, as he always said one year had been enough for him . . . he accepted their offer, leaving me not a leg to stand on" (n.d.:202). Arriving with Leavitt in Barrow in the fall of 1886, Brower established what was to be his home base for the fifty-nine remaining years of his life. In 1889 he took over from Leavitt as manager of the station.

For nearly thirty seasons following, Charlie Brower went "out on the ice" as a commercial whaler. By 1893 Brower had become dissatisfied with the Pacific Steam Whaling Company and persuaded H. Liebes and Company of San Francisco to back him and fellow trader/whaler Tom Gordon. Liebes was to handle the furs and baleen and to outfit a trading company, managed by Brower and Gordon, which they dubbed the Cape Smythe Whaling and Trading Company . When the price of furs declined dramatically during the Depression, Liebes was forced to let the company go, and in 1938 Brower scraped up enough of his savings to buy them out and take it over. The Cape Smythe Whaling and Trading Company, now a general store, has remained in the hands of the Brower family ever since.

The indefatigable Charlie Brower was well suited for the role of self-designated "northernmost American." He was not only whaler and storekeeper but also welcoming committee for arriving teachers, missionaries, and explorers; resident authority on native culture and language; amateur archæologist; natural historian; and lay physician and surgeon in the days before Barrow's hospital. He also eventually became the U.S. Government's representative in Barrow in the appointed roles of postmaster, U.S. Commissioner, and wildlife agent. He is seen through the eyes of several of his Outside friends in their writings. Wrote C. L. Andrews in The Eskimo and His Reindeer in Alaska *(1939:75–76), "Brower was a royal host, keen, traveled, competent, with a fund of experiences from sailor days in Amsterdam to this farthest corner of the Northwest. He was equally at ease, in San Francisco, New York, or in the Arctic." Mollie Greist, nurse at Barrow from 1921–37, remarked similarly about Brower in a letter to her brother: "Mr. Brower himself is a remarkable man in many ways—well read, cultured, educated, a man of means, a great museum man, a lover of natural and ancient history. . . . [he is] full of information if you know how to get it out of him. . . . He belongs to the big clubs in New York—Explorer's Club and National Geographic Club, etc.,*

and he is somebody when he hits New York. He travels all over when he goes out and spends all the money he wants and has his whole family taken care of in case of his death. . . . A good talk with Mr. Brower can be of more interest to you than if I wrote steady for six months" (Greist 1968:131).

Because of his many-faceted occupation and his place of residence, Brower had important and powerful friends Outside. On his periodic year-long trips south, he would call upon them. During one such trip in 1905 he managed a private audience with Theodore Roosevelt, with whom he exchanged big-game hunting yarns. Most of his Outside friends, though, were explorers, adventurers, or scientists who had ventured into his Arctic outpost. Brower claims to have been the first to greet Roald Amundsen in 1906 when the Norwegian completed his historic voyage through the Northwest Passage. He staked out an airfield for the first airplane-landing in Barrow, made by scientist Hubert Wilkins and aviator Ben Eielson in March of 1926. Wilkins and Eielson's historic flight out onto the polar ice the following year landed them at Barrow for an extended period, when Brower housed them at his station and repaired their damaged propellor.

Young Sadie, an incidental child-witness to these historic events, made the rounds of the laps of famous men. She remembers sitting on Ben Eielson's lap as the engine oil for their airplane was being heated on the station's cookstove, and, from the vantage point of Amundsen's lap when he visited in 1923, she reminisces: "His nose was so big; I used to marvel at that nose."[3] Others came by plane. Brower, en route home from a trip Outside, just missed Charles and Anne Morrow Lindbergh, who flew to Barrow in August of 1931 (Sadie's older brother David photographed them). Wiley Post and Will Rogers were on their way to pay a visit to Brower in 1935 when they crashed at Walakpa, twelve miles to the southwest.

Because of his knowledge of and close relations with the native people, Brower had contacts with many museums. His numerous collections found their way into the Smithsonian Institution, the National Museums of Canada, and the American Museum of Natural History. He assisted in archæological excavations and provided ethnographic information to various individuals and institutions. Brower also collected ornithological specimens for Alfred M. Bailey at the Denver Museum of Natural History, sometimes sending Sadie off into the tundra with lunch and a shotgun to look for birds. Bailey, a naturalist who later assumed the directorship of the Denver Museum of Natural History, spent 1921–22 in the north collecting mammal and bird specimens for the museum. In fact, he made a trip to Barrow specifically to enlist Brower's

assistance in collecting natural history specimens for the Denver museum. The young naturalist became good friends with Brower, describing him as "the most interesting person in the entire North Country." Bailey taught Charles Brower and his sons how to prepare bird and mammal specimens, and "as a result in the ensuing years the Browers added greatly to the knowledge of the range of Arctic birds, doubling the number of species known from the Barrow region" (Bailey n.d.).

Brower's closest and longest friendship, however, was with explorer and scholar Vilhjalmur Stefansson. They met in 1908 when Stefansson stopped at Brower's station stock up on supplies; when Stefansson returned in January of 1909 and began collecting folk tales at Barrow, Brower served as his interpreter. "I stood it as long as I could, then turned him over to the assistant school-teacher, an Eskimo girl who had been Outside for a number of years. I never got a chance to read and hardly any time to attend to my own affairs" (n.d.:628). Stefansson and Brower remained in close contact until Brower's death in 1945.

It was Stefansson who persuaded the busy Brower to write his memoirs. Between 1927 and 1938 Brower typed 895 manuscript pages, mailed in installments to Stefansson in New York.[4] Stefansson lined up a potential publisher and supplied encouragement to Brower who, though he continued to churn out pages, had little self-confidence in his writing, describing his own words as "trash." Brower depended heavily on Stefansson's help, remarking (2/25/28): "Just finished my writing, from 1877 to 1925. And am mailing to you the last installment. . . . I realize that it is bum, the spelling bad and the punctuation worse, and that to be of any value it will all have to be rewritten by someone that knows how, and that I will have to be along with whoever does it." A month later (3/15/28) he again wrote Stefansson, "I thank you for the interest you take in my poor effort to become a literary person. . . . If you have read what I have written maybe you could tell me what more there is I can write about, I know there is much that I could elaborate and have not done so because the words do not come to me quick enough." Brower evidently decided on his own what to add, commenting to Stefansson in July 1928, "The last two years many interesting things have happened that may be well to have along with the other manuscript."

Throughout, Stefansson was enthusiastic about the manuscript, prodding Brower, "Your manuscript is awfully good stuff" (5/11/30). Publication, however, was a long time coming. Stefansson urged publication of sections of the manuscript first in a magazine series, and Alfred Bailey, who had received a

copy of the manuscript from Brower in 1929, rewrote from it "a series of first person True Life Adventure publications under Charlie's name in the Blue Book, *then one of the popular magazines of the McCall Company" (Bailey n.d.). The four articles appeared between 1932–34.*[5] *It was another eight years before Charlie Brower's life story was published in book form by Dodd Mead. Four months before he received a telegram informing him of its acceptance, Brower had reported to Stefansson (2/22/41), "My book has been to allmost* [sic] *all the big publishers in New York and for some reason they have all turned it down so have just about given up hopes that it will ever be published. There is something I can't figure out. They like the mss but not the way it is written or something to that effect." The final publication,* Fifty Years Below Zero, *was rewritten and condensed from the original manuscript, entitled* The Northernmost American.[6] *The Introduction to the book was penned by Stefansson, who describes it as "the life-story of one of my oldest and dearest friends." He adds, "in subscribing myself a friend I speak for most of the explorers, whalers, traders and missionaries who have reached or passed the north tip of Alaska since 1884" (Brower 1942:viii).*

The unedited version, The Northernmost American, *is a curious memoir. For those who would wander through all 895 of its pages, it is a treasure trove of ethnographic and historical data. Yet while it provides a personal history of Brower, it reveals little of Charles Brower, the man. The author portrays himself as having trod through life with a determined optimism; his disappointments, misfortunes, failings, and passions are smoothed over with understatement. Of the death of his first wife and baby in the measles epidemic of 1902, for example, he writes simply: "Christmas was not so cheerfull* [sic] *this year." The narrative is strictly chronological, and soon the reader can forecast the unfolding of each year: Christmas and New Year's at the station occur "as usual" with a big dinner and party attended by the community's white residents; summer is heralded with the arrival of the first of the season's ships; people of note arriving at Barrow for that year are duly chronicled; the biennial appearance of new schoolteachers and missionaries to replace those who have become Arctic-worn is faithfully noted along with Brower's evaluation of them—Richardson, Hawkesworth, and Spriggs were fine fellows, respected throughout the community, while Cram was a ne'er-do-well.*

Brower has an incredible memory for the whales taken by his outfit, recounting how each was pursued and who did what in the chase. He has an equally good recall of the year-to-year availability of other game, recording the abundance or scarcity of polar bears and foxes, the taking of caribou and eider

ducks, and the cycling of wolves, lemmings, and snowy owls. Brower's comings and goings during his periodic year-long visits Outside are recorded in similar detail: he stops in on the Liebes and Company headquarters, visits a daughter in San Francisco, another daughter in San Diego, a son in Corvallis, Alfred Bailey in Denver, friends in Chicago and Ohio, parents and siblings in New Jersey, and Stefansson in New York. He takes in the Rose Bowl and other football games, stays at New York's City Club, dines at the Explorer's Club, and, at the end of the year, retraces some of his steps, making his way back to San Francisco in time to sail north in the summer. Regardless of how each year develops, Charlie Brower never seems to sit still. Mostly his time is marked in travel—if he's based in Barrow, he's out on the ice hunting whales, inland hunting caribou, or out tending the trading stations to the east or west. And when he travels Outside, he spends his year crisscrossing the country.[7]

Besides its predictable and somewhat pedestrian structure, there is a peculiarity to Brower's autobiography. As well as providing little insight into his own character, the manuscript is striking in its omission of his Barrow family.[8] *His second wife of forty years is never mentioned; neither are Sadie and her siblings Maria, Arnold, Harry, Kate, and Mary. Older siblings Tom, David, Robert, and Jennie are mentioned, but only in passing as they are taken Outside for schooling and/or medical attention. Tom eventually becomes part of the cadre of employees at the Cape Smythe Whaling and Trading Company and appears later on in that context. The four older children from a previous marriage, all of whom were eventually sent Outside to be raised by Brower's sisters, merit more discussion. Brower takes daughters Flora and Elizabeth to the White House when he has his audience with Roosevelt; he worries over Jim's schooling; later he spends time with Elizabeth and her children in San Diego; and he enjoys football games with son Bill in Corvallis. Brower's own parents and siblings also enter the manuscript on each of his Outside visits.*

Judging from those mentioned in The Northernmost American, *it is easy to conclude that Brower's "families" comprise his birth family, his four oldest children, and the men who bunked at his Cape Smythe Whaling and Trading Company. His diaries do not alter this view. Preparatory to writing his manuscript, Brower kept what appears to be a retrospective "diary" for the years preceding 1928; from 1928 on, some of the diary and events reported appear to be concurrent.*[9] *Brower's Barrow family fares little better in the diary, though Maria and Sadie, who don't make it into the final manuscript, are mentioned when their father takes them Outside. Sadie appears very briefly in the context of her voyage to San Francisco to attend high school (see p. 79, below).*

Perhaps, in the final analysis, Brower's memoirs are not so peculiar after all. As Sadie remarks, his interests were in telling his "stories." Brower's focus, particularly in the edited version of his autobiography, is on his adventures in the Arctic: the remarkable sled dogs he owned; the whales won and lost; the explorers he met and helped; his close calls with death; and interesting Iñupiat he came to know. This is the autobiography of a man's man. Children, wives, home and hearth are not the stuff of men's adventure stories.[10]

Charles Brower, like other resident traders of his time, married an Iñupiaq woman. This surely was one of the keys to his successful long-term adaptation to Arctic living. Toctoo,[11] *from Point Hope, met Brower in 1884 when she was just a young girl. She rescued him when he became lost in the fog on a hunting expedition; Brower was not only impressed but grateful. He writes in January 1888: "Just before starting [to Point Hope] Toctoo . . . told me that she wanted to go along, saying that as she was now matured the Eskimo here all wanted her to take one of their young men for a husband. She didn't want any of these men here, the only one she wanted was me. I thought it over for a long time, and finally took her with me, and married her the next summer [1888] when the ships arrived" (n.d.:304).*[12] *Toctoo appears from time to time in the manuscript after that, finally succumbing in the measles epidemic of 1902; Brower's final entry reads: "Soon she sickened and a few days later she died, her young baby dying the day after."*

As Sadie notes, a few years later her father married the baby-sitter he had engaged to look after his four young children.[13] *The four children were eventually sent Outside to be educated and to live with Brower's relatives, while Asianggataq, or "Bones" as he affectionately called her, bore him ten more children between 1904 and 1929.*[14] *Why this accomplished woman has escaped mention in his autobiography is an enigma. Asianggataq is most distinctly remembered by Sadie as a humanitarian who helped Barrow's needy. She was also a hunter who taught her sons (and daughters) to hunt and fish; she had her own large dog team, and Brower entrusted her with her own whaling crews. When it came to duck hunting, Asianggataq was remembered by Sadie as a "dead shot." "Mom could do most anything!" Sadie exclaimed. "She could shoot a gun and get her own game." Her aim apparently translated well to new activities, for Asianggataq loved to play pool at the table Brower kept at the station. "Mom was an ace at pool," Sadie remembered.*

Asianggataq lived a somewhat separate life from her husband, going off to camp while he kept the store, eating her Eskimo-style meals with her friends while Brower and the children ate white-man's meals at the station, weather-

ing Brower's periodic year-long absences when he went Outside, and suffering—not silently—his infidelity. Nonetheless, she was there when he needed her, making his skin clothing and mukluks, listening to him tell of his day at the store when he returned home at night, playing cards with him, preparing his midnight snacks. She bore and reared ten children by Brower,[15] *accepting the fact that her husband wanted to send them Outside to be educated for a life different from hers.*

The only place Asianggataq appears in Brower's copious writings is in his correspondence to Stefansson and Bailey. In a letter to Stefansson (5/17/23), Brower writes, "My wife wishes to be remembered and says if you are coming back some time to let her know a few years ahead and she will have boots for you." Brower also mentions her in the context of having to let his station cook (Fred Hopson) go. He tells Stefansson, "I am living home [;] Bones does the cooking and things while not so fancy nor abundant as they used to be answer the purpose, in fact I sometimes think I like it better now I can get my deer ribs and breast bones boiled as I like them. . . . I am eating more frozen meat and fish this winter than for a long time. It makes me think of the early days when everything tasted good away from the houses" (12/3/28). Stefansson mentions her, too, sending his regards to "Bones" in closing his letters to Brower. In his correspondence to Bailey between 1923 and 1944, Brower mentions Asianggataq just once, in connection with her death, beginning, "I as a general rule don't get down very often, but things have not been going well with me personally" (Brower 1943).

For whatever reasons, Brower's writings present a limited perspective of the Brower family personae: he speaks sparingly of his children; he never reveals himself; and his wife, for all intents and purposes, is nonexistent. Sadie, of course, sees neither parent through her father's writings, but speaks of both from the perspective of a daughter. In different ways they loom equally large in her life; Sadie expresses great admiration for both parents and believes that she, in her choice of careers and commitment to her community, has followed each of their paths. Sadie appears to have been closer to her father than to her mother—a bit fearful of him at times, but ever eager to fulfill his expectations of her despite her occasional defiance of his wishes.

My dad was a known whaler from way back, and he was the sole survivor of a shipwreck which was found by Point Hope people. Dad was in one of those whaling ships in the fall at age nineteen. He got

caught in an ice crush. The ice coming in caught their ship in early fall, in October near November, and when the weather was getting really extremely cold and they couldn't get it out of the ice, it froze in. Dad said he had no more idea of where they were when this happened, but later on I used to press him for information. . . . There were twelve men on that whaling ship that got caught in the ice, and he was the sole survivor. The others froze to death or starved to death trying to find ways to come ashore, and Dad said he had no idea where he was when he must have passed out, just half-frozen. He started to walk towards land, they thought, and that girl, Taktuk, and her two brothers, they found him. The next thing he says he remembers, he was in a sod house and a young girl [Taktuk] and two of her brothers were in it, and they cared for him. This was down in Point Hope.[16]

He first landed there in Point Hope and was finally accepted, after many attempts on his life (because the chief of that town thought that he was bad—could be because he was a white man). But he'd made friends with the people that had found him, the young lady and her two brothers that had brought him into their home. Later on, he wandered off up here [Barrow] looking for a favorable spot for whaling. It was in 1882, he first came up here for that. So he married the girl that found him, Taktuk. He brought her up [here] and they had four children, but three only survived.[17] During the black measles epidemic, she died along with the child who was born, and then our mother came into the story. My mother was young and also married and had a baby girl; and when her husband died and Charles Brower's wife died, he needed a baby-sitter for his four kids. He picked our mother, and she was baby-sitting for four years until they decided they might as well get married. So, there were ten of us out of that mother, out of Asianggataq. And here I am right in the middle. I had five brothers and four sisters.

Dad's four older children were taken away from here when they were barely ten, to live with their aunt, because their mother had died.[18] He had no way of taking care of them. He talked to his sister and bought this piece of land down in San Diego, an orchard farm, and made it a home for Uncle Fred and Aunt Jennie. So I never met them until I was sixteen. They were all born in the 1800s; the youngest one was born in 1898, I think. There's a big gap between

us. But we knew each other. They never regretted coming to visit, but were sorry they were sent out so young and didn't know all about this northland, their original home, where they were born.

My grandfather on my mother's side, Aluiqsi, was from King Island, and my grandmother was from Shishmaref. I have the name—Tagiagiña—of my great grandmother, I understand.[19] But I never knew her. I never knew my grandfather. They died before I was born. My grandparents were looking for a good place to hunt, and they wandered off way up here. My mom's maiden name was Asianggataq. She had no English name. She had four brothers older than her. When they started migrating north after some sort of information reached them that living was better around Barrow area, this northern area, her mother, Aluiqsi's wife Kupaaq, came down with some kind of influenza—probably pneumonia—when she was giving birth to my mother, the only girl born into that family. And she died right there, after giving birth to our mother.

But it was the custom in those olden days that if the father or the family did not want to take care of that child, it was buried alive with its mother. And this is what they did. And in those days, all they did was use skins or old boat covers to tie the body up and leave it on a stilt. Their burials were more like the Indians' that you see in shows today. It was something to that effect, but they said it was more sanitary than to try and dig them in the ground, let them surface.

And so when the older brother, Ugiagnaq, came back from a hunting trip, he'd heard his mother died. But he'd also heard that there was the delivery of a girl. And he asked the people, the rest of the family, what they did with that baby, because he couldn't see it around their home, their camp. And he was told that it was buried with the mother alive. And he took all his clothes off, the ones he hunted with, and went to the grave, took it apart, and found the baby girl, who was still alive. And he took her out of there and raised her, which was, I guess, out of love—and that was our mother. And we used to try and pump my uncle to tell us the story about it; and it was such a sad affair, he didn't want to live through it again. But anyway, we got the story out of him. So, our mother was Asianggataq; she was given the name of Asianggataq. "Asiang" is a berry, and "Asianggataq" means "a sweet berry." It was something he could think of, I guess, a name for a little girl, loving her so much. He raised her.

Well, we had to give Mom an English name when we went Outside to school, and so we chose the name "Mary," my sister Jennie and I. When Jennie first went to school, she couldn't even spell "Asianggataq Brower," Mom's name, so she put "Mary Brower." So, when I went out there, I followed in her footsteps and I put "Mary" down, too, and the name Mary stuck. And then we came back and told Dad that we had given Mom an English name, Mary. Later it was given to our sister, our youngest sister Mary.

They used to call us *umialik*, the rich family of the north. In those days the store and prices didn't mean much to my mother; money didn't matter to us. My mother was the social worker of this town when we were growing up. She was a very busy woman—concerned, loving. There wasn't anyone in town that didn't look up to her.[20] And our mother, I can remember, did so many things for this community when it was small, young, and so poor. The town wasn't very big—some four hundred people—and she was always out there. When she went and heard that some family was in need of food, she'd take a sack and run down to my dad's store. I can remember her going into the store; Dad would be sitting there in his chair. She was so skinny, my dad used to call her "Bones." And he'd say, "Bones, who is it for this time?" Then she, in her native tongue, would tell him, "Oh, so-and-so needs this and that." And Dad would sit there and just say, "Go ahead." Mom would start picking up stuff from the shelves and putting it in her bag.

More than once I saw her do that, help out with the welfare. She was brought up to share if you had more than you need. She didn't care about the price—she'd take those and take them to the family; there was never any charge. It never went on the books, no matter how much it cost. Because my mother was a good hunter, too. She'd go fishing, she'd go caribou hunting or seal hunting, when I could remember, until the boys were big enough to go out and hunt for her, bring what was needed.

Dad pretty much kept the store, and there were many hunters that were out that brought food and their catches and traded off for what goods he had and wares, so we always had enough, more than enough. My mom was the hunter of the family, when I remember. She had her own dog team; Dad made her sleds, and she would make these sleeping bags out of caribou hides sewed together, which were the warmest things that you could get into. You could never feel

cold weather even on a forty below day or night. You were sleeping snug inside that big two-inch-thick winter fur.

And the first tents I remember—people from inland used to come in trying to trade off with some of the people living on the shoreline that could never go up inland. These willows, long willows that bent easy, and the covers for those were caribou hides sewed together. They put this thing together and just cover it with fur; but later on they used cloth, this white canvas. And then the ready-made tent came about.

So we went out with the dog team. I would go with my mother and learn to fish—under-ice fishing, in the fall, when the ice is not too thick, and the river was sturdy enough to walk on the ice—and sit there and fish. Parents of the children at those times knew how to put their nets under. They were homemade—"knitted" from twine or linen. You didn't own too many of these nets; people didn't own too many of them. But they whittled soft wood for floats. And I remember in the summertime after a big storm, the old people used to tell us to pick these bark that—what they call *qasalluq*. It's bark—tree bark, pieces of tree bark—and it's orange colored, very soft to whittle for floats on the nets. And we'd look for old solid bone for sinkers; as kids we used to beachcomb and look for these to help the old people out, so that they could fix their nets. They weren't able to walk too far, and we used to just walk after a big storm, sometimes finding old ivory tusks, or whatever. In those times they were just of no value to us; they were just a piece of ivory.

❖

My dad learned to speak Iñupiaq. He had to learn to communicate. At first, he said, it was all Greek to him, just like the expression goes. . . . Even with signs, find some way with trying to make someone understand what you're trying to say to them. And finally, word by word, he had to learn and pick up the language and what it meant. And when it was my time, and Nate and I got married, I remember Nate and I came home, and we were warming ourselves by the fire. And my dad and my mother were playing solitaire, and I guess Mom was cheating a little bit, and Dad was talking to her over the table. And my husband Nate, the first time he ever heard my

father speak, just quietly said, "Is that your father?" "Yeah." He said, "I didn't know he could talk like that."

When Dad would sit in his store—it was a gathering place for old people—and they'd sit there and tell their stories and laugh, and Dad never spoke a word of English. He spoke their language, he had learned it so well. You wouldn't think, when you had your back turned and listened to him talk, that he was a white man. He talked the language so fluently.[21] My mother said she communicated with him when she married him—she never had to speak English to him at all. And my mom couldn't read or write, but she could say a few English words. But my dad spoke to her always in the native tongue. When we were in school we had to take certain English words home and teach them to our parents. Try to teach it to my mother—oh goodness! She was interested, but she was on the go all the time.

❖

Dad started baleen basket making here at Barrow. He was the first one to teach the Eskimos to make baleen baskets. He knew that he could strip the baleen and scrape it down to the right size he wanted for threads and make them. He made his own homemade tools and carved his own ivory. The first baleen basket Dad made, it didn't come out too good, and he gave it to my sister. And then he carved a Viking ship, put a salt and pepper shaker in there and they started cracking, and he didn't want it as a show piece and he gave it to me. I had that one—oh, I was just tickled pink with that. I kept it for many years until Nate and I were in need of money, and the kids were kind of wrecking them; then I sold them off to the workers up here at the base, the commanding officers that were there. Dad just gave his baleen baskets away to friends. Then he showed his brother-in-law, Taalak, how to make baleen baskets. Dad also carved ivory; he made beads for us girls out of ivory, and necklaces, and pendants, bracelets, and little jewelry boxes where he'd dig out a little stem like—oh, it was so neat. My sister may still have some of hers, but I sold all of mine.

❖

There were no marriage ceremonies in the old days, and if an old

couple with a daughter saw a man that they'd like to have in the family, then they would invite him: "Here is our daughter; you can have her." And there were never any objections to it. But as we grew older we saw how that type of marriage as arranged by parents failed. Divorces started occurring, and it was strange, but we had to live through it, when people realized that they didn't love each other and lived all these years and finally separated, went their own way. In those days, too, the girls were so young when they were given to a man to marry; it would be their first menstrual period—age thirteen, fourteen. I used to listen to Dad tell about those—"Gosh, how could they stand it? You didn't do that to Mother, did you?" "Oh no. She came willingly, even though she objected there for a while, that I might leave her," Dad would say. And he promised her that he would never leave her, except when he would go Outside. That would be the only time he would leave her, and then he would come back. She understood that for many years and always looked forward to Dad coming in.

There was a writer, though. When I was around ten or eleven years old, [Miss] Wallace came up; she was a writer, and Dad took to liking her, and Mother didn't like it. And she used to sit at the table where Fred prepared our supper at night, and I used to sit next to her.[22] And we detested her, knowing that Dad paid more attention to her than he did Mother in that time then. How we hated her. Anything, anything that we could make miserable for her, we did. She would try and send one of us kids over to her place to get her cigarettes, and we would get something and deliberately spill the cigarettes all over the floor, or when we were passing the food, dump it—just "accidentally" dump it or pour it on her lap—and Dad saw it. He knew we were disturbed. I guess I was about the worst one out of the bunch, because I sensed it and I was very hurt. She was here for two or three years writing a book. I don't know if anything ever came of it. I never did ask. The thing that we didn't dare ask Dad about, you know. She stayed in the little house where Dad's former clerk had lived, and Dad used to spend evenings there and come home late, and pretty soon Mom just wouldn't let him in.

Later on, Dad found out about her . . . what type of a woman she was, just living off of men. It wasn't just Dad, it was just any man that she could hook up to, where she wouldn't have to have any expenses.

She did it with Jim Allen down Wainwright and with others, after Dad. Dad got rid of her the year before I left for San Francisco. Well, we were all glad to see her go and wondered when Dad would come around and we would have our parents back the way they were. . . . I remembered telling Jim [Sadie's half-brother] that that woman had almost spoiled our family. She showed up in San Francisco, in our hotel room. She knew she wasn't wanted. I remember Dad getting after me for my attitude, showing so darn much, and then I told my sister Jennie about it. And boy she stepped in there, she was worse than I was, then. But those things come up, you know, if you think about it. And then you don't see it anymore. By then I had my own life to live, trying to be independent Outside, with my family away, no brothers or sisters around.

Brower's mention of Edna Claire Wallace no fewer than eleven times between 1923 and 1926 might go unnoticed in an autobiography the size of Brower's were it not for the omission of his wife and family. Given his propensity for understatement, one suspects he was smitten by Miss Wallace — at first, anyway. She is present at his birthday party in March of 1924 along with other whites in the community; he relates her near-disaster on the ice at Wainwright ("for a white woman not used to this traveling, it must have been hell"); she joins him and others going south on the Teddy Bear *in 1924. They party together in Seattle, and when they meet again several months later Brower invites her to Barrow for the year. "She was working on a novel, but thought she would like to go north again for a year, to get more material and wanted to know how she could get up.*[23] *We talked things over and she finally decided if possible to come with me . . . to Barrow where I had plenty of house room for her" (n.d.:768). By the following summer, Brower's fascination with the aspiring authoress had waned, a change undoubtedly expedited by his wife's outrage and the pranks his children played. He finally shipped her out on the revenue cutter* Bear, *noting, "I had enough of her as well as the others and did not want her around any longer." Although Sadie remembered seeing Miss Wallace in San Francisco in 1930, she does not reappear in Brower's life story.*

❖

Mr. Brower, although he lives far from civilization, lives well. The Cape Smythe Whaling and Trading Company have, besides numerous storehouses, a commodious and substantial building known as the "station,"

> which contains not only their workshops where boats, sleds, and other needed articles are made and repaired, but also living rooms, of which Mr. Jack Hadley and myself were the sole occupants, and a well-equipped kitchen, presided over by a man who is the master of his profession. But it was not so much the excellence of the table and the comfort of the house that made Cape Smythe attractive, but rather the quality of the few white men and women who were gathered there together. [Stefansson 1912:85]

> In the front of the building [station] was the storeroom. The shelves were piled with prints, factory cloth, and calicoes in bolts, blankets in bales, cartridges in stacks on the shelves, steel traps hanging by their chains along the wall in heavy bunches, the cases of well-oiled rifles and shotguns, in the corner shoulder guns and darting guns for the whale hunt, flenzing knives, all the paraphernalia of the world in which they lived. Primus oil lamps, dog harness, and thermos bottles for the trails, fur *arteegees* [parkas], bales of sox, Eskimo mukluks. [Andrews 1939:76]

The Cape Smythe Whaling and Trading Company carried a full line of groceries for the time, supplied by a wholesale grocer in San Francisco whose invoices record items such as dried figs, canned oysters, sliced pineapple, Campbell's soups, string beans, bacon, and pickles. At Cape Smythe one could also buy ladies' cotton dresses, long underwear for the entire family, knitting worsted, and just about any over-the-counter drug. "[I]t was boasted that one could buy here [at the height of commercial whaling] almost anything that one could ask for, at prices no higher than in San Francisco" (Stuck 1920:211).

For a long while Brower lived at the station, but in 1905 he built a separate dwelling. "Leaving San Francisco," he says, "I had brought along lumber to build myself a house. I was tired of living in the station, wanted some place where I could have some time to myself away from everyone coming to the station. . . . Just before the ground froze I had the place completed, and moved in" (n.d.:620).

Our house had this cookstove and a big table on the bottom floor, chairs, and paper, Dad's easy chair when he came home, and a small table for Dad and Mom to play card games or sit together and visit. Dad would tell what went on at the store and Mom would relate who she visited with and what they talked about. But half the time, it was looking into the past and asking each other, just conversation—till bedtime, because Dad used to turn in quite early and read a book. Around 10:00, if he wanted his "midnight" snack, then he'd call on Mom or somebody to go get whatever he wanted. It was one big

room where there was a cookstove in the middle and shelves, like cupboards and stuff, where we kept our dishes and our needs in the house, pots and pans.

The second floor of the house was everybody's sleeping quarters. Mom and Dad had theirs towards a window, and the cribs were on the opposite side when I can remember Mom and Dad still had little ones. The bigger kids were in the back; there was a partititon between where Mom and Dad had Mary [the youngest] and the younger ones. And all the grown ones sometimes slept at the store, like my older brothers did; they started living on their own. They didn't stay in the house. But later on, when we were quite grown, Dad made an addition, a wing to the house, and put two rooms in it—on the side, yeah, on the side, more like a storm shed—and put our girls [there]. Most of the boys stayed on upstairs; the girls had their own room. After I came back—the wing had been built in the five years I was out—then there was another wing built on this side, like the one where Dad and Mom had their bedroom.

So there were additions to the house, wings. One [wing], the bedroom for Dad and Mom, was started by our brother Tom, mainly because he was interested in a girl and he would have a separate bedroom. But later on he built his own house and moved in there. This was my mother's house. She bought it off of Dad with fifty white fox skins. Her brother had given her all these skins and she didn't know what to do with them, so Dad said, "Well, Bones, I'm going to let you have that house, let you have it for fifty white fox skins." This was after they were married. There's a legal record, in the commissioner's office where all those old records were, that Dad sold the house to Mother for fifty white fox skins.

❖

Our mother died in 1943. In those times any ailment that came about was quite serious. There were no doctors, no surgery done, and people just died off. Mother had this gall bladder infection and died. . . . My mom was around in her early sixties when she died, though no one really knew. Dad guessed at her age. There was no doctor available, and she had gallstones. There was no one to operate. Couldn't get a doctor up here early enough. When one did arrive, the operation never was successful because of poisoning or

infection. It didn't last very well. But Mom had gone down so bad that nothing could save her then. I was there by her side all the time. . . . She was in the hospital constantly. And then we'd report back to Dad, because he couldn't walk. There was no transportation. Dad had broken his back and had to be tied down with silver wire or something. He couldn't walk any distance. He could walk through the flat boardwalk. But he made it from the house to the store, and some days he didn't hardly go there . . . because he was in such poor health. Dad had a heart attack soon after Mom died, but he came out of that one. He was just lucky they were just going into the store when it happened. They got him to the hospital and he got out of it. But he never went back Outside again after that.

As Charles Brower indicated to his friend Alfred Bailey, things did not go well for him in the summer of 1943. "I reached home in the middle of May and when I did get here I found my wife a very sick woman and in a few days I could see that she was not likely to live for very much longer. I had her taken to the hospital where she passed away Sept Third" (Brower 1943). He added, "Shortly after that I was unfortunate enough to break a small blood vessl [sic] *in my heart and I have been on my back ever since."*

Right after we lost our mother, the will that my mom wanted after Dad died was read early. Dad told Maria that she'd inherit the house and everything in it, and my sister Maria started carrying it out to where she wouldn't let any of us use the stuff inside the house.[24] It was meant for us girls to be used equally, and I continually got in trouble with her; we argued, and it just got so uncomfortable. And so my husband Nate and I talked it over, and we went and talked to Dad and told him we were going to go away up inland to a cabin and live there by Tom, my brother who had the reindeer herd, and maybe help out up there. Dad just couldn't see why I wanted to leave. I was the only one that he could depend on at the time, and I said I would be back at Christmastime. We left in the fall of '44, and I remember my brother Bob and his wife Berna came down here [from the reindeer herd] for Christmas because Berna was due to have this baby, and they stayed at the house. Dad was guarding himself because he had had a slight heart attack, and the next one,

his doctors said, would be fatal. But at Christmas we couldn't make it. Dad left a place open at the table for Nate and me; he wouldn't let anyone else sit there, because he thought we were coming in. I didn't see him again.

Though Brower was guarding his health, he still held hopes of making a trip Outside. He paid his $10 dues for 1945 to the Explorers Club, writing, "Give my regards to all the Club that remember me. I would like to drop in for afternoon tea but that is out for me until things get more settled here [referring to the Navy activity] and when that will happen no one can tell at present" (Brower 1944).

He died on February eleventh, 1945, and I remember the next morning, February twelfth. We were with my brother's reindeer herd at Alaktak, known as Half Moon Three by the oil company. They put a wireless station there, to communicate, for people exploring this northern area. Tom had this two-story house and he built another one, a little larger one, and that was where he was communicating that morning. The radio message came up, and his wife was reading over his shoulder, and he was trying to make these letters, you know, not realizing what he was writing: "Your father passed away at five last night." And his wife looked over his shoulder and said, "My God, your dad is dead."

And it hit him like a rock—just about knocked him out cold. She said, "Tom, look what you are writing!" And he threw those earphones down, started getting ready to go back down to get our family up there. And he didn't realize what he was writing until his wife pointed to it. I can remember those words were so abrupt. But he took the message. Somebody from out here at the base had sent the message, the first group of people that had CB's. Sad, sad day. Unbelievable.

They said he was sitting like you and I here talking, and just slumped over, and that was the end of him—just nodded off in his chair.[25] He had one big easy chair that he used to just sit back in and yarn away with the old folks and people coming in and out. He had a lot of visitors then, from the base, asking him questions and listening to his stories. That was my joy, too, in being with Dad. I could

remember evenings when he would come home. I would pump him for stories and sit there, and not a sound, just listening to him relate some of those stories. I was so interested.

Dad was eighty-three years old when he died.

⁂

Charles Brower's obituary appeared in the New York Times, *and Vilhjalmur Stefansson (1964:353) lamented his friend's passing: "At Edmonton we received news of the death of Charlie Brower of Point Barrow. It had been my dream to introduce our party*[26] *to him and for as many as possible of them to hear his fascinating narratives and philosophizing. . . . Most of our interest of a Barrow visit disappeared with Brower, so we gave up our planned trip there and headed northwest toward Fairbanks.*

3

Growing Up

1916 was a difficult year in Barrow, at least according to the white people who wrote about it. T. L. Richardson, the village schoolteacher, reported to his superior: "The loss of the whalebone market and the low price of fur until Christmas, combined with the small catch has made financial conditions of our village very bad. Unusually high prices have prevailed as a result of the European war and a scarcity of supplies at Barrow. The larger part of the supplies for one of the traders failed to get here and this has caused a shortage of all the staple articles of food" (Richardson 1916).

Reviewing his early years in the Arctic preparatory to writing his autobiography, Charles Brower jotted down the following highlights of 1916, the year of the birth of his sixth child. "Whaling this spring for the last time. . . . Dr. Spence comes as missionary. . . . I buy Hanson's store. . . . Fall whaling. . . two whales." He later elaborates (n.d.:680): "1916 in the spring I built three canoes in the station to amuse myself. After we quit whaling as a business I had sold most of the oomiaks the station owned, those left were all badly used up. I wanted too, to have one more spring on the ice then if things were not picking up I thought I would quit the spring whaling and hunting. It took up a lot of time that I could give to something else. I enjoyed the excitement as much as ever, although I was getting older and could not get around as well as I used to." A month before spring whaling began, Sadie Brower was born.

Earliest Memories

The earliest memory that I ever had was being on my baby-sitter's back, and I don't remember how big I was; she was packing me. I must have been crying. That was the first recollection I ever had,

being in some woman's parka trying to look out, and crying, probably trying to say something, because I saw my mother hanging up some meat on a rack. But I couldn't say anything. . . . Later on when I asked my mother, "Where were you that time, hanging up meat when I was real small and I felt like I was on somebody's back?" She said I was barely a year old. She said she was hanging some *ugruk* meat by my uncle's sod house, his rack. He'd gotten an *ugruk* and she was helping him. . . . That was the one that raised her from when she was a little girl.[1]

My mother used to have me on her back when she would go to Hanson's store[2] looking for whatever, even though Dad had that store over there. It would be something that caught her eye that she wanted from Hanson's store, and I can remember a little bit of those. I can remember the year. We were all in this great big building; Mom said I was barely two years old, and it was in 1918 when the war ended, and all that stamping and noise and after that I don't remember anymore. And then we were in a church. I saw these two men walk in through the door, when the news [of the end of the war] came in; the two men were all frosted, coming in around Christmastime from being out on the trail, bringing the message in, because we got mail every three months.

And oh, visiting people with my mother, hanging onto my mother's hand; she was probably dragging me. I can remember her hanging on to my hand and I was going with her to somebody's house. And I remember sitting down to eat something, but I don't even remember whether I ate or not. . . . And at that time I was probably about two or three years old, between two and three. And so on, till I was able to fully remember a whole day going to school, seeing my teacher, and sitting there.

A Carefree Life

[In 1921 in Barrow] there was nothing to break the horizon of the broad expanse of tundra to the south except the white-painted church, the schoolhouse and scattered buildings of the trading post, and the inconspicuous sod igloos of the natives. The site was one of the most desirable locations of the whole coast for hunters because of the Arctic foxes, polar

> bear, walrus, and bowhead whales taken each year. . . . The trading post "station" was built on a little knoll and adjacent were well-filled warehouses where a line of general merchandise was handled, while half a mile to the south, separated by a salt lagoon, were a school building, the church and manse, and a modern hospital. [Bailey 1971:88]

In the summertime after *Nalukataq* the families split. There was hardly anyone left in town when school was out. They all took their families and went off to some good hunting area. All summer long we never saw each other, until such time as school started. But we were with our mother who always had a way of going off to camp, and we'd all go with her along with some other kids. Sometimes up to the point, sometimes where that Brant Point is, where they duck-hunt. Dad [also] used to take us out camping the month of July when the ducks would start returning back. We'd camp up at the Brant Point, make a tent . . . and hunt for ducks along with him and his old store worker, the one who used to keep the store clean. My mom, she'd top them all with her shotgun; and this is where I learned to shoot a shotgun, real early, about age eleven.

There were no movies, no games or basketball of any kind like that when we were growing up. All we grew up with were games brought down by our ancestors. In the summertime, after we did our chores, we'd all gang up down on the beach with all kinds of competitions done with bones or old spike nails, heavy objects. It was like playing horseshoe, but there was a scoring system. You each had five pieces of stick or five rocks that, every time you win or come closer than your opponent, then that rock went to your side; you play until all the rocks are on one side or the other, then a new player, or a couple of players, takes over. There would be four of us sitting down about, say, ten feet apart, with stakes, you know. And then, too, we played a guessing game, where you have two groups of young people, and you try to guess what they are doing by their actions, and if you guessed it right, then you go try and grab however many [kids] from the opponents and bring them back to your side until it eliminates the other side. We also would get an old can or something that won't break and try to hit the target, and then we had our own old homemade bows and arrows made from this drift log, which is quite hard. Whoever made your bow had to soak it

after making it, so it wouldn't break up kept its spring; your arrows are homemade, too. You have a target, whether it's a can over there, or something that you can make with a piece of cloth and hang up. And one-base baseball, where we had one base and everybody lines up—I can't remember the scoring system on that. And then a free-for-all football game, where you have goals on each end and players on two sides.

Usually the grown-ups would join us, the marrieds against the singles, or something to that effect. All of us boys and girls played it together. Mostly it was the kids and young people, but the old people would join too. It went on through wintertime, that type of game. Sometimes we played without goals to see how far you can run away with the ball, and win for your side. And there was—if you could have a bouncy ball, we used to walk by bouncing it, kicking it, and see how far you could go. Those games among the girls, and jump-rope. We played jump-rope, only in numbers, you know. We would line up and try and beat that rope and go through it without fumbling within it. There were songs to jump-rope to. And songs with string games, certain little songs. Put your finger in between and wind it according to the words you had in your little song, and, if you let it go, if you hit it right, the string was free.

We had some old people that would teach us how to play those string games, which were quite popular in our time. We were warned not to play them at a certain time, in the fall, I think, when the days got dark,[3] or else a boogie man would come in and spook us. *Ayaqhakkiiq* men, they were called. He would come in through the doorway, playing with his intestines [mimicking the making of string figures]. The blood would be streaming down, and he'd keep on playing. It was said just to scare us.[4] In the summer we had no care in the world; you didn't have to do certain things at a certain hour, and you ate when you got hungry.

In winter, we were mostly in school. We would walk to school and stay there from 9:00 to 4:00. Those of us that lived in Browerville sometimes brought our lunches, and we would go to the nearest house or stay out there and eat our lunches with families we knew. And after school, then, pretty much taking care of what we were supposed to do—empty the slop bucket, clean the house, for the girls. And boys brought in the wood, or go get some ice or snow, a

box of snow, and put it by the house for water. But it wasn't every day. We sometimes did all these and just played when we were kids. But on Saturday and Sunday . . . Saturday was a work day for all of us, because we helped around the school, too, those that wanted to help . . . and around where that mission hospital was. We helped to bring in whatever was needed—wasn't much—or entertain some of the patients or go visit them. We did that mainly on Sunday.

Stories were told in the wintertime—only in the wintertime, never in the summertime. Storytelling was done on long nights when we couldn't go out and enjoy ourselves in the dark, and it was mainly old people that had hand-me-down stories, legends, or where they came from and how they got here. Stories were told during hunting season; if you were a successful hunter or had a good hunting trip, you were entitled to invite some storyteller to your house. And it was an honor, like giving out candy to a bunch of kids if you were successful. Whoever was successful would pick out his favorite storyteller and say so-and-so is going to tell a story at so-and-so's house. It didn't matter where. The houses were small, but those of us that could get in, we could sit there and listen until it was time to go home.

Mom used to invite this one old man, Suakpak. That was because my brothers used to go out trapping and hunting. And if they were successful, they would bring in that old man to our house and we'd sit all evening, listening to his yarns and stories and hand-me-downs and all types of stories about animals and about boogie-men; the boogie-men stories would scare us half the time. I remember him so well—and we'd sit there along with some of our next-door neighbors' kids and listen to this man tell his stories. We were given dried fruit—raisins and dried prunes—saying this was the part of the catch that was to be given to him. We enjoyed it. Pass the evening listening to that old man. And we were supposed to learn those stories. I don't think I even remember one whole one.

Dad used to tell stories to us kids, too. I used to just sit there by the hour and pump Dad about his life, and it was so interesting. The others weren't as interested as I was. I was more attentive and curious. And then my mom would be sitting there, be playing solitaire, and let him tell his stories in the evening when he came home from the store and have his midnight snack, whatever he wanted. He'd just talk away [in English], and when he would say

names, Mom would want to know what he was talking about. She would ask questions in her native tongue, and Dad would answer back, verify in Eskimo, and then she'd frown: "It wasn't quite like that; it was this way." "Aha, aha, aha," and they would agree it was like that. Oh, it was interesting!

Dad didn't think it was proper to tell about the shaman, their activities that he had witnessed. Some would tell them, the old people would relate some of them, but as young kids we never heard too much about it [shamanism]. Dad always told us never to shun those stories. "Don't think they didn't have any power in those days. They did." And he had seen it, but he wouldn't tell us about those kinds of stories.

I was a tomboy, and I could lick any boy my age at that time who came near, mistreating some of my girl friends. Boys were afraid to cope with me. I can remember that I was somehow bold enough to get a big enough stick if I didn't think I was going to beat that boy that was after us. And when I actually used the stick, they went and told their parents that I did this, and their parents would come over and talk to my mom. "Your daughter did this—such an unladylike act." But Dad always said if you never learn to defend youself, you would never learn to stand for whatever your beliefs. And Dad said, "If you get hurt, don't you ever start feeling sorry for yourself. That's the worst thing you can do." Dad used to talk to us about those kinds of things when we were kids. He encouraged me to take care of myself, and he would send me out on the tundra with a .410 shotgun or light caliber rifle to pick specimens because he used to stuff birds and send them out to museums.[5] I'd have a basket on my back, with only one sandwich in there and a jar of water, and I'd roam all day.

Dad had a flower bed, about twenty by twenty [feet] where he planted all these Arctic flowers, and some came from maybe ten, twelve miles up—little forget-me-nots. And anytime when he wanted flowers for his garden, I can remember I'd go out with the spade, and he'd instruct me how to take the whole flower or certain type of plant, get it way down in the roots and bring it back. When spring came on, he would have some old men shovel out the snowbank so it would melt and start getting thawed out, prepare the

plants to start growing. We used to take pictures of Dad's garden. Usually he had a fence around it, where us kids couldn't get in, so we would peek in and watch him putter around in it.

When we did something out of line, Dad would have to give us a punishment of some kind for it; he would explain that he was doing it for the love that he had for us, to make us understand—not because of hate. He said if he didn't care and didn't love us, he wouldn't give us that kind of punishment, and because he loved us he had to do it, to teach us and make us understand. When he punished us he used to tell us that, which I thought was very good. I use it on my children if they need some kind of punishment for something they do. We never got real harsh spankings from Dad. Mom was the one that did that. She brought out the broom or the stick or whatever, but not too many times. One time I was playing outdoors and we had this one young man that was older and bigger than we were, and I got a stick and hit him on the head, and I remember that boy's dad chasing me right into the home, and old man Okakok said that I clobbered his son. And then Mom really took my pants down and gave me a whipping. But that boy was a bully. . . . And then, too, Dad knew I was using his pet dog to scare kids. He had a white collie that he kept tied up, and I knew if that thing ever got loose, he would tear some kid. Well, I always had a way; if I couldn't win whatever I was trying to do, I'd sic the darn dog on him. Boy, was Dad mad about it. I really got it. Dad sat me in a chair inside the house and he wouldn't let me go out for two or three days; it was in the summertime, and that was bad. That's the worst punishment, to sit there in a chair and do nothing.

It was a carefree life when I was growing up. No rules or regulations or ordinances or curfews. It didn't matter what hour of day you got home, you ate; there was no set time among the young people. They just came home when they got hungry, or go with their friends and eat there. But because my father was a white man, he had hours for us to come home, and it was different from the other kids. That was hard to do. And if we ate some of our native food with our friends, we still had to eat the plate of food that was set before us. Sometimes we'd sit there, just halfway swallow it; you're already full, but you had to learn the hard way to do it, because Dad had all that good food on the table for all of us. We

usually had dinner between 5:00 and 6:00. We had to be home and couldn't play out after 8:00. Dad relaxed the curfew in the summertime, up to 9:00. It was hard on us, and we got spanked more than once for coming home late.

Our mother didn't necessarily agree with Dad's curfew, but she was always there hollering; you could hear her calling our names way over there if we were over here. She was like a big horn: "Time to go home." I can remember Mom hollering at us: "Time to go home." We always knew our mother's voice. Up to about twelve years old, we had this curfew of 8:00. We had to be home and be cleaned up and brush our teeth. And when we weren't doing anything else, our mother would have something else for us to do before Dad came home from his trading post at 9:00. In the summertime, if we were with our mother,[6] we didn't have to go to sleep. We could stay up all night if we wanted to . . . free type of life.

Our mealtime was different from the other kids' because, when Dad was home, there was a certain hour we had to have our breakfast, certain hour we had to have our lunch, and certain hour we had to have our dinner. When my father was away,[7] there wasn't a time set aside when we should eat with our mother. My mother never got after us, because that's the way she was brought up. In those days it was invite whoever was there to eat.

> Connected with the establishment as cook was an old shipmate of Mr. Brower's, Mr. Fred Hopson, with another batch of assorted half-breed children, and the two families lived together in a sort of patriarchal plenty and simplicity, and with an absence of bickering that was very pleasant and unusual. Fred Hopson's most prominent mark was a carefully cultivated ferocity that did not deceive anyone as to his kind and indulgent nature. When the children came trooping in from school, their appetites sharpened by a walk of half a mile, perhaps against a blizzardlike wind, they would invade the kitchen, and the most explosive and alarming fee-fi-fo-fum threats and growls would immediately proceed therefrom. "Get out of here, you young wolves, or I'll kick the left ear right off you!" "Where's the ramrod. . . . " The children, quite undismayed, issued forth munching slabs of cake or sections of pie, or, at least, hunks of bread and jam. [Stuck 1920:212–13]

As far back as I can remember, there was a cook that used to take

care of my dad's family. His name was Fred Hopson. Fred Hopson also had a native wife, and Dad had this big store, this trading post, with a big kitchen where he fed our family. My mother didn't know how to cook—she could boil meat for her own consumption; she hardly ever ate with us, but we were required to go down to the kitchen area, the dining room, and eat what was there on the table for us. After you're used to your own native food, white man's food is not too interesting. We would sneak out and eat from my mother's food and learn to like it.

In the summertime there was a lot of seal meat, and whale meat if there was a successful whale hunt. Mom would go to her cellar and bring out some *maktak*, boil some of the meat and whatever she had—bread and biscuits and fried crackers, sugar. She would always have that. She had one of those old pump-type Primus stoves, like a big motor roaring . . . heat the water, make tea. We kids loved to have dried meat, when it was available, and frozen fish and seal oil—dunk it in seal oil. And *maktak*, oh, our favorite food. Mom would make her own caribou soup or reindeer soup the way she wanted, not fancy, like with vegetables or stuff like old Fred used to make, meat pies and stuff. She didn't like them; she was brought up on just plain, like Nate. Whenever we ate with her, Mom always said to us, "Don't eat too much now; you are going to get it when you go down [to the station] to eat." Sometimes it was sad. We couldn't miss going down there. Dad always knew if we missed. If we got caught not hungry at the supper table, we really, really suffered. Because Dad said, "You eat or you sit!" We had to sit there and try and down whatever was on the plate. We were taught to not throw away food or play with it.

Our family would come in and eat first, and then Fred's family—wife, children, grandchildren—would come in on the second table, but it was the same overall meal. Our mother would rather stay home and eat with her friends and eat her native food. But Fred used to make a big panful of food, in case she and her friends would like to have some of it.

Fred cooked anything, you name it. He was a wonderful cook. In fact, after I came back from high school and Dad had retired him from cooking and told us girls we had to learn how to cook, we were forever running over to old Fred Hopson and letting him write

out a recipe, or going out on our own and trying something, a new recipe on Dad, from old cookbooks that were there. And most of the time, Dad would ask us, "Have you tried this kind of food before?" Dad would say to us, "Well, if you live through that meal, I guess maybe I'll try it too." He used to tease us about that. But overall, he knew what he wanted.

Fred used to prepare Christmas dinner and invite the whole white population to Dad's house, but everything else was done at the church for all the needy people. It started out one year as a Thanksgiving ceremony by everybody bringing in what they were able to bring, like a big potluck supper. What Dad had was inviting the teachers, the doctors, the wireless people, whatever white people were up here. They would come in and enjoy turkey and big roast and cakes and, oh, everything was put out on the table. We dearly loved Christmas dinner, and then we were left out after supper, the kids out on their own and the grown-ups on their own to play their games or whatever.

The small white population of Barrow apparently gathered frequently, oftentimes at Brower's trading station. Alfred Bailey had especially pleasant memories of such gatherings in the winter of 1921–22. He wrote in his field notes:

> We found thirteen white people living here, as one happy family, for without exception, they proved congenial and hospitable and had their weekly get-together meetings. We were dined . . . and wined for a week, till I often wished for two stomachs instead of one. Every night the entire [white] population got together. . . . We ran the gauntlet from whist to penny ante . . . then music and dancing, and finally to playing pool on the portable table. Life in this little northern city is not full of the tragic hardships that are usually visualized in thinking of Arctic wastes, for although the sun is gone two months of the year, the mercury goes into the bulb and forgets to come out again for weeks at a time, and the winds blow so that no one dares venture forth, there is usually plenty of coal to keep warm, an abundance of grub, and a few congenial companions. [1921–22:7–8]

❖

We didn't know anything about money. We never knew what money meant. We didn't know what stealing meant, taking somebody

else's stuff. If somebody left something valuable and a kid found it, it was returned to them, automatically. There was no stealing. . . . We never had candy or fruit. The only time we ever saw fruit was when the boat came in in the summertime, and each child was given an orange or an apple—and oh, how we treasured that. And candy. You had to earn your candy by chopping wood, or kindling wood, bring it in, and when the storekeeper or somebody gave you a handful—oh, that was a treasure. But sometimes your mother took it away from you and just gave you one little piece. I can remember my mom used to get it in a little cup for each of us, with our names on it, and put it by our bed on Saturday night. And in the morning we would wake up and there would be a piece of candy or something in there. Usually candy was for special occasions like Christmas. The mission would have the women go in, the mothers go in, and pop some corn and make out all these bags of candy and popcorn and cookies. One for each person—children, adults alike.

These sailors or people out of the boats that used to come up here, when they'd come ashore, they'd give us these little round metal pieces, and we didn't know what they were. They were money—five-cent pieces, ten-cent pieces, quarters. And when our mothers found out, they took them away from us and put them in the church offering. So we never had any use for money when I was growing up. I never realized what money was, even at twelve. And money was nothing to our people. It had no meaning—that green paper, or whatever—because of the cooperative conditions in trading.

The Only Place to Go

A plank sidewalk led to the two-story white frame building facing the salt lagoon and bearing the words "U.S. Public School" across its facade. The ubiquitous school bell stood at the entryway to signal the beginning of the day and call the village children in from recess. Less a part of the expected milieu was a crow's nest, salvaged from one of the many shipwrecks in the area and tethered in the schoolyard. At the sign of the season's first ship, a U.S. flag was hoisted from the flagpole atop the crow's nest, and undoubtedly the perch was also used as a lookout by eager whale hunters in the spring.

Besides its three classrooms the Barrow school housed the white schoolteachers, in many ways effectively segregating them from the rest of the community. The one native schoolteacher who was employed, if not from Barrow itself, was usually also quartered here. Beyond their classroom duties, the schoolteachers were responsible for the Cooperative Native Store (one of several established in northern and northwestern Alaskan villages) and the village reindeer herds. In their classrooms, English was given top priority, particularly in the lowest grades. During Sadie's elementary school years, the school day would begin at 9 A.M. and progress through singing, English conversation, geography, arithmetic, dictionary study, dictation, reading, history (for fourth and fifth grades), composition or letters, and, in the third grade, hygiene (Evans 1931).

A few teachers had apparently effective ways of introducing and adapting the alien school materials to native life. Fred Ipalook, a native teacher from Barrow, for whom the present elementary school is named, reported to his fellow teachers in the district in 1931 a particularly effective drill in arithmetic which he called "Trapping with Numbers":

> To play the game, the class is divided into two teams. Each team is working hard to get the most foxes for the store he traps. A line of 36 traps, which a child goes to see each day, are represented by 36 combinations of numbers on the blackboard. When a child from one of the teams goes through his traps, the other team watches his adding very carefully and counts how many mistakes he makes. When a child goes through his numbers in less than 60 seconds and without making any mistakes he has gotten 36 foxes for his team. When he makes several errors, the number of errors are deducted from 36. When 60 seconds elapse while the trapper is out on his traps, it means that the trappers have walked slowly all day and when he saw it was getting dark he left his team. The team that traps the most foxes wins the game. When the children have acquired speed in adding, we will cut the time limit down to 50 seconds, 40 seconds, et cetera. [Evans 1931]

Contests seem to be endemic to American education, and they were single-mindedly applied in the government-run schools in native villages. In northern and northwestern Alaska, contests were held in every subject from arithmetic to English word drills to geographic locations. Results were collected from each grade and compared across schools in different villages. Although Sadie indicated that such contests were enjoyed by the students, it is difficult to imagine how the Iñupiaq child of the early twentieth century might apply the skills he or she had gained from contests like the "geography speed map." The instructions

for this particular exercise indicate how far the system went in emphasizing speed and competition:

> First have them draw the continents for speed. As soon as they have gained a required amount, have them draw the six continents on one sheet of paper, three continents on each side. Give the time required to draw. The names should be written in after the time is taken. As soon as this has been sent in, have them work on the countries within the continents. As soon as they have acquired skill in drawing any one continent with its countries, submit the best of each grade. [Morlander 1931]

❖

I can remember my first day in school, because this teacher that I had was an Eskimo, Roy Ahmaogak. I truly loved that man, as a teacher. He was so gentle with all the children. I thought he was the kindest person—and such a pleasant face. He never spoke harshly. But he would show us these on the board, these curlicues, which were alphabets. My first recollections were of him writing numbers and ABC's, and we tried to make copies of these and learn them, go back to school and see how many we could say.

We didn't have any sandwiches to take from home for lunch, and there were no school lunches prepared, so we'd run home or go to the nearest house. Our mother would tell us to go to so-and-so's house and have lunch if we don't want to come home, or if it was a windy day. Somebody would automatically be there at the school, some adults, to take us home on a blizzardly day, so we wouldn't get lost. Today, when the wind is blowing and you can hardly see your next-door neighbor, the school is cautious about children going to school. But in those days, even from Browerville, there'd be an adult with a rope, who'd tie us all up so we wouldn't stray off from each other and get lost, and he'd take us to school. And after school he'd be there to guide us back home. But on days when it was nice, he didn't need to.

School was something we really valued and wanted; we were just happy to be in school. There wasn't a kid that didn't want to go to school, because that was the only place that we could go. Most of us loved learning. There were never more than two or three in a class in the same grade when I went to school. There were only three classrooms—one for the beginners; one for the third, fourth,

and fifth; the sixth, seventh, and eighth were in another room. The main subjects that you had to take were English, writing, arithmetic, and geography. If you took those and passed them, then you were ready for whatever higher education there might be. When you completed eighth grade, that was all the schooling that you had up here. No high school. So you had to go out and learn to make a living, or, if a girl, learn to make clothing and tan caribou hides, or whatever; at about twelve or thirteen years old you were a learned, skilled sewer, because you were taught that. But when you finished eighth grade, that was it. You had no more schooling. So my father was good enough to take me Outside to high school. When I came back in 1934, there was still no high school here.

When we started school, we were not allowed to use our native language in the BIA school. We had to answer back in English, and we got reprimanded for using our native language in the schoolground, even in those years, those young years. From the time we left home and got into the schoolground, we couldn't speak our language. We'd get caught speaking Eskimo; we'd be out in the playground at recess time and accidentally speak it. Somebody would be sure to report you. Then you didn't attend the party at the end of the month.[8] All BIA teachers were instructed not to use the native language among the children, and when Roy did use a native word, it had to be guarded to where it was for making the kids understand what he meant, if they couldn't catch on. But it wasn't too often he did that, because he was very clear on making us understand what was there in school for us. We didn't tell our other teachers about it, and we got away with it. He was good with that, but later on when I started teaching school, even though the rule was there, I couldn't help it. Because it was pathetic for a student when, no matter how hard we try to explain, they wouldn't get the meaning of a sentence until you spoke it in our language. They needed that in order to get ahead.

Our last two years in school here, as seventh and eighth graders, we were given a word each week to take home to teach to our parents. If you knew a word and could spell it and knew the meaning of it, then you could explain it to your parents—kind of teach them what the English language was about. That was just an added item on our school curriculum. If we were successful, we got a prize or a

mark, a credit for doing it, and some of the teachers were good enough to visit and talk to the parents and be very surprised at what advance we got from bringing the information across to our parents. It wasn't much, but I know we did help to bring the English language to our elders.

I had it easier than some of my friends because I was so far advanced in English. The assignments with reading and words, the English words, I was way ahead of the schoolchildren. There were many children who didn't know the English language, so they had to redo and redo the next year, according to what the teachers would evaluate.

When Dr. Greist and Mrs. Greist[9] were here they had a son, David, about our age, and he was determined he was going to learn the Eskimo language. And he got more marks against himself than we ever did, that Greist boy, because he was trying to learn the Eskimo language; he didn't care where he did it. Towards the last, though, it wasn't all that strict. I think they realized that they had started to take our native language away, make the kids forget it. And even today, some don't even know how to speak Eskimo, and then their kids are learning the Eskimo language in school.

There was only one teacher I didn't like, a man by the name of Mr. Sylvester. He always had a ruler in his hand, and he was so determined that he was going to make each child learn not to make a mistake. If they did, then he got their hand slapped, or they stood in the corner for the longest time, and no one liked that teacher.[10] That's the only one that we never did like. His wife used to have so much pity on the children; you'd see her actually crying for what her husband was doing.

Sundays

And on Sunday, there was Sunday School and church. Still, no matter how many times you went to church, it didn't matter, that was the only place you could go. Unless it was a nice day and you could get the whole town to turn out for a free-for-all football out on that flat lagoon. There were no goals. You could run with that ball until you got tired.

But most of the time, church was the only place we could go, and we never thought anything about it. In the morning, 9:00 would be Sunday School, and about 10:00 would be for the adults; if our mothers couldn't take us back home, we sat there and listened to what was going on. But 11:00 was the actual sermon, up till 12:00. And from then on there were other little groups that would meet—Bible classes and stuff. So all day long we could spend our time in the church if we wanted to. And prayer meeting at night, from 7:00 maybe until 9:00, because of the interpreter. The sermons were long. They seemed long, because there was an interpreter that had to be there to interpret for people who didn't know how to speak English or understand English.[11]

Sunday was quitc strict, because in those days our old people were so strong in their Christian way of life. You couldn't hunt, you couldn't work on Sunday. All you did was go to church or play games or visit.[12] So it was quite different than what it is today. It was a must with you; you went with your parents to church or to visit a patient in the hospital, ask him what he'd like to have, or talk to the missionary doctor. He did the preaching and the doctor work.

Sewing

When we were little, Mom made all our clothes. Sometimes she would sit us down and see if you could sew this or that on. I remember sewing or patching because I was always tearing my clothes, my snow cover or my pants covers, because I was such a tomboy. When we were growing up, a young girl had to stay home and learn to sew your own clothes when you were old enough, like eleven, whether you wanted to or not, because, if your mother didn't sew for you and you didn't learn, then you went without. If our mother made a pattern, we had to go by it and cut our own clothes and make them—patch whatever holes were in our clothing.

It was hard, because by age eleven you were quite an ace at sewing; I was. I was crimping, with my teeth, the boot sole—we didn't have these pliers they use today—[13]and I wore my teeth out. Some of these older women that you see today, where their teeth are real straight and worn, this is what happened. They're crimping

the boot sole for their husband and children, and maybe their next-door neighbor—who knows? I used to see that, and I was doing a lot of that until my father got after me and said that I would have to take care of my teeth, because he was taking me Outside. You could see where they were worn off even when I went Outside, as young as I was. A girl at eleven or twelve knew how to make her own mukluks, using her teeth to crimp that *ugruk* [bearded seal] hide, or whatever.

And worst of all, because Dad used to have some of this tar paper—this thick tar paper—my sisters and I used to practice on the tar paper and chew it, learning how to crimp. And we'd get some other girls interested and take some of that tar paper and hide—well, we didn't think we were stealing it, because sometimes when Dad found out, he'd ask, "Who's been into my tar paper?" And then we had to tell. We could never tell a lie. How to make the skin pliable was something that was taught to us; we had to learn. And the nearest thing to *ugruk* hide was this tar paper we used to get out of Dad's warehouse. The sealskin, which was bleached in the wintertime and dried in the spring, was very popular and was easier to work with than *ugruk*.

The half hour we had with Mother before bed was something else. She'd cut out some material or give us something to do to teach us how to sew and make patterns. How to make our mukluks and mittens, and maybe help out patching mukluks for old people who didn't have anything to put on. We never had any rubber boots or ready-made shoes. We had to make our own mukluks. Summer-time mukluk was out of sealskin, and the winter ones were from caribou or reindeer legs. So we had to learn to make our waterproof boots, and our winter boots, which were different. And clothing—your parka was made of reindeer hide. My mom did most of the cutting, and my sisters and I, we did the sewing, but when it was skin sewing for mukluks and stuff, well, we had to be by her side for her to continually teach us how—which way to put the mukluks together, or your snow shirts—otherwise we would put it backwards, and it didn't fit.

We didn't have sewing classes at school.[14] Mainly at the mission, they had sewing classes and cooking. Mrs. Greist did most of that, the missionary's wife. These boxes of surplus clothing, boxes and

boxes of donations, would come in every summer by boat. Mrs. Greist tried to interest women into cutting up some of that clothing and making it into clothing that would fit their children; it was free, and she used to call them in every week or every day that she had time for, and work with the women, because there was nothing else for the women to do but tend to their kids, and they take their little ones over there to the mission and make clothing. We were asked if we wanted a new dress for Christmas; we'd get fitted, sew them with the help of our mothers, and get a new dress for Christmas. That was interesting. An old dress or something that was good, we'd redo it—make it smaller, or make it into something for our brother. This was all under the supervision of Mrs. Greist, and under what was known as the Presbyterian Mothers Club.

Mollie Greist, a nurse and wife of the missionary doctor, organized the Mothers Club shortly after her arrival in Barrow in 1921. She placed a notice in the church bulletin "asking all women with babies who would like a mothers meeting club to come to the manse on a certain day." The Mothers Club began with twenty-eight mothers and their babies and within six months had increased to sixty-eight. Only one woman spoke any English, so Nurse Greist communicated with them through Helen Suvlu, her interpreter and health aide.

At club meetings they served tea and pilot bread to the mothers and milk to the children; they sang hymns and prayed; and Mollie Greist instructed the women in sewing calico and in "proper" childcare. Greist tried to picture for them "the life we live in civilization," showing them magazine pictures of homes, schools, and so forth. Of the homes, Greist reports the Eskimo women remarked, "Ah, too big—clean all time." And about the schools—"Too many children . . . [our children] were plenty happy when they could go hunting with bows and arrows, take care of babies and puppies all day—no bells ring!"

Through Helen, Mollie Greist tried to obtain the Barrow women's perceptions of white women. Helen dutifully reported: "Some of them think white women are good to them and work plenty but worry so much." Another stated, "White women work hard too much but they don't do things—you don't make boots for family, no make parka, scrape skins, cut up seals and walrus and whale . . ., cover boats and many things Eskimo women must do."[15] *Nonetheless, Greist had the respect and friendship of the people, and her Mothers Club still plays an important role in the Barrow community today.*

That was the first organization of mothers, and it was done by Mrs. Greist, the missionary doctor's wife. She taught how to make patterns for kids; well, most of the women knew, because they sewed most all of their children's clothes. We didn't have any order catalogues to order from in those days. There were very few sewing machines, too, and they had to wait their turn. I don't know just how many there were in the mission—two or three sewing machines. Most of it, though, was done by hand, which they were used to. Then, when I was around nine or ten years old, the missionary's wife started teaching us in school how to make our mittens with yarn. And there weren't enough knitting needles in town, so she used to get these big nails and polish them up, and we'd use those to knit with.

Chores

Young kids had to learn to chop wood, because if you didn't, then the chore would fall on your parents, who were already busy trying to make a livelihood for you. As far back as I can remember . . . first I learned how to chop wood, because that was an easy item. I must have been around six or seven years old when it was a requirement on Saturdays, when we weren't attending school, to chop all the wood we could find, get our friends in there, fill up I don't know how many bins with wood. And some had to be chopped very fine, because they were the ones to start the fire in the morning—kindling wood.

We'd take a dog team and bring in drift logs gathered from along the coast. We'd saw them, chop them on Saturday for a whole week at a time, trying to get the fuel when we were able to go out and bring drift logs. Most of the time it was in the spring—well, warmer days, like in May and June—before the ice deteriorated, or what we used to call "melt away." We'd go out with the dog teams and sleds, pile all the driftwood we can find and bring it in, put it on racks during the summer months, and dry it out for winter use. And if some family was unfortunate enough not to be able to go out, we shared what we had, and take it to the homes and saw it. Each kid, it didn't matter whose house you went to, we were taught to share and help out the older people, and this is how we grew up—being concerned about our own people. And then, aside from that was

shoveling snow, and keeping our storm shed clean in the wintertime from snow, and helping people out—melting snow, getting water, which was very hard to get for people in those times.

One thing I never learned to do was to piggyback, because at age twelve I was the chore girl, it seemed like, out of the family, and my sister Maria was the little mother. She carried all the babies, our younger brothers and sisters; she took care of them while I did all the work. Maria was always packing while my mom worked. And I helped Mom with all the chores, and she wore Mom's packing parka and slapped the baby on her back when she wanted to be out. Later I carried my own kids on my back; I worked with a baby on my back; I had to work with them on my back and carry them while I worked.

On the weekends Mother always had us wash up, and we couldn't go play outdoors for a couple of hours because we were cleaning up and washing our clothes and hanging them up. And we didn't have any washers or dryers; we had to use the old scrub boards to clean our clothes. We had to wash our brothers' clothes, too, my sister Maria and I. Kate was too small to do any of that work, but she helped chop kindling wood. Then later on, when I was about eleven years old, Dad bought one of these wooden tubs where you operated it with your foot. The whole tub had grooves on it where you could put your clothes in it there, wash them, and if the dirt didn't come off, you had to rub it off. Mom would inspect the cuffs and the necks and the fronts to see if they were actually clean, because with the scrub board you could really get all the dirt out. Dad was the only one that brought one up, one of those newfangled washing machines, hand-operated, foot-operated. So we had it a whole year before I went Outside. Then when I came back, they had the washing machines with [gas] motors to run them. You had to start it, but you couldn't hear a thing going on inside the house because of the noise.

Reindeer

In 1916 reindeer looked like a promising solution to Barrow's economic problems. The schoolteacher wrote in his annual report: "The reindeer business

seems to be the only thing that will enable the Eskimo to meet the changed conditions that are coming and when means of disposing of the butchered meat is furnished, the deer business will at once become the main industry and will mean independence to these people" (Richardson 1916). He added that 122 owners, herders, and apprentices owned 2,107 adult deer and 915 fawns. In 1914 Diamond Jenness had commented upon the economic value of reindeer at Barrow:

> At this period the live animal was valued at $25; its hide is from $2.50 upward depending on its size and quality; and a "slab" of sinew from its back, which furnished thread far superior to either linen or cotton for the sewing of fur, $1.00. It required from seven to eight reindeer skins to clothe a man completely. [1957:24]

Reindeer herding never lived up to its promise at Barrow, though reindeer continued to increase until about 1935.

As far back as a I can remember, the reindeer herds came into town in the fall. I was barely able to walk, but I remember seeing Mom at the house cleaning all those guts and hearts and livers. I can't even remember whether there was any caribou when I was young. My mother used to tell us that when she was younger there used to be nothing but caribou. When they [caribou] migrated on this side from Canada, they could get them out there. And they roamed where these animals were, for subsistence.

But we always had the reindeer herds in the fall. It seemed like every older adult native was a reindeer owner, shareholder. And it was exciting for us children to see the adults make a corral, or we kids would hold hands so the reindeer wouldn't stray off while they were putting them in the corral and looking for which ones to butcher. Sometimes we'd be scared and let loose, you know. But we were asked to help out. When I first became aware of that and was old enough to know when they used to bring the reindeer herds in, they would build a big corral where that lagoon is,[16] after freeze-up in November, and the whole town would get us kids from hand to hand while they were putting the herds in the corral, and there, after they got them in there, then we could watch them—they were like cowboys with lassos.

When I was a little older I can remember them using these poles, wooden poles made from drift log and some kinds of wire attached to it, so the reindeer couldn't get out. It was right in town. They never shot the deer that they butchered; their method was either to cut the throat and hang them up, or puncture the heart, which was much easier than shooting the animal. There were some reindeer corrals built with wood and wire. Before, they used to take ice blocks, and they would make a chute when it was time to mark the reindeer company's mark on the ears. They had to mark them because, during the fawning season, they left the reindeer herds unattended so they could roam and graze. Then they would try to round them back in the fall. Reindeer would mingle together from each group of herds, and then they had to be sorted out because there were about five or six herds here in town. But it was an exciting day; we never went to school when that happened, because the teachers were just as curious as we were and there was a lot of meat. As far as I can remember, it used to last a couple of days, and the butchering was another one.

And it was interesting to see the herders come in with a reindeer trained to pull a sled. They were the fastest thing, I thought, that anyone could ever see in those times. Because they had reins and special sleds made with a top railing where you could hang on, because reindeer didn't start out gently. They just went like that! And you had to hang on for your dear life to that sled railing until you got to your destination. They never use dog teams around the deer—because it scared the herds—but a sheep dog, or what we called a reindeer dog. Talk about smart dogs, they were the biggest help to the reindeer herders.

The herds were locally owned. You had shares and you were allowed, if you had ten heads, you were allowed two reindeer to butcher out of the herd, because there weren't very many caribou roaming up in this area at that time, hardly any. Each herd had their grazing grounds; each was assigned a boundary where they can graze. There were thousands of acres allotted for each herd to graze in and the reindeer herders, who guarded it in that area, so they don't wander off. The deer can recognize the voice of a herder, and they come towards you, they are so happy to see you. Then the caribou started migrating back from the Canadian side. When the NPR

[National Petroleum Reserve No. 4] opened up in 1950 or late 1949, the reindeer wandered off and they never came back.

We see stray reindeer today among the caribou. Some men will go out there and hunt and, among a herd of caribou, they will see a spotted one, and they know that's a reindeer, because there are no spotted caribou (they are all brown and gray). And they blame the oil reserve, the tractors, the roaming. All that activity going on—with tractors, and cat trains, and stuff—drove them [the reindeer] off from this northern area. Because there was so much activity with drilling, and so many people going back and forth—machinery, noise.[17] And then the caribous—I can remember seeing some of the first caribou coming in, and we used to think they were reindeer.

Siblings

> About him now were half-a-dozen [children] by a second wife, sturdy, wholesome-looking half-breeds, the blood mantling their cheeks with rosy bloom. The bitter winds of this coast bring the colour violently to the children's faces, and some of the mixed race that I saw had the richest complexions imaginable. Mr. Brower's Bobby, about six years old, was my special pet, an affectionate little chap with coal-black hair and eyes, small regular features, cheeks like poppies, teeth white and regular enough for a dentifrice advertisement—as pretty as any picture—and with a shy manner and engaging smile that took me captive at once. [Stuck 1920:212]

Sadie had nine siblings: Tom (1904), Dave (1907–85), Jennie (1909), Robert (1912–84), Maria (1914), Kate(1919), Arnold (1922), Harry (1924), and Mary (1929). Jennie at this writing still lives in California; the remainder, regardless of any Outside education and experience, chose to return to Barrow to live.

I remember Mary was very small; she was going on six months when I left to go Outside to high school. She was born in March and I left in September. She was a preemie, but Mom made her live with a medicine dropper. Even the doctor didn't think she was going to live. She was probably five months, very small. Mom had a ring on

her finger, and when Mary was born, that ring would go all the way up to her shoulder. That's how small she was.

Some were given a chance to go Outside, but they came right back, within a year or two. They couldn't stand it out there. Well, the four older ones from the first wife never did come back, but Tom and Dave went out there; they didn't stick it out. Dad was kind of disappointed. It was understandable, I guess. He needed them home, too, with the work, to teach them the management of the store. Dave tended the store,[18] and Tom and Robert took care of the reindeer herd, away from the community. But they had a chance to come in every so often, driving the herds in for butcher in the fall; they would stay a while, and they would go back out again. But we looked up to them.

Jennie, my older sister, left before I could really remember many things about her. In 1927 she left home and went through high school and entered nursing at Alta Bates Hospital in Berkeley. And there was another girl, Kate Allen from Wainwright, whose father was a white whaler.[19] Jennie and Kate both went to nursing school. Jennie kept right on going until she went up to the top with hers, and [she] was a nurse in the war and came back and got married and settled out there. She did visit maybe a couple of times, but none after that. And her kids, her two boys, have lived out there. One did come in and visit last year [1983]. But it was rather hard for him, I guess, because he wasn't built for this area.

From Bob on down, we were close-knit brothers and sisters. Mom was very sick at the time when she delivered Maria.[20] There was a Diomede family here at the time, and he married a woman from Point Barrow [Nuvuk], and they adopted Maria, raised her while Mom was convalescing from whatever she had. But when they both died with TB, then—well, old man Kunniaq first died, and then a year later, her mom, Mary, died, and she [had] requested that Mom take Maria back, if she wanted to, and both [had] agreed.

She belonged to that family; she still does. She thinks of them; she grew up with them away from our family, and when she was brought back to our family, she was so shy. Maria was around eight, I guess, going on nine and I was around seven when she came back. She came between Robert and me, it seemed like, and I was very jealous of her for a while. But we were close. Mom would instruct Bob and

me to try and bring her back into our family. She had a poor heart to begin with, and then Mom instructed me to trail her. And everywhere she went, I would be her shadow, it seemed like. It was hard for me, because I was just a carefree, happy-go-lucky kid roaming whenever I wasn't doing my chores, because that's the way we lived during the summer months when there was no school. When she would fall down or something and she couldn't get up, I would run over, go home and get Mom, tell her Maria was down on the ground again, and she would come running. Later on, we found out these were mild epileptic fits. This is how we understood the way my mom used to explain it to us, that we had to be very careful and watch her that she didn't go way off and lose her breath with it.

When she was around fourteen and I was going on twelve, she had her menstrual period, and we used to hide it and wonder what that was, and she would ask me, "Can you see where I cut myself?" Later on we laughed about growing up because Mom never told us anything about it. After she started having her menstrual period, she stopped having these attacks.

Our mom used to make our snow coverings. Maria had the women's piece [ruffs]; I used to have the men's, the boys' leftovers. I always got the hand-me-downs and she got all the good ones! I got most of my brothers' hand-me-downs; Mom didn't care how I looked, I guess, but Maria had to be a pretty one, get all the pretty ones, because she missed out on so much. My mom favored her[21] with whatever clothing she made and just pampered her more than she did me, because I was a roughneck, grew up with my brother Bob.

Bob and I were close. He was Dad's favorite, too. I couldn't do anything mean to Bob or say anything mean to him without Dad getting in there and reprimanding me or giving me a nice whack on the butt for doing what I did, and all because of Bob. And I'd sulk for a while and wouldn't talk to Robert. But it wore off.

I guess Maria was about the closest to our mother. Mom lost her once, sort of, for a while and then, I think, was making it up to her when she came back—and it was noticeable. But Mom cared for all of us; she never neglected any of us. My brothers, even after they married, she was always making them warm parkas, and mukluks, and stuff, mittens for travel, something to wear when they went out hunting—and keeping their hunting gear in order. She did it with

Nate, too, and she tried to do it with Joe, my sister's [Maria's] husband, but he was used to having certain styles that his mom made him.

Maria went [Outside], but not to school. She went out there and lived like a little princess, going around with my father, and then eventually ended up down in Los Angeles staying with one of the older [half] sisters, Elizabeth and her family—Elizabeth Kelley, who also had two daughters about the same age as Maria and I. But I was rather jealous because she could just roam all over. . . . She took the grand tour while I had to trudge through school; she made the newspapers while everybody just forgot about me, even though I had been out there for about three years when she came. They put her in the newspaper as "the uncrowned princess of the north," and there I had been all this time, and nobody had noticed what I had gone through. But I made it, you know, and I was busy with my education. Sometimes sad, sometimes happy, but I had to learn to live and be independent out there.

Utqiagvik. This first photograph of the village was taken during the International Polar Exploring Expedition, 1881–83. Courtesy of the National Anthropological Archives.

Barrow, looking south, 1930. (Hospital, church and manse, school and teacherage.) Courtesy of the Federal Archives, Seattle.

Barrow, 1988. Photograph by Bill Hess.

AGVIK ST
1888
1892
TUTTU

Point Barrow school house, 1912. Courtesy of the California Academy of Sciences, Liebes Collection.

The Station and Brower's house, 1917. Courtesy of the California Academy of Sciences, Liebes Collection.

A successful whaling crew returns, 1988. Photograph by Bill Hess.

H. Liebes Company's trading station at Point Barrow, 1917 [Brower's station]. Courtesy of the California Academy of Sciences, Liebes Collection.

Interior of the trading station at Barrow, 1923. Courtesy of the California Academy of Sciences, Liebes Collection.

Eskimo whaling camp with victory flag. Photograph by R. W. Hendee, 1921. Courtesy of the Denver Museum of Natural History.

Children playing on the back of a whale at Barrow, 1988. Photograph by Bill Hess.

Transporting shares of the whale to Barrow, 1988. Photograph by Bill Hess.

Nalukataq, 1920s. Photograph by Fred Hopson. Courtesy of the Denver Museum of Natural History.

4

An Outside Education

Sadie had a wonderful experience coming up the Bay. Had her first ride in a car going to the hotel and watching the cars and people on Geary Street. [Brower 1930:36]

A Wonderful Experience

Looking back, I don't think I ever really thought of what I wanted to do as an adult. It was such a carefree life. You just accepted what came; it was your life. And some of my friends, their marriages were arranged, and eventually when they grew up, they'd get together and get married. Some of them would be so young, and they were having kids already at age fourteen and fifteen. I never thought about it. I wasn't interested in boys then; I was so young, twelve.[1] We had friends that we played with, but other than that, I was too young to even get interested in any boys. And when I went Outside, I was very shy. I couldn't look at a boy in the face, let alone talk to them. I was so conscious of myself.

As we were growing older and going on to having a first period, my mom explained these many things about it, a woman's life. In those times we didn't have any big toilets; we had to go out in the snow. It was soon after my thirteenth birthday when I saw this red stuff on the ground in the snow and came in and told my mom that I must have cut my back somewhere. She had a big smile and cornered me and took me to her room and showed me how to put a pad on. And then, later on, she talked to us about having a good life, not mess around with boys. I guess it was very shameful if you were caught in those days.

I really didn't have any choice in the matter of going Outside,

because I had nothing else to do at that early age but to go along with what Dad wanted me to do—get an education and eventually come back and do what I could here if I wanted to, or find a new life out there. I eventually came back and put my education to use. My mother went along with my father. She missed me, and I felt like I was being taken away from whatever life I had, but I was also very anxious to see what the other life was all about. I had a lot of tutors along the way to bring me up to date about what goes on.

Dad had a clerk named Harry Riley. His wife used to tell me all about the schools and fixed up some clothes for me to take out and fitted me, but we never could find a pair of shoes that would fit. I had these high-top leather boots that belonged to my brother Bob and were about three sizes too large for me, but it didn't matter because style was nothing to me, I was so young yet. When my dad decided to take me Outside, he sent for some clothes. And they were saved until I was ready to go out. They were placed in the suitcase. Mrs. Riley also put all these pads [sanitary napkins] that I had never seen in my suitcase, and I thought, "Well, gee, what are those for?" My mom had showed me how to use this flannel—put it on your belt, and then soak them the way they used to—but these were the right size for my foot, and I thought they were for my insoles! I kept using them because I didn't have another period until it was near Christmas.

We left September third [1930] from Barrow; we made a stop around the fifteenth in Unalaska in the Aleutian Islands, and from there on to San Francisco. Dad said it took us twenty-three days to reach there on a trading boat, the old *Patterson*. That was the first time I had ever seen those big freighters. I thought we were on a big ship, that old *Patterson*, and then I woke up one morning, saw this big wall, and wondered where we were. We were in Unalaska and were tied up to a big barge.

That was also my first time to pick blueberries. All over the side of the hill was blueberries. I had a light tan outfit on with a big pocket, and I put those blueberries in my pocket. I didn't know any better. Dad had said, "Be sure to bring me back some fresh blueberries," and that is how I tried to bring them back home. But there was hardly anything left by the time that I got there—just the biggest mess in my pocket that you'd ever want to see.

I never did get seasick. Here when we were going through the strait [Bering Strait], the boat would go down and then you would see the water up there, and come up to the top [on deck] and you could see everything, even over to the Siberian side. You could see land over there, and I would just sit there along with the captain's son, Walter Pedersen, about two years older than I was. We became real good buddies on that boat. We had a lot of things to do on board. I would help him steer the boat on nice days, and we'd watch the sea gulls and albatross, and the cargo of silver foxes [destined for a fox farm]. I didn't have any shoes, but I wore my sealskin boots. "What are you going to wear when you get to San Francisco?" Walter would tease me. "You can't wear those things. They'll think you're a primitive person."

I remember when we were coming into San Francisco Bay; I had never seen so many lights. I could see all these lights as far out as you could see on that coastline, and the masts would get closer and closer. And then when we landed, and all these things that were writing by themselves in the air—these neon signs. I had never seen electric lights, I had never seen cars, I had never seen streetcars, that or anything run with electricity. I thought that was a miracle. I just looked. . . . I think if somebody had put their hands over my eyes, I don't know, I'd have bit him or something. And to get inside a car—my first car ride. A taxi took us to the hotel. Oh, the bumps, because San Francisco is hilly. Going over the streets to the hotel I thoroughly enjoyed myself and I didn't want to get out of that taxi; I wanted another ride.

And such big buildings. I was just looking and marveling. I was so awed with the hotel I almost got lost. How pretty the lobby was! There were big windows and colorful pictures and designs—colored glass windows. Dad had to look for me because I was just looking at the inside of that hotel. Oh gosh, I don't think I could hear my father speaking to me: "C'mon, young lady!" I don't know how many times he said that, but I was still looking, and everybody had their eyes fixed on me because I was a strange-looking character. I was partially dressed in Eskimo clothes and had this big stocking cap on and my big high-top boots that went flop, flop, flop all over the place. I still had my sealskin mukluks on when I landed in San Francisco, but Dad had told me to put my boots on, and I did.

I knew that hotels were places where people stayed, not a home. And I'd read about elevators, but I didn't know what they were or what they looked like. So when this young man took our luggage and put it in this little room, this elevator, I looked at my father and I said, "Where's our beds?—Is this the room we're going to have?" So little—it looked like a six-by-six [foot] room. And this young man that was running the elevator said, "She must be new around here." Dad told him I was new, and I came to find out it was an elevator. That's how dumb I was. And I can remember my dad saying soon after we got placed in that hotel that he was going to call my sister and tell her that we were there. "Would you like to say hello to your sister?" I took the phone and she told me to "hold the line for a minute." I looked at the phone and there was this "string," so I rolled it up on my finger and held on to it. I was hanging onto it until my dad said, "What are you doing?" "Well, Jennie said to hold the line, and that's what I'm doing."

How dumb I felt, not knowing what these things were when I went Outside! But I soon learned. It's very different from how you were brought up. . . . You read about these things in school, but to actually see them the way I did was a great experience. How important I felt, just being there; it was just like a dream. So strange, like going from a dull area to something that's so wide awake. I don't think I ever slept that first night, because I was looking out the window, seeing so many people. And then when my sister came in that night, she asked me, "Aren't you going to sleep?" "Well, don't these people ever go to sleep in towns?" Because I saw people going all night long in the streets from my window. And they were different people—they were not the same people.

❖

When Dad gave me this piece of paper with this green stuff on it, I didn't know what it was—it had a five on it. I took it to a Martha Washington Candy Store. I went in there, and this lady asked me what I wanted. I said I wanted some candy, and I gave her this green piece of paper. She said, "All of it?" I said, "I guess" (whatever it was). And she gave me this box filled with candy. I could barely carry it. So, when I took it back to the hotel I forgot all about it, because there was this "shelf" by the window, and I left the candy

on top of it; it was a radiator—I'd put my candy on top of a radiator! So, later on that night, one of my sisters [Jennie], who was a graduate nurse across the bay in Berkeley, came over, and my dad asked me, "Aren't you going to treat your sister to some candy?" "Oh, yeah." "Well, where's the change?" "Well, what's that?" "Didn't she give you any money back?" "No." And Dad said, "You mean to tell me, you spent that whole $5 for candy?" "Yes, it's right there by the window." And the minute I said that, oh-oh, the disappointed look on my sister and Dad; they knew it was soup inside that box, because all the candy had melted. I didn't know what I had put it on; I thought it was just a shelf to lay things on. That's how dumb I was.

We stayed about a week at the hotel.[2] I had to have my eyes tested, and while I was at the hotel I had an operation on my eye because I was crosseyed. [During that week] my dad wanted my sister [Jennie] to take me to these fashion places to get me proper clothes. Oh my, how unhappy I was! Style never meant anything to us, so when my sister told me that I had to be in style, it took me quite a while to learn what being in style was.

She took me and she put a pair of three-quarter heels on me, which I never had before. Then she bought this beautiful coat for me; it was green felt with black fur on it. I don't know what kind of fur it was. My shoes were the hardest for me to get used to. I had never worn anything with heels, so I had wobbly ankles until I got used to it. And then too, my feet, having worn mukluks for so long, were spread. Your feet are loose in mukluks, and when I had to wear shoes, we had a hard time finding a pair of shoes wide enough to fit my feet. I wore a pair of flat shoes, leather ones, that I finally got.

The style that year was these tight hats with the feather sticking out, ostrich feather or whatever, and Jennie got me this hat. She said it was a beautiful hat, and she stuck it on my head and told me that whenever I went out, all dressed up, I can always wear it. Well, I tried to once. I looked at myself in the mirror with this feather over my head. Well, it seemed so ridiculous to have a feather on my cap, or whatever it was—the "hat" as she called it—that when I got home, I got a pair of scissors and cut it off. And I had these chiffon dresses—oh my goodness, Dad had me so well dressed out there; he was so proud. When he came to San Francisco, he'd go out and take

my sister, as usual, and pick out these outfits, because he didn't trust me with the right type of style, and he could trust Jennie.

Then, at Christmastime this storekeeper that Dad traded with [Liebes] had these beautiful furs. My sister and I each got a white fox fur neckpiece. I said, "What's that for? I don't want that darn thing around my neck." It was supposed to be in style—expensive fur, $600 skin, but I didn't want it. And instead, they had us try out some coats, fur coats, because I didn't want that [fox] fur. And I don't know how much those things cost in those times, but I still have the pieces of muskrat fur out of my first fur coat my dad gave me in San Francisco a long time ago.

When I look back, it is interesting, because I never could pick out my own clothes, except my blouses and skirts and my flat shoes that I wore, the kind that were comfortable. And the day that my sister wanted me to have plucked eyebrows! She said, "We're going to the beauty parlor and we're going to have your face fixed over. Your bushy eyebrows don't look right. See all these girls with these pretty arched eyebrows." They used this wax or whatever that dried, and [they] just pulled the hair right out. I wasn't going to have them do it on the other eye. But my sister said, "That's the style. You have to." And then she bought me a pair of tweezers to pull all those stubs out when my eyebrows started to grow back, and I didn't like it one bit, but I got used to it. Those types of things that I had to go through that I never thought you did to your face; my dad never wanted any of us girls to use makeup, so I never wore lipstick or rouge or powder on my face—just soap and water, just natural. That same week I had my hair curled and permed in San Francisco, too. I thought they were burning my brains out, it got so hot underneath there! But I went along with whatever my sister wanted done to get me in style.

I started gaining an awful lot of weight the first two years I was out there. It got to the point where I couldn't buy any clothes that would fit. Too much sweets—candy—and I didn't know what diet was. I just ate anything that they gave me, ate candy and candy and candy bars, which I had never had. I soon found out where to buy candy, found all the candy stores. Then I started realizing that there were people who would reduce; about my fourth year, I started to take notice, to fully grasp what style was about and to look neat and

be trim. And then I went down from 180 to about 150 pounds at the middle of the year, and I kept working on it. We went through exercises and stuff. The lady that I stayed with and her daughter were helping to get me down to where I would be comfortable with dresses bought in a store. We had to make my clothes, because she couldn't find anything to fit. That was the oddest part of my stay out there, gaining so fast and becoming really fat.

Family Life

The first year I was quite homesick. I waited for the snow to fall that winter, which never came. I missed the atmosphere—the cold, the snow. There was day and night all the time in San Francisco, and how strange it was to be living in an area where winter just never came. And to see these trees blossom and grow fruit, that was really something to me. Most of the people in that area had gardens, so I could see blackberries growing over a vine and just pick one off the vine instead out of a can—you know, eat the fruit and find out which trees thay came from, which was very interesting to me.

There was a German family that had a son Dave's age. When Dad took him Outside, Dave started school in San Francisco and met this boy and got to "palling around" with him. Dad met them and left Dave in the charge of his family. And so when I went out, I was given a choice to stay over in Berkeley with another family that had been up here, or with the German family in San Francisco. Because the Berkeley family was near where Jennie and Kate Allen[3] were, I decided to stay with them. Jennie and Kate lived at the nurses' dorms about three blocks away, so I could get to see them, but I wasn't comfortable with that family. There wasn't anyone near my age to talk with. I tried, but it just didn't work. It was awfully hard. The times when I would be closed into my room all by myself when something else was going on in the other room, that was what I didn't like. They didn't include me. They had parties quite a bit, and I didn't know what it was all about, with all the noise and stuff. I didn't even know what a drunk man was, or what liquor was. Even though I didn't know anything about drinking, I didn't approve of the way the daughter of that woman was running around and bringing

drinking into the home. I felt like I wasn't good enough for them. But I stayed out in Berkeley about eight months, I guess, until I moved over to San Francisco to live with the Waldas.

The Waldas had been in the city for many years.[4] I guess they relocated there from the old country. They had a girl about my age. Her interest was in music, and from the time she could remember, she had played the piano. She was taking piano lessons, and I'd never heard anybody play the piano before. Oh, I just marveled at what she could do with that piano. We were close because we were the same age. And I used to be so surprised because she was so talented. I used to just sit there and marvel at her playing the piano, just sit there while she went through all her practice runs. I would even say, "Don't bother about cleaning up. I will do all the cleaning if you will promise to play the piano." We got along real good. There was an older brother, but he was about five years older than she was.

My dad and Mr. Walda talked and they made some ground rules about what they would allow me to do and what they wouldn't allow me to do, and where I could go and where not to go. I had to ask permission to go various places. And if my guardians would approve, then I could go, and if they didn't approve, then I had to stay home. Which was sad, because up here you don't have any restrictions growing up—except for my dad's evening curfew. In the summertime, if we were with our mother, we didn't have to go to sleep. We could stay up all night if we wanted to. And then suddenly to find yourself with all these rules you had to abide by. . . .

They accepted me as one of the family. I had to do a lot of learning, you know. They would tell me what to do, and I would learn it. They had a car, and whenever we wanted to go out anywhere, it was available. Homer [the brother] would drive us here and there, over to the park or the zoo, and places where I enjoyed, and they were very good about it. Their concern for me was good. They never left me out like that other family did.

I saw my father every so often. Every other year he came out, and one time he brought out Maria with him. How I envied her! I'd been out there three years, trudged myself through school, and here comes my sister, and some newspaper outfit interviews my father and names him as the "uncrowned king of the north" and my sister as "princess" Maria on the front page. And I looked at it and said,

"Gee, no one ever noticed me like that. . . ." Oh, I think I was so jealous. But I had to get rid of that feeling—how she could enjoy herself without having to go to school, travel with my father, be in these areas where he was visiting, and here I'm stuck in school. But later on, when I had a little more sense in my head, I began to work things out.

Galileo High School

As an Eskimo transplanted from a BIA schoolroom in Barrow to an urban San Francisco high school, Sadie did remarkably well. Although she failed bookkeeping, she earned above average grades in all the rest of her courses, including A's in algebra. Unfortunately, her high school transcript offers no clues to the personal adjustment Sadie had to make, nor, beyond the letter grades they gave, to her high school teachers' evaluations of her performance in school.

It was so different, so different from what I knew in Barrow. My first day in school, I was asked what studies I wanted, and all I could say was geography, arithmetic, English. And there was a whole line of subjects that I could choose from, but I was told that the basic needs would be English, math, and some kind of language, like Spanish, and whatever was there—Latin, German, and I can't remember what else there were, there were so many that you could take.

And there were so many nationalities in that school, Galileo High School. I didn't class myself as being good enough, equal to the white children that I was placed with in that great big school. But I made friends, because there were a lot of Chinese, and Italians, and Mexicans, and Japanese. Most of my friends were the Chinese. I got so I could communicate with them, and I thought they were the most polite people that I had ever met at my young age. Some would invite me to their homes—and how different life was for them from the house that I was staying in, the German family. And then they'd take me through their town, which was classed as being very dangerous in those days. There were hidden speakeasies, and many crimes [were] committed in that area. But it didn't scare me,

because none seemed to apply to me. I was accepted in Chinatown with my friends, and I didn't think it was dangerous. In fact, when I had been out there a whole year, I even invited my father into a home of one of my girl friends, and we got accepted.

My language [English] bothered me, because it was sort of half broken. And the inferiority complex—when I first went out there to high school, I couldn't bring myself to think that I was as good as the white kids. But after four years that feeling came off, and I was just as good as any of them. Math I never had problems with. I could work out a problem any time. It was my English, and studies about government. I didn't know what a president was, or his cabinet, Congress, all those things. It was hard for me to learn and remember "important" dates . . . [they] had no significance to me; why should I remember all these? These were people and events that had no bearing on my life, and I used to just about fall off to sleep when the history teacher would recite these things we had to learn, because I could never make heads or tails of it. But for the kids who lived there, it was an easy subject. For me, it was trying; it was really hard—but I made it.

My English teacher said that I would have to study in front of the mirror to learn how to speak. "And if you learn to take that lump out of your tongue and learn to speak English, you'll do good." He used to have me in front of the mirror saying words—he'd give me words to pronounce. And I'd sit there in front of the mirror, talking to myself—learning to talk these phrases that he would give me. So this was part of my education.

I didn't speak my language for a few years. Then Jim Allen's daughter Alice went Outside and was in a convent in San Francisco. On weekends, the mother superior would allow me to go and visit her or take her to my home for a weekend, and there we could talk our native language. It was fun.

I was always so afraid to talk in class. In those times you had to be able to give an oral speech in English class. And I got tongue-tied. When I had to get in front of the class. I couldn't speak. But when I'd look up in the ceiling and start telling stories about this northern area, you could hear a pin drop, because they didn't know anything about life up north. I talked about what life was like up here—dog teams, my people hunting, somebody going seal hunting, or making

a snow house. And then the questions would start, and more and more I would get bold, until I felt by my fourth year I was just as good as they were.

What was my happiest time? When I was able to go out to the zoo and these recreational areas—the ocean park, where you'd see all the marine animals and go swimming; being with my sister who was in nurses' training at Alta Bates Hospital over at Berkeley. She used to come over and take me out to the Presidio where she'd made friends with the Army personnel there. They had horses. Try and go horseback riding, as scared as I was to get on top of one of those things! But it was fun. And you soon learn; you just class yourself as good as those kids out there and you make it. But most of all, my interest in school. I was trying so hard to make it good. I had this inferiority complex so bad, I couldn't ever put myself up to the level of the white kids. My speech was sort of broken, though I could speak English and understand. With my subjects, my main problem was the government, how a government is run; because I came from a place where there was no government. Finally, my third year Outside, I began to catch on to what the government meant. Even in college, when I went to college here at the University of Alaska, I took government. By that time I thought I knew a little bit more about it; even then, I just barely passed it.

How Dad used to egg me on, bribe me with this and that, trying to make me finish high school. I remember that my last year in high school, he'd been out to San Francisco. "I'll give you this car if you finish the whole year." Because I was belly-aching about coming home with him. I didn't want to stay out there anymore. And he said, "I'll leave you this car." All I did was maybe take three rides one year when he left it; the family I stayed with had the use of it. I didn't bother to take driving lessons. I just didn't want to bother. I didn't think it would be any help even if I did; I was afraid of machinery.

Hollywood Beckons

Igloo life in the Arctica for the mass film mind is as unappealing as the title . . . "Eskimo." The label militates against any and all yeoman efforts by the exploitation department in selling this picture away from the frozen north locale.

> Yet the film holds a lot. There is adventure and the basic elements of struggle for existence. There are sympathetic leads and villainous menaces. There is a caribou stampede, a hand-to-hand fight with a polar bear, another life struggle with a wolf, the walrus hunt . . ., a whaling hunt . . . that are beautifully caught for the screen. . . .
>
> Mala, the male lead, turns in a swell performance. The two femme leads, one particularly a looker, are excellent, and both suggest a trek to Hollywood away from the Arctics—in truth the souvenir booklet confesses that much of the frigidaire cast has already had its baptism of cactus and palm trees for the added scenes, process shots, etc.
>
> The cast is all native, save the heavy, played by Peter Freuchen, the author. [*Variety Film Reviews* 1930–33, *vol.* 4, *November* 21, 1933]

My biggest disappointment was in my last year. When I turned seventeen, some outfit from MGM came up here and scouted this northern area for characters to play in Peter Freuchen's story, *The Eskimo*. They picked Ray Wise from Prince of Wales and Gertie Becker from Nome to act in this picture. I had an offer to play a small part, but my father wouldn't allow it.

It all happened the summer that Alice and I got left alone. Both our dads went home at the same time, and we didn't know what to do with ourselves. I believe it was 1933. We talked it over, and we talked our guardians into making this trip down to Los Angeles where my cousin Edith was staying, my dad's old cousin. We worked it out to where we could make the trip down there, and they could meet us, but we could still go together down there and enjoy our summer vacation in a different place. So I stayed with Aunt Edith, and Alice stayed with the Kramers. They were some old teachers from Wainwright who lived near Hollywood. But what we didn't know that summer was that we were going to meet some Eskimos from the north.

They were making that Peter Freuchen movie. They had started making it, coming up here to take scenes and stuff; the rest of it they filmed in Hollywood. Alice's sister Kate, who was a nurse then in Wainwright, got in that film. And we met Gertie Becker from Nome, Ray Wise from Wales, and Evrulik Rock, an Eskimo from Point Hope; they all had this long hair because of the film that they were making. We were out on this long beach area, sunning

ourselves, when we saw these odd-looking people. "Gee, they sure look like Eskimos," we thought, but we didn't know.

Well, the Kramers were saying, "Oh, you see all kinds of people here. They are film people." We were sitting and talking in Eskimo, and this one man, Evrulik Rock, looks around and says, "Oh, I hear somebody speaking Eskimo." And it was Alice and me. He came over and introduced himself and later on brought Ray and Gertie Becker around, and we started "palling around." We got into the Hollywood studios and got guided tours around it that summer, just thoroughly enjoyed ourselves. Occasionally we met—because we stayed there for almost four weeks—and we got to be good friends, and we'd laugh, we'd talk the Eskimo language out there; it was fun.

To our surprise, Evrulik Rock said he had some dried seal meat, but he didn't have any seal oil. Well, it didn't matter, we would like to have some anyway. So he brought some of this black dried meat out to where we [were] picnicking one day, and the Kramers were there as usual. This *ugruk* tasted so familiar and so good. Evrulik Rock had taken some of his native food down there with him, because he couldn't cope with the white man's food. They were finishing off the Peter Freuchen movie down there. After we went back to San Francisco that fall, I got a letter from Ray and his wife Gertie. They had gotten married in the meantime. (Later she got so she was drinking quite a bit, and Ray couldn't stand it. He eventually separated from her, maybe three or four years later.) Ray wrote and said how thoroughly he enjoyed our company, and he had shown pictures of us that Gertie took at the beach to the movie studio, and there were some scenes missing that they wanted to do. Would I be interested in acting some parts of it? Wow! Me, an actress—oh! What could be better than for a young girl to be offered something like that! When you're young, you're foolish—you never value anything, it seemed like—and I was at that age when they asked me.

My dad's permission was needed, so when he came to San Francisco that fall, I showed him the letter with all the enthusiasm in me. Gosh, I was in seventh heaven with that—getting a chance to go down to Hollywood and play in a picture. Well, you can imagine what Dad thought of it. "That trash," he said. "I wouldn't think of my daughter going to Hollywood and ruining herself, throwing away her education for a little two-flit bit. You are not

going to leave school." Oh, what a setback. And I think I didn't speak to my father for about two weeks—properly, anyway—I was so disappointed. How long I moped, because Dad wouldn't even think about it; he wanted me to continue my education so bad. He had these high hopes for me—just making something of myself, how far I could go with it. A young girl's dream, with prospects of becoming a movie star or taking a part in a movie. That was the biggest grudge I ever had. But I got over it. If I could have been in it, I don't know what would have happened to my schooling. Probably the end of it. I had a good, sensible father, I guess. I can understand my father's feeling. I guess he knew all about Hollywood, because later on it kind of ruined Ray's life and Gertie Becker's, having been out there and gone through so much.

They got hold of a Japanese girl who looked like an Eskimo, dressed her like an Eskimo. Well, when we saw the movie, it showed, because you couldn't understand what she was saying. She couldn't speak a word of Eskimo, but she was in the scene. I was so excited when the picture came out, I couldn't wait to see it and recognize all the people from the north in it, and all the drumming, the Eskimo dances.

It was a popular film for a long while; we still see it every so often. And Ray—when he separated from Gertie Becker, he married a Russian actress and he became a movie director. They had a son, and he calls himself Mala (the doctor). He roams around this area and he's got that film with him. He shows his dad's picture, *The Eskimo*, all over wherever he goes. Ray died not so long ago in Hollywood, but his son, a part-Russian Eskimo, has been up here several times. This young man comes in to my home; I don't have any idea who he is. "Somebody informed me that you know my dad well." (That was last year [1984] when he came and introduced himself as Ray Mala.) "You mean Ray Wise?" Then I showed him a picture of his dad, and some of the pictures taken down along the beach. I still have them somewhere among my pictures in there.[5] They had their hair tucked inside because they didn't want to show all that. They couldn't cut their hair because of the movie; they had to finish it first.

Southern California

After the first year I had been out, my dad then took me down to Los Angeles and San Diego to have Christmas vacation with my aunt. And that was the first time I had seen trees that grew fruit. And I was afraid to pick, because my older brother[6] was teasing me and I didn't know any better. . . . "Well, do you think I could pick a fruit and eat it out of the tree?" He said, "No. Uncle Fred will know right away what fruit you took out of the tree." And I believed every word he was telling me. And then, I can remember, I dearly loved to eat olives, and I thought you could pick one out of the tree and eat one, but I soon found out it was different, because they're very bitter. I chased my brother for pulling that stunt on me.

Uncle Fred and Aunt Jennie didn't have any children; their only child had died. But they used to say I so looked like the daughter they had lost. My older brother [Bill] had told me, "Well, you are going to have to guard yourself before Aunt Jennie, because she is very strict and you have to use the proper language. You can't say 'ain't it so,' or 'ain't that right,' because that's not proper." And gosh, I got the biggest surprise of all my life when I got down there and they took me just like I was one of their kids, all because I looked like the child that they had lost. I was very popular and could get away with anything. My brother Bill was a lot of "help," teasing me, teaching me the wrong things, just so I could get in hot water with Aunt Jennie. I was so young and so green, not knowing anything, and I believed every word they told me about Aunt Jennie and Uncle Fred because I had never seen them.

Because of what Bill had said about my aunt and uncle finding out if I picked any fruit, I was afraid to go near an orange. Finally, Uncle Fred said to me, "How come you just never go over there and pick an orange for yourself? I'll show you how." And I looked at my brother Bill—"What have you been telling me?" Then he'd laugh, and later on I would have to tell what he told me, because Uncle Fred always wanted to know what my brother Bill was telling me. One day Bill took me to this brown cow and said, "Would you like to milk it?" It was a bull. I didn't know any better. That was Bill. And then one time I was going to show off this beautiful dive I had

acquired in swimming, after I had lost all that weight. Dad was there that time, too. I said, "Dad, let me show you how well I can swim." And just as I got ready Bill got on the back of the board, and I belly flopped. Oh gosh, I was so mad at him. And Dad was there laughing, in stitches because I was telling him what a great graceful dive I was going to show him. Bill was always doing those things to me, but we got along. I loved Bill.

Jim wasn't like that at all.[7] He was very serious, with his family, too. So gentle, so different than Bill. His wife Catherine was a wonderful woman. Bill and Marianne, his two kids, live out in the Seattle area today. When I was in San Francisco, during the summer months when school was out, one summer I stayed with Jim and Catherine. And Billy was only about three or four years old—before Marianne had been born yet—and I used to take care of him. They were in Coronado, California, [on] Catalina Island. Down there. He was in the Army then, a captain in the Army; and then when he became a major, he gave me his first oak leaves. I still have them.

Jim spoiled me though. He had never had a little sister around to pamper, and his little son just loved me so much that by the time I was ready to go back to school little Billy was in tears; he didn't want me to go, and we promised that maybe next summer, if we were lucky, we would go down and see him. I got to know my other two sisters too.[8] We all met at Aunt Jennie's. Daddy paid for all the trips, and we got there all together.

College Plans

I wanted to be a teacher; I was going to take education and go back to Barrow to teach. That was the only way to come back home. I had made preparations to enter Stanford. I had made the grade, and I was all set to enter Stanford that fall; my papers and everything were ready for Stanford. That was something to be proud of, I guess, but I didn't value it in those times. Just after graduation from high school, I got sick—actually, it was a ruptured appendix that put me in the hospital; I was in serious condition, the doctor said, for three days. But my brother Dave and Jim Allen, another whaler whom we called Uncle Jim, came down for the summer.

While I stayed in the hospital, my brother gave me a whole mess of pictures of home. How changed some of my friends looked, and the family! I got so homesick looking at those pictures in the hospital that I wired my father that I wanted to come home. He got the wire, but I never got the answer, which he sent to Arnold Liebes, his partner in business in San Francisco. Arnold never told me anything about it, so I talked Uncle Jim and my brother David into bringing me up here.

There was a big ship strike in '34, out of Seattle Harbor, and we had to sort of hide around to get on the Alaska steamship. It was a happy trip; some of the old Alaskan friends that knew Dad were on board, and I got to know everybody on board. But once we got to Nome it was another problem. I found I had no passage to go up north, so I had to wire my father again and let him know that I was in Nome. So, this was the first that Dad knew that I was actually on my way home. He had wired me that he was coming out that fall with my sister Jennie,[9] and he told me to hang on. Well, he wasn't very happy; he was very disgusted, because he had put his heart into my schooling. Dad really was resentful of my coming back, but that was hardly my fault, because I never received his answer. He wanted me to stay and go to Stanford, because I had done so well and made the grade to enter Stanford, and here I was in Nome, asking Dad to help me out with passage all the way to Barrow. And he had to wire Washington, D.C., so I could get on an old Coast Guard cutter that came that summer. So I boarded her and got up here. By the time I arrived in Barrow, Dad was in no talking mood to me; he was so disappointed that I had come back home. I guess he had such high hopes for me because I had done so well in school.[10] But his feeling didn't really matter then, because I was already home and in my glory, seeing my old friends. Two weeks after I came back, Dad made preparations to go back Outside with Jennie.

I never knew I was so homesick until I saw those pictures. I couldn't shake it off.

5

Going Home

[In Nome] I stayed with a family, the MacGregors, who [had] lived up here [Barrow] for maybe three or four years before going back to Nome to run the weather station. I was introduced to them when I got stranded down there in Nome. Jim Allen had known them and found them. Dave, I, Uncle Jim, and this Ada Thompson, who was part Indian, were all on the same boat, the Alaska steamship, and we all stayed at the MacGregors. And Mrs. MacGregor made sure that we were going to have a good time while we stayed at her house. She was the daughter of Judge Cochran of Nome. Dad knew him well, Judge Cochran. He used to come up on the old cutter *Bear* and stay at our place, maybe two weeks at a time every summer, to take care of any pending cases that might be here, under the old federal law violation. Mrs. MacGregor had a little daughter that I used to baby-sit; I have forgotten her name, though. And I couldn't do enough; I would clean house whether the house was clean or not, doing it just out of habit and not knowing what else to do. Nome wasn't all that big, and if I wanted to meet some of my dad's old friends, I could go to the Pioneer Home and see some of the people that knew Dad. I introduced myself as Charlie Brower's daughter, and they would talk. Dad saw them every so often when those liberty ships would anchor down there and come in. Dad knew some old-timers all along the coast.

There were many things that a girl at age eighteen could do in Nome. I found that I could mingle, being half native. I never knew that there was this thing about segregation. There was a definite line between the natives and the whites.[1] If it was a white man's dance, no one with native blood could go in there. Well, a whole plane load of Army boys came in to town, and there was a big dance going on,

and there weren't enough white girls to go around. Ada and I both wanted to go to this dance; she was a half-breed like me and looked between native and white, but we were both "dark-complected." Mrs. MacGregor got hold of some peroxide and started rubbing Ada's and my hair—so it would be lighter, you know—and we just let her. She made us up, and we dressed up in our fancy clothes from Outside.

Well, anyway, we got ready and went to the dance with these [Army] Air Force officers and really had a beautiful time. There was no drinking at that time. And when the dance was over, some of the boys walked us home. And that was the last that we ever saw of them. They left the next day, and all for that one night's doing we had bleached our hair. We began to worry about it when it was time for us to make the trip home.

Well, we started looking for berets to cover our hair, because the roots were starting to come out black as you please, and there was no hair dye available in Nome then, no way to color your hair. So my hair was like that when I got off the boat in Barrow. Dad took one look at me and said, "Foolishness. How foolish can you get!" "But we had a good time, Dad." Didn't do much good, and I had a long wait before it grew out. Talk about being young and foolish. Gosh! That was a one-time deal.

Homecoming, 1934

The people were different. The kids that I was kids with were no longer kids; they were grown up. All my friends that I pictured growing up were grown like me. They were so different. They were already married because, at that time, their parents would give them away when they were fourteen or fifteen years old, because they had nothing else to do; there was no more schooling. So, [if] a suitable young man [was] interested in a girl, they got married; they had families. Some of the girls my own age had two or three kids already when I came back. I knew a couple that got married when the young man was seventeen and the girl was thirteen. By the time they were fifty, they had twenty-four children, but due to health problems, only about seven lived out of that many. That's how many deaths there would be in early births up here.

The houses that I used to think as a kid were quite large didn't seem that way when I returned. I remember my impression of our house. I used to think it was such a large two-story house, compared to some of the little ten-by-twelve family houses that were built by whatever salvage lumber they could get, and out of drift logs covered with sod, with a skylight. But our house didn't seem big after what I had become accustomed to Outside. The little houses built of sod or scrap had begun to disappear when I came back, because the BIA had taken over and brought in a shipment of some freight-free lumber for housing, donations for this northern area.

From the time I was young until I left, Barrow was a happy town—no care in the world. And I never noticed how poor the town was. I never experienced it except when I saw my mother being very concerned about who was short of this or that and helping herself to goods from my dad's store. It didn't sink in that these were needy people. After I had my education and came back—oh, the different feelings I had. I was so happy to be back because I had been so homesick. But seeing my friends, I started to notice how they were dressed, and their home conditions, where there was no constant heat. And this I never really noticed when I was young, visiting, because it was the only way of life I knew. People had to scrounge for whatever they could burn in their stoves, and cook with it, and share the blubber of any animal to heat their home. They never had enough water to wash what little clothes they had, and there [were] no such clothes you could order. They didn't know how to make out an order for clothing, and money was hardly known to them. People were so poor—but high in spirit, never sad or complaining. They had learned to accept that type of life.

I noticed many things about sanitary conditions here in Barrow when I returned: filthy clothes, smelly clothes, and kids going to school in the clothes that they slept in. Some of them would have the urine smell from the bedding—stuff like that—which I had never noticed before as a child. Those things just stood out because of the education that I had, and being away.

When I came back, the territorial school under the BIA had made a rule that each child should have an education. And they started congregating into this community here. Not very many of them, but

the young people who had the children left them pretty much in the hands of the grandparents, so they could have an education, while the younger couple would go out and look for subsistence food. Because there were no jobs—the only places one could get a job would be the hospital and the school, which would hire janitors and cleaning women, and the ACS [Alaska Communication System], the wireless station. And Dad had in his store two men who were employed and working for wages. These were the only people out of some maybe three hundred or four hundred people at the time, in 1934, when I came back. And I don't think there were more than ten white people in Barrow, heading these programs.

The first thing my friends noticed, they started calling me *tanik*, "white lady," because of the way I dressed and how I conducted myself. I was being very sanitary, too; things that I never knew were unsanitary when I was young stood out, and I went out of my way to say that I was going to make a better situation. Evidently they looked up to me as though I was a white girl, but I classed myself as one of them. Just my clothing was a little more conspicuous than what they were wearing, until I got my own native clothes again and dressed like everybody else. Getting back into native clothes was sort of essential because it was cold up here, windy. I couldn't rough it with just a little coat and scarf around my neck, or a cap. I had to have something with a hood and fur around it. It did take getting used to the weather again, but it was so welcome, so different from California. In fact, I don't think I ever had the urge to go back to California after I came home.

There were certain things that I had forgotten that I had learn to all over again, like I was pretty rusty with my own native language, but it came back, because after hearing it so many times, it just came right back. I was saying some of the words a little off key from what was supposed to be said, and I was corrected; the names of people that I used to know, I thought I could remember what they were like, but I couldn't say them right. It felt like my tongue had gotten stiff. My friends started laughing at me because I was talking broken Eskimo. "Eskimo slang," they called it. And it wasn't all Eskimo. I would say the English word for something, and they knew what I meant because they had gone through school, some of them as far as the eighth grade.

Now I was home among my own people and friends, and my concerns were so many. Trying to put my education to use was the hardest thing. I was working so hard to put it across to my people. I was just never idle, I guess. I was putting everything to use that I had learned, and passing it on, and helping people—writing letters for people and all kinds of other things. When I came back to Barrow in 1934, that's when I found out what education was—communicating to the people that I grew up with, and they started looking up to me because, in their minds, I knew so much. I was educated.

Putting an Education to Use

That year after I came back, I just didn't know what to do with myself; so I put my education to use, helped out with programs here in the community. We had a wireless station here, we called it the ACS station. When they started broadcasting news in 1934, I was the first announcer who gave out the news to people in our native language. About once a week, in the evening when I wasn't working, I put out the news to people who had radios and could listen in. They were battery-operated radios in those days. You had to go out and charge your battery, because if it ran out, that was it.

A little later on, the Bureau of Indian Affairs got a hold of my name and wanted to know if I could scout this northern area for prospective high school students for Eklutna Vocational School outside of Anchorage. I went from house to house recruiting and wrote letters. Lord only knows how many letters I wrote. From Barrow I found six students, and then two from Wainwright, one from Point Lay, one from Point Hope, and we picked up four or five more in Kotzebue. Some were older than I was. I was just going on nineteen, and some were twenty, twenty-one. I guess my sister Kate was the youngest one who enrolled (she was two years younger than I was).

I was then ordered to take these young people all the way down to Kotzebue, and then from Kotzebue to Anchorage. And that was a big job. We had to take the *North Star*[2] as far as Kotzebue. That boat stops at every port, and it was interesting for those young people to

see what they did at other communities—their first time out of their home villages. We were lucky because Mr. Lopp, who had been active in the reindeer business, and Mr. and Mrs. Hawkesworth, who had been schoolteachers here, had come up. They were senior citizens by then. And you can imagine our interest in their stories about this north, how they first came up—Mr. Lopp with his interest in the reindeer herds, and Mr. Hawkesworth with the schools. In the evening, after supper, we'd get out on deck, and they'd tell a story about their experiences, and old stories they had heard from the native people. And we stopped at Kivalina and watched them butcher some reindeer.

We got to Kotzebue, and then from there we went by plane. That was the first plane ride these kids had ever had.[3] At first, when we were taking off, the kids were scared, but after we got in the air, they were quite satisfied, but so guarded for fear they were going to fall down any minute. Scary for them—and a relief when we landed. We went from Kotzebue to Anchorage by way of Bettles in a DC-3. At Anchorage, the principal of the school was waiting for us with a bus and took us to Eklutna, which was some twelve or thirteen miles from Anchorage. Eklutna had just opened; that was its first year. It was an old Army barracks that had hardly been renovated; it still had concrete floors, no rugs. And when we got there, there were some three hundred girls and about the same amount of boys, most of them older than what you would expect to see in a high school.[4]

Eklutna was a vocational school. The boys did all the farming and killing of animals for food there, and the girls took care of the gardens, where they grew vegetables. There was also this orphanage—I guess it had been there for two or three years before we got down there. About twenty orphans there needed care, and this was part of vocational training for the older girls—how to care for kids. The students had a chance to work on something on different educational levels—learn to do a job and be responsible for it. We had tractors there for the boys to study machinery and farming. They had carpentry, and the children that weren't too bright or couldn't cope with the school program, they were given just vocational training. But there were some smart students there, too, out of the bunch—college material. And you could just tell who stood out, too. They screened the ones who were capable of

handling the whole academic course. Students were also assigned to do certain jobs in the school area, like seeing to it that the laundry was done, and keeping the floors, the hallways clean, and mopping, working in the kitchen. . . . They switched around, twenty students at a time. Clothing was issued to all the students who needed it, boys and girls alike. They were all the same, just different colors. They were issued to the young people who needed shoes, coats, which made them a little happy.

My job was to escort the students to the school and then return home, but when I got there I learned that they needed an assistant dorm hostess, or matron, or whatever they call them at a high school where you had a dorm. I offered my services and sent a wire to Dad not to be expecting me. I was going to spend the year brushing up on some of my high school, if I needed to, and be there to assist Miss Harper, the dorm hostess for girls—but I didn't realize what I had gotten myself into. I thought I could do it—take care of some three hundred girls in a dorm. And over half of them were older than I was, and they had gotten into a habit of having their own way at age twenty and twenty-one; but they went along with what I said because I seemed like the boss there. Most of the students were very shy to make requests, and they looked up to me as a big sister or somebody who could solve their problems.

I had to see that they were in their rooms and stayed out of trouble, because the kids had a habit of congregating in some of the remote areas of the school and smoking—or sniffing this pyrene. Some that came from Nome and Kotzebue had had experiences with drinking. Whenever they got the urge to get high, they [had] found out somehow that this pyrene in the fire extinguishers could make them really high when they sniffed it. This was my first knowledge of things like that. The years I stayed out in San Francisco, I'd known about liquor and wines, and I'd tasted them because this family I lived with would have a weekend party. They'd leave their glasses lying around, and my curiosity would get the best of me, and I would taste some. In fact, one Monday morning I went to school with the smell of liquor because of my tasting it, and one of the teachers smelled me and sent me to the office, and so—what a predicament that was! But I had never experienced being drunk. My problem there at the school was to keep these kids from getting

high, but I never knew what made them high until one of the security officers that we had there at the school described it as pyrene from those fire extinguishers. We used to have a laundry bin at the school that opened up. When I heard these noises coming from there I opened it, and this bunch of kids was inside.

There were many other problems. That first year there were so many homesick children—away from their homes for the first time. It was a long 185-day year for the students. I started writing letters to parents telling them not to write to the children that they missed them real badly, because that would start a whole chain reaction among the children who were really homesick and didn't want to be in the classroom. They sulked. They would be in their rooms, and you would have to talk to them. There was no way they could go home until spring came and school was out. Some students, though, really liked it and stayed on during the summer to tend to the farm and the gardens and earn summer money at salmon canneries.

Also, for the first time, the Indians, the Aleuts, and the Eskimos were mingling in one area. It was hard to make them come together, the Indians and the Eskimos, because there had been so many stories told about their earlier grandparents' way of life—about why they had wars, and so on. And for the first time these young people experienced that that type of living no longer existed. And then we started to get along, and be like one people, exchanging information about our way of life.

And *complain* about the food! There was a farm where the young women tended the vegetable garden, and the young men cared for pigs and chickens and learned to milk the cows. Most of the diet that year was pork meat. And the kids got tired of it; they weren't used to pork and the conglomeration of food put together called a goulash. And when they added beets to it, we had a pink or a rose-colored meal, along with your pork and gravy. It wasn't like their native food. And when the food got to where the kids couldn't stand it anymore, I helped complain. The principal of the school approached me and said, "Miss Brower, do you have any experience with cooking food?" I said, "Sure, I know a lot about cooking." Well, I had to meet with the students, and then the area director came up from Juneau and fired the cook and stuck me there in the kitchen for the duration of the year and gave me four or five of the oldest women students,

some of whom had more experience than I did in cooking. We took over the kitchen and had to get up at 4 A.M. to start the bread and peel the potatoes. To prepare food for six hundred students and the teachers, I had to be on my feet from early morning until about 6 o'clock in the evening. But the help from the students I got was really good.

When that spring [1936] came, Dr. Gale and Dr. Butler, the area directors, came up and started asking what would make the students happier. So we had a big meeting with the students, and the bolder ones would get up and say, "It would be nice to get some of the native foods." And they started naming the kinds of food that they wanted. The food arrived by the *North Star* and through the rail belt from Seward. There was *maktak*, dried seal meat; there were whole reindeer carcasses we had to store, moose meat from the interior, and, from the Aleutian Islands, fish. Our main problem was how to preserve it all. So when all that got settled, we had to decide what days these native foods should be served. We had to figure some way, because students and teachers all ate in the same mess area. And when we served the first native food, the teachers couldn't stand the smell in there. So we had to choose a day when there wouldn't be any complaints from anyone. And they chose Saturday—the day when there was no school—and the teachers prepared their own food in different quarters or another building. It was buffet style. They kept that tradition even for a while after I left.

I wonder how that old place is. I wonder if those old Army buildings are there that we used as school.[5] I never saw Eklutna again after I left it. But old memories of it still linger.

University of Alaska

> The late thirties were pleasant years on the University of Alaska campus. Enrollment was increasing each year, the faculty was stabilized and enthusiastic about their opportunities, not only in teaching but in applying their specialities to the "Alaska Scene," and the student body was a closely-knit group of highly self-reliant young men and women, mostly from Alaska's scattered communities, who saw nothing but better times and unlimited opportunities ahead. [Cashen 1972:275]

In the fall of 1936[6] I enrolled at the University of Alaska [at Fairbanks]. I decided to go there because I was working just below that area at Eklutna [Vocational] School. And I had made enough money to make my entry, and I was going to pay my own way, being very independent. At that time tuition was $600, but my dad paid most of the way. He flew into Anchorage when he learned I had enrolled myself in college. And I think he bought out all the stores down there. I never wore all those clothes, there were so many.

There were only twenty-five of us girls—and about two hundred men. There were two men's dorms quite filled, and only one women's dorm. I've got pictures of them. There was only a dirt road between the college and the town. Classes were so small, not like they are today. When I go to see those grounds, it's so complicated. I can't even recognize the university, it's so big. And I guess we knew most all the professors there. If a girl, or a young man, was willing to help out on weekends or in the evening and earn their spending money, they offered it. Like, I baby-sat for three or four professors' families, Dr. Ryan, and Dr. Southwick, and two others.[7] I used to take care of their children at night and in the afternoons when I was not having class. I was very trusted, because I was a good baby-sitter. They used to call for me all the time.

Anyway, I enrolled in education classes because I wanted to be a teacher. I had to take physics, government, and English, of course, and I took German. Physical education was added; sports went with it. I was on the archery and ski teams. And I played basketball. Imagine me, the shortest member of the basketball team! It was never a dull moment for us; there was always something doing if you weren't in the dorm, or baby-sitting and studying. I kept myself plenty busy.

My roommate was Gladys Hall, from the Bethel area. She had buck teeth and was part Indian. She was brushing up on some of her high school. There was a program there where you could prepare yourself for college at the university if you weren't fully qualified to become a student. Our room used to get a banner for being the neatest.

That first year I had a closetful of stylish knit garments. That year,

knits were the style. Dad went through Anchorage on his way out and picked out all these outfits—my ski outfit, my hiking outfit—you name it, it was there. And shoes galore. No room in my closet for all the clothes he got me. I never wore half those clothes. Some I had no intention of wearing because I just didn't like the looks. The ones I wanted most I shoved to one side, and all the girls that were down there [came to my room] . . . and, "Could I borrow this? Could I borrow that?"

And I didn't want any of his [Dad's] money that year, because I was well paid for helping out at Eklutna School. And I could see that sparkle in Dad's eyes when he came in, and I said I was going to enter myself at the University of Alaska. That old spirit came back to me; he was no longer disappointed in me. But then, he was like that.

After I finished my second year, the BIA stepped in again. The area director in Juneau had found out that I had completed my second year of college, and first he contacted my father, and then me, and asked if I would be interested in coming back to Barrow to teach. Barrow badly needed teachers. He told me that I now qualified to become a BIA teacher. So, I asked him, "Well, what about my next two years? How will I get that in?" And they said it can be done through the summer months. "Well, who's going to pay for my way?" They said that by the time I was ready to return, I would be earning enough. You thought you were earning a lot of money, but it was $52 a week. When everything else was taken out, the full amount was probably $40 a week. But in those years, that was big money.

So when Dad came through, I told him about it, and he said, "It's up to you." We went over to talk to Dr. Bunnell, the university president, and tried to arrange for further education. No student was allowed to eat at the president's table, but when my father came, they asked President Bunnell's daughter and myself to come over and sit at the president's table and eat.[8] Talk about being conspicuous from the other students! I left school that spring on my second airplane flight, from Fairbanks to Barrow with a stopover in Allakaket. It cost Dad $900 one way, in that small plane, to get us home.

University of Alaska was much easier because of my San

Francisco experience, but I had a hard time with government and education. I never had any problems with math, even way up through geometry; I loved to figure out problems with numbers and distances, but my English still needed work. I guess just trying to take too many subjects was my main problem, because it didn't leave me any free time; all I did was study, trying to keep up.

I remember my old physics professor. He had occasion to come up here on a trip that took some scientists through ARL [Arctic Research Laboratory]. Nate had been out earlier and brought home some fresh caribou meat with his old weasel [an early all-terrain vehicle] that he bought and put together, and I was still cutting up all that caribou meat at four in the morning. That was when we had that big underground cellar. I was getting it ready for the boys to put it down there so it wouldn't spoil, and some of it I hung up. This man in Army khaki clothing was walking at 4 A.M.—the sun was shining and I was tired and I sat down out there to rest—and he kept loitering around on the road, as if he wanted to come over and talk to me.

So I said, "Come on over. Don't be shy." I hailed to him and we started talking, and something about him looked a little familiar, but he had that Army cap on. He came over and said, "This is the first time I've come to Barrow." And he mentioned that he used to teach at the University of Alaska. And after he said that, I started smiling. He had been my physics professor, and he'd made the trip down to the Antarctic with this group of people, and when they came back, he got stationed in Washington, D.C., to document what they went through on the trip. And he said his name, and I remember there was one girl that used to keep after him, one of the students, a girl by the name of Florence Walker. And I had a yen to ask him if he ever saw Miss Walker, you know, but I didn't get a chance to. He told me he had married this Florence Walker, and they had two sons and were now living outside Washington, D.C. So she really got to him, I guess, and that was nice.

And he started to mention that there used to be a girl from up here in his class. "That's me." "You mean to tell me you are Sadie Brower?" "Yes. Used to be. But I am married and have my own family, and that's my house there, and this is the doings of my husband that I am trying to store away." And he started taking

pictures, and later on he sent me some copies of them. And then we talked about Professor Robe, because I used to have such an awful time with my government studies.[9] Later on, Professor Robe came up after I became a magistrate, and [he] started to laugh: "You mean to tell me that here you are, advising peoples of their rights and what this Constitution is all about?" He remembered all right. And he was very surprised that I was a judge.

I worked at the University Museum that second year, cataloguing artifacts, because of Dad. Later on, when the Arctic Research Lab opened up, Dr. Geist[10] from the museum had occasion to come up here, and they told me about the experimental farm that I helped start with them and Dr. Bunnell. I used to go around with him and see how the potatoes got that big, and cabbage got that big. This was at the first experimental station for growing vegetables. They were huge vegetables because of the constant daylight in the summer.

Going to school in Fairbanks was good because I got letters more often than in California. I couldn't make any phone calls or anything like that, but planes were now going back and forth maybe twice or three times a week. And I could write to my dad, and he would write back to me. It wasn't quite so lonely, because it seemed like I was with my own people, Alaskans. Some of the whites were just as bad as I was, because they never been out of Alaska; they were self-conscious, too.

My second year at the university was my last. When I left to become a BIA schoolteacher, I planned to return to complete my education, but that chance never came around because there was so much more to do here than going back to college.

❖

Sadie's interrupted education was brought to an unexpected and formal closure for her in the spring of 1987, when the University of Alaska voted to award her an honorary doctorate of laws at its May commencement.[11] *I phoned to offer congratulations in February, bringing Sadie away from a seal she was cutting up. She expressed some concern about what she perceived as the responsibility such an accolade might carry with it, adding, "When I received the letter, it didn't hit me as exciting, you know. 'Gee, at my age, I would get a letter like this? Seventy years old going on seventy-one—why would they want*

to bother with me?'" Of equal concern to Sadie was that commencement fell right in the middle of whaling season during which time she, as the wife of a whaling captain, would be very busy.

As commencement drew near, Sadie also worried about the cost of going to Fairbanks. "I almost backed out of it until my sponsor, who was my niece Edna MacLean (Maria's daughter and one of the professors down there at the university), called me almost every other hour: 'Have you made up your mind yet? Have you made up your mind yet?' 'Well, it seems that we are just sort of short of funds, and it is ridiculous for me to be begging for a ticket just to receive that thing.' And first thing I know, here comes the mayor's[12] secretary with a ticket, a round-trip ticket: 'After we submitted your name for this doctorate, and backed you up, we can't let you off.'"

Sadie attended the graduation ceremonies, along with her husband Nate, her daughter Donna, and assorted relatives. A few of her old classmates were also there, as well as some of the Alaska Court System judges with whom she had worked during her years as magistrate. "We thoroughly enjoyed ourselves," Sadie confesses. And, yes, she reflects, the celebration did make her feel as though she had finally brought her education to a finish.

6

A Teacher and a Student

School was out, and I returned with my father to Barrow. The cook from the hospital, Mrs. Bailey, had quit. She went back on the same plane that we came in on. So the hospital was left without a cook. Dr. Sheer, from the hospital, approached my father and asked if I knew anything about cooking. I told the doctor that I couldn't take the job permanently but could fill in for the summer until he got a regular cook. I wanted to be independent and earn money, and then, too, I saw how poor some of our people were. Dad used to get after me because I used to hide some food [from the hospital] and feed poor families. So that was the first job I did when I got off that plane that spring. But I wasn't just a cook; I was the night nurse. There was only one doctor and one nurse at the time. They badly needed an anesthetist; so the doctor showed me how to give anesthetics. Picture me after an operation, with all that ether in me, trying to cook over a hot stove! We had an old coal stove with an old boiler that used to heat the hospital.

Oh, I didn't think I'd make it, but I did. There was a lot of work. I did the laundry, you name it, cleaned in the hospital, until they allowed me to get help and they hired Rebecca [Panigeo] Hopson. She cleaned the kitchen and did half the work that I did, and we got along so well. But that bachelor doctor and I forever fought, chewed each other. He insisted on bringing his poker gang and letting me work through the night to get their midnight lunches and clean his clothes. I used to chew him out for it, and when I refused to do it one night [make snacks for the poker players], he almost set the hospital on fire trying to light one of those Primus stoves to heat water. If he were still alive and read my book, he'd remember. At the end of the summer, the cook assigned to the hospital came in

from Nome. So that was actually my first job, before my teaching job came on in the fall. I enjoyed it.

Teaching School

There was no training, just two years of college education was the requirement to be a teacher up here. So all I had to do was sit down with the principal of the school, see what my duties were and what grades I would teach. The rest was worked out as we went along. Evaluations were done by us on each student, and the grading system was based on how well they handled themselves and did their work. Their citizenship standing was not evaluated then, but their attitude towards learning was. And if one student lacked ambition, or learning abilities were declining, then we were to encourage the child and talk to the parents. I was assigned to teach third to fifth grades. By the time I got to teaching, there were maybe seven or eight kids in a class. That schoolhouse only had three classrooms. Flossie Connery[1] had from the first to the second grade in one room; I had the third to the fifth grades in another room; and Mrs. Williams, the principal's wife, who had more knowledge of teaching school, had the sixth, seventh, and eighth grades. Fred Ipalook was in what was an annex to the school that was just above my house. It was sort of a shop. He taught the little kids, the beginners, and the kindergarten, getting them ready for the grade school. Fred always had a noisy kindergarten, but he was patient. Fred was so good with kids.[2]

The only problem I had was with Mrs. Williams. She had her classroom right next to mine, and any time my students made a little noise, like in a spelling bee, she was inside my schoolhouse, saying I was disturbing her work with her class. That was hard, because I couldn't stand her interference, and it bothered the children, too. They loved to get up and have their spelling bees and do their math at the board. When they used erasers at the board it made noise, and when they checked their work by exchanging places there was this shuffling on the floor, and she couldn't stand even those noises. So we guarded from making any disturbance for her. That went on for one year.

Trying to teach in a classroom where you had all three grades, and

trying to get the interest of the children. . . . It was difficult for the other classes not to listen even though you gave them assignments to finish. And trying to keep them happy was another thing in the school, because if one sulked and you had to get after them, you had to do it in a manner without the others hearing what you were doing. If you think that student might be drawing back, you try to encourage him without pointing him out right in front of the class. It was hard for me to do that, but there weren't very many times it happened.

We never assigned any homework for the students in those days. While we were teaching one grade, the others had a chance to do the work that was assigned to them the day before. So it was all done in the schoolhouse. But the kids all liked to get together and have a spelling bee or math tests. It seemed like all the native students were good in math. And spelling was good, because it helped them to see the words. We used to try and have the students get the meaning out of the words that we were going to use for spelling. It wasn't just spelling; it was a requirement that you had to learn the meaning of so many words and be able to explain and use each in a sentence.

We were instructed not to speak our native language or use our native language in the school, and to instruct the children that they can't use their native language, even on the schoolgrounds at recess time. But some kids would talk to each other, and we never said anything. The ones that got found out used to be reprimanded. They got left out of the school party, which came at the end of the month. They'd invite their parents from 7 to 9 P.M. to take part in games. The end-of-the-month party was mostly games—like musical chairs, drop the handkerchief, competing for prizes, and singing—and then refreshments after that. The parents loved to come in when they weren't doing anything at night and just watch their kids play these musical games. Flossie started it. And if it wasn't the kids, then she would have just the parents come and enjoy themselves and do whatever. If they wanted to sit and watch, and tell stories or visit with each other, a chance to be at one area where they could mingle together and exchange stories—more like a get-together. The people dearly loved to laugh or just enjoy themselves being happy. They were a happy bunch of people. I

don't know what would happen if you got a group of people like that today; they'd be so bored that they would just probably walk out. But in those days, we had no radio. There were a few phonographs here and there, the kind that you wound, and a few old songs people got to learn by playing the records over and over and over again.

For entertainment we used to have a little Christmas plays, and the Sunday School would put on an Easter play or little programs where the children learned parts that they dressed up for. That was really something. If they did well, the audience clapped and had smiles all over their faces. I never really remember having long holidays; it was usually a day or two at Christmastime, and right back to school again, because at the end of the school, it meant more to the kids to be with their families and to go off hunting.

Sometimes school ended a little before whaling and then started early in the fall, and the families would come in little by little. We'd have more students as each family would come in, but I can't remember anyone lagging behind. They caught up with the schoolwork. It was required that they do a little extra studying until they were up to date with what the rest of the class was doing. We gave tests each month, and it showed up on some of the kids who never paid too much attention. But overall, they were pretty much all the same caliber. There were hardly ever any fights among the children, because disagreeing about things was unusual.

Our rule was that each child should sit in their place and not walk around or talk to the next one. Chewing gum was not allowed; no candy was allowed. The only time they would be free to talk to each other was at recess time. Then they played a free-for-all football game or threw the basketball around. This was when the kids were first starting to introduce basketball. There was just one basket, and the kids took turns throwing the ball. There were no rules, but it was basketball—one sided. The whole class would play.

The education kids got then wasn't related to life up here, because you taught geography about places Outside, where they would just see the pictures. Students would have to learn what people did in those countries and compare it with what we had here. There was no form of government up here, and history was a very dry subject for the children because they had to remember dates and who was president. It just had no meaning to the children. Still today

they have a hard time, even in high school. Kids would just fall off asleep, while their teachers would try and pump them with information. Even down as far as Mt. Edgecombe, when the kids would go out there to high school, there still wasn't much difference; it was an isolated area. But they all had to use the textbooks that they had assigned to them.

At first I didn't notice how bad the textbooks were. Then I started observing how backwards some of the school material was. It was really old stuff. My biggest problem was to try and upgrade the schoolbooks. Nobody heard me at first, but I was determined to get better books and material for school. The BIA said the children are so slow in learning that they had to buy these books, which were on the level of the children. They were cheap, old, old-fashioned grammar-school books that were no longer used in modern schools. The children accepted them; these were their books. A sixth grader was trying to read the third grade book. . . . "Well, that's to his level." They were using that excuse, and oh, how I disliked it. They didn't even test the children to see what their learning capacity was.

Later I tried to get two of our teachers interested in putting our views across to the heads of the BIA education. And that's when I started to travel, from Alaska to the states, talking my head off, trying to get better school material. And when I finally got it across, then this land claim came through, and our school system changed again.[3] I can remember going down to Juneau and getting thrown out of the BIA. I was merely down there because we were having such a time with teachers up here. We had no screening process for teachers, like the BIA did. I was sent down there to ask about it and learn how we could screen. I got thrown out because I was trying to ask for help, and they said, "Well, I don't think we can help you. We're no longer involved up there. There is no BIA connection." Well, you can imagine how I felt. By that time, I was a magistrate; that was in 1960.[4]

You couldn't determine what students were interested in becoming at that age. And with no prospects of high school, you could only think of preparing them for whatever comes next. Since I had been involved in scouting for high school students, when they weren't doing so well I stressed that if they were ever to go a higher place of learning, they would have problems if they didn't study or

talk to their parents. But at that time, the people were still subsistence hunting most of the time. Families would go looking for a more prosperous area to hunt in, and they wanted to take their children; so there wasn't much you could do to hold back. And that was part of their future, too, learning from their parents how to survive. When I was teaching school, I couldn't somehow see what to stress in their education; everything was laid out for them, and the only thing we could ask was that they do their best. There wasn't much of a future for the students beyond eighth grade, then, though we had high hopes of sending them out to high schools. They were told that there would be schools available if they wanted to go. But that was the extent of it.

What the white teachers said was law in the school. After that first Mr. Williams, we got along beautifully with the others, because they had seen what we had started. Things didn't work with the first Mr. Williams who was principal, but the second one listened to all of us. He would have us sit there, and we would talk the problems over. That was when he tried to get a Parent-Teacher Association started, and just the women would show up. The men were out hunting or working. The Parent-Teacher Association never succeeded until we got the high school for Barrow.[5]

I was interested in how the parents felt about their children being in school and how much they encouraged them. It wasn't much, because the kids were all eager and happy to go to school on their own. The kids were enthusiastic about school in the 1940s and 1950s, because their goal was only up to eighth grade. When I began teaching school, there were no jobs for families. Menfolk still hunted and trapped, and the womenfolk took care of the children and tried their best to get them to school. There were hardly any problems taking the kids to school, because that was the only place that was of any interest to the children. They had nothing else to do. School was a warm place—even though we didn't serve any lunches to the children. It was hard, because some of the kids would come into school with no breakfast. They'd come in wearing the clothes that they had slept in, because it was cold and they had no fuel in the homes. Today things are different. There is a lot of interference; there's TV programs and what have you. The kids today are harder to put through school. Some, when they get older, if they are not

getting any encouragement from the parents, become dropouts.

When I first started teaching, some people still lived in sod houses. They were crowded. Families with seven or eight kids lived in a ten-by-twelve [foot] building. We showed them how to air their bedding. In the wintertime lice infested some of the homes, and we didn't know how to get rid of them. Kids brought them into the school, and when they hung their parkas up, the lice would transfer onto others. Then we got a method where we could freeze this pest, get a stick, and pound it out. When they froze, you could get them out. We also started using disinfectant and finally won—we never found one louse anymore.

In homes, cleanliness wasn't taught until the Mothers Club took over. The doctors were concerned about health conditions, but there was no way they could be made better until proper diet and cleanliness were taught. Oh, it was a terrible mess when those first white teachers used to come in. They couldn't stand the smell of some of the younger ones, who would have that urine smell clinging to their clothes from their little brothers, because they were all in one bedding. The teachers put clothespins over their noses so they couldn't smell the kids. And that hurt. It hurt my feelings, because I was a native and Flossie was a native.

We had to do something for our people, and the mothers were eager to help out. On Fridays, twice a month, we had this meeting with the mothers—the Mothers Club—to talk about problems in the school. The health methods were being introduced to the homes, and we had a flag or banner—"Clean Home for the Week"—that one house was entitled to. The Mothers Club visited each home and picked out the neatest house.[6] We'd take two or three mothers and check the cleanliness and neatness of a home on Saturday. Were clothes washed, kids bathed, and was there water and food in the house? They had quite an inspection; there was a check list they had to go through. And one house would get that banner and be very proud of it—have it hanging all week in their home. That was quite an honor, to present that to a home. Then, too, there were some prizes. Little bit, maybe, but not too much, went to that house for being the cleanest home for the week. The next week it would be changed to another home. More and more we could see the change in the cleanliness of the kids. Even though I wasn't married, I was

quite active among the teachers in the Mothers Club. We were all involved—all the teachers and all the mothers that were able to come in.

The second Mr. Williams and his wife were just beautiful. Before, the principal had never really responded to some of Flossie's requests, like getting water in the school in order to give the kids a bath, and allowing mothers to wash clothes there because at home they couldn't melt enough ice in the wintertime for washing clothes. The new Mr. Williams went along with most of our requests. Flossie and I talked him into turning the schoolhouse into a laundry house over the weekend, so the kids could have some clean clothes. And this stayed on until 1941 or 1942, because there was hardly any fuel in the home to melt enough water to even wash clothes. He put in cookstoves to heat water for washing clothes. The menfolks were entrusted to bring in ice and snow after school hours to fill that one big tank we had in there, and melt it down before Saturday.

On weekends the mothers with tubs would come in and wash their children's clothes and hang them up. There was a partition that you could open, and lines could be put up where the mothers' washing could dry overnight. And there was space where they could give their kids a bath. There was hardly any privacy, but little curtains here and there. Kids were very shy when their clothes were taken off, because they hardly ever took them off. But when they had to start introducing taking baths even just once a week, that was something. In most families, there weren't any baths. Some people even went a whole year without taking a bath. And this was something that we had to teach the children, that a bath was needed. Before I went Outside, it never bothered me, because I didn't know any better. But when I had lived Outside and came back—ah, I was a sad person.

The hardest part of coming back and relearning when I became a teacher was visiting the homes of my people and observing how poor they were, how much was needed in their home to make it better—to find out that some homes didn't even have any fuel to melt water to wash their kids' faces in the morning. The best thing about teaching was the children, because I love children and they're eager to learn. They were entirely different from what students are today, because they were learning to speak English and [were] very

much interested in learning the meaning of words they were studying. Kids would follow me home, come into our house after school and visit for a while, and then they would go back out and play. You get attached to them, and there are some that just look up to you and say, "Can I go with you?" There is so much—I can't explain. It's the way you get so attached to the children, the same ones every day.

From 1947 through '52 I substitute taught.[7] I quit because I couldn't handle my baby-sitter with the pay we were getting, and we weren't earning very much money, and Nate was just starting to work out at the base. So we talked it over and decided I would do better staying home than to dish out every bit of money I was earning, because that's what it came to.

An "Eskimo Education"

The traditional nuliariik [husband/wife] relationship can be described as one characterized by moderately intense positive sentiment, coupled with restrained expression of that sentiment. It was moderately intense because, although spouses were expected to be fond of one another, the Western concept of "love" simply was not a feature of this relationship in its institutionalized form.

[It was restrained] because, regardless of the nature of the intensity of the sentiment in any given case, spouses were expected to keep their feelings to themselves. . . . [W]hen spouses were angry with one another, they were more likely to express their emotions than they were when the opposite situation obtained. [Burch 1975:93]

There was little by way of instruction of any kind given either to the boy or to the girl before marriage. It was understood that the skills acquired during the socialization process were applicable to adult life. . . . There was little or no mention of sexual practices or expectations. If a boy and girl were known to be engaged in a sexual relationship, some gossip might arise. On the whole, however, sex was commonplace. There was no sense of artistry in it nor was it felt necessary to explain to the young person anything relating to sexual mores.

There was no attempt at intellectual intimacy and no overt sign of affection. No person could relate his own aims, ambitions, or hopes to another. . . . In short, a young couple did not discuss their marriage beforehand and settled domestic problems as they arose. [Spencer 1959:248]

There was a young man from a family here; we were born about the same time, and it was a custom in those years to make a match for your children such that they should know that they were chosen for each other from the time they were born. This was the situation with me. I was aware of this from an early age, and I accepted anything that the boy's parents gave me, and he did the same. And we had never felt any discomfort with each other. But then after my dad said that I should go back out [to college] and educate myself, I had to start thinking about making decisions about the situation. All my friends and even the whole town knew and accepted that the situation with this boy one day would somehow be resolved. And this boy had been there and accompanied me wherever I went, and I accepted it, but I didn't know how far it would be carried. He was getting more interested in other girls and getting jilted [by them] at the same time. But he would always come back to me and try and make amends.

Somehow, I just couldn't take it anymore. So, when my dad started after me again about my education—this was back in 1935—I didn't want to go.[8] Then I approached this boy, which I thought was part of my duty to do, and said if he was willing to marry me, then we would settle down and I wouldn't have to go to college. But it didn't work out that way. He told me that he was sorry but he had an eye on another girl whom he was courting at the time. And so I took it. I said, "Well, I won't interfere with your life; this is a new world that we live in today. You can choose your own partner; we don't have to live the way our ancestors prepared it for us."

I had to make my parents understand, because he was still kind of close to Dad at the time. I made it be known that I wouldn't have anything to do with him anymore. And then I went back out to school, came back [to teach], and found he wasn't married at all. Then he started after me in a manner like a he-wolf would chase a mate. And I ran around and avoided him, and finally I found some interested boys who were willing to protect me, just to keep him away so he wouldn't be near me. I got so I just didn't want to be near him anymore.

I knew Nate all this time, but I never thought I'd get interested in him. He had never been to a day of school, but we grew up together here and there; we were the same age group. He lived at the Point with his parents and, when they came in, or we

got to this camping area at Brant Point, then we were together. It was like a little village up there; we played and were carefree during duck season. But when I came back in '34, the whole town had moved in here from the Point so their kids could go to school. There were tractors available so they could move their houses down here on skids. There was maybe one or two still up there, but the families had moved in with relatives and there was hardly anyone. They were using it as a stopping-off place for travelers going east of Barrow. Nate and his family moved down here, lived with their in-laws for a while till they were able to get their own place. They lived in a sod house, too; I remember that. So, Nate started escorting me here and there.

Dad knew I had a new boy friend, because whenever Nate was in town he was at our house. But we had hours; we had to be home by midnight, because we were now "young ladies." During the summer months, Mom would go off to her camp and Dad would tend to the store, and I was there to cook for Dad. So, more and more Nate and I saw each other, and then Dad started getting after us. "When are you two going to get married?" "Oh, we're going to have to stand on our own two feet, be able to afford our own stuff before we get married; we are going to prepare ourselves." And so, when my sister Maria got married in the fall, Dad wanted a double wedding. And I said, "No, we are not ready. We are going to wait this year out and maybe by summer."

Nate and I were ambitious. We were going to save enough, and the only way you could get your supplies and orders that you needed was to make an order into Montgomery Ward or Sears Roebuck. And it came on the summer boat, in July. We had started to order through catalogues things that we might need when we got married, and they were to come in on the boat. We were waiting to be married in style. Nate's parents knew and his sister knew; she was around me quite a lot. By summer Dad got restless. It was about fifteen more days until the boat would be in, bringing our order, and he needed Nate's help. So he wanted me to talk Nate into making our marriage earlier, so he could send him out on a boat to help out the family.

Finally, we were out all night one night and just enjoying ourselves on a sunny day and didn't realize what time it was. I

remember there were four of us couples out there,[9] laughing it up and not realizing what time it was. This boat was turned up and we were all sitting around in a circle. That morning, Dad came down before he opened up his store. He was furious, and he said, "Well, if you kids can stay up all night and make a night of it, maybe it's time I should start handing out some marriage licenses. You could just as well spend your time getting married, making some use out of yourself." And I remember it was July seventeenth, that morning. So we all looked at each other, and the others got cold feet. The boat still hadn't come in yet with all our stuff. So, when all the others went home, Nate and I sat there and we talked, and I said, "Why don't we take up Dad on his word? Let's go get married." Well, we didn't even know what it took to get married. We didn't have an available minister at the time, but Dad was commissioner; he could marry people.

I took Nate home, and we got cleaned up. I had made him a nice fancy white shirt. So Nate put it on, and we walked down to the store. Dad was all alone and he was doing something at his desk with his back to us. Nate's heart must have been pumping when it came right down to it, standing in front of Dad. Dad acted like he didn't know what we were there for. He turned his swivel chair and said, "Well, what can I do for you kids?" So I was bold and I spoke up. "Well, you said since we are able to stay all night together, it's time for us to get married; so that's why we are here." Dad turned around, a smile on his face, and asked Nate something, I don't quite remember what. But I remember Nate said, "Yeah," and that we were going to get married. "Well, I'll tell you. You're going to have to go out and get your witnesses if you want to get married." I said, "What's that? How many?" "Two will be enough."

The only witnesses I could think of were Maria and Joseph Ahgeak, my sister and her husband, who were at the house right next to the store. When I was leaving, Nate was getting kind of shaky because he didn't want to be left alone with my dad, because in those days I guess we were just kind of afraid of our elders. If we thought we made a mistake, it would be pointed out, because the church program was so strong. If you were found to make a sinful act or something, you got expelled from the church. So we honored the rules of the church and the rules of our elders in those days. If

you broke one of the church's moral rules, you could be barred from the community for life.

As I was leaving, I met Dave[10] on his way to the store on the boardwalk; I smiled at him and I didn't say anything. I told my sister Maria we needed her and Joseph down there. "Do you want to be our witnesses? Dad's going to marry Nate and me." My sister looked at me and said, "Why not?" They already had a child, and so we went out and got a baby-sitter. We didn't even know how long the marriage was going to take. So we went back down there, and Dad prepared all our papers and married us right there in his office. We had boasted so much about having our stuff together before we got married, but the boat was late. So on the seventeenth of July, 1940, Nate and I got married.

Nobody in town knew we were married, because it was so early in the morning; it was on a Wednesday, I remember. That night we didn't want to stay at the house, so we got a tent. We pitched it and put a bed in there, and while we were doing that, some old lady came around. She had been expecting her son, who was one of the reindeer herders, to come in on a boat any time from my brother's [Tom's] camp over at the reindeer herd. It was a dark foggy day; she saw us in silhouette pitching our tent, and her vision wasn't that good. She came down, expecting she might find her son, and asked if we had just come in from somewhere since we were pitching our tent. We told her we had just gotten married and we were trying to pitch this tent up so we could sleep in there, and she sat down and she talked to us like an adult would about being married. I guess she must have been around sixty or seventy years old. I can still remember her.

And the next morning, there was a prayer meeting going on, so we went hand-in-hand to the prayer meeting. We didn't think it was strange; we were already married, but people didn't know, and one of the elders approached us: "I don't think you should be seen in public holding hands like that coming to church." And I looked at Nate and I told that elder that we were already married. "Oh, then, it's all right." So old-fashioned. Those people had such strong ties to the church that they thought it was wrong before you got married to be seen holding hands.

We saw Nate's mother at the prayer meeting. She had come in

from camp, but Mom hadn't come in yet. Mom didn't know we were married till we went up there and told her about it. It was a week later when the boat came in with all our stuff. My wedding things were in the trunk for many years until one of my nieces who was getting married used them.

Later on, when the people in town had gotten so religious, this one minister we had said those that were married by commissioner weren't really sanctified by the Lord, and would they be willing to go through a church marriage? Nate and I decided maybe we should do it, stand in good faith. But I got cold feet. I could see all my children tagging behind while we were at the altar. So we never did it. But we have been married ever since.

We never knew anything about marriage licenses and how much they cost. We never paid any fees, but after Nate and I had been married for about six months, Dad mentioned the fee. By then, it was trapping season. That year I didn't do anything. I just went with Nate, went out with him to his hunting grounds. Nate caught I don't know how many foxes. When he came back, we were quite rich with furs, and Dad surprised us. "Well, now that you've been married this long, I think it's time that Nate bring in a whole white fox for your marriage peformance." And we looked at it, and I looked at Nate, and we kind of laughed; but we laughed more after we got out of Dad's view. To think that here I was a free wife for six months. These matters never occurred to us.

At that time, a marriage license and the marriage ceremony was only four dollars. But Nate paid a whole fox skin, which was worth about $50. And my mother got amused after we told her that Nate finally paid for our marriage. She looked over with a smile on her face and said, "Well, the only thing expensive about you is your teeth." Before I came home I had my teeth worked on and had gold crowns, quite an expensive amount of gold in my mouth. I can remember that remark my mother made, pointing to the gold fillings that I had in my teeth. Those things cling to your mind; you never forget them.

❖

I marveled at the things that existed up here that I missed in my growing years. And when I married Nate, he took me all over with

the dog team, to his hunting grounds—how I valued all of that, because I was such a greenhorn. I was born into Eskimo life, I knew what it consisted of, but I was so young when I was taken out to school. So, I had to learn it all over—learned to sew all over again, how to make clothing, mukluks, parkas, tan hides. Some of the life of my people just really sank into me that first year of our marriage, because it showed me how much I had missed, and how much I didn't know that existed in our native way of life. Nate was a hunter; it was his livelihood. He never went to school, but he knew more than I did, a college student, a teacher. From him I learned how to be an Eskimo all over again. So that was my marriage to Nate.

7
Family and Community

After we'd been married a month, my dad asked for us over at his store, and Nate and I looked at each other and wondered, "What did we do wrong this time?" We were always thinking something like that, because we thought he wanted to get us down there and scold us. We were both twenty-four years old; we weren't really young. When we got there, he told us to sit down, and, "Oh gosh, what's coming?" Then he walked back and forth in front of us, which made matters worse. And pretty soon he turned around and said, "What would you kids say if I gave you an *umiaq*?" "A skin boat? For a present?" "Then you could travel wherever you want this summer."

Oh, my Lord, we thought we were the richest people when Dad gave us that present of a skin boat. Right away we started making plans. Nate said we should go up inland, and I should forget about teaching for a while; so I went along with it. Ernest Kignak and his wife, with their seven kids, were thinking of going up the river. So we asked them to show us the way. They went, and every ten miles or so I think we camped, because we didn't have any motor. We put all their stuff on our boat. Well, in the meantime, before that month was over, after we got married, the boat [barge] came, and we had all this stuff we had ordered. So we had most everything; we were really fortunate.

The First Year

It was a new kind of life that year, because I didn't teach school. That fall we were up inland after freeze-up. We had some lumber and fixed up a sod-covered cabin, and that's where we wintered, up

the Chipp River. It was an exciting year for me, because I learned what living was all about, being an Eskimo. Oh, I was just in my glory, and everywhere we went, Nate had his dog team, and we were never in want. Nate and I were just in our glory and carefree that first year. We traveled all over the tundra and trapped; we lived in makeshift snow houses, snow block houses, which were surprisingly warm. I had never lived in one before, and I was curious. I was going through a survival training myself that year with Nate.

The cabin we fixed up belonged to Nate's parents, and it was still standing when Nate and I got married. I remember cleaning the inside of it and fixing it up, putting bunk beds in there. It was built from drift logs, and in between the logs we filled with dirt, pounded it in so the wind wouldn't come through. And it was warm in there. It was a large cabin, twelve-by-eighteen or sixteen-by-eighteen [feet], and it was very roomy. I made a cupboard out of some of the old boards we found, and little curtains—things that that cabin had never seen. We had our own utensils, plates and cups and stuff. We were all prepared when our order came in on the ship. Dad teased us, "What are you doing? Are you going to start a store and compete with me?" "No, that's all our stuff." And when it came, it was all there. And I remember Nate's mother coming over—how wonderful for her to see all that. There were sets of heavy aluminum cooking ware, and our blue willow cups and saucers, service for eight, all ordered from the catalogue. I remember packing some of it when we went out; we just took what we needed out of it, and then later on, when we got our own place where I could place them, then we took them up to Cape Simpson to the cabin and they were there.

Nate was a good hunter; he never came home empty handed when he went out hunting or trapping. Nate showed me how to trap. I wasn't observant. When a fox is caught in a trap, the animal would go around in a circle and make sort of a round mound in the middle where it would dig, trying to get out. By the time we approached the trap, Nate knew there was a fox in it. I had to learn all these signs that he showed me. I learned which way the caribou went by the tracks. If we saw a polar bear track, he could put his hand down and feel how long ago those tracks were made. If there were a lot of fox tracks in the soft snow, then Nate knew there was

some type of dead animal like a seal or walrus that they were going to, and we could find it through those tracks. There were a lot of things like this that he taught me.

We were married in July, and the last week in August I missed my period. I was pregnant then. Right away! When we came back for Christmas someone started a rumor that Nate and I had been playing around and we were going to have an illegitimate child, and that's why we got married.[1] Waggy tongue, that's what it was. But Nate never touched me before we were married. And I found out who that woman was who started it, and I marched right over to her house, and I can remember the look on her face when she saw me. "Oh, you got back from your camp," she said. How sweet she pretended to be! And then I told her why I was there, because I had heard that she started a rumor that Nate and I were playing around and I had gotten pregnant before we got married. I told her, "Now you start counting the months to when my baby will be born, and satisfy your curiosity and figure out for yourself that I'm having a legitimate child." Middle of April, Billy was born, so that screwed up her story. Oh, gosh, the rumors would start a little bit over here, and by the time they reached over here, they would be a mountain. It's still sometimes that way.

At Christmastime we came home. We brought a load of fat caribou meat and fish from our cache, and it was a happy reunion. My mom had made all these warm clothes, and when we came back, she had these real long caribou legs with fur inside for me to wear and a brand-new spotted skin parka.

In April Nate was out. He had gone off to go fetch our boat, which was up at Chipp River, and during his absence I started having these stomach-aches and ended up in the hospital. I had a bad case of diarrhea. I was running upstairs, because we had a pot upstairs, and I'd sit there. And when it wore off, I would come downstairs again. Mom kept seeing me more often going upstairs, and finally she asked me if everything was all right. I said, "Well, I got this awful stomach-ache." And then she had that smile on her face, telling me she knew that it was time for me to go over to the hospital. That was when they were starting to have deliveries at the hospital. They didn't use midwives anymore.[2] I was eight hours in labor. Nate came after Billy was born. When he saw the boy there

was a beam all over his face. He wondered, looking at the size of him, how I could deliver such a baby, because he was pretty big, about eight pounds. My parka was big enough to put him inside, and we went everywhere with Billy on my back. The first time I did that, I remember they were whaling. And they got a whale out there, and I wanted to go so bad, but here was this newborn baby, barely three weeks old. I put him on my back, but we stopped at every rough edge of the road to see if he was still breathing, and Nate would be down there and open up my parka and see if he was breathing in there. "Oh, he's okay."[3]

Packing kids I had to learn, because my sister did most of the packing when we were young. Maria was the little mother when Mom was working, and I was there helping Mom out with all the chores and stuff. From Billy on, I learned to work with a baby on my back, which was much better than leaving it where I would worry. We would wear a work parka. We used to have several of them—thin ones, and heavy ones for traveling. And then, too, I always had a big winter skin sleeping bag for Billy—just tie him in there like a little papoose, so when we were traveling I would be free to help Nate with whatever was needed on the trip. How active we were in those days!

We got the urge to leave again when Billy was small. I ran out of breast milk, and that fall I remember I had to feed Billy fish roe and broth. Nate was also able to come into the village and get some milk and groceries, after the ice got thick enough for him to go over with the sled.

We were known as inland people then. They called us inland people because we hardly ever stayed here in the village.

Family Life

I have very pleasant memories of those early years. When Billy was about a year and a half, I was beginning to notice I was pregnant with Margaret. Nate took us all the way up to the edge of the mountains that year, and we hunted all the way up there. I shot my first caribou up there with Billy on my back. He could talk a little by then, and he said "Mama, puppy?" when he saw the caribou.

We were with another family, the Oyagak family, Lora and Roxy. They had three kids with them. When the boys went off hunting, they left this one female dog that had a litter of pups, and we wanted to raise them. That's how Billy learned about puppies.

Nate and I grew up in sort of different environments; mine was a strict one, while Nate never had any restrictions. He roamed freely and learned the way of life that his father wanted him to. His only schooling was learning to live from the land, learning to survive. He went to school for maybe a total of a week. His parents couldn't stay in the community because family life was getting so poor—no food—and his father had areas where he wanted to go to and live.

So, when we got married, we talked it over how we were going to raise the kids. We wanted to raise them as free as possible, but teach them what's there for them, what not to do, and how to treat people—to help old people, to share—things like that, that we were brought up with. But if our kids did something [wrong], we used to have a little council. The kids would all be present when we punished one for doing whatever was against our rulings, and they all listened, and then we talked to them. We weren't doing this to embarrass them; we were doing it to show them that it was wrong and to let them all know. We didn't want the kind of situation where each of them would point to one and say, "You did this; you did that," or, "He did it; why can't I?" So, whenever we were talking to the kids and other kids came in, we sat them down like they were part of the family, too.

The minister's daughter got so she would be over here a lot. I never sent any kid out. I never told her, "You have to go home and eat with your family." What was here was available, because it didn't matter in those times where the kids were, just so they ate and were warm. They were not in danger, and if any kids stayed too long, Nate would walk them home. We never had too many troubles with the kids because when they did something, they were never afraid to tell us. At least they knew they weren't going to be punished severely for it. Then, in the 1960s, the community had police to see to it that they didn't get out of line. We had curfews, and the Mothers Club used to come in and act on behalf of the school to carry out the curfew, sending kids home by 9:00.

Dad was happy with my marriage; he liked Nate, but he often

teased me about that other boy I was supposed to have married. He was concerned that I might not put my education to use when I quit teaching. After we lost our mother [1943] Dad didn't want me to go out again; he just wanted me to be around. We were very close, and he showed it, too, always asking if Nate and I needed anything. If I was closer to him than the other kids were, I guess it just happened that way. He couldn't keep us there, though; we wanted to go away. Mainly, we went away because we just couldn't stand the bickering and the hard feelings that sometimes worked up between my sister Maria and me. She and her husband and kids were living in the house then, too, and she pretty much took care of Dad. She knew, too, that after Dad passed away, she would inherit the home and surroundings.

In 1945 I went back to teaching because there was nothing else for me to do, and I kept myself busy; I never stayed idle. I never liked being idle, and it was a waste of time for me to sit home and do nothing. I liked teaching, liked being with kids—and so did Nate—and living that close to the school, you can imagine what a crowd of young people we used to have in the house all the time. And Nate would come in and the older boys would come in and spend the evening with their friends, and they felt at ease, knowing Nate and me. Laugh, oh! Happy bunch of young people!

When I started teaching in the fall of 1945 I was pregnant with Charlie. I was having a hard time, and I started missing quite a bit that year because of hemorrhaging. I'd had a miscarriage earlier, and the placenta never came out. And that was what was causing all my problems. Charlie was born in December, and after his birth I started thinking about being home most of the time. I hired a baby-sitter, though, and I went back to school until the end of the school year. And it was about 1946 I finally quit and didn't teach any more, just took substitute work whenever any teacher was unavailable. I enjoyed substitute teaching. I taught all grades and the kids accepted me. Some kids would be so happy because I would be substituting, because I wasn't as strict as some of the teachers.

When I was teaching, it was on weekends that I did my baking for the whole week, because in the wintertime you could freeze the bread and then take it in as you needed it. We had lots of kids. They knew where my bread box was, and they knew that on Saturdays I

baked. And the kids would smell it. Not just my kids, but the town kids were all over here, all eyes. My own kids would say, "Oh, Mom's baking cookies today," and they would bring all their friends. I made lunch for everyone, including the baby-sitter and her family. I'd come home from school to eat lunch, because it wasn't very far. Nate ate out at the base after he started working out there. I never had to worry about him. I would prepare most everything the night before for the next day; then all I had to do was heat it up and have it ready.

Towards the last there, it was just a little too much, expense-wise. When my baby-sitter started wanting more than I made teaching school, I told my husband, "Well, it's ridiculous for me to keep working and just turn over my whole paycheck to this baby-sitter." Nate and I used to feed them with what extra we had, because Nate was a good hunter. He would go out and come back with his sled loaded. So it seemed kind of ridiculous for me to be teaching school, working so hard, and then come home and just sign my check and give it to my baby-sitter. And, too, there was a lot of work for me when I got home, so I got no rest. My baby-sitter got so she would bring her whole family in, her brothers and sisters, and I would have to feed them. So Nate and I talked it over, and since he was working and making money, I quit teaching in 1952. But I was a substitute teacher, whenever they needed me, for a long time.

We had an active house; kids just played in it. Then Nate acquired friends where he worked, and he used to bring them home, and I would take pains to amuse them. At first he wouldn't stand for his friends to even look at me. He'd be very jealous. I noticed this and started guarding myself, where I wouldn't be too friendly, or I'd sit by his side. But it wore off. He saw that I would never change. It's terrible, because I remember how uncomfortable it is to have a jealous husband. I could never picture Nate like that when we lived without any Outside visitors. But white people started coming in and making a fuss over our family and the kids. When they would come back, they would always have something to give the kids, or something for our table that we had never had, like fresh watermelon. It took a long time for Nate to acquire a taste for watermelon. And fresh fruit—he was just amazed how different it was from canned fruit. When that base opened up, it was more education for us.

At suppertime, I made it a point to have a nice full table of prepared foods, and Nate never complained. After about ten or fifteen years, he had nerve enough to tell me that he was sick of my cooking, and how I spoiled the taste of meat. When we first got married I was so green about preparing food the native way, because I had grown up with nothing but Fred Hopson's cooking, and then being Outside. . . . I never realized that Nate had never had any Outside contact. I know he dearly loved baking powder biscuits, and I was forever making those. Sometimes I'd make biscuits with fresh seal oil, or I'd make fried bread or donuts. Well, after he complained, I began to cook something else for him. I learned to ask what he would like to have for supper that he would enjoy. So, I prepared something different for him the way he liked it. There was nothing hard about it, but it had never dawned on me that all those years I went through to please him with food and stuff, he ate it but didn't like it. Or sometimes he would look at it and go out and get a frozen fish or something, and take his seal oil and stuff and eat that, but he never told me anything about it. How patient he was to put up with what I brought into his life.[4]

After we settled in Barrow, we only left in the fall at fishing time. We put all the kids on the sled—we didn't have any snow machines then—dressed them all up, got their clothes prepared, and took them all out. We camped near a lake, and the ice was only about five inches thick. Nate chopped some blocks up and stood them up for a windbreak, and we pitched our tents inside it. Put a top over it—warm! We stayed about a month, then we came back after fishing was over. That fall the kids had a chance to see some reindeer herders bring in their herds, drive them through; they got all excited. One time our dogs got loose and our leader got shot. Oh, was I ever mad! We had had that lead dog for about four years. I remember I got after that herder for driving that herd too close to our camp and exciting our dogs, which were naturally wild anyway. We finally had to kill our dog, and that man tried to give me two fat reindeer—he butchered them and put them by my tent. I said, "Take them away. That's not going to replace my dog." Nate had the fastest team in the whole town, too.

Children

We didn't figure on having so many, but there was no birth control pills or anything. Overall, there were big families up here. I came from a big family. I remember, when Nate and I got married, my mom said, "The work you have, you shouldn't have more than three. You can control it." And I said, "If you can have ten, I can have twelve." And I did. Twelve are alive. I lost one. He would have been the fourth one, a boy, way back in 1948. I was helping out with the health problems in the community. Even though I changed my clothes after taking care of some of the people very sick with TB, I was a carrier I guess, and I got my little year-old boy infected with TB. When a child gets sick with TB, they call it meningitis, because he doesn't get it through his lungs; he gets it through his spine,[5] which leaves him helpless and very pathetic. There was no cure for them in those days. So all we did was just watch him just pass away.

So, other than that, Nate and I have twelve children alive.[6] William Neakok, the oldest, was born April 10, 1941. And then the next one I had was Margaret; she's married to a young man out of Kotzebue, Ray Ferguson, and she lives in Kotzebue. She was born on Memorial Day—May 30, 1943. And Charles, named after my father, Charles DeWitt Brower Neakok, the third child, born December 18, 1945.

After that we had another son, James Neakok, born in '48. He had a couple of months of fever when he was young, when there was no doctor here, and he ended up retarded. He spent six years in a school in Oregon, and when he came back he didn't know us at first. The next one was the boy that we lost, Robert; he was a year old on May 9 [1950], and his sickness was noticed in October, when he became very listless. We took him over to the hospital. They diagnosed it as [tubercular] meningitis, and we lost him on December 4, [1950]. Our next was Ronald, born 1950, August 1. [And then] Danny, 1952, July 18; he just missed our wedding anniversary, which was July 17. And then Donna, who is Donna Miller now; she was born in 1954, August 25. Then Pat was born December 19, 1956; he just missed Charlie's birthday by one day.

Glenn Neakok was born August 5, 1957. And then Dora in 1958, on November 8. And then George was born in 1960, on June 14. I had been traveling and was in seminar in Nome to learn more about being a magistrate. I came home, and three days later George was born.

I thought George was the last one, and I didn't figure I would have another child. But I had heard about how old people would come to you and say, "How come you never named a child after me?" And then give you some kind of prediction that this would happen to you. And so that happened to me.

When I was growing up, I was very attached to one of the reindeer herders and his wife. I stayed with them and slept in the same bed with them, even though I had my own parents. My parents were jealous because I wanted to stay with these people all the time. I loved them dearly. And so this old man, William Leavitt, came to me one day and said, "How come you never named one of your sons after me?" "Well, you're still alive. If you were dead, maybe I would have named a child after you." But about a month later he died, after telling me that I was going to be pregnant again, and it was going to be a boy. And I laughed inside, thinking, "Well, it will never happen." But come that winter, my health was such that I kept going to the hospital. I was forty-eight years old, and I thought I was going through the change of life. So I kept on going over to the hospital, back and forth. And pretty soon this old lady who was a midwife came over. She'd heard I was having problems, and that I was going to be sent down to Anchorage to see some doctors down there, to see what was wrong with me. "You know," she says, "I bet you're pregnant." And I looked at her and said, "Me?" Here it had been almost four years since George was born, and George was quite a big boy. And I said, "No, not on your life." "Well, lie down anyway." So I lie down on my bed. She poked around inside and said, "There it is. You're pregnant, all right."

So about that time I was still lying on the bed and talking to her when my husband comes in. And he'd gotten the word that I was going to go out of Barrow down to Anchorage to be checked for my health. And he came over kind of sympathetic and asked, "Well, what did the doctor say?" "Well, the doctor didn't say anything, but Ena here says I'm pregnant." He looked at me and said, "Whatever

for?" He didn't want another child; we had many. But that was it. It was Robert. And we called him Robert, because we already had a William. That was the middle name of that old man; we also gave him the name Inurok. It makes you think that there is something to the words the old people tell you. I never forgot that. And it's so funny at times. . . . We've never told him the life story of this old man. Every so often he'll come around like he was that person. "Didn't I used to do that?" We'd look and ask, "Why, how did you know that?" "Well, I just knew." It's kind of an uncanny thing sometimes. And that was Robert—November 4, 1963.

I breast-fed my children. In fact, later I had so much milk [that] I used to breast-feed other babies whose mothers weren't as fortunate as I was. Then, from Danny on, most of them were bottle-fed, because of my work. Then, when I became a magistrate and George and Robert, the two younger boys, were born, I was out of the house most of the time, but I had a baby-sitter, a woman much older than I was. In fact, Lena had been my baby-sitter when I was growing up. She was very good, and I allowed her three kids to come in. They were quite grown, but they had lost their father. Lena and her children were part of our family. In those days we didn't have disposable diapers, and I used the regular cloth ones. I used to clean the mess, and then boil them, and then rinse and dry them. When we were first married, Nate used to be happy to help with the diapers when they just urinated. We shared everything.

We raised several other kids—never actually went through adoption procedures, but had them in our home for six months or a year. They were kids who were unwanted by their parents. You get so attached to them. Finally the welfare department would make a placement, and we would lose them, but they never forgot us. We would often get some abused children for two weeks or one month, until I was able to talk to the parents [and] to return their children. We had a lot of traffic with children like that when drinking started here in Barrow. There were very many children neglected and abused because of their parents' drinking. A mother brought her kids over because the father was drinking. She would want to know how long I could keep them until she could straighten him out and then, if she couldn't, have him arrested. She would come and sign a

complaint. They'd sleep upstairs. I always had mattresses—about three or four mattresses on the floor where they could sleep—[and] clean bedding. . . .

I remember there was one deformed kid whose parents thought that he wasn't a human being, and they starved him to where it stunted the growth of that young man. But I took him in and told the kids that this would have to be their little brother for a while, until we find some place to place him. "Because he is this way, you will find that he is different; but don't tell him; don't point at him. Mom and Dad love all of you kids, and here is a boy who is very strange because he is like this. He is a cripple; his parents don't want him." The troopers found him naked—must have been twenty below—in the fall, in the snow, and there a female dog with pups. He was huddled in there by that female, and I guess they put him out so that he would freeze to death or something. . . . I kept him for over six months and got so attached to him. I'd take him to school, and he was bright. The parents said he was like a little animal. . . . How else would he be after they starved him! At first he was like that when we tried to feed him. He would grab everything, just like a little animal. But after a while, he knew that he could have all that he wanted.

But what he used to do when Nate and I would sit down on the couch, he would wiggle himself between us and say, "My mamma; my daddy." And I guess we were trying to win him so much that we forgot all about our kids, until one of them—it was Glenn—[said]: "That's not your mom and dad; that's my mom and dad!" "Oh, Glenn," I said, "We are your mom and dad. We love you. But we are trying to make a special effort to give this little boy what he needs. We didn't know how you felt. Now we know." You never think about it. Trying to teach a kid that there is different way of life, you forget about your own family. At least I used to get carried away with it. We didn't have homes for kids then. And nobody else offered, because I was the magistrate and the welfare worker at the same time. Everything came [to me]. But we always had plenty, plenty to eat. Nate was a good hunter.

The old people would know [that we had] more than what we can have when he comes home with a sled load. We'd have a full house, and [they'd] sit there after I set down their food. (They didn't like to

eat at the table.) They would put a big tablecloth in the middle of the floor [and] set their food down; they would squat down and, after they ate, they would tell their yarns. I wish to goodness I had a tape recorder in those days! And they would laugh. They would remind each other, "You remember when . . . ?" And somebody would remember and they would tell about . . . "Where were you that time?" And I would have a whole house full of old "fogies." Some would take a nap, if they overate or something, until they were able to wake up and go home. It was always so darn pleasant. I was so used to them, just so happy, not a care in the world. Some of them felt they were useless to their families because they were so old, and they would come over here [and] they would feel different. Try and encourage them to bring whatever they wanted to do, or ask me what they could help with, and they would be happy even it was just shredding sinew for braiding and stuff. Or they would see an old man whose clothing was ripping, and they would offer, "Take your boot off; let me sew it."

I took in this old man that I found dying, brought him into my home and nursed him to health, and later sent him out to sanitorium. [I] didn't know what happened to him for four or five years. When he came back, I promised I'd have him live in my home. And I kept that promise and had old David Otuana for over twenty years, until he decided he wanted to move up to Nuiqsut when it was opening up in 1973.

We were a close-knit family. We pretty much stayed together. We went camping; we helped the kids to school. Once they got older, Nate taught his boys to go out and hunt, and to learn to save money and put it away. When Billy was around thirteen or fourteen he got a job shoveling coal from the Meade River coal mine. When the coal "train" came in after school, any child that wanted to go earn a few dollars could go shovel all this coal into the bin and earn some money. It was a mess. They'd come home looking like little Negroes from the coal dust, but it didn't matter to them because they'd earned some money.

And we went to church as a family. Church and prayer meetings were about the only place you could go on a Sunday to see your friends. Everybody went to church in those days because there was no show house, no bingo, no distractions of any kind. The only

church we had was this Presbyterian church. These other churches didn't exist.[7] Or we went to school parties. If our kids qualified to be at a party by doing well and not breaking the language rule, at the end of the month, from 7 to 9 P.M., we went to to a party and watched the games.

I was really involved with my children's education. I was there pushing them through and helping them out when they first started bringing in their homework. But most of the time I'd let them try, and then I'd read and let them read to get the meaning of what was there. We pushed for high school education. The kids were screened in eighth grade for high school, for which school they wanted to go to. All my kids went to Mt. Edgecombe in Sitka. Because their oldest brother went, the next one wanted to go to Mt. Edgecombe. So, as close as they were, there'd be three of our kids in school at a time. And it was hard on the children. But we had the telephone system then in Barrow. We could talk to our children when they got quite homesick, and have a big telephone bill to pay. But we didn't mind because the government paid for the fare then.

When we first started sending our kids out to school, when high school was becoming compulsory, I remember paying Billy's and Margaret's fares down to Sitka and their return tickets. And it was hard on your pocketbook. Something like $800 each. Kids started dropping out even though they wanted to go, because their parents couldn't afford to send them out. So, after so many complaints, then the government stepped in and started paying their way out. So, today, we don't have that. We have a nice high school now. When the school opened up in Barrow, then the younger ones went to high school here. We pushed for college, but the girls were the only ones; Donna and Dora tried their luck with college. Dora kept running out of money. She spent her sophomore year, which was her last, down in Maui, in the Hawaiian Islands. That was when Nate start whining for his favorite daughter, so we scrounged up enough money to send him down and take a trip to Hawaii for three weeks.

By my house there was a big snowbank. The kids used to come down there, because it used to be the biggest snowbank. Get them to playing out there with whatever they could find to slide down. And they played one-base baseball where you have a whole line of batters behind you. There's a catcher and a thrower, and there's only

one base. So this line of kids bats, but there's no sides to it. It's individual scoring. Whoever makes the most score wins. They also played at throwing balls at objects to see who's the best shot; and in the summertime, they played with heavy bones, throwing them like horseshoes at stakes. But today, I don't think anybody even remembers how to play those kinds of things anymore. There's so much going on—arcades, and show houses, TV; nobody wants to play out, squat down in the sand and play those games anymore. Kids used to love boats and kayaks. They learned to use them from their fathers. Even my sister and I used to go out and get the ducks that our father shot in those things. Once you learn how to maneuver yourself in a kayak, they're pretty good. Some of the bolder ones, older kids, used to do stunts with them—turn around, get under the water and then come up again.

After school was out, most families would camp out and, at first, we used to go up to the point and down the coast by dog team on the ice—take our stuff, summer grub and bedding, or whatever we were going to use. We took our boat on top of a sled and towed it down with a dog team. And when the ice broke up, after hunting, then we could come back in the boat. The only time hunting is good is when the ice is breaking up, or after that time. When there was little snow on the ground, we could use our dog team to travel inland. When the rivers started to flow we'd put nets in for fishing. We never used to go very far, because you could never travel very far with a dog team with big families. We used to go down maybe about ten miles and thought that was a whole day's journey. We would stay two or three months until school started again. But when this base opened up and Nate started working, they used to have auctions of some of the old machinery—like weasels for $300. We got one that used to pull our family, plus whatever other kids wanted to go, up inland some twenty to twenty-three miles by a big lake, Tulurak.

Public Health Volunteer

After I quit teaching full time, I worked as a volunteer public health "nurse."[8] I was shown how to take off the clothes that I wore when I visited the sick and the ones with TB. I had a special area

over at the hospital where I could disinfect myself before I came home. TB grew after people started living together in these small homes. Not knowing that some of their family members were active with TB, it spread to others. Later on, the doctors started separating man and wife who were carriers—it was a pathetic deal, but they had to start somewhere. Little separate homes were built to place those people with active TB nearby their own family. They could meet outdoors with family members, but their kids couldn't go inside the little huts and be exposed to TB. That was before anyone was ever sent to any sanitorium. It wasn't until around 1949 or 1950 that they started sending people out to a hospital with sanitoriums. Before then, the sick people infested with TB couldn't be sent out. We had no way to carry them out to sanitoriums until we started getting these planes in the early fifties, when this base first started opening up. Even so, though, there was quite a bit of meningitis[9] among some of the children. There was a new drug being introduced to fight meningitis.[10] My little son got meningitis from my visiting patients who had it and then, too, by my bringing in that old man who had active TB, old David [Otuana]. That old man still lives today.

I visited homes as a public health nurse, seeing to it that they took their medication, that their places were cleaned, and making things a little more pleasant for the patient in the home, cleaning for them and bringing them food. It was not really a full-time job; I did it on certain days. Barrow wasn't all that big, so there were about ten to fifteen patients I had to tend to. Sometimes the nurse from the hospital went with me. But her place was at the clinic, along with the other doctor, making referrals to the doctors. I was also writing letters here and there, because we were researching areas where there might be sanitoriums where people could be sent. Dr. George at the hospital was about the first one aware of that, and he helped us.

Church

In 1958, I became the first woman elder in the Presbyterian church here. I guess the church had a meeting, and because of the way I worked at the church and helped out, they wanted me to become an

elder. After talking with the Reverend Wartes I felt that there should be another woman, so Lucy Aiken was chosen. The elders in those times were known to be very sober men; they didn't go out and have a good time, or you never saw them mingle and gossip. But here are Lucy and I, two happy-go-lucky ones, no care in the world when we got together. It's a wonder that they never threw us out, but there were rumors, and even people from the congregation had things to say about Lucy and me. "How can you become elders? You're so happy-go-lucky." "Well, there won't be a sober-looking elder when you two get in there and mingle with others."

Later on, after we heard those things were said about us, we had our meeting with the minister. We asked how we should act in front of the public and what should we do, and he said: "You don't have to. Just be yourselves, but do the work of the Lord—and show it, that you are good people, that you are not straying to something foolish." We were chosen because we had common sense and good minds in working for the Lord and teaching others. We were elders four years in a row, and then they appointed another woman and a man out of the deacon section. My name is still in the church, but I'm not active anymore. I'm on the inactive list, but when I am called upon to do a sermon, then I respond to it.

The church is still involved in welfare work today. If there are any families going hungry, and they have no funds and no immediate help is available, then the church will step in and ask for donations for hungry families or the people in need. But not so much anymore. The church realizes that people are now working for wages, and if they mismanage their money, or whatever, then it's not a long-term deal until the next paycheck comes around. But they are not neglected. And then we have the Mothers Club, too, that looks into the needy families. They'll go out and donate or buy certain things and keep on until the people get on their feet, especially a family where they have lost a family member, a mother or a father.

The church has been important in my life; I have accepted my religion. I taught it to my kids, but when they were old enough to choose what they wanted to be, then I didn't press them.

Sewing

For a while I made parkas for sale, for about a year, until I just couldn't handle it anymore. I was making a lot of money. I was doing welfare work, most of the time out of my home, and in the meantime, when people weren't keeping me busy, I sewed. I got started because we had some teachers here from back east, and when they went back to Maine, they worked the ski resort and they showed off their parkas that I had made for them. Then they kept ordering and ordering for people who wanted them there. And then for a while, when Wien [Airlines] first started bringing in tourists, we made parkas for the tourist group, too, and then somebody else took over and bought ready-made ones and put trimmings and ruffs on them. I got to where I was making quite a bit of money. I could make one parka a day, $150 for one, and by the end of the year we were pretty well off with what I made.

I was also still sewing for my family. I enjoyed it; part of my hobby was sewing. My free time was sewing and fixing up people's clothes that needed it. I'd see somebody's clothing that really needed to be sewed, and I would take them under my wing, take their measurements, and put together all the scraps that I used to have and make a parka for them. It was much easier when all this fabric started coming in to Barrow, because you could just go out to the stores and buy it and charge people who wanted a parka for just sewing it. I quit doing parkas for others because my sewing load with my own family was getting too heavy, what with grandchildren. Our family was dependent on me with their clothing. That's what I am going to have to start to do before winter sets in. I do that every year. Nate's clothing comes first. But then the kids would get hold of his clothes if he wasn't using them. He would get too many of them, because he didn't wear them out as much as the kids did. Now I make about twenty or more parkas a year, and a pair of mukluks occasionally.

Umiat

During the course of oil exploration in National Petroleum Reserve No. 4 a supply and operations base was established on the Colville River, at a place

called Umiat ("boats") by the Iñupiat, who traditionally cached large skin boats there. Located southeast of Barrow and some seventy-five miles inland, Umiat comprised an airfield and camp. At the height of oil exploration in the late 1940s and 1950s, some thirty men were based there.

In early 1954, the base at Umiat was being decommissioned and left to the new construction of oil companies. While they were pulling out, somehow our family got picked to take care of that base up there before everybody was fully out. So in October, we had to pack up and move our family up there to take care of that camp. They swore Nate in as a commander, and I was by his side interpreting all this. I used to tease him about my rights, saying I swore in the same as he did because I had to interpret everything.

Puget Sound and Drake was the first outfit to come in with a plane load of men. I had just fixed a big supper in the mess hall and made a cherry pie, in one of those Army-type ovens, with the pans that are this big. I had a pan full of that cherry pie, and a stewing chicken that I had boiled for about four hours and drained and then rolled in flour and made fried chicken out of it, and vegetables, and hot biscuits.

I can remember they brought a professional cook with them who was supposed to cook for the outfit. Another man we had known when he worked out here; he was half-white and half-native from Nome—Donald Buck. Don came in with that group, and he was to be foreman for as long as they were stationed there, and Nate showed them to their quarters. All they had to do was turn the heat on and fill the water tanks. All the silverware and eating utensils I had boiled, and rolled in a clean sheet, and stored them away in shelves. Oh God, that was a lot of work. And trying to get the grease out of that kitchen, the way the Air Force left it. . . . It took me about two weeks to clean it. The floor was wooden, and they had some crystal lye, which I was going to use to clean the floor. I made the mistake of dissolving some of it in an aluminum container, and it started to boil and eat the aluminum. I almost poisoned myself until I moved it to a steel container and started cleaning the floor with it. Got that kitchen all spic-and-span, and the tables in the dining room area were covered and ready for use so they wouldn't be dusty when people moved in. All the sanitation knowledge I had, I put to use.

Well, that cook, I remember his remark. The name Neakok was

Eskimo, but I was Sadie Brower at one time, and Donald Buck knew it. I was from Charlie Brower's family, but this cook didn't know who I was. When I told him that everything was pretty well sanitized for use, he remarked, "Yeah, I can just bet how an Eskimo can sterilize and sanitize anything up here." I didn't say anything, and then [I] announced, "Well, we ate already, but if you men would like to eat, we have a lot left over from supper which is good and hasn't been touched. There is cherry pie for dessert with whipped cream, and chicken, and vegetables, and mashed potatoes and gravy." And the cook looked at me—"Well." Don said, "Let's all sit down. Sadie, put the food on." So I put it on buffet style—heated these big pans up in the ovens and laid it out. Everybody went for it. They ate till they were filled, and they praised my biscuits, saying how tender and good they were.

Don Buck came to my rescue, and he looked at me and said, "Are you going to take that remark?" "Well, I guess I will have to accept his opinion about my people, if that's how much he's learned, being up here, about the Eskimos." Don Buck knew my background, so he goes up to the cook who made that remark, and said, "I will have you know that this is Charlie Brower's daughter. Have you ever heard of Charlie Brower?" "Oh yes." And he looked at me and said, "You do look like one of the Browers. Well, I will take back everything I have said. Your cooking was delicious, I'll admit; maybe better than my cooking. And everything you say turns out to be true. It's all so clean and sanitary."

We had another family with us—Luther Leavitt's—to keep us company, and I taught school to all the kids in my spare time. We took some books from the school, so the kids could keep up with their studies, and they had pretty much stayed around in our quarters while I did all the cleaning and working and Nate did the overhauling of the trucks.

We were there from October until about the first of January. We had every building in order, so anybody could just walk in and light the stoves and get the water. Nate even got offered a job by the outfit [Puget Sound and Drake] if he wanted to stay, but he was still a commanding officer up there, so they couldn't put him to work until they released him from it. The kids pretty much knew that whole area. We knew where everything was kept. Billy and

Margaret Leavitt were both about fourteen, and they were great help with running the machinery. Except when Billy started one of the weasels and ran it right through the mess hall. Right through the wall! He didn't know how to stop it. Luther and Nate patched it up. Cora [Luther's wife] and I laughed so hard over that. She was pregnant and had to leave around November to come back to Barrow to deliver her baby. And while she was gone, then we got busy. When the plane came in [in January, with Puget Sound and Drake personnel], they asked if we wanted to go out on that plane. So we had to gather our belongings, from one end of the building to the other. One box would be filled with whatever, then tied and taken to the truck, and we were ready to leave in two hours. Nate stayed up there to be in charge until he got released [of his command].

We had let somebody else use our house while we were gone, and it was a mess when we got there! Terrible. No heat. Frost all over. The carburetor in our oil stove wasn't working, and they didn't know how to make it work, so they half froze and were getting ready to move out. They had used all our supplies, the stuff we stored upstairs; they helped themselves to whatever. And our gas lanterns were barely alive. I remember we had a flashlight. I had to work fast with those kids, but I had learned how to take care of those types of problems—fix the carburetor in our stove and get it going, fix the gas lanterns, clean the generators out and get them to work again. Then when the heat started hitting our house, water started to drip from all that frost. So that night we had to make do. But the kids were so happy. All our stuff was dumped by the truck right out there, and the kids were bringing it in. Then the next-door neighbors found out we were back, and Cora found out we were in, and pretty soon you could hardly move inside the house. Our friends, who we hadn't seen for four months, just started coming in, and that was our homecoming.

A Public Welfare Worker

My welfare work in this community really started in the early fifties, while I was teaching school. Seeing the children so poorly dressed and undernourished, the principal gave me the job of looking

into the family life of those kids that weren't doing too well in school. In those days there were no more than 150 houses in Barrow, and it didn't take long to make the rounds, talking to parents of children and finding what their needs were. And then the BIA in those times had emergency help for destitute families. They could help out when the parents were unable to hunt, or had no means of going out and hunting, and were running out of food. I found and wrote down the needs of a family, and if they qualified—if the man was not trapping, not bringing in any kind of income to trade—then I would turn over all these reports to the principal who was in charge of the BIA monies and grants.

I became a full-time social worker after we came back from Umiat, taking care of that Air Force base. Before I had been doing it on an application basis, and then when I came back in '54, there was a man who was trying to do the welfare work. He wasn't digging around to see if people qualified; he wasn't doing background work on them. And they wanted to let him go and get somebody else. The principal, knowing that I had done well while working for the school, submitted my name, and I got appointed in February of 1954.

Welfare work involved the old-age program and the dependent children and widows, filing their applications each month. I had to try and establish age groups and verify the age of each person. This meant looking through medical records and school records, and, oh gosh, it was a whole-day deal to research one family at a time, because they were all big families. There were six or seven kids in the family, and if their births were not recorded, then you had to write to Juneau and wait six or seven weeks, sometimes. Meanwhile, the person needs assistance, but they had to wait. So Nate and I helped out with what we made, feeding people and going to the church and getting donations for families who were in need until such time as they could get help. That was a lot of work.

At that time no one knew about Social Security benefits; no one had Social Security numbers, so we started giving them out. The commanding officer [at the base] was informed that no one from Barrow had Social Security numbers, and they started giving them out. I remember one day was picked for every worker to come in and put in an application for a number. I remembered Nate's so well I never forgot it. Then I tried to explain to people that they should

memorize the number in case they should lose it.

Then there was income tax. I had to really make the people understand that if they worked for wages and they had a Social Security number, there was a tax that had to be paid. I used to work until 3 A.M. with people. I didn't do the itemized deductions; I did just that short form. But when people wanted the itemized deductions, try to make them produce all their receipts and they couldn't find any. And then there was unemployment compensation. My house was like the post office, with people lined up who didn't know how to fill their forms, or how to go about making applications. I filled out a lot of forms and wrote a lot of letters as a social worker. I would write the letter in English and then translate it into Eskimo, to see it if met with their approval. And then they would sign it. I didn't mind it; I started it all and had to carry it through until somebody else could take over. After I became a magistrate, people still trusted me with their taxes. Then, I started teaching some of the high school students how to do taxes, so they could help out. People were thankful, and when their returns would come in, they would give me $10 or $5 saying "Thank you for making this money available to me." They never knew about deductions, or that they were entitled to that tax return.

I worked for Social Security, did social work—you name it, I came under it. And then, by 1960, there were problems between the base and here to the extent that a line was drawn between the village and the base. People were starting to drink; our young people were beginning to wander up there, learning how to drink and getting in trouble. [Hugh] Saltzman, the commissioner there, would approach me about how to handle some of these cases. I served as counsel, and we would have a little powwow about this thing before the case would come up. We would have full knowledge of the whole thing, because our people just never denied whatever action. If they could remember, they were truthful. And they weren't ashamed to tell it; they didn't keep it back.

Saltzman found out that everybody was very truthful with me in relating what happened, so when complaints regarding our people were brought before the commissioner by the territorial marshall, I would sit in, like I was acting as a lawyer defending these people. I was called in for advice and I would give it, and also I would inter-

pret the law to my people. Kids never thought they broke the law, because they had never lived under it; they didn't know anything about rules and regulations. Then Saltzman would search me out about what type of punishment would be appropriate. Then we sat down and reasoned it out and found that there could be a solution to the problem, that if they lifted that restriction between the village and the camp [base], we couldn't have all this. And so I started standing up for the rights of my people, even though I wasn't a lawyer.

8

Farthest North Judge

In the mid-1970s just about anybody in the state had heard of Sadie. She had been a magistrate up there for a long time and had an excellent reputation. [Judge Robert Coats, March 6, 1986]

If it hadn't been for Sadie and Charlotte Brower [her law clerk], the whole system would not have functioned at all. [Judge Michael Jeffery, August 5, 1985]

Sadie Neakok's small frame house stands in the shadow of the ultramodern, three-story Alaska Court System building, two ends of the quarter-century continuum of modern law for Barrow Iñupiat. In 1960 arraignments and sentencing were conducted at Sadie's kitchen table; her kitchen filing cabinets bulged with dockets and the vital statistics she was required to keep for the North Slope; she had no law clerk or even a typewriter; jail was a spare room at the school and later a two-cell holding facility that she often had to clean herself on the weekends; the state trooper flew in to investigate serious cases, as there were no resident police; court was held after hours in a schoolroom, and juries deliberated in the church. Felony cases weren't even heard in Barrow; there were no resident lawyers and none flew into town. Instead, Sadie, the defendant, and the witnesses would board a DC-3 for a long, circuitous flight to the headquarters of the Second Judicial District of Alaska in Nome, where the case would be tried.

Today there are eight attorneys in Barrow (none of them in private practice), five law clerks, a magistrate, and a superior court judge.[1] *Thirteen borough police (most from Outside), a state trooper, an investigator, and eight correctional officers staff the Public Safety building. Although completed just five years ago, its nine-cell jail is already inadequate for community needs. Department of Public Safety statistics indicate that most crimes in Barrow today are alcohol-related; rape and sex offenses, assault, liquor-law violations,*

and domestic violence are on the rise (Alaska Consultants 1983:69–70).

Across the street from Public Safety is the new Alaska Court System building. A plaque in the building's foyer "commemorates the distinguished services of the Honorable Sadie Neakok . . . as a magistrate in Barrow from 1960 through 1977." The carpeted district and superior courtrooms are appointed with cushioned theater-type chairs, oak-paneled benches, and simultaneous translation facilities, enabling jurors or witnesses to speak in Iñupiaq. According to Michael Jeffery, the superior court judge for the North Slope, the Barrow courts have the highest trial rate in Alaska today.

The U.S. federal legal system is barely one hundred years old in Arctic Alaska;[2] *the more directly felt state system is just over a quarter-century old. In traditional times, authority and adjudication were relatively informal, residing first in the male head of a nuclear or extended family, and, beyond that, in the* umialik, *the leader or headman of a collection of related families. In northern coastal Alaska the position was often conterminous with the whaling captain.*[3]

Although there was considerable individual variation, within the family the husband ideally had authority over his wife and children, deciding "where they should live, when they should move, and how they should deal with any crises and problems that developed" (Burch 1975:91). A wife's opinion was usually solicited in important decisions, the husband's power resembling that of a benevolent despot (Burch 1975:91). Neither husband nor wife had recourse to legal sanctions enforced at a higher level, so family conflicts were worked out between spouses, each calling upon close consanguine kin for assistance as needed. Husband or wife could terminate the union at any time by simply packing up and leaving.[4]

Beyond the nuclear family was the local family—a large, bilaterally extended group, up to four generations in depth, comprising several nuclear families and occupying adjacent dwellings in a settlement (Burch 1975:235–38). Larger settlements like Barrow were inhabited by several local families, ranging in size from thirty to sixty individuals. The local family was headed by an umialik. *Although an* umialik *was recognized as such because of his personality, hunting skills, and wealth, the position tended to run in certain family lines.*

The umialik, *according to Spencer (1959:179), was characterized by dignity, modesty, circumspection, popularity, generosity, and great wealth. He exercised authority by virtue of his personal magnetism, his skill in manipulating people, and the promise of his prosperity. While people might be readily attracted to an*

umialik, *he still worked hard and continually to maintain the loyalty of his followers, particularly his whaling crew members. The* umialik *and his local family were affiliated with a* qargi, *commonly glossed as a "dance house," or "men's house." By day the* qargi *was a place where men and boys gathered to work and eat and socialize; on nights when ceremonies were held, the* qargi *was open to women and children of the community.*

Charles Brower, who visited the qariyit *in Utqiagvik in December of 1884, counted three in the village. He commented (n.d.:146): "These dance houses were supposed to be the community property but the head men each claimed one and speaking of where the dance was, a native would say, 'in Mungies or Ah-kuz-ige' or whoever was giving the dance." Brower also suggests a ranking of* umialit *when he remarks that "Mungie was at that time chief headman here . . . a fine native, the richest man (or Omalik) in the north" (n.d.:146). A man of influence and power, the* umialik *commanded the respect of the people, and though the ethnographic literature is not explicit about his judicial role, his advice must have been sought in the settlement of disputes and conflicts.*[5]

Restitution, reprimanding, teasing, shaming, and—in extreme cases—ostracism were all employed as sanctions for misbehavior. Serious crimes such as murder, wife-stealing, and rape were generally handled by revenge, with mediation attempted at some point. Crimes were dealt with at the family level, though the number of individuals involved might grow as relationships between kin required that an individual fight for his relatives and avenge them (Spencer 1959:73). Revenge could lead to protracted blood feuds, but attempts were made to end the cycle by mediation and payment of blood money. Charles Brower describes a situation that began in 1894. Although the precipitating causes for the initial murder (drunkenness) and the participation of a white man in adjudicating the conflict were not traditional, the structure of the crime and its denouement were. The murdered man, "Baby," from Point Hope, was the brother of Brower's first wife and, in Brower's estimation, "a mighty fine fellow when sober, and a good friend to me" (n.d.:450).

> Two nights after our return Baby got drunk in the village. As usual the drunks wound up in a row, Baby beat up two of the village men so badly they could not see. Some time later he did the same thing [;] this time he got drunk with his father's friend, almost killing him. When Baby left the house to come home his friend also came out at the same time, taking along his rifle, coming up the trail ahead of Baby. Just at the last house in the village he shot him through both legs, leaving him where he fell. One

of the men Baby had beat up some time before saw what happened, going to where he lay he stabbed him through the heart, then tying a rope around his neck he dragged him some little distance from the track and left his body. At daylight someone saw him there and reported it to me. I told his family who went for the body, bringing it to the station [Brower's trading station] where he lived.

One of Baby's younger brothers was going to kill the old fellow that had done the shooting. I tried hard to make him let things rest saying Baby brought it on himself and no man would stand for what his brother did to the other men. I thought for a time there was to be a general killing match. The old fellow heard what the boy had said, sending him word that he would kill him on sight if he even made a move against him. He was willing to pay the Baby's mother for her son's death. Finally it was compromised, the man paying to the Baby's mother a new sled and four dogs [and] agreeing to leave the village at once so there would be no chance for the boy to change his mind. [Brower n.d.:449–50]

Unfortunately, the payment of blood money did not end the conflict. The older man left but the next summer some of Baby's relatives killed him and his two sons at Kivalina. Brower does not say if the feud went any further.

In their discussion of the changing legal culture of the Iñupiat (1974), Hippler and Conn argue that the basic Iñupiat personality structure has had a direct bearing upon the operation of the Anglo-American legal system in Iñupiat communities. In particular they note the negative value placed on the direct expression of anger, a point emphatically made also in Never in Anger, *Jean Brigg's study of Eskimo interpersonal relationships. Noninterference and the avoidance of conflict are also traditionally valued behaviors, though one might try covertly to intervene in a situation if one could get away with it. Spencer (1959:249) elaborates in discussing another aspect of Eskimo personality: "The culture made no provisions for expressing 'feelings.' No one could feel free to indicate to others that he might be out of sorts. This was true in all interpersonal relationships. People talked, and still do so, of weather, hunting, food. There was no attempt to evaluate situations or to pass judgement on them." For the most part these personality qualities did not bode well for the successful adoption of the Anglo-American adversarial legal system. Other legal problems were created by cultural differences in the definition of crimes, stemming, for example, from divergent concepts of property ownership. To the advantage of the Anglo-American legal process, but not necessarily to the advantage of the Iñupiat, was the native value placed on honesty; defendants, perhaps all too willingly, admitted guilt.*

The imposition of U.S. federal law in native Alaska began in 1867 with the United States Revenue Cutter Service, whose ships plied Alaskan waters from the southeastern extremity of the territory to Demarcation Point, some two hundred miles east of Barrow at the Canadian border. The revenue cutters were charged with regulating traffic in firearms and liquor, preventing smuggling, protecting merchant vessels from piracy, aiding vessels in distress, looking after commercial whaling interests, removing shipwrecks, and so forth. In addition, their commanding officers were empowered to grant marriages or divorces, to make arrests for violations of federal law, to pass sentence when sitting with their officers as a court, and, in extreme cases, to impose capital punishment.

In some instances the native people looked to the revenue cutter personnel as a higher legal authority. Spencer (1959:113) describes a case where an Iñupiaq man died of apparent poisoning, and neither of the two suspects—his wife and her lover—would admit to any knowledge of the event. When the government cutter came shortly afterwards, the officials on board were informed of the death by the deceased's relatives. All parties involved were brought on board ship and, in the absence of any evidence, the only sanction imposed was the removal of the female suspect to Barrow. In other instances, cases were brought to the attention of the revenue cutter authorities at the instigation of white traders, whalers, and later, teachers. The legal system that the U.S. Revenue Cutter Service represented, however, was ephemeral, for its ships were present in the vicinity of a village for only a few days per year, and only the most serious violations were brought to their attention.

Eventually, federal lay judges—commissioners—were appointed for larger Alaskan settlements, native and non-native alike. Commissioners might be assisted by federal marshals who policed vast areas of territory. Barrow's first commissioner was a schoolteacher and, not surprisingly, Charles Brower eventually fell heir to the job, which he held until his death in 1945. Brower doesn't comment on his commissioner's position in his autobiography, suggesting perhaps that it didn't consume much time, thought, or energy. Sadie recalls helping him with his commissioner's work in his last years, and she remembers well the fact that, as commissioner, her father conducted her marriage. The federal judicial presence was probably not all that significant in Barrow, because neither the funds nor the logistics were provided for jails, the setting up of trials, or the transporting of offenders to them (see Conn 1977). A commissioner remained the only judicial officer in the Barrow area until after statehood, when the present magistrate system was put into effect.

Far more important than the commissioner as a judicial authority from the

early twentieth century through the 1950s was the village council. Village councils were introduced to Alaskan native villages by schoolteachers and missionaries, and although they operated on an unclear legal basis, they came to be supported by the U.S. legal institutions that extended to bush communities, that is, by the commissioner and the federal marshals. Comprised of native men and women, the council was a dispute-settling body that acted by consensus; it heard complaints, lectured wrongdoers, and occasionally reinforced its decisions by invoking the authority of the church and the United States.[6] *Rather than taking punitive measures, council actions were directed towards "an admission of wrong and a promise to correct conduct in order to live more compatibly with other villagers" (Hippler and Conn 1975:33). The village councils were successful in their administration of justice because they avoided the confrontational posture of trials, allowed for group decisions in which no single individual had to take the responsibility, and found solutions for misbehavior which were models of correction and deterrence (see Hippler and Conn 1974, 1975).*

This all changed following statehood. The federal commissioners and marshals were replaced with state lay judges or magistrates who were appointed by the Alaska Court System and selected from the native community. The result, though a far cry from what it aspired to, was the imposition of procedures more closely resembling those of the Anglo-American legal system, undercutting the adjudicative role of the village councils. Hippler and Conn in the mid-1970s commented on the effects of the magistrate system:

> Eskimo magistrates and citizens alike disliked the idea of a single Eskimo authority sitting in judgement. They disliked and felt uncomfortable with the requirements of formal complaints, written accusations, and the like. They further disliked the often tedious delays between offense and resolution. . . . More and more complaints and action were left to the (nearly always white) state trooper, who would . . . use his greater knowledge of law and procedures to elicit a preferred judgement from the magistrate. . . . Pleas of guilty to any and all offenses charged by the trooper and automatic maximum sentences became the rule. In contrast, the magistrates, who wished still somehow to ameliorate the uncomfortable situation facing the community, would suspend imposition of sentence in 40–60 percent of all cases before them. Thus effectively the law was not interpreted and was not enforced. [1974:183]

Though Barrow faced all of these problems with the institution of the magistrate system, the law was enforced and interpreted in Barrow owing

almost single-handedly to the forceful personality of Sadie Neakok, who was determined to make the system work for her people.

In the four-tiered court system in Alaska, the district court, within which the magistrate and the district court judges operate, has the most restricted jurisdiction. Magistrates are limited in the kinds of cases they can hear and the amounts of money involved.[7] *District courts, for example, adjudicate misdemeanor cases, but handle felony cases through the preliminary hearing only; felony trials are held in superior courts before superior court judges. Nonetheless, because the magistrate is the only judicial officer in bush communities, the responsibilities and pressures of the job are substantial. In addition to issuing warrants for arrest, summons, and search warrants, conducting arraignments, preliminary hearings, trials, and sentencing, the magistrate is expected to perform coroner's duties and marriages, and to record vital statistics. Magistrates may also be appointed to hear certain kinds of cases for the superior court—usually cases involving divorce and children's proceedings.*

Today there are some sixty magistrates in the state of Alaska, most of them in bush communities like Barrow. Since Sadie's time on the bench, a special division of the Alaska Court System has been created to administer to magistrates. Magistrates are trained mostly on site today, by "training judges," though some of their preparation takes place in Anchorage or Fairbanks. They are also assisted by a field auditor, who gives on-site instruction in the bookkeeping required by the job. The new magistrate receives from Magistrate Services a Magistrate's Handbook *and a set of seven lessons which, in plain English, lead the novice through the Alaska legal system. Other essential reference material for the bush court includes the five-volume set of* Alaska Rules of Court Procedure and Administration, *the Alaska Administrative Code—a four-volume set of executive branch rules and regulations—and the eleven-volume set of* Alaska Statutes.

The amount of written legal material to absorb and apply in practice is staggering, and were the body of case law available to bush courts, it would be even more so.[8] *The job requires only a high school education, but the unwritten criteria include the ability to withstand the loneliness of being an airplane flight away from anyone else in a similar position, the strength to disentangle oneself from the loyalties of kinship and friendship in imposing sanctions, and the endurance to suffer being viewed as a judge twenty-four hours a day, three hundred and sixty-five days a year. Perhaps most important, those magistrates like Sadie who have made the system work bring to the job common sense, creativity, determination, and bicultural understanding.*

❖

When Alaska became a state, the state wanted the magistrate system in all the largest communities. So they went to city councils and important people of each community to select that person who they might think would make a good magistrate. They didn't need any law background because they were willing to train them for their position. Eddie Hopson was appointed magistrate at first, and for almost four months he held the title of magistrate, but he didn't know how to make it work. He didn't know about the law or the procedures. He couldn't figure out how to go in court and have an arraignment, and he never had one. So, when they started asking him for records and his proceedings, he had nothing to give them.

Because I had been a welfare worker and I had worked with the general public in this community for so long, he started coming over here sometime in March [1960], trying to convince me that I would do a better job than he had done in the position. The whole town knew that I was doing all the work for it, and since I had so much experience working with people's problems, he said I would fit in as magistrate. I said, "Well, let's hope a man will respond." And Eddie answered, "Well, I did respond and I couldn't make it work." Then the village council approached me and said, "You've been working with the commissioners here and there; you've been working with the general public; you have their trust in you; you know about the law from your father. We think you'd make a good magistrate." Well, gee, be a woman magistrate? I just didn't think a woman's place was in the courthouse, so I didn't think too much about it.[9] And I kind of refused it for a while, until the whole town was on top of my head to make me the magistrate. So, I finally gave in.

At the time I was very pregnant with George—very big because he was due in June and here it was April. "Well, what's required to become a magistrate?" I asked Eddie Hopson. He said, "If you are appointed, you will have to go to Nome or headquarters and learn to be one." He had gone there, but I guess he couldn't get head nor tails out of it. So I went, even though I was uneasy that close to having a baby. I didn't want to leave Barrow and be in the air somewhere in an old DC-3 having a baby.

I went down to Nome to a seminar, and this highfalutin lawyer who wrote the *Magistrate Handbook* to be used by all appointed magistrates in the state of Alaska got up and lectured us. The training seminar was two weeks, but it wasn't complete. They didn't teach me coroners' duties, or how to perform marriages, and lots of other things that were included in civil cases. We were just taught the criminal law and how to cope with it: how to talk to a person standing before you; and if a man standing before me did not know the English language, then my native language was [to be] used to explain to him; and a whole page of rights that we were to read to this defendant [to] make him understand before [we] went ahead and started. Does he want a lawyer? If he said no [I would ask], "Do you fully understand what your rights are?" If he said, "Yes, I just want to plead my case," then I would explain what the different pleas were that he could give. And when the defendant admitted to a charge, then he was given a chance to talk about the problem—if there were some important information he might give me to show leniency, or if he could make me understand why this happened. Then you gave your sentence.

We were also taught how the police are connected with our work, with complaints and so on, but I didn't have a policeman to work this northern area; it was too soon after statehood. The old [federal] marshals used to scout the North Slope area. They were here with the commissioner, but when the commissioners were relieved, they had to do away with the marshals; that's why I had no policeman in town. When I was appointed, I had Wainwright, Point Hope, Point Lay, Anaktuvuk, Barter Island, and the places in between; and then when Prudhoe opened, that was part of my district, too. So, it was really a full-time thing, and I saw why Eddie didn't want the job, but I was already in it and I had to do the best that I knew how.

New on the Job

When I first started in 1960, I didn't know one thing about the law. I had to read it, get myself versed on what the law was about. Later on, when I learned a little more, it wasn't as hard because I just

guarded myself trying not to make a mistake. But when I did do something in court that needed a decision, and I would call my superior in Nome, I didn't get very much help.

At first I had to answer to any complaint. If there was a fight I was in the middle of it, as big as I was, pregnant with this baby. You can picture me in action. But people started trusting me, and no one would touch me, even though I might egg them on. I walked right in the middle of situations—like a man beating up on his wife and just about killing her and abusing the children. The person causing all the problems would take one look at me and say, "I could never do that to you." No one laid a hand on me. There were always curious crowds around, so I would pick a man and deputize him right there to help me out on the spot. If they refused, they landed in jail. At first I didn't do that when people refused, [but] later, when I told the court system of my problems, they advised me to.

So I would arrive on the scene in answer to a call, and if whoever made the complaint was willing to sign it, I would write it out. But if they refused, then it got thrown out of court. We had to arraign within twenty-four hours. So half of the time in the early days, I was witness to a case, wrote out the complaint, then held the arraignment and the trial. If the person pled not guilty, then automatically the case went into trial. If it was a jury trial, I had to select the jury by myself.[10]

Well, what would you know, my first case for Barrow I had to call in for a state trooper because we didn't have any investigative police up here. There was a break-in at the Wien [Airlines] terminal where all this booze was coming in. Alcohol was the main thing that led them to break in. [That was the] first time stealing other people's property started occurring; and there was assault and battery where they would get a little too much to drink, get wild, and get into a fight, and someone would make a personal complaint. It wasn't easy, because so many of the complaints I would get were alcohol-involved—two people getting drunk and in a fight and coming into my court in a complaint. I used to get those, too, that flocked together and made a complaint, get them in front of me before I would hear the case, and try to talk to them. Counsel them that they had to live in this town; are they going to be mad at each other forever? And then when they made up, I tore up the complaint and threw it away—it never came to my court.

I didn't think cases like that should go to court, because there were so few people in Barrow, and being mad at each other wouldn't help. So I solved many problems by talking to the people. I think I did more preaching in that courthouse than I did anywhere else, trying to keep peace in this town. So, if people forgave each other, then I threw the case out. Or if somebody charged somebody for stealing their stuff: "Well, did you try to talk him into bringing it back?" If he said, "No, I didn't," then I would call the person that was charged with stealing something: "How come you have so-and-so's possession," whatever it was. "Oh, I just never thought to take it back. I'm always doing something else, and by the time I'm ready to take it, I forget and just leave it there. It's still in my house." And I would call that person that made the complaint: "Because you didn't go and ask him, and just got mad at him for holding onto your stuff—the man is not angry at you at all." And these types were excused out of my court. So many of them like that.

When people learned that they could make complaints, some were made while a person was drunk. And when they sobered up, they automatically came over when I called them: "So you still want this complaint to go on before court? Are you still mad at so-and-so?" "Oh no. Please tear it up." Or, "I don't want any charges against my friend." And they were not heard. But other matters, like if someone—a woman—was really hurt, we had no shelter for women whose husbands got violent. The women didn't want to make complaints against their husbands, but if it was a repeated type of offense and the woman got tired of it, then she was placed in my home along with her kids. And the man automatically went to jail or paid a fine when the city adopted the ordinances for disorderly conduct, or for possessing and transporting liquor.

During my second year the city council trained two young men out of this community, sent them down to Sitka for six months, and then when they came back, they were my city policemen. We didn't have a state trooper up here, but if there was enough trouble that required a state trooper's investigation, then I had to call Fairbanks and have them send one up. The city police were a problem because they didn't want to involve themselves; they were members of the community. It was hard for them because they knew everybody. Sometimes they could have the courage to bring one of their relatives in. I remember one young officer had to

handcuff his father and bring him in. They were pointed at; they were threatened. But I soon got to the community; I had meetings to explain all this, that if these policemen are threatened, then anyone who threatened them can go to jail. We were never very successful in keeping a local person as a policeman in town even though they would be trained. They were better off working in another community.[11]

For a time, I had to educate this whole community, make them understand the basic meaning of the law. So we had town meetings, and then I brought my problems over to the council members, too, about what kind of time I was having. I knew I could go before the city council and have them listen to what types of problems I was having and that, since they're the councilmen of our community, they should help resolve some of it, take it upon themselves to talk about it and help me. For a while, too, we had an IRA [Indian Reorganization Act government] within our community, and their council would be the recommending body. . . .[12] My main part in trying to educate this town was to make them aware that these laws did exist, and so it wasn't easy in the courthouse—my five-, ten-minute arraignments would turn into half hours or more trying to explain their rights. So the first three years I didn't know whether I was coming or going, because it was so hard, and I was trying to do so much to make it work. When I finally got the respect of this whole town, then my problems were resolved.

Problems

> She was terribly busy and used by the court system. The court system uses all their judges, and especially the magistrates, unfortunately. They don't pay what they should, they expect miracles, and they don't give them the recognition that they deserve. [Stephen Cline, March 7, 1986]

There was no jail here in Barrow. We had to select a vacant house or an area where we could hold prisoners; sometimes one of the school principals allowed me to use one of the enclosed kitchen areas to keep a prisoner in there with a guard. Later on, we got just a two-cell jail, but it was more the type where we would put in

drunks to sober up. I would deputize a guard to watch over the prisoners, to leave the hands of the policemen free to do his scouting during the days and nights. For a while there I was cleaning the jail cells myself. Some prisoners chose to stay in jail instead of going out and doing the work program for the community. You know how drunks, when they get thrown in, will pee all over their clothes and on the wooden floors. No matter how much disinfectant you put in there, that odor still permeated. And using ammonia sometimes made it worse, because you can't keep your eyes open without letting them smart. I even talked to Max Brewer [head of Arctic Research Laboratory] to get these mattresses that I could put in the jail. So it was that I took it upon myself to clean the jail, because we had so many complaints from there, and no matter how hard we tried to sanitize it, it was never very sanitary; that odor just clung. And then, too, we tried it with paint, which helped. Then they made additional cells for women, and then later on, one was built for children, away from that area, the holding facility for minors.

Stephen Cline, a Fairbanks attorney who traveled to Barrow as a public defender in the early 1970s, recalls visiting clients in the jail. The jail was off the courtroom area in the fire hall and was guarded by a very old man who was hard of hearing and nearly blind:

> When court wasn't in session, the jail wasn't warm. The cells were constructed out of corrugated landing-strip material, with locking doors. The commode was down the way. It was dark back there; the whole thing was lit by a sixty-watt bulb hanging down. If you went in to see your client, you could either yell through the bars or try to get this old guy to let you in. It was always cold if you went in the wintertime, and if the prisoners wanted out to go to the commode, they had to try to get this old man's attention by yelling until he could hear them. I remember one time I went in to see my client in there, and he was lying on the floor; they didn't have any place to sleep. He had his coat, and it was quite a choice, because he could either take his coat off and lie on it or he could wear it. I asked him what he had for breakfast. He said. "I didn't get breakfast." I said, "What did you have for lunch?" He said, "Hamburger." I said, "What did you have for dinner?" He said, "Hamburger." [March 7, 1986]

My kitchen was my first courthouse. I made sure no one was here

except my small kids, and I would hold court right over my table.[13] If my little kids needed me, then I would have to excuse myself, tend to them, and come back. Give them something to keep them quiet while I was having an arraignment. There would be a state trooper in here, or an arresting officer, sitting on this side of the prisoner and me on the other side. And my files were over by the kitchen door. People had to leave, or sit in the other room and not make any disturbance. They were my audience. I would have loved to have had a public place where people could come in and anyone curious enough could listen. Early on I talked to the principal of the school to get permission to use one of the schoolrooms as my courthouse for some of my jury cases, which I couldn't hold in my house, but it still didn't work. It was such an inconvenience, because I had to wait until after 5:00 P.M. to get in there, and then if I had more than three or four cases, it went until about 8:00 P.M.

Sadie worked in a succession of "courthouses," beginning with her kitchen. From there she was given a room in the community center which also housed the fire equipment, police station, and the jail facilities described above by attorney Stephen Cline. This setting proved difficult because of the juxtaposition of courthouse and police facilities—"I was seeing my cases come in," Sadie remarked—and because the quarters were too cramped to run jury trials properly. During recesses the jury, witnesses, defendant, judge, and clerk all crowded cheek by jowl into one small area to drink coffee and smoke. An exceptionally noisy heater that obliterated the court recordings had to be turned off during trials; when the temperature fell to an uncomfortable level, court was recessed to reheat the courtroom. To make matters worse, the honeybucket nearly overflowed whenever jury selection or trials took place.

A negative evaluation of the facility of the state resulted in removal of the court to the more spacious quarters of a former game parlor. This building served as Barrow's court for some six years. But as the number of jury trials increased and the size of the jury pool grew, this courthouse, too, became obsolete. "When we summoned some twenty jurors to come in to select out of, they couldn't all go inside the building. Some had to be outside and stand by a loudspeaker where they could hear my voice during jury selections," surely an uncomfortable proposition during most of the year. In 1978, court moved to the still larger remodeled quarters of Shontz's General Store. (The store's sign remained above the door for a long time afterwards, drawing surprised tourists

during the summer months.) In August 1985 the Alaska Court System finally moved into a facility designed and built specifically as a courthouse.

I used my kitchen for about four or five years, until the files started taking too much of my kitchen room. Then the city allowed me to move into their community center and made a small courtroom. But what I didn't like was the heater above my head. Used to rattle so bad I couldn't even hear the people talk in front of me, and on days when it was cold, we had to recess to put that heat on until I was ready to resume again. But it was a working courthouse for quite a while. When I moved to the courthouse over across from the school [the former game parlor], one of the teachers asked if they could bring some students in from the school to observe. I said, "Sure. Let them see what I go through." At arraignments I used to put a robe on and walk in the court, and then the policeman would bring in the prisoner, and the children would be sitting back there in the audience watching me with their small eyes. And they were taken back to school and asked questions. It would scare some of them. But, it never failed, when I walked out to the street, the kids all said, "Hi, Sadie." They all knew me, and people would greet me, and I would loiter, stop long enough to talk to people if I went to the store, take my time. If I went to the store now, I probably would never come out, so many people there.

The hours that I worked were not to be over seven and one-half hours a day, but sometimes it went over, because I had to do the written dockets and we had no recorder. I had to take notes on what went on and, if we had lawyers, write down what the lawyers would say. Usually there was plea bargaining between the lawyers, and if it was agreed upon, then that was it. And the defendant was involved in the plea bargaining deal, and then the sentence would be explained to him; and if they accepted it, then that's how it went. That was spelled out for you, but they don't do that anymore. Plea bargaining is not allowed anymore except in civil cases, where both parties can agree on settlements. And I had to write the disposition and what type of reprimanding. I had no clerk to help me in those days. I had to do all the recording and docketing by hand. The dockets we used were handwritten, and I would write out the whole case, what happened, because we had no recorder. If I had four or five cases,

I stayed on after working hours at the courthouse until 9 or 10 o'clock, writing these cases up, and then finally came home and just flopped into bed. And I stood it, not knowing any better, and because the state refused a clerk for me.

And so, after almost a whole year of working late, I couldn't take it anymore. It was in '68. We had a death out at the base. There was a state trooper in town, and I was called in on the case, and I tried to get the state trooper to go out there and investigate it. I had to be on the scene because he didn't respond. And all that was Sunday morning, of all days to have something happen like that. And it was a heart attack victim, but I had no help. I had no way of removing that body out of that base until I could get somebody's attention to help me. I called the doctor, and he said he would try to help me, but we would have to get the body over to the morgue [the hospital]. And so the next best thing was to contact Max Brewer or John Schindler, who headed that area program at the base. Well, that was a relief. Anytime I needed help with vehicles and stuff, they said, "Just let us know." Because they were working for the state, too, and they would authorize it. So I would let them know whenever I needed transportation, because the airport was up there and we didn't have any [state vehicles] here in town.

That was some problem. I stood through all that until I just couldn't take anymore. I don't know why I never went nuts with it. But I think there was some help from above that kept me sane. And then finally I said, "I am not going to go back to that courthouse if I am not going to get any kind of assistance up here in this court." Well, the information reached to the administrator of court, and they disregarded it, saying, well, for a court that size we didn't need a clerk. "Well," I said, "you may not need one, but I do."

No one seemed to hear me. Justice [George F.] Boney was our chief justice then, and I told him that I had too much of a backlog of cases, and I wasn't going to the magistrate's seminar that year [1972]. Magistrates from all over Alaska were meeting at Eielson Air Force Base in Fairbanks. I just couldn't keep up [with the work]. And with all incoming other work, like recording, which needed to go out every month, and vital statistics, adoptions, marriages, small claims courts—I was just such a mess. And when I refused to go, they wanted to know the reason why. I said, "If no one is going to

wake up to the fact that I have many requests for this Barrow area, I don't think I want to keep going on. I just want to quit. The pay isn't enough for all this trouble that I am going through, and I need a clerk. My caseload is getting heavy, and even though I am sending in all of my cases, the calendaring, and how many cases I am hearing, no one is responding to it." So I called in and I said, "I am not coming." And Justice Boney called me and said, "We need you here, Sadie." He even tried to tell me that Nora Guinn [native magistrate from Bethel] was there, and I said, "I don't care who's there. I am not coming, unless you call the Judicial Council[14] and explain my problem and let them decide whether I get higher pay and a clerk and this equipment in my courthouse that will cut my caseload down, my work." And I left it at that.

Finally, Chief Justice Boney, without any help from his secretary, got on the phone. "Sadie, you've got to come. The Judicial Council wants to hear your case. You have to appear before the Judicial Council to decide whether we will give you a clerk or raise your salary; so you'd better come."[15] So I got on the next plane, but there was a trooper taking out a prisoner at the time, so we both left on the same plane, and we all ended up at this state trooper's office in Fairbanks at the same time. And I wanted to play a joke on the whole group that were there at the seminar. They were all at the police station getting their new ID's when I walked in. I had this trooper walk behind me. Nora ran and hugged me, and said, "I am glad you're here; you got us worried there." Judge [Hugh H.] Connelly was there, and I said, "Well, I finally had to be arrested and be brought in." They all looked; you could hear a pin drop. After, I presented my case to the Judicial Council, and it didn't take them twenty minutes to decide. They came back in, and I was all smiles because I knew it was something good. So they raised my pay and allowed me to have a clerk. They also said that the copy machines and the court recorders would be there in my courthouse.[16]

When the recorders came into our court, things were much easier for me. And when I first started complaining, then other magistrates all joined me to improve the situation. Magistrates who lived in Anchorage were using recorders, so they sent us portable recorders that used little tapes. And then finally we got the regular court recorders. When you're talking in court, there are recorders

going with numbered tapes. And you can just sit there and, for a certain case, look at the number, and just say the important highlights of the case—a docket. You just write the number of the case—what you said, or what the D.A. said. And then anyone wants to know about a certain case, all you had to do was turn the recorder back and just go to that number and just listen to what they said. The whole thing was recorded. I still didn't have a clerk then, though. I would start the tape with that number, and then when I was through, I would look at the number and put: "Court adjourned for this case." But in the meantime, if I wanted to log the whole thing, I would have to listen to that tape again that I did all day, and make out these logs with earphones, and listen and keep watching the numbers, and that was a lot of work.

I was given a part-time, fifteen-hour-a-week clerk, and I used up a whole week's time in two days. I was in the courthouse all day, and when the troopers would bring in a defendant from outlying areas, I was in the courthouse when it was midnight, or four o'clock in the morning, because we had to have arraignment within twenty-four hours of the arrest. When I finally did get permission to hire a clerk, they wanted me to hire an older person, someone with a mature mind that I could work with. My first clerk was killed in a three-wheeler accident about her second year, after I'd trained her fully, and then a trooper's wife, Jean Rowe, was the only one available; so I had her. There was so much conflict between his arrests and her being the clerk, that sometimes I almost disqualified myself from hearing a case, because she would know it all. But we took precautions, and she promised that he wouldn't talk about these cases to her when they were brought in. It was all right, because she would know all about the case after arraignment; so we got along here for two or three years, and then they decided to move out. Then [1974] I got Charlotte Brower.[17] She was an ace. You couldn't get anyone better. She had been an accountant and a clerk in one of the main offices [in Barrow], and she had secretarial training. By then, we had our recorder and copy machines, which made it really easier.

I traveled a lot after I became a magistrate, because Nome was our district headquarters, and any prisoner that needed to be escorted out, I had to be the escort. And I was in and out. Finally I got so

tired of that, because it took a week to get from here to take the prisoners down; and so, after about four years [c. 1964] I started complaining: "Why can't Fairbanks take care of some of our load?" And then they said, "Well, they have their own load." But then we went to the legislature, and I went before them and talked the situation over to see if it could be worked out to where we didn't have to go by way of Fairbanks and Kotzebue to get to Nome. There was no straight flight from Barrow to Nome. You had to stay overnight sometimes in Kotzebue, and then to Nome, where you would have to stay another night, take care of your matters, and talk to whoever authority was there, [and] then come back the same way. My job was being in the air half the time. And when I got back, there would be a backload of cases waiting for me. In the early days I transported all the prisoners to Nome; then when we got state troopers they took over the job.

When I needed assistance with a decision and I would call my superiors, I didn't get very much help. They would say, "Well, you have been appointed because you have a good head. Use your common sense to solve the cases up there the best you know how." So that was the only advice I would get. As I went on, then I understood a little more each year. But there were also changes to where we couldn't use Anchorage's system, because it was so different up here. The main thing that bothered me was when somebody got arrested, and I just never knew when to calendar the case to come up. We didn't have any system whatsoever. Whenever anyone was put on bail, and they couldn't post bail, they had to go all the way down to Nome, our Second [Judicial] District headquarters, and be jailed there until such time somebody wakes up to the fact that they were there.

We had no calendaring system up here to set up trials. We never knew when the superior court judge might be in to help us set up these trials, because the lawyers came only when the judge came, and having no lawyer, you couldn't proceed. Some would stay in jail five or six months awaiting trial for a minor violation.[18] Sometimes they served more than the maximum sentence for the violation. I was disturbed with that, and I started presenting it to whoever would listen to me. And then when Nora and I were called into the Judicial Council, the body which made changes in the law, I talked freely

about the problem. It wasn't long, possibly two months, before the chief justice and a team of people came up to have a conference with me. I wanted to send people pending trials to Fairbanks instead of Nome, because it was closer and less expensive for the state. But Fairbanks had opposed me sending my prisoners over there for some reason. They said they were too crowded to have Barrow traffic, and that we should still use the Second District headquarters in Nome for this northern area. I also felt that it would be better to use Fairbanks, because some of the superior court judges assigned here would come from Fairbanks.

When Judge [William H.] Sanders, who was the superior court judge in Nome, could not make it up here because it was too inconvenient for him to take maybe a week or more to come up here and handle the cases, I talked it over with the chief justice. There were four district attorneys, four public defenders, four superior court judges and two supreme court judges that came up to decide this matter for me, to hear me present the situation. I was very happy and very proud that they responded to my problem, because I felt it was serious enough for somebody to wake up to the fact that I needed somebody's direction.

Finally, the supreme court made it a ruling. The chief justice[19] appointed Jerry Van Hoomissen from Fairbanks to be at my beck and call whenever I had a case, which wasn't very popular with Judge Van Hoomissen. But he accepted it, and I was talked about quite a bit because of it, but I couldn't see how else we could handle some of our cases. So the system got a little better and started to work to where we were able to calendar cases. If I calendared a case, or sent the pending case file to the presiding judge, the superior court judge, he would get hold of a district attorney who might be coming up and a public defender to represent the people that can't afford lawyers.

Once a month the plane from Fairbanks would transport to Barrow the necessary outside personnel for the proper operation of the legal system in bush Alaska. On board might be some or all of the following personnel: the superior court judge; his law clerk; the prosecuting attorney; the attorney representing the attorney general's office who represented the state in children's proceedings; an attorney or two from Alaska Legal Services who represented parents in

children's hearings and indigent clients in civil cases; the public defender, who represented criminal defendants; and the social worker for the North Slope who was based in Fairbanks. They didn't really know the community, they didn't know who their clients were or what they were like. After they were met at the airport by the police, who transported them in the paddy wagon to the courthouse, they depended upon Sadie to orient them to the local community, to provide information, and to give them credibility in a community where they were perceived as part of a bad system.

❖

In 1978 after Charlotte had taken over as magistrate, I went back into the courthouse to help out when she was having health problems. And I had to straighten all the files, because they had recently moved in to that courthouse [a remodeled store] and all the files were in a heap. They weren't even sorted out; no one had checked the pending files and the disposed of files, or the records being sent. I walked into that [office] and there was no copy machine working, and when I made my complaint that I needed a new copy machine or to have this one serviced, the new administrator from Fairbanks said, "I don't want to hear anymore complaints from Barrow. That place costs too much for the state to pay and to have all the equipment."

Well, that was some answer, so I went over his head and called Anchorage, to the magistrates' supervisor, and I reported what had happened. I started beefing about a clerk. "Send me an ace clerk to come up here and help me." They sent Marjorie Lori, who was the head clerk out at the court system. And Ed Crutchfield, who was a magistrate [from Fairbanks], also came up to help me straighten out the mess. There were backlogs of dispositions, some two hundred cases that had to go out. "How are we going to do this?" And I said, "Ed, I know the people in town. If we can't find it on the record, I will go directly to the person." And he looked at me and said, "Oh my God, you mean to tell me you would go and ask these people that have been out of court for a year or two what the disposition was on their cases?" "Sure. That's the only way we are going to get it." And in two-weeks' time we did it. And Marjorie put all the case files together, numbered them, and put them in the new cabinets.

Then there was a gas leak in the courthouse which made us all

sick. I reported that to the administrative office. They had a lawyer, and he wouldn't hear of it. "Do you know how much it costs to run that courthouse up there!" "Well, then maybe you better close it down, if that is all the concern you have!" So when I hung up, I went right over his head. I called the Department of Labor in Anchorage. I found out that they did all the testing for this type of complaint, so I directly made my complaint to them. So they came, but not for a couple of months. I was still working [for Charlotte] and I remember I had this little trainee, Sarah, doing some of the work to get credits for school. She got the worst end, because she did her work at that area where the leak was the worst, and she landed in the hospital. My skin was beginning to peel off, and I didn't know what was causing it, and then the doctor said it was that irritation from the gas leak.

When we finally did get the man to come in and check it out, one of the superior court judges had come in to try a case, and we had to open the doors every fifteen minutes to air out the courtroom. During the trial I peeked in there, and I could see the jurors just about falling off to sleep and the judge getting listless. So I went in through the judge's door and told the clerk that I think we should recess and air the courthouse. And about that time, after we had had the doors open, this investigator comes in, and says, "I don't see any immediate danger in here." He wasn't even going to bring in his instruments to measure how bad the gas leak was. I persuaded him to let me break one of those test tubes that turn brown if there is gas noticeable in the room. I broke one, and he couldn't believe it; it turned brown immediately. And so he let me do another one, and the same thing happened again. Meantime, there's court going on, and we closed all the doors in that area, which we usually keep open, and he brought his instruments in and found that over 90 percent of the air, if we left the area closed for any length of time, measured over the allowable amount of gas, and he started immediately to close the courthouse down. And I called that lawyer [in the administrative office] and said, "We are out of a courthouse." He said, "What happened?" "I told you about the gas leakage in there. So I went over your head and called the Department of Labor. They came up to check the building, and they closed it down. So there!" He had to come up then.

Our next problem was: "Where are we going to arraign any cases

that we might have?" So we had to rent the front room of *Stuaqpak*.[20] There was one area that we could use to arraign in. It was all right from 9:00 A.M. until 3:00, but after school was out, you couldn't hear anything when the traffic started coming in, with kids whooping and hollering and everything—that recorder picked it all up. If we had to hold a trial during that period, then the next best place was the bingo hall. But if trials lingered on beyond 7:00 P.M., then it was a mess. [Bingo took precedence over the trials.] So we had to make another arrangement. For thirty days the courthouse was closed. Took that long to fix it up and get it checked out before we moved back in.

But there were other problems when we moved into that building. The tourist season had started, and we still had that Shontz's General Store sign. So tourists kept wandering in—"Is this the store?" One of them slammed the door, and what should happen, the ceiling in that front reception hall caved in on us! That was the second disaster with the ceiling. Before that, Judge [Warren William] Taylor from Fairbanks had come up to hear a case and, at recess time, he went back into the area that had been made into judge's chambers to lie down on the couch, and the ceiling caved in on him. Fell right on him! He came into the courtroom all speckled with plaster dust. Finally they got it to where we didn't have anymore uncalled-for accidents in there.

❖

In 1965–67 the case loads started escalating, because of so much drinking and people moving up here from other areas, looking for work. The town doubled, tripled. We didn't even have enough housing for people. I was forever looking for homes for these people that got caught with no homes, and the families that had them got tired of having them in their homes. We had people coming in from Outside, too, that had never been to school—and dropouts—what the trooper called "white trash." They were uneducated people who bucked the law, making it hard for me, because when they were brought into my court, some of them would look down on me—"What can that little Eskimo judge do?" But there would be some that would be civil, and they listened to me when I arraigned them.

Any problem that arose came to me, whether great or small; and

then, if there were children who were abused or unwanted, they landed in my home. I wasn't a licensed foster-home owner but, because of my work, there was nowhere else for them to go. The relatives didn't want to get involved because they didn't want to get in a fight with a friend or a relative for keeping that child, because the parents sometimes wanted these children. With repeated abuse, we had to take custody of that child and place it somewhere else until court trials were over. And then probation officers would be brought in. Homes would be checked for placement, but no one came forth to be foster-home parents until a couple of teachers responded, "Why don't we try?" And after that it started to work, but I had to be continually on top of them to keep the parents away before the case was settled. If I didn't have Nate for a husband, I don't think it would have worked, because he loved the kids just as much as I did.

My job disrupted my home life a lot. I would take my feelings home, and Nate would be so understanding. I confided in him, saying, "This is confidential. But if I get it out of my mind and you carry part of it, maybe I won't feel so bad." By 1965 my two workloads conflicted very badly. If, as magistrate, I had to send a man out for getting in trouble, I had to deal with his wife and kids as a social worker. In order for them to be eligible for welfare, I had to sentence him to a minimum of ninety days. Then, mad as the family was at me for sending their father out to a jail, I had to make out their application for welfare. That caused so much conflict that I no longer felt I should hold both jobs. They couldn't doubt my word, because I was the magistrate. If a man was sentenced, all I could do was just get the judgment out and say, "Here's proof," then get the ages of the children so they could get some type of support. But some of them would turn around when they came back from jail and thank me for putting them through that. It would awake them to the fact that I meant business.

Interesting and Difficult Cases

After I had city policemen, there were times when a policeman would be so proud of the arrests that he made that he would

celebrate his night. On one such occasion two young people had broken into the Wien [Airlines] terminal, where orders of liquor were kept, and they felt their way through in there. Through the packing lists and a carton that was found, we could trace who might be drinking certain brands, because it was stolen out of that terminal, that freight office. I had one policeman then, a native boy who had never been trained. I picked up the receipts from those boxes and left the boxes there and called the city policeman. "Anyone who went through that, I don't think they had time to drink all that liquor. So here is the list, and if you find anyone drunk, make sure what type of bottle they are drinking from, and bring them in as a test. I will type out the complaint, and you will sign it." So he made two arrests, brought them to me, and we had an arraignment. Bail was set somewhere around $500, and we ended up holding them in lieu of bail. This was a felony-type complaint, where I could hold only the preliminary hearing on it.

Well, that night the arresting officer was so proud of himself, having made this arrest, that he got a hold of his girl friend and started drinking that night. We had a guard to watch over the prisoners, who were in that two-cell jail we had here just above the school. And, lo and behold, at four in the morning, I get a knock on my door from this guard, and he is telling me that he has got my policeman and his girl friend over there. He had released the two who were already in the cell and [had] put my policeman and his girl friend in one cell. This I had to see; so I got dressed and I went over there. One of the boys who we'd previously put in had a guitar (they let him have his guitar), and he was sitting and strumming the guitar and singing away. The other one is there, too, instead of trying to run away. With no one tending to them, these two were sitting there in the jail. I checked the noise coming from the back room, and there was my policeman and his girl friend in one cell. The guard didn't know what else to do.

What had happened, I made a mistake in showing the policeman the combination of that safe where we kept the evidence. The policeman got into the evidence after he'd had a few drinks and wanted more, and [he] had taken the liquor out of there and was drinking it. This I couldn't believe. And he admitted to it. I had borrowed a jeep from the base to transport the prisoners to the

airport, and when I asked the guard where the jeep was, he said, "We don't know. The city policeman had it last night and he was in no shape to tell me."

Well, the first thing I had to do was to release them, so I went back home and I got Nate out of bed. "You're going to have to help me find that jeep. First, take the policeman home, and I will take the girl friend home." The jeep was stuck in the mud between here and the base. Nate brought it back in. I washed it, because somebody broke a whole bottle of whiskey inside that thing and it scared me. "What is Max Brewer going to say to me when I return this vehicle?" Then we went back to the jail area, and I talked to the guard there. Well, he said he didn't know what to do when he caught the policeman getting into the evidence box and starting to drink right there. He had to do something; so he locked him in the cell along with his girl friend.

That was about the oddest case that ever happened. I had already sent word that I had two prisoners who needed to be shipped out, but I didn't know what to do with the situation with the policeman. Who's going to make the complaint? So I sent for a state trooper to come in and do the investigating of this whole thing. Well, when the plane was coming on I had to transport those two prisoners out to the airport, and since I had no driver that morning, I deputized Nate to drive the jeep and take these prisoners over there, and I had to accompany them. When the plane came in, Trooper Monacle, I remember him, he was smiling at me when I told him the story. I told him that I didn't know what to do with this whole situation, because my policeman was involved in it. He went ahead and took the prisoners all the way to Nome, then came back and did the investigation, but nothing ever came of this. We had a meeting, and it ended up that that city policeman was fired.

Then another time, we had a bail jumper and failure to appear in court. And this was happening around July fourth. It was warm, but quite cold if you didn't have heat in the house. So there was a warrant out for pick up on this one person, and the police arrested him on this warrant and called me up on it. I said, "Well, I guess we are going to have him overnight. Tomorrow I will arraign him

Facing page: Sadie Brower Neakok, 1986. Photograph by Edwin S. Hall, Jr.

The North Slope Borough Field School, 1984. Bottom, left to right: Kate Mary Solomon, Josephine Nashaknik, Andy Conception, Sheila Leavitt. Second row: Cliff Anderson, Patty Coumbe, Laura Pederson, Sylvia Leavitt, Florence Long. Third row: Ian Trent, Matt Davis, Ray Atos. Top row: Edwin S. Hall, Jr., Margaret Blackman, Craig Gerlach. Photograph by John Trent.

Fred Hopson and Charles Brower, Point Barrow, 1917. Courtesy of the California Academy of Sciences, Liebes Collection.

Asianggataq, c. 1940.

Charles Brower and family, 1921. Clockwise, from left: Brower, Jenny, David, Asiang-gataq with Kate in parka, Sadie, Maria, Robert. Photograph by Alfred M. Bailey. Courtesy of the Denver Museum of Natural History.

Dinner at the station, 1921. Clockwise, from left: David Brower, A. M. Bailey, Russell Hendee (?) (photographer accompanying Bailey), Mr. Nichol (schoolteacher), Henry Greist (physician and minister), Charles Brower, Fred Hopson (standing), unidentifiable person, Mrs. Dakin (nurse), Harry Bloomfield (Brower's clerk), Mrs. Nichol (schoolteacher), Jim Allen (whaler and trader from Wainwright), Mollie Greist (nurse). Courtesy of the Denver Museum of Natural History.

Sadie, Robert, and Maria Brower, 1923. Courtesy of the California Academy of Sciences, Liebes Collection.

Panorama of Eklutna Industrial School. Courtesy of the Federal Archives, Seattle.

Dorm
Gymnasium
ware house
Boys Dorm
School Rooms

Sadie and Nate, c. 1960.

Sadie being congratulated for her honorary doctorate by her granddaughter, Aqpauraq Miller, May 1987. Photograph by Bill Hess.

Left: The Neakok family in their living room, 1971. Front row, left to right: Darryl (grandson), Cheryl (granddaughter), George. Second row: James, Dora, Robert (in Sadie's lap), Sadie, Nate. Third row: Pat and Glenn.

Sadie's house (far left) and Alaska Court System Building in background, 1987.

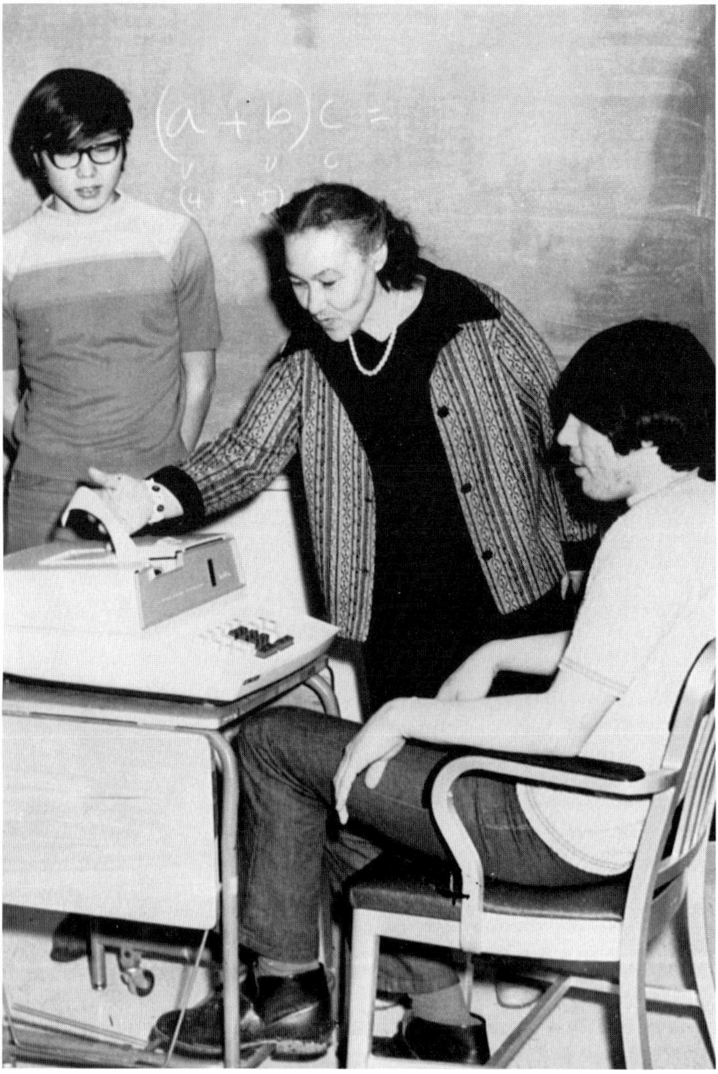

Sadie at Chemawa school, Oregon, 1971.

Left: Sadie and state trooper Parker in her kitchen courthouse, 1960s.

Sadie at Kaktovik, 1975. Photograph by Stephen Cline.

Dedication of the Alaska Court System Building, Barrow, August 1985. Left to right: Magistrate Gates, Judge Turny, Superior Court Judge Michael Jeffery, Chief Justice Jay Rabinowitz, Sadie, Charlotte Brower (former Barrow magistrate), Jennie Cross (former Barrow magistrate), Art Snowden, Administrator of All Courts. Photograph by Dave Libbey.

Left: Sadie speaking at the 1986 North Slope Borough Elders' Conference. Photograph by Bill Hess.

Sadie during an interview in her kitchen, 1986. Photograph by Edwin S. Hall, Jr.

before the twenty-four hours is up." And, as usual, I accompanied the policeman over to the jail area, and they put the prisoner in. He was sober, but picked up on a warrant, you know, and he was advised of his rights at the time of the arrest.

We had a little oil stove in the jail; sometimes it worked and sometimes it didn't. I had checked the stove earlier, and it was working okay. So I go in the jail area and I know something is wrong, but I couldn't figure what was wrong when I was trying to light the oil stove. Well, anyway, the carburetor wouldn't work. So I took it apart, cleaned it all out, got the water out, put it back together—I had learned to do that living up here. So I lit it. Then, whatever was wrong finally came out. The room started to fill with smoke. Some pranksters had pulled that flue out of that stove. Lord only knows where they put it, but they played this prank on us by climbing on top of this little jail and pulling the whole flue out.

And so I come home and I am looking for a flue, because usually when we went out camping with a tent, we had a set of, say, like three or four stove pipes that we could put together and use for our camp stove. I found what I was looking for, went back and put them up [and] solved our problem. But in the meantime, the prisoner is offering his help. "Sadie, if you let me out, I'll help you with that stove." But I didn't dare let him out. So I went ahead with the help of the policeman and solved that one.

Another time, after freeze-up, there was a gun call. An old man was being threatened by his son-in-law with a gun. And I was big—I was pregnant and could hardly walk. It was my last month. It was in October [1963]. So I responded to that and, knowing the people, I could get away with solving the problem before it materialized. That morning we didn't have any police, so I went over there and I responded first to the house where the old man was being threatened, and then when he said his son-in-law went home with a loaded gun, I went over and knocked on his door. And he admitted right there during my investigation that he had pulled this gun on his father-in-law, because he was disturbing the family somehow. The younger man and his wife had been in a fight and the kids were there [at his father-in-law's], due to drinking. And now that he was

sober, he wasn't about to follow through what he had threatened this old man with.

Well, anyway, I had enough evidence there to book him. So when he walked out, I said, "Well you might as well let me have those guns, because I don't think you should have them in your possession if you are going to threaten people with them." And even though he tried to tell me that he would never do it again, I didn't trust him, because he was one of those people that flared up every so often and got in fights—a hot-headed type. So he reluctantly finally produced those guns, and I took them in my custody. The ammunition was still in them, by the way.

I started walking towards the jail carrying the loaded guns, and it's slippery. Picture me trying to walk and my prisoner hanging on to my arm, walking with me to the jail area. He was talking to me all this time, "Sadie, you shouldn't be out alone. You are so big, you are going to drop that baby." So I let him help me where walking was hard. We had our arraignment, and nothing really serious came of it, but he was warned about threatening this old man. We didn't have any phones in those times, so I had to respond to it by somebody's word who was very scared. I look back and see that prisoner hanging on to my arm, helping me to get to the jail area, helping me to walk. But people respected me so much that whenever any problem arose, I knew practically everybody in town, and they knew who I was. So when I appeared on the scene, they knew what I was there for. After I got my policeman, then I got away from it.

❖

The most difficult case that reached me was a suicide case. They found the girl overdosed on some INH [Isoniazid] pills—TB medication—along with some other medication. She left a note, but it was too late when they found it. She had already gotten unconscious, and no matter what the doctors did, we just lost her. We never did find out what her motive was. She had lost both parents that winter, so probably depression over losing both of them. She was quite young, about sixteen or seventeen. We hadn't had any cases of that type, where people were beginning to take their own lives, or threaten and shoot somebody, or stab somebody to death with a knife.

And the other was a murder. And I remember that boy [murderer] being drunk and coming over to my house that morning. He was a young man I knew real well, and he knew we were quite close friends with his parents. They were gone somewhere out on a camping trip and left the young people alone in the house. And they had been drinking in that house, and somewhere else too, but when the report came to me, one of the brothers, when he woke up, he heard someone come in and go upstairs. There was a little scuffle (which he never heard) where this girl was staying, and when he came downstairs, there was a pool of blood over the body of his young brother; he had been stabbed to death. The investigators found the suspect; they picked him up. The girl that was there in the house where this boy was stabbed to death told who all had been in the house, and through her story they figured out who had done it. It was jealousy over this girl that caused it, we later found out. I had to arraign the young man and set bail. I was constantly on the phone. We had phones by then, and I was getting directions from the district attorney's office—asked what to do—and then he was taken out until such time a preliminary examination could be scheduled to be heard. But that was the first murder we had here, about 1966 or 1967.

❖

The coroner cases were my hardest ones, they hit me worse than my criminal cases did. About the last two years I was magistrate, we were being ordered to take blood samples off of dead bodies. We had heart attack victims, and unknown cause deaths where we had to send bodies out to be examined and let the examiners determine what the cause of death was. Then we had several overdose cases that were alcohol-related. Mainly the check for blood was to see if we could draw alcohol contents in the bloodstream of the person. It took me just two tries to find out that I wasn't made for doing that. It was too much. Well, if you've never had any experience in dealing with bodies, even to just poke them and try to get the blood out, that's something.

As coroner you see bodies in the worst conditions. And the worst one I ever had was a plane crash with five state workers and one Army officer. Bobby Fisher's plane crashed taking off. Oh, my Lord.

There was one survivor; the plane was upside down and he was breathing when the skidoos responded to the scene, and I was already at the hospital where they were bringing the bodies in. We couldn't identify them. All I could do was number them—the first body brought in number one, number two, number . . . until we got six of them. The hospital assigned this one area where we could do the work, take each body and take the belongings out and try to identify them so we could notify the government, because these were people sent by the governor's office.

I remember, I was getting so many orders from different high officials that I couldn't properly do my work, until I contacted the governor's office and told them, if they were sending a group of investigators, I would just as soon be left out. I did the initial step in the investigation. So what the governor's office did was to send a whole plane of workers to identify each person. We knew the pilot all right, but we had to deal with the families, and, oh God, pathetic. One woman wanted to see her husband; all we could show her was his hands, because some of the faces were not there, parts of their bodies were missing. It was a relief when that plane of investigators came in.

❖

There were some graveyards towards the point, and after a big storm in October 1963, several bodies got washed out of their graves—that sand—into the inlet where people duck-hunt. Some of the hunters found them—here are these partial bodies that had decayed. Some were in a frozen area; some had remained where you could see the skin and all. Some young men called me after they found a body up there in the spring of 1964—and I went out and I got in a car and I called Max Brewer up and I said, "Well, I've got to go up to the point and view this thing." When I got there, they fished it out of the water. There were no hands on it. And it was the body of a woman, and before I could do anything and decide, the police had taken the darned body into the morgue, and it was up for reburial somewhere. We didn't know whose relative it was; it looks like it's been in the burial ground for many years.

I tried to get the minister to help me: "Well, I don't know if I can help you or not. There must have been a burial service at one time

for this person. I don't think we should get involved." So, there is your answer. I go through the law about unclaimed bodies and found that maybe the state has funds to rebury an unclaimed body. So, I send my wire to the state. And, lo and behold, they had no help for me because the body had deteriorated. They no longer wanted any part of it; they didn't know whose relative it was. Then I called the welfare department and told them that I had this body, and I needed some funds to pay off some people who might help with the burial. No can do. They never responded.

So what did I do? Nate was out with the weasel up inland somewhere—this was in July. The city policeman had gone off, too, over the weekend. The doctor over at the hospital said, "We can't keep this thing in here any longer. We better find some way to get rid of it." "Well, since no one is going to help me, I might as well make the casket." So I go to Nate's leftover lumberyard, and I try to measure how long to put it and how wide to make it after I viewed the body. I had some white material I was planning on making a tent with, so I go over to the hospital, to the morgue, and I wrap the body up in that canvas. And then [I] proceeded to go home and get all the tools and make the coffin myself. I am out there by my house, after I measured the body, and I am making a coffin, and I line it with this white material that I had.

I got halfway through when my brother Bob comes along. He says, "What the hell you making?" I said, "I'm making a coffin." "Well, you don't look too sad about it." And I said, "Well, there's no reason to be sad, because I don't know who I'm burying." And then he asks me, "Who's going to dig the grave?" "I guess I am, but with whoever's help." By that time it got to be a joke with me; but it wasn't a joke. I was really serious. So my brother helped me. He worked in the hospital. He finished off the coffin, and we put a cross on the headline, and I said, "Which way do you bury these people?" I hadn't noticed, actually. Well, some old man came to us, and he said, "Well, towards the north; the head goes to north. That's always a custom of our native people." And so my husband is away; I have no help; the chief of police is out on a case; and there I am. I don't know how to drive. So I asked Max Brewer and John Schindler if they could supply me with a vehicle with a flat back on it, so I could drag this coffin up to where the graveyard was. So, you see me there

on Saturday morning, digging a grave, no help.

Nobody else would help me, so several of the older kids start helping me until we got to the frozen ground and we couldn't use the ice pick. I was so tired. I was exhausted. I didn't want to sit on the ground; so I sat down on the coffin and lit a cigarette until I decide what to do next. How I was going to put that coffin down there was my next question.

Right then some curious kids came by. "Say, what you doing?" And the coffin is right there, you know. "Who is it?" "I don't know. Just somebody that needed to be put away again." "Whose relative is it?" So we decided it was somebody from Point Barrow, long time ago, and proceeded to tell the story of it. Whoever was from Point Barrow, it might have been one of their relatives. And here comes one of the Leavitt girls—her father was from Point Barrow. And she comes around with two little kids . . . this curiosity brought them. And I'm sitting on one end of the coffin, and my two helpers are sitting on the other side. The young boys that asked the question must have been four or five years old. They said, "Who do you have in that?" "Well, if we knew, we'd tell you, but we don't." Then one of the two boys, who was about eleven or twelve, said, "Maybe your relative—you're from Point Barrow, aren't you?" The kid looked up and said, "Yeah, my father's from Point Barrow." "Well, maybe it's your relative." The little boy looked at us and said, "Well, if that's the way you treat dead people, I sure wouldn't want to die."

By that time Nate comes in from his hunting, and then my policeman comes after. They both come in and help me, and we buried it. We just stuck a cross on it; I don't know if it still exists up there. It's in the graveyard—no name. I was so disgusted with everybody that time. That happened in 1964. From there on, after I coped with that, everything was possible.

Barrow Duck-In and Subsistence Law

If no whale is caught, other hunting for game and birds must be doubled in effort to obtain the much needed meat for our survival. Also during this month [May] the eider ducks arrive and they are hunted and taken for food because they are virtually the only source of meat we can get during this

> month and through the major part of June. [Eben Hopson, state senator from Barrow, quoted in the Fairbanks *Daily News Miner*, June 16, 1961, p. 3]

> As it is now the federal government won't let the natives take ducks and geese while the ducks and geese are in the arctic, but after the birds go south, where they are killed by the thousands by white sportsmen, the government says to the hungry native, "Now you can hunt." [Rev. John Chambers, Presbyterian missionary, quoted in the Fairbanks *Daily News Miner*, May 31, 1961, p. 1]

When Alaska became a state, they adopted these many rules that the federal government had and applied them as they saw fit for the state, making new regulations. And this is where we had a hard time. They made criminals of all our people breaking the law. Eben Hopson was our senator and I was magistrate when the state made compulsory that anyone who hunted waterfowl out of season would have to be put in jail.[21] And the state didn't realize that from May until September was the only time we had the waterfowl—the ducks, the geese that came up here. Or they didn't research it, when they made it compulsory. We only saw waterfowl from the latter part of May until the latter part of September. And, according to the treaty, this was the closed season for waterfowl. From September until May would be the open season. And so, Eben and I knew every man, woman, and child who was able to hold a shotgun was guilty of hunting ducks that spring.

The game warden at that time had originally worked out at NARL, on NPR [National Petroleum Reserve No. 4], and he knew how we hunted ducks and geese. When he quit work out there, he became one of the game wardens, and he was up here when the state wanted to enforce waterfowl regulations among our people. He was unfair; he knew this area, and then he had the gumption to come over to my office and try to talk to me: "Well, you can talk to your people and tell them they can hunt when I am not around, but don't hunt when I am in town." I said, "What kind of a situation are you inviting? You mean to tell me that you want my people to deliberately break the law when you are not around? They shouldn't do it in your presence? What if someone told you so-and-so came home with a whole sled load of ducks? Then what do you do? You

would have to go and investigate that, wouldn't you?" "Oh, I suppose." "Well, you are some person! You're trying to make me feel like I am being bribed to my people. You want me to tell them that they can hunt when we have no game warden, but not when you are around. How are we going to know if you are going to be around? Who's going to tell us?" "Well, I usually send word that I am coming." I said, "That's unfair. If you are sworn in to do a job, and you come over and try and talk me into something like that, you're as guilty as we are. You do your job or else!"

So Eben and I had a general meeting with all the people of Barrow. The only way we could solve the problem was for every man, woman, and child that had shot a duck, or gotten a waterfowl, to go and stand in the front of the game warden when he made an arrest. And I would know when the game warden would come over and make his complaint and bring that guilty person before me. And Eben would have a watcher out at the airport. We did this for our own good, to make the state understand that we meant business. So each man, woman, and child got a duck from his next-door neighbor, or from the [ice] cellar even, a year-old duck.

We were waiting for the arrest that he made. The game warden was good enough to let him go, but he took his gun and his bag of ducks and told him as soon as he got into town to report to him, and he would be brought before me. But then Eben said, "How are we going to know who got arrested?" "Well, I'll have the name for you through the game warden's complaint. And you have a watcher—make sure you have a watcher out there. So when this man comes in with his dog team, just let me know, and we will alert the whole town, and they can go stand before the game warden."

That's how it came about. When the game warden made the arrest, they all went over there.[22] And I'm sitting home (I'm not supposed to know about this). I'm drinking tea at my table and looking out the window to see when that game warden would be coming in after I had called Eben. Sure enough, here comes the game warden. Just about knocked my door down when he was knocking. I'm trying to stay calm. I say, "Come in. Tell me all about it. What's going on?" "What's the meaning of that crowd in front of my office down there?" "Well, come in and tell me all about it"—as

if I didn't know. I asked him first, "What do you see in front of your office?" "Every man, woman, and child standing in front of my door with a duck in his hand." "Oh, you mean you don't know, as an officer, what to do about a person in possession of a waterfowl?" "Oh, yes, I do. But I can't handle that much paperwork." "Well," I said, "There is that form; and before you can have people sign, you can keep on pasting until you get everyone's name, regardless of how long that paper gets. All you need is that one little form, and if they're going to self-commit, let them sign; whoever is guilty, let them sign."

But in the meantime, before the evening was over, Eben had sent a wire to Governor William Egan, asking him to be prepared to send a welfare person out to Barrow, because we would not be able to handle children whose parents were being picked up and taken to jail for violation of this waterfowl law. And that night, the game warden wrote everybody's name down that was standing before him—took their statements, some 148 to 150 people. Nate was right in the middle of the AP photo when it showed in the newspaper—had his jacket on with this duck in his hand, as big as daylight among all those people being arrested.

We had to open up the old theater when they got through, to bring everybody in out of the cold that night. It was cold—sometime in May. And when all the ducks and waterfowl were picked up, there were about ten big sacks of ducks. And the game warden came over and asked, "Would you mind holding on to all this evidence?" I said, "No, I don't want any part of it. You can take care of it." So he had to fly twice to Fairbanks to take his evidence in. Our people never got taken out. The two trips he made with those ducks were enough. The governor's office called in a special meeting, and they decided our hunting of waterfowl would be made neutral to where our people could hunt ducks for food anytime they wanted. So that was the one area that we resolved on our own.

The controversy waged for weeks following the duck-in. The natives of Alaska took their appeal to the governor of Alaska, and 300 Barrow natives signed a petition sent to the White House. On June 10, 1961, eleven days after the incident, Secretary of the Interior Stewart Udall upheld the law, and Eskimo women vowed to continue hunting ducks if their husbands and sons were

transported out to federal court. A letter to the Barrow Village Council, explaining the Interior Department's decision, concluded: "We are not unsympathetic with the native problems in Alaska . . . but we are responsible for the protection of a great natural resource, and if we are going to have waterfowl on the North American continent we are going to have to manage this resource wisely" (quoted in the Fairbanks Daily News Miner, *June 23, 1961, p. 7). With the support of the United Presbyterian Church and Governor Egan of Alaska, Alaskan natives eventually won special dispensation to hunt migratory waterfowl between May and September.*

❖

They told us before that subsistence hunting would not change in Alaska among our people. The state took over and started enforcing all these rules and regulations. I said, "I am going to have to disqualify myself from hearing any violations, game violations, because these are my people." And I had it be known. I talked to the judge in Fairbanks; I told him I wanted to disqualify myself from hearing any of these game violations. And they talked it over with the supreme court, the chief justices—and then when the complaints started coming in, with me out, they couldn't very well send somebody up here who wasn't prejudiced against this thing. And it came to the attention of the governor.

Other game regulations were being changed by the state. The state wanted to regulate these federal laws regarding caribou, walrus, and so forth. And it was hard for me to try and hear any case saying that so-and-so broke the law because he got a caribou or a duck out of season—these types of things were very sad for me. Before '65, if they were found guilty and I had to confiscate the meat, I could take it into custody and give it back to the people who needed it, because I was a welfare worker. I could also excuse myself from the bench in such cases. I would ask to be excused, and [my request would] be honored. If these laws were to exist among my people, I said I would exempt myself, because these included me. When I had no other, better solution, I would step down and let some other judge come up. And I would have to give them my reason why I did not want to hear the cases. And my reasons were that we had lived so long under the federal government, under territorial law, that when Alaska became a state, the state promised that life for our

native people would not change much. But it did. They started accepting federal laws into their hands and applying them as they saw fit.

And then they started enforcing limits on how many we should catch . . . on ducks, fish, polar bear—when you can go out fishing, how many a day you can get. They treated Barrow like down south, in Anchorage and Juneau areas, and disregarded our subsistence hunting up here. Caribou—each man could get no more than five for the whole winter to feed his family. Our family could use one caribou a week. We didn't have anything else. If whaling was bad, and other seasons are bad, then we have only caribou.

There was a case where a man from Barrow shot a moose out of season and was good enough to report it because we don't usually have moose up here. He injured it before he found out it wasn't a caribou, and he had to kill it. He was active with the game warden commission rules up here, so he reported himself, but they never gave him any warning that they were going to come up and make a charge against him. When I found out, right there at the hearing, that he did report it, I asked the arresting officer, "Is this true?" "Yes, it's true." "Well, why wasn't he warned? Why didn't you take it upon yourself to warn him, when he was good enough to report it and we don't get moose up here all the time?"

Well, it went through my court, and the instructions were already given to the game warden that if that meat was confiscated, no fine should be issued, but he should be reprimanded or get some type of suspended sentence. I think it was a year's suspended sentence that he was supposed to be given, with warning from the court that it is against the law to get moose up here unless it was in season. And I guess the season in those times was sometime in August and September, and you had to get in a plane to get a permit to shoot one, go out maybe four hundred and five hundred miles from here, shoot a moose, and bring it back. That was legal. White hunters got most of the moose; they could afford plane rides out there and get themselves a moose.

Well, moose wasn't included in our diet until they started wandering up here, maybe only one or two a summer, but someone was sure to shoot and kill them. And then we had musk ox wander up here, two of them one time. And they got shot down the coast

sometime, and the game warden heard about it, and he confiscated every bit of the meat.

Oh, it was pathetic. How could you deny a man from hunting to support his family? You couldn't do that; so I discussed it with the judges, and at the seminar that was my main priority. Nora Guinn at Bethel was having the same problems; so we paired off and went before the Judicial Council who made the rules and regulations for Alaska in regard to adopting laws.[23] And they heard us. At that time, I was already refusing to hear any more game violations, and they had to be heard; the person had to be taken out, or the case be dropped. So we have had that type of problem with our game laws.

Alcohol: *A New Understanding*

It was going on the third year as magistrate that my husband was bringing in friends to have a drinking party, and I was pretty much getting after them. It usually happened over a weekend, and so at one occasion, I was really coming down on him quite hard with bringing home all these drinking friends from the base. They were usually happy ones and never in trouble, but it got too much for me; I wasn't a drinker; I didn't touch the stuff. On one of the occasions where I told Nate he had to cut down on his drinking and parties because of my work,[24] he remarked, "Well, why don't you learn how to drink?" "Why, if I could find a drink that I might be able to take, maybe I'd try it. Why don't you order me a bottle?" And so he took me up on that, and along with his order, he ordered me a bottle of Southern Comfort. Those times, all you had to do was get on the phone and order from liquor stores in Fairbanks, and your freight could come in on the plane because, even though we were dry up here, the liquor was still coming in plane loads, and no one could touch the freight.[25] Well, anyway, the order came, and the following weekend his friends came again. There's this bottle that they had ordered for me. I had no idea what it was like; I didn't know any kinds of drinks. I said, "Well, I will sit over here at my kitchen table, and you folks sit over there [in the living room]." I had a pot of tea, and I had some coffee made, and I started drinking by adding whatever—orange juice or pop—trying to make that liquor to my

taste. I had pretty much drunk half of it, and my husband I guess was curious to see how I was doing over there.

Nate said when he came over to check me out with drinking that bottle, I was actually pouring it straight into a cup and I was drinking it, and I wouldn't let anybody else touch it. I was determined that I was going to drink that whole fifth. So, the night went on, and I must have gotten talkative, too, because I remember remarking how people like to go to the dance after a few drinks, and I said, "Why don't we go to the dance?" "Well, we are not dressed for it." "Well, I've got a good dress; I will put it on." And I tried. I walked out that door with whoever wanted to go to the dance, and we had this little [ice] cellar. It was a mound just quite a ways from our doorway, and there was snow still on the ground, quite slippery, and I was determined I was going to go over that mound, which I never made. I kept falling back, and I had no coordination whatsoever, but I still knew what I was doing. I had my mind set that I was going to go over this mound. There was a way to go around it, but my mind was set. I was going over that mound. But I didn't. I kept slipping back, and I could go no farther, and nobody was helping me. So I came back inside and flopped on the bed. And that was the last I could remember that night.

I had never, ever, felt what it was like to have a hangover. I would see these people come before me who had been picked up for drunkenness or involved in excessive drinking, and they used to look really bad; some of them would faint trying to stand up before me in arraignment. But I never had any sense of how they felt until I tried it myself. The next morning I heard my nephew, who was living with me at the time, saying, "Oh boy, my poor aunt! She's going to have a hangover and be sick." I didn't know what a hangover was. So the next morning when I woke up, I was okay. I did my work. But towards the evening, my mouth kept getting dry, and I went to the water tank and filled a large glass of water and I drank it, and I got drunk all over again just by drinking water. By that evening, I couldn't make it. I just had to lay my head somewhere. And by the next morning. I couldn't even lift my head. The smell of any type of food turned my stomach and I was hollering "Quit that noise!" to the kids. They just thought I was sick, because they were asleep when all this happened. And oh my, for the next two weeks!

About Wednesday the superior court judge from Nome was coming in to hear some felony cases, and that morning I remember I couldn't even lift my head. This was about the fourth day. I was miserable and still throwing up anything that I drank or ate, and for two weeks it was like that. And the judge came over when he heard that I wasn't feeling well and sympathized with me, but I didn't let him know that this was the result of my drinking. Finally it passed, but oh, after that I knew how these people felt standing in front of me, and I began to sympathize with them. My approach to them changed extremely, because before I never sensed how they felt. But that was a one-time deal. Never again! When we are out of town, we go to these big restaurants to eat, and I will occasionally take a glass of wine or something, but nothing stronger. So that was my drinking, and it has lasted me a whole lifetime. I didn't realize it at the time, but I was just going to satisfy Nate, show my husband that I could drink. I guess I didn't show him too well, but after that he started sobering up and didn't indulge in drinking to where it was excessive anymore.

Further Training

About 1966 I was appointed, along with Nora Guinn and Judge Connelly of Fairbanks, to be an instructor for newly appointed magistrates for the state of Alaska. We were called in whenever new magistrates were being sworn in, to be there to train them for two weeks at a time. Those sessions were held sometimes in Nome, sometimes in Anchorage and Fairbanks, wherever was the appointed place to have the training. I quit when the court system wanted to train newly appointed magistrates in their own area, and they got somebody else in that area to train them, four at a time. But the three of us would each be assigned to present a mock trial, and to perform marriages. Also we just to talked to the people, to see how well they would fare when they went back. But most of the newly appointed magistrates were not trained for the coroners' duties like we were.[26]

I was sent to paralegal training at Antioch College in Washington, D.C.,[27] to learn the basics of the law—back in 1966 or 1967. And

then in 1976 I went to a judicial college in Reno, Nevada [National College of the State Judiciary Institute]. It was a one-month course and sort of mandatory to go. There were other judges from all over the United States—county judges, those from the lowest court in any state. I was the only one from Alaska that year. We compared how we handled arraignments and other parts of our jobs. They test you out, observe you, grade you on your approach to the people. The dean of the college is right there, watching you, evaluating you, taping you. My arraignment procedure stood out so that they asked if I wouldn't give permission to show on videotape what my method was in dealing with the person standing before me—my way of showing interest and not reading from a book.

Adapting the Law to Native Culture

There were blunders, too, in my work, where I got so scared, going forward on my own without any orders. Like we were instructed to never use our native language in court, but here was this man who couldn't speak a word of English. The state trooper brought this charge before me, and I arraigned the man. What had happened was that he was charged with petit larceny, taking something away from the base area that was surplus, that to his mind was good stuff that he was going to put to use with his family who needed it. But he didn't tell the superiors that he was going to take some of the stock, and when the state trooper apprehended him, he knew he had made a mistake, and he returned everything that he had taken.

But here this case came up, and the trooper never told me anything about him returning the stock, and he pled guilty. I was speaking my native tongue all the time. I advised him of his rights, and he said he didn't want to use his rights, he wanted to waive them and admit to the charge that was before him. We did it in such a manner it was on record—tape—and I had to interpret the whole thing so the court system would know what the case was all about. But I didn't know that base up there was federal property, and the trooper made a state charge instead of a federal charge out of it. So four days later the federal authorities arrest this man and take him to

Anchorage before a federal court. I got this phone call over at the Wien [Airlines] terminal from the chief justice of the Alaska Court System about that case.[28]

I was asked to come to Anchorage and demonstrate how I arraigned this man. "Did I, in fact, have so and so in my court on a charge?" "Yes. The state trooper brought the charge, and I heard it, and this case was disposed of." "Well, we want you to come down and demonstrate before the federal courts how you did it." I had to go down there. And I had never been in a big courthouse, let alone in a robe.[29] And they railroaded me into this big courthouse and put a robe on me, and as the prisoner was being brought in, we all had to stand for the gavel. This we did in my court when I came in, but not that formally. My heart was in my throat. I explained that I did it all in my native tongue because there was no alternative. There was no way that I could make this man understand what his rights were until I used his own native language.

So they bring in the prisoner, and who it should it be but that same man I had arraigned who didn't know one word of English. As they brought him in he was looking down, and he looked up and he recognized me and you should have seen the beam on his face: "Hi, Sadie!" Right there in the courthouse. No formality of any kind, not knowing why he was being brought there, but recognizing me. He didn't even know I was there, but when he looked up and recognized me, the smile on his face, and then for him to say, "Hi, Sadie!"

And then I demonstrated. Well, after I demonstrated to them, I told him in Eskimo, "We have to go all through the same thing we went through in Barrow." And he did beautifully. He pled guilty. And then I asked the state trooper what was the charge there, was this true? Because when someone gives himself up to me on a plea of guilty or admission of guilt or *nolo contendere*, then you ask the defendant if he has anything to say where we might show cause for leniency. He came up with the statement that he did let the trooper know that he [had] returned all the items he was charged with, and [that] they were back at the base. And then I asked the trooper, "Is this true?" He said, "Yes, it is true." "Well, why didn't you mention it?" And then they knew what kind of a person I was. I wanted the full information on any case that came up before me. I told them I was stumped: I couldn't read his rights in English; he

couldn't make head nor tails out of it; and he didn't know anything about the law, nor did he know that he stole. He was just taking something that was going to be thrown away—he just took advantage of it—and so, all those things, they [had] never [come] out.

The court system had planted some people in the back, listeners who were from my town, to record and to translate back in English what I had said in court about the man's rights. When it was all over, I was told, "The chief justice would like to see you in his chambers." My heart is still in my throat, and I thought, "This is where I get thrown out." I was so scared. But when I got to his door, there he was in a white shirt, just relaxing, smoking his pipe in his chamber. And he said, "Hi, Sadie." The voice that he greeted me had no hurt in it whatsoever, and he said, "That was the most wonderful demonstration you performed. From now on, it will be rule of the court to use the language of the people." So from there on [c. 1964], they started using the native language.

Having been born and grown up here, there was a time when there wasn't drinking. It started coming up after the base was settled. Our menfolks and our young people started consuming alcohol, and I could see where the fights were coming from—assault and battery, assault with dangerous weapon, or whatever. The laws say that you cannot use alcohol as an excuse and bring it into court—"Because I was drunk, I don't remember doing it." Well, you can't use leniency, because he was drunk and did this. In evaluating cases, most of the time, if that type of complaint came in and it was signed by some member of [the] family caught in the same situation [also drunk], automatically when they sobered up, they were no longer fighting, they were friends again. If they had broken anything, if they had wrecked something, I would take the criminal charge away, and let them pay restitution, and just let them go—with warnings that they could go to jail for a certain amount of months or days the next time. And it worked. So, much of my feeling went into my work, and I talked to my people. And knowing them was even harder, because I couldn't believe some of the charges against my own people, when the law says drunkenness is no excuse to do an act. That was even harder for my people to believe, when they sobered up, that they did something like that. Shameful.

My main concern in that job was to make my people learn about the law, and to learn about what rights they had. Some would be mad at me, because they were held in jail and didn't know what their rights were. At arraignments they would ask, "What is that?" And it used to take me fifteen or twenty minutes longer to try and explain and make my people understand what their rights were—rights to a lawyer, rights to remain silent, and oh, they had many rights that I had to read to them. And when that initial period was over, then it was much easier for me to hold court. And when the city adopted all the misdemeanor laws as city ordinances, on Monday mornings my courthouse was like a schoolhouse. I had so many the police had picked up over the weekend, when liquor first came into Barrow in the early sixties, and I had to find out a system to take care of each and every one of those as fast as I could. So I used to let them line up in front of me, and I divided them into who could understand English and who could not understand English. I was asked to use my native tongue to make them understand what their rights were. So, I could read their rights to the ones who were able to speak English and understand it, and have them line up. And then the ones who were not able to understand fully what the English language was all about, then I would do it in my native tongue. And then their charges are right in front of me; so like a school roll call, I would call each name and ask them, one by one. And when a person admitted to the charge before me, there were set fines. If it was an ordinance-violation [that] the city had given me on a first offender, it was a suspended sentence. If the same offense was committed for a second time that month, then a $10 fine. The third one, the fine tripled, until you had five or six charges against you. Then it became a state matter, instead of a city ordinance.

I was in the habit of searching for solutions to better our situations, because by Monday I would have thirty or forty cases in the morning—the same alcohol-related charges. The police that we had there would just throw them in jail. Or, if they were transporting liquor while under the influence, that was another charge—one of the ordinances, too. You could just walk out your door here with a can of beer and get arrested. Your property didn't mean that you were in your own private property—didn't mean a thing to the police, because we didn't own our property then. We were

squatters on the land until BIA decided they would give us the lots and area where our houses were, and they were sectioned off. But before that it was such that you were a violator under the city ordinances, and I was collecting all these fines and making some six or seven thousand dollars a month at the time for the city through their ordinances, because the fines stayed in the community. In those days the menfolks and most everyone in this community were earning big wages, and those fines didn't mean a thing. It wasn't a punishment to them. They would go back, walk out of the courthouse and do the same thing, and they would be right back in my courthouse. They just handed the fine over, and the city was getting richer fast from those ordinance violations.

So, when that didn't seem like a punishment to the people, then I went to the council and asked if there were some way we could put these people on a work release program, clean up program, or help out somebody in need with building their home, or whatever. And oh, you should have seen the effects of that one. People who came from well-respected families said, "Oh, I'm not going to be seen out there doing silly work—clean up, or. . . . " "Either that, or you sit in jail." It was a choice. And that jail we had wasn't a very pleasant place to be. The solution wasn't very popular, and people hated me for that, because people who classed themselves well-to-do did not like to be seen out there in the street, cleaning up because they had been picked up. That was the most effective sentencing in those times, to put somebody on a work release program. People didn't like it, and they started thinking about themselves.

❖

Basically when it came to sentencing, the prosecutor and I would generally just say, "Okay, Sadie, do your thing." And it was strange. A lot of times she would do sentences that I didn't understand. I would go in there with somebody who I thought hadn't done much and she would really bring the hammer down. And I wouldn't know why. And Sadie would explain, "He comes from a really good background and he has had an opportunity to know right from wrong and this is the first time he had been in trouble; if I come down hard on him now, he won't be back." Or I would go in there with somebody who was really bad and deserved to have the hammer fall and maybe she'd be light on him. And afterwards I would say, "Sadie, why did you let that guy off?" She would say, "Well, you know he comes from a

really bad situation. His wife just left him and his dad was never home when he was being raised, and his mother had a hard time with all those kids. Right now, given the situation, he's doing the best he can." She was always thinking in terms of where did these people come from, what was their background, which is more than any judge can do in a big city. [Stephen Cline, March 7, 1986]

In the matter of sentencing, I waited until I looked into the family situation. Sometimes this is [unorthodox], but it was my practice. I knew the people, but I had to get more information—why this was happening, if it was a repeated offense. If I had to sentence a person on their plea of guilty, or if they were found guilty, I had to look into the background of the family, or ask questions of the defendant after the case was all formed, that might allow me to show leniency or give me an idea what type of sentencing would be proper. Then I would have to explain why I am giving it. It helped to look into the family matters at times.

I always tried to get to the bottom of the problem when it came before me, whether it was a criminal complaint like assault and battery or a small claims. If it came through my court as a small claims to get the amount of the money for making a parka, because the person who intended to buy had never paid the seller, I would ask, "Have you ever talked to that person, to find out if they were able to pay, instead of making this small claim in court?" And sometimes it just was a matter of not communicating, and working up to a frenzy to where you were forced to make this complaint. After talking with both parties, then sometimes it was resolved.

In areas like Fairbanks and Anchorage my system would never work, because I wouldn't know the people. But I made it a point, if I didn't know the person standing before me, to ask them questions—where he is from, and how long he has been here, and how long he expects to stay, and what type of work he is doing—those types of questions. I wanted to know the whole story so I could evaluate the case properly before me and get to the core of it, what caused it. And after a plea of guilty or a no-contest plea, then I could ask that person to give me his views, what he felt, talk to me freely so it wouldn't happen again. They did talk freely; they never kept back. And later on, some of the whites who were

looking down on me got to know me better. They didn't shun me anymore. That was quite hard to come to, and they found me a different person. Sometimes they would knock on my door and come in and apologize for their attitude.

Speaking Out

I really fought to make that courthouse work up here, that court system, it didn't matter who was before me, trying to question me. If I felt what I had in my mind was right, I just spoke it whether they fired me or not. And that's how I guess I got noticed. But whenever I was asked to go up here before the chief justice, I would think, "What did I do this time?"

Well, at one time, I got mad at Justice [Jay] Rabinowitz. At the time I wasn't aware that, after Boney, he was acting chief justice before the vote. We were having a seminar, and I was asked to instruct the police and the magistrates, both at the same time. My God, there must have been over a hundred policemen assigned to training, and I had to explain what the connections were between the magistrates and the policemen at that time. And I was trudging along when we heard that the supreme court judges were going to swerve from Fairbanks into Nome and visit the seminar where I was doing all of the instructing. And when they came in, they closed the meeting down to take us out to lunch. Nora Guinn was there, and Judge Connelly was there, and Justice Rabinowitz.

I had heard that the appointment of magistrates should come from the supreme court level, and I wasn't in favor of it, because we were never in contact with that level at all with our work. The superior court judges and the district judges are our main contacts. Justice Rabinowitz asked me, "How do you feel about this appointment situation coming from our level?" "What do you mean, what do I think of it? You ever come to Barrow to see what I do?" I went like that, and Nora nudged me. "Well, let me finish. I think that is ridiculous. You are never interested enough to come over and see what we do in our own area. It's the superior court judges and the district judges that come to our area, and they see what we do,

especially the superior court judges. I wouldn't even consider it." And I was talking like that to Rabinowitz, not knowing he was a chief justice. And he said, "Well, I am glad that somebody like you can.speak up." "Well, it is the truth! How many of you ever come to our areas to see what we do? All you do is hear the appeals. And whatever you make law in your appeals, your decisions, your opinions, we follow. That is the only contact we have with you—when we refer to you through your opinion on cases, your decisions."

And then it wasn't long, come November of that same year, we were asked to go and talk about the law before the Judicial Council. And I was called upon, Nora was called upon, and several of the lawyers that came up here were called upon to come in for about two weeks. All the supreme court judges attended. Well, by that time I knew that he had been appointed chief justice and that he was the keynote speaker. And he was looking around, and he looked at me, and he said, "Well, I am glad that we have somebody here who is outspoken and can decide for herself among us," and he called me by name. He thoroughly embarrassed me, "Now what did I do?" "Well, if it wasn't for her," he explained, "I think we would have made it law for magistrates to be appointed by the supreme court judges. But as it stands, with her outspoken statement on that matter, it still stands that the appointment should come from the superior court!"

I took it the wrong way; I just felt like I was abused. I was laying for him when Judge Connelly said, "You'd better not say anything. That's the greatest honor any person can obtain from a chief justice." Steve Cline was there, too. I asked him, "Why am I always getting picked on whenever something comes up?" "Because you are outspoken; you speak the truth. And what you say is noticed. So, you just sit back and take it all."

Mayorhood and Marriages

I was mayor at one time because the city council felt that, being magistrate, I should be the mayor of the town. We had the city council with their president, vice-president, and so on, and they took

care of all the city matters. And I was only taking care of court matters. I felt that it wasn't fair for me to be called that, because I had no knowledge of city matters; questions that were coming in, I couldn't answer. So I went to the council meeting and told them that by rights the president of the council should be the mayor. So around 1962 I was mayor, but not for long, because I couldn't handle the position and answer all questions. So from then on, the president of the chosen council, he's the city mayor.

As magistrate I was in charge of vital statistics;[30] the originals were sent down to Juneau and the copies kept here for our files. Marriages, too, were part of my job. I performed most of them. Then one year I got quite popular by request. A grandmother who was not able to understand English wanted me to perform this marriage all in Eskimo, and I appeared in the newspaper, and after that I was often asked to do weddings in our native tongue. And people getting married started to really understand what their vows meant. Then one year Charlotte lost quite a bit of the files—moving in to the new courthouse they got blown off, so she was caught without marriage forms and a copy of the ceremony. So, I wrote one up for her. I still have that. And I remember Ed Crutchfield, magistrate up at Fairbanks, was here when I wrote it, and I said, "Ed, you want to read this thing and see if it contains everything a marriage vow should have? And maybe we could make it a little more personal, a little advice in there to the newly married couple." Then we submitted it to the magistrates' office, who evaluates some of that material we use, and it was accepted by the state and it is being used in magistrates' courts now. And then, too, "Wilt thou obey?" was deleted out of the marriage ceremony, because women were beginning to feel that they were equal to their husbands.

We always called it the ten-minute marriage ceremony. But when I had to use it to the church's order, it was much lengthier. I used that when somebody wanted to get married in church and there was no minister available. Being an elder and a member in good standing, I could perform church marriages. I'm the marriage commissioner yet. But I haven't performed any marriages for a couple of years because of my health.

I performed the marriage ceremonies for two of my children—Pat and Donna. And I had requests from Outside—letters, saying they

were coming up and wanted to be married under the midnight sun, or out at the point—but it got to be too expensive to try and travel to the designated areas. I remember this one couple wanting to get married. They wanted an Eskimo-style marriage, so we had to get the drummers in. They didn't know anyone here, but they requested the general public to come. Everyone sat there on all this deerskin listening to all the drumming before the ceremony started. Then the man was required to bring the woman in. That one was a lengthy one. They were both college professors.

Another time I had a request for a marriage to be done out on the Arctic ice. This happened to be in June, and by that time you had to have a pair of hip boots to get out there, or a boat to go stand in the Arctic ice. So here comes the woman, all dressed up in her wedding gown, and we had to put a pair of hip boots on her. If someone had taken a movie of it, it was ridiculous. But we all got out there on the ice, and I performed the marriage out there. And another couple, we had to find warm parkas for them because they wanted to get married out at the point in December. They hired people with skidoos to take them up there.

So I have had a very interesting part added to my being a magistrate. I had so much traffic, the only time I could perform those types of requests was on a weekend when I was off. I honored most of them; except towards the last, I started turning them over to the minister to see if he would perform rituals like that.

A Busy, Lonely Job

Back in 1975 this whole town, in order to show honor and respect, chose my birthday and celebrated it with me right in the midst of it. The whole town showed up, and I can remember how surprised Nate and I were, because they said we were needed over at the town hall and we walked over there into the party. I got railroaded over there. My brother came in—said that they had some type of controversy that they wanted me to listen in on, things that needed to be ironed out. I responded like I always do, just closed up my courthouse and started walking over there. I stopped by home first, because they said Nate should come along too. So we went over

there, and the whole town was in that building— "Surprise! Happy Birthday!" They started singing. All the heads of the community were there, and they honored me with speeches, and it was so heartfelt that when it was all over, I told our policeman, "I think that even if you make an arrest this week, I am not going to have an arraignment!" After that, things were much easier. But the respect of these townpeople was so great that I never forgot it.

❖

In addition to being magistrate she would also come in and act as interpreter. I mean they never considered the fact that she may need the time to review her cases. Her job never stopped. Twenty-four hours a day you get phone calls. And faithfully she's at work at 8:30 in the morning, and I don't hear any gripes from her. [Charlotte Brower, August 5, 1985]

Reflecting on a typically busy day as magistrate, Sadie remembers what it was like:

Well, I was still taking care of the family here, too. By then I had about six or seven kids at home, and I would be in the courthouse until 4:30 and then come home. Or if I got off early, I just closed up the courthouse until a policeman would come in needing this and that; then I would go back with him. But I would inform them that I would be home because I didn't have any more traffic. I had done my paperwork and would be home if they needed me.

The hours in those days were serious; I was running the courthouse all by myself. I didn't have anybody to leave in there; I didn't have any help. Then when the base up here started closing down on some of their constructions and people needed money, then I started spreading the word that there was work compensation, unemployment. And I started writing letters for people—they would come in, and I would write letters. And then, too, Social Security spliced in on that.

I was still a social worker when I did it, and my busiest days would be coming home from court and finding a house full of people waiting for me to answer these [letters] or fill these forms out for them. Then, besides taking care of some of those foster kids that I had taken in, I had to try and cook a supper. Too, being a welfare

worker, I got all the indigent people that were hungry. They would land in my house because Nate was a good supporter and went out and hunted. We always had lots of meat and fish. So, my busiest days were when I did all that.

After '65 it started to slacken, because I was no longer doing welfare work. But my criminal case load started coming up, and civil cases, too. Then when we got the dirt roads and started getting cars in, the state trooper that was up here started enforcing traffic, and I used to set Wednesday afternoons aside for traffic violation tickets. I couldn't work traffic violations in along with my criminal cases by recessing to take care of them, so I figured there had to be a special day to take care of all of that, and I chose Wednesday to do it. That was a lot of work, too.

I would be tired at the end of the day, but in those days there was nothing wrong with my health. I really never noticed it until a real heavy case came on and I was involved in my mind. My mind made me more tired—thinking of it, because I couldn't talk about my cases—and I would sit there, and Nate always knew when I had a hard day in court. "Look at me. You must have had a hard day in court." He always noticed. He was always by my side—made things a little easier—and then, too, when I didn't feel like cooking, he was happy to eat frozen food. We'd just chop it off, bring it in and have a meal, which was more like a meal to him than my cooked ones. If I had enough water, on Saturdays I did the wash when I was able to, or assigned my baby-sitter to do it. Happy times were when I was able to be with my family over the weekend.

I did bear the town's burdens; everything, it seemed like. And I made it work. I had to make it work, otherwise there wouldn't have been any sense in my being there.

However poor the fit between traditional Eskimo law ways and the American judicial system, Sadie by all counts made it work in Barrow for twenty years. She attributes her success to several things: to knowing the people and their background by virtue both of her birth in Barrow and her social work; to winning the trust and respect of the people through her years of public service; to settling cases out of court by counseling; to applying liberally her own common sense; and to making use of her fluency in both Iñupiaq and English.

Representatives of the judicial system who have worked with her speak uniformly highly of Sadie's work as magistrate.

Judge ROBERT COATS, *Alaska Court of Appeals; former public defender in Barrow: "She seemed to have tremendous concern for everybody. I felt like she cared about all the court system people and she cared about all the defendants and all the jurors. She just really had a tremendous amount of compassion. The defendants always felt better pleading guilty or whatever in front of Sadie, because they understood Sadie and she understood them. My impression is that the defendant standing in front of her was totally ashamed and that she got more mileage out of a suspended sentence. She had an incredible impact in terms of probably changing peoples' behavior without having to put them in jail for a long period of time. She gave the system a tremendous legitimacy. As an attorney, you had a real comfortable feeling with Sadie doing a sentencing; she had very good judgment. She was so willing to learn and lacked arrogance. But the important thing with Sadie is that there was this bit of steel or something that the good ones have. They realize almost instinctively it seems, 'Hey, I'm the judge. I've got the information at this point; now I have to make a decision. And I don't like having to send this person to jail for ninety days, but damn it, that's the job and I'm going to do it.' And they do."*

Superior Court Judge MICHAEL JEFFERY, *Barrow; former legal services attorney: "Sadie is a very determined individual. And very sensitive not only to the local situation but to the wider situation in the state. She was also quite capable of just laying down and delivering an ultimatum [to the court system administration]: 'I'll leave unless you do this and this.' And that's what it took. And then also [she was] that kind of real pioneer who held this thing together at the beginning."*

Field Auditor MARJORIE LORI, *Alaska Court System: "She was really fabulous on the bench. You could feel the rapport between Sadie and whomever was in front of her. She always looked at whomever she was talking with, which many judges don't do. She had a sixth sense to know when the local people could and could not understand English, and frequently she would lapse into Iñupiaq because she knew that even though they might understand, they couldn't translate rapidly enough. She talked to defendants like she really cared about them, and I think they knew it, too.*

Magistrate CHARLOTTE BROWER, *Barrow (1977–81); former law clerk for Sadie: "No one could ever really replace Sadie. Barrow hasn't been the same since she retired. She was stubborn. She has a way of bringing things across to people. People listen. For the defendant, it's bad enough that he got charged with a crime, but to get a lecture from Sadie is the worst punishment!"* M. BLACKMAN: *"So if Sadie were still magistrate today, she really couldn't operate in the same way she did back in the seventies?"* C. BROWER: *"I think she would."* M. BLACKMAN: *"Could she? Would the system allow it?"* C. BROWER: *"I think she would. And who would refuse her?"*

Attorney STEPHEN CLINE, *former public defender and magistrates' training judge: "She was always fair. She is the only judge that the prosecutor and I regularly entrusted without trying to influence her. I never knew an attorney to take a sentence appeal from anything that Sadie did. I'm not saying that it never happened, but I can't think of one. She had a lot of empathy. She felt genuinely sad at every sentencing. There was no vindictiveness; there was no routineness to it; it was a personal sad thing she had to deal with. She took care of her people. She knew they had certain rights and she knew what they were, and she didn't run roughshod over them. She didn't go into court with an air of authority at all. She went in there like a mother."*

9

A Matter of Survival

The hunt represents tradition, and to engage in it means preserving the core of Eskimo life. There are more crews and probably a greater percentage of men engaged in whaling today than ever before. Most of the Eskimos now and in the future will be part-time hunters. They will hunt less intensively, but that will not make their hunt less important. [Boeri 1983:227]

In May of 1986, I phoned Sadie to discuss a couple of matters relating to the life history. It was a bad connection, with static and a worse than usual echo, but good enough to communicate the excitement that day in the Neakok household. "We've having 'Nalukataq' *right now," Sadie shouted.*[1] *"Nate's crew got a whale, and we've been up all night cutting meat!" The phone conversation came to a close as the household scrambled to welcome the returning whalers who had, just at that moment, come into the house.*

This pattern of expectation and triumph has been repeated among North Slope Iñupiat for almost 1,500 years. Although whaling today is dominated by technology introduced by New England whalers in the nineteenth century, and by more modern conveniences such as CB radios, the customary laws governing the taking and division of whales, the involvement of kin and community in the sharing of the catch, the responsibilities of the whaling captain's wife, and the joyous celebration known as Nalukataq *all have ancient roots.*[2]

Preparations for the annual spring whaling began during the dark months of deep winter, as they still do today. The umialik *and crew spent long hours in the* qargi, *the former conferring there with shamans regarding the coming hunt and preparing the whaling charms and other regalia needed. Much time was given in the evening to talk of whaling, and the old men retold accounts to whales won and lost. Preparations intensified in early March as thought was*

given to the location of the whaling camp. Roads out on the ice were prepared, and, most important, the gear itself was readied.

Respect for the whale was shown in the new clothing and boots worn by the whalers and in the new skin cover on the umiaq. *A shed, attached to the* qargi, *was erected. Here the women who sewed the new* umiaq *cover gathered to work. Here, too, the women came to sew the whalers' parkas, mittens, and waterproof boots. The boots of the* umialik *were specially decorated with white stitching to record the number of whales he had taken, and special mittens were worn by the* umialik's *wife when she poured fresh water on the whale that her husband's crew caught. For the period of the hunt, she gave her husband her left-hand mitten (along with her belt), symbolizing the crew's ties to the land.*

Many ritual acts governed the progression of the hunt. The umialik *and his crew spent the four days and nights preceding their departure in the* qargi, *in solemn contemplation. The ice cellars were cleaned of all their contents by the women, and the remaining whale meat was fed to the crew and distributed to townspeople. Once out on the ice, the men observed numerous eating taboos and were enjoined from building any fires for cooking. The* umialik's *wife spent the duration of the whale hunt quietly at home, refraining from work of any kind.*

During the six to eight weeks of the hunt, the crew was supplied from the umialik's *house. Since the* umialik's *wife was required to remain inactive, other women in the household made the trip out to the whaling camp with food and supplies. In earlier times they had to trek to the camp on foot, for dogs were not allowed on the ice at whaling time. Women were free to come and go out on the ice to the whaling camp except during menstruation and childbirth, at which times they were confined.*

The whaling crew comprised eight or so men, plus a young boy or two, who, as apprentice crew members, ran errands and assisted at the camp. In addition to the umialik, *specialists in the crew included the harpooner, the steersman, and the person who sat near the harpooner and fed out the line of floats attached to the harpoon head. The harpooner occupied the bow position. In addition to throwing the harpoon, he afterwards thrust the stone-bladed lance into a vital organ. The steersman sat in the stern of the* umiaq. *He was, as the name suggests, responsible for piloting the boat with his stern paddle. Often the* umialik *was also a harpooner or steersman. The remainder of the crew served simply as paddlers.*

Despite the relative docility of the bowhead, whaling was an extremely dangerous venture, and the whale had to be carefully approached to avoid capsizing the boat. Whales were harpooned from distances as close as ten feet

and were preferably approached so the float lines could be played out over the starboard side. Sometimes more than one boat might chase a whale at the same time, and often two or more harpoons from different boats would be put into a whale.

Iñupiat custom dictated that the whale belonged to the boat whose harpoon first struck the whale. All boats in the vicinity, however, joined together to tow a whale to shore. Once a whale had been taken, a runner was sent to notify the umialik's *wife, who bore the responsibility for formally greeting the whale with a "drink" of fresh water and offering it thanks for allowing itself to be taken.*

The entire community turned out when a whale was killed. The maktak *and much of the meat was cut off while the whale was still in the water, attached to long ropes, and was pulled onto the ice by groups of people. (Later, the introduction of block and tackle by commercial whalers allowed the whale to be landed before butchering.) Division of the* maktak *and meat was governed by traditional laws, with certain parts falling to the boat owner, the* umialik *(if not the boat owner), his crew members, and to the other crews that had assisted. When those parts had been secured, the entire community was allowed to cut away at the* maktak *and carry away what they could. The meat and* maktak *were cut up and stored in the ice cellars, but enormous quantities of meat were also cooked by the* umialik's *family for immediate consumption by the community.*[3]

Nalukataq, *the whale festival, marked the formal closure of the whaling season. This outdoor festival, held in June, was hosted cooperatively by the crews of a* qargi *and was attended by the entire community.* Nalukataq *featured games and competitions between men of different* qariyit, *the distribution of* maktak, *and the "blanket-toss," which was the culminating event of several days of celebration.*[4]

Commercial whaling in Arctic waters attracted not only coastal Iñupiat but also people from the interior, as large numbers of natives began to be hired by the shore-based stations in 1880s. The attraction of commercial whaling is not surprising given the recompense of a year's supplies, including a gun and ammunition, and the practice of allowing the natives to keep the meat and maktak *(see p. 12). It was probably at that same time that women became full participants in whaling crews. John Murdoch (1892:273), naturalist with the International Polar Expedition of 1881–83 at Point Barrow, commented in this regard: "Men are preferred for the whaling crews when enough can be secured, otherwise the vacancies are filled by women, who make efficient paddlers." In 1884 Charles Brower (n.d.:182) observed similarly: "The*

women were out in the boats same as the men, doing the same work . . . and they seemed just as efficient. When the time of menstruation arrived they had to go ashore, [as] the whales would know immediately if they stayed on the ice."

Acculturation in whaling practices from the coming together of commercial and native whale-hunting cultures was mutual; the setting up of shore-based commercial whaling stations, for example, depended upon the adoption of native methods of whaling. The most noticeable changes effected in native whaling were technological. The harpooner took up the darting gun—a harpoon with bomb attached, fired from a gun and attached to a line of floats—and a new specialist was added: the shoulder gunner, who sat in the mid-section of the boat and fired a bomb that exploded deep inside the whale. Although the shoulder gun, but not the darting gun, could be effective from a distance, the two weapons had to be used in tandem, for the bomb alone merely blew a hole in a whale. The darting gunner did not need to have the same degree of skill or strength as the traditional harpooner, for as long as he shot the harpoon into the whale, attaching the floats, the killing bomb could then be dispatched from the shoulder gun.

One of the more dramatic alterations in native whaling was the relaxation of taboos. Charles Brower himself broke the taboo against cooking in camp [at Point Hope] by building a fire and heating a pot of coffee out on the ice during the whaling season of 1885. The Iñupiat dismissed his activities for a time, rationalizing his behavior as acceptable for a white man but not for them. Finally, a native woman who had built Brower's fire for him agreed to have a cup of coffee, even though the others said something bad would befall her. "The others looked on with great concern for some time, then as nothing happened, several others did the same." Brower adds (n.d.:279) that "that was the first I ever saw any Eskimo do anything to break their taboo regarding their whaling customs." During the 1889 whaling season Charles Brower hired a man from Point Hope who, because of the death of a close relative, was under a ritual prohibition from whaling with a native crew. Although he couldn't hunt at Point Hope, the man apparently had no fear of violating the taboo in another community under a white umialik.

Other aspects of native whaling suffered a gradual erosion; adoption of the new technology also met with an occasional setback. After the Eskimos had embraced the white man's whaling gear in the 1870s, during the 1883 season "it was decided that they would have no luck whaling unless the first harpoon darted was of the old fashioned stone-headed kind" (Ray 1885:101). But according to Brower (1942:124), the spring of 1888 "marked the last season in

which many of them kept to their old whaling customs. After that the younger crowd began more generally to adopt our whaling gear, tackles, guns, bombs and all. They even insisted on hard bread and tea out on the ice. Tents, however, were not to be used for many years yet; not until we began to hire Eskimos to whale regularly for the station." The assault on shamanism was aided when commercial whalers with Eskimo crews paid no heed to shamans' advice, and the whaling activities associated with the qargi *came to an end in Barrow with the destruction of the* qariyit *in 1900–01 (see p. 19).*

Following the demise of commercial whaling after 1910, whales were scarce and ammunition was precious. Whaling became once again a subsistence enterprise, and the number of crews declined. Beginning in 1907, at the apparent instigation of a white whaler, Barrow natives took up fall whaling in addition to the spring hunt. Between 1928 and 1934 fall whaling was almost as important as that in the spring. The whale count kept by David Brower, Sadie's brother, shows an average of 5.8 whales per year taken at Barrow between 1928 and 1954.[5] *By the mid-1970s the number of whales taken annually had increased dramatically.*[6] *Several factors contributed to the intensification of bowhead hunting—a sudden decline in the caribou population (1975–76); an increase in North Slope village populations, due both to a high birth rate and to the establishment of local high schools; a revival of cultural identity, which is closely associated with bowhead whaling; and increasing affluence among Iñupiat, enabling them to outfit more crews (Alaska Consultants 1984:A-53).*[7] *The quota on whales, imposed in 1977 (see below), may bear a relationship to the growing number of crews. Whaling captains have encouraged the formation of new crews in the hopes of reducing the number of struck and lost whales (Smythe, personal communication). Several crews will assist in pursuing a struck whale, and thus more crews can mean more assistance and less likelihood of losing a whale.*

Today the Barrow Whaling Captains Association meets each spring to review the rules governing the hunt and the distributon of the whale, to discuss any problems from the preceding year's hunt, and to distribute a list of property marks. They are also responsible for construction of the ice road out to the leads. Snow machines now transport the crews and their gear out to the campsite, though once the whales are running they are not used near the camps because the noise frightens the whales. Citizens' band radios allow crews to keep in touch with one another and have brought the excitement of the hunt into virtually every native home in Barrow. The link between land and sea once symbolized in the sharing of mittens by the umialik *and his wife has been*

replaced by radio communication; today the whaling captain's wife monitors the home-base CB, receiving word on the progress of the hunt, taking requests for supplies, and offering encouragement.

In 1977, the International Whaling Commission (IWC) voted to halt all subsistence whaling of bowhead, basing their decision on low population estimates. In response, the Iñupiat banded together to form the Alaska Eskimo Whaling Commission (AEWC).[8] *With the backing of the U.S. delegation to the IWC, they successfully lobbied to obtain a small quota of eighteen whales struck or twelve landed.*[9] *Since that time, the quotas have been gradually raised,*[10] *owing largely to whale population research sponsored by the AEWC and the North Slope Borough working in conjunction with the National Marine Fisheries Service. When the last organization suffered cutbacks in funding for the 1982 year, the financial responsibility for conducting the spring census of the bowhead fell upon the North Slope Borough. In 1982, funding of the census project approached the $1 million mark. As part of this ongoing project, the North Slope Borough also sponsors a "Biology of the Bowhead" conference held each year in Anchorage. Current concerns of Eskimo whalers are reflected in the agendas for the annual AEWC meetings which have included discussion of the meaning of "strike," the quota and its defiance by one whaler in 1985, reduction of whales struck and lost, and workshops on the biology of the whale.*

In recent years there has been a concerted effort on the part of whalers to improve their efficiency so that subsistence hunting of the bowhead can continue without harm to the bowhead population. Research sponsored by the borough is directed towards aiding both the whalers and the whales with new technology that will result in fewer whales struck and lost. For example, ballistic research resulted in improved bombs, introduced in 1985, and researchers have been testing the feasibility of installing radio transmitters in floats to aid in the tracking of harpooned whales. Such inventions have met with mixed reactions among whalers; as Sadie commented, "When these people hunt they don't want any kind of interference with their traditional hunting." "Interference" in the form of quotas has had a significant impact on recent Iñupiat bowhead hunting. The quota system has resulted in a shortened whaling season, for once the quota is met, whaling ceases. Until 1985 this also meant the abandonment of fall whaling in Barrow, as the quota was met in the spring. The long-term effect of quotas and the resultant shortened whaling season[11] *will have a major impact on the transmission of whaling to a younger generation.*

Whether the relatively small quotas will allow all the aspiring young men (and perhaps women) sufficient experience and the opportunity to became skilled and successful at whale hunting is questionable. Nonetheless, evidence of the enduring cultural significance of whaling is easily seen, from the ice cellars full of meat, to the high school basketball team dubbed "The Barrow Whalers," to a mayoral reelection campaign slogan of "Keep on Whaling." Regardless of the changes imposed from outside on Iñupiat whaling, it is clear that the Barrow whalers intend to "keep on whaling" for a long time to come.

❖

Being a whaler's wife is just as much work as preparing to go out with a crew. Once your crew members are named, you have to see that they all have warm clothing, because they are outdoors all the time. So your husband buys all the fur. In the olden days, it was caribou hides, ruffs, fur socks, fur pants. We didn't have down clothing, so everything was made out of caribou hide or reindeer hide and sealskin for waterproof boots. New clothing is made every year because it's tradition. You started sewing in March if you knew who was going to be in your crew. The men had to have white canvas parka covers and waterproof boots. When you had to sew boots out of sealskin, that was a lot of work. If there's a person on the crew and no one to prepare their clothing, they asked the captain's wife. Our crew is mostly our boys, our two next-door neighbors, and our son-in-law, John. They had ready-made clothes and these big bunny boots that take the place of mukluks, but I had to make all new snow covers, white ones, to wear up there.

If you want a good skin on your husband's boat, you have to hire several women to sew together six or seven *ugruk* hides with waterproof seems and stretch them over a frame. That's prepared first. The boats suffer wear and tear because they have to drag them back and forth over the ice all the time. So the skins have to be replaced every year, though some who are careful can have theirs two or three years. And there are certain women who have the knack of sewing hides together so they don't bunch over the seam. I found that out about 1954 when my girl friend Terza [Hopson] and I tried our luck at sewing covers. Her husband's crew needed one, so we said, "We'll see. Maybe we could sew a seam." But when the

skin got stretched out on the frame, it didn't look at all like the work of the other women who are noted for their sewing of this type of skin. There was a whole groove across the skin where we failed to do like they did. We just sewed it without stretching it as we sewed. So we knew that you had to have the skill of sewing *ugruk* hides together.

The sewers also have to know how to make the thread; it's braided from caribou leg sinew, and then the part where you put the needle [i.e., eye of the needle] is made from the back sinew. You sit there and shred this before you start sewing [to] get it to the size and thickness you want. And it is hard on your lips. You have to wet it, and then if you twist it, it is ready for use. Younger women are starting to learn [to sew *ugruk* hides]. I was surprised this spring [1986] how many are asked to come in and observe to try to get the feel of sewing it, and to ask questions about how to sew the hides and how tight you have to pull your thread.

We had women here this spring [1986] sewing on hides to cover our boat. There's eight women. You pay them $50 [each] for one sewing of a skin, cutting and the inside. Pay them, feed them while they are sewing, and get their tea or whatever. We buy them their thread—$100 a set for one boat, and it costs $75 for one skin if you have to buy them. A set for one *umiaq* consists of five to six *ugruk* hides. Pretty expensive stuff. That's why they call the boat owners "*umialgich*."[12]

You also have to clean out your ice cellar where you keep your fresh meat; take the old stuff out and share it with whoever wants to come and take it. Because you're hoping that some new stuff will come in. A whale is so sacred with us that we listen to all these tales that say if you never share at least some of it in your cellar, and you say you don't have any more, it will show in your catch. It will be a part of that whale, where it looks as though it's rancid when you take it out. And on several occasions, I guess that has happened. Today nobody watches out for it, but the tradition is that you clean out all your storing area and prepare all new clothing when you go out whaling.

Sometimes you buy a new tent, or, if you can't afford it, you wash the old one. I called that laundry over there [Iñupiat Cleaners] and asked them if they would be able to wash a whole tent. They said,

"Well, let's see it first." So we took it over there, and they said they'd attempt to do it. They did wash it, but all the soot and stuff from the Primus stove never came out, but otherwise it got clean. Before that I used to rip apart the tent and sew it all over again, because it was much easier to wash in sections. The material shrinks when you do it that way, and you have to add on. It's a big tent—ten by ten [feet] with a three-and-a-half [foot] wall.

I sewed that tent on my Singer sewing machine—easy. Just have to know how to hold that bulk. And then you reinforce by hand where the ropes go to tie it. Otherwise they'll tear off. Because out there it gets wet, and you've got your Primus stove on. If there is snow falling on your tent, then when it freezes, it tears easy. So you have to reinforce your seams where you stretch it out. At the corners, and at the tips where you have your poles, you double the material. Then you have to sew another one for a cover. I found time to do all those things even while I was magistrate.

Then all the time the crew is out there, you fill all of their requests for food and cigarettes, and if their clothing needs mending or cleaning, you do it. In my spare time I would make them their bread and cook beans—freeze them, so they can chop them up into a fry pan. I'd prepare fish—take the fins off so it would fit in the pack and not take up so much room. You tried to use the smallest space possible—put everything in there for their needs and keep it light as possible. We used to then take it out to them with a dog team.[13] We didn't have any CB's then. Now we keep in touch with crews all the time. We're the Neakok base, and they're the Neakok crew. They call, "Neakok base; Neakok crew." Then you know you are being called. The others, they have their own calls—Half Moon Three base and crew; Igloo base and crew.

You stay close to your CB. We know when they catch a whale, who's got it, and what is needed out there. It's exciting. I can sit here and realize I'm inside the skin boat with the whalers. When they put a bomb in there, you sit there like you are inside the boat, just waiting for them to hoot and holler when the whale is dead. In the earlier days, you never knew who got a whale until some observer would say, "There's a runner coming in," and everybody would get out of their house to look. You knew who it was when you could recognize the design on the homemade flag the runner

was carrying. Each crew selects its own design for the flag. Ours is the black with a white diamond in the middle. We wanted something that will show. I made the flags. The big one stays with the boat, but there is a smaller one that the runner brings in to put on top of the house.

Nate has been a whaling captain for quite a while. He was a crew member for a whaling captain when he was much younger, but after we got married we had our own skin boat that Dad gave us. But we always traveled and let somebody else use our skin boat for whaling, and we'd get a big share out of the whale catch.[14] Nate decided to get his own crew after we had lived in this house for maybe five years. And in his time, I guess he has gotten about five whales. The last one was in 1984.[15] And you could see him cutting it up, measuring it for the various parts that go to certain people.

The fluke area is for the whaling captain, and then there's a belt of about eighteen to twenty inches wide which is for the captain's pleasure. It's up to the captain whether he wants to sell it; he talks with his crew whether they want a share of it for their own consumption or to sell it. And the captain's part is set aside by itself, to give to people at the whale catch celebration—*Nalukataq* time—and Thanksgiving and at Christmastime.[16] We cut it up in thirds for all the people. That's a lot of work, cutting it up. They put rings, rope rings, around the *maktak* that comes from the flukes, so they will know that it is part of the tail end of the whale. The meat, too, you put a certain color ribbon around each sack of meat; so we always know, when we get the sack out, what it's for.

In 1984 I came home from the hospital for Christmas. I wasn't home Thanksgiving, and the kids did it themselves and found out how much work there was. They had to bring in all that meat and halfway thaw it out, so they could cut it and freeze it over again to be ready for Thanksgiving. But at Christmastime, I came home and started to work. Nate got after me; the kids got after me. "Mom, you shouldn't do that." "Well, I am able to sit down and use my *ulu*, I'm not straining myself." So I helped cut up some of the meat. The Thanksgiving and the Christmas feast is a tradition started with churches by the missionaries, where we share our catch with everybody. The first one we share is at *Nalukataq*, which comes in

about a month after whaling season closes, usually in June on a warm day.

Mounted on Sadie's kitchen wall is a plaque presented to Nate Neakok by the twelve members of his whaling crew to commemorate Nate's catch of the first whale of 1984. Sadie provided the following account of the event:

The ice was breaking up, and the next day it turned out to be real nice, favorable weather. When Nate called me on that CB and wanted the menfolks out there, there was just Jimmy, and Robert, and George Zaya (a Cheechako [newcomer]), Dora, and Nate out on the ice. And Dora was still in the tent when the boys pulled the canoe out. I was talking to him, and then all of a sudden everybody got quiet on the CB, and some of the men even remarked, "Don't use the CB. We are in a serious situation. Somebody just put a bomb in a whale." And I listened here, and pretty soon a crew said, "Nate just put a bomb in, and it's got a float on it. Let's get to it." Then everybody started, all excited. They went after that, and before they could tow it in, then my brother Arnold, he gets another one and it's right next to his camp. So they get in before ours did. And one of Arnold's sons—Arnold, Jr.—said he hesitated putting the flag up on top of his house, because when he looked over across, we didn't have our flag up yet. They had quite a time bringing in Nate's whale. Two days later, Jake Adams, and who else [Eugene Brower], each got another one—two whales. And there was a fifth one, a wounded whale that they went after.

We waited. We wanted to know who was bringing our flag in. And then somebody, as though they heard us, yelled, "Hey, Tagiagiña, here comes your flag!" And we all ran out, and it was Robert who'd come in with a skidoo. We all had to go down over on that side quite a ways to see him coming from the ice. And I wanted to ask so many questions, because Nate was the only one that knew how to whale, and he had Jimmy, Robert, and this George, who had never had any experience with whaling. And when he told the story, I tell you we almost split apart laughing at what they went through to get that whale.

Nate said, "Now, when I look back, you boys shove the boat and get in there, because I will be right on top of the whale." Well, he said he had the harpoon ready. And he got in the front when half of that boat was in the water and half was on the ice, so when he turned back, he figured, well, they understood. When the boat didn't move, he looked back again, and there's the boys sitting in the canoe on top of the ice instead of shoving the boat out. And then when they actually did get in the water, and Nate put the bomb in the whale, this boy George had never been around where a bomb exploded inside of the whale. It jarred them when it went off. And then the gun, shoulder gun, was right there, and Robert was sprawled out, trying to get to it, and his foot is caught on one of the ladders [thwarts?], and when he shot it, it didn't go off. So Nate got the harpoon in with the float, just barely made it, and it went in the whale.

And when George came in, I said, "How do you feel, catching a whale, my crewman?" And he laughed; he said, "I am ashamed of myself because I didn't even know which way to paddle the boat." And he sat at the rear end of the boat, where he is supposed to make the boat go this way or that, as steersman. And so when Nate would go this way, then he would start going the other way and paddle away from the whale. Nate said he looked back, and Jimmy was the only one doing it for all he was worth, right in the middle. But we all laughed when they told their story.[17] It was some experience for the boys. We got some pictures of the whale when they were towing it in.

You have to feed the whole town; that's the custom. We had people waiting here; we had water boiling, but no meat had come in yet. So we got on the CB: "When do you think you might bring us the feast for the whole town, the meat for us to cook?" "Well, we are in the process of doing it, but we need some help." All the boys at work got off work to help. Some of our crew members—the people next door, Mark and his son—had given up and were going to go up inland, and they said they got halfway up there when somebody told them that our crew got the whale. They came right back and went out to help bring it in and cut it.

My friends, my old friends, came in and helped me cook it. Half the time I never knew who I was giving the meat to; I was so busy

trying to do it as fast as I could, because we had so many people. They were even upstairs; they'd go upstairs and sit down, and some would put some *maktak* in a little bag and then go out. One of my old friends, Flora, cooked up a whole batch of fried bread and brought it over; so we were serving that, too. Everybody enjoyed our whale. There are so many people in town now—even our whites have acquired the taste of fresh *maktak* and meat, and they mingle in with our people—and feeding some three and four thousand in one day out of that whale, by 10:00 P.M. we were all in.

Then you do it all over again at *Nalukataq* time. You have to cut up meat and *maktak* and put it into containers to age. It's known as *mikigaq*, sweet meat. Whale meat is the only meat I know that will ferment and sweeten like berries. It has a lot of sugar in it. You cook the heart, and the kidney, and the intestines at *Nalukataq* time.[18] You start cooking the day before, and then you start serving. They start gathering early. If there are people out there in the windbreak, where *Nalukataq* is going to be, you go and serve them their breakfast—coffee, donuts, or whatever you have, cereal. Then at lunch time you serve your soups, your hot soups, then your fried bread again. Oh, that's a lot. We had box after box of bread, and sack after sack; the table was filled with donuts made the day before. Cases and cases of "Sailor Boy" crackers to go with their soup—goose or duck soup. I was up at six o'clock in the morning making soup.

[At *Nalukataq*] they throw candy for the kids and whoever wants it. It's thrown from behind the windbreak; when they use [transparent sheets of] plastic visquine you can see the people throwing. Before, when they used the boats [*umiat* on their sides] and the old tarps, you couldn't see anyone; you didn't know until it hit you. Oh, it's a lot of excitement when it happens. Then there's the blanket toss and the dances, but it's not like the old days anymore. People didn't work in those days when I was young. Now we have to wait till everybody gets off work to serve our big portions of whale. It starts at five.

✣

As far back as I can remember, in the old tradition, women were out there on the ice with the men. They could go out and hunt with

the menfolk; they would cook for them, or sew, or tend to their men's needs out there. But we are shying off from that today. There's not very many women who would go out and stay out there, but Nate gives our girls a chance to be out there. Margaret, our oldest girl, and Dora, our youngest daughter, were out there in 1984.[19] The only time women weren't allowed on the ice was if they were menstruating or having a baby; besides, the grunting and moaning would scare off the whales! It was taboo, for you were unclean at that period in your life.

When you're a whaling captain's wife, your part is just as important as the men's because you're entrusted with keeping your husband's crewmen out there comfortable and fed. You're in charge of all of their care, preparing their food. . . . While they're out there, you don't want to do anything else but listen to the CB, though there is lots of work to be done. When the boats start chasing a whale, all you do is just listen to see who is catching it. It gets so exciting, like you are inside of the boat yourself. It's an exciting event when your crew gets a whale, a lot of work, but when all the women's work of feeding the whole town is done, then you feel like you have shared in the whale catch.

10

Retirement

> In the case of old women, the transition [to old age] was somewhat more dramatically marked [because of the cessation of the menses]. The old woman was as active as she chose, the work habits of a lifetime probably being too well engrained to ignore. . . . The old woman was regarded as endowed with rather pronounced supernatural powers. These they could use to their own advantage, causing illness and death of those who offended them. But an old woman could also be friendly and could use her powers to the advantage of others, particularly of children. As is so often the case in societies where the work load is so well defined, the grandmother, and to a lesser extent, the grandfather, become guardians of the young.
>
> Old women also busied themselves about the house or camp. When their place as cook in the household had been taken by a younger woman, they continued to sew, to make bags, to gather feathers and willows for bedding, and the like. [Spencer 1959:251–52]

It is only with retirement and illness that Sadie has had the leisure to reflect upon her busy life—to devote the hours to interviewing that she did in 1984 and 1985. Even though she considers herself retired from the white man's world of government employment, she is by no means retired from her other roles. In April of 1986 she went with a group of North Slope Iñupiat to Greenland on a two-week cultural exchange program—"My first trip, with a passport, out of U.S. territory," she remarked. In May her reading of the manuscript was put aside during whaling season, and, since Nate and his crew had taken a whale, in June there were preparations for Nalukataq.

During the fourth week in June, 1986, the North Slope Borough hosted the Elders' Conference, focusing this year on native law ways and the white man's legal system. Sadie, not surprisingly, was selected as a keynote speaker. July, she hoped, would bring a trip upriver with Nate to retrieve a boat that a son had cached the previous fall. Added to these activities is the daily rhythm of keeping

a household for a still large family. Even when she was recuperating from surgery in the summer of 1985, Sadie was active—cleaning out her freezer, searching for pots and pans misplaced by household members during her hospitalization, cutting ugruk, *baking bread each morning, and preparing daily lunches and dinners for ten or so people.*

❖

I officially retired in '78, but actually I was in and out of that courthouse whenever I was needed until 1980, when I started getting problems with my health. I would be judge for a day, judge for a week, maybe a couple of months. Jeannie Cross was magistrate until she started having problems with her pregnancy, and then I responded because I didn't know what else to do. Another time I stepped in for three weeks to give her a chance to go to the Magistrate Seminar for her training, and when she came back, I pulled out again. It was like that when she was not able to hear cases; I was right back on the bench. Until, finally, I got this sickness and I just refused to go back anymore.

I was under such heavy medication, I wouldn't have been any good anyway. This medication I had for blood clots left me so drugged that I couldn't have worked in there. I had to take it all the time. Two hours after I took my medication, I could never function as a normal person because I was so drugged. I just wasn't myself. It was like dreaming and listening to people talking way out. They would be very close to me, but their voices would be over my head somewhere. It affected me like that. Then it would start wearing off after two hours, and I would break into a sweat. It was miserable. I had to take that heavy steroid medication for two years. After the first year, they tried to take me off of it. And then I had a relapse—I started getting these episodes of blindness—and they put me right back on it again. I was taken out of any strenuous work, and I couldn't read anymore because it affected my eyes; then, because of the steroids, cataracts started forming.

I got in an accident last year [1984], in October. I got thrown off the sled with such force that I ruptured my stomach; I just about tore it in half. I lost so much blood with it. I don't even remember going to the hospital. And then, when they finally operated, I came out of it. They didn't realize that my whole intestinal area was

swollen. They fed me too soon, and I started throwing up and just ripped all my stitches. And that's when they knew that I couldn't heal up because I had so much steroids in my system. And that was a mess. So they put me on an IV—fed me with that for six weeks—and finally I started healing up.

But then, when I started having problems with walking—I couldn't walk anymore—the doctor tried me with sixty milligrams of steroids for a week, and then I went back and had my test, but it didn't do any good. So I got sent out in June [1985] to the hospital in Anchorage. The arteries had closed at the base of my legs, and I had no circulation in my legs. So they put a new artery in me. And then I had an eye operation for the cataracts that were caused by steroids, so I'm really a newly manufactured person. Even the doctors joked with me about it and said all that was missing now was for me to get a face lift. I had a new stomach, I had new arteries, and I had new eyes.

Nate and I both retired at the same time. He was a heavy-duty mechanic and machinery operator at the base. When that base first opened he trained on the job until he became an ace mechanic. Any outfit that wanted to sell tractors or machinery that had broken down, they used to get my husband to come and check the machinery before they would sell it. And if he okayed it, then it went on sale. Responsibilities like that he had for many years. Then when the gas well opened, he was entrusted to watch the gauges, the pressure, and keep check on how much was coming into the community. He had to record that with numbers, by looking at those gauges out there at the gas well.

Finally he retired due to the deterioration of his limbs. He couldn't work with heavy machinery anymore. That was caused by a drug, they say. In 1969, when he punctured his lung on the job, for fear of TB they sent him down to Anchorage and had him treated. And they used this new drug on him which eventually deteriorated his legs. They stopped it all right with medication of some kind. All they use now is this electrode of some kind to check him once a year.

We didn't know any hobby when we retired. We looked at each other just sitting there and got on each other's nerves. This went on for a long time until we talked it over. We had to learn something

and do something to get out of each other's way, so Nate started doing carving, and I started sewing, making garments, and working with baleen.[1] I also began drawing or making sketches on paper, which I used to be very good at when I was younger.

When I fully recover from my surgery, Nate wants to take me off inland somewhere for about two or three months and see how good we are at our age doing the things that we used to do. So, that's coming yet, maybe within a month or so. We will have to take all of our winter clothes and a boat. A tent with an outside covering of maybe plywood or something to give a windbreak. We'll go to the river, where there is good fishing. The fish-runs in the river start around the latter part of September—the big white fish we call *aanaakliq* in Eskimo. In certain lakes, we fish for trout, too, and Nate knows where all of those are. So when we camp, then he will point the direction which way and how many miles it is from where we camp to a certain lake where there is trout or burbot.

Right now I don't have too many plans for the future. But once I respond to help out with a problem, then my phone is going to start ringing. If word gets around that I helped out at the school[2] other outfits are going to start asking me—the ones I had refused earlier. But since I've had my health go back on me, I've learned to say no. Even the court system has tried, and I'm proud of myself when I say no, for my health's sake. It's not a very proud thing to do, but when people of your community know what you're capable of doing, they'll keep asking, regardless of how old you are.

I got a call the other day from a woman who was just about giving up everything. Her husband has found somebody else in Fairbanks. I told her to go talk to her lawyer, and if she's not making enough, to go and see legal service personnel over here, get their advice. So that type of thing still comes to me. And people who are already in jail, writing me letters: "Can you help me somehow? Get a copy of my whole case or something?" Sometimes I go to the lawyers direct with the letters, show them what their former clients are going through—what they are feeling. And I kept getting summons to jury duty. The poor prosecutor never won any of his cases when I got on. When I came back after my operation [1985], I got summoned again, but I got excused. I told them, "I don't want to be a juror. I am seventy years old now, and I don't want to be a juror."[3]

What they want me to do now is to represent Barrow as a delegate to the ICC [Inuit Circumpolar Conference, held in 1986 in Kotzebue]. I just don't want to go. There should be some other person. I think I put enough input in my life for whatever, and I want to just go out and be free and do what I want to do. And it's hard. I want to just go gallivanting while my health holds out, go with Nate and be with him, hunt and be where we used to be. I want to be free with my own kind of work, no supervisors—go out fishing, get the fish and strip it, dry it, store it—no pressure anywhere.

In July of 1986, Sadie and Nate left by helicopter to retrieve the boat their son had left inland. They planned to spend a leisurely month working their way back to Barrow, camping and fishing. The Inuit Circumpolar Conference took place as scheduled in late July and early August, without Sadie Neakok as a Barrow delegate.

During the three summers of our interviews, Sadie offered two comments on growing old. As she and Nate waited in their kitchen for a helicopter ride in the summer of 1986, she joked about what might befall them at their ages [70] should they wrench their backs trying to move the boat they hoped to bring home. "We might just end up lying there not able to get up," she laughed. "Let me tell you, growing old is the pits!" After assuring me that I could quote her, she added, "But I intend to keep active to the very end." In addition to her commitment to physical vigor, Sadie offered the field school students in 1984 the following perspective on aging: "You learn everyday. It seems like, even as old as I am today, I learn new things. You don't cease to be a student."

Epilogue

"There's So Much More"

> The perceptions of any people wash over the land like a flood, leaving ideas hung up in the brush, like pieces of damp paper to be collected and deciphered. No one can tell the whole story. [Lopez 1986:272]

It is difficult to bring to closure a life story such as Sadie's; the ending is always arbitrary, for the life, if not the telling of it, continues. It is difficult, too, for there is a certain seductiveness to storytelling—the desire to hear one more story, to do one more interview before considering the project "complete" enough to commit to the printed word. Other obligations, financial constraints, and promised deadlines, if nothing else, draw such projects to their inevitable conclusions. Still, one muses how subsequent life experiences might affect the telling of the story, could the life history enterprise be indefinitely continued. Thus, I was eager to see what new perspectives Sadie might offer in 1987, after a year's hiatus in the telling of her story.

July fourth, 1987, found me back in Barrow with my husband, preparing to do another field school for Barrow high school students. The previous October, part of an archaeologically rich mound on the bluff facing the Chukchi Sea had washed into the sea during a storm, and the remainder of the mound was in danger of further slumping. Field school students would be learning culture history while doing salvage archaeology on the bluff and at the nearby site of the North Slope Borough's proposed museum. They would be interviewing elders, too, but interviews would concentrate this time on studying artifacts from the dig, learning native skills that are still practiced today, and finding out about the site of the archaeological excavation.

Before the field school began on July sixth, we treated ourselves to Barrow's Fourth of July festivities, watching the parade from Browerville to Barrow: the color guard, the fire trucks, the search-and-rescue unit, and restaurant owner

Fran Tate throwing candy to eager kids from Pepé's "float." Friendly competitive events followed the parade on the playground below Sadie's house: the egg toss, the kids' bike race, the cutest baby contest. When the wind got too cold, we left to pay a visit to Sadie. Nate had been out videotaping the festivities with the video camera she had bought him for Christmas, but Sadie was inside, and she warmed us with hot tea and coffee.

The holiday had not kept her from her work; in fact, she remarked how thankful she was for the three-day weekend because she had decided to wash the family's work clothes and parkas (which required dismantling). To my mind, washing the clothing of six men in a wringer-washer without the luxury of running water was no small order. But Sadie matter-of-factly dismissed the magnitude of the chore, remarking that all one had to do with the parkas was reattach the fur ruffs and the zippers once the garments were clean! As we drank our tea, we discussed the status of the book. We made plans for an afternoon's interview to address issues raised by reviewers of the manuscript and to talk of her life since the last time we had met.

On that visit as well as each of the previous times I had interviewed her, I found myself marveling at Sadie's energy. Sadie is a "doer," readily confessing that she can't stand to be idle; her life history is ample testimony to that confession. Even just home from the hospital in 1985, under doctors' orders to take it easy, Sadie was far from inactive. One day that summer when we began our interview, she informed me she had spent the morning cleaning out a deep-freeze full of spoiled meat. During the course of another afternoon's interview, Sadie remembered that she had forgotten to get out meat for dinner. Hurrying to the freezer, she returned with the hindquarter of a caribou, grabbed a large saw, and began vigorously cutting the frozen roast to fit the pan, speaking all the time to my tape recorder across the room.

In the interim between our visit on the Fourth of July, 1987, and my interview with her three weeks later, Sadie had come and gone to her fish camp and had processed large quantities of meat and fish. When I arrived for our interview with my daughter just after lunch on a slow afternoon, freshly cut fish hung on the rack above Sadie's kitchen stove to dry; she had just folded a large stack of laundry belonging to one of her children and had baked two long loaves of bread and two dozen rolls. I wondered aloud if the baked goods would last the family two days. Sadie laughed, assuring me they would likely be gone by dinner that same night.

My first question that day, addressing her comment after reading the manuscript that "there was so much more . . . ," did not elicit the elaboration I

had expected. Instead, Sadie recounted major turning points or marker events in her life: Maria's return to the Brower family when her adoptive parents died; what Sadie had learned of value from her parents which she did not appreciate until later; how difficult it was going Outside to San Francisco, and how she saw the world through new eyes when she returned home; leaving for Eklutna and college; her welfare work; and her career as a magistrate. The life story was retold, in abbreviated form, and I had the comfortable feeling of one who had listened before and could anticipate the narrative. It was not important that I had already heard the story; like all stories, Sadie's is meant to be retold. I did learn "more" that afternoon, but not necessarily in answer to the specific question I had asked.

As Sadie retold her life story, and as she later related how she had spent the past year, I was struck with her "public" focus. Because Sadie spent more than forty years as a public servant, it is not surprising that Barrow and the changes that have been visited upon the community and its people should comprise the context of her story. Much of Sadie's life has been of and for the public; her repeated use of the phrase "my people" reminds us of this fact. Moreover, in her narrative, Sadie's public role takes precedence over her familial role; husband and children become the backdrop to Sadie's busy public life as welfare workers and magistrate.

In this respect, her life as told bears a striking similarity to Charles Brower's account of his life on the North Slope. In The Northernmost American, *Brower is the focal point around which Barrow's history unfolds. His personal life, as noted previously, is far more minimized in his account than Sadie's is in hers. Like her father, Sadie has helped bring the Outside world to Barrow, turning her newly found knowledge to improvement of the standard of living and health conditions, and ever instructing. Reciprocally, she has introduced Outsiders to Barrow. As Outside visitors found their way to Charlie Brower's "station" in the early years of the twentieth century, so more recent ones have called upon his daughter. Sadie recounted in some detail a two-week visit from Naomi Uemura, a Japanese adventurer-explorer who made a solitary journey to the North Pole.*[1] *Her description of Uemura's visit recalled Charles Brower welcoming Amundsen, Eielson, Wilkins, Stefansson, and Rasmussen on their travels. Judges and college professors visiting Barrow have dropped in on Sadie from time to time; Alaska Court System personnel routinely have depended upon her when they have come to town; and today, tourists and journalists, not to mention anthropologists, find their way to Sadie's two-story green house.*

Throughout her adult life Sadie has been caught up in Barrow's growing pains, and communitywide problems have seemed to loom larger to her than any personal misfortunes of her own. In seeking an accommodation of her people and community to the white man's ways, Sadie has seen herself engaged in a perpetual struggle. She has battled tuberculosis, poor sanitation, alcoholism, the inefficiencies of the trial courts in bush Alaska, the BIA school system, infringements on subsistence hunting, and more.[2]

Because she is capable and because she is a Brower, Sadie has been called upon to do virtually everything. If someone else bungled it, Sadie could straighten it out, as she proved with each new assignment undertaken. Sadie has seen herself as privileged because of her education, and I think she also has seen herself as privileged simply because she is a Brower. The Brower name has carried weight and has opened doors, not just in Barrow but throughout Alaska where Charles Brower is known. At the same time, privilege carries with it enormous responsibility to community; accordingly, Sadie appears to have seldom turned down requests for help. As a result, Sadie has worked multiple jobs—teaching and welfare work, welfare work and magistrate—a situation not uncommon in changing cultures where a handful of talented native people have acquired skills outside that setting.

Eventually, and inevitably perhaps, Sadie's multiple roles began to conflict. Being the welfare worker to a family whose breadwinner she'd sentenced to jail became unbearable. Other conflicts arose on ideological grounds. One of Sadie's more difficult tasks as magistrate was grappling with the subsistence laws that impeded the livelihood of her people. Although she was able to manipulate the system to serve their needs on occasion—such as the time she confiscated the evidence (a moose killed out of season) under her authority as magistrate, and turned around and distributed it to the needy (the hunter's family) as welfare worker—there were other times when she simply had to withdraw by stepping down from the bench.

One of the most intriguing aspects of Sadie's multiple roles is the balancing act she has had to perform between careers and domestic life. One wonders how she found time for family when she spent all day in the courthouse and came home to a lineup of people outside her house requesting assistance in filling out various government forms. The modern urban woman managing one or two children and a full-time career must give pause to ponder what it would be like with twelve or even eight or six children, never mind two full-time jobs, and the occasional foster child.

Sadie's older children did look after the younger ones, probably in much the

same way that Sadie's sister Maria as a young child packed her younger siblings on her back, and there was a baby-sitter to watch over the household during the day. Also, Barrow was then a very small community, where neighbors were kin and where the mechanics of commuting to work and back involved walking out the door and over to the courthouse a few blocks away. Still, the sheer amount of laundry and simple provisioning which fell upon Sadie's shoulders must have been staggering. Would that one could conduct a retrospective time-motion study that would reveal, moment to moment, what a typically busy day for Sadie was really like. As an Iñupiaq in a community of large families, bearing and mothering thirteen children was matter-of-fact for Sadie. And, coming from a culture where adoption of children was routine, taking in foster children as part of her job was also not unexpected. Thus, it is not surprising that the domestic aspect of her life was, to Sadie, not nearly as worthy of comment as were her public roles.

Yet Sadie's parenthetical comments during our afternoon interview confirmed that, at age seventy-one, she continues to play an active role as mother and provisioner to her still large household (four sons and a grandson). "Oh, that's an endless job," Sadie remarks of her family. "And at this time, right now, from April on, it's a busy, busy time, because the men are out hunting and they are forever bringing in their catches. . . . Mealtime," she muses, "is a free-for-all for everybody. They gang up on me—get off work—'Mom, what you got for supper? You got enough if we come?' 'Sure, always enough for everybody.'" Although Sadie is helped from time to time by her two daughters who live in Barrow and a daughter-in-law living next door, as the only woman in a household of active male hunters (and unmarried sons), she may well be busier preparing meals, sewing, and processing food than the average Barrow woman her age.

In discussing her family in 1987, Sadie elucidates her role as family disciplinarian. Because of medication prescribed years ago (see p. 219), Nate has problems with loss of strength in his hands and relies on his sons for help with heavy work. "He comes over and cries on my shoulders," Sadie admits, "[saying] 'I need this and I need that.' Then I get after the boys . . . he hates to chew them out and he lets me do all the chewing. One day I got so mad at him and [at] chewing out the boys and talking to them. I look at him and, 'Nate, how come you are not opening your mouth?' I bet he's just listening to me, keeping it closed. I was so mad at him. Then he smiled. He said, 'You do more than I do, putting your point across.' Always been like this—mothers. . . ."

As a mother, as one who voluntarily took on foster children to mother, and as

a magistrate who even approached the bench "like a mother" (see p. 202), it may seem unusual that Sadie speaks so sparingly of her family in her life history. Perhaps, as noted above, to Sadie, her public role, not her life as a mother, is the stuff of life stories. In Barrow, while mothering is an expected part of every woman's life, playing a leading role in directing the history of the community and the North Slope is not. Then too, Sadie has had the model of Charles Brower, who hardly acknowledges his family in his autobiography. When I have asked her about her apparent silence regarding her children, she does draw a parallel to her father: "Well, like Dad, too. He didn't say a whole a lot about his children." But, in response to this omission, Sadie elaborates on her family:

They were born, every one, eighteen months apart, and they are different. There's no two alike, and they have different ambitions. Most of them [the males] are mechanics, because their dad was a mechanic. And Donna is with the health board; the oldest girl [Margaret], her husband flies a lot, and she goes wherever he goes. Dora just went up to fish camp. She told her boss she wanted a week off to be with Mama and hunt and fish. . . . She's the hunter, of the girls, and carpenter. The boys . . . Billy was a mechanic and worked at the weather bureau for many, many years. Then he got interested in law in '72; he went to paralegal training in D.C. Ronald's the mechanic. He's the stripper on the sand spit down there and is always coming in with fossilized bones and old ivory and stuff. And Danny, he went to Seward to train as a mechanic, but he had an accident and broke his temple. . . . It still bothers him when he is doing any strenuous work. Robert, the youngest one, he is a laborer; he's with Public Works. George is with GSI [Geophysical Service, Inc.], the clean-up crew. They fly with the helicopter and they clean up the tundra where the Navy had distributed drums and stuff. Charlie is with the water plant.

Three sons are not mentioned in Sadie's enumeration of her children. I suspect the omission is because of her focus on activity and work as opposed to character or personality traits. Jimmy, who is retarded, lives at home, helps out about the house, and goes hunting and camping with the rest of the family. She had previously discussed the illness that led to his brain damage and his return to the family (see p. 133). Pat is currently in prison, serving time on a

manslaughter sentence in the killing of his brother Glenn in October of 1985. Sadie had said little of this tragedy in 1986, except to speak of how the family had pulled through it. She elaborated when we talked in 1987. "Well, I was never asked about it until I heard the whole thing in court. I have always felt that one day, somewhere, with our family as big, that an accident was bound to happen. All these young men, when they get together when I am away, I guess it just had to come true. But he wasn't the only one, I tell you. There were four accidents like that [shootings in the fall of 1985]. They charged him with manslaughter, which has a sentence of up to no more than ten years, and five of that was suspended. So when the judge came out and said, 'You can appear for parole in '88,' he asked me—I thought that was very strange—'How do you feel about your son?' 'Right now I feel numbness, the only way I can describe it.' I had no feelings of blame towards Pat, but I thought that was kind of—I think he [the judge] wanted to feel me out about parole."

Sadie sat through the whole trial, mourning one son, wondering at the fate of another, and learning things about both that she would rather have not. "I was so surprised to hear they were smoking marijuana, and one of the boys had cocaine, or something, that night. And it really hurt me to hear that. They had been pretty honest with Nate and me growing up."

In the face of this recent tragedy, Sadie balances a certain fatalism with her optimism. She seems to have done so throughout life. Just as Vilhajalmur Stefansson once described Charlie Brower as a cheerful optimist, so does Sadie appear throughout her life history. While "problems," "burdens," and "struggles" are recurrent in Sadie's characterization of her public service in Barrow, she has nonetheless acted on the conviction that she could make a difference.

If she was optimistic, she was even more determined, taking on the job of magistrate, for example, after one person had already failed at it, and at a time when she was just weeks short of delivering her twelfth child. Sadie's efforts to become educated marked the beginning of her lifelong determination to accomplish, a determination undoubtedly nourished by the high hopes her father placed in her. Only one out of the four siblings that preceded her Outside had stuck it out and pursued the education that Brower so desperately wanted his children to have. Though she completed high school and was accepted at Stanford, Sadie saw her Outside education as a lengthy struggle. Forced to repeat the eighth grade and to practice her English daily in front of a mirror, Sadie was almost five years in becoming convinced that she "was just as good as they [the white students] were."

The struggle was more than an academic one, as Sadie several times wished

for the freedom that she perceived her sister Maria to have, who did not go Outside to school. Furthermore, she would have thrown over school in a moment to be in a Hollywood film, had her father allowed it. Charles Brower, it seems, tried almost everything to keep Sadie in school, from putting his foot down, to bribery. Whether his tactics worked or Sadie finished school out of love and respect for her father, or both, is not known; what is clear, though, is the sense of accomplishment she derived from completing something that was personally as well as academically difficult.

Sadie's parents were particularly important in nurturing her commitment to community, and Sadie herself believes that she has taken both of their places. "Mom used to tell me that one of these days I would follow in his footsteps, taking care of this whole community, along with keeping people, because I had a tendency to make things work right. I was sort of 'domineering,' or whatever she called it. I wasn't that at all. But I was there to help people, like she was. I got it from her, I guess, and my dad, his nature, helping people out with the law." Charles Brower filled several important roles in Barrow open only to one who was educated—storekeeper, commissioner, postmaster, game warden, census taker. Native people looked to him as a source of information on, and as their intermediary with, the culture that was increasingly impinging on their world. Brower was a powerful figure in Barrow, and, in her several leadership roles, Sadie does seem to have stepped into his shoes.

But it is to Asianggataq that we must look for the source of Sadie's humanitarianism. The Iñupiat prescription to share overrode the operating rules of the Cape Smythe Whaling and Trading Company. Asianggataq routinely raided the store's shelves with impunity to give to Barrow's needy. And that is how Sadie remembers her mother—sharing, doing for the community, caring. Like her mother, there is much about Sadie that is unselfish; she, too, has often fed the less fortunate—from Nate's larder of game and from leftovers at the hospital when she worked there as cook. We see Sadie in her roles as teacher, welfare worker, and magistrate not so much powerful (though she is) as caring.

Her success as a magistrate, in particular, had much more to do with her compassion and understanding than with her legal mind. Sadie's involvement went beyond the duties of the job itself; the townspeople called on her when they had family problems, marital problems, and financial problems. She listened to them all, and because of her caring, she bore individually and collectively the town's burdens, suffering, according to her colleagues in the Alaska Court System, each time she imposed a sentence.

Today, Sadie's warmth and compassion are readily evident to the Outside visitor in her home: She drops whatever she is doing to reach for a visiting grandchild, engaging the baby in an exchange of coos and smiles; she talks long distance to two of her sons, her closing message—"We're thinking of you; we love you." It is her compassion, her understanding of the human condition, and her lack of pretense that make Sadie such a comfortable and open life history subject.

❖

We talked, too, that July 1987 afternoon, of how Sadie spends her days now. "I have been busy," she began.

I was selected to go down to the [Inuit] Circumpolar Conference, and then Nate and I were invited up to the Fairbanks Correctional Center to visit with the inmates up there and talk to them and join their potluck and see what they go through, because we are sort of suppliers for them, knowing that the kids need baleen, ivory, and bones. And we just send it up when they need it, and they wanted us to go up there and see what the boys make out of them. So it was enjoyable. Then I got invited to the AFN [Alaska Federation of Natives] Convention, to take part in the senior citizens program and talk about many things that are with subsistence, and hunting, and what our people are going through with these laws. My part with that was to introduce to the senior citizens what the law was all about, you know, when it comes out from the legislature, and explain to them, and so on and so forth. Then, too, I have been quite active when they call me over at the court. Lately I've been interpreting for the defendants and their lawyers, and [also] being guardian *ad litem* for children's matters.

Although the present magistrate has resigned, Sadie refuses to go back to the bench even on a temporary basis. She does do the occasional arraignment, but not trials, saying she's been away from the law too long and doesn't know the new laws.

Sadie and Nate had a whaling crew out this year, she relates, and yes, graduation ceremonies at the University of Alaska, where she received an honorary doctorate, did take Nate away from whaling camp.

But we were in communication; the boys took over for us. We came back, and then the quota had already been met and all the boats started coming in. But some stayed out there, hoping to get ducks and seals and polar bears, but not the whale. Quota was done, and that's it. And by July, after the whale, *Nalukataq*. Then the people scatter, go to their hunting grounds while there's still ice on the ocean to travel on, and go way down with their skidoos. Or those where there is camp, where there is a place to land, they will take the small plane and go to their fish camps or hunting areas—like us, we go with our skidoo up to our fish camp for two weeks. Just got back. By August, when the caribou start fattening up, then we take our big boat and we go up the rivers, the mouth of the rivers, and then go in one of the leading rivers—the Meade, or Chipp River, or Topagoruk, and Alaktak, they are all up there—but you have to know which one to take. If the hunting is good on the Chipp River, then we go on the Chipp River. I feed the family, as usual. We close up the house and just go. Everybody goes. Unless somebody wants to be left behind.

Comings and goings are recurrent themes in Sadie's life history. Her progression through life is seen as a series of leavings and returnings—leaving to learn, returning with new knowledge which she eagerly applies. Following childhood in Barrow, Sadie leaves the small Iñupiat community at the top of the world for urban San Francisco, then comes home with new perceptions of her old world. She leaves again, this time for a less exotic setting closer to home, to put her education to use among natives in a vocational residential school, and she seeks further education herself, again within Alaska. She returns once again to Barrow, this time for good, and applies her education in the classroom. Marriage brings a leave-taking of a different sort, as Sadie and Nate travel and live off the land; Sadie returns with a knowledge no school could impart to her.

Becoming a magistrate requires her temporary absence once again, for one must go afield of Barrow to learn the white man's legal system. Throughout her years as magistrate, Sadie travels between two worlds: going out for training to Nome and Reno, touring Alaska as the state's "Mother of the Year," flying to Washington, D.C., to serve on a White House committee, and always back again to Barrow. Now in her retirement, Sadie enjoys the kind of leave-takings

of her early married years with Nate. Her comings and goings are not the prescribed travel of a government employee but are her own purposeful journeys, expressive of her freedom and of her connection to the land and to Iñupiat traditions.

Sadie's connection to Iñupiat traditions has always been strong, despite the influence of the world her father represented and to which he introduced her. As the offspring of a bicultural family in a native settlement, Sadie was somewhat unusual, particularly in the opportunities afforded her as she grew older. Her bicultural upbringing, however, is by no means unique, either on the North Slope or in Alaska generally.[3] *While Sadie is clearly comfortable in both white and Iñupiat worlds, her self-identification has always been "Eskimo." The differences she saw in childhood between herself and others were largely reflected in the rules imposed by her father—the nightly curfews and the required appearance at the dinner table—the kinds of annoying infringements that set one apart in minor ways from one's peers. Other differences gave her a decided advantage in a changing Arctic world. In particular, Sadie's knowledge of English—however "broken"—from earliest childhood put her ahead of other Barrow schoolchildren.*

Eskimo or not, it was clear that Charles Brower believed his children could and should adapt to life Outside, and he sent them south with that in mind. It seems that he wished Sadie to remain Outside, attend Stanford, and go as far with her education as opportunities would permit, despite the fact that she had tentatively been promised in marriage to a native Barrow man. When, to her father's exasperation, Sadie did return home, her friends called her a tanik*—white person—because of her strange accent, her halting Iñupiaq, her San Francisco clothing, her bleached, permed hair, and her newly acquired attitudes about health and hygiene. Although well aware of the gap between herself and the friends to whom she returned, Sadie certainly did not count herself among the "*taniks.*" If Sadie saw herself as Eskimo, however, she has always seen her husband Nate as much more so. He became Sadie's teacher of forgotten native ways, her bridge back to the Iñupiat world of her childhood, as she, reciprocally, became his window on the white man's world.*

Sadie used her skills to help Barrow people cope with the intricacies of the white man's world that had penetrated their Arctic outpost—unemployment forms, welfare regulations, Social Security. She became a cultural broker[4] *in her role as magistrate. She explained the legal system to Barrow people in their own language; she explained Barrow people to those with power in the court system; and, as much as she could, she adapted the legal system to the cultural*

realities of Barrow. The formalities of arraignments and sentencing were personalized, and the sentences imposed were not standardized but were derived from Sadie's personal knowledge of the individuals, their families, and the cultural milieu of the North Slope.

Though a lowly magistrate in an extremely hierarchical system, Sadie was important as the only legal officer serving an area the size of the state of California. And, as a native who understood the people with whom she had to deal as no other court-system person could, Sadie eventually did effect change. Winning the right for the native language to be the language of the court in cases where defendants did not speak English was probably her most significant victory, but she also successfully fought a protracted campaign for better services and equipment for the Barrow court.

Sadie brought to her campaign years of speaking out on matters of importance to her. Long before she gave a piece of her mind to the chief justice of the Alaska Supreme Court, or went over the head of her immediate superior when she did not get results, Sadie had confronted the town bully, had delivered an ultimatum to her affianced, had spoken up to her father when she and Nate approached him regarding marriage, and had told off the town gossip for accusing her of becoming pregnant before marriage.

In some respects Sadie's accomplishments are all the more noteworthy because, unlike the typical cultural broker, she is female. Sadie is a diminutive, unassuming woman who could easily have spent all her time mothering her large brood of children, preparing food for her family, keeping house, and sewing winter garments for her hunter husband; in addition to these full-time jobs, she became a key figure in the introduction of the American legal system to bush Alaska as well as an advocate and spokeswoman for her people.[5]

❖

Our interview came to an end in the late afternoon, as the time drew near for Sadie to begin dinner preparations and for the men of the household to return home from their various jobs. We had covered much ground in three hours, some of it familiar, some of it new territory: the retelling of Sadie's story; her childhood relationship with her older sister Maria; the mother of Charlie Brower's first child, Elizabeth; Sadie's children and foster children; the untimely death of her son in 1985; her activities during the past year, including her receipt of an honorary doctorate; and Barrow's new senior citizens' home. I left, having learned more, but knowing there is much more to learn about Sadie Neakok and her times.

During my month in Barrow in 1987, incidental conversations with others offered more perspectives on Sadie's story. Our translator for the field school project remembered when she, along with other Barrow youth (including one of Sadie's sons), appeared for the first time before Magistrate Sadie Neakok for arraignment; she was young and afraid, and, worst of all, Sadie made her move to the front of the courtroom. One of Sadie's nephews remembered a fight with one of her sons over a basketball, and the resolution imposed by Sadie, who cut the contested ball in half, resewed it, and made it into two "footballs." Additional perspectives could be obtained on Sadie's life, but, like most life histories, this one, for a variety of reasons,[6] has focused almost exclusively on the subject's own perspective. How would Sadie be seen by her sons and daughters? by patient, reticent Nate? by her rival sibling Maria? by the odd individual in the community who does not like her? Sadie's life story could also be cast against the experience of other Iñupiat women of her generation as well as those of prior and succeeding generations. And how similar is her life experience to that of other bicultural women and men of the North Slope, many of whose fathers, like Charles Brower, were Yankee whalers? In the near future we can begin to address some of these comparisons. The North Slope Borough's Commission on Iñupiat History, Language and Culture, recognizing the importance of life history as a medium for recording Iñupiat tradition, has sponsored and encouraged research. Genealogical information is collected at the borough's Elders' Conferences; an individual in each of the borough's village communities has been entrusted with taping elders' stories and brief life-history data; and Sadie's niece, University of Alaska professor Edna MacLean, in 1985 directed the collection of six Iñupiat life histories. Of these, the life history of Waldo Bodfish, son of a New England whaler and an Iñupiaq mother, is being prepared for publication.[7]

The life history is always a partial story. Parts of the story are inevitably withheld, consciously or unconsciously, and a series of transmutations occurs from the actual telling of the story to the printed word: the translation of experience to words, the selection of words appropriate to the audience, and the rearrangement of those words by the interviewer/collaborator for publication. It is not necessarily the same story that would be told were the account strictly autobiographical; nor is it identical to the story that would be told by the same subject to a different collaborator; nor is it the same as that told at an earlier or later point in time. The life history is a singular creation, born of the collaboration of two[8] unique individuals, working together at a particular time and place. Yet there is a structure to the story that transcends audience, place,

and time. When I listened to tapes of Sadie speaking at the 1986 Elders' Conference, when I watched a video of her presentation in 1986 to the borough's new Public Safety officers, and when I listened to her 1974 interview with Neville Jacobs,[9] *I recognized the stories that she had told to me over the four summers of our collaboration.*

Like all life histories, Sadie's offers a window on her era and the culture of her people, but, as Barry Lopez contends, no one can tell the whole story. There is no singular life history of an individual. There are, instead, many variants of the same life, each reflecting the time and context in which they were collected and retold, each expressing many of the same stories, but each also revealing experiences that both the interviewer and the life history subject bring to their collaborative effort. As the native people of the North Slope continue to probe their own cultural heritage, and as they begin to explore in depth the lives of their own people, we look forward to the new dimensions they will add to the life history enterprise.

Appendix
The Examined Life

A properly constructed life history reads with an immediacy that makes the reader feel like the exclusive audience to a well-told story. In actuality, however, a life history culminates a complex series of interactions between life history subject and interviewer(s). Describing the permutations of a life story, Edward Bruner (1984) distinguishes between the life as lived (reality); the life as experienced, with all the richness of images, feelings, and meanings that the individual imparts to it; and the life as told (expression), the attempt to represent the richness of the experience through the limited medium of language. In eliciting the life history, we have access to only the third order, the life as told or represented.

But the transformations do not end with the life history subject's representation of his/her life. A life history is the outcome of a dialogue—an interview—in which questions are asked and answers (the life history narrative) are proffered, though it seldom appears this way in final form. The life history text is influenced by numerous factors: the social/cultural context within which the interviews take place; the conventions of storytelling within that context; the audience to whom the text is related (interviewer and future readers); and the subjective world of the life history subject at the time of the interviews. At the same time, the life history text is ontological, negotiated consciously or unconsciously as the teller expresses and the interviewer experiences that expression and responds to it.[1]

The interviewer, having received the story, shaped it through inquiry, and recorded it, inevitably retells it—the expression of the expression, as it were, or, as Bruner (1984) puts it, the interpretation of the interpretation. The retelling ranges from simply producing verbatim transcripts of oral history, to editing and rearranging text in a form that is meaningful to both the intended audience and the life history subject, that follows certain literary conventions,[2] *and that meets the implicit or explicit goals of the author/editor.*

Frequently, text is rearranged in chronological order so that it follows the natural life cycle. Few life histories comprise solely the words of the life history subject. The retelling usually includes some interpretive commentary upon the narrator's life story.[3] *Because the life history is a collaborative product and not strictly autobiographical, it is important to understand, at the least, the circumstances under which the material was collected, how the data were processed, and by what steps the life history has achieved its final form.*

The Telling and Retelling of Sadie's Story

As noted in the Preface, Sadie's life story was elicited in chronological order. She would likely have narrated her story largely in chronological order regardless of who had elicited it, given her own western education and her familiarity with her father's memoir (which was monotonously chronological in detailing each of his years from age thirteen to sixty-five). In Sadie's case, the constraints of the field school required an expedient and structured approach to the life history, and for the sake of convenience, the life cycle was chosen for a frame of reference.

Each student group of three or four had an opportunity to work twice with Sadie—to ask basic questions and, later, to ask follow-up questions on the same material. Since there were four groups of students it seemed most expedient to divide Sadie's life into four segments: childhood, teen-age years, early adulthood, and later years. With some coaching, students composed questions that we wrote on the blackboard for easy reference. To provide more context for their interviews, I filled students in on what the preceding group(s) had learned of Sadie's life before they composed their interview questions.

When Sadie arrived at the high school for the interview sessions, we all gathered around a library table, the students positioned so they could see their questions on the blackboard. The tape recorder and microphone were centrally placed on the table, an ashtray was fetched for Sadie, and each student in turn asked her a question selected from the list on the blackboard. At the second meeting with Sadie, each group continued to explore with her that same segment of her life. Sadie's and my interviews in the summers of 1985 and 1986 also proceeded chronologically, beginning with childhood and working toward Sadie's years as magistrate and her retirement.[4]

In 1984 and 1985 Sadie spoke to two very different audiences in two very different settings. At the high school in 1984 her interviewers (excepting

myself) were local high school students ranging in ages from thirteen to eighteen years. Some were Iñupiat whose families were well known to Sadie, some were relative newcomers to town of other ethnic backgrounds, and two were the children of a white schoolteacher. Sadie spoke to the students as a member of the community, sometimes as a teacher, and most of the time as an elder. She referred frequently to local landmarks or institutions—the point, the cemetery, and the community hall and other buildings which had housed the court in the past. She showed her awareness of their time frame, asking if they had ever seen DC-3s, trying to describe what growing-up years had been like with no Arcticade, three-wheelers, or television.

With Iñupiat members of the class, references were made to Iñupiaq personal names, to kinship ties—as in her reminder to one class member that he, like her, had relatives in Nome—and to aspects of Iñupiat heritage. Iñupiat students drew upon their own knowledge of their cultural heritage to ask Sadie questions—What are imiññauraq?[5] *Did women really have to leave the house to give birth in the old days? What did she remember about reindeer herding?*

Sadie had spoken differently when I had interviewed her alone in the summer of 1985 at her home. Some of the differences had reflected my adult status. Also, because I was an Outsider, she had clarified matters for me that she did not for locals. In our conversations, Sadie attributed to me a general knowledge of the North Slope region, and probably a greater knowledge of the Alaska legal system than was warranted.

All interviews were conducted in English. Sadie speaks English fluently and, listening to her today, one would not be aware of her childhood struggles with the language. Her style was informal and conversational. Sadie is loquacious and at times made it too easy for the students; if there was a lull in the questioning, there was never an awkward silence for the interviewers because Sadie had plenty to talk about on her own. Her conversation was expressive, punctuated with "My gosh!" "Oh my!" "Oh Lord!" She laughed readily as she related particularly amusing incidents, and her hands were usually in motion, adding emphasis to her words.

Regardless of who they were, Sadie involved her audience in the telling of her story. Frequently she used expressions like "you can imagine how I felt," or "picture me doing this." Instead of simply reporting events, she would often reenact them, assuming the attitude of a mischievous child or the sober but kindly demeanor of Barrow's magistrate; examples in the text include her trip to the candy store in San Francisco (see pp. 82–83), getting married to Nate (see p.

121), and her reburial of a corpse that had washed out of a grave (see pp. 179–80). As is typical of people whose thoughts get ahead of their ability to express them verbally, Sadie often interrupted herself, leaving hald-completed thoughts to tend to one that was more pressing.

It is difficult for me to ascertain specifically what of Sadie's narrative style is reminiscent of Iñupiat narrative; someone more knowledgeable than I of Iñupiat forms of expression might be able to discern the similarities and differences. Today the oral tradition, in both Iñupiaq and English, is very much alive in Barrow. Though the winter gatherings around native storytellers are a thing of the past, elders come to the classrooms on a regular basis, and many have been videotaped by the high school students. There is the North Slope Borough Elders' Conference; and, for several years now, the borough has been compiling an oral record of traditional land-use areas within the North Slope. Sadie's style is undoubtedly informed by the stories she knew from childhood—those she heard from Iñupiat storytellers during the long winter months, as well as those she and her siblings teased out of their father, whose capacity as a storyteller was renowned across northern Alaska. Sadie's oral style also reflects both her past as a teacher to her people and her present status as elder. Because she taught not only in the BIA school but also as a welfare worker, health worker, and as magistrate, her public posture for many years has been that of a teacher. Equally, as an elder she is regarded as a holder of knowledge and a communicator of values. Not only did Sadie instruct when talking with the students, but she took advantage of the situation to offer advice, urging them, among other things, to value their education and make the most of it.

Sadie brought to the interviews a remarkable presence. Though I had talked with her only once prior to her first appearance at the high school, there was no apparent awkwardness or discomfort on her part as we began the first interview session. Following my explanation of how the project was to be structured, Sadie began, "Well, I'm Sadie Neakok. I was born up here in 1916, and that's sixty-eight years ago, going on sixty-nine. So my growing up was entirely different from you kids. There wasn't always Barrow. . . ." She began with the arrival of her father, "a known whaler," in Barrow in the 1880s and worked forward to her own appearance some thirty years later.

Sadie was direct and forthright in answering questions. She seemed not the least bothered by talking about herself to a group of students nor to an anthropologist in the presence of family members in her own home. The only issues Sadie would not discuss became evident in 1985, when she mentioned

phone calls she had recently received from newspaper journalists. She had been asked to comment on the investigation of the former mayor of the North Slope Borough (see p. 32) and on a whaler who had violated the quota in taking a whale in the spring of 1985 (see p. 208). Her feelings about those issues, she said, she was keeping to herself. Sadie's ease in telling her story can be attributed, in part, to her public role in life. She has led the "examined life," and her story, though not without its intimate moments, is a public story. She has put her life experiences together for the public before—though never so thoroughly as now—as is evidenced in the several magazine and newspaper articles about her since the late 1960s.

Seventeen hours of interviews with Sadie resulted from the field school in 1984; twenty-one hours of interviews were recorded in 1985, seven in 1986, and three in 1987. Interviews from all summers were transcribed verbatim.[6] *Because they had been typed on a computer and saved to disks, organizing and editing the transcripts was made considerably easier. New files, identified as "narratives," were created on disks; text from the original transcripts from 1984–85*[7] *was copied and moved to these files. The questions were deleted and, where needed, explanatory parentheticals were added to Sadie's narrative.*

As the narrative was copied from the original, it was organized chronologically and topically and was assigned to one of ten headings: Childhood (birth through eighth grade); San Francisco Years (high school); Eklutna School and College; Teaching School and Marriage; Marriage and Children (the early years); Welfare Work and Becoming a Magistrate; Magistrate; Magistrate and Retirement;[8] *Parents; Barrow History.*

Because this organization of material resulted in the juxtaposition of narrative from two summers, narrative material was referenced by its tape- and page-number in the original transcripts. With the material now organized topically, I could compare discussion of the same events with different audiences at two different points in time. Contradictions, particularly in such obvious features as dates of events, could be readily identified. By retaining printed copies of the original transcripts, the intermediate narrative as just described, and the final manuscript, it became possible to retrace with considerable exactness the editorial steps in production of the final manuscript.

In brief, the narrative as it appears here represents a combination of the narratives collected in 1984 and 1985, with addenda from my 1986 and 1987 follow-up interviews and some material from Sadie's interview with Neville Jacobs in 1974. The narrative was edited for redundancy and clarity; personal references to student interviewers or to things exclusively local were deleted, as

were false starts and the ever-recurring expression "you know." Where the narrative switched directions dramatically, the question eliciting that response was noted either in brackets or in a footnote. These changes were minor and conventional in anthropological life history writing; essentially, the narrative remains faithful to the original. Roughly ninety percent of the transcribed interviews were used in the final narrative. The nine chapters of Sadie's narrative in the book follow closely the organization of the first editing of the transcripts.

In some respects Sadie's life history is unorthodox. Anthropological life histories have generally been collected following intensive field research in the life history subject's community and, thus, only after one has amassed considerable first-hand data on the people and their culture. Most often, life history subjects have been native consultants or teachers for the anthropologist on previous projects and, thus, life history subject and anthropologist usually know each other well. Often the life history itself has evolved over a lengthy period when the anthropologist was doing other research in the community.[9]

None of the above describes the circumstances under which Sadie's life history was collected. I first met her in 1984, when we invited her to work with field school students; that summer marked only my second visit to Barrow. My summer's research with her in 1985 was equally brief and intense, and although I spent a month in Barrow in the summer of 1987, my time was consumed with another project. As a result, although we compiled an impressive forty-eight hours of taped interviews focused on Sadie's life, I do not know her as well as I would like. I met all of her family (during interruptions and other breaks in our interviewing), but I have engaged in nothing more than casual conversation with them. I have not seen Sadie in court (she still does some court work today), visited her fish camp, or traveled the land with her.

There is no doubt that being with Sadie in her various environments and gaining the views of her immediate and extended family would have enriched the manuscript considerably. As a contract researcher for the North Slope Borough, however, I did not have the luxury of long-term residence in the community. But it was essential to Sadie's account to interview at least some of the significant individuals in the Alaska Court System who had known Sadie in her capacity as magistrate. Doing so not only helped me to understand the very important role that Sadie has performed but also gave me insight into the Alaska Court System, particularly as it operates in bush Alaska. I was further assisted in the latter task by a copy of the magistrate training materials from Magistrate Services in Anchorage.

While the field research for this book might have been more extensive, I was aided by the considerable literature that exists on Barrow, much of it in unpublished reports funded by various government programs in the wake of oil exploration and development on the North Slope. In addition, there are considerable ethnohistorical materials for Barrow and the North Slope which are cited throughout the text. The most important historical source was, without doubt, Charles Brower's own autobiography and his correspondence with various individuals.

Because a number of people have engaged in anthropological research on the North Slope, I was able to benefit from the commentary of those who have done more field research in the area than I. I was also fortunate in that my life history subject was literate. Sadie read the entire manuscript, making marginal comments, in a record three days. "I just buried my nose in it," she explained.

Much could be written about putting together a life history. First-person narrative is essential, and oral historians and anthropologists alike agree on the importance of letting the life history subject speak for him/herself.[10] *But where are the author/editor's comments best placed? For example, does the reader want to get to Sadie's story right away (at least two reviewers did) instead of first wading through a history of Barrow and its people? Might it be preferable to see Barrow simply through Sadie's eyes? Do more voices provide more context, or do they confuse and interfere? Are there too many outside experts peering into Sadie's story and interrupting her narrative? Are those outside voices needed at all? There are no clear-cut answers to these questions. Past authors of life histories have taken varying approaches to these issues.*[11] *Obviously this author is one who subscribes to the importance of placing the life history subject within a larger cultural and historical context; the success of this approach will, of course, have to be decided by the reader.*

For all who read them—social scientist and lay person alike—life histories carry an inherent and obvious value. They invite the individual reader to act as analyst in the most fundamental of ways, comparing and contrasting the life depicted with his or her own life experiences. Beyond this self-examination, the curious reader is inevitably led to examine further the life within its own context. To what extent is this person like other people of her generation in her community, her culture? And, more broadly, what does she share with others of her time and gender, beyond her community and culture? Surely one of the great attractions of life history is the potential it offers for discovery and rediscovery of the common threads of our gender, our stage in life, our humanity.

Bibliography

Alaska Almanac

1983 Anchorage: Alaska Northwest Publishing Company.

Alaska Consultants (with Stephen Braund and Associates)

1984 *Subsistence Study of Alaska Eskimo Whaling Villages* (249 pp., plus appendix and bibliography). Report prepared for the U.S. Department of the Interior.

Andrews, C. L.

1939 *The Eskimo and His Reindeer in Alaska.* Caldwell, Idaho: The Caxton Printers, Ltd.

Abe, K.

1893 Letter to Sheldon Jackson, August 19, 1893. Microfilm. Alaska State Historical Library. Sheldon Jackson Correspondence Transcripts, vol. 15, 1885–96.

Alaska Consultants

1983 *North Slope Borough Background for Planning: City of Barrow.* Prepared for the North Slope Borough by Alaska Consultants, Inc.

Alaska Consultants (with Stephen Braund and Associates)

1984 *Subsistence Study of Alaska Eskimo Whaling Villages* (249 pp., plus appendix and bibliography). Report for the U.S. Department of the Interior.

Allen, Jim

1978 *A Whaler and Trader in the Arctic.* Anchorage: Alaska Northwest Publishing Company.

Bailey, Alfred M.

n.d. *The Charles Brower Journal Preface.* Mimeographed. Denver Museum of Natural History. Archives.

1921–22 *A. M. Bailey Field Notes*, vol. 3. *Arctic Alaska (1921–22).* Denver Museum of Natural History. Archives.

1936 Letter to Charles Brower, August 5, 1936. Denver Museum of Natural History. Archives.

1971 *Field Work of a Museum Naturalist 1919–1922*. Denver Museum of Natural History, Museum Pictorial No. 22.

Bataille, Gretchen M., and Kathleen M. Sands
1984 *American Indian Women: Telling their Lives*. Lincoln: University of Nebraska Press.

Berger, Thomas
1985 *Village Journey: The Report of the Alaska Native Review Commission*. New York: Hill and Wang.

Bockstoce, John
1977 *Steam Whaling in the Western Arctic*. New Bedford: Old Dartmouth Historical Society.
1979 "Arctic Castaway: The Stormy History of the Pt. Barrow Refuge Station." *Prologue*, vol. 11, no. 3:152–69.
1980 "Battle of the Bowheads." *Natural History*, vol. 89, no. 5:52–61.
1986 *Whales, Ice, and Men: The History of Whaling in the Western Arctic*. Seattle: University of Washington Press.

Boeri, David
1983 *People of the Ice Whale: Eskimos, White Men, and the Whale*. New York: E. P. Dutton.

Briggs, Jean
1970 *Never in Anger: Portrait of an Eskimo Family*. Cambridge: Harvard University Press.

Brower, Charles
n.d. *The Northernmost America: An Autobiography* (895 pp.). Typescript. Dartmouth College Library. Stefansson Collection.
1923 Letter to V. Stefansson, May 17, 1923. Dartmouth College Library. Stefansson Collection.
1928*a* Letter to V. Stefansson, February 25, 1928. Dartmouth College Library. Stefansson Collection.
1928*b* Letter to V. Stefansson, April 15, 1928. Dartmouth College Library. Stefansson Collection.
1928*c* Letter to V. Stefansson, December 12, 1928. Dartmouth College Library. Stefansson Collection.
1930 Diary of Charles Brower. Dartmouth College Library. Stefansson Collection.
1936 Letter to A. M. Bailey, June 7, 1936. Denver Museum of Natural History. Archives.
1940*a* Letter to A. M. Bailey, February 20, 1940. Denver Museum of Natural History. Archives.

1940*b* Letter to A. M. Bailey, August 13, 1940. Denver Museum of Natural History. Archives.

1941 Letter to V. Stefansson, February 22, 1941. Dartmouth College Library. Stefansson Collection.

1942 *Fifty Years Below Zero*. New York: Dodd, Mead and Co.

1943 Letter to A. M. Bailey, November 7, 1943. Denver Museum of Natural History. Archives.

1944 Letter to the Explorers Club, October 30, 1944. Explorers Club Library. New York.

Brumble, David

1981 *An Annotated Bibliography of American Indian and Eskimo Autobiographies*. Lincoln: University of Nebraska Press.

Bruner, Edward M.

1984 "Introduction: The Opening Up of Anthropology." In *Text, Play, and Story: The Construction and Reconstruction of Self and Society*, edited by Edward M. Bruner, pp. 1–16. *1983: Proceedings of the American Ethnological Society.*

Burch, Ernest S.

1975 *Eskimo Kinsmen*. American Ethnological Society, Monograph 59.

Cashen, William R.

1972 *Farthest North College President*. Fairbanks: University of Alaska Press.

Conn, Stephen

1977 "The Extralegal Forum and Legal Power: The Dynamics of the Relationship—Other Pipelines." In *The Anthropology of Power*, edited by Raymond D. Fogelson and Richard N. Adams, pp. 217–24. New York: Academic Press.

Dubay, William

1981 "Women Support Whalers." *Tundra Times*, vol. 18, no. 8:3, 16 (February 25, 1981).

Evans, Ben F.

1931 Newsletter to teachers in the Northwestern District, Alaska, October 24, 1931. Alaska State Historical Library. BIA General Correspondence, Alaska Division, 1908–35: District Files—Northwestern.

Ford, James A.

1959 "Eskimo Prehistory in the Vicinity of Point Barrow, Alaska." *Anthropological Papers of the American Museum of Natural History*, vol. 47, part 1.

Gallagher, H. G.
1974 *Etok: A Story of Eskimo Power*. New York: G. P. Putnam's Sons.

Greist, Mollie
1968 *Nursing under the North Star*. Privately published manuscript.

Hall, Edwin S., Jr.
1981 "Post Depositional Factors Affecting the Formation of the Utqiagvik Site." In *The 1981 Excavations at the Utqiagvik Archaeological Site, Barrow, Alaska*, edited by Albert Dekin, Jr., et al., vol. 4, chap. 22. Binghamton: Public Archaeology Facility, Department of Anthropology, SUNY.

Hampton, Nan
1971 "Farthest North Judge." *Alaska Magazine*, vol. 37, no. 7:26–27.

Hawkesworth, Charles
1908 Letter to Harland Updegraff, June 30, 1908. Alaska State Historical Library. BIA Alaska Division, General Correspondence, 1908–35: School Files.
1910 Annual Report of the Barrow School, June 30, 1910. Alaska State Historical Library. BIA Alaska Division, General Correspondence, 1908–35: School Files.

Hippler, Arthur E., and Stephen Conn
1975 "The Village Council and Its Offspring: A Reform for Bush Justice." *UCLA–Alaska Law Review*, vol. 5, no. 1:22–57.
1974 "The Changing Legal Culture of the North Alaska Eskimo." *Ethos*, vol. 2, no. 2:171–88.

Jenness, Diamond
1924 *Report of the Canadian Arctic Expedition, 1913–18*, vol. 13: *Eskimo Folk-Lore*. Part B: *Eskimo String Figures*. Ottawa: F. A. Acland.
1957 *Dawn in Arctic Alaska*. Minneapolis: University of Minnesota Press.

Jones, Wendy
1976 *Women Who Braved the Far North*. 2 vols. San Diego: Grossmon Press, Inc.

Kennicott, Donald
1931 Letter to A. M. Bailey, September 26, 1931. Denver Museum of Natural History. Archives.

Lopez, Barry
1986 *Arctic Dreams: Imagination and Desire in a Northern Landscape*. New York: Charles Scribner's Sons.

MacLean, Edna Ahgeak
1980 *Abridged Iñupiaq and English Dictionary*. Fairbanks: Alaska Native Language Center, University of Alaska. Barrow: Iñupiat Language Commission, North Slope Borough.

Maynard and Partch, Woodward Clyde Consultants
1984 *North Slope Borough Coastal Management Program Background Report*. Barrow: North Slope Borough.

Morlander, George A.
1931 Memorandum to Teachers, Northwestern District (Subject: Contests), August 16, 1931. Alaska State Historical Library. BIA General Correspondence, Alaska Division, 1908–35: District Files—Northwestern.

Muir, John
1917 *The Cruise of the Corwin: Journal of the Arctic Expedition of 1881 in Search of De Long and the Jeanette*. New York: Houghton Mifflin Company.

Murdoch, John
1892 "Ethnological Results of the Point Barrow Expedition." *Ninth Annual Report of the Bureau of Ethnology*. Washington, D.C.: Government Printing Office.

North Slope Borough Planning Department
1986 *North Slope Borough Semi-Annual Economic Profile*. Barrow, Alaska.

Paine, Robert
1971 *Patrons and Brokers in the East Arctic*. Memorial University of Newfoundland: Newfoundland Social and Economic Papers No. 2.

Peacock, James L.
1984 "Religion and Life History: An Exploration in Cultural Psychology." In *Text, Play, and Story: The Construction and Reconstruction of Self and Society*, edited by Edward M. Bruner, pp. 94–116. *1983: Proceedings of the American Ethnological Society*.

Peat, Marwick, Mitchell & Co.
1978 *Beaufort Sea Region Socioeconomic Baseline*. Alaska OCS Socioeconomic Studies Program, Technical Report No. 11.

Pospisil, Leopold
1964 "Law and Societal Structure among the Nunamiut Eskimo." In *Explorations in Cultural Anthropology*, edited by Ward H. Goodenough, pp. 395–431. New York: McGraw-Hill.

Ray, Lieut. P. Henry
1885 *Report of the International Polar Expedition to Point Barrow, Alaska*. Washington, D.C.: U.S. Government Printing Office.

Richardson, Jeffrey
1978 "My Kitchen was My Courthouse." *Tundra Times*, vol. 15, no. 1:1, 8 (January 4, 1978).

Richardson, T. L.
1916 Annual Report of the United States Public School at Barrow,

Alaska. Alaska State Historical Library. BIA Alaska Division, General Correspondence, 1908–35: School Files.

Schneider, William
1986*a* *The Life I've Been Living, by Moses Cruikshank*. Fairbanks: University of Alaska Press.
1986*b* "Some Considerations about the Oral Tradition and Writing." *Alaska Quarterly Review*, vol. 4, nos. 3 & 4:16–18.

Shostak, Marjorie
1981 *Nisa: The Life and Words of a !Kung Woman*. Cambridge: Harvard University Press.

Simpson, John
1875 "The Western Eskimo." In *A Selection of Papers on Arctic Geography and Ethnology*, pp. 233–75. London: Royal Geographical Society.

Slaughter, Dale
1982 "Post-Contact Changes in House Form." *Anthropological Papers of the University of Alaska*, vol. 20:157–58.

Smythe, Charles W., and Rosita Worl
1985 *Monitoring Methodology and Analysis of North Slope Institutional Responce and Change, 1979–83*. Alaska OCS Socioeconomic Studies Program, Technical Report No. 117.

Solomon, Alice
1985 "Women and Whale Hunting." *Alaska Native News Magazine*, vol. 3, no. 9:6–7.

Sonnenfeld, Joseph
1956 *Changes in Subsistence among Barrow Eskimo* (589 pp.). Mimeographed. Report for the Arctic Institute of North America.

Spencer, Robert
1959 *The North Alaskan Eskimo: A Study in Ecology and Society*. Bureau of American Ethnology, Bulletin 171. Washington, D.C.: U.S. Government Printing Office.

Stefansson, Vilhjalmur
1912 *My Life with the Eskimo*. New York: Harper and Brothers.
1930 Letter to Charles Brower, May 11, 1930. Dartmouth College Library. Stefansson Collection.
1964 *Discovery: The Autobiography of Vihjalmur Stefansson*. New York: McGraw-Hill.

Stevenson, L. M.
1892 Letter to Sheldon Jackson, September 17, 1892. Microfilm. Alaska State Historical Library. Sheldon Jackson Correspondence Transcripts, vol. 15, 1885–96.

Stuck, Hudson
1920 *A Winter Circuit of Our Arctic Coast*. New York: Charles Scribner's Sons.

Titon, Jeff Todd
1980 "The Life Story." *Journal of American Folklore*, vol. 93, no. 369:276–92.

Tundra Times
1969 President Nixon Calls Barrow's Sadie Neakok." Vol. 7, no. 230:1 (October 10, 1969).

U.S. Bureau of Education
1893 "Education in Alaska, 1890–91." In *Report of the Commissioner of Education for 1890–91*, chap. 25. Washington, D.C.: U.S. Government Printing Office.

VanStone, James W.
1962 *Point Hope: An Eskimo Village in Transition*. Seattle: University of Washington Press.

Variety Film Reviews
1933 1930–33, vol. 4. New York: Garland Publishing, Inc.

Wells, Ken
1985 "Scandal Gives Eskimos Quick, Painful Lesson in 20th Century Ways." *Wall Street Journal*, June 21, 1985:1, 23.

Worl Associates
1981 *Beaufort Sea Sociocultural Systems Update Analysis*, Alaska OCS Socioeconomic Studies Program, Technical Report No. 64.

Worl, Rosita
1978 "The North Slope Iñupiat Whaling Complex." *Senri Ethnological Studies*, no. 4:305–20.

Worl, Rosita, and Charles W. Smythe
1986 *Barrow: A Decade of Modernization*. Alaska OCS Socioeconomic Studies Program, Technical Report No. 125.

Notes

Preface

1. *Iñupiat* (*Iñupiaq*, singular), sometimes written without the tilde, is a term of self-designation, meaning "real" or "genuine" people, used by North Alaskan Eskimos. *Inuit* is the counterpart term in Arctic Canada and western Greenland. In 1977 the Inuit Circumpolar Conference officially adopted *Inuit* as a designation for all Eskimos regardless of local usages. *Eskimo*, a term of Algonquian origin, is still used as a generic to refer to aboriginal inhabitants of Arctic North America, Siberia, and Greenland. Older Iñupiat people, when speaking English, often use the term *Eskimo* instead of *Iñupiat*, as can be seen from Sadie's account. (see *Handbook of North American Indians*, vol. 5, *Arctic*, pp. 5–7, for a discussion of synonymy). The orthography here is that used by the North Slope Iñupiat (see MacLean 1980:xviii–xix). Most of the letters in the Iñupiaq alphabet also are found in the English alphabet; there are six additional sounds represented in Iñupiaq, only two of which appear in Sadie's life story. These are the palatal nasal, *ñ*, and the voiced velar nasal, ŋ. The latter is rendered here with two letters, *ng*.

2. Roxy Ekowana, now deceased.

3. "Outside," as used by Alaskans, refers to the lower forty-eight states.

4. Jennie, Sadie's older sister, who trained as a nurse in California, resides in San Francisco.

5. The Soroptimists are a service organization of professional women.

6. The details of the life history research are discussed in the Appendix.

7. David Brumble (1981) lists forty-eight Eskimo life history accounts, ranging from brief narratives to book-length publications. Thirty-six are of males and twelve of females.

1. Home: The Northernmost Outpost

1. North Slope Borough Planning Department (1986:8); this is an increase of 18 percent from the 1980 census.

2. The more familiar spelling, *umiak*, is defined by Webster's as "an open Eskimo boat made of wood and covered with skins." In Iñupiaq, *umiaq* [present orthography] means simply "boat." In her narrative Sadie uses *umiaq* (plural:

umiat) in the former sense, as have I. *Umiapiaq* is the proper word for skin boat.

3. By the summer of 1987 both the Arcticade and photo concession were no longer in business.

4. The building is the oldest in the Alaskan Arctic. Constructed by the U.S. Government in 1889 as a refuge station for stranded whalers, it was sold in 1896 to the Pacific Steam Whaling Company, and a year later to the Cape Smythe Whaling and Trading Company, owned by H. Liebes and Company in partnership with Charles Brower (see Bockstoce 1979).

5. As noted later, when first established in 1947 under the Office of Naval Research, the facility was known as ARL (Arctic Research Laboratry); in 1967 it was redesignated the Naval Arctic Research Laboratory (NARL). For many years it was operated in partnership with the University of Alaska.

6. Before any formal archaeological excavation took place in Barrow, John Murdoch in 1881–83 collected archaeological specimens from native people, and Charles Brower amassed a large collection, most of which Stefansson took to the American Museum of Natural History. In 1912 Stefansson and Brower dug at Birnirk, and Brower arranged for the hiring of native workers to dig "wherever there was a ruin or kitchen midden" (Stefansson 1912:388), while Stefansson paid them off in chewing gum. Their efforts resulted in 20,000 artifacts for the American Museum of Natural History. There were at least six other archaeological excavations conducted in Barrow and environs between 1912 and 1981, when the "Utqiagvik Archaeological Project" began a three-year excavation of the old settlement of Utqiagvik itself.

7. He says "Cape Smyth," but all indications are that the village at Cape Smyth itself was much earlier, and that he means Utqiagvik (see Ford 1959:18).

8. This discussion of subsistence and much of the succeeding discussion on changes in subsistence are drawn from Sonnenfeld (1956).

9. Brower provides no description of the *Nalukataq* at Utqiagvik, though he does describe the first one he saw, at Point Hope in 1885 (n.d.:187–91). Spencer (1959:350–53) provides a general description of *Nalukataq*.

10. Data on the commercial whaling period is drawn primarily from Bockstoce (1977, 1979, 1986), Sonnenfeld (1956), Stefansson (1912), and VanStone (1962).

11. The *Mary and Helen*, built in 1879, was the first steam whaler constructed specifically for the Arctic fishery (Bockstoce 1977).

12. A detailed account of shore-based whaling is given in Bockstoce 1986, chap. 11.

13. The Pacific Steam Whaling Company and H. Liebes and Company, which had gone into partnership with Charles Brower in 1893.

14. According to Charles Brower, in an unpublished paper entitled "The Bowhead Whale," located in the H. Liebes and Company records in the California Academy of Sciences. Bockstoce (1986:345) gives $5.38 as the peak wholesale price of baleen (1891).

15. In 1897 more than one hundred men from seven wrecked whaling ships were stranded in Barrow for the winter.

16. In 1871, thirty-three whaling ships were abandoned in the ice, and in 1876, twelve more (Bockstoce 1979).

17. Sadie confirmed this, adding that he didn't discuss this aspect of his career in his autobiography because he soon saw the damage alcohol caused.

18. Regarding the composition of the Barrow population, Stefansson (1912:66) remarks: "The village of Cape Smythe contained probably about four hundred inhabitants in 1880, and contains about that today [1908]. But only four persons are now living who are considered by the Eskimos themselves to belong to the Cape Smythe tribe, and only twenty or twenty-one others who are descended from the Cape Smythe tribe through one parent." Jenness's (1957) observations corroborate those of Stefansson.

19. At Point Hope in 1885.

20. The darting gun was more like a harpoon than a gun, as it was hurled. A bomb was released when a metal rod came in contact with the whale. The shoulder gun was a gun that shot bombs (see glossary, Allen 1978).

21, The Pacific Steam Whaling Company prohibited its ships from engaging in the liquor trade (with questionable success). Charles Brower's attempts to eradicate hootch-making have already been noted.

22. The U.S. government took over schooling in 1894, while continuing to rely for several years on the Board of Home Missions of the Presbyterian church for recommendations in the appointments of schoolteachers.

23. The relief measure proved unnecessary as the Iñupiat had, through their hunting, kept the whalers supplied with provisions (see later discussion).

24. The following year, management and supervision of the herd was transferred to the schoolteacher at Barrow; the management of native reindeer herds remained with the Bureau of Education until 1929, when the Reindeer Service was placed under the governor's office.

25. The authority of the shamans was undercut somewhat earlier as commercial shore-based whalers, in hiring Eskimo crews, ignored many of the traditional taboos, and still managed to take whales. Brower (n.d.:474) noted, "So many things turned out good in the whaling industry that never were used by their ancestors, they were losing faith in their devils."

26. Other criticisms of Marsh included his encouragement of Sabbath-breaking and his endorsement of immodesty by taking off his coat in native houses (Stefansson 1912:92). Marsh did leave in 1903 but returned a few years later in the capacity of physician. Upon his return he fell under the criticism of schoolteachers and missionaries for his lack of commitment to the new religion and housing as well as for what were regarded as his slothful personal habits. He left permanently in 1911.

27. This statement gives credence to Stefansson's claim about the spread of Christianity. It also suggests that it occurred within a couple of years of the missionaries' arrival and was spread through personalized contact among natives.

28. By 1906 all the dwellings in the vicinity of Brower's station were frame houses; in 1928 the sod house was pronounced by a teacher to have "disap-

peared almost entirely." In the early 1940s, however, a survey of Barrow revealed fifteen to twenty sod homes and approximately fifty frame ones. Perhaps the use of sod houses was a result of the Depression and lack of fuel (Sonnenfeld 1956:503–4). On the other hand, the sod houses that had all but "disappeared" by 1928 may well have been just those with the traditional subterranean entrance tunnel. The sheet-iron stove, which became widely used around the turn of the twentieth century, eliminated the need for the tunnel cold trap. The modified sod houses opened directly to the outdoors or into an above-ground entry corridor (Slaughter 1982).

29. Today the Mothers Club contributes services and money to some eighteen community organizations and social events, ranging from the Barrow search-and-rescue, to the high school athletic teams, to the Arctic Women in Crisis Center (Smythe and Worl 1985:283).

30. Jenness (1957:42–43), referring to the situation in 1914, remarks: "from mid-November to the end of March . . . a skillful trapper might hope to kill as many as fifty white foxes and perhaps two or three white bears. With Brower paying $15 apiece for the fox skins, he anticipated that the income from his four months' trapping would purchase not only all his necessities for the coming year, but a number of luxuries besides."

31. Caribou had begun to decline during the commercial whaling era and were reported to be scarce between 1890 and 1920.

32. Poor herding, lack of markets for reindeer meat, increase in wolf population, mingling with caribou, opportunity for wage labor in the 1940s, and incompatibility of herding with whaling are all given as reasons for the decline of the reindeer herds (Sonnenfeld 1956:371 ff.). Tom Brower (Sadie's brother), owner of the largest Barrow reindeer herd, noted in an interview with William Schneider and Wendy Arundale that Navy personnel doing seismic work had stampeded his herd in the summer of 1951 He recounts a series of difficulties in acquiring new stock to replenish his herd.

33. Undoubtedly because caribou were beginning to increase again.

34. The airfield and "camp" are all part of what is known today as NARL or "the base."

35. This was some six years before an aggressive chemotherapy program against TB was begun in Alaskan native villages.

36. An early tracked vehicle for all-terrain use, the weasel was first used at the Navy base. Surplus vehicles were later auctioned off and purchased eagerly by villagers. Nate's old weasel, for which parts are no longer obtainable at reasonable cost, still sits outside the Neakok house.

37. *Maktak*, also known as *muktuk*, consisted of chunks of bowhead blubber with skin.

38. In the 1950s a Catholic church and an Assembly of God church were established in Barrow. The latter continues to have an active membership today. The Bahai also have a church in Barrow today.

39. When the Arctic Slope Native Association opposed ANCSA, they were the only regional group to do so.

40. Only those born on or before the date the act was signed into law, December 18, 1971.

41. For the time being, anyway. In 1991, according to the original act of 1971, corporation lands will become taxable and stock can be alienated from native shareholders through general sales.

42. Major concerns addressed in the Alaska Native Claims Settlement Act Amendments of 1987 include protection for undeveloped land; the exclusion of traditional and subsistence lands from business risk; the exemption of native corporation lands from taxation; indefinite extension of village and regional corporation stock restrictions (the stock remains natively controlled unless shareholders vote to remove restrictions); and the enrollment of natives born after 1971 as shareholders in the native corporations. The Alaska Native Review Commission's report was popularized in Thomas Berger's 1985 book, *Village Journey*.

43. The 1980 census listed the borough population at 4,199, which did not include non-resident workers at Prudhoe Bay and other industrial sites. The figures cited above reflect both the village and industrial-site populations as of 1985 (North Slope Borough Planning Department 1986:6).

44. Federal government positions accounted for only 11 percent of the government jobs in Barrow, state positions only 1 percent. The next largest employer to government was contract construction with 20 percent of the jobs, followed by transportaion, communication and public utilities, services, trade, finance insurance and real estate, and mining (Alaska Consultants 1983:13).

2. The Northernmost American and His Family

1. "Whalebone,"as opposed to "whale bone," refers to baleen. The Pacific Steam Whaling Company had a one-year patent on the coal mine, which did not prove profitable for them to mine. The coal, however, was used over the years by U.S. revenue cutters and other ships. It was named after the revenue cutter *Corwin*, which coaled there.

2. Also known as the International Polar Expedition (see chap. 1).

3. Sadie was not alone in remarking on Amundsen's nose. He was known among the Eskimo as "King-ok-puk," or "Big-Nose" (Andrews 1939:18). After an unsuccessful test flight at Wainwright of a plane he had hoped to take over the pole, Amundsen was thwarted in his second attempt to cross over the pole by air, when Richard Byrd beat him to it in 1926. Nonetheless, in 1926 Amundsen made the first dirigible crossing from Europe to Alaska, sailing the *Norge* from Spitzbergen along the north Alaska coast and down to Nome. Sadie says, "I can remember that day so well, because we were all looking at it going slowly on the horizon. It was so big that you couldn't help but see it on a clear day."

4. According to Bailey (n.d.), Brower "in about 1927 brought a typist to Barrow who compiled the extensive account of Brower's most unusual experiences." Brower doesn't mention the typist in any correspondence or in the manuscript itself, and Sadie could not recall any. The original manuscript appears more likely to have been typed by Brower himself, as the typographical errors, punctuation, and lack of capitalization in the manuscript are typical of correspondence he typed himself over the years.

5. About 1931 Brower signed an agreement with Bailey, turning the manuscript over to him "for publication in serial form or in a book, as he sees fit." The agreement provided for an equal division of profits from publication between Brower and Bailey.

6. Bailey did quite a bit of editing on the original manuscript, but the published version is much more condensed than that, resembling the editorial style of the *Blue Book* articles. At Brower's request, the informal agreement regarding publication of the ms was terminated in 1936. He wrote Bailey: "From what you write I imagine that you are getting tired of fooling with that story and I can't say I blame you. All along I was of the opinion that it would not go over and what you did get for what was published was more than I expected" (Brower 1936). Also at Brower's request, the original ms held by Bailey was sent to Phil Farrelly in Los Angeles for editing. Bailey concurred with Brower's decision, noting that Farrelly "is in a good position in Los Angeles to get in touch with writers and he will possibly be able to do something with it" (Bailey 1936).

7. As suggested in Sadie's narrative, Charles Brower probably spent a great deal of time in his store, at least during the years she knew her father. In fact, he is seen in her narrative usually seated in his big chair, tending to his commissioner's or other records, or yarning with old-timers who come in and warm themselves beside the stove. The action-orientation of Brower's narrative makes him appear to be constantly on the go.

8. Sadie comments about this omission: "That didn't seem strange to me because, well, knowing Dad, he never made too much fuss about anything, except to tell his stories as they happened in the years he was up there." Brower must have had his family in mind, at least later, for he "affectionately dedicated" *Fifty Years Below Zero* "to My Devoted Wife, My Fine Sons and Wonderful Daughters."

9. The "diaries" come from the Stefansson Collection at Dartmouth. The nature of the entries suggests they were written long after the fact, for they appear simply as a jot list of events and people, each year comprising less than a handwritten page. Sadie could not remember ever seeing her father at work typing his manuscript or writing in a diary, though she remarked, "I know he did a lot of writing . . . I knew he had a diary; it was all handwritten." The "diary" to which she refers was about 5 or 6 inches thick (more voluminous than the Stefansson Collection "diaries") and was in the possession of her sister Jenny when Sadie last saw it in San Francisco in 1969. In the original typescript to "My Arctic Outpost," the first in the series of *Blue Book* articles, Brower is

quoted as saying, "I went to sea at the age of thirteen years, and since that time I have always kept notes. Fortunately, these have been saved through the years, and as I work through them, I realize that a great deal of ice has piled along the shores." Perhaps these "notes" were the volume Sadie saw. Brower's remark about the notes, however, never appeared in the published version of "My Arctic Outpost," probably because "Stefansson . . . read the introductory page, and complained [to *Blue Book* editor Donald Kennicott] about Brower's statement that he kept notes. He (Stefansson) says he knows very well that Brower never did any such thing" (Kennicott 1931).

10. The very readable account by close colleague and fellow trader Jim Allen, however, manages to present a more rounded view of life as a trader/whaler in the Arctic (Allen 1978). Allen writes quite comfortably of his wife and children. There is a curious unpublished piece in the Bailey collection of material at the Denver Museum of Natural History, entitled, "Fifty Years among the Eskimos North of Sixty-eight." Bailey edited this from, he says, "Brower's journal" [*The Northernmost American*? the "diaries"?]. It contains an account of the birth of Brower's last child, Mary, but the account shows up neither in Brower's autobiography nor in the Dartmouth "diaries."

11. Brower's spelling. "Taktuk" in the current orthography.

12. Thus, he was married to her officially by a ship's captain or other person authorized to perform marriages.

13. According to Sadie, the oldest child, Elizabeth, was the offspring of Brower and an Iñupiaq woman from Nuvuk, whom he had planned to marry, but who, during Brower's absence (perhaps between 1885–86 when he returned to San Francisco), had married another man. Elizabeth was apparently born in 1886. Ties between the two families persisted, however, and Sadie recalls Elizabeth's real mother: "she was my real aunt, and we dearly loved her, but we were never smart enough to make the connection; then her kids, by her marriage, we called them our cousins. One of the sons, I can't remember which, used to [say], 'Hi, little sister.' But I never knew the connection until I was fully grown." Neither, apparently, did Elizabeth, who had been adopted by Taktuk. Charles Brower does not mention his relationship with Elizabeth's mother in his autobiography.

14. So called, according to Sadie, because she was so skinny when Brower first married her. An anonymous explanatory note penned on a letter from Stefansson to Brower indicates just the opposite—that she had received her nickname because she was so fat. Photographs of her taken in later years do show her to be somewhat heavy.

15. Another daughter—Dora—by her first husband, was taken in by Brower and raised with the older Brower children.

16. There is a discrepancy between Brower's and Sadie's versions of the story. Brower did land at Point Hope that first trip, but his autobiography describes only his shipwreck of 1897, when he led most of the crew from the drifting steam whaler *Navarch* on a twelve-day trek over the ice to eventual rescue. Half the party perished en route. On the other hand, in the typescript to a

1931 radio interview (in the Liebes Collection materials, California Academy of Sciences), Brower states that he was shipwrecked six times. Brower describes meeting Taktuk and her brother under different circumstances than Sadie describes, though Taktuk did later come to his rescue when he became lost while out hunting.

17. Brower came to Barrow in 1884.

18. Elizabeth and Flora went out to Ohio with the missionary I. M. Stevenson and his wife when they left Barrow in 1898. When Brower visited his parents in New Jersey that year, they complained that he had not brought his daughters with him, "saying if they were to be left in civilization they wanted them. They were so insistent I had to send my sister for them. They stayed with my father and mother until I came north in the summer then she [Brower's sister] took them and raised them in West Orange, until one married and the [other] became a teacher" (n.d.:537). In 1904, Charles Brower took Jim out with him, leaving him with the same sister to attend school while he traveled about the country. Brower had planned to take Jim back north with him when he returned to Alaska in the summer of 1905, but the San Francisco earthquake altered his plans. Jim was left, happily, according to Brower, in West Orange, New Jersey. Bill Brower was sent out with missionary Samuel Spriggs and his wife in 1908, the last of the four children to be delivered to Charles Brower's sister in New Jersey. Sometime later Brower purchased a farm outside of San Diego for his sister and her husband. Sadie visited this aunt when she was attending school in California (see chap. 4).

19. The name means "one who roams wild."

20. This remark was prompted when I asked Sadie how she would describe her mother to someone who didn't know her.

21. In an interview on March 25, 1925, Brower noted that "I can now speak it [Iñupiaq] better than I can English. I had no white man with me and had either to learn the language or do without talking. I had to make myself understood the best way I could. They [Iñupiat] could not understand English at all in those days."

22. Fred Hopson, Charles Brower's cook, who, from 1911–28, prepared and served meals at the station (see chap. 3).

23. The novel, if there was one, was never published.

24. Maria's daughter, Edna MacLean, concurs that Maria inherited the house and its ice cellars from her mother, adding that Maria, unlike the others, was not offered the opportunity for an Outside education, because her mother needed her at home to help with the younger children. Perhaps, too, Asianggataq was reluctant to let Maria go because she was her favorite child. See Sadie's discussion of her sibling's in chapter 3.

25. The final entry in Charles Brower's diary, perhaps penned by Tom or Dave, into whose keeping it was entrusted, reads: "C. D. Brower passed away Feb. 11, 1945, 3:30 P.M. Heart Attack."

26. A team of historians who had been charged to write a human-interest history of the armed forces in Alaska during World War II.

3. Growing Up

1. Ugiagnaq,the brother who rescued Asianggataq when she was left to die at birth.

2. A trading post established by a whaling captain and trader, John Backland, some years after Brower's. It was managed by Charley Hansen. Although Brower bought out Hansen in 1916, the building continued to be known as "Hanson's Store."

3. According to Jenness (1924:181B), there was a taboo against playing string figures *except* in the winter when the sun was beneath the horizon. Concern about the taboo was still expressed in 1915–16 when he did his research on the topic. Evidently the taboo was no longer adhered to in the 1920s, as Sadie distinctly remembered playing string games in the summertime and thought that fall and winter were the taboo times.

4. Jenness (1924:182–83B) notes that belief in the spirit of string figures was widespread in Alaska. The spirit revealed its presence by making a sound like the crackling of dry skins, and it made string figures with its own intestines or with invisible cord. To drive the spirit away, it was necessary to make a certain string figure, or pretend to make it. If this gesture were not made, "every inmate of the house would be paralyzed and die."

5. To A.M. Bailey at the Denver Museum of Natural History.

6. Out camping.

7. Brower was often away for the entire year, as he periodically made trips Outside.

8. A party was given one evening each month at the school for parents and children (see chap. 6).

9. Greist was a physician and missionary, and his wife Mollie was a nurse. They worked in Barrow from 1921–37.

10. The "Teachers' Efficiency Record" of 1927 notes the following "habit or idiosyncrasy interfering with success": "Mr. Sylvester is a little impetuous which I think interfered with his success the first year."

11. Although earlier ministers learned Iñupiaq, by Sadie's time they spoke only English.

12. See discussion of the Sabbath taboo in chapter 1.

13. The use of pliers for crimping the rounded toe portion of the soles was introduced in Barrow in 1940 or 1941 by a woman from Noatak, according to Sadie.

14. In response to a question I had asked, based on knowledge of the sewing classes that Annie Coodalook had taught some fifteen years earlier in the Barrow school.

15. The quoted material comes from Greist (1968:58).

16. Isatkook Lagoon.

17. See note 32, chapter 1, regarding the demise of reindeer herding.

18. Sadie added, "Now Tom has the sole responsibility; he inherited all that from Dad."

19. Jim Allen, referred to earlier.

20. Sadie's discussion of her siblings closest in age was prompted by a photograph of Sadie, Maria, and Robert taken in 1921 by Arnold Liebes, the furrier in partnership with Charles Brower. Liebes had visited Barrow and his other stations that year.

21. Favored children are common in Eskimo families. Burch (1975:140–41) elaborates: "Ideally Eskimo parents were supposed to view each offspring with equal affection. . . . In fact, parental sentiment was frequently allocated differentially among children, one or two being favored over the others. In the majority of cases, the child favored by the mother was not the same one favored by the father, although favoritism did not otherwise correlate with sex. In addition, each parent pressured the other to treat his or her favorite in an approved way. In traditional times, when most couples had only two children living with them, the net effect was that the overwhelming majority of children were favored by one parent or the other, hence were treated very well. . . . With the great increase in the number of children per family, however, the result was a marked distinction between a few favorites on the one hand, and many non-favorites on the other. Upon the favorites were bestowed the best clothes, the most and best food, and the greatest attention. . . . A favorite child could do just about anything and get away with it. Non-favored children . . . were treated quite differently. They had to run errands, do the dirtiest chores, wear the ugliest clothes, and eat the worst food."

4. An Outside Education

1. Sadie was actually fourteen; according to her father's diary, they left on September 3, 1930, from Barrow.

2. Brower's diary notes that Sadie was taken the next day to Mrs. Bloomfield's (in Berkeley) to begin school as soon as possible.

3. The daughter of Jim Allen, manager of the H. Liebes and Company station at Wainwright.

4. The family with whom David had lived.

5. Unfortunately, Sadie was unable to locate the photograph. It had been in an album that was destroyed during a period when the Neakoks were absent from home.

6. Bill, Sadie's half-brother.

7. Another half-brother.

8. Flora and Elizabeth, half-sisters.

9. The wire that Sadie never received. Jennie had spent the year in Barrow, helping out at the hospital.

10. Sadie added, "I disappointed him so bad that he never wanted to send one of us out again." Tom, David, and Robert had already been taken Outside for medical treatment and schooling and had returned to Barrow without completing high school.

5. *Going Home*

1. Segregation between whites and natives was common in Alaskan towns then.

2. The BIA ship.

3. Sadie had flown at least once before, from San Francisco to Los Angeles.

4. This was actually not Eklutna's first year; the school had been in operation since 1928. Although there are no enrollment figures for the year Sadie was there, later enrollment figures are considerably lower than her estimates.

5. Sadie's query was prompted by seeing a sign for Eklutna when out on a Sunday drive during her hospitalization in Anchorage in June of 1985.

6. Records from Eklutna list Sadie as entering that school on August 23, 1936. In the June 30, 1937, report for Eklutna, neither Sadie nor her sister Kate are listed among the students; neither, however, are they included in the list of students who had returned home. When I questioned Sadie again in 1987 about her date of entry at the university, she replied: "I went to the University of Alaska, '37. Yeah, I think so; either '36 or '37. I'm forever getting mixed up, because it was in the fall of '35 that we took those kids out [to Eklutna]. I guess it was '36, fall of '36." University of Alaska records show Sadie entering on September 14, 1937.

7. James C. Ryan was director of athletics and professor of education, and Charles U. Southwick was professor of English and French.

8. According to Cashen (1972:221–22), "Dining room service was 'family style,' with co-ed waitresses bringing the filled serving dishes to the tables. Each table had six or eight students. . . . Each week a new seating schedule for dinner was posted. There were usually a number of single faculty members who lived in the dormitories and each of these was assigned a permanent place at the head of a particular table. The weekly seating assignment gave the students an opportunity to get acquainted with each other as well as the faculty. . . . President Bunnell took his meals in the dining room and the president's table was strategically located so that he could see just about every table and everyone in the room. . . . At dinner hour, 6:00 to 7:00 P.M., the entire campus population, excluding the four faculty families occupying private homes, would be gathered in the dining room, affording Bunnell a captive audience when he wished to make announcements or pronouncements. . . ."

9. Cecil F. Robe, professor of history and civil government.

10. Otto William Geist, head of the University Museum, paleontologist and natural historian.

11. Sadie was one of two Barrow natives recognized at the 1987 University of Alaska commencement. Harold Kaveolook, Iñupiaq educator at Kaktovik and Barrow, received a doctorate in education.

12. Mayor of the North Slope Borough.

6. *A Teacher and a Student*

1. Flossie was a native teacher from Barrow.

2. Fred was also a native of Barrow. Educational specialists who made periodic supervisory visits to the Barrow school agreed with Sadie's evaluation of Fred Ipalook. He is described in their reports as a "versatile man able to do almost anything that needs doing," an "outstanding" and "natural born teacher," and a man of "quiet dignity."

3. During the 1950s, the BIA and the state worked out an agreement under which the BIA, through its Johnson O'Malley program, would subsidize schools in native villages and the state would operate them under its rural school program. In 1975 responsibility for the schools was turned over to the borough.

4. Evidently, though still subsidizing Barrow schools, the BIA had bowed out of any administrative assistance.

5. Ninth grade classrooms were opened in Barrow at the beginning of the 1969–70 school year, and high school through twelfth grade in 1974.

6. Sadie notes that Mrs. Greist, the minister's wife, had begun home visits before.

7. Sadie taught full time from the fall of 1938 through the spring of 1940, then from the fall of 1945 through the spring of 1947.

8. This was evidently just before Sadie went south to Eklutna, for when she returned from there she had decided to enter the University of Alaska.

9. Eddie and Alice Hopson, Noah and Molly Itta, and Tommy and Dorcas Simmons (none of whom were married at the time).

10. Sadie's older brother.

7. *Family and Community*

1. This conservatism of the community regarding illegitimate children is a product of Christianity.

2. Mollie Greist (1968:114), nurse at Barrow from 1921–37, described childbirth prior to hospital deliveries: "I found that an Eskimo woman gave birth to her baby on the floor or wall bed, on her knees on a new deerskin [caribou or reindeer] if it was possible to obtain one. Her mother or midwife would tie off the cord and dispose of the afterbirth. Then the mother cleaned up her own baby with seal oil and she put it to the breast. She spent the first 10 or 12 or more hours nursing her baby and holding it on a can or tin cup every fifteen or twenty minutes until she got the first urination. After that she had no trouble for as soon as the baby squirmed, she would put it on the cup. This she continued night and day until the baby would not urinate until it felt the cup on its bottom."

3. Women's parkas are cut large enough to accommodate babies up to two years of age. Very small babies are secured by a belt worn outside the parka.

Sadie noted that there had been cases of infants smothering inside their mothers' parkas.

4. The reader may find it equally remarkable that Sadie apparently accepted his criticism with equanimity and altered her meal preparations accordingly.

5. Tuberculous meningitis.

6. In the fall of 1985 Sadie and Nate lost another son, Glenn, the victim of an alcohol and drug-related shooting.

7. Assembly of God and the Bahai.

8. Actually she was a nurse's aide. Sadie, despite her earlier experience in the Barrow hospital, did not have the formal training to be a public health nurse. In 1954, when the chemotherapy program was introduced in bush Alaska to treat TB, natives were trained as "chemotherapy aides." The period to which Sadie refers is earlier.

9. Again, here and in the following sentences, she is referring to tuberculous meningitis.

10. She may be referring to INH (Isoniazid) or PAS (para-amino salicylic acid), both of which were used in the treatment of tuberculosis beginning in 1954.

8. Farthest North Judge

1. There are four levels of Alaska State Courts: the supreme court, court of appeals, superior court, and district court. The district court (in which magistrates serve) has jurisdiction over misdemeanor violations. It can hear civil cases for the recovery of money or damages not to exceed $10,000 ($35,000 as of 1987). The district court can also establish death. It can issue marriage licenses, summons, writs of *habeas corpus*, and warrants for search and arrest. The superior court is the trial court of general jurisdiction and the appellate court for district court cases. It has exclusive jurisdiction in probate and in cases involving minors. The state is divided into four jurisdictional districts (Alaska Almanac 1983:46).

2. The Organic Act of 1884 created a judicial system for the territory of Alaska.

3. An *umialik*, Sadie explained, is "a well-to-do man, a man with many properties, a leader with everything going for him. It's [*umialik*] got lots of meanings. *Umialik* also means a headman, or someone who owns a boat; also the head of a whaling crew, or the man who owns the [whaling] boat."

4. The most common sources of conflict in marriage were infidelity and sexual jealousy (see Burch 1975:95 ff.; Spencer 1959:99).

5. Pospisil (1964:414,423) provides more detail on the powers of the *umialik* in northern interior Alaska, noting that he planned the hunt and the construction of corrals used in taking caribou, assigned and coordinated hunters' activities, and supervised the division of the catch. During periods of leisure following a successful hunt, he adjudicated and resolved controversies

among his followers, relying almost exclusively upon verbal and psychological sanctions, the most serious of which was ostracism from the band. Given the fluctuating Iñupiat populations and their areas of exploitation from the third quarter of the 19th century on, it is difficult to know to what extent these characteristics applied to the *umialik* in the Barrow area.

6. Hippler and Conn (1975:36) note that "where the church was powerful and disputants were church members, the cases were usually referred to the church board of elders." This was evidently true in Barrow, for Sadie noted that the church "was strong; they gave out the punishment. Become a member, and if you were known to be loose or whatever, they really got you in there and chewed you out in front of the church."

7. Magistrates can hear cases involving no more than $5,000 in money or damages. (At the time that Sadie was magistrate the amount was less.) They cannot hear cases regarding disputes over real property, liens against property, cases regarding false imprisonment, libel and slander, or malicious prosecution.

8. The magistrate training materials recommend that magistrates request information on specific cases from Magistrate Services in Anchorage.

9. Sadie said her feeling was based largely on the fact that she knew of no women commissioners. She soon discovered that there were many women magistrates (all of her successors in Barrow, except one, have also been women), and she believes that her sex had no real bearing on the job. She notes, though, that there were very few women in leadership roles in the community (none, for example on the city council) when she became magistrate. She believes she was accepted as a leader because of her proven efforts on behalf of the community since 1939.

10. Taking on these various roles was illegal. Without police, however, Sadie had no choice.

11. The same pressures that make it difficult for a policeman to be a local person also apply to magistrates. Many in bush communities have quit because of these pressures. Sadie notes, though, that such pressures have been greater on the policemen, and that hiring native police in Barrow never has worked.

12. Under the Alaska Reorganization Act of 1936, the provisions of the Indian Reorganization Act of 1934 were extended to Alaskan native villages, so that they might incorporate for business purposes, borrow money from the revolving Indian credit fund, and adopt a constitution and by-laws for self-government. Barrow incorporated under the act in 1940, and the village council fell under the jurisdiction of the new corporation.

13. Sadie's kitchen courtroom was not all that unusual. Marjorie Lori, field auditor for magistrates, remembers that the magistrate's office in Kotzebue was in his kitchen: "He had one file cabinet, and you absolutely could not open the drawers because they were so full. And the vital statistics for that area and the land recording office were in cardboard boxes. He had a marriage while I was there which he conducted in his kitchen." Dillingham had an even more unorthodox setup. "Arraignments in Dillingham, the first time I went over there, were held on the beach on a boat that had been turned upside down."

14. The Judicial Council is a constitutional state agency comprised of three attorneys, three non-attorneys and the chief justice of the Alaska Supreme Court as the chairman *ex officio*. The council nominates candidates for judgeships, evaluates judges standing for retention elections, and does research on and makes recommendations about the justice system. During Sadie's tenure as magistrate, the council was called upon more for advice in court administration than it is today.

15. Teresa Carns, senior staff associate of the Judicial Council, noted that the council did not have the authority to provide a clerk or equipment or to alter a magistrate's salary. She suggests that Sadie may have been meeting with the Supreme Court, sitting as an administrative body. Or she may have met with the Judicial Council, and the chief justice may have taken some action in his capacity as chief justice, rather than as chairman, *ex officio*, of the Judicial Council.

16. Up to that time, if anyone wanted a copy of a docket, it had to be written out by hand and certified.

17. Sadie's niece, married to her brother's son Eugene Brower. Charlotte served as magistrate after Sadie, from 1977–81.

18. This was apparently before the "120-day rule" went into effect. Under Alaska law—absent delay occasioned by the defense—if a criminal case does not come to trial within 120 days after the complaint is filed or after arrest, it is automatically dismissed.

19. Chief Justice Jay Rabinowitz, who succeeded George Boney.

20. The main grocery/department store in town.

21. The federal law that was being upheld was the Protection of Migratory Birds Treaty of December 8, 1916, which was signed by Canada, the United States, and Mexico.

22. On May 20, a Barrow resident had been arrested at Meade River and had been charged with taking three geese out of season. On May 29, State Representative John Nusinginya from Barrow was apprehended with a duck in his possession. On May 30, 138 natives carrying ducks turned themselves in to the game warden in Barrow.

23. Contrary to Sadie's statement, the Judicial Council did not make "rules and regulations for Alaska in regard to adopting laws."

24. That is, it reflected poorly on Sadie as magistrate.

25. Bringing liquor into the community for personal use was [and is] legal.

26. Sadie noted that, under the present system, no bodies are examined in Barrow; they are sent to Fairbanks or Anchorage to be dealt with by special examiners.

27. The Antioch School of Law.

28. At that time the only phone in town was at the Wien Airlines terminal. Wien Airlines allowed townspeople emergency use of the phone.

29. This was before Sadie began wearing a robe in her own court.

30. According to Marjorie Lori, field auditor for the Alaska Court System,

3. Because Barrow is a fairly small community with a very high trial rate, people get called upon frequently to serve as jurors.

Epilogue: "There's So Much More"

1. Not included in the life history text.

2. She was not alone. Others fought the battle for native rights on these and other fronts. Eben Hopson, the first mayor of the North Slope Borough, and Charles Edwardsen, Jr., among others, led the fight for land claims and for political recognition of the North Slope area as a municipality.

3. One reviewer of the manuscript personally recalled at least five families along the Kuskokwim Valley who had a white trader father and Eskimo mother, noting that the achievements of first-generation offspring included well-known bush pilots, a member of the state legislature, a successful store owner, and an admired artist. Some of the earliest "bicultural" individuals in Alaska were the Russian Aleuts, who held the official designation of "Creole."

4. Paine (1971:21) defines the cultural broker as "one who, while purveying values that are not his own, is also purposively making changes of emphasis and/or content."

5. Long before I became involved in Sadie's life history, others had been captivated by her story—she appears in at least three articles in the *Tundra Times*, Alaska's native newspaper (Anon. 1969; Dubay 1981; Richardson 1978), in an *Alaska Magazine* piece entitled, "Farthest North Judge" (Hampton 1971), and in a book, *Women Who Braved the Far North* (Jones 1976).

6. These are discussed further in the Appendix.

7. Edited by anthropologist William Schneider.

8. Or more, if more than one interviewer is involved.

9. Neville Jacobs, who has a background in anthropology, did a series of oral history interviews with Alaska pioneers in the early 1970s, including several with Barrow people. She interviewed Sadie in September 1974, and the tapes were later deposited in the University of Alaska's Oral History Archives.

Appendix: The Examined Life

1. Bataille and Sands (1984:14) add, "the narrator and recorder-editor remain in a continual present as the content of the narrative recreates the past; the process leads to a double narrative stance that allows simultaneous exposition of event and evaluation from temporal distance. Like all literature, the as-told-to autobiography creates an enduring present within the illusion of temporal sequence."

2. A life history, for example, has an ending, while the life as told may not.

The life history is brought to some sort of closure—either by the selection of text elicited from the life history subject or through the words of the author/editor.

3. Elaborating upon folklorist Jeff Todd Titon's (1980) distinction between life story (a personal narrative) and life history, William Schneider (1986*a*:121–22) describes the latter as based on life stories, but analytic and interpretive. "[Life histories] are derived from the narrator's experiences but are evaluated through the lens of the writer whose training enables him to point out how the facts presented by the narrator enhance our understanding of areas such as history, culture, or personality."

4. In 1986 the interviews were structured by the chapter organization of the manuscript which we were then reviewing.

5. Sadie responded, "Mainly what we know as the *imiññauraq* was something that they used to scare you which would rise out of the water after dark and come chase you. . . . I remember we used to really think they existed. Because if we were playing outdoors and somebody hollered '*imiññauraq*!' we all ran home." According to Sadie's niece, Edna MacLean, an *imiññauraq* was the ghost of a person who had drowned at sea.

6. Although the 1986 and 1987 material was transcribed and incorporated into the final life history narrative, the rough narrative was compiled prior to my 1986 return to Barrow.

7. Copies of all tapes and transcripts are on file at the University of Alaska's Oral History Archives.

8. The different "Magistrate" files reflect the sheer volume of material on this topic.

9. I am speaking here of full-scale life history research; most anthropologists in the field collect some life history information from each of their native consultants as a matter of course.

10. William Schneider (1986*b*:18) speaks to the importance of this issue in Alaska: "I think we'll also see a continuing interest in producing written works which emphasize first person narration as opposed to works written about Alaska Natives. This trend has been facilitated by the tape recorder, but the origins of the movement go back to a discontent by Natives with outsiders who came in, collected stories and then interpreted them incorrectly. The fallout from this has been very healthy for all of us. I suspect it will continue as we balance the need for explanation/interpretation and the vividness of reading the stories of an elder speaking in his own words."

11. For example, William Schneider (1986*a*), in his recent life history of Athapaskan elder Moses Cruikshank, plunges the reader immediately into Moses's narrative; the cultural-historical context and discussion of life history methodology follow the narrative. Marjorie Shostak's (1981) account of a !Kung woman, Nisa, also separates the author's commentary from Nisa's narrative, but Shostak prefaces each chapter of the narrative with introductory remarks on aspects of !Kung culture dealt with by that portion of Nisa's narrative.

Index

About the Author

Margaret B. Blackman is professor and chair of anthropology at the State University of New York, College at Brockport. She is the author of *During My Time: Florence Edenshaw Davidson, A Haida Woman* (1982), the first life history of a Northwest Coast Indian woman; and a co-author, with Edwin S. Hall, Jr., and Vincent Rickard, of *Northwest Coast Indian Graphics* (1981).

"Sadie was a tremendous boon to the court where vital statistics were concerned."

9. A Matter of Survival

1. Not literally. *Nalukataq* proper is the celebration in summer hosted by the successful *umialgich* (see page 205). Sadie is referring to the quantities of meat and *maktak* prepared by each *umialik's* family right after the whale catch.

2. The material that follows draws upon several sources. Spencer (1959) gives the most detailed account of traditional whaling. Bockstoce (1977, 1980) traces the changes in whaling from the commercial era to modern times and discusses the issues surrounding Iñupiat whaling in the late 1970s. Worl's accounts (1978, 1981) focus on the socioeconomics of contemporary whaling, and Braund (1984) presents a profile of present-day whaling practices in Alaska. David Boeri (1983) gives a personalized, journalistic account of whaling seasons spent at Gambell on St. Lawrence Island and at Barrow. Charles Smythe (personal communication) provides field data for the brief sketch of contemporary whaling presented here. The role of the contemporary whaling captain's wife is discussed by Solomon (1985).

3. This preparation and consumption of meat was the *Nalukataq* to which Sadie referred earlier.

4. The blanket toss is commonly misrepresented to tourists by Outside tour guides in Arctic towns like Barrow and Kotzebue. Sadie, who has long been involved with tourists, commented," The information they give out for that *Nalukataq*, it disgusted me so I got after that tour guide. The tour guides [in Barrow] were telling the people that this was a means of looking for a person that got lost. Can you imagine using the *Nalukataq* for something like that? That was so ridiculous, I had to chew him out and tell him that this was just recreational. . . . *Nalukataq* was never used to search for people. It was used in celebration of a whale catch." Another misconception perpetrated by tour guides is that people were tossed in the air for the purpose of scanning the horizon for whales.

5. The range was 1–17. The count was recorded at the request of Joseph Sonnenfeld, who reproduced it in his report (Sonnenfeld 1956:277).

6. Boeri (1983) reports an average for Barrow of sixteen whales between 1970–77 but does not cite a source or give annual counts. Braund (1984:A–56) gives annual counts for all the whaling villages (not separated by community) from 1962–82. The years 1972, 1973, 1976, and 1977 all had significantly larger than normal takes of bowhead.

7. By the mid-1970s, when it became possible to secure high-paying jobs in Barrow in the wake of the oil boom, the number of whaling crews in Barrow had increased by 50 percent over the preceding decade, reaching thirty-six by 1979. Braund (1984:29) recorded twenty-seven crews in Barrow in 1982; Worl

and Smythe (1986:157) report thirty-three registered in 1985. The cost to a whaling captain of outfitting and operating a crew was estimated at $16,090 in 1984, up from $10,361 in 1978 (Worl and Smythe 1986:156).

8. Each Whaling Captains Association elects a commissioner to the AEWC to represent the whalers of that village.

9. This was divided among eight villages; Barrow was alloted three whales.

10. In 1985 the IWC increased the quota to twenty-six whales struck for each of the years 1985–87. Strikes not used in one year, however, might be transferred to a subsequent year, providing no more than thirty-two whales were struck in one year.

11. Worl and Smythe (1986:155–56) comment: "Prior to the IWC quota the average time spent in harvesting whales was four weeks. Today that is constricted to less than four days. This does not include all the preparation time needed for cleaning of the ice cellar, constructing and repairing the *umiaq*, and all the other equipment, and surveying and constructing the ice trail to the open water. All of these jobs must be done even if to spend only one day on the ice."

12. Thus, covering an *umiaq* could run upwards of $950 plus the feeding of eight women.

13. Snowmobiles began replacing dog teams in the mid-1960s.

14. According to Spencer (1959:345), the flippers and heart comprised the boat owner's share.

15. Nate and his crew took a whale also during the 1986 whaling season.

16. The belt or ring around the entire whale replaces the now-worthless baleen, which was formerly shared by the crew. Sadie noted that the heart, liver, kidneys, intestines, and tongue, in addition to the flukes, went to the whaling captain. Worl (1978) discusses bowhead distribution patterns.

17. Although this episode ended positively, inexperienced crews can cause innumerable problems.

18. Sadie later explained that one-half of the heart, kidney, intestines, tongue, and meat for distribution was cooked when the whale was first brought in; the other half was prepared at *Nalukataq*. If there was any left over, it was prepared for a feast at Thanksgiving. She added, "There's hardly ever enough to cook at Christmastime, so we just share the fluke, the *maktak*, and the frozen [raw] meat."

19. Worl and Smythe (1986:159) note that the primary role played today by women who go out on the ice is to serve as spotters watching for migrating whales.

10. Retirement

1. Incised drawings on strips of baleen.

2. That is, she worked with field school students on the oral history project.

Printed in the United States
by Baker & Taylor Publisher Services